Der

CW00731135

richard x

West Ham United

includes Thames Ironworks 1895-1900

West Ham United

A COMPLETE RECORD

John Northcutt and Roy Shoesmith

The Breedon Books
Publishing Company
Derby

First published in Great Britain by
The Breedon Books Publishing Company Limited
44 Friar Gate, Derby DE1 1DA
1993

ISBN 1 873626 44 4

Printed and bound by Butler and Tanner Ltd, Frome and London.
Jacket printed by BDC Printing Services Ltd of Derby.

Contents

Acknowledgements

A number of fellow statisticians have assisted in the compilation of this book and the authors would like to express their thanks to them and others who have contributed to it. Tony Hogg wrote several match reports and loaned a number of photographs; Trevor Smith, Sports Editor of the *Ilford Recorder*, also helped with photographs; Jack Rollin provided wartime statistics, and Andrew Ward gave timely help with players' biographies. John Powles supplied new information on Thames Ironworks. Others, like Mike Davage and Douglas Lamming, will recognise their contributions of dates of births and deaths. The staff at the British Newspaper Library at Collindale have also been extremely helpful. Not least, the authors' wives, Marian and Janet, also made vital contributions of encouragement and practical help.

Photographs were supplied by Allsport, EMPICS, Colorsport and the Hulton-Deutsch Picture Library.

Introduction

THE formation of the West Ham Statisticians Group in 1980 helped contribute new information about the club, and its many members were pleased when the first edition of *West Ham United: A Complete Record* was published in 1987. Fresh material has been included in this new edition which is updated to the end of the 1992-3 season and which we believe to be the most exhaustive and accurate work ever published on the Hammers.

Since the last edition six years ago, it has been an eventful time at Upton Park. The team has played in three major semi-finals, been relegated twice and promoted twice. We hope that this book gives pleasure to all supporters of West Ham United Football Club, the pride of London's East End.

John Northcutt
Roy Shoesmith
May 1993

The West Ham Story

WHEN Dave Taylor, a foreman at the Thames Ironworks shipbuilding yard, suggested the formation of a works football team in 1895 he received all the backing he needed from the firm's chairman, Mr Arnold Hills.

The Ironworks, situated at the mouth of the River Lea in East London, had manufactured scores of ships during its long existence, many for the Royal Navy and for overseas governments. And Mr Hills was a very enlightened Victorian employer who took a genuine interest in the welfare of his workforce.

Taylor, a local referee, found a willing ear and the company journal announced the scheme in the next available issue. Before long, would-be players were subscribing their half-crowns towards a year's membership.

Taylor spent the summer of 1895 planning the new club's first season. In that inaugural campaign Thames did not join a league, although whether that was a conscious decision, or whether they were unable to gain admittance to a competition, is not clear.

Affiliation to the Football Association was seen as a useful step, however, and in consequence Thames entered the FA Cup for 1895-6, as well as the Essex and London Junior Cups and the local West Ham Charity Cup.

Before the new season got underway, Dave Taylor resigned his post to resume refereeing and Mr A.T.Harsent, a Thames employee who lived in nearby Mary Street, became the club's new secretary.

For their first three years of FA Cup matches, the Ironworks made no impression on the competition, apart from attracting 3,000 to the Chatham ground for their first-ever FA Cup tie. The Ironworks were first out of the hat, but waived the right to stage the game at their Hermit Road ground.

In the West Ham Charity Cup, however, Thames Ironworks carried off their first trophy when they beat Barking 1-0 at the third attempt.

The infant club could always rely on help from the parent company and in December 1895, the shipbuilding department provided equipment to stage a match under artificial lights.

Apparently, the game against Old St Stephen's was not a success, although the fact that it was refereed by Lt W.Simpson, who was to take charge of that season's Sheffield Wednesday-Wolverhampton Wanderers FA Cup Final, underlined the status of the occasion.

For subsequent matches the lighting system was considerably improved and, in March 1896, two Football League clubs were to visit Hermit Road. Both Woolwich Arsenal and West Brom, who fielded the legendary Billy Bassett, scored comfortable victories but at least the Ironworks were getting themselves noticed.

But friendly games were not enough and two months before the end of the club's first season, the committee were planning the second. The newly-formed London League voted Thames into its Second Division but, when Royal Ordnance withdrew, Thames found themselves in the First Division without kicking a ball.

Thames Ironwork's first league match of any kind was staged on 19 September 1896 when a 3-0 win over Vampires gave them a splendid start to their season in the London League. The Ironworks finished their very first league campaign as runners-up, although they were well behind the champions, 3rd Grenadier Guards.

Their position was all the more commendable for the fact that they had been evicted from their Hermit Road ground in the autumn of 1896 and had been forced to play all their games away for several weeks before finding a temporary home in East Ham.

Predecessors of the Hammers. The Thames Ironworks team of 1895.

Ironworks' cup form was not nearly so satisfying and in an FA Cup qualifying round match at Sheerness they crashed 8-0 to Sheppey United.

The West Ham Charity Cup was surrendered to West Ham Garfield in the Final at the Spotted Dog, and Leyton eliminated them in an early round of the Essex Senior Cup.

There was, however, lengthy involvement in the London Senior Cup and Ironworks played seven matches before Bromley, a London League Second Division club, knocked them out.

During the close season Arnold Hills financed the construction of a magnificent new stadium at Plaistow. It was opened in June 1897 and called the Memorial Grounds to commemorate the 60th year of Queen Victoria's reign.

With facilities for cycling, soccer, athletics and, later, swimming, it was capable of accomodating 100,000 people, a fact which the FA undoubtedly considered when nominating it for a possible replay venue for the 1901 Cup semi-final between Spurs and West Brom.

The Irons had a splendid second season of league football, winning the London League title in a close finish with Brentford. The issue rested on the final match when Thames defeated 2nd Grenadier Guards, 3-1, a result which meant that Thames had surrendered only five points in 16 games and averaged just under three goals per game.

The Irons also won their first FA Cup match and Redhill and Royal Engineers were both defeated at Canning Town before a trip to St Albans proved the Irons' undoing.

Thames had by now recruited some very useful players. James Reid joined them from Reading, Henry Hird from Stockton and George Neill from West Norwood. Neill was to become club secretary for a short time.

There were some pleasing London League results and Bromley were beaten 7-3 and 5-1, ample revenge for the previous season's London Cup defeat, and 3rd Grenadier Guards were also beaten twice, thus reversing the previous season's fortunes.

The only real shock was the 3-1 defeat by Ilford at the Memorial Grounds in the London Senior Cup. The Irons had scored seven in two games against Ilford and were expected to go through.

A.T.Harsent was succeeded as secretary by Francis Payne for the 1897-8 season. Payne was to continue for 1898-9, although he was to create serious problems for himself and the club.

In September 1897, Millwall, a strong, professional Southern League side, managed only a 2-0 defeat of the amateur Irons to further underline Thames' progress. In goal for Millwall that day was Tommy Moore, whose erratic skills were to serve Ironworks for the next two seasons.

Another measure of the Irons' growing status came in April 1898 when Woolwich Arsenal, highly placed in the Football League Second Division, found themselves trailing 2-1 to Thames with ten minutes to play. Arsenal fielded nine of their regular League side plus two new signings and saved their blushes only with a last-ditch effort.

The splendid facilities at the Memorial Grounds made the committee ambitious. Better quality players were enlisted by the club which now felt that the time was right to embrace professionalism and fill the vast open spaces of Thames' home ground.

The committee approached Arnold Hills who, as an advocate of 'sport for sport's sake', must have found the suggestion that players should be paid quite unpalatable. In the end he agreed, most reluctantly.

Thus fortified, Thames Ironworks applied for entry into two new leagues for 1898-9, the Southern League Second Division and the Thames and Medway Combination.

New players arrived, too, including Millwall's erratic goalkeeper, Tommy Moore; David Lloyd, a 6ft 4in, 13st giant who came along with three others from 3rd Grenadier Guards; and Roddy MacEachrane, who stood 5ft 6in and made a journey of almost 500 miles from Inverness to play for Thames.

A hitch in the fixtures saw that the Irons' only home game in their first six of the season was a friendly against 1st Coldstream Guards. Thus Brentford's visit on 24 September was Thames' first home Southern League fixture, whilst Chatham, on 6 October, were the first visitors in the Thames and Medway Combination.

Both competitions expected their member clubs to field first teams, but the better class of club in the Combination made that Thames Ironworks' obvious target. By the New Year, however, with only three wins in nine Combination outings compared to a 77 per cent success rate in the Southern League, Thames readjusted their sights.

The Irons went from strength to strength and took the Southern League title. They won their remaining 11 matches in that competition, culminating with a splendid 10-0 win over bottom club, Maidenhead United. Their Combination results also took an upturn and only one defeat in their last seven games enabled them to gain a respectable position.

In the FA Cup, the Royal Engineers Training Battalion waived home advantage and the Memorial Grounds staged a double bill that afternoon by putting on an athletics meeting as well. The Ironworks met the Royal Engineers three times in 1898-9, winning every game, and in the Cup they got through with goals from Gresham and MacEachrane.

Three thousand people saw them hold Brighton United to a goalless draw in the next round and many of them had paid the 4s 2d (21p) fare to travel from Plaistow to the seaside town. Brighton, from the Southern League's First Division, found Moore, Dove and Tranter outstanding for Thames but in the replay the Irons were outclassed and lost 4-1.

Despite winning their league section by nine points, Thames still had to take part in a play-off to decide the title because a little-publicised six-club section of the Southern League, representing the South West, had produced an equally decisive champion.

Cowes, from the Isle of Wight, had won all their ten games but they could hardly have been pleased when the neutral venue for the play-off turned out to be Millwall — 100 miles from the Solent and three from Canning Town. Ten thousand spectators saw Lloyd put the Irons ahead. Cowes, who had scored 58 goals in their ten league games, pulled one back but second-half efforts from Henderson and Leonard gave Thames victory.

In the end it was all quite meaningless. Winners and losers qualified for the Test Matches, Ironworks were sent to play Sheppey United, who had finished 12th out of 13 clubs in the First Division, and then the senior section was enlarged for 1899-1900, so the four Test Match combatants, plus QPR and Bristol Rovers from outside the league were granted places.

In the closing months of the season former Manchester City player, Patrick Leonard, made an immediate impact with a hat-trick against Upton Park in his first game. Chatham full-back Tommy Dunn, who had played for Wolves in the 1896 FA Cup Final, was another newcomer but the biggest haul of talent came from Bristol.

In February 1899, the Warmley club folded and Francis Payne, the Ironworks secretary, secured the services of three leading players, Henderson, Peter McManus and George Reid.

McManus had won a Scottish Cup winners' medal with Edinburgh St Bernard's in 1895 and had also played for West Brom; George Reid had played with Reading, although he was no relation to Jimmy Reid who had served the Berkshire club at the same time; and McManus was serving a two-week suspension when he signed for the Irons.

Two other interesting characters to join Thames at this time were J.Reynolds, a right-winger from Gravesend United who could 'bend' dead-ball kicks, and Alf Hitch, a particularly fine header of the ball he had only a short stay at Canning Town who took part in an England trial match two years later.

Francis Payne was still not satisfied with the Irons' playing strength, however, and that proved his downfall. Through an agent he misused a large sum of money given to the club by Alfred Hills.

Payne was trying to lure well-known players to Canning Town but the agent's activities were uncovered in Birmingham and when Payne failed to attend the FA hearing into the matter he was suspended until he did appear. In addition, the club was suspended for two weeks from 1 September and fined £25.

Shortly after the FA ruling, Payne announced that he had resigned as Ironworks' secretary at the close of the previous season. A new secretary was appointed in the form of George Neill, who had played his last game for the club only six months earlier. Neill was then 25 and during his term of office he strengthened the playing staff, particularly prior to the start of the 1899-1900 season. Sadly, Neill was dead by the time he was 30, a victim of consumption.

Among the arrivals in the 1899 close season were Albert Carnelly, a much-travelled forward from Bristol City, and E.S. (Syd) King, who had played for Northfleet. As player and the secretary, King was to serve the club for over 30 years.

Neill's most outstanding coup was the signing of three established players from Spurs, Harry Bradshaw, Bill Joyce and Kenny McKay, but there was some disquiet amongst the opposition and when the Irons travelled to Reading on 16 September, immediately after their ban was lifted, they found plenty of critics.

The *Reading Standard* commented cynically that Thames Ironworks, lining up for the first game in the Southern League Division One, 'had a familiar look about them'. The newspaper suggested that 'anybody can get up a good team with plenty of 'ready' behind them'.

Reading won by the narrowest margin but it was seven weeks before Thames next tasted defeat and hopes rose, only to be dashed when, early in November, the Irons conceded seven goals on a muddy Tottenham pitch.

Up until then Thames had been playing well and four FA Cup games had produced 21 goals including seven past Dartford when Charlie Craig, a tall full-back from Scotland, began a career that saw him become one of Thames' most popular players.

Undaunted by the Tottenham disaster, the Irons hammered Grays United 11-1 in the Thames and Medway Combination with Bradshaw and Carnelly each netting four. By the New Year, however, the Irons had suffered five more defeats and been knocked out of the FA Cup by Millwall in front of 13,000 spectators, then the largest attendance ever seen at the Memorial Grounds.

Defeat denied Thames a place in the hat with the Football League clubs but, worse, it proved to be skipper Harry Bradshaw's last appearance on a football field. Capped by England in his Liverpool days, Bradshaw was a key figure for Thames and his death, on Christmas Day 1899, stunned the club.

In the aftermath of Bradshaw's death, Thames scored only three victories in 15 games and the 16th game was against Cup Finalists, Southampton, just 12 days before their encounter at the Crystal Palace with Bury.

Maybe the Saints were conserving their energies but Thames won 4-1 and the hero was Bill Joyce who scored a hat-trick and was chaired from the field by Irons' fans grateful for two badly-needed points.

Jubilation was cut short when, the very next day, Brighton United announced their resignation from the Southern League, leaving Thames in an even more vulnerable position. With two games to play they were bracketed with Sheppey United at the foot of the table.

If Thames won their remaining games then they could possibly overhaul both Chatham and Gravesend but, although the Irons did indeed win both games, so did Chatham and Gravesend and for the second season in succession Thames found themselves involved in Test Matches.

This time it was to preserve their status and at neutral Tottenham they met Fulham, the Second Division runners-up by a narrow margin from Chesham and Wolverton.

Former Thames forward, David Lloyd, was now a Fulham player, one of only six survivors from the previous meeting between the clubs. Thames won that game 1-0 and they went several goals better this time. Four goals ahead at half-time, they won 5-1 and Bill Joyce was again a hat-trick hero.

The emphatic win justified the Irons' claim to a place in the top division but off-the-field activities were making Thames' victory seem purely academic.

In an effort to finance a takeover, the Thames Ironworks Shipbuilding Company was forced to go public and the outcome had a profound effect on the football club who had to act likewise.

Four thousand, ten-shilling (50p) shares were issued and Arnold Hills, anticipating that they would be under-subscribed, generously offered to match the sale by buying one for himself for every other one purchased.

Shares were offered, first to staff at the Ironworks and then to the general public, but there was no rush to buy. In 1900, any typical East End working man would have been hard-pressed to find the money for even a single share.

In late June 1900, Thames Ironworks Football Club resigned from the Southern League and was wound up. Almost immediately, however, on 5 July, it was relaunched as West Ham United Football Club and was offered the Southern League place vacated by its predecessors. A new secretary, Swansea-born Lew M.Bowen, a clerk at the Ironworks, was appointed.

Events at Canning Town in the summer of 1900 could not be regarded as a parting of the ways. The new club and the shipbuilders maintained a relationship, albeit an uneasy one, for some years afterwards.

The owners of the Memorial Grounds allowed West Ham United full use of the facilities under a tacit agreement and for a nominal rent, although Arnold Hills still required a sports ground for his workers and in 1904 the association was finally broken.

By then he had given the new club some breathing space and vital time to establish itself. Indeed, had he withheld any of the assistance he gave unstintingly in its earliest years, the Thames Ironworks FC itself would have foundered. His encouragement and funding ensured its survival.

New men arrived to reinforce the team for 1900-01, amongst them the Bristol City goalkeeper, Hugh Monteith, and Billy Grassam, an inside-forward from Burslem Port Vale. Both men were Scots and on the first day of the new season, Grassam scored four goals against Gravesend United, still the best start by a Hammers' debutant.

Yet attendances were still disappointing for anything but the visits of clubs like Spurs and Millwall. On 5 January 1901, however, the visit of Liverpool for an FA Cup intermediate round game gave an excellent opportunity for the fans to come flocking to the Memorial Grounds.

Liverpool were on their way to the Football League Championship and were competing at this early stage of the competition only because of their secretary's error. They might have been expected to set a new attendance record but the Hammers' directors decided to cash-in and double the admission prices which deterred thousands of casual supporters.

A significant event occured later in the month, however, when the London, Tilbury and Southend Railway opened their new station at West Ham's Manor Road. This was expected to be the salvation of the football club, yet it served only to prove just how limited interest in Hammers really was.

At the end of the season, Billy Grassam was Hammers' leading scorer with 12 goals, and as four of them were scored on the opening day, it can be seen that the West Ham attack was hardly in form. They managed 40 goals in 28 League games to finish sixth in the Southern League.

The club once again dipped into the market-place for unemployed footballers and brought Bill Linward, from Doncaster Rovers, and Bill Jenkinson, from Burnley, for their second season. Linward played in the opening game which, because of the late arrival of opponents Wellingborough, was abandoned because of bad light. It was replayed a month later and Hammers won 4-2 with a hat-trick from Corbett.

In November, the club found itself engaged in two first-class matches on the same afternoon when an official's blunder forced Hammers to meet Tottenham in a Southern League game and also cope with the visit of Leyton for an FA Cup third qualifying round match. The prospect of handsome 'gate' receipts for the visit of Spurs could not be ignored and Hammers solved the problem by waiving home advantage in the Cup and dispatching their reserve team to Leyton where they won 1-0.

Having done the difficult bit, West Ham then turned out their full Southern League Second Division team against Grays and made a complete hash of a fog-shrouded contest at the Memorial Grounds. Frustrated by the heroics of Grays' goalkeeper Tommy Moore — dismissed by Hammers the previous season after some fickle performances — they went down 2-1 to the Essex 'village' side.

Halfway through the season Hammers exchanged reserve centre-forward Peter Kyle for Kettering Town's Welsh international centre-half Bill Jones. It was a splendid piece of business and in his 15 appearances that season Jones, who was capped

West Ham pictured in 1901-02. Fred Corbett (centre of the front row) scored a hat-trick against Wellingborough in the Southern League, but it was Billy Grassam (on Corbett's right) and George Ratcliffe (on his left) who ended the season as joint top scorers with ten goals each.

again whilst in Hammers' employ, was on the losing side only twice.

After finishing fourth in 1901-02, the fine team assembled by Syd King was broken up and for 1902-03 King, still a relative novice as secretary, had to start almost from scratch. Billy Barnes, Jack Farrell and John Campbell were the pick of his new crop of players, Barnes having scored Sheffield United's winner in the FA Cup Final replay a few months earlier.

Yet for all these new signings, and the fact that Grassam scored over half the Hammers' League goals, the season was a disappointment. Arch-rivals Millwall completed the double over West Ham who conceded six goals on visits to both Reading and Southampton. Exempted until the intermediate round of the FA Cup, Hammers made a fruitless trip to Lincoln, then sixth in Division Two, and were beaten 2-0.

The disappointing results of 1902-03 saw the departure of trainer Jack Ratcliffe who had succeeded Abe Norris only 12 months earlier. Ratcliffe's position was filled by Bill Johnson, a well-known figure with Sheffield Wednesday and Spurs. Billy Grassam was also on the move. After being Hammers' leading scorer for the past three seasons he signed for Manchester United.

The line-up for the opening match of 1903-04, against Millwall, contained few familiar faces. Charlie Satterthwaite, of the thunderbolt shot, was Grassam's replacement and he proved an ideal choice by finishing leading scorer before moving to Woolwich Arsenal at the season's end.

Charles Cotton began the season in goal, but the 6ft 2in Welsh international Fred Griffiths — first choice the previous season — won back his place in November and retained it for the rest of the season.

Millwall again achieved a League double over West Ham, as did four other sides. One of them was Swindon Town who won the last-ever Southern League game to be played at the Memorial Grounds. Their outside-right, E.Toombs, had the honour of scoring the last Southern League goal there with his only goal of the

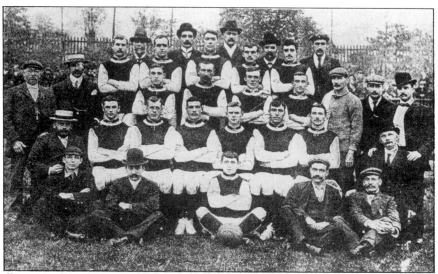

Hammers' staff for 1903-04. Back row (left to right): J.Caerns, G.Fundell, J.Moss, G.Handley, T.Williamson. Fourth row: G.Eccles, A.Kaye, F.Griffiths, C.Cotton, A.Fair. Third row: G.Hone, E.S.King (secretary), J.Bigden, E.Watts, J.Blythe, T.Allison, W.Johnson (trainer), T.Tappin, A.C.Davis. Second row:J.Grisdale (chairman), T.Duckworth, H.Lyon, J.Butchart, W.Kirby, C.Satterthwaite, W.Barnes, W.White. Front row: C.Paynter, J.Johnson, W.Ingham, G.Davis, H.Simms.

Plymouth goalkeeper Pinnell fists away from a West Ham attack during the Southern League game at the Memorial Grounds in January 1904, when a crowd of 8,000 saw a 1-1 draw.

season. Another curiosity of this historic match was that the referee allowed both teams to wear exactly the same colours for the first half.

The more pleasing features of the season included three points won from Southampton, and Hammers' first-ever Southern League win over Portsmouth.

15

The summer of 1904 saw a number of changes for West Ham United. Virtually the whole playing staff was dismissed and only Billy Bridgeman, Charles Cotton, Aubrey Fair, Tom Allison and Len Jarvis survived the clear-out. Trainer Bill Johnson was another casualty and his job went to 55-year-old Tom Robinson who had been connected with the club since its formation and who was the Thames Ironworks trainer. His assistant was 26-year-old Charlie Paynter.

The most important change of all, however, was that West Ham United moved home. There was a steadily deteriorating relationship between the club and the owners of the Memorial Grounds and, as it showed no sign of improving, Hammers' board decided to seek alternative accommodation.

They quickly agreed to an offer of land from a Roman Catholic reformatory school at the Boleyn and by July, contractors were making it ready for Southern League football.

New players included three former internationals and when the fixtures were arranged so that Millwall were the first visitors to the new ground, some 10,000 spectators turned up, although some felt that this figure would have been doubled had the game been played on a Saturday.

Billy Bridgeman was credited with two goals as Hammers beat their local rivals for the first time since 1901, although some historians claim he netted all three, a fact unsubstantiated by contemporary newspaper reports. There is no doubt, however, that Bridgeman scored a hat-trick in the first public trial match a few days earlier.

Scottish international left-back Dave Gardner, was Hammers' new captain. Gardner, who had won his sole cap with Third Lanark, had a wealth of experience and had captained Newcastle and Grimsby before coming to Upton Park.

By mid-November, West Ham were third in the table with only two defeats in 12 matches, but an appalling run saw them lose their next nine games, including an FA Cup match at Brighton. Six of the games were settled by the only goal which must have been particularly galling.

A saviour was at hand, however, in the form of Chris Carrick who came in at outside-left. His presence saw Hammers score 30 goals in their remaining 15 games compared to only 18 in the first 19 matches.

There was an ugly incident in the Southern League match at Brighton in March when goalkeeper Matt Kingsley was sent-off after a bout of fisticuffs with the former Hammers' player, H.Lyon. It proved to be Kingsley's last game in West Ham's colours and, after his suspension was served, he signed for Queen's Park Rangers in the summer.

Despite the presence of so many marksmen recruited from outside, it was local product Bill Bridgeman who topped the scoring charts with 11 goals. His Marner Street school chum, George Hilsdon, weighed in with four.

Attendances took a giant upward leap in 1904-05, due almost entirely to the change of venue, and five crowds of 10,000 plus were recorded whilst another nine topped 5,000.

There was a further improvement in 1905-06 with seven home 'gates' in excess of 10,000. By now, George Kitchen had succeeded Kingsley in goal. The well-known former Everton man was considered the best uncapped 'keeper in the country.

West Ham had also secured the services of Fred Blackburn, an England international forward from Blackburn Rovers, and midway through the season Billy Grassam returned after spells at Manchester United and Leyton. At the same time amateur centre-forward Harry Stapley, who had so often promised to assist West Ham, finally signed for the club.

Hammers' disappointing 11th place stemmed from their poor away record with only three victories on opponents' grounds whereas only three visiting teams were

West Ham in 1904-05, their first season at Upton Park. Back row (left to right): H.Bamlett, A.Fair, M.Kingsley, D.Gardner, E.S.King (secretary). Middle row: T.Robinson (trainer), F.Branston, T.Allison, F.Piercy, J.Russell, L.Jarvis, C.Messer, C.Paynter (assistant trainer). Front row: W.McCartney, C.Simmons, W.Bridgeman, J.Fletcher, C.Carrick, J.Flynn.

West Ham in 1905-06. Back row (left to right): S.Hammond, A.McCartney, G.Kitchen, C.Cotton, D.Gardner. Middle row: W.White, E.S.King (secretary), T.Allison, H.Hindle, F.Piercy, L.Jarvis, T.Robinson (trainer). Front row: W.Ford, H.Winterhalder, S.McAllister, C.Mackie, G.Hilsdon, W.Bridgeman, H.Wilkinson, L.Watson, F.Blackburn, A.Winterhalder.

successful at Upton Park where Hammers conceded only nine goals. Reading scored three of these and then hit West Ham for six at Elm Park.

For the first time in their history, Hammers began their FA Cup campaign in the first round proper. They ended it there, too, when Woolwich Arsenal, aided by ex-Hammers players Bigden, MacEachrane and Satterthwaite, won a muddy replay at the Boleyn.

Stapley headed the scoring list with nine goals from only 13 games, and he was to be top-scorer in the following two seasons as well.

West Ham pictured with the Western League trophy which they won in 1906-07. Back row (left to right): W.Wildman, G.Kitchen, S.Hammond. Middle row: T.Robinson (trainer), T.Allison, F.Piercy, L.Jarvis, E.S.King (secretary). Front row: D.Lindsay, W.Grassam, H.Stapley, L.Watson, F.Blackburn.

In 1906-07, West Ham improved to finish fifth. They beat the champions, Fulham, twice — each time by 4-1 — as well as defeating the Cottagers in the Western League Championship play-off. Hammers enjoyed meeting the top clubs and 20 of their 60 League goals were registered against the top four teams.

Stapley scored six goals in the first eight games but it was Lionel Watson, signed from Blackburn Rovers over a year earlier, who grabbed the headlines with hat-tricks against Luton and Fulham. Grassam scored a hat-trick, too, but finished on the losing side when Portsmouth won 4-3 at Fratton Park.

Another hat-trick hero was Arthur Winterhalder whose three against Spurs marked the first time that Hammers had scored more than two in 15 attempts against their North London rivals. There was another Winterhalder on Hammers' books at this time, Herbert, but the two were unrelated. Arthur became the outstanding character in West Ham's attack. He was quick, had a good shot and possessed boundless energy. All this did not go unnoticed by Cup opponents, Everton, who signed him at the end of the season.

A violent Western League match against Millwall in September almost resulted in the FA closing Upton Park. Len Jarvis, who had not been dismissed during the game, was found guilty of violent play and suspended for 14 days, both teams censured, and warning notices were posted around the ground. The severest punishment was reserved for the referee, Mr E.Case, who was suspended until the end of the season for failing to maintain order.

Four more Scots, making seven in all, joined Hammers in the 1907 close season. The most famous was Brentford's tough-tackling full-back Archie Taylor who had

18

also played for Dundee and Bolton Wanderers. All four had extended runs in the first team and at Swindon on 14 September, West Ham fielded six Scotsmen.

In the FA Cup at Newcastle, some 47,000 spectators, the biggest crowd West Ham had ever played before, saw Hammers lose the game and the services of George Kitchen who was injured and missed the rest of the season. Frank Piercy took over between the posts at Gallowgate and conceded both Newcastle's goals. For the rest of the season, Hammers used the former Bristol Rovers and Glossop goalkeeper, David Clarke.

West Ham slumped to 17th place in 1908-09. Not a single away win was recorded as Hammers drew three and lost 17 of their games away from Upton Park and recorded their worst Southern League season since moving from the Memorial Grounds. Attendances were good, however, and eight 'gates' each yielded more than 10,000, whilst over 120,000 fans saw Hammers in six FA Cup games covering three ties, each of which went to a replay.

Another pleasing aspect was the continued emergence of local talent. Already Danny Shea and Tom Randall had followed in the footsteps of the long-established Len Jarvis. Occasionally, George Chalkley and H.J.Eastwood, from neighbouring amateur clubs, would assist Hammers, and before the end of the season George Webb played his first game in a West Ham shirt.

Southampton, who finished third that season, attracted 15,000 people to the Boleyn where Hammers inflicted Saints' ninth defeat in ten visits to the ground. A fortnight earlier, West Ham had led 3-1 at Norwich, only to lose 6-3.

Jack Foster signed from Sunderland during the season and was soon on his way to Southampton; but Herbert Ashton, from Accrington, remained a good deal longer and, with Danny Shea, formed one of the most formidable right-wing partnerships in the land. With Stapley gone to Glossop, Shea made the centre-forward spot his own and in his first full season he finished top-scorer with 16 goals. For the second year running, Hammers' FA Cup hopes died at Newcastle.

Following their flirt with relegation, Hammers climbed to a respectable ninth place in 1909-10. The contingent of locally-produced talent had increased dramatically and Randall, Shea and Webb were now joined by Bill Whiteman, Dan Woodards, Fred Massey and Albert Scanes.

Shea, who scored six goals in the first three games, including a hat-trick against Brentford, went on to set a new club record of 29 League goals in a season. Tommy Caldwell, an outside-left from Southend United and soon to become an Upton Park hero, was next with eight.

The team was virtually unchanged for the first 19 matches with Webb occasionally replacing the injury-prone Vincent Haynes and Dawson deputising for Kitchen in one match. A home defeat by Portsmouth was the only set-back in the opening 12 games but a poor spell in November and December, when Hammers gained only four points from eight games, dropped them to eighth. By the time the slide was halted with a 5-0 defeat of Norwich, the leaders, Crystal Palace and Southampton, had got clean away.

Carlisle United, then of the Lancashire Combination, were beaten 5-0 in an FA Cup replay at Upton Park after a financial inducement had tempted them to stay in London following a creditable draw on the same ground. Danny Shea's second hat-trick of the season helped West Ham to an unexpected win at Wolverhampton in the next round and Hammers were through to the third round proper for the first time.

The result at Park Royal was a repeat of the 1909 drawn game, although this time each side managed a goal. An unusually large attendance (18,000) for a midweek game at Upton Park saw the action held up for four minutes when a fence collapsed

West Ham staff in 1909. Back row (left to right): S.Hammond, F.Shreeve, C.Dawson, G.Kitchen, R.Fairman, H.S.Bourne. Middle row: C.Paynter (assistant trainer), R.Whiteman, R.Stanley, W.Lavery, D.Woodwards, E.S.King (secretary-manager), E.Wagstaff, F.Piercy, T.Rands, F.Rist, T.Robinson (trainer). Front row: H.Armstrong, H.Ashton, D.Shea, F.Cannon, G.W.Webb, W.F.White (chairman), V.Haynes, C.Carvossa, D.Waggott, F.Blackburn, Caldwell, W.Silor.

although no one was hurt. The only goal of the game came from Rangers' amateur centre-forward, W.O.Steer, who netted three minutes from the end of extra-time.

A week before the first match against Rangers, the Hammers' directors had paid Reading's travelling expenses to Upton Park after the Berkshire club announced that they could not afford the trip to London. They promptly repaid West Ham's generosity with a savage performance which saw them have a player sent off and then concede two penalties. Fred Shreeve missed one and scored the other to salvage a point.

Over Easter, Hammers became the first side that season to inflict two defeats on Crystal Palace, and at the end of the campaign, Danny Shea's 29 goals made him the first West Ham player to top the entire Southern League's scoring list.

West Ham's moderate season of 1909-10 was the first under new chairman William White. White, a barge-builder from Blackwall, East London, had joined the West Ham board in the club's Canning Town days. In May 1909 he succeeded Joseph Grisdale, who had been elected president, and he was the chairman who steered Hammers through the difficult years of World War One and the hectic season of 1922-3. He was still in office at the time of his death in 1934.

The headlines of the 1910-11 season were undoubtedly made in the FA Cup. In succession, Hammers entertained four Football League clubs in reaching the quarter-finals. Nottingham Forest were beaten and then made an unsuccessful appeal about the foggy conditions; Preston went down to a George Webb hat-trick; and Manchester United, League Champions that year, were knocked out by a last-minute goal from Caldwell which provoked many of the 27,000 fans to invade the pitch at the end and the former Southend United winger was carried shoulder-high from the field.

West Ham and Swindon were the Southern League's survivors in the quarter-final. Hammers met Blackburn Rovers at the Boleyn, but this time the home magic failed, although there was the consolation of taking part in what the *Athletic News* called 'the best Cup tie of the season'. Bob Crompton's men won 3-2.

Danny Shea's 25 goals made him the Southern League's leading marksman that season although he failed to score when Herbert Chapman's Northampton Town were the only successful visitors to Upton Park.

An explosive start to the campaign saw Hammers three goals ahead after only 12 minutes against Southend before they allowed the Shrimpers off the hook to draw 3-3. At Bristol in November, Harry Lauder, the great music-hall performer, considered Hammers' visit worthy of his attendance, but was rewarded with a dull 1-1 draw. Boleyn patrons were given an early look at a 19-year-old centre-forward called Charlie Buchan. He failed to impress as his side, Leyton, went down 3-0, and the fans could hardly have imagined that Buchan would one day become a household name, playing for Sunderland, Arsenal and England.

During a lively October encounter with New Brompton, a section of the Upton Park crowd took exception to the treatment being meted out by the visitors' defence to little Herbert Ashton. An ugly situation was defused only by the intervention of Hammers' chairman, William White, who left his seat to speak to the fans.

No significant signings were made for 1911-12, although Vic Glover, a 28-year-old full-back from Southampton, was enlisted to understudy Jim Rothwell and Bob Fairman. In fact, Glover finished the season with more appearances than either of the men he had been bought to cover.

The most important event of the 1911 summer was the departure of goalkeeper George Kitchen. The influential skipper of the side, Kitchen was to be sorely missed. Indeed, goals-against increased by 50 per cent and Hammers dived to 13th place. Happily, Danny Shea maintained his scoring ability and 24 goals put him second on the Southern League list behind J.Smith of Brighton.

Fred Harrison, previously with Southampton and Fulham and signed late the previous season, contributed 13 goals and they compensated in some part towards those that might have been expected from George Webb, had he seen the season out. Webb did not appear again until a brief spell with Manchester City at the start of the following season.

Shea and Bill Kennedy each scored hat-tricks when Hammers beat Brentford 7-4 at Upton Park on 21 October 1911. Rippon got three for the losers and the 11-goal aggregate is still the highest for a first-class match involving West Ham. Another goalscoring record was set on 3 December when Crystal Palace became the first Southern League visitors to score six at Upton Park.

A knee injury to Kennedy in an FA Cup third-round replay over Middlesbrough ended his promising career but West Ham managed to win the game and then faced Swindon Town. It was Hammers' sixth home game in seven ties and 20,000 people paid £1,200 to see them entertain Swindon Town, Southern League champions and, for the last four seasons, the competition's highest scorers.

The first game ended 1-1 and for the replay, Hammers were forced to play Joe Miellear at centre-forward because of injuries. Swindon romped home 4-0, helped by two own-goals from Hammers' full-back Vic Glover.

Some self-respect was regained that weekend when Southern League champions-elect, Queen's Park Rangers, were beaten 3-0 at Upton Park, all the goals coming in the last 12 minutes. On their first visit to Millwall's new home at Cold Blow Lane, however, West Ham crashed 5-1 in front of 28,000 fans, the largest crowd ever to watch a Southern League match involving Hammers.

In a League match at Leyton in April, West Ham goalkeeper Jack Geggus walked off the field in a huff after conceding three goals and being subjected to some uncharitable remarks from his club's supporters. He was persuaded to return and Hammers lost 3-1. At the end of the same month Tom Randall was the only West Ham player in the League XI which met Kent in a match for the Titanic Disaster Fund at New Cross.

Supporters arriving for the first public trial match of 1912-13 found the South Bank newly terraced. This end of the Boleyn was now as sound underfoot as the North Bank which had been similarly treated 12 months earlier.

On the field there were several new faces but the one that everyone especially wanted to see belonged to George Hilsdon who returned to Upton Park after six successful years at Stamford Bridge. Just as noticeable, however, were the absentees,

Bill Kennedy, George Webb, Tommy Caldwell, Bob Fairman, the enigmatic Jack Geggus and popular skipper Frank Piercy. Piercy had retired as a player and had succeeded Charlie Paynter as assistant trainer; Paynter, in turn, had taken over from Tom Robinson who had retired. As it was to turn out, the most significant new player was Syd Puddefoot who came from Limehouse Town.

After losing twice in their first five home games, Hammers went on to enjoy one of their best seasons and they were undefeated by any of the top seven clubs, performing a double over champions Plymouth, and taking three points from Swindon. West Ham suffered only one defeat in the second half of the season. During the season Coventry City added two victories to their already impressive record against Hammers.

By far the most important event of 1913 was the sale of Danny Shea to Blackburn in January. A tempting offer, coupled with the fact that Shea wanted to play First Division football, left the directors little option, but Shea's transfer was not a popular move with supporters. However, in the 16 games remaining, Hammers lost only once — and that when King rested players for a Cup match and fielded reserves at Merthyr.

The bitterly cold January of 1913 played havoc with West Ham's FA Cup programme. Their first-round tie against West Brom, runners-up the previous season, was postponed and the eventual drawn game played in several inches of snow. The Upton Park replay proved indecisive but at Stamford Bridge they won easily and George Hilsdon scored twice on his old hunting ground. Aston Villa, on their way to another Cup Final triumph, were a different proposition, however, and they beat Hammers 5-0 to end any dreams of glory.

After scoring 25 goals for the reserves, Syd Puddefoot was given his debut against Norwich at Upton Park on 1 March 1913. Finding the net in the first team proved more difficult and Puddefoot's first goal came after five hours' football, against Brighton on Good Friday.

Despite leaving halfway through the season, Shea retained his title as Hammers' leading scorer with 16 goals. A 'reborn' George Hilsdon netted 13 and Albert Denyer, snatched from Ilford 12 months earlier, contributed ten. The side was now dominated by 'home-grown' talent even if one or two were native to other parts. In addition to Denyer and Puddefoot, Dan Bailey, Frank Burrill, Jack Mackesy and Harry Caton were all local acquisitions. And in 1913 were added the names of Jack Tresadern and Arthur Stallard.

That year West Ham's shareholders were paid a dividend for the first time, whilst during the summer, a new grandstand was erected, further proof of the club's growing prosperity.

At the start of 1913-14, Hammers included only one new professional with any experience. He was Boston-born Alf Leafe who had spent the previous two seasons with First Division Sheffield United. A big man, Leafe scored in each of his first four games and in November his hat-trick ended Coventry's recent dominance over West Ham. His 20 goals made him Hammers' leading scorer for the season although he was overshadowed once Puddefoot was given an extended run in the team.

Puddefoot opened his account against Gillingham in November, but after receiving a bad injury in an abandoned game at Watford, his tally was restricted to 16. He had scored five against Midland League Chesterfield in the FA Cup game — including a seven-minute hat-trick — but his two goals against Liverpool could not halt the Merseysiders' march towards their first-ever FA Cup Final.

Attendances again improved, largely due to the more comfortable facilities on both North and South Banks, and a huge 25,000 crowd saw the first home game of the season against Swindon. Including Cup games, 17 games topped 10,000 each. In October, Tommy Lonsdale, a new goalkeeper, arrived from Grimsby Town to

Chesterfield's goal comes under attack during the Hammers' 8-1 drubbing of the Derbyshire club in the 1913-14 FA Cup, when Puddefoot hit a hat-trick inside seven minutes and finished with five goals.

become Hammers' fourth claimant in three years to Joe Hughes' place. Like Geggus, Carter and Beale before him, Lonsdale was seen off by Hughes and not retained for 1914-15.

In January 1914, West Ham turned down Sunderland's offer which would have taken Syd Puddefoot to Roker Park. Hammers might have been tempted because they had an option on centre-forward Arthur Stallard who had been playing as an amateur with Chatham. He turned professional as soon as Chatham's FA Cup run ended — coincidentally at Sunderland — but his association with the Boleyn club was sadly brief and he was killed in World War One.

Stallard's entry into first-team football with West Ham also marked the beginning of Tom Randall's decline. Long-serving Randall, now Hammers' captain, was injured in an Easter game against Southern League newcomers, Cardiff City. West Ham's balding captain would never recover from the leg injury which dogged him for the rest of his playing days. He took part in the 2-1 home win over Gillingham that kicked-off the 1914-15 season, but the leg had not improved and, after three matches in November, he called it a day and did not play first-class football again.

When the playing staff gathered for training in preparation for 1914-15, the future looked very uncertain. War clouds which had gathered over Europe burst in early August and unleashed the beginnings of a conflict, the like of which the world had never before seen. Yet the FA decided that football could continue, although the 1914-15 season was the last 'normal' campaign for four years.

The previous season Hammers had conceded still more goals and this time Joe Hughes' position came under threat from Derbyshire-born goalkeeper, Joe Webster, who had been Watford's regular 'keeper for the previous four seasons. At full-back, the experienced Bill Cope was bought from Oldham. Cope, although he was a shade slow and inclined to be somewhat unscrupulous to compensate for that lack of pace, was second only to Puddefoot in the list of Hammers' wartime appearances and he was made skipper for West Ham's first season in the Football League. Hull City provided a lively wing-half in Alf Fenwick who, despite sometimes being caught stranded because he loved to attack, was nonetheless a fine capture.

Hammers conceded 11 goals in their first five games, but after Frank Burton was installed at full-back they let in only 36 goals in their remaining 33 matches. The improvement was not all down to Burton, of course, and when Joe Hughes was recalled he was beaten only 22 times in 21 games.

At the other end, West Ham scored at least once in every home game and of Puddefoot's 18 goals — which saw him top the club's list — all but two came at the Boleyn. Crystal Palace, who did the double over Hammers, were the only successful visitors to Upton Park.

In the FA Cup, West Ham faced Newcastle United for the fifth time (including replays) in seven years. The Hammers team that met Newcastle on that February afternoon in 1915 contained eight local men, compared to only two in 1908, which bore testimony to the development of soccer in the area in the intervening years. In the Newcastle team was Billy McCracken, the only member of either side to have played in the previous encounters of 1908 and 1909.

Two costly errors by Joe Hughes gave Hammers a daunting second-half task, but Alf Leafe's goal gave them hope. By now the Magpies were opting for defence and four footballs were employed as one after the other went sailing out of the ground as the visitors hoisted every clearance long and hard. With ten minutes remaining, Leafe saved the game with his second goal. A wartime ban on midweek football meant that the replay had to be staged the following Saturday, when Hammers went down 3-2.

Watford, who in 13 previous seasons had never finished higher than ninth, took the Southern League title, but not before West Ham became the only side to take four points from them.

Hammers' final match that season, at home to Norwich City, signalled the end of first-class football for the next four and a half years. Regionalised football was introduced and West Ham's part in it is told elsewhere in this book. Suffice it to say that two men, secretary-manager Syd King and trainer-caretaker Charlie

Paynter, saw the club through those difficult times. The success they helped West Ham achieve gave the club impeccable credentials when the time came for them to argue their case for admittance to the Football League in 1919.

"The greatest pleasures I have experienced in my career were when West Ham United secured election to the Second Division at Manchester in March 1919 and their ascent to the First Division four seasons later." These words were written by Syd King for the *Athletic News* in November 1929, three years before his death.

Less than one year after the end of World War One, 20,000 expectant followers assembled at Upton Park for the very first Football League match. Visitors Lincoln City registered the first goal — a penalty by Chesser — but Jim Moyes levelled matters before the end.

Seven goals were conceded in the second match, at Barnsley, but the defence eventually settled down and proved one of the most stubborn in Division Two. Sixteen sides failed to score against the Hammers, who finished a respectable seventh with the fourth-best defensive record in the section.

Twenty-six thousand fans saw a 3-1 FA Cup win over Southampton in a first-round replay and a similar figure watched as Puddefoot's hat-trick helped remove Bury in round two. The end was nigh, however, and Hammers bowed out at Tottenham, 3-0.

Dominating the scoring, Puddefoot notched hat-tricks against Port Vale and Nottingham Forest in addition to the one against Bury. His efforts earned him a place in the international trial match at West Bromwich and subsequently, the England centre-forward spot in the Victory International at Cardiff.

After an excellent showing in the latter half of 1919-20, the complete defence of Ted Hufton, Bill Cope and Frank Burton was re-engaged for 1920-21. Other notable recruits were Danny Shea, returning to Upton Park after eight war-interrupted years in the north, and Jim Simmons, possessor of an FA Cup winners' medal earned with Sheffield United in 1915. New youngsters included Vic Watson and Syd Bishop.

Kicking off the new season with a visit from Hull City, Hammers dropped a point in a 1-1 draw. After winning at Wolverhampton with two goals from Puddefoot, defeat at Hull in the return game proved to be the only blemish in the opening nine games.

The fixtures in the period 1919 to 1924 were arranged so that, on Saturdays, the same opponents were met in consecutive weeks. The November games against Sheffield Wednesday produced five goals and all were scored by Puddefoot. But the Yorkshiremen had the last laugh, for when the teams met in a January cup-tie, an own-goal by Ted Hufton decided the issue.

At St Andrew's on Boxing Day, the gates were closed on 60,000 customers as Hammers were beaten 2-1 by Birmingham. Twenty-four hours earlier, Syd Bishop had scored in a Christmas-Day debut against the same opposition; and in January, Wilf James, bought from Portsmouth, scored against Clapton Orient on his debut.

Danny Shea went to Fulham before Christmas, leaving Dan Bailey, Syd Bishop and Les Robinson to battle for his place.

The 1921-2 season is often overlooked when assessing Hammers' achievements, yet it deserves close examination. Never out of the top four after December, West Ham occupied second place throughout January and February. Points were won off both promoted clubs, Nottingham Forest and Stoke, but a poor spell of only three points from the final seven fixtures denied the East Enders promotion. Before the season had started, Frank Burton went to Charlton Athletic and George Butcher joined Luton, but Syd King was confident that the replacements were adequate. Jack Hebden, later to captain the Boleyn men, was brought from Bradford City but he broke an ankle at Derby in December. Several different men filled in during his absence, namely Turner, Cope and William Waugh, a youth from Bedlington, County Durham. But it was not until Billy Henderson arrived from Aberdare that a satisfactory replacement was found. Apart from an eight-match absence at the start of 1922-3, the Whitburn-born full-back filled the spot for most of the time until 1925-6.

Two other newcomers worthy of note were Jimmy Ruffell and William Brown, both going on to make significant contributions the following season. Syd King was also particularly pleased to have captured the services of Billy Williams, the East Ham boy who was captain of the England Schools team.

West Ham's part in the 1921-2 FA Cup competition was another disappointment. After the previous term's defeat in the first round, Hammers failed at the same stage again, although this time they had three attempts. A drawn game at Upton Park against Swansea Town was followed by another deadlock at the Vetch Field. A third game, at Ashton Gate, Bristol, was won by Spottiswood's goal for the Third Division club.

At the end of the season, skipper Billy Cope said goodbye to Upton Park and joined Wrexham. His place in the side for 1922-3 was at first filled by Tommy Hodgson. Alhough the teenager promised to solve one of the full-back problems, he never quite established himself at Upton Park. He did, however, later become an important part of Luton Town's set-up.

In February 1922, the most disturbing event of the season occurred when Syd Puddefoot was sold to Falkirk. It was a most unlikely destination for such a talented Englishman and the sale caused a good deal of bad feeling between supporters and the club. The fan's anger soon subsided when it was realised that, in Vic Watson, there was a ready-made replacement. Watson scored in each of the three games following Puddefoot's departure, dispelling any fears supporters might have had about his ability.

Both Billy Brown and Jimmy Ruffell were given a few outings in the second half of the season so, by the end of 1921-2, the following term's successful side was almost assembled.

Summer signings included Crossley (from Everton), Dick Richards (Wolves) and Billy Moore (Sunderland). The new skipper was George Kay who took over from the departed Billy Cope.

Defeated at home by Bradford City in the first match of the new season, Hammers suffered six other reverses in the opening 13 fixtures. Pairing Jack Young and Billy Henderson at the back, Syd King stopped the slide. The pair had represented Whitburn, their home town, as full-backs in earlier years, but Young had since been used as a winger during a spell at Southend United.

By the time the FA Cup first round was due, the Londoners had recovered from their disastrous start. At the time of the tie at Hull, the Boleyn men were enjoying a splendid sequence of only one defeat in 11 games — and the next defeat was still 20 matches away.

Goals from Vic Watson (2) and Billy Moore ended Hull's Cup hopes for another season and earned Hammers a trip to Brighton. Brighton, highly placed in the old Third Division South and defeated only twice at home that season, were held to a 1-1 draw at the Goldstone. Jack Tresadern was the outstanding Hammer in the replay, but it was Billy Moore, stabbing at a hard cross by Ruffell, who got the winner.

Returning to the League, West Ham were held to a goalless draw by Leicester City at Upton Park but, five days later, they staggered City by winning 6-0 at Filbert Street. This unexpected lapse by Leicester almost certainly cost them promotion. Back in the Cup, Hammers had a comfortable 2-0 success at the expense of old Southern League rivals, Plymouth Argyle.

The attendance of over 30,000 at this match showed the East End was beginning to take the Cup run seriously. One League match separated the third round from the quarter-finals where West Ham's progress was temporarily halted at Southampton. Hammers were held to a draw at The Dell where they had lost a League game in October. Saints proved a hard nut to crack in the replay and surrendered an early lead only after a fierce struggle.

The second replay was initially scheduled for Stamford Bridge but, as the winners would be playing Derby County in the semi-final at that venue, it was switched to Villa Park. Hammers' previous visit to this ground in February 1913 had ended in a 5-0 defeat.

This time West Ham enjoyed control of almost all the proceedings and cruised home, albeit by the narrowest possible margin. Billy Brown diverted a Dick Richards free kick past Lock, the Saints' goalkeeper. Having taken so long to dispose of Southampton, there was no time for West Ham to fit in any League matches before the semi-final against Derby.

It was an all-Second Division tie and the League games between the clubs had provided Derby with three points. Those games, though, had been during West Ham's black period at the beginning of the season. To reach the semi-final, Derby had beaten Blackpool, Bristol City, Sheffield Wednesday and Tottenham Hotspur, and in doing so had not conceded a goal.

Yet within seven minutes of the start at Stamford Bridge they were two goals down. In West Ham's most impressive display of the season, the Rams were swept aside, 5-2, in front of 51,000 spectators. Billy Brown and Billy Moore each scored twice, and Richards once, in helping the Upton Park side become only the third of London's professional clubs to reach the FA Cup Final.

In the other semi-final at Old Trafford, a David Jack goal ensured Bolton Wanderers a place in what would be the first FA Cup Final to be staged at Wembley.

A backlog of League fixtures now meant that the East Enders had 11 games to play in the remaining six weeks of the season. In addition, of course, to their appointment at Wembley.

Hammers played nine League matches between the Cup semi-final and the great day at the Empire Stadium. Five goals were scored in two consecutive away games, at Crystal Palace and Bury, but the 23-match unbeaten run came to an end at Barnsley when the home side won 2-0.

Refusing to rest any player, King fielded his strongest team right up to the Final. As the big day approached, there were fitness scares over Jimmy Ruffell, Vic Watson, Jack Young and Ted Hufton, but all reported fit by 28 April. In the week leading up to the Final, the players were taken to the brine baths at Southend, the races at Epsom and a show at the Adelphi Theatre in the Strand.

Syd King made what was probably the most interesting contribution to Cup Final week when he made a radio broadcast from the '2LO' station at Savoy Hill, his subject — 'Our Prospects at Wembley'. Of events on the day itself, they were described by the contemporary press as 'a fiasco' and 'chaotic' — and those were the kinder comments.

The match was ruined as a spectacle by the proximity of the huge crowd. Once or twice the match was halted as the vast sea of spectators spilled on to the playing area. There is little doubt that, but for the presence of King George V, the contest would never have started.

At the end of the day, the Boltonians handled the conditions better, scored enough goals (one after only two minutes), and carried off the Cup.

With the big event out of the way, Hammers rejoined the scramble for promotion. In a desperate finish that went to the very last day of the season, they edged home in second place behind Notts County, with Leicester City third.

The 'White Horse Final'

THERE MUST have been a thousand words printed for every one of the estimated 200,000 fans who turned up to witness Wembley's first-ever FA Cup Final, since that dramatic April day in 1923.

Uncovering unpublished details and anecdotes of the match and the unprecedented events surrounding it becomes harder as time goes on.

We have, however, been fortunate to find one grand old man who witnessed at first-hand the chaos and near-catastrophe which took place over 60 years ago.

Previously unrecorded in print, Albert York of Dagenham gives us a fascinating insight to what it was like on his trip to Wembley that day, recalled in his own words . . .

"I'll never forget that match because I set off in the early hours of the morning to walk to Wembley.

"After tramping several foot-weary miles I noticed a barrow-boy pushing a cartload of fruit, apples and pears and the like. So I fell in behind him.

"Every now and then an apple or pear would tumble from his overladen cart, and my they tasted good! Helping to sustain me on the journey which, by the time we neared Wembley, had begun to take on the look of a procession.

"By this time I'd got friendly with the barrow-boy and helped him to sell his wares to our hungry fellow-travellers. A farthing an apple, halfpenny a pear! When everything was sold we went into the match through a broken gate and joined

Happy Hammers fans on their way to Wembley.

28

the heaving, sweating cloth-capped mass of humanity, but hardly saw a thing of the action because of the immense crowd."

A moving account, but what of this game of which Albert saw so little? When the pitch was finally cleared of the vast crowd which had spilled almost involuntarily over the barriers, 'Olympian' filed this report for the *Bolton Evening News*:

"Joe Smith won the toss from George Kay and set West Ham to face the wind and sun, and before the crowd had settled down to enjoy the game, the Wanderers were well on their way to victory.

"It was a dramatic start, and the goal which David Jack scored after only three minutes had its influence on the subsequent play. It is easier to play a game fraught with vital issues when you are a goal to the good, and it says much for the morale of the West Ham players that they made the contest interesting, and never caused to try to discover a weakness in the Bolton rearguard.

"There was a ten minutes' stoppage early in the contest in consequence of the crowd again encroaching.

"The ball control, the method and the craftmanship of the Wanderers' players were superior to that of their opponents; who had plenty of pace, swung the ball about with good judgement, and never spared themselves. Twice in the first-half, the Wanderers, who kept the ball on the ground with rare discretion, might easily have lost the lead. From a corner placed nicely by Ruffell, Pym and one of his colleagues both failed to get away a high ball, and Watson, in his eagerness to make the most of a gilt-edged chance, propelled the ball over the bar.

"The other attack which placed the Bolton goal in jeopardy emanated from the

Near kick-off the crush outside the ground intensified.

More fans trying to escape the hordes and see the game.

Mounted police hold back part of the huge Wembley crowd.

right-wing, Richards, cutting in towards goal and smartly making his way past Jennings and Finney, shot obliquely when everyone expected him to centre; and Pym, who advanced, pulled up just in time to thrust out his right foot, and so arrest a ball that would have otherwise gone into the net.

"But as against these escapes must be set the goal which John Smith obtained

Kick-off is still some time away as the stadium authorities ponder their next move.

from a centre by Butler after 38 minutes. Butler dribbled to within two yards of the line before he delivered a square centre, and racing in Smith just got his outstretched foot to the ball, which Hufton touched on its way into the net. The referee gave Smith offside, a palpably wrong decision for the simple reason that the scorer was always behind the ball. A Liverpool and a London pressman agreed with me that the Wanderers had been deprived of a perfectly legitimate goal. Happily, it did not effect the issue.

"In the early stages of the second-half, West Ham certainly played well enough to inspire amongst their followers the hope that they would make a fight of it, but that hope vanished within nine minutes of the cross-over, when J.R.Smith got a second goal for the Wanderers.

"From that moment West Ham were a beaten team. Such method as they had shown in the early stages gradually died away, and playing well within themselves the Wanderers finished the game confident and comfortable winners."

There can be little doubt that had it not been for the good-humoured nature of the crowd the game would never have started. Certainly, a match held in similar circumstances today would never get underway. The cheerful mood spread to the players, too, for when the teams tossed up for the delayed start Hammers captain George Kay shouted out, "What about the white horse on the penalty-spot, ref?" He was referring to the famous steed, Billie, mounted by Constable F.A.Storey and which symbolised for everyone the way in which order was restored out of total chaos.

31

West Ham players look bewildered as play is suspended.

But West Ham's legendary trainer and later manager, Charlie Paynter, had a different view after the match.

"It was a pitch made for us until folks tramped all over the place and that white horse thumped its big feet into the pitch. When the game started it was hopeless. Our wingers, Ruffell and Richards were tumbling all over the place, tripping up in great ruts and holes".

But George Kay remained onwardly philosophical: "The better team won, we did not touch our real form." Although Hammers' inside-forward Billy Moore agreed with his trainer about the reasons for defeat, "Ruffell and Richards could have won the game on the flanks. We really fancied our chances."

Both teams had had a hard slog to the final, Bolton disposing of Norwich, Leeds, Huddersfield (after a replay), Charlton and Sheffield United in the Old Trafford semi-final for a goals total of 9-2.

West Ham put out Hull City, Brighton and Hove Albion (after a replay), Plymouth, Southampton (after two replays) and Derby County in their semi-final at Stamford Bridge for an aggregate of 15-7.

After the Final victorious Bolton left with a horde of their delirious supporters for a London banquet and later a reception at the House of Commons, addressed by David Lloyd George. And at Piccadilly Circus that night, the roads were impassable

At a later commemorative dinner given by the club, each of the regular first-team players was presented with a gold watch acknowledging their contribution in Hammers' promotion to the First Division of the Football League in 1923.

As a reward for the splendid endeavours of 1922-3, West Ham United earned themselves nine seasons of First Division football. Never threatening the supremacy of the Northern and Midland clubs, the Londoners only twice ended a season in the top half of the table.

The match is under way and West Ham's Moore receives a pass from Ruffell.

because of the noisy celebrations of the northern visitors.

Despite their defeat West Ham had dinner at Brent House, Golders Green and then made their way by an illuminated and claret and blue decorated tramcar to Canning Town where they met the Mayor and Councillors of West Ham and thousands of celebrating supporters.

Bolton Wanderers: Pym; Haworth, Finney, Nuttall, Seddon, Jennings, Butler, Jack, J.R.Smith, J.Smith, Vizard.

West Ham United: Hufton; Henderson, Young, Bishop, Kay, Tresadern, Richards, Brown, Watson, Moore, Ruffell.

Referee: D.H.Asson (West Bromwich)   *Attendance: 126,047*

Footnote: All gate records were broken at the match, but no correct return was possible, owing to the crowds breaking in. The official figures returned by the Empire Exhibition authorities were that 90,520 persons paid through the turnstiles and 35,527 ticket holders were admitted, making a total of 126,047. Various estimates were made of the crowd, whose actual number will always remain a mystery, but it is probable that 200,000 persons were at the stadium on that memorable day. The gross gate was £27,776. The amount paid in entertainment tax was £4,206. The British Empire Exhibition share was £4,714. West Ham United, Bolton Wanderers and the Football Association each received £6,365 1s. 8d. The FA refunded to ticket holders, who were unable to get to their seats, £2,797.

FA Cup tournaments told a similar tale. Following the glory days of 1923, Syd King's men failed miserably in attempting to recapture the Cup form of that year. Two appearances in the quarter-finals in nine attempts, plus three defeats at the hands of clubs from a lower division, made it a depressing period.

Despite their failings as a team, the players received plenty of recognition as individuals. Eight Hammers won international caps in the years 1924 to 1932.

Jim Barrett, albeit for only eight minutes, appeared in an England shirt, as did

Leeds United' defence is in a mess: George Kay has just scored West Ham's goal in the FA Cup second-round game at Upton Park in February 1924.

Billy Brown, Stan Earle, Ted Hufton, Jimmy Ruffell and Vic Watson. The most capped player at this time was amateur centre-forward Viv Gibbins, who turned out eight times for his country. Meanwhile, Wilf James and Dick Richards earned five Welsh caps between them. At a slightly lower level, Jim Barrett, Albert Cadwell and Jimmy Ruffell each appeared for the Football League.

Life in Division One began at Roker Park, Sunderland, where a goalless draw earned a point. Hammers' first goal in Division One was scored by Albert Fletcher, against Arsenal at Upton Park in the second match. It was Fletcher's only goal for West Ham.

Hammers found goals hard to come by and they scored only four in the next nine games, and only 19 up to the New Year. The Boleyn men could claim, however, that their leading goalscorer, Vic Watson, had been sidelined for most of that time with a foot injury. Attendances showed a vast improvement on any previous season and only four Saturday games failed to attract a 20,000-plus crowd to the Boleyn.

Hopes were raised in the FA Cup when West Ham thumped Third Division Aberdare Athletic, 5-0, but Leeds United, the Second Division leaders, then eliminated the Londoners at the second attempt.

For the last engagement of the season, a railway accident delayed visitors Manchester City for two and a half hours. Eighteen thousand spectators waited patiently, amusing themselves in song, but their wait was in vain. City's ordeal did not affect their performance and they won 2-1.

During the season, Billy Brown left to help Chelsea avoid the drop into Division Two, and Percy Allen, not a first-teamer, went to Northampton Town.

To offset the loss of Brown, Hammers gained the services of Stanley Earle, an amateur from Clapton with experience of First Division soccer at Arsenal. Another newcomer was Sam Jennings, a centre-forward from Reading, brought to understudy

Hammers' chief goalscorer; but Vic Watson remained fit and kept the Nottingham-born man in the reserves. Jennings, however, did have the distinction of scoring West Ham's opening goal of 1924-5, against Preston. Curiously, his only other goals that term came against Nottingham Forest, who accompanied North End into the Second Division at the end of the season.

Watson's presence in the West Ham forward line certainly improved matters. There was a 50 per cent increase in goals scored but, unfortunately, the defence was 'leaking' at a similar rate. Five goals were conceded at both Burnley and Bolton, whilst Newcastle United, West Brom, Bury and Notts County managed four.

An end-of-season flourish saw Syd King's men hit Sheffield United for six, beat Everton 4-2, and then grab a point in a 1-1 draw at Roker Park.

The highlight of the season was the 2-1 win at Huddersfield in January, Hammers thus becoming one of only two clubs to record two goals against the First Division Champions in a match at Leeds Road.

In the FA Cup, West Ham beat Arsenal at the third attempt, and Nottingham Forest at the City Ground, but were then unexpectedly knocked out in a replay at Blackpool who were, at that time, close to the bottom of Division Two.

All told, Arsenal were beaten three times by the Hammers in 1924-5, a rare demonstration of East London's superiority over the northern district. It was in this campaign that Jack Tresadern's ability at last began to desert him, and the 4-1 defeat at Newcastle in September proved to be his last outing for West Ham. In November, the popular wing-half moved to the claret and blue of Burnley.

George Carter played at right-half for most of the remaining matches and began the following season in the same spot.

That summer saw the completion of the new West Stand, providing seats for 4,800 and cover for a further 10,000 standing.

The new season also saw a change in the offside law that now required an attacker to have two, not three, opponents between him and the opposing goal-line to avoid infringing the law.

The old law had inhibited forwards, thanks to some intelligent tactical moves led by the Newcastle defender Billy McCracken, and the change appeared to have the desired effect when Aston Villa managed ten goals against Burnley on the first day of the new arrangement. Hammers scored only one, however, against newly-promoted Manchester United. Conceding only one goal in the opening five games, the Boleyn club's defence seemed to have got it right, but five goals by Leeds United on 19 September opened the floodgates and 49 were in the 'against' column by the New Year. Seven were contributed by West Brom where George Kay made his only appearance in the first half of the season.

On Christmas Day, Stanley Earle got a hat-trick against Aston Villa, and on the last day of January, Jim Barrett did likewise in the 4-2 revenge over Leeds. Played only three times at centre-forward, Barrett scored on each occasion.

George Kay's return stemmed the flow of goals against and only 26 were conceded after the re-instatement of the skipper.

The FA Cup was a one-match affair, a rampant Spurs assisted by Bill Kaine, the former Hammers' goalkeeper, won 5-0 at White Hart Lane. Jimmy Dimmock, hero of Tottenham's Cup triumph of 1921, scored a hat-trick.

Hammers' final League placing was 18th in 1925-6, but the season had been crowded with injuries. Suffering a broken nose, followed by complications, during the club's close season tour of Spain, George Kay was unable to take part in the opening games of 1926-7. Syd Bishop took over the captaincy but his form was so inconsistent that when an offer for him was received from Leicester City, the board allowed him to leave.

Unable to call on Tommy Hodgson, Albert Cadwell or Alf Earl, for one reason or another, the Boleyn side were severely handicapped from the start. Stan Earle suggested he was ready by scoring three goals in the second public trial match. He scored in the opening fixture, against Leicester City, as well, but then had to wait several weeks before finding the net again.

The defence was 'meaner' than the previous season, and the attack more enterprising. Hammers' away record was a revelation. By the season's end, ten wins on opponents' grounds had been achieved, a figure bettered only in the promotion season and one which would not be passed again until 1958.

Syd Puddefoot made a three-goal return to Upton Park in September — but he was wearing a Blackburn Rovers shirt. Jack Hebden was carried off, badly concussed, in the same match, but the full-back was sufficiently recovered to report for training the following Monday morning. Hebden was made skipper after the departure of Syd Bishop.

One of the quickest goals ever scored by a visiting side at Upton Park was netted by Armand of Leeds United in December. The goal, inside 30 seconds, did nothing to help Leeds to victory, however, and West Ham won 3-2.

A double over Birmingham at Christmas was followed by a massive 'gate' for the Cup tie against Spurs in January.

The interest in this match was enormous. Queues began forming outside the Boleyn Ground at 6am. At 12.30pm, the gates were opened, then closed again at 2pm with a crowd of 44,417 inside. Police reported not a moment of unrest or discord from the huge gathering, and Watson's three goals ensured ample revenge for Spurs' ruthless mauling of the Hammers a year earlier.

In successive weeks in February, Syd King's side defeated Championship hopefuls, Huddersfield Town and Sunderland, both by 3-2; then they lost at home to bottom club, West Brom, 2-1.

Sixth place was a big improvement on the previous year's 18th. Vic Watson's 34 goals placed him high on the First Division list, but equally pleasing was the fact that two others, Jimmy Ruffell and Stanley Earle, also got into double figures.

The 1927-8 First Division Championship was won by Everton, for whom Dixie Dean scored a record 60 goals. Hammers' top scorer was Jimmy Ruffell with a mere 18. At Goodison in October, both teams were weakened by international calls, but the Merseysiders overcame the problem best, winning 7-0. The defeat equalled West Ham's previous worst scoreline, at Barnsley in 1919.

In a season that saw some massive attendances at Upton Park, the visits of Arsenal, Spurs and Everton all threatened the record 'gate'.

A Boxing Day fixture at Bramall Lane saw Harry Johnson, Sheffield United's centre-forward, hit five goals against Hammers to establish the best individual scoring performance against West Ham by an opposing player. After disposing of First Division newcomers, Portsmouth, at Fratton Park in the FA Cup, Syd King's men were eliminated at Huddersfield.

Opening the 1928-9 season with 14 goals in four games, the Hammers piled up 86 in the campaign to equal their previous best, set two seasons earlier. The defence, however, also reached new 'heights' in conceding 96 goals. Alf Earl and Tommy Hodgson were the regular full-backs but occasionally Cyril Norrington deputised.

Vic Watson fell just short of his best total in netting 29 times, but in one splendid display, he hit six of West Ham's eight goals in the game against Leeds United.

A rather fortunate victory over Sunderland in the FA Cup third round was followed by a much more convincing 3-0 triumph over the amateur Corinthians. The largest Boleyn crowd of the season, some 42,000, saw Earle, Watson and Gibbins score the match-winning goals.

West Ham survived a tough trip to Third Division Bournemouth in the fifth

West Ham goalkeeper Ted Hufton, a mainstay of the side in the 1920s, with over 400 senior appearances for the club altogether.

round when a Tommy Yews goal earned them a replay. The same player scored one of the goals in Hammers' 3-1 success at Upton Park.

Big Jim Barrett filled the inside-left berth in the Bournemouth replay and he continued in that position for the sixth-round tie at Fratton Park. Two goals by Barrett were not enough, however, and Hammers went out after a gallant fight. Portsmouth eventually reached their first Wembley Final.

A heavy reduction in West Ham's goals-against column accounted for an improved League position at the end of 1929-30. Once again, 86 goals were scored, 42 of them coming from Vic Watson, who thus set what is still the best total by one Hammers' player in a single season. Watson scored hat-tricks against Aston Villa, both home and away, another achievement still unmatched by any other West Ham

Another Cup game against Leeds and this time it is the Hammers' turn to look in disarray as Hufton is bundled over the line for a goal to the visitors at Upton Park in January 1930. But West Ham went on to reach the quarter-finals before losing to Arsenal.

player. But his real venom was saved for Leeds United, against whom he netted nine goals (five in the League and four in the FA Cup) in three games.

The highest attendance of the season at Upton Park saw a sixth-round FA Cup tie against Arsenal. For the third successive season, Hammers were defeated by a team destined for Wembley.

For the closing match of 1929-30, West Ham faced a Newcastle United side doomed to relegation unless they could take both points from the Londoners. After a tense struggle, Devine's second-half goal sent 48,000 Geordies wild with delight and saved Newcastle from the Second Division. Returning from their exertions at St James' Park, West Ham defeated Brentford in the London Challenge Cup Final to record their third success in the competition in five years.

A serious injury to Vic Watson, at Newcastle in September, forced the centre-forward to miss more than half the 1930-31 season. The amateur player, Viv Gibbins, proved a useful deputy but could not match Watson's scoring record. At the back, nervous defenders gave weak-hearted supporters palpitations as opponents pumped 94 goals into the West Ham net. Ted Hufton was absent for most of the campaign, but when he was available, the goalkeeper, now 38, was conceding goals at no less a rate than his young deputy, Rob Dixon.

In the FA Cup, Hammers failed to progress further than the third round for the first time since 1926, their involvement beginning and ending at Stamford Bridge, the venue of the club's great semi-final triumph of 1923.

West Ham's 7-0 thrashing of Liverpool in September 1930 equalled the club's previous-best winning margin (against Coventry in January 1921 and over Arsenal in March 1927) but the impetus was lost at Villa Park five days later when Billy Walker's side crushed the Londoners 6-1. If the 1930-31 season had been disappointing, then 1931-2 proved disastrous. After a promising opening spell in which Hammers recorded their first-ever victory at Bolton, the team began a steady decline. By the middle of March, the club was in desperate trouble. Not even the return of former idol, Syd Puddefoot, could halt the slide.

Constant team changes and permutations of established players failed to prevent the drop into the Second Division. The win against Derby County in March 1932 proved to be the club's final First Division success until the defeat of Portsmouth in August 1958. Gathering only one point from the concluding ten games, the Boleyn side slid down the table at an alarming rate.

The irony of West Ham's situation was that in 42 First Division games they had failed to score on only four occasions. They did however have 'their day' and it came on 5 December when Champions-elect, Everton, were tormented by the magic of Jimmy Ruffell. West Ham's England winger tore the Everton defence apart, scoring a hat-trick in a 4-2 triumph. After an away win at Charlton in the third round, the Boleyn men went out of the FA Cup at Stamford Bridge. It was the second year running that they had failed in the Cup on that ground. Back in the Second Division after nine years in the top grade, West Ham made a dreadful start. Two wins in the opening 13 fixtures saw them firmly placed at the wrong end of the table. Such poor form may have been due to the constant changes in the staff. Long-serving goalkeeper Ted Hufton had gone to Watford, and Stanley Earle to Clapton Orient, whilst Vivian Gibbins now wore the colours of Brentford. New arrivals included Albert Walker, Arthur Wilson, a goalscorer from Southampton, and the Mills brothers, Hugh and George.

From the middle of November, results improved slightly and by February, a relatively respectable League placing had been attained. In the meantime, events off the field captured the attention. Syd King, the secretary and manager for almost 30 years, was under strain following the depressing results of recent months. At a board meeting in November 1932, he allegedly used abusive words in a clash with directors and was immediately relieved of his duties. Charlie Paynter, long-time trainer and a highly-respected individual in the football world, was put in charge, and the whole affair had a sad ending. In January 1933, Syd King died in St Mary's Hospital, Plaistow. An inquest returned a verdict of 'suicide while of unsound mind'.

The Hammers go behind following a corner at Molineux in the 1933 FA Cup semi-final against Everton.

On the day after Syd King's tragic death, Hammers began an FA Cup run that took them to within 90 minutes of their second Wembley Final. In turn, Corinthians, West Brom, Brighton (after a record attendance at the Goldstone, and then a replay), and Birmingham were eliminated before Everton barred Hammers' way in the semi-final at Wolverhampton. East London's dreams were ended at Molineux where goals by Critchley and Dunn, against one by Vic Watson, sent the Toffees to Wembley. Returning to their problems in the League, a 3-1 defeat at Charlton pushed West Ham into 21st place; and a defeat at Chesterfield on Good Friday sent them to the bottom.

Then a splendid recovery took place, and by winning four of the last five matches — which included a fine victory over Tottenham — the drop was avoided by a single point. Twentieth place in Division Two in 1932-3 is the lowest final position occupied by the Hammers since gaining admission to the Football League in 1919. The most notable newcomer for 1933-4 was the stylish Joe Cockroft from Gainsborough. He quickly established himself in the side and in one spell, played in more than 200 consecutive matches. Both Ted Fenton and Len Goulden had made their League debuts in 1932-3 and in 1933-4, the youngsters totalled more than 50 appearances between them.

As the Hammers set about re-establishing themselves, Preston North End, the League leaders, received a taste of West Ham's new-found determination. Within the first 12 minutes of their fixture at Upton Park, the visitors were 3-0 down and eventually conceded six.

Vic Watson scored a hat-trick against Preston, a feat he repeated against Lincoln City and Fulham. Earlier, Len Goulden had netted three goals at Plymouth; and in March, Ted Fenton hit three against Bury, his first goals for the club. For the fourth time since World War One, West Ham and Spurs were paired in the FA Cup; and for the third time Tottenham came off best, winning 4-1 at White Hart Lane. By August 1934, West Ham had made a complete recovery from the ordeals of 1931-33 and were seriously anticipating a return to Division One. Although well-blessed with capable goalkeepers, George Watson, McMahon and John Rutherford, Hammers bought Herman Conway from Burnley. Always a fruitful source of talent in the past, Gainsborough Trinity allowed Stan Foxall to join former colleagues, Jimmy Morton and Joe Cockroft, at Upton Park.

The new season began untidily. First, the opening match was postponed due to a closure order on the Hull City ground; then four of the next six fixtures were lost. Seventeen goals were conceded in those first matches, but Hammers persevered with Conway and his defensive colleagues. At the end of the campaign, Paynter's confidence had been rewarded and 63 goals against was the best since 1925. Up front, Hugh Mills scored goals in every one of nine consecutive matches between September and November, and Jimmy Ruffell did likewise in all seven matches in December.

Dick Walker, who was to become one of West Ham's long-serving players, made his debut against Burnley in 1934-5, but the Upton Park regulars were witnessing the twilight of the popular Vic Watson's career with West Ham. In March, he played his final League game in a Hammers' shirt and started the following campaign with Southampton. As Watson moved out, Dave Mangnall (from Birmingham) and Dr James Marshall (Arsenal) moved in. Both men were much in evidence for the rest of the season.

A fine sequence of results during February and March carried Hammers into second place, but a 3-1 defeat at Bolton a month later, condemned the Londoners to a further term of Second Division soccer.

West Ham's interest in the FA Cup lasted a brief three hours. At home to Stockport County of the Third Division North, Hammers were leading by a goal until Jim

Barrett headed past his own goalkeeper in the last minute. In the replay at Edgeley Park, a third-minute goal by the home side was defended gallantly for 87 minutes to see the County into the fourth round.

Returning from a summer tour of Sweden, West Ham were reinforced by the signing of Crystal Palace's 28-year-old record scorer, Peter Simpson. Among the younger intake was Benny Fenton, a former pupil of Godwin Road School and a brother of Hammers' half-back Ted Fenton.

After an indifferent start, West Ham finished a creditable fourth behind Manchester United, Charlton Athletic and Sheffield United. They did, however, out-gun all three clubs in scoring 90 goals, a total bettered only by Blackpool (93) and Spurs (91). Manchester United, Division Two title-winners in 1935-6, were beaten 3-2 by Hammers at Old Trafford, but United then won at Upton Park. The second promotion place virtually hinged on the final game at the Boleyn, against fellow candidates Charlton Athletic. A 43,000 crowd saw Charlton, who a year earlier were playing in Division Three South, prevail over West Ham's greater experience. In a third round FA Cup tie, another huge attendance at Upton Park saw Jimmy Ruffell save West Ham's blushes when he scored a late equaliser against Third Division South leaders, Luton Town. On a frost-bound Kenilworth Road pitch, Luton won the replay 4-0.

An important signing in the latter weeks of 1935-6 was Charlie Bicknell, a full-back from Bradford City. In Charlie Walker he would find an able full-back partner and the two, with goalkeeper Reg Weare from Wolverhampton Wanderers, would form the Hammers' defence for most of 1936-7. Fred Dell was brought from Dartford and billed as the 'new Charlie Buchan', and Norman Corbett was recruited from Heart of Midlothian. The loss of Dave Mangnall to Millwall forced Paynter to seek a replacement. He bought Sam Small from Birmingham before Tudor Martin became available at Swansea. Both came to Upton Park and although Martin made the bigger initial impact, Small proved more durable. Martin's three goals on his debut at Newcastle was the only hat-trick by a West Ham player all season.

There was no flirting with promotion this season, although Hammers finished in storming fashion. Conceding only three goals in the last nine games, Paynter's men gathered 14 points along the way. In the FA Cup, Bolton inflicted a third-round knock-out in a Burnden Park replay, Hammers failing to score in either match. At the end of the season, Len Goulden was West Ham's top-scorer with 15, one ahead of Jimmy Morton.

West Ham's 1937-8 season was disappointing and home attendances slipped significantly. Poor away form, though, was mainly responsible for the club's mid-table position and it was in the very last trip, to Chesterfield, that a victory was finally achieved.

Dr James Marshall chose the summer of 1937 to retire and take up a post with Bermondsey Borough Council; and Peter Simpson decided a move might help his career and joined Reading.

The most exciting newcomer of 1937 was Archie Macaulay, an inside-forward from Glasgow Rangers. Experiencing trouble with the centre-forward spot, Paynter experimented with Macaulay in a Combination game. The Scot duly obliged by scoring six times against Queen's Park Rangers Reserves.

For the fourth time in as many years, West Ham made an early exit in the FA Cup, this time at Preston where George Mutch's hat-trick went unanswered. Three months later, Mutch would score the most important goal of his life and win the Cup for Preston.

Following several years of neglect, a West Ham player, Len Goulden, was selected for the Football League team and he scored in the 3-0 success over the Irish League.

West Ham United, 1938-39. Back row (left to right): Corbett, Bicknell, Conway, R.Walker, C.Walker, Proudlock. Front row: Foxall, Macaulay, Small, Goulden, Cockroft, Morton.

A new goalkeeper, Harry Medhurst from Woking, was signed to understudy Herman Conway in what was to become the last peacetime season for seven years.

Medhurst, who was then 22, shared the goalkeeping duties throughout the season, conceding 18 goals, whilst the experienced Conway let in 34. The two Charlies, Bicknell and Walker, were still first-choice full-backs, with Alf Chalkley their deputy. Steve Forde, from Rotherham United, had been added to the staff in January 1937 and a year later, Arthur Banner joined from Doncaster Rovers. The high-scoring amateur forward, George Foreman of Walthamstow Avenue, was induced to sign professional forms and he played regularly throughout the war. Within a week of playing on the losing side in the 1939 Wembley Cup Final, Stan Burton, the Wolves' winger, signed for West Ham. Burton played for three clubs during that season, having started it with Doncaster Rovers.

The opening match of 1938-9 was a Football League Jubilee Fund Game against Fulham at Upton Park. Hammers won 4-2, but a week later were defeated at Fulham in the season's first League game. Losing their first three League matches, Hammers soon settled down to occupy a mid-table position. Occasionally sparking to life, they ran up scores of six against Tranmere (of which Macaulay netted three); five against Swansea Town; five against Nottingham Forest; and six at Norwich, where Sam Small got three.

The feature of the season, however, was the FA Cup battle against Spurs. Drawn against the North London side for the fifth time since World War One, Hammers were taken to three matches. Stan Foxall was the hero of all three games. Two

When West Ham equalised in their FA Cup tie against Tottenham Hotspur at Upton Park in January 1939, a spectator ran on to the pitch and kicked the ball back upfield.

late goals from him at Upton Park wiped out a two-goal Tottenham lead; and in the replay, he notched a second-half equaliser. But on a muddy Highbury pitch in February, he crowned all that with the goal that finally put Hammers through. A total of 150,000 people witnessed the three ties and the manner of the victory made up for all the disappointments suffered at the hands of Spurs in earlier years. The effort was all in vain, however, for at the next hurdle, First Division Portsmouth comfortably defeated the Londoners 2-0. It was the sixth time since 1928 that West Ham had been eliminated by a side on their way to a Wembley Final.

"In 1939, we really and sincerely thought we were going to do it. We had the balance, the power and the experience necessary. We saw it as our season of fulfillment". They were the words written by Ted Fenton in his book *At Home With The Hammers*. Regretably, his hopes, and those of many others, were dashed by World War Two.

On a Saturday afternoon in August 1946, normal peacetime soccer was welcomed back. West Ham's senior side kicked off again at much-blitzed Plymouth, while the reserve team played before a crowd, some of whom watched from under roofless stands at Upton Park.

Of the side beaten 3-1 at Plymouth, Medhurst, Attwell and Macaulay would shortly be on the move; and while Sam Small started the campaign at centre-forward, he would soon be shifted to inside-left to make way for Chelsea's prolific scorer, Joe Payne. By the time 'Ten-goal Joe' arrived, in December, the Hammers had been defeated ten times. Payne scored six times in ten games including a goal on his debut, before injury forced him to retire.

Charlie Paynter replaced Payne with the signing of Frank Neary from Queen's Park Rangers. Neary, who arrived during that year's atrocious winter, was a 'physical' player with a fierce shot. He netted two goals in a game on five occasions, plus a first-half hat-trick against West Brom before moving to Leyton Orient shortly after the start of 1947-8.

In the FA Cup, Hammers met Leicester City for the very first time. The Filberts won all three encounters with Hammers in 1946-7.

The heaviest defeat of the season was saved for the last home game, when beaten Cup Finalists, Burnley, fielding ex-Hammer Reg Attwell, won the points needed to ensure promotion with a 5-0 victory.

Dick Walker, skipper of the side since the appointment of Charlie Bicknell as manager of Bedford Town, scored the opening goal of the new season, 1947-8, at Park Avenue, Bradford. The Yorkshire team contained 25-year-old Ron Greenwood, and George Wilkins, whose son, Ray, later played for England. West Ham's new full-back, Jack Yeomanson from Margate, made his debut in that match.

Another new signing, Tommy Moroney from Cork, quickly established himself in the team, as did Eric Parsons, once he got a chance.

Hammers drew 14 League matches, nine of which ended 1-1, but Yorkshire venues became unpopular as defeats were suffered at Doncaster Rovers, Leeds United and Sheffield Wednesday, as well as Bradford.

There was an unexpected success at St Andrew's where Richard Dunn's only goal of the season embarrassed Birmingham's promotion bid.

At St James' Park, Newcastle, the post-war boom in attendances was highlighted when 55,000 watched a goal by Jackie Milburn beat Hammers 1-0. Seven days earlier, Ken Tucker, a week past his 22nd birthday, scored a debut hat-trick against Chesterfield.

Paynter still considered the forward line understrength and bought J. (Bill) Stephens from Swindon Town. Stephens broke a leg playing for West Ham but not before he had scored a hat-trick in a Good Friday fixture at Cardiff.

In the Cup, Hammers drew a third-round tie at Blackburn, who were 21st in Division One, after extra-time. It was a rare occurrence of the additional 30 minutes being used in a first match, the replay also required 120 minutes before Rovers won 4-2.

A minor 'invasion' by the Irish marked the close season of 1948. In May, Fred Kearns, Johnny Carroll, and Danny McGowan arrived to supplement the Republican presence of Tommy Moroney, Jimmy McGowan and Frank O'Farrell.

In the autumn of 1948, Scottish inside-forward, George Dick, a Cup Finalist with Blackpool a few months earlier, joined the Upton Park staff; and in January, Paynter signed 28-year-old Bill Robinson from Charlton Athletic. Robinson was a member of Athletic's successful Cup side of 1947.

Only one victory was recorded in the first eight games — over eventually promoted West Brom. Eddie Chapman, later to become West Ham's secretary, netted on his debut, against Coventry City. A goal in the following match at Plymouth made Chapman joint top-scorer at that point.

A double over Leeds United at Christmas was followed by a Cup defeat at Luton. Robinson scored on a losing debut at West Brom, but his presence visibly strengthened the front line. At White Hart Lane, 63,000 spectators — the largest crowd ever

Tottenham's Ted Ditchburn grabs the ball from West Ham centre-forward Bill Robinson at White Hart Lane in February 1949.

to watch Hammers — saw the improving visitors snatch a point. Robinson netted ten times in 17 outings in 1948-9, improved both those figures considerably the following term.

Among the 33,000 crowd for the Good Friday fixture at Upton Park was the Wolves team, 'Spying' on their Cup Final opponents, Leicester City.

Despite Robinson's increased output, Hammers finished 19th in 1949-50. The Second

Division title went to White Hart Lane where Hammers were beaten 4-1 in March. Spurs had won 1-0 at Upton Park earlier in the season.

After winning at Griffin Park in November, West Ham won only two further points away from home. Their home record was not much better, although Ipswich Town went down 5-1 at Upton Park in the Cup. Everton, a poorly-placed First Division side, did better, winning 2-1 to keep intact their 100 per cent Cup tie record over the Londoners.

Eight months after scoring his lightning goal against Barnsley, Ken Bainbridge played his last game in a West Ham shirt. A month later he was a Reading player and enjoyed a 'second career' at Elm Park.

Played at full-back Fred Kearns made his initial appearance against Chesterfield; and in the last days of the season, Jim Barrett junior made his debut at Blackburn.

In March 1950, club chairman, Mr W.J.Cearns, died. A hard, but fair man, he had guided West Ham through the difficult war years and during most of the frustrating time in the Second Division. He was succeeded by Mr Reg Pratt, a board member since 1941.

Another important administrative change took place in the summer when the highly-regarded Hammers' manager, Charlie Paynter, retired. Employed by the club in one form or another, Paynter's service stretched back to the early days at Canning Town. Widely known and very popular in the soccer world, the 72-year-old would be difficult to replace.

Ted Fenton, not unknown to Hammers fans, was the man chosen to take over and in anticipation of Paynter stepping down, Fenton had spent several months at Upton Park preparing for that eventuallity.

In September 1950, a testimonial match was staged for Paynter's benefit and many important dignitaries from the Football Association and the Football League attended.

An own-goal after only 30 seconds, by Hull City full-back Vigo Jensen, gave West Ham their opening goal of 1950-51. In the visiting side that day were Raich Carter and Don Revie.

Bill Robinson's hat-trick in September's game against Sheffield United included two penalties. Three times West Ham led in this extraordinary match which eventually went Sheffield's way, 5-3, helped by two own-goals by Ernie Devlin and a Furniss penalty. Sunderland-born Tommy Southren made his West Ham debut in this game.

After the match against Notts County in November, Eric Parsons joined Chelsea, with whom he was to gain a First Division Championship medal in 1955.

At Rotherham in October, Terry Woodgate put a blemish on Hammers' excellent disciplinary record when he was sent off.

Ted Fenton had by now sown the seeds of the youth policy, but he still had to seek talent in the transfer market. Albert Foan made his debut in the Hull City match, and before long, Harry Kinsell, Harry Hooper and Malcolm Allison would also make their first appearances. In the meantime, Frank O'Farrell at last got an opportunity when fellow countryman, Tommy Moroney, temporarily lost his place.

A disputed goal ended West Ham's Cup hopes at Stoke after a third-round home win over Cardiff City. John Bond, who came to Upton Park at the same time that Ted Fenton returned, made his League debut in the 2-1 win at Coventry City in February.

The 19-year-old Bond was one of two debutants that season. The other, Silvertown-born Roy Stroud, was an England Amateur international from Hendon FC, who turned out in the match at Notts County on Easter Monday.

A splendid crowd of 38,000 saw the Cup game against Blackpool at Upton Park. The Seasiders, a star-studded squad of entertainers in those days, boasted names

at Upton Park, for he joined Leyton Orient that summer. No other West Ham player has signed off with two goals in his final match for the club.

West Ham turned a surplus in the goals account (74-69) in 1955-6 into a defect (59-63) the following year and yet rose eight places in the table. Hammers and Fulham had provided the only Second Division London 'derbies' for the previous two seasons, but the promotion of Leyton Orient added another to the schedule. Fenton's men won all the points off their Brisbane Road neighbours in their first meetings since 1922-3.

Frank O'Farrell left for Preston in November 1956, in a deal that brought Eddie Lewis to Upton Park. Lewis made a scoring debut in the 2-1 home win over Leicester City, and he also scored in the third round Cup win over Grimsby Town, a match which saw young John Smith score twice — his first goals for the club.

Bob Wyllie, a Scottish goalkeeper from Blackpool, was drafted in for 13 mid-season games and was on the winning side in ten of them. Hammers won only 19 games all season.

The early games of 1957-8 gave no indication of what was in store. Five matches were lost in August and September, and included in those was a double by Sheffield United. Vic Keeble's signing from Newcastle United in October, changed all that. A former Colchester Grammar School boy, Keeble was good in the air and his deft flicks from head and foot added penetration to Hammers' front line. After a debut goal in a drawn game at Doncaster, Keeble went on to score 18 more, plus four in the Cup. John Dick, the chief beneficiary of Keeble's subtlety, matched his output with 23 League and Cup goals. Billy Dare was next best on 14, and the versatile John Smith also reached double figures. By Christmas 1957, Hammers had won 31 points and scored 47 goals. The defence, though, was far from impregnable and only two sides, Charlton Athletic and Stoke City, had so far failed to pierce it. The attack went from strength to strength, however. Eight goals were hit against a Rotherham team who were unlucky to meet West Ham in such rampant form. Six each were conceded by Lincoln City, Swansea Town and Bristol Rovers, and five by Huddersfield. Seven doubles were achieved, the last of which, at Middlesbrough, sending Hammers' large travelling contingent of supporters for that match wild with delight as it clinched the Second Division title.

The 101 goals which West Ham scored in 1957-8 is still their best total for a single season and is likely to remain so, but in terms of results alone, the side did less to get promotion in 1957-8 than to finish third in 1934-5.

The FA Cup provided some exciting entertainment. A Vic Keeble hat-trick helped beat Blackpool in the third round, but Stockport County, of the newly reformed Third Division, gave Hammers a scare before going down 3-2 at Upton Park in front of 36,000.

In a curious way, the fifth-round defeat by promotion rivals Fulham, increased Hammers' prospects of First Division football. Fulham became involved in a Cup run that went to a semi-final replay with Manchester United. The resultant backlog of fixtures and Fulham's hectic finish (six games in two weeks) saw the Cottagers fail.

In a triumph that was completely a 100 per cent team effort, Andy Malcolm's consistency was rewarded when he was chosen as the local newspaper's 'Player of the Year'.

West Ham were welcomed back to the First Division at Portsmouth on 23 August 1958. A large number of the 40,000 crowd were Hammers' fans who went into raptures when Keeble and Dick scored to start West Ham off with a win.

Within a week, defeats had been inflicted on both Wolves (the eventual champions) and Aston Villa (7-2), but Luton Town put a stop to Hammers' advance by winning 4-1 at Kenilworth Road.

Noel Dywer saves spectacularly from Nottingham Forest's Stuart Imlach at the Boleyn in December 1959.

An eagerly-awaited fixture with the rebuilt Manchester United side, decimated at Munich seven months earlier, was played on 8 September. After leading by three goals, Hammers only just scraped home on an exciting night that saw the debut of 17-year-old Bobby Moore. Moore was in the side because Malcolm Allison was ill. Club captain for the last four years, Allison had been sidelined by tuberculosis since early the previous season. In October 1958, following an operation to remove a lung, Allison retired and decided to go into coaching. A testimonial match was played at Upton Park in November and a 20,000-plus crowd were treated to 13 goals and a splendid evening's entertainment by some of the country's greatest talents. Jimmy Scoular, Ray Barlow, Brian Clough, Don Howe, Peter Brabrook and Bobby Charlton were in an All Star team. An injury to Graham Shaw resulted in young John Lyall being called upon to deputise for the All Stars.

Shortly after this event, the club announced its costliest signing when Phil Woosnam, a Welsh international was bought from Leyton Orient.

By the end of the season, doubles had been achieved against Spurs, at Christmas; Blackburn Rovers, against whom Vic Keeble got five in two games; Aston Villa and Portsmouth, the two relegated clubs; and Bolton Wanderers. The Cup, though, was destined elsewhere when Spurs defied their League form by beating West Ham 2-0. It was the seventh FA Cup meeting between the sides since 1920.

John Dick found goals as easy to come by in the First Division and he netted 27 times. Keeble scored 20 and the third man on the list was John Bond who, together with Cantwell, made occasional appearances in the forward line. By the beginning of 1958-9, Hammers' youth policy was beginning to bear fruit. Although a few youngsters like Alan Blackburn, the unfortunate Geoff Hallas, Terry Matthews and Fred Cooper, had preceeded him, Bobby Moore's inclusion at senior level opened the floodgates. In Moore's wake followed Tony Scott, Eddie Bovington, Martin Peters, Peter Shearing and Geoff Hurst; they were just some of a seemingly endless stream of Boleyn products. To stiffen this young team, players of some experience were drafted in, notably Noel Dwyer, Dave Dunmore, Lawrie Leslie, Johnny Byrne and Peter Brabrook.

A promising 3-0 home win over Leicester City kicked off the 1959-60 season. Following this with a draw at Preston and a 3-1 win at eventual champions, Burnley, the Hammers were off to a flying start. In November, the Boleyn men were getting close to the top of the table and a 3-1 win at Highbury, followed by a 3-2 victory over Wolves, put them there.

In November, a delighted Ken Brown donned an England shirt for the only time, but his, and West Ham's world came crashing down a few days later. At Hillsborough on the last Saturday in November the elusive Johnny Fantham scored twice as Sheffield Wednesday enjoyed a 7-0 thrashing of top-of-the-table West Ham. The season turned into a nightmare as 91 goals were conceded. In losing 16 games after November, Hammers tumbled from top to 14th in the table, and at the finish were only four points above a relegation place.

Burnley avenged their early season reverse by Hammers, winning 5-2 at Upton Park in January. On a bitterly cold Thursday afternoon two weeks later, Ted Fenton's men went out of the Cup when Huddersfield Town, inspired by Denis Law, beat them 5-1 in an Upton Park replay.

A recurrence of an old injury kept Vic Keeble out of the side, and a number of deputies were used. One of the most successful was John Bond, who in making six appearances at centre-forward scored six times, netting a hat-trick against Chelsea in February.

In the same month, there were newspaper reports suggesting that the result of West Ham's match with Newcastle had been 'fixed', but the rumours proved to be unfounded.

A straight exchange deal brought Dave Dunmore, of Spurs, to Upton Park and sent John Smith to White Hart Lane. Dunmore failed to improve the scoring rate in 1959-60, but he did better the following season. The departure of Smith gave Geoff Hurst a chance to gain a place at wing-half, but he soon had to make way for Bobby Moore.

John Dick for Andy Smillie was manager Ted Fenton's only change from the final line-up of 1959-60, as West Ham went down 4-2 at Molineux in the opening game of 1960-61. Only one away victory was recorded all season as Hammers dropped a little further down the table to finish the campaign in 16th place.

All the best days were at Upton Park where the home team scored five against Aston Villa, Preston and Wolves and, most satisfying of all, hit six past Arsenal. One of the largest crowds of the season, some 46,000, saw Mike Beesley score in a losing debut at Goodison Park, but that figure was topped when West Ham visited White Hart Lane.

The Football League introduced its own cup competition in September, and Hammers took part in one of the two ties that kicked off the event which some other First Division clubs ignored. Now captained by Phil Woosnam, they overcame Charlton Athletic in the first round but fell at Fourth Division Darlington in the second. Interest in the FA Cup also ended in the north when Stoke City won a third round replay.

Malcolm Musgrove, who in 1959-60 had become the first winger to top the club's post-war scoring chart, repeated the achievement in 1960-61.

In March 1961, Ted Fenton staggered the football world by announcing his resignation. The reasons have never been made entirely clear and many believed, at that time, his relationship with the club would be 'till death us do part'.

Fenton's departure resulted in the appointment of Ron Greenwood, hitherto Arsenal's assistant manager and coach to England's Under-23 squad.

Ken Brown heads one way, Fulham's amateur international centre-forward Bobby Brown heads the other, and the ball is no where to be seen. The game at Craven Cottage in October 1960 ended in a 1-1 draw.

In Greenwood's first complete season of 1961-2, the Upton Park side climbed eight places up the table. Edinburgh-born Lawrie Leslie, a Scottish international, took over between the posts from Brian Rhodes; and another Edinburgh recruit, Ian Crawford, played some early games on the right wing.

John Dick, re-discovering the target, netted 23 times to head the scoring, but he and the others failed miserably at Home Park where Plymouth Argyle stopped

West Ham parade the FA Cup around Wembley after their victory over Preston.

With the last League match ending in defeat at Everton, only the Cup Final remained. Preston North End, winners of an all-Second Division semi-final with Swansea, had just missed promotion and were worthy Finalists, having eliminated Nottingham Forest and Bolton Wanderers, both from the First Division, in earlier rounds. At left-half in their team was Howard Kendall, at 17 the youngest-ever performer in a Wembley Cup Final.

Despite having fewer chances than the Lancashire team, it was a West Ham effort that decided the destination of the Cup in 1964. Twenty-one-year-old Ronnie Boyce wrong-footed the Preston 'keeper with a close-range header in the last minute and the trophy was Hammers' for the first time in their history.

Bobby Moore (6) and Ken Brown (5) watch Leeds United's midfield master Bobby Collins in action at Elland Road in April 1965.

Before the new season began, West Ham took part in the FA Charity Shield match. Two goals, by Hurst and Byrne, earned the London team a 2-2 draw at Anfield and a share of the trophy with League Champions, Liverpool.

A two-match winning start to 1964-5 was followed by a 3-2 home defeat at the hands of Nottingham Forest. At the beginning of October, Johnny Byrne was the First Division's leading marksman, but in the League Cup at Sunderland, the home side nullified his threat and went on to win 4-1

The FA Cup slipped from West Ham's grasp in front of the best home crowd of the season when Bobby Tambling's tenth-minute goal for Chelsea proved to be the only one of the match.

Qualifying for the European Cup-winners' Cup by virtue of their Wembley success in May, Hammers had two-leg aggregate wins over La Gantoise (Belgium), Sparta (Prague) and Lausanne (Switzerland) before meeting the Spaniards, Real Zaragoza, in the semi-final. West Ham won the first leg 2-1, but before the second leg was played, Hammers had their Easter League programme to fulfil.

In a remarkable match against West Brom, on Good Friday, Brian Dear set up a West Ham record for rapid scoring with five goals in a 20-minute spell either side of half-time. The Londoners won 6-1, but the rest of weekend was a failure as Greenwood's men failed to pick up another point.

Despite winning at Upton Park, Hammers were clearly underdogs for the second-leg of their European semi-final and the Spaniards underlined that with an early goal which put them level on aggregate. In a nail-biting second period, Hammers were put under severe pressure and listeners to the radio commentary might have

Frank Saul of Tottenham gets to the ball despite the close attentions of Martin Peters and Dave Bickles at White Hart Lane in April 1966.

got the impression that Bobby Moore and Jim Standen were the only West Ham players on the field. Although all of them did their bit, it was the youngest member of the side, Johnny Sissons, who got the equaliser on the night and the winner on aggregate.

The venue for that year's Cup-winners' Cup Final had already been chosen and West Ham knew that victory over Zaragoza would give them a Wembley game. It was Alan Sealey's night. Two goals by the former Orient man — who did a somersault as the first one hit the back of the net — won a marvellous match against TSV München 1860. Accolades poured in praising the two sides for the superb entertainment and J.L.Manning of the *Daily Mail* called it "the best soccer match I have seen at the stadium in its 42 years."

A Football League decision to allow substitutes for injured players in matches under its jurisdiction came into force for 1965-6 and when Jack Burkett injured a leg against Leeds United on 28 August, he was replaced by Peter Bennett who thus became the club's first-ever League substitute.

Hovering around the foot of the table for most of the season, Hammers improved near the end of the campaign to finish a respectable 12th. Only five teams won at Upton Park — Leicester City, Liverpool, Fulham and Nottingham Forest. The fifth side was Borussia Dortmund who thereby effectively released West Ham's hold on the Cup-winners' Cup. Their 2-1 win at Upton Park was followed by victory in West Germany.

In the League, five goals were conceded at Forest, Leeds United and Sheffield United; and Chelsea managed six in a Stamford Bridge fixture prior to which Bobby Moore had been stripped of the Hammers' captaincy.

A splendid 10-3 semi-final aggregate over Cardiff City (5-2 and 5-1) won West Ham a place in the League Cup Final against West Brom. It would be the last of the two-legged Finals and subsequent Finals would be staged at Wembley. Goals by Bobby Moore and Johnny Byrne, in a 2-1 win, gave Hammers a meagre advantage to take to The Hawthorns where goals from Kaye, Brown, Clark and Williams put the trophy beyond the Londoner's reach.

West Ham played their final League match of a long and exhausting 1965-6 season at Leicester on 9 May. For Martin Peters and Bobby Moore it was their 63rd first-class match, and Geoff Hurst had played 62. With the World Cup just around the corner, there would be no respite for the Hammers' trio.

Although Moore, Hurst and Peters helped England to glory in the summer of 1966, they could not prevent West Ham's poor start to the new season when the club went five games without a win. As the season developed, West Ham's form became increasingly eccentric. Whereas points were readily picked up away from Upton Park, the team did not record a home League win until the end of October.

The ability to score goals was still there and in September, Johnny Byrne (4) and Hurst (2) netted in the Football League's 12-0 defeat of the Irish League.

Tottenham Hotspur and Arsenal were beaten in the League Cup before Hammers faced a formidable Leeds line-up at Upton Park in November. Before the match, Don Revie announced: "We shall be playing for a draw." His tactics went awry somewhere and West Ham won 7-0. A fifth-round win at Blackpool, then bottom of Division One, set Hammers up to avenge the previous season's failure against West Brom. History was repeated at The Hawthorns when Albion went off at half-time four goals ahead. At full-time the score was the same, and the second leg was a formality. A week after the League Cup semi-final disappointment at Upton Park, Johnny Byrne returned to his former club Crystal Palace.

In the last weeks of the season, a number of youngsters were given first-team chances. From the performances of these players, who had graduated from the junior ranks, it was evident that the signing of some experienced defenders was to be a priority if First Division soccer was to be maintained at Upton Park.

During the summer of 1967, Billy Bonds, a rugged full-back, was purchased from Charlton Athletic; John Cushley came from Glasgow Celtic; and Bobby Ferguson, a Scottish international goalkeeper, from Kilmarnock.

Jim Standen had to make way for Ferguson, but Cushley was filling a place vacated by Ken Brown who had joined Torquay United. All three newcomers played in the opening fixture which Sheffield Wednesday won at Upton Park.

A meagre three points were won from the first six games, but then a 5-1 victory at Roker Park, where Bobby Moore scored for each side, and a 5-1 League Cup win at Walsall seemed to spark a temporary revival. However, by Christmas, Hammers were still in the lower reaches. Then six points were taken from three games, and Brian Dear netted five times in two games against Leicester City. Trevor Brooking and Frank Lampard each received their First Division baptism in the opening half

John Charles battles it out with two Arsenal players at Highbury in October 1968.

of the season, and at one point, Geoff Hurst was the division's joint top-scorer with Peter Lorimer of Leeds United.

Against Fulham in February, they scored five goals in 22 minutes to win 7-2; and in the same month, two goals in the last ten minutes helped Hammers to a 3-0 FA Cup win at Stoke City. Sheffield United's unexpected fifth-round win at Upton Park saw Hammers lose confidence and sink to within a point of 21st place. Wins over Newcastle United, Forest and Liverpool recovered the situation.

Alan Stephenson, signed from Crystal Palace for a big fee in March, was at the centre of the defence for the first game of 1968-9, at Newcastle where a last-minute goal from Brian Dear saved a point. Martin Peters netted a hat-trick in the 4-0 defeat of West Brom, and the unbeaten away sequence continued until West Ham visited Turf Moor on 8 October. The League Cup, meanwhile provided a nine-goal thriller at Upton Park when Hammers defeated Second Division Bolton Wanderers, 7-2. The next round, however, was a 'no-score bore' when Coventry City earned themselves a replay which they won 3-2.

Later that month, Geoff Hurst hit the jackpot with six splendid goals against Sunderland. The double hat-trick equalled the club record set in 1929, but Hurst, it was alleged later, admitted to using his hand in scoring one of them. November saw the opening of the new East Terrace at Upton Park, and two months later, the seating area was in use for the third-round FA Cup tie against Bristol City. The whole complex replaced the wooden terracing called the 'Chicken Run,' which had stood since the club's very early days at the Boleyn.

Thirty-two thousand saw West Ham's Cup match against Bristol City. It was the first-ever Cup meeting between the sides, although, Hammers had played an FA Cup first-round second replay against Swansea on the Ashton Gate pitch in 1922. In the tenth minute, Galley put City in front, but after Martin Peters had equalised, West Ham went on to win 3-2. After a two-goal victory in the fourth-round, at Second Division Huddersfield Town, Hammers were drawn to visit Third Division Mansfield Town on 8 February.

The day was a disaster for football as severe weather conditions curtailed the entire Cup programme of eight games, plus all but four League matches. Rearranged for 19 February, Hammers' tie was postponed again. Postponed yet again five days later, it finally got underway on 26 February, when West Ham went down 3-0. Hammers finished eighth in 1968-9, and their 50 goals against was the club's best since 1923-4. Hurst finished the season as leading scorer with 25 goals, whilst Peters was second with 19. Both players, and Billy Bonds, were ever-present.

The following campaign failed to see a continuation of that trend. Hammers conceded ten more goals, scored 15 fewer than the previous season, and ended 1969-70 in 17th place.

New players were signed in the form of Peter Eustace from Sheffield Wednesday and Jimmy Greaves from Spurs. The cost of bringing Greaves to Upton Park was the loss of Martin Peters who went to White Hart Lane. Clyde Best, a 19-year-old Bermudan, made his debut against Arsenal early in the season and went on to play in over half the matches. Middlesbrough beat West Ham in the FA Cup, and Nottingham Forest knocked them out of the League Cup after Hammers had faced Third Division Halifax Town for the first time in any competition.

A promising start deteriorated into another season of struggle. Poor results in early December threatened Hammers' First Division status but nine points from the last seven games salvaged the position.

Fifty-eight thousand fans saw West Ham's 5-2 defeat at Old Trafford, but when they next visited Manchester, the Londoners won 5-1 at Maine Road. Everton's victory at Upton Park in December was their seventh win in the last nine matches between the clubs, and the Merseysiders' third double over Hammers in four seasons. At the end of the season, Everton were crowned Champions.

Without a win until the 11th game of 1970-71, West Ham continued to disappoint well into the New Year. In an effort to stiffen the defence, Tommy Taylor was bought from Orient and John McDowell promoted from the reserves. Both made their debuts in October. Results were still worrying when 'Pop' Robson was purchased from Newcastle in February. He cost a new club record fee, but Greenwood was confident that he was the man to lead a recovery and Robson's influence was such that in ten of his first 14 games, Hammers gained at least a point.

In the League Cup, a Peter Eustace goal saw Hammers through at Hull, but an ugly incident in the same game earned Billy Bonds a hefty fine and a long suspension.

There were further internal troubles following the FA Cup exit at Blackpool.

Jimmy Greaves scores one of his two goals against Manchester City at Maine Road in March 1970, when the Hammers won 5-1.

A breach of club rules on the eve of the game cost four players a fine, and two of the group were suspended. Hammers ended the season in 20th position, seven points ahead of relegated Burnley.

West Ham made another dreadful start to a season in 1971-2. Almost seven hours of playing time had elapsed before they scored their first goal, when Clyde Best's effort beat Everton on 28 August.

Best scored six out of 12 goals in the subsequent five matches. Among them was one at Old Trafford, but a hat-trick by George Best kept United at the top of Division One. Although undefeated throughout October, Hammers lapsed into another five-match goal famine in November. Meanwhile, League Cup progress was made at the expense of Cardiff City and Leeds United. Each required a replay, but Liverpool were eliminated at the first attempt in front of 41,000 fans at Upton Park. Sheffield United, beaten 5-0 in the fifth round, conceded the only goals scored by Hammers in November.

The semi-final paired West Ham with Stoke City and their 2-1 first-leg win at the Victoria Ground, could reasonably have provoked the belief that the hardest part had been accomplished. Yet five and a half hours of this tie had yet to be played. In the second leg, Ritchie levelled the scores. At Hillsborough in the replay, extra-time was again required but Gordon Banks and Bobby Ferguson kept their goals intact.

The tie, already seen by over 120,000 people, was watched by another 48,000 at Old Trafford where Stoke finally settled the issue 3-2. One of their goals was

Dudley Tyler gets in a shot past Liverpool's Larry Lloyd at Upton Park in January 1973.

netted past West Ham's substitute goalkeeper, Bobby Moore, after Ferguson was concussed in a collision early in the game.

In the Boxing Day match at White Hart Lane, Hammers spoiled Spurs' unbeaten home record; four days later they upset Manchester United, 3-0 at Upton Park.

Goals from Best and Hurst knocked Luton out of the FA Cup, and three more from England's 1966 World Cup hero put an end to gallant non-League Hereford in a fourth-round replay. A sequel to the Cup meetings with Hereford was the transfer of Dudley Tyler, their midfielder, to Upton Park later in the year.

In the fifth round, Hammers failed at lowly Huddersfield Town, but a week later they comfortably defeated the Yorkshire side in a League match at Upton Park. Clyde Best's 23 League and Cup goals, of which 14 were scored at home, placed him high among the First Division's leading sharpshooters.

Apart from a three-match goalless spell in February and March, West Ham's strike-rate improved dramatically in 1972-3. An increase of 20 goals on the previous season saw the club rise to sixth, equalling their best-ever final position in Division One. Not since 1958-9, and before that 1926-7, had they ended a campaign so highly placed.

There is little doubt that Robson's contribution made the difference but, significantly, only five of his 23 goals were scored away from Upton Park. Hammers won only three points from the five teams that finished above them. One of those points cost West Ham dear when Bobby Ferguson had a spell in hospital after

Bobby Moore was back to lead the Hammers against Leicester City at Upton Park in September 1973. The previous week he had been dropped for the game at Old Trafford and there were rumours of a transfer. It was indeed Moore's last season with the Hammers and the following March he moved to Fulham.

he was knocked out in the match against Leeds. That game featured Ted MacDougall, who once scored nine goals in a match for Bournemouth and who Hammers had signed from Manchester United in March. Before the season began, Geoff Hurst joined Stoke after a distinguished career at Upton Park.

Limehouse-born Pat Holland, who had made his debut back in April 1969, was the only goalscorer in the Port Vale-West Ham FA Cup tie in January. In the next round, a Hull City team which contained player-manager Terry Neill and 23-year-old Stuart Pearson, scored a memorable victory over West Ham. Fourth Division Stockport County beat Hammers in the League Cup with the help of a second-half penalty. It was a most embarrassing experience but Greenwood, maintaining his confidence in the side, made only one change for the drawn game at Ipswich Town three days later.

Yet another appalling start was made to a season in 1973-4 when Hammers went 12 League matches before recording a victory. John McDowell ended the sequence by getting the goal that beat sixth-placed Coventry City at Highfield Road.

It was a transitional season. Departures included long-serving Bobby Moore, whilst Bobby Ferguson went out on loan and Dudley Tyler returned to Hereford United who were now a League club. Ted MacDougall was another departure, leaving to join Norwich City in an exchange that brought Graham Paddon to Upton Park. Other newcomers included 18-year-old Mervyn Day, a Chelmsford-born goalkeeper; two 23-year-olds, Keith Coleman and Mick McGiven from Sunderland; and the much-travelled Bobby Gould.

Never out of the bottom-four between September and the end of February, West Ham's highest placing all season was 16th. Billy Bonds, appointed skipper after the transfer of Moore to Fulham, was top scorer with 13, one better than Clyde Best.

League Cup dreams were ended at Anfield where a John Toshack goal won the replay for Liverpool. The FA Cup provided revenge for Hereford United. Now members of the Third Division, Hereford almost won at Upton Park where a Pat Holland goal saved the home side's blushes. The *coup de grace*, however, was only delayed and West Ham went down 2-1 at Edgar Street.

Even by the standards of recent seasons, the start to the 1974-5 campaign was hardly tolerable. A win and a draw, both against newly-promoted Luton Town, punctuated seven defeats as West Ham plunged to bottom place. Then a remarkable recovery started with a 6-2 victory over Leicester City. It continued until the Saturday after Boxing Day, when Stoke City ended Hammers' run of nine wins, seven draws and one defeat. Thereafter, they slumped again, winning only three of the next 18 League games. But there were distractions in the FA Cup as West Ham went into the quarter-finals at the expense of Southampton, Swindon and Queen's Park Rangers. Drawn at Highbury in the quarter-finals, where they had not won for ten years, Hammers saw 21-year-old Alan Taylor, a November signing from Third Division Rochdale, score a goal in each half to put them into the semi-final.

Their opponents were Ipswich Town, who needed four games to beat Leeds United in the other quarter-final. The Suffolk club boasted six internationals and a high level of consistency that had maintained a place in the top three virtually all season. They were also favourites to win the Cup. In the first match, at Villa Park, injuries to two of Bobby Robson's key players frustrated their attempts and the untidy semi-final ended goalless.

John Lyall, who had been Hammers' team manager for eight months, made no changes for the Stamford Bridge replay four days later. Enjoying far more of the proceedings than at Villa Park, West Ham took the lead midway into the first half, through Alan Taylor. Just on half-time, Billy Jennings inadvertently helped Ipswich to an equaliser. Speculation on the venue for a second replay was ended

West Ham pictured before the 1975 FA Cup Final. Back row (left to right): Robson, Best, Brooking, Bonds, Ferguson, Day, Lock, Holland, McDowell, McGiven. Front row: Taylor, Curbishley, Gould, Lampard, Taylor, Paddon, Jennings.

when West Ham's lethal opportunist, Alan Taylor, netted his fourth goal of the competition ten minutes from time.

For their second post-war appearance in an FA Cup Final, West Ham faced Fulham. The Craven Cottage side, managed by Alec Stock, were making their first Wembley appearance but they were reinforced by two former England men, Bobby Moore and Allan Mullery. It was, however, largely the efforts of Pat Holland that decided the issue. Twice escaping the attentions of his marker, he provided the telling passes (once via Billy Jennings) from which Alan Taylor scored. Taylor's goals brought his total in the 1974-5 competition to six — all scored in the concluding rounds, and equalling Peter McParland's achievement for Aston Villa in the 1956-7 season.

West Ham got the 1975-6 season underway with a return to Wembley where League Champions, Derby County, beat them 2-0 to take the FA Charity Shield. Putting that disappointment behind them, Hammers made their best start to a League season and were undefeated until their tenth game.

Alan Taylor picked up where he had left off the previous May, scoring in each of the first three matches, including two at Anfield where West Ham stole a point. Hammers climbed to second place after a brilliant recovery at Leicester, where goals from Bonds, Lampard and Holland, retrieved a three-goal deficit; and a draw with Coventry finally saw them to the top of the First Division.

When West Ham had reached top spot in November 1959, their season abruptly fell away, and so it was in 1975. Their next 14 League games yielded only two points and at home, Alan Taylor's goal against Queen's Park Rangers on 24 January, provided Hammers with their only League win after Christmas as they finished 18th.

In the League Cup, Tottenham won a fourth-round replay at Upton Park, and the Hammers' interest in the FA Cup ended at the Boleyn where goals from Keegan and Toshack saw Liverpool through.

Charlie George comes close to beating West Ham goalkeeper Mervyn Day in the 1975 FA Charity Shield game at Wembley. The other Hammers defender is John McDowell.

Yet West Ham looked to be on target for a European success in this otherwise dismal season. They reached the Final of the European Cup-winners' Cup — after two second-half goals by Bill Jennings had helped them through against the Dutch club, Den Haag in an earlier round.

Eintracht Frankfurt brought a slender 2-1 advantage to Upton Park for the semi-final second-leg, and Trevor Brooking (2) and Keith Robson ensured Hammers' second appearance in this particular European Final. They faced Anderlecht, the Belgian Cup winners who had the advantage of the game being staged at the Heysel Stadium in Brussels.

A full house of some 58,000 brought the attendance for West Ham's games in the competition to 340,000, but although Pat Holland put Hammers ahead, an uncharacteristic slip by Frank Lampard set Anderlecht on the road to a deserved victory.

Second-half goals by Andy Gray (2) and Ray Graydon (2) shattered West Ham in the opening game of 1976-7 at Villa Park where Bill Green, Hammers' expensive signing from Carlisle United, endured a torrid debut. Green eventually made way for Alan Devonshire, who appeared for the first time in the 3-0 defeat at The Hawthorns. Eighteen-year-old Alvin Martin joined West Ham during this depressing season. Although he had to wait 12 months for his first chance.

Hammers looked set for the drop, but when all seemed lost, they put together a run of 13 games with only one defeat. Nine goals from 'Pop' Robson, who returned from Sunderland in October, included two in a superb 4-2 win over Manchester

Trevor Brooking slides the ball past Eintracht Frankfurt's Peter Kunter's diving body and West Ham are through to the 1976 European Cup-winners' Cup.

United in an all-ticket last match of the season which helped West Ham to 17th place.

West Ham were quite active in the transfer market that season. Graham Paddon returned to Norwich in November, for a fee that financed the signing of Arsenal's 30-year-old striker, John Radford. An earlier bid to bring Bristol Rovers' prolific marksman, Alan Warboys, to Upton Park foundered when the player refused to move.

Queen's Park Rangers dumped West Ham out of the League Cup in a fourth-round match at Upton Park, and Aston Villa recorded their third win of the season over the Hammers when they knocked them out of the FA Cup fourth round.

The 1978 close season was a quiet summer at the Boleyn, but soon after the start of the new campaign, Keith Robson was sold to Cardiff City, and John Lyall brought Derek Hales to Upton Park. Hales had proved a successful marksman with Charlton, but his career at Derby had been singularly unsuccessful by comparison.

Another poor start to a season saw Hammers score only one goal in their first three games — and then, Robson's penalty failed to stop John Bond's Norwich winning at Upton Park. Boleyn fans had to wait until 10 December for Hammers' first home win, by which time the side was firmly entrenched in the relegation zone once more.

David Cross was signed from West Brom in December and made his debut in Hammers' defeat at The Hawthorns, but his overall presence steadied the side which failed to score in only five games after his arrival. Hammers almost repeated their Houdini act of 12 months earlier, needing one point from their last game to stay up. Unfortunately, their opponents were Liverpool, who also needed a point to finish runners-up. A crowd of more than 37,000 — West Ham's best of the season — saw the Merseysiders win comfortably.

So, West Ham were down at the end of a season which had also seen them crash 5-0 to Brian Clough's Nottingham Forest in the League Cup — Forest would

QPR's Ron Abbott rises above West Ham's Derek Hales in the FA Cup fourth-round replay at Loftus Road in January 1978, when the Hammers crashed 6-1.

take that trophy and the League Championship — and then go down 6-1 in an FA Cup fourth-round replay at Loftus Road.

During the season, John Radford's 14-month stay at Upton Park ended when he joined Blackburn Rovers, and full-back Kevin Lock, out of the side for a long spell, was sold to Fulham.

The most significant change, however, had come in December when John Lyall was elevated to team manager following Ron Greenwood's appointment as England manager. It was a popular move on the part of West Ham's directors, to return to the club's tradition of employing former Hammers players as managers.

Back in Division Two after an absence of 20 years, Lyall's team made an explosive start. Four first-half goals in the opening match against Notts County signalled their intentions. West Ham were in second place early in November, but then — as has so often happened in the past — their season fell away with only 15 goals scored in the final 15 games. Cross, who had scored a hat-trick in the opening match, had netted 17 by February, after which he failed to find the net again. Hammers' most successful striker was Robson, whose 24 included three against Millwall, in the first match between the clubs since 1948.

Hammers' confidence had been temporarily dented following a League Cup defeat by Third Division Swindon, early in the season; it was more severely damaged after Fourth Division Newport County secured a shock FA Cup win over West Ham at Somerton Park early in the New Year.

Whatever the reason for the lapses after Christmas, it left Hammers six points short of promotion after such a splendid start. Lyall used three goalkeepers during the season: Mervyn Day returned to replace Bobby Ferguson; then Day himself had to make way when Phil Parkes was signed from Queen's Park Rangers in February.

Despite the fact that in 1979-80 Hammers again failed to win promotion, the club's supporters have every reason to remember that season because it was brought to a magnificent climax when West Ham scored a memorable victory over old

Sunderland goalkeeper Barry Siddall looks cross after Alvin Martin's equaliser in the League Cup game at Upton Park in November 1979.

73

Frank Lampard takes a tumble with Arsenal's Liam Brady in the 1980 FA Cup Final. The other Hammers player is Billy Bonds.

rivals, Arsenal, in the FA Cup Final. Trevor Brooking's 18th-minute header settled the issue, and Hammers might have made it 2-0, had Paul Allen — the youngest man ever to play in a Wembley Final — not been cruelly hacked down by Arsenal's big Scottish centre-half, Willie Young, when the teenager appeared to have the goal at his mercy.

In the League, however, West Ham again disappointed, finishing seventh, despite being the only team to beat the champions, Leicester, twice. Home form let Hammers down and six clubs won at Upton Park in a season which saw Alvin Martin now established in the centre of the defence following Tommy Taylor's return to Orient. Robson returned to Sunderland in a move which surprised many, and newcomers included England player Stuart Pearson (from Manchester United), full-back Ray Stewart (Dundee United) and forward Jimmy Neighbour (Norwich).

Billy Jennings and Mervyn Day had joined Taylor at Brisbane Road where the manager was former West Ham player, Jimmy Bloomfield. And the 1975 Cup Final hero, Alan Taylor, went to Norwich with John McDowell. Altogether, Hammers

Phil Parkes is beaten but Terry McDermott's effort went wide in the 1980 FA Charity Shield match between West Ham and Liverpool at Wembley. The other Hammers defenders are Ray Stewart and Billy Bonds.

played 58 'first-class' games in 1979-80, including nine in the League Cup before going down in extra-time to Forest.

The signing of Paul Goddard from Queen's Park Rangers, for a Hammers record fee in the 1980 close season, proved a fine investment. Goddard turned out to be one of several West Ham successes in a record-breaking season which they started as firm favourites for promotion following their heady Cup triumph over First Division opposition.

This time, Hammers did not disappoint their fans. After a poor start — only two points from their first three games — West Ham drove relentlessly towards the title and were assured of promotion long before the season was over. David Cross top-scored with 22 of Hammers' 79 goals, and in April he netted a brilliant foursome at Grimsby. Ten days later, Goddard hit a hat-trick against his old club, Queen's Park Rangers.

West Ham ended their season top of Division Two with 66 points, but the most exciting times were not restricted to the League. In the League Cup, they went all the way to Wembley — and also reached the European Cup-winners' Cup quarter-finals.

The League Cup trail began with a handsome aggregate win over Burnley, then followed defeats of Charlton Athletic and Barnsley before a particularly satisfying victory over Tottenham Hotspur in the quarter-finals.

Before the first leg of the semi-final against Coventry City, the Boleyn club found themselves involved in an awkward FA Cup tie against Wrexham. The Welsh club won the right to stage a second replay at the Racecourse Ground, where Hammers went down 1-0.

Seven days later, they led 2-0 at Highfield Road, only to see City's spirited second-half performance edge the West Midlands side into a 3-2 lead. It took a late Jimmy Neighbour goal at Upton Park to decide a hard-fought semi-final, 4-3 on aggregate.

Hammers' Wembley opponents were Liverpool, who beat Manchester City in the other semi-final. A capacity crowd at the Empire Stadium saw a goalless first half before Alan Kennedy shot Liverpool ahead with a disputed goal in extra-time. They were already celebrating on Merseyside when Ray Stewart's last-ditch penalty saved the day for West Ham.

The replay at Villa Park was delayed for three weeks, and it was something of an anticlimax. Liverpool had lost at Highbury the previous Saturday, and a week later they were to face Bayern Munich in a European Cup semi-final, all of which may have explained their lacklustre performance. Nevertheless, Liverpool found enough spark to recover from Paul Goddard's ninth-minute goal. Dalglish equalised and three minutes later, Hansen's header found the back of the West Ham net via Bonds.

West Ham reached that season's Cup-winners' Cup quarter-finals with aggregate wins over Castilla — the second leg played in an almost deserted Upton Park stadium after a UEFA ruling following crowd disorder in Spain — and then the Romanian Cup holders, Poli Timisoara. David Cross had scored five goals in the tournament so far, including three in the ghostly atmosphere of the Boleyn when Castilla were beaten 5-1 on the night, and he managed another against Dynamo Tbilisi at Upton Park.

But the Russians were a much more formidable proposition than Hammers' previous opponents and they cruised to a 4-1 win. West Ham faced an impossible task and they failed — but not before they achieved victory on the day, beating Tbilisi with a goal from Pearson in front of their 80,000 spectators. Of course, those fans were unable to travel to see their team collect the trophy later that season when the presence of another Eastern Bloc club, Carl Zeiss Jena of East Germany, restricted the attendance at the Final in Düsseldorf to only 9,000.

By then, West Ham were savouring the prospects of a return to First Division football and they began 1981-2 by going nine games before tasting defeat. The highlight of that sequence was undoubtedly a 4-0 win at White Hart Lane where Cross scored all the goals. Bad weather badly affected the League programme in December, by which time West Ham had won 20 points from 16 games, scoring 33 goals in the process.

In other times, Hammers' final tally of 58 points might have won them the title, but this was the first season of three points for a win and they finished ninth, still a creditable position in their first season back in Division One. Cross (16 goals) and Goddard (15) headed the scoring chart, followed by Ray Stewart who scored a remarkable 13 penalties, only two short of Francis Lee's record.

Belgian star, Francois Van der Elst, made his League debut when he came on as substitute in the defeat at Brighton in January, but he missed the final matches of the season because he was required to join the Belgian squad preparing for that summer's World Cup Finals in Spain.

A Cyrille Regis goal dumped West Ham out of the League Cup in a third-round second replay at Upton Park, and Watford, that season's Second Division runners-up, ended Hammers' FA Cup run after the Boleyn club had scored their second Cup win over Everton in three seasons.

West Ham improved their League position by one place in 1982-3, yet the average attendance at Upton Park was down for the third successive season — a common trend amongst almost all clubs in the late 1970s and early '80s.

Before the season began, David Cross left for Manchester City, for whom he scored in each of his first two games, and Hammers had an indifferent start with home defeats and away victories coming in the first few matches.

Alan Devonshire battles away with Swansea City's Neil Robinson at Upton Park in April 1982.

Then the team settled into a run which brought five consecutive wins, including successes over Arsenal and Liverpool, and goals from new man Sandy Clark (from Airdrie) and central defender Alvin Martin. Early in September, Billy Bonds passed Bobby Moore's record of 544 League appearances, and four days later, Frank Lampard reached 500 games for the club.

Hammers moved into second place in October and, apart from an indifferent spell in February and March, they maintained their high place and finished eighth. In contrast to the long-serving Bonds and Lampard, Hammers gave 18-year-old Alan Dickens his debut, against Notts County, and a little while afterwards, blooded Tony Cottee, a Chadwell Heath youngster, against Spurs.

In March, Clark left for Glasgow Rangers, confessing that the pace of the English First Division was too hot for him, and West Ham replaced him with Dave Swindlehurst from Derby County.

Paul Allen, goalless in 33 League games, saved his scoring shots for the League Cup — now restyled the Milk Cup — and his goal against Notts County helped West Ham into the quarter-finals where Allen netted an equaliser at Anfield. Two minutes from time, however, Graeme Souness hit Liverpool's winner. Another northern giant, Manchester United, beat Hammers in the FA Cup with goals from Coppell and Stapleton.

In the 1983 close season, manager John Lyall signed Steve Whitton from Coventry City, and Steve Walford from Norwich City. Whitton, a six-foot 23-year-old, was in fact an East Ham boy who had been snapped up by the Highfield Road club as an apprentice. Walford had served Spurs and Arsenal before joining Norwich.

The Hammers could hardly have enjoyed a better start to 1983-4. They won their first five games at the gallop, netting 15 goals in the process before West Brom halted their charge at The Hawthorns. This time, however, Hammers saved their usual lapse until the end of the season when four defeats in their last six games saw them finish in ninth position.

The most pleasing aspect of the season had been the form of young Tony Cottee who, in his first full campaign, finished top-scorer with 15 goals in the League. And when West Ham created a record by winning 10-0 against Fourth Division Bury in the Milk Cup, Cottee was on hand to grab four goals. Everton were less impressed with the Hammers' fire-power, and they won a fourth-round replay 2-0 at Goodison Park on their way to the first all-Merseyside Wembley Cup Final.

Paul Hilton, a member of the Bury side devastated by West Ham, signed for the Upton Park club in February. He played a few games as replacement for the usual wearer of Hammers' number-six shirt, Alan Devonshire, who was sidelined with a serious injury.

Devonshire was hurt in the FA Cup third-round match at home to Wigan, a match in which Ray Stewart scored the only goal with a penalty. Dave Swindlehurst scored a second-half equaliser at Selhurst Park against his former club, Crystal Palace, and Hammers went through in the Upton Park replay with a goal from Bobby Barnes — his only FA Cup goal for the club — and a goal from Geoff Pike.

Two first-half goals at St Andrew's put Birmingham City well on the way to a place in the quarter-finals, and the Blues netted a third after both teams were twice forced to leave the field after pitch invasions by a hooligan minority amongst the crowd.

The end of the season brought two landmarks for West Ham. Ray Stewart made his 200th League appearance for the club in a midweek game at Highbury, but that was overshadowed a week later when Trevor Brooking played his last game in the home defeat by Everton. Brooking, one of the game's major figures, announced his retirement after more than 500 appearances in the claret and blue of West Ham United.

When the Hammers began the 1984-5 season, they were not only without Brooking. Goalkeeper Phil Parkes was injured, but the much-travelled Tom McAlister proved an able deputy as the side suffered only two defeats in their opening 11 League and Milk Cup games.

The latter competition saw West Ham get off to a promising start by crushing Bristol City 8-3 on aggregate — Goddard and Cottee scored two each when City were beaten 6-1 at Upton — but then Second Division Manchester City scored a surprise win at the Boleyn.

Fulham had reluctantly parted with Tony Gale, who proved to be Hammers' only cash buy that season, but before the campaign had ended, Potts, McPherson and Parris were blooded in the first team.

That promising start was not maintained and at the end of the season, although they finished in 16th place, Hammers were only two points better off than Norwich who were relegated. They could be thankful, therefore, for the goal by Barnes which gave them victory over the Canaries in the 37th League game of the season.

That success was one of only seven League wins at the Boleyn, where Hammers scored only 27 goals and six visiting sides took all the points; six away victories, however, restored some balance to the club's overall record and when goals from

West Ham's Tom McAllister saves from Stoke City at the Victoria Ground in October 1984. The other players nearest the camera are Steve Bould and Ian Pointer of Stoke and the Hammers' Alvin Martin.

Cottee and Goddard gave Hammers a win over Nottingham Forest at the end of March, they were the first goals that West Ham had scored at the City Ground since 1969.

Cottee again ended the season as West Ham's leading scorer with 24 League and Cup goals. And Hammers welcomed back Parkes for the last ten matches in which his giant presence between the posts helped in the fight against relegation.

In the FA Cup, it was the goalscoring powers of Cottee and Goddard, yet again, which helped Hammers into the quarter-finals. Goddard's hat-trick helped beat Port Vale in the third round, and Cottee netted three times against Wimbledon in a fifth-round replay at the Boleyn. Manchester United, however, proved too strong a challenge at Old Trafford and they eventually went on to win the Cup with subsequent victories over Liverpool and Everton.

The summer of 1985 proved to be a busy time at Upton Park. After an unsuccessful trip to the Far East to play in the Japan Cup — Hammers won only one of their five games in that competition — they returned home and sold Paul Allen to Tottenham Hotspur for a new West Ham record for an incoming fee.

The money financed the summer signings of Frank McAvennie, St Mirren's exciting young striker, and Mark Ward, the Oldham Athletic midfielder. McAvennie's arrival allowed the club to part with Dave Swindlehurst, who was sold to Sunderland, whilst long-serving Paul Brush moved to Crystal Palace. Other faces leaving Upton Park included Keith McPherson and Warren Donald (both to Northampton Town) and Bobby Barnes, who had a short, temporary spell with Scunthorpe before signing for Aldershot.

McAvennie, little-known outside his native Scotland, took the First Division by storm in 1985-6. He was young, strikingly blond, and an exciting player who netted 26 times in his first season to finish second in the First Division list, behind Everton's Gary Lineker.

McAvennie's presence helped West Ham to achieve their best-ever placing in the Football League. They finished the season in third place and only two clubs —

79

Chelsea and Luton Town — were wholly successful at the Boleyn where Newcastle were particularly unfortunate to catch the Hammers in rampant mood. In a midweek game near the end of the season, the Magpies went down 8-1, when Alvin Martin scored a hat-trick with one goal past each of three different goalkeepers after Newcastle's Thomas was injured.

Indeed, at one time it looked quite likely that the Hammers would win their first-ever League Championship — until a storming finish by Liverpool (11 wins and a draw in their last 12 games) took the title to Anfield in Kenny Dalglish's first season as manager, and set the Merseysiders on course for a League and Cup double. Liverpool took four points from West Ham.

After Ray Stewart had scored three penalties over the two legs of a Milk Cup second-round tie against John Bond's Swansea City, Manchester United again proved Hammers' stumbling block in a Cup competition, this time winning with a Norman Whiteside goal at Old Trafford.

Revenge was West Ham's later in the season, however, when a brilliant goal by Geoff Pike, and another penalty from Stewart gave Hammers victory at Old Trafford in an FA Cup fifth-round replay.

West Ham had got that far after taking three matches to beat lowly Ipswich in the fourth round, but they were denied a place in the semi-final when Sheffield Wednesday won at Hillsborough. The Londoners trailed by two goals at half-time but fought back and could count themselves unfortunate not to have earned a replay. A few days later they beat the Owls in a First Division match at the Boleyn with a goal from McAvennie.

The Scottish striker missed only one match in 1985-6, when he played for Scotland in their World Cup play-off game in Australia. Upon his return, McAvennie scored the only goal of the game at Loftus Road.

Confidence was high at the start of 1986-7, and when West Ham faced Coventry at home in the first game, they fielded the same 11 players who had taken part in the final match of the previous season — the first time that had happened in living memory.

An 84th-minute goal by Gale — his first for the club — defeated Coventry, and 48 hours later, McAvennie's two goals helped Hammers to a fine win at Old Trafford. But this was a season in which Manchester United were to make an appalling start — one that would eventually cost Ron Atkinson his job — and West Ham's success there did not signal the start of another title-chase.

Home defeats by Nottingham Forest and Liverpool (who scored four goals in a 19-minute spell at Upton Park) checked their progress, although by 29 November, Hammers were still undefeated at home. The next day, however, in a live-televised Sunday game, they crashed 4-0 at Newcastle where Paul Goddard, recently transferred to the Magpies, collided with George Parris and required five stitches in a head wound.

From that moment on, Hammers' League season fell away and although Cottee was still finding the net, McAvennie, in his second season of English football, struggled to repeat his success of 12 months earlier.

The Littlewoods Cup (the new title of the Football League Cup) saw Cottee record another hat-trick, this time in the second leg of the game against Preston, and then Hammers beat Watford and Oxford — against whom Cottee netted a penalty in Stewart's absence — before they were drawn against Tottenham.

Sandwiched in between the latter stages of the Littlewoods Cup were two FA Cup games against neighbours, Orient, and League games at Liverpool, Spurs and Coventry where yet another Cottee hat-trick gave West Ham a double over the Midlanders. The Boxing Day clash at White Hart Lane must have dented Hammers' hopes of Littlewoods success when Spurs won 4-0.

The League's leading scorer, Clive Allen, gave Tottenham the lead in the first leg of the Littlewoods Cup at Upton Park before Cottee levelled the scores. Clive Allen was again the scourge of West Ham in the replay. His eight-minute hat-trick denied West Ham a Wembley place against Arsenal.

In the FA Cup, Hammers played five games and yet failed to reach the sixth round. First Orient held them 1-1 at Brisbane Road before three goals in the last ten minutes of the replay saw the Upton Park side through; then Sheffield United were beaten when two goals from McAvennie helped West Ham to a 4-0 win in which Stewart Robson, an expensive signing from Arsenal, scored his first goal for the Hammers.

In the fifth round, West Ham looked set to avenge the previous season's defeat at Hillsborough when a battling display earned them a 1-1 draw on the same ground. Sheffield Wednesday, however, chose the Upton Park replay to end their four-year famine in London and won 2-0.

With their season rapidly disintegrating, Hammers brought the former Arsenal midfielder, Liam Brady, back to English football from Italy. The Republic of Ireland international made his West Ham debut against Norwich City on 14 March, but the 21,000-plus crowd saw Brady's new team fail again, this time by 2-0. Indeed, Brady had to wait until his fifth appearance for Hammers before he was on the winning side, and his presence failed to check the club's slide down the First Division table.

It was the old war-horse, Billy Bonds, who finally helped the East Enders to pull clear of the danger zone. Recalled to the side, Bonds fired the team at a critical stage and they eventually finished 15th — the first time they had occupied that particular position in 61 seasons of League football.

By the time the 1987-8 season got underway, West Ham had already been involved in eight matches. A five-match tour of three European countries had been followed by three engagements in the UK, one of which was a testimonial for long-serving Eddie Chapman.

The serious business began on 15 August, when Hammers received an early shock as Queen's Park Rangers won 3-0 at Upton Park.

Further set-backs were in store and none came bigger than that which arrived on 6 October. In a Littlewoods Cup second-round second-leg tie against Second Division Barnsley, Hammers held a two-goal half-time advantage and appeared a safe bet to progress into the next round. But the Yorkshiremen had other ideas. In a bizarre late spell, Barnsley levelled the scores then proceeded to blast Hammers from the competition with three goals in six minutes during extra-time.

Barnsley's success ended a 20-match sequence of fruitless visits to Upton Park going back to 8 September 1919.

Contrary to expectations, West Ham's League performances improved and only two defeats were suffered in the 11 games following the collapse against Barnsley. During this period Hammers reached ninth spot, their highest of the season.

In October an unhappy and out-of-touch McAvennie departed for Glasgow Celtic. The Boleyn club allegedly reaped £800,000 from the deal.

During the same month, 18-year-old Stuart Slater made his debut, albeit the final two minutes of the home game against Derby County.

Another debutant with a far more impressive impact was Leroy Rosenior. The 6ft tall coloured striker, formerly with Fulham and Queen's Park Rangers, marked his arrival with a goal in each of his first three games.

Two of his goals, against Chelsea, at Upton Park, saved Hammers from the drop but at the same time condemned the Stamford Bridge side to the play-offs.

Rosenior's five goals in nine appearances placed him second among the club's scorers. Top of the list was the only ever-present Hammer in 1987-8, Tony Cottee.

Alas, Cottee's 13 goals would be his last in West Ham's colours.

The lack of fire-power undoubtedly contributed towards an unwanted distinction — for the first time in the club's history West Ham failed to win two consecutive League matches.

After defeating Charlton Athletic in the third round of the FA Cup, the draw for the fourth round paired Hammers with Queen's Park Rangers at Shepherds Bush.

There was drama when the holders of over 2,000 forged tickets gained admission. In the resultant crush, hundreds spilled over on to the Loftus Road pitch and the police were forced to halt the game.

By the time order was restored over one hour had passed. Both managers, Jim Smith of Queen's Park Rangers and the visitors' John Lyall, paid tribute to the splendid behaviour of the crowd.

Witnesses to the afternoon's events were six high-ranking officials of the West German police. They were monitoring British crowd conduct, mindful of the coming European Football Championships in their own country.

The outcome of the afternoon's main attraction was West Ham's elimination from the FA Cup, on a ground they had won a League match on just a few days earlier.

Shortly before the 1988-9 season began, Hammers made soccer headlines when they sold their England striker Tony Cottee to Everton for £2.2 million.

The massive cash inducement proved impossible to refuse but, at the same time, it presented the club with the major problem of finding a replacement for a proven goal-getter.

David Kelly, a Birmingham-born Irish international, appeared to have the right credentials and was signed from Walsall. His seven goals in Walsall's end of season play-off games had helped the Midlanders into Division Two.

Goalkeeper Allen McKnight was, like Kelly, an international but the former Celtic 'keeper could not halt the trend that began with the defeat at Southampton on the season's first day.

When thes opening 23-match spell came to an end, Hammers were bottom of the First Division where they remained anchored for the next 14 weeks.

Anxious to recover a safe League position, John Lyall restored 38-year-old Phil Parkes into goal for his first extended spell for two years. Lyall also spent the club's record outlay in bringing back Frank McAvennie from Glasgow Celtic.

Neither move brought the desired outcome, but it was close.

A late flourish saw maximum points won at Newcastle, Sheffield Wednesday and Nottingham Forest, where Rosenior recorded a 20-seconds goal, but the damage had already been done.

Had Hammers shown the same determination in League games that they displayed in Cup ties, then the struggles of 1988-9 would have been at the other end of the First Division.

Between late September and the end of March, West Ham were engaged in 14 Cup ties. And despite some atrocious League form progress was made to the latter stages of both competitions.

Hammers saved their best displays for Cup ties against the League's leading clubs. There were victories over Liverpool, Derby County (after three games) and Aston Villa in the League Cup, whilst Arsenal were accounted for in the FA Cup.

Eight clubs achieved a League double at West Ham's expense but Hammers' two included a satisfying one over Millwall.

On 9 May, West Ham's visit to Sheffield Wednesday reopened the Hillsborough ground following the horrendous tragedy of a few weeks earlier.

In November 1988, a new name was added to the club's directors. Mr Charles J.Warner, a Tonbridge solicitor and great-grandson of Arnold F.Hills, who was

Paul Ince beats Stuart Ripley of Middlesbrough at Ayresome Park in 1988-9.

instrumental in the formation of the Thames Ironworks FC and consequently of West Ham United.

For a club unused to being the subject of controversial debate, West Ham United received more than its share before and during 1989-90.

In July, a decision by the club's board not to renew the contract of long-serving and popular manager John Lyall sparked a chorus of protest that could be heard almost everywhere East Enders gathered. Only the continuing 'inquests' into Hillsborough managed to divert attention away from Upton Park.

Eventually, commonsense prevailed as loyalty to the club claimed priority over the individual. Most felt that John Lyall would not have argued with that.

In the same week that BAC Windows succeeded AVCO Trust as club sponsors, Lou Macari was lured from Swindon Town to become John Lyall's replacement.

Macari, who had an outstanding soccer pedigree, turned out to have links with the district, having been a resident of Forest Gate when he was very young.

From the moment of his appointment there were whispers of 'unease' at the club, whispers that refused to go away.

Later in the season, an act of waywardness in Macari's past was revealed which ultimately led to his resignation.

In the meantime West Ham's return to Division Two had begun tragically when Frank McAvennie broke his leg in two places after a tackle by Stoke City's Chris Kamara. Mac's next first-team appearance would be on 31 March.

Over £600,000 was spent in bringing Martin Allen, Queen's Park Rangers' aggressive midfielder to Upton Park, and he made a scoring debut against Plymouth Argyle in August.

Top of the Division at the end of that month, Hammers soon slumped to eighth following a 3-0 defeat at Brighton.

A further plunge to 14th followed the departure of Mark Ward to Manchester City, but the slide was halted when Ludek Miklosko's work-permit problem was solved and he took over in goal at Swindon on 18 February.

The seven days that followed saw the departure of Lou Macari and the installation of Billy Bonds in the Upton Park hot-seat.

Unanimously supported by those on the terraces, Bonds' appointment was greeted with a huge ovation when he appeared at the tunnel entrance prior to the start of the Blackburn Rovers game.

By the season's end Bonds' influence had helped recover some of the dignity lost at Torquay and Oldham in the early weeks of 1990.

On the pitch, violence flared-up in a Littlewoods Cup tie against Wimbledon. Seventeen players got involved, West Ham won the game but the cost was a red card for Julian Dicks and a hefty FA fine for both clubs.

In August, Paul Ince, Hammers' talented but unsettled midfielder, finally got his wish and joined Manchester United. The fee was a reported £2 million. His final few days as a Hammer were marred by an incident in which he was photographed wearing a Manchester United shirt.

In January, the board recruited yet another new face when locally-born Hammers 'fanatic' Peter Storrie became a director.

The last words on 1989-90 must belong to Liam Brady, whose wonderful playing career was brought to a close in the final match of the season against Wolves at the Boleyn. A goal in the last minute of a 500-plus match career was a splendid way of saying goodbye.

Encouraged by the team's form in the latter half of 1989-90 West Ham's followers were highly optimistic regarding promotion in the coming campaign.

Early results confirmed that their hopes were well founded. Apart from a lapse at Oxford in the Rumbelows Cup, Hammers remained undefeated for 21 games, until a trip to their 'bogey' ground, Oakwell, on the Saturday before Christmas.

Despite an injury list that did not seem to shorten and at one time almost forced Billy Bonds out of retirement, the side retained a place among the promotional hopefuls.

No visitors were successful at Upton Park until March, when Sheffield Wednesday

Ian Bishop celebrates a goal against West Brom in 1989-90.

snatched three priceless points with a well-earned victory. A list of the vanquished included First Division sides Luton Town and Everton, both beaten in FA Cup ties.

Luton, though, twice came to the rescue as Hammers were forced into the transfer market. Tim Breacker, a full-back, was secured in October as Bonds' defensive resources began to thin out; and in March, Ian Dowie joined the Upton Park squad to deputise for Trevor Morley, who was injured in a domestic incident.

Dowie was Cup-tied but Breacker was able to appear in all the FA Cup ties leading up to that highly controversial semi-final against Nottingham Forest at Villa Park.

In a match televised live by the BBC, Hammers and Forest were expected to provide their usual high level of entertainment to an audience of millions. But it was not to be.

In the 27th minute, a harmless-looking tackle by Tony Gale on Forest's Gary Crosby earned the Hammer a red card and referee Keith Hackett a permanent place in West Ham's history.

Ironically, Gale's column in a local newspaper that week was headed, 'Semi-Final Day . . .could prove my worst'. How tragically prophetic that turned out to be.

Tony Gale's dismissal, the second for a Hammer in less than a month, had a profound effect on the match. It meant the Londoners could have little hope of containing an accomplished First Division side for over an hour. In the event the Nottingham men moved smoothly on to Wembley with a four-goal victory.

To compound a cheerless 24 hours, West Ham's Youth Cup endeavours came to an end at Millwall on the very next evening. A week later, however, the smiles were back when a 2-0 success over Glenn Hoddle's Swindon ensured Hammers' return to Division One.

Newcastle United, unbeaten by any of Division Two's top three sides, kept that record intact when they came to Upton Park. Fielding two 17-year-old defenders, Ossie Ardiles' men deserved all three points but left with only two.

At Ewood Park, the Blackburn hoodoo was active once more as Hammers conceded an early trio of goals and failed yet again on the Lancashire ground.

Despite these slips, however, Hammers kept their heads in front. The championship was now the target but more frustration lay ahead. Two precious points were lost in Charlton Athletic's farewell game at Selhurst Park, and Bristol Rovers' gallant resistance was cracked only by Stuart Slater's first League goal since Boxing Day.

Only a mischievous mind could have contrived Division Two's final day's fixtures: Oldham Athletic v Sheffield Wednesday and West Ham against Notts County. The top four teams paired together.

In front of their largest home audience of the season, Bond's men chose to put on their weakest performance. Within the hour they were two goals down, both substitutes on, and Colin Foster on the treatment table.

Hopes rose dramatically as news spread that Oldham's situation was much the same. They, too, were two goals in arrears. In the 77th minute, Hammers recovered a goal through George Parris, but Oldham had already done so up at Boundary Park.

On 80 minutes, Oldham drew level against Sheffield Wednesday but at Upton Park the scoring was over. Referee Brian Hill sounding the final whistle with Notts County 2-1 ahead.

At that moment West Ham were champions but celebrations were put on 'hold' for only a few more seconds.

Only another goal by Oldham could stop West Ham taking the title and the Lancashire side had less than a minute to get it.

Then, in the Latics' final fling, Wednesday midfielder John Sheridan tripped Barlow

Ian Bishop battles with Neil Adams of Oldham in March 1991.

in the penalty area and Neil Redfern stepped forward to blast the Second Division championship trophy from West Ham's grasp.

Nobody was predicting great deeds by the Hammers in 1991-2, but the club's disastrous adventure in the Makita International Tournament at Highbury failed to create any optimism in the side's ability to make itself felt in the higher section.

Recruiting during the close season brought Mike Small, Mitchell Thomas and Kenny Brown to Upton Park, whilst Ray Stewart and Jimmy Quinn sought new employers. Before the season was a few weeks old, Ian Dowie left the club for Southampton. Brown, the son of a former Hammers favourite, was purchased from Plymouth Argyle.

Apart from a dizzy spell at the end of October, when points were gained off Arsenal, Spurs and Liverpool in successive matches, the Boleyn men found themselves up against it. By Christmas, Billy Bonds' side had only Southampton below them. But if the fans were disenchanted with the Hammers, they now had the option of watching their tenants, Charlton Athletic, doing considerably better in Division Two.

The launch of the 'Bonds' scheme in November disturbed what had once been a happy relationship between Hammers fans and the club's directors. In subsequent months this developed into anger, then into hate as supporters threatened to boycott home games.

Frustration became an ingredient in the side's performances and Martin Allen suffered the loss of a week's wages as a result of a reckless tackle on Sheffield Wednesday's Carlton Palmer. Mitchell Thomas, too, appeared to be attempting a record when he collected his sixth yellow card of the season at Everton . . .in December!

In the FA Cup, Vauxhall Conference Leaguers Farnborough Town waived their right to a home tie and succeeded in earning a replay . . .the 1-1 result was courtesy of Julian Dicks who had a hand in both goals, particularly Farnborough's. Hammers went on to defeat the Hampshire non-Leaguers with Trevor Morley's last-minute goal saving considerable embarrassment. Wrexham, who had put paid to Arsenal's hopes in the previous round, couldn't reproduce that form but still took Bonds' men to a second match. Sunderland proved Hammers stumbling block, but only after the Londoners had done the hard bit in forcing a replay. Despite Martin Allen's two goals at Upton Park, Sunderland survived and went on to Wembley.

Early January brought the sad news of the death of Hammers' popular historian Jack Helliar. Jack's family's connections with the club went back to Victorian times.

After the home defeat by Arsenal on 14 March, Hammers reached rock bottom. Having been goalless for six of their last seven games, Bond's invested a quarter of a million pounds in Chelsea's Clive Allen. After serving a suspension, Clive's first match proved to be a goalscoring debut against his former club. But he was incapable of preventing the Boleyn side's relegation.

Two significant results in a final flourish were the win over Manchester United, which virtually ended Old Trafford's hopes of the Championship, and Frank McAvennie's parting shots against Nottingham Forest which brought him a hat-trick in his last appearance for the Hammers.

After an absence of a season, Hammers were back in the lower section but because of the restructuring of the Football League due in turn to the formation of the new FA Premier League . . .they were still a First Division club.

Season 1992-3 could be remembered for a number of reasons. Most important, the club won back its rightful place among the country's top teams, although there were some heart-stopping moments at the back end of the season as the race with Portsmouth went to the wire.

Bonds brought his old pal, Harry Redknapp, back to Upton Park as assistant

Stuart Slater is toppled by Arsenal's David Rocastle at Highbury in November 1991.

manager and gave Ronnie Boyce the position he had always sought . . .chief scout. Eddie Baily got a well-earned retirement.

Dagenham Motors took over the sponsorship in a £200,000 deal, plus extra awards should the club do well.

During the close season the newspapers reported Hammers' interest in Gavin Peacock and Robert Lee, but both ended the season as winners of Second Division championship medals with Newcastle United. However, the arrival of Peter Butler from Southend United, for £170,000, and Mark Robson, on a 'free' from Tottenham Hotspur, proved more than adequate consolation.

Trevor Morley scores West Ham's second goal at Derby in January 1993.

In one region or another, West Ham were given plenty of TV coverage and their first-ever Sunday kick-off to a new season was broadcast live from Oakwell. Although the three points were won, the occasion was blemished by the sending off of Mike Small. His dismisall was the first of several that season. Dicks led the way with three, but was many times Hammers' saviour. Following his 30th-minute departure at the Baseball Ground, West Ham still continued to threaten the home goal and went on to an epic victory.

After dropping points in three of their first five home games, West Ham off-set the loss with splendid victories at Bristol City and Rovers, Portsmouth, Derby County and Peterborough. But the most significant point was probably the one brought back from Grimsby, who had been victors over Newcastle and Portsmouth in recent games. Five League matches in December produced only six points, but January was better. Leaving aside the unexpected FA Cup defeat at Barnsley, Hammers recorded five wins that included the scalps of Derby, Portsmouth and Leicester. As expected, the visit of League leaders Newcastle United attracted a full house, despite the match being broadcast live by London Weekened Television. But the viewers saw no goals.

February was oveshadowed by the death of England and West Ham hero Bobby Moore. Hammers' games at Sunderland and at home against Wolves were turned into occasions of tribute to a man of great stature.

Three odd-goal defeats, at Notts County, Oxford and Southend, temporarily lost Hammers the automatic promotion place they had held for some weeks. The absence of Clive Allen, out injured since January, was now being felt and David Speedie was brought on loan from Southampton. The little Scot's previous visit to Upton Park had been in November, when he was wearing the colours of Birmingham

Celebrations after the Hammers promotion to the FA Premier League in May 1993.

City. By scoring in the vital games against Leicester City, Cambridge United and Bristol Rovers, Speedie silenced a hostile section of the West Ham crowd.

In the Cups, Hammers made very little impression. Their quest for the Coca-Cola trophy was ended by Dario Gradi's Crewe, who scored twice in the dying minutes of the second leg. In the Anglo-Italian Cup, West Ham failed to better the record of Derby County against the Italian clubs and so did not qualify for the final stages.

Three Hammers, Miklosko, Keen and Steve Potts, played in every League match and Trevor Morley finished the term as the club's leading scorer on 20. Just prior to the March transfer deadline, George Parris ended nearly 15 years at Upton Park when he joined Birmingham City for £100,000.

After a hiccup towards the end of the season, Hammers faced Cambridge United in their last game needing to win, although their nearest rivals, Portsmouth, could overtake them if they won and overtook Hammers' goals-for total, for both sides were on the same number of points with West Ham having scored one goal more. It could hardly have been tighter, but Hammers won through to take their place in the Premier League for 1993-4.

The club that grew out of Thames Ironworks has proved one of the most enduring features of British football and West Ham United will surely set the East End alight once more. If they are looking down, the ghosts of those early Hammers will heartily approve of the way their infant club has established itself as one of the most famous names in the game.

The Boleyn Ground in 1905, showing the original West Stand and the directors' box which also housed the Press facilities.

Home of the Hammers

TO MOST football supporters, outside London at least, West Ham United play at Upton Park. And indeed they do, but if one wishes to be accurate about the matter, then the home of the Hammers is the Boleyn Ground in the *district* of Upton Park.

The club moved there from the Memorial Grounds in 1904, when the rift between the club's erstwhile benefactor, Arnold Hills, and the professional Hammers became too great.

The Boleyn Ground takes its name from a sixteenth-century house which stood close by on Green Street. West Ham moved there in May 1904, to a piece of rough land rented to them by the authority which was then using the Boleyn Castle (as the house was known) as a school.

West Ham United set about the task of preparing a ground suitable for staging Southern League football and on 2 September the same year, Millwall were the first visitors, watched by some 10,000 spectators. There was a small grandstand on the west side, and some covered terracing backing on to Priory Road. A directors' box stood in the south-east corner, and the dressing-rooms were on the north-west corner beside the North Bank.

In 1913, a new, improved West Stand was built; and in 1925, an even more substantial stand rose up on the west side. It had seating blocks, a directors' box and press facilities. The roofing from the old West Stand was then used to cover the South Bank. The new West Stand was a major improvement to the Boleyn Ground and came in the wake of West Ham's rapid success after World War One, when they were admitted to the Football League and then won promotion to Division One and reached the first FA Cup Final to be played at Wembley.

Perhaps the most famous feature of the ground in those days was not the improved facilities on the west side of the pitch, but the primitive timber and corrugated-iron covered standing accommodation which ran along the east side and which was known for years as the 'Chicken Run'.

A crowd of 13,400, many of them in uniform, watched the last League game at Upton Park before World War Two. The Hammers lost 2-0 to Leicester City on 2 September 1939.

During the 1930s, five FA Amateur Cup Finals were played at the Boleyn, involving famous London clubs like Dulwich Hamlet, Ilford and Leyton. On 18 April 1936, when Charlton were the visitors, a crowd reported to number 43,528 spectators crammed into the Boleyn to set a record 'gate' for the ground. The figure cannot be verified from club records alone, however, because they were destroyed during World War Two.

In 1944, a V1 flying bomb fell on the ground, extensively damaging the South Bank and forcing West Ham to play a number of 'home' games on other grounds. During the earlier London Blitz, the ground had also suffered and the club offices in the West Stand had been evacuated as the Hammers moved to a temporary administrative home in the Boleyn Castle, which was then known as Green Street House.

Floodlights were first installed at the Boleyn Ground in 1953 and the first visitors for a match under lights were Tottenham Hotspur, who played a friendly there on 16 April that year.

Floodlights apart, there was no real improvement at the Boleyn Ground between the re-building of the West Stand in 1925, and the 1960s. In 1961, a roof was added to the North Bank, which meant that the ground was now covered on all sides; Four years later, the West Stand had a new block added; and in 1968, the Boleyn Ground lost its most nostalgic feature when the 'Chicken Run' made way for a £172,000 East Stand with a covered standing enclosure in front.

West Ham find the net against Castilla in the 1980-81 European Cup-winners' Cup but there are no supporters to cheer the effort as the match had to be played behind closed doors.

The East Enclosure was opened on 2 November 1968, for a League game against Queen's Park Rangers; and the East Stand had its first paying customers on 4 January 1969, when Bristol City were the visitors for a third-round FA Cup game.

On 17 October 1970, the official record attendance was set when 43,322 saw Spurs draw 2-2 at the Boleyn. In contrast, when Hammers played Castilla in a European Cup-winners' Cup game on 1 October 1980, the only people who saw the game live were staff and pressmen, who numbered just 262. The first leg of the game in Spain had been marred by the behaviour of a hooligan minority allegedly supporting West Ham. UEFA therefore ordered the second match to be played behind closed doors.

In 1982, however, the Boleyn Ground was chosen as the venue for the England-Poland UEFA Under-21 Championship match, so the club had apparently purged its 'guilt' for the Spanish incident.

Today, the Boleyn Ground — like most stadiums since the implementation of the Safety of Sports Ground Act — has seen its capacity reduced. The current ground capacity is set at 28,000.

Work has now started on the new two-tier Bobby Moore South Stand with executive boxes. The stand will hold 7,600 people, all seated, and should be ready around Christmas 1993. Final conversion of the ground into an all-seater stadium will take place during the summer of 1994.

Hammers' Managers

NLIKE most football clubs, West Ham United has not had many managers. Indeed, since 1900, when the club first assumed that title, only seven men have been in charge of team affairs. In the earliest days of Thames Ironworks FC, football managers in the sense that we understand today were a still-to-be-born species. In those times, the club secretary was the man charged with running almost everything, with team selection probably a matter for a committee.

The Irons' first 'unofficial' secretary was Dave Taylor, the man responsible for the club's formation. Taylor, a foreman in the shipbuilding department of the Ironworks, was a qualified referee and because of that — and possibly due to the fact that the post of Irons' secretary carried little in the way of financial reward — he stood down once the club's first season was underway. From time to time, Taylor would referee matches involving Thames Ironworks, although the games were friendlies.

Ted Harsent, who lived near the Ironworks, in Mary Street, Canning Town, and who was also an employee, took over for the first season and was in office at the time of the dispute over the tenancy of the Hermit Road ground in October 1896.

It is known that Harsent gave up the post at about this time because the local press announced that Taylor had, in fact, been persuaded to take on the job after all. Taylor, whose home was in James Street, near the Greengate, held the post of Ironworks' secretary during the club's 'homeless' period following their eviction from Hermit Road.

There was speculation that the club might move to Harold Road, Upton Park, but nothing came of it and Taylor eventually located a ground at Browning Road, East Ham. Thus, Thames Ironworks played out the 1896-7 season in 'foreign' parts.

At the start of 1897-8, Francis Payne, hitherto secretary of the Thames Ironworks' Federation of Clubs, took on the task of running the football club. He was secretary when the club moved to the spacious Memorial Grounds and became a professional organisation. Payne's tenure lasted for just over a year before he was suspended by the Football Association following allegations of 'player poaching'.

The club was also suspended and began the 1899-1900 season later than the other clubs. Before his departure, however, Payne had brought several players to Thames Ironworks and he left the club with men of the calibre of Harry Bradshaw, Kenny McKay, Bill Joyce and Syd King.

George Neil, a 24-year-old full-back with the club, took over the secretary's job and inherited a good team. Neil, a native of West Norwood but then living in Dewberry Street, Poplar, relinquished the job midway through the 1899-1900 season, probably because of ill health, for he died before he reached his 30th birthday.

The manager of the Memorial Grounds, which were used for several sports besides soccer, at this time was Lew Bowen, and upon Neil's premature retirement, he assumed responsibility for the football club. Bowen was in office at the most significant period in the club's history. Thames Ironworks FC broke away from the parent company, went public, and changed its title to West Ham United FC.

At the end of the first season under the West Ham banner, the new directors appointed Syd King as assistant to Lew Bowen. King had made a rapid recovery from a broken ankle the previous season and went on playing after his appointment to the club's administration. In 1902, he reclaimed his amateur status as a player.

E.S. (Syd) King
1902-1932

SYD KING was born at Chatham in August 1873. Educated at a grammar school in Watford, he was later employed at an ordnance depot in his home town and also developed into a full-back of considerable experience by the time he arrived in East London in 1899.

He had played for Northfleet and once claimed that he had scored a hat-trick of own-goals for that club against Swindon Town. In 1897, he transferred to New Brompton (now Gillingham) and spent two seasons there before joining Thames Ironworks in the summer of 1899.

King was a flamboyant character and he formed a well-known full-back partnership with Charlie Craig, the lanky Scotsman who moved to Nottingham Forest in 1902. King himself was destined to stay with Hammers for many years, and in 1902 he became secretary.

He made it a rule to maintain good relationships with the press, being fully aware of the benefits that could result. And when West Ham applied to join the Football League in 1919, they found support from the sporting papers readily forthcoming.

King thus guided West Ham United from the Southern League and into the First Division of the Football League, as well as to the club's first-ever FA Cup Final. In those golden Upton Park days of 1922-3, he realised many of his ambitions in the game, and having steered the Hammers into Division One, he kept them there for several seasons, and saw several of his team win full international honours.

But that team eventually grew old as King failed to acknowledge that although ability may linger, its effectiveness becomes diminished with passing years. In the side beaten at Chelsea in the last First Division fixture of 1931-2, there were still three members of the side that had steered Hammers to Wembley in 1923.

As performances deteriorated, so did Syd King's health. The board of directors, who had once thought so much of Syd King that they paid him a bonus of £300 after he had managed to get a good price from Falkirk for the transfer of Hammers' most saleable asset, Syd Puddefoot, now regarded the manager as a drunken insubordinate, and responsible for the club's unhealthy position.

In 1931, the directors gave him some shares in the club, but the following year, at a board meeting on 7 November 1932, it was recorded that: "It was unanimously decided that until further notice, C.Paynter be given sole control of the players and that E.S.King be notified accordingly."

Behind that terse sentence lay a sad, pathetic story. King, who was well-known for his fondness for ale, had arrived at the board meeting drunk. He had made insulting remarks to at least one director, and so his career in football — and, as it would happen, his own life — was almost at an end.

The following night, West Ham United held an emergency board meeting at which it was decided to suspend King for three months without pay and to ban him from the Boleyn Ground. Thereafter, if the directors could be satisfied that his behaviour had improved, he might be reinstated as secretary only and his salary reduced to £8 per week, accordingly. Certainly, his days in charge of the club's playing staff were over.

At another meeting, on 3 January 1933, the directors decided that King should not, after all, be employed in any capacity. The secretary, now Alan Searles, was instructed to write to King and inform him, and the directors also agreed that, in recognition of King's previous service to the club, they would pay him an *ex gratia* payment of £3 per week for 'as long as the company sees fit'.

King saved them their money. Less than one month after his dismissal, he committed suicide by lacing an alcoholic drink with some kind of corrosive substance. By a strange coincidence, Charlie Craig, his old full-back partner in the days of Thames Ironworks, died on the same day. An inquest jury recorded a verdict that King had taken his own life 'whilst of unsound mind', after his son had told them that the Hammers' former manager-secretary had been suffering from paranoia. He was, however, said his son, quite satisfied with West Ham's offer of a £3 per week 'pension'. A decade earlier, the *East Ham Echo* had stated in its FA Cup Final issue: 'West Ham is Syd King'.

Charlie Paynter
1932-1950

CHARLIE PAYNTER, was six years younger than Syd King. He was born of Welsh parents at Swindon, and brought to London at an early age. Paynter attended Grange Road School, Plaistow,

and after leaving there, he was offered an apprenticeship with the City of London Electric Light Company.

He was keen on all sports and when the Memorial Grounds were opened in 1897, Paynter began to spend most of his spare time there, competing in athletics events and coaching others. Perhaps he spent too much time at his sport, because eventually his employers cancelled his apprenticeship, which at least left young Paynter free to concentrate on athletics.

Inevitably, he became involved with the Hammers and after a season helping Abe Norris as an unpaid 'assistant trainer',

Paynter was put on the club's staff as assistant to trainer Jack Ratcliffe. He survived Ratcliffe and had a spell under Bill Johnson before West Ham removed from the Memorial Grounds to Upton Park in 1904.

Secretary-manager Syd King had been impressed with Paynter's work and he recommended him to another new West Ham trainer, Tom Robinson. That partnership was to last until 1912, when Robinson retired and Paynter was made trainer, with Frank Piercy as his assistant.

Charlie Paynter was trainer to West Ham for 20 years, and was looked upon as a kind of 'father figure' by the players. He was an ideal link between the players and the manager, and if the players had any genuine complaints, then they could be sure that Paynter would bring them to Syd King's attention. Such was his stature in the game that in 1924, he was appointed trainer to the England team for the first international to be played at Wembley.

In 1932, following King's tragic demise, Charlie Paynter was appointed manager of West Ham United. At first, there were some board members who did not want to see Paynter's appointment, in the wake of King's suspension, made permanent, but gradually everyone felt that he could bring together a team good enough to win back Hammers' place in the First Division.

Perhaps he could have achieved that, had not war intervened in 1939, when West Ham had a side which looked good enough for promotion. In 1940, he saw the club win a Wembley Cup Final, but by 1946, when League football resumed, too much had happened and the team brimming with potential in 1939 had broken up.

Paynter, now 67, knew he would be unlikely to take Hammers into the First Division and he told the board that he would soon be thinking of retirement. He recommended that Ted Fenton be engaged as his heir apparent, and the board wisely agreed. They had grown to trust a man who had spent 50 years with West Ham — nearly 20 of them as manager — and his advice was readily accepted.

Charlie Paynter lived into his 90s, long enough to witness his beloved West Ham United return to the First Division in 1958, under the guidance of the man he had said ought to have his job.

Ted Fenton
1950-1961

TED FENTON was born at Forest Gate in 1914 and was a prolific scorer for the Oddessa Road School team, an ability he carried into the West Ham Boys eleven. He was denied an England Schoolboys cap when an outbreak of smallpox resulted in the game being cancelled, but eventually won one against Scotland at Ibrox in 1929.

Fenton joined West Ham as a youngster and one of his earliest memories of Upton Park was being sent to fetch beer for manager Syd King. He made his League debut for Hammers in 1932-3, when he was on the losing side five times in six outings, but his second season was more successful with six appearances on the winning side and a hat-trick against Bury.

He played regularly right up to the outbreak of World War Two, during which he served as a PT instructor with the army in North Africa and Burma. When the war was over, Fenton became manager of Colchester United, who were then a Southern League club, and he brought that club national fame when he steered them to the fifth round of the FA Cup where they were beaten by First Division Blackpool.

Shortly afterwards, Fenton was enticed to Upton Park as assistant manager, with the knowledge that when Charlie Paynter retired, he would take over. Under Fenton's leadership, West Ham set up a youth policy and the team was also strengthened with ventures into the transfer market. The youth policy soon began to produce results and in 1954, Hammers reached the FA Youth Cup semi-final.

Fenton's greatest achievement, however, came in 1958 when he guided West Ham back to the First Division after an absence

Ron Greenwood
1961-1974

RON GREENWOOD was born at Burnley in November 1921 and played as a centre-half for Bradford, Brentford, Chelsea and Fulham, appearing in Chelsea's League Championship winning team of 1954-5.

Whilst still a player, he qualified as a coach and after retiring became manager of Eastbourne United. Success with the England Youth team brought him the offer of a job as chief coach at Highbury and he combined the job at Arsenal with that of looking after the England Under-23 team.

of 26 years. In 1959, the club finished sixth in Division One, but two years later, Ted Fenton was no longer the manager.

In March 1961, he left in circumstances which have never been satisfactorily explained. Admittedly, Hammers had slipped from the heady days of 1959 — 14th and then 16th places in the two subsequent seasons — but there was nothing to suggest that anything was wrong at Upton Park.

Nevertheless, the board issued a statement that Ted Fenton had been suffering from strain and had been granted 'sick leave'. Eventually, Fenton left and both he and the board of directors had made up their minds that what had gone on behind the scenes at Upton Park during those final few weeks of his managership would remain confidential. Eventually, he became manager of Southend United. Ted Fenton died in July 1992, aged 77, following a car crash near Peterborough.

In April 1961, he became the first West Ham manager to have had no previous connection with the club. During his time at Upton Park, Greenwood bought a number of expensive players to the club, including Johnny Byrne, Peter Brabrook, Billy Bonds, Alan Stephenson and Peter Eustace; and there were notable departures like the World Cup trio of Moore, Peters and Hurst — although only Peters was sold when still in his prime.

Greenwood cared little for people's reputations, withdrawing Moore's captaincy after the man who had led England to World Cup glory was one of several players found guilty of indiscretion on the eve of an FA Cup game at Blackpool.

He was also in charge of West Ham when they won the FA Cup for the first time, in 1964, and a year later saw his team triumph in the European Cup-winners' Cup Final against TSV München 1860 at Wembley.

In 1974, Greenwood was made general manager of West Ham United, and his assistant, John Lyall, was appointed team manager. Three years later, Don Revie's shock departure for the Middle East left England without a team manager and Greenwood emerged from a pack of contenders which included Brian Clough, to take on the job of picking up the pieces and trying to get England into the 1978 World Cup Finals in Argentina.

Greenwood's immediate task was quite hopeless, for England were as good as out of the World Cup, but he later guided them to the Finals of both that competition and the European Nations Championship before retiring after five years in charge of the national team.

John Lyall
1974-1989

THOUGHT by many to be a permanent fixture at Upton Park, John Lyall's dismissal from the club in 1989 came as

a colossal shock. Taken on as an office boy in August 1955, he had served the Hammers on and off the field for 34 years.

Lyall was born at Ilford, Essex, in February 1940 and played for England Youth against Luxembourg at Upton Park in 1957, in a team which included Jimmy Greaves and Barry Bridges (both of Chelsea) and fellow Hammer, John Cartwright. The same year, Lyall played in the West Ham team beaten by the all-conquering Manchester United team in the FA Youth Cup Final.

Although he signed professional forms shortly afterwards, Lyall had to wait three years for his League debut. It came against Chelsea in February 1960, but signalled the start of a spell of troublesome injuries. His final outing was against Blackburn Rovers, in the last game of 1962-3, a match that marked the debuts of John Sissons, Martin Britt and John Charles.

After returning to office duties for a spell, Lyall redirected his career towards coaching and under Ron Greenwood's guidance soon qualified. He then became the manager's right-hand man, and in 1974, was appointed team manager.

Greenwood's appointment as England manager in 1977 left the way clear for John Lyall to take over and he brought several honours to Upton Park, notably the FA Cup (twice), and perhaps more significantly, the FA Youth Cup. Under him, West Ham also reached their second League Cup Final and their highest place ever (third) in the First Division.

Following his depature from West Ham, Lyall spent a year scouting for Spurs before being appointed manager of Second Division Ipswich Town in May 1990. After Town had finished 14th in his first term, Lyall recruited several former Hammers into his squad and a strengthened team was able to win a place in the new FA Premier League.

Lou Macari
1989-1990

CHOSEN to succeed following the shock dismissal of John Lyall, Lou Macari took over the unsettled East Enders in July 1989. On his arrival at Upton Park, he found Alan Dickens bound for Stamford Bridge, whilst Mark Ward and Paul Ince were making similar transfer-seeking noises.

Within a few weeks, Ince was on his way to Manchester United, one of Macari's former clubs, for a flat fee plus premiums. When Ward eventually departed to the other Manchester club, Macari managed to capture Trevor Morley and Ian Bishop as part of an exchange deal.

These Macari signings played an important part in recovering Hammers' position in the latter half of the 1989-90 season, following a slump to 12th place in December.

Macari was born in Edinburgh on 7 June 1949, of Italian parents, and the family moved to London when he was still a schoolboy. For nearly six years he lived in Forest Gate, at the other end of Green Street from Upton Park.

Once back in Scotland, Macari began to take soccer seriously and after spells with Kilwinning Rangers and Kilmarnock Amateurs, he was signed by Glasgow Celtic and the Parkhead club won the Scottish League title in every season he was with them. Although his contribution was just 26 goals in 50 games, it earned him two championship medals. He twice won Scottish Cup winners' medals but his three League Cup Final appearances brought only runners-up awards.

Macari played for Scotland at every level from schoolboy to full international and in January 1973 moved to Manchester United and in an 11-year stay at Old Trafford made 400 appearances and collected further Cup winners' medals and a Second Division championship medal.

In the summer of 1984 he was appointed manager of Swindon Town and during his time at the County Ground he helped take the Wiltshire club out of the Fourth Division (with a record number of points) and into the Second. Unfortunately he also became associated with a betting scandal — his part was described as 'minor and foolhardy' — which cost him a £1,000 fine. There followed a more serious charge of illegal payments to players and Swindon were denied another promotion already won on the field. All this came to light after Macari's move to West Ham and he did the honourable thing and resigned. His last signing for the Hammers was Ludek Miklosko, the Czechoslovakian international goalkeeper.

Within a year, Macari was back in soccer as manager of Birmingham City and guided them to victory in the 1991 Leyland Daf Final at Wembley. Three weeks later, however, he parted company with the troubled Birmingham club and joined Stoke City.

In his first season at the Victoria Ground, he improved Stoke's League position by ten places and in addition the Potters captured the Autoglass Trophy (the re-named Leyland Daf Cup). The little Scotsman's success continued and in 1993 Stoke romped away with the new Second Division title.

Billy Bonds
1990-

NOW about to start his fourth season in the Upton Park hot seat, Billy Bonds must by now be accustomed to the ups and downs of League football. In every season he has so far been in charge, Hammers have been involved in either a promotion or a relegation struggle.

Bonds virtually got the job by popular demand, for in the days following Lou Macari's resignation, there was so much speculation that the clamour for his appointment could not have failed to reach the ears of the Hammers directors.

It is easy to understand the appeal that Bonds has for the Upton Park faithful. He talks like them and plays the way they would, if they were able. The word 'bucaneering', for so long applied to him, is apt, for he would not look out of place beneath a 'skull and crossbones' flag. On the pitch, he played with a zeal that inspired others and his robust competitiveness was never described as dirty by opponents.

As a mark of his standing in the game, the Nottingham Forest club presented him with a Royal Doulton vase after the League fixture at the City Ground on 14 February 1987. The Forest chairman, Maurice Rowarth, said it was in recognition of Bonds' contribution to the game of football. Some ten months later, in January 1988, Bonds was summoned to Buckingham Palace to receive an even higher award . . .the MBE.

Billy Bonds began his managerial career in February 1990. His first match in charge was a home fixture against Blackburn Rovers and there were emotional scenes as he emerged from the tunnel alone to acknowledge the tumultuous reception of the crowd.

The club's League position before kick-off that day was 14th — their lowest placing of the season. When the season was over, Hammers had accumulated another 33 points and had missed the play-offs by just two.

Under Lou Macari, the side had reached the semi-finals of the Littlewoods Cup, but at the time Bonds took charge they were facing Oldham Athletic with six goals to make up. In the event, the gallant Hammers clawed back three in the second leg.

Starting 1990-91 with a clean sheet, Bonds took Hammers to within a minute of the Second Division championship — sixty seconds being all it took Oldham Athletic to gain and score a penalty in the dying seconds of their final match of the season. About a month earlier, Bonds' team had, by general consent, been cruelly treated when a harsh refereeing decision deprived them of Tony Gale at a crucial time in an FA Cup semi-final.

Since Bonds has held the reins,

Hammers fans have witnessed a fair number of staff changes: Liam Brady has retired, or rather gone into management; David Kelly has found the success some thought he was capable of, culminating in his achievements at Newcastle United; and others making the outward trip have been Stewart Robson, Leroy Rosenior, Frank McAvennie, Ray Stewart, George Parris, Stuart Slater, Gary Strodder and Simon Livett.

Among the imports have been Tim Breacker, Chris Hughton, Mitchell Thomas, Ray Attveld, Mike Small, Clive Allen, Peter Butler, Mark Robson, Matt Holmes, Kenny Brown (son of a 1960s Upton Park favourite), David Speedie and Ian Dowie, who has since moved on to Southampton.

West Ham's return to what was still the Football League's First Division in the 1991-2 season was not a happy one. Goals were the problem and how to get them. In only eight games did West Ham score more than once and their final aggregate of 37 was the third smallest total in the entire Football League.

Near the close of the campaign, Bond reacted and pressed Alvin Martin back into service. And he also convinced his directors that Clive Allen would be a useful acquisition. The moves were a partial success, but too late as two victories were recorded in the final three games.

Billy Bonds' men started the 1992-3 campaign as joint second favourites, but some poor home results lost them ground early on. His old friend and former West Ham winger Harry Redknapp was now his assistant. Although the team recovered the lost ground, it developed a unenviable disciplinary record. When Julian Dicks was shown the red card at Derby County on 10 January, he became the seventh Hammer to be disciplined in this way. Bonds' reply to an obvious question was an emphatic "We're not kickers."

In the same month, Bonds won the Barclays Manager of the Month award. It was the fourth time since becoming a manager that he had done so.

Following a string of good results, his team stumbled at Notts County — "We could have played all night and still not scored" was his reaction. When his lads comfortably beat Brentford 4-0 in April, he told a reporter, "We could have had eight." But he must have been reasonably satisfied with his club's position, for in programme notes later that same month he said: "If somebody had said to me at the start of the season that we would have 79 points in the bag at this late stage, I would have been delighted." He pointed to the fact that Portsmouth were having a splendid run but predicted that they would come unstuck . . .and they did.

Having succeeded in getting Hammers into the Premier League, Billy Bonds commented on the stiff competition that would make up the First Division next term. "It's a good job we're out of it!" he said.

Hammers Stars A-Z

A member of the Allen clan that has been so prominent in British soccer in recent years, Paul Allen became the youngest player ever to appear in an FA Cup Final when, aged 17, he helped Second Division West Ham beat First Division Arsenal in the 1980 Wembley game. He might have marked the achievement with a goal, too, had he not been cynically fouled by a defender when clean through and bearing down on goal. Born at Aveley, Essex, in August 1962, Allen won a record 23 England Youth caps and skippered his country to victory over Poland in the 1980 UEFA Youth Tournament Final in Leipzig. After being on Queen's Park Rangers' books for a short time, Allen joined West Ham in the summer of 1978, signing professional forms on his 17th birthday and making his Football League debut a month later, on 29 September 1979, against Burnley. He played in most of Hammers' games that season, including all the FA Cup matches on the way to Wembley. He was still young enough to win an FA Youth Cup medal in 1981, when Hammers beat Tottenham Hotspur in the Final. Following a long lay-off through injury, Allen made a great impact on

his return and soon attracted the attentions of other clubs. In the summer of 1985, he joined his cousin, Clive, at White Hart Lane — Clive's father, Les Allen, was a great Spurs favourite in the 1950s. A tireless worker, Paul's career already spans 14 seasons and over 500 senior appearances.

PAUL ALLEN

	LEAGUE		FA CUP		FL CUP		EUROPE		TOTAL	
	App	Gls	App	Gls	App	Gls	App	Gls	App	Gls
1979-80	31	2	7/1	1	7	0	0	0	45/1	3
1980-81	1/2	1	1	0	1/2	0	1/1	0	4/5	1
1981-82	27/1	0	0	0	0/2	0	0	0	27/3	0
1982-83	33	0	1	0	7	2	0	0	41	2
1983-84	19	0	1/2	0	1	0	0	0	21/2	0
1984-85	38	3	5	2	4	0	0	0	47	5
	149/3	6	15/3	3	20/4	2	1/1	0	185/11	11

Malcolm Allison, who was born at Dartford in 1927, was one of the most colourful footballers ever to wear the claret and blue of West Ham United. He arrived at Upton Park from Charlton Athletic in February 1951, replacing the ageing Dick Walker. The fact that he succeeded such a popular figure as Walker perhaps worked against him, for Allison never quite established himself with the Hammers' supporters. There was no question that he was a talented centre-half, but he was also something of a 'character'. One of his favourite tricks was to feign injury during a practice match, then from writhing in agony he would dart into place for the resultant free-kick. One undying memory of Allison comes from a friendly match against AC Milan in 1954, when the Italian club's great hulk of a centre-forward, Gunnar Nordahl, literally dragged Allison — who was hanging on to the Swede's shirt — with him past several defenders before lashing a shot into the roof of the West Ham net. Milan won 6-0 that night and, curiously, a fortnight prior to his move to Hammers, Allison had taken part in a friendly at Upton Park when he played in the same side as another Swede, Hans Jeppson, who netted four times in Charlton's 5-1 win. Allison had a keen tactical mind and he was probably a great influence on Hammers' promotion season of 1957-8. Sadly, he lost a lung after being ill with tuberculosis and was denied a single First Division appearance for the club. Thereafter, he made his name as a coach and his greatest days were spent with Joe Mercer at Manchester City where the duo lifted City

to the greatest days in that club's history. Allison also courted controversy and his private life sometimes made as many headlines as his football career. Nevertheless, the game has been brighter for his involvement. His most recent post was at Bristol Rovers.

MALCOLM ALLISON

	LEAGUE		FA CUP		TOTAL	
	App	Gls	App	Gls	App	Gls
1950-51	10	0	0	0	10	0
1951-52	38	0	3	0	41	0
1952-53	39	2	1	0	40	2
1953-54	42	0	3	0	45	0
1954-55	25	0	2	0	27	0
1955-56	40	3	6	0	46	3
1956-57	39	4	2	0	41	4
1957-58	5	1	0	0	5	1
	238	10	17	0	255	10

Born in Edinburgh in 1875, Allison spent three years with New Brighton Tower, then in the Second Division of the Football League. When that club disbanded in 1901 he joined Reading in the Southern League and helped them to their highest placings, in 1901-02 and 1902-03. In an exodus of Reading players, Allison, along with Cotton, Lyon and Watts, joined Hammers for 1903-04, the last season at the Memorial Grounds. Allison became a regular for the next five years, appearing in 150 Southern League and FA Cup games. On 14 December 1908 he was awarded the proceeds of the Western League fixture against Portsmouth, thus becoming the first West Ham player to earn a benefit. Allison, who won a Scottish junior cap with Strathclyde, often skippered Hammers when the regular captain was not available. He made his debut on 7 September 1903, in the 4-1 Southern League win over Kettering Town when he marked his first-team baptism with a goal. Allison, who played all his games for West Ham in the half-back line, managed seven League goals altogether. His best season was 1906-07 when he missed only two games as Hammers finished fifth in the table.

	LEAGUE		FA CUP		TOTAL	
	App	Gls	App	Gls	App	Gls
1903-04	28	2	4	0	32	2
1904-05	30	2	1	0	31	2
1905-06	28	1	2	0	30	1
1906-07	36	2	2	0	38	2
1907-08	29	0	0	0	29	0
1908-09	5	0	0	0	5	0
	156	7	9	0	165	7

He made his last appearance in the first team against Watford in April 1909, playing his part in West Ham's 3-1 victory which helped the club struggle to 17th position. In his early days at the club, during the summer of 1904, Tom Allison was one of the few players who survived a purge on the Hammers' playing staff when several were released.

THOMAS ALLISON

Ashton was a diminutive winger with clever ball-control whose partnership with Danny Shea was often compared with the famous Swindon pairing of Jefferson and Fleming. Born at Blackburn in 1887, Ashton first played senior soccer for Accrington, whom he helped win the Lancashire Combination in 1905-06. He joined West Ham in the summer of 1908 and made his Southern League debut in September that year, against Queen's Park Rangers. One goal in 27 outings that season underlined the fact that he was not a prolific scorer but his successful efforts always received an over-enthusiastic reception from the Boleyn crowd. Indeed, as far as Hammers' fans were concerned, Ashton could do no wrong, even on bad days. He married a local girl, from Forest Gate, and his best man was Danny Shea, even though Shea was by now a Blackburn player. Ashton served as a mechanic in the Royal Flying Corps during World War One but remained on Hammers' books throughout the conflict. His final appearance in a West Ham jersey was in May 1919, in a charity game against Arsenal at Upton Park. He could then look back on a career which had seen West Ham finish quite high in the Southern League without ever making a real challenge

for the title. His best season was probably 1912-13, when Hammers finished third in the table and Ashton missed only two games. For certain, Herbert Ashton was that relatively scarce commodity — a player who people would flock to watch. His last two games in the Southern League were at centre-forward when he took over from the injured Dan Bailey.

	LEAGUE		FA CUP		TOTAL	
	App	Gls	App	Gls	App	Gls
1908-09	27	1	2	0	29	1
1909-10	42	4	5	0	47	4
1910-11	37	6	4	0	41	6
1911-12	33	3	5	0	38	3
1912-13	36	6	4	0	40	6
1913-14	35	3	4	1	39	4
1914-15	14	0	1	0	15	0
	224	23	25	1	249	24

HERBERT ASHTON

On Saturday, 27 August 1949, winger Ken Bainbridge scored the quickest goal ever seen at Upton Park when he netted within seconds of the kick-off against a Barnsley team that included Danny Blanchflower. Bill Robinson, the West Ham centre-forward, side-footed the ball to Gerry Gazzard, Hammers' new inside-right; he transferred it to Bainbridge who took it forward a few yards before crashing his shot into the back of the Colliers' net. There have been some quite outrageous claims over the timing of the goal — one report of only two seconds is clearly a physical impossibility — but there is no doubt that the Boleyn has never seen a quicker strike. Born at Barking, Essex, in January 1921, Bainbridge came to prominence during the war with amateurs, Leyton. They shared Upton Park in 1943, and Charlie Paynter was quick to spot Bainbridge's talent. He signed professional forms for 1946-7 and his speed and hard shooting earned him a regular place. Thereafter, he struggled

somewhat and after a further three seasons in and out of the side he moved to Reading in an exchange deal which brought centre-half Vic Niblett to Upton Park. In his first season at Elm Park, Bainbridge scored 17 goals, the best by a Reading winger for many years. In February 1953, he signed for Southend United for whom he scored 24 goals in 78 League games before leaving the Football League.

KEN BAINBRIDGE

	LEAGUE		FA CUP		TOTAL	
	App	Gls	App	Gls	App	Gls
1945-46	0	0	3	1	3	1
1946-47	35	9	1	0	36	9
1947-48	4	0	0	0	4	0
1948-49	16	2	0	0	16	2
1949-50	25	5	0	0	25	5
	80	16	4	1	84	17

At 5ft 11in tall and weighing 14st, the figure of Jim Barrett dominated the West Ham team between the wars. Barrett, who was born at Stratford, East London, on 19 January 1907, played as a forward during his schooldays, although he was capable of giving a sound performance in any position. It is claimed that in two seasons with the Park School team he scored some 200 goals. Young Barrett also found time to win a district boxing title but football was his first love and he won two England Schools caps, scoring against Scotland on the old Third Lanark ground at Cathkin Park in 1921. Barrett joined the Fairbairn House Boys' Club team that had produced footballers of the calibre of George Barbour, Jack Townrow and Ted Fenton. He signed professional forms for Hammers in 1923 but had to wait for the departure of George Kay to Stockport before he could establish a regular first-team place. In 11 seasons between 1925-6 and 1935-6, Barrett made 400 League appearances. His international career was much shorter: injured after only eight minutes of

England's game against Northern Ireland at Goodison Park in October 1928, he was never given another chance. Barrett's next appearance at Goodison was a much happier occasion. Hammers' 4-0 win there in April 1929 is still their biggest victory on Merseyside. He had a fierce shot which brought him nearly 50 League goals, some from the penalty spot, and he played centre-half more times for Hammers than any other player between the wars, although he was adaptable and in a seven-match spell in January and February 1926 he played in five different positions. His last game for Hammers was a thrilling 5-4 win over Brighton during the war — West Ham had trailed 4-1 with 30 minutes remaining and Brighton missed a penalty in the final minutes. Barrett was in charge of the juniors at Upton Park and had the satisfaction of seeing his son, Jimmy, graduate to the senior team. Jim Barrett senior died, following a long illness, on 25 November 1970.

	LEAGUE		FA CUP		TOTAL	
	App	Gls	App	Gls	App	Gls
1924-25	5	0	0	0	5	0
1925-26	42	6	1	0	43	6
1926-27	42	1	3	0	45	1
1927-28	34	5	0	0	34	5
1928-29	22	1	2	3	24	4
1929-30	40	7	4	1	44	8
1930-31	40	4	1	0	41	4
1931-32	38	3	2	0	40	3
1932-33	40	8	6	0	46	8
1933-34	38	5	2	0	40	5
1934-35	41	5	2	0	43	5
1935-36	40	2	2	0	42	2
1936-37	11	1	0	0	11	1
1937-38	8	1	0	0	8	1
1938-39	1	0	0	0	1	0
	442	49	25	4	467	53

JIM BARRETT senior

Until Bobby Moore lifted the FA Cup in 1964, full-back Charlie Bicknell was the only Hammers skipper to have led them to a major trophy. Bicknell's big moment came when he received the Football League War Cup after Hammers had beaten Blackburn Rovers in a Wembley Final in 1940. Born at Pye Bridge, near Chesterfield, in November 1905, Bicknell was a coalminer before taking up full-time soccer. His first club was the local village team, Tupton, and in 1927-8 he spent the season as an amateur on Chesterfield's books before signing professional forms with them. He spent two years at the Recreation Ground before moving to Bradford City in 1930. At Valley Parade he set an extraordinary sequence of consecutive appearances that stretched over five and a half seasons. He was transferred to West Ham towards the end of 1935-6 and made his debut in March that season, in a 4-1 win over Newcastle. Up to the outbreak of war, Bicknell made more than 100 appearances for Hammers and became club captain. A special policeman during the hostilities, his 200-plus wartime appearances are a record for a West Ham player. Although he began 1946-7 as captain, Bicknell was then 41 years old and his final appearance was at Leicester on 4 January 1947, after which he retired. He later managed Bedford Town in the Southern League.

	LEAGUE		FA CUP		TOTAL	
	App	Gls	App	Gls	App	Gls
1935-36	7	0	0	0	7	0
1936-37	28	0	2	0	30	0
1937-38	42	0	1	0	43	0
1938-39	41	0	5	0	46	0
1945-46	0	0	4	0	4	0
1946-47	19	1	0	0	19	1
	137	1	12	0	149	1

CHARLES BICKNELL

A legacy of the short Macari era, Bishop's capture from Manchester City was instrumental in the revival of Hammers' flagging fortunes midway through 1989-90 as the classy Liverpudlian with the distinctive hairstyle became the driving force of the revitalised West Ham side. In a career that spanned all four divisions, Bishop gained early experience of the ups and downs of the game, when he was twice a member of Carlisle United teams relegated during the 1980s. More recently he was a major contributor to West Ham's successful promotion bid of 1990-91. In addition to spells at Brunton Park and Maine Road, Bishop had a short stay at Crewe Alexandra, on loan from Everton, his first club. His only other Football League employer was AFC Bournemouth, under the management of former Hammer, Harry Redknapp, and in a career already spanning more than 250 League games he has scored 24 goals. In May 1991, the FA recognised Bishop's talents when he was capped for England 'B' against Switzerland at Walsall.

	LEAGUE		FA CUP		FL CUP		TOTAL	
	App	Gls	App	Gls	App	Gls	App	Gls
1989-90	13/4	2	1	0	0	0	14/4	2
1990-91	40	4	5/1	2	3	0	48/1	6
1991-92	41	1	3	0	4	0	48	1
1992-93	15/7	1	0	0	0	0	15/7	1
	109/11	8	9/1	2	7	0	125/12	10

IAN BISHOP

A versatile half-back or inside-forward, Syd Bishop was a valued member of Hammers' team in the early 1920s. He made his first-team debut against Birmingham on Christmas Day 1920 and marked his first appearance with a goal. Born at Stepney, East London, in February 1900, he served in the RAF during the latter months of World War One and it was in the services that his football career blossomed. After his demob he joined Isthmian League club, Ilford, and also played for Crystal Palace Reserves before signing for West Ham. He was an important member of the Hammers' team that did so well in the Second Division and he played in the 1923 FA Cup Final. His form declined in the aftermath of those West Ham glory days and in November 1926, after a long spell of reserve-team football, he signed for Leicester City. The move did him good and at Filbert Street he recaptured his old form to such an extent that he was playing for England against Scotland at Hampden Park the following April. Three more caps followed on England's European tour, but illness robbed him of another appearance against Scotland and he thus missed the 1928 thrashing by the 'Wembley Wizards'. After 18 months with Leicester, Bishop moved to Chelsea and went on to make over 100 appearances for them, helping the West London club to promotion from Division Two in 1929-30. He retired in 1933 and died in April 1949, aged 49.

SYD BISHOP

	LEAGUE		FA CUP		TOTAL	
	App	Gls	App	Gls	App	Gls
1920-21	21	3	1	0	22	3
1921-22	36	4	3	0	39	4
1922-23	34	2	8	0	42	2
1923-24	31	0	0	0	31	0
1924-25	14	0	0	0	14	0
1925-26	14	1	1	0	15	1
1926-27	9	0	0	0	9	0
	159	10	13	0	172	10

Fred Blackburn was born in Blackburn in 1881 and, not surprisingly, his first club was Blackburn Rovers. He was capped three times for England between 1901 and 1904 and arrived at Upton Park in May 1905. A frustrating player whose clever ball skills were sometimes wasted by wild shooting, Blackburn played most of his career at outside-left although he began as an inside-forward. In 1911-12, Hammers converted him to wing-half with some success. Blackburn made his West Ham debut in the home game against Swindon on 2 September 1905 and his final appearance was at Merthyr on 18 January 1913 when Hammers were defeated 6-2. In 1911 he had shared, with George Kitchen, a benefit game against Coventry City. His brother, Arthur, was a full-back with Blackburn Rovers and Southampton. Fred Blackburn later spent some time in the Merchant Navy and in the early 1930s he was engaged as a coach by Barking FC.

	LEAGUE		FA CUP		TOTAL	
	App	Gls	App	Gls	App	Gls
1905-06	30	5	2	0	32	5
1906-07	29	4	0	0	29	4
1907-08	36	4	2	1	38	5
1908-09	40	6	6	3	46	9
1909-10	42	3	5	0	47	3
1910-11	16	2	0	0	16	2
1911-12	22	0	5	0	27	0
1912-13	2	0	0	0	2	0
	217	24	20	4	237	28

FRED BLACKBURN

People following the merry-go-round managerial career of John Bond are apt to forget that almost 16 years of his playing career were spent at one club — West Ham United. Born at Colchester in December 1932, Bond played for North-East Essex Schools and Essex Army Cadets before joining Colchester Casuals. Even at this early stage of his career, he had already caught the eye of Ted Fenton, then the manager of Colchester United, who were still a non-League club. When Fenton returned to Upton Park to take up the position of assistant to the ageing manager Charlie Paynter, he induced young Bond to go with him. It was a decision which Bond never regretted. Turning professional in March 1950, he remained a Hammer until 1965. Making his debut in a 2-1 win at Coventry in February 1952, Bond went on to make 428 senior appearances for West Ham and although used mainly as a defender, his name appeared regularly amongst the scorers. In March 1959 he was tried at centre-forward against Bolton Wanderers and promptly obliged with two goals. On another memorable occasion about a year later, he netted three times against Chelsea. Bond missed only one game in the Hammers' Second Division championship season and was ever-present in their first season back in Division One in 1958-9. Forced to share the right-back duties with Joe Kirkup during the 1963-4 season, Bond nevertheless played in every FA Cup game that season when West Ham beat Preston in the Final. A year later he found himself left out of the side for the European Cup-winners' Cup Final against TSV Munich at Wembley. In January 1966, Bond became a Torquay player and at Plainmoor added another 129 games and 11 goals to his career tally before obtaining his first job in Football League management at Bournemouth. He took over from Freddie Cox at Dean Court in 1970 and soon regained for Bournemouth a place in the Third Division. After three seasons at Dean Court, he went to manage Norwich City, taking his star pupils Ted MacDougall and Phil Boyer with him. Norwich were relegated to Division Two in his first season at Carrow Road but within 12 months they were back in the top flight and also reached the Football League Cup Final. Early in 1980-81, Bond went to manage Manchester City. They were bottom of the First Division but he lifted them out of trouble and into the bargain took them to the FA Cup Final and a League Cup semi-final that season. After two and a half years at Maine Road, Bond resigned after a 4-0 FA Cup defeat at Brighton and since then has been in charge at Burnley (where he proved so unpopular that police recently advised that he should stay away from Turf Moor), Swansea City and Birmingham City. His up-and-down career in the Football League continues with Shrewsbury Town.

	LEAGUE		FA CUP		FL CUP		EUROPE		TOTAL	
	App	Gls	App	Gls	App	Gls	App	Gls	App	Gls
1951-52	2	0	0	0	0	0	0	0	2	0
1952-53	14	0	1	0	0	0	0	0	15	0
1953-54	18	0	3	0	0	0	0	0	21	0
1954-55	25	1	1	0	0	0	0	0	26	1
1955-56	34	1	6	0	0	0	0	0	40	1
1956-57	30	1	2	0	0	0	0	0	32	1
1957-58	41	8	3	1	0	0	0	0	44	9
1958-59	42	7	1	0	0	0	0	0	43	7
1959-60	35	7	2	0	0	0	0	0	37	7
1960-61	34	4	1	0	2	0	0	0	37	4
1961-62	37	2	1	0	2	0	0	0	40	2
1962-63	14	0	0	0	2	0	0	0	16	0
1963-64	26	0	7	0	6	1	0	0	39	1
1964-65	29	1	2	0	1	0	4	1	36	2
	381	32	30	1	13	1	4	1	428	35

JOHN BOND

It seemed a lot of money in May 1967 — £50,000 for a Second Division wing-half — but it must have been one of the best signings of all time. That month saw the start of over 20 years association of Billy Bonds and West Ham. And for much of that time Bonds proved an inspirational leader. Appointed club captain in 1973, he made ridicule of the oft-remarked hypothesis that West Ham were a soft option. Bonds had ferocity and fight. Socks down, hair flapping, with or without facial hair, he was a tough, spidery customer, biting in the tackle and blistering in his runs from midfield. An England Under-23 international, Bonds was chosen for the full international team but was forced to withdraw with injury. He twice captained West Ham to FA Cup Final successes, and was involved in the chases for two other major trophies at the turn of the 1970s. Perhaps the most staggering achievement of Bonds' career, however, has been his soccer longevity. Having passed his 40th birthday, he was able to re-establish himself in the Hammers' team. He took his West Ham League and Cup appearances on towards 800, having passed Bobby Moore's club record in the 1982-3 season. Added to this were his 95 League games with Charlton, the club he joined in September 1964. Bonds, who was born at Woolwich on 17 September 1946, made his first League appearance in a West Ham shirt in the opening match of the 1967-8 season, against Sheffffield Wednesday at Upton Park. His progression to club captain after Bobby Moore had been transferred to Fulham in April 1974 was a natural choice. That season he had fought almost a one-man rearguard action against West Ham's relegation from the First Division, scoring a hat-trick against Chelsea at Upton Park and ending the season as Hammers' leading scorer. Even after he had relinquished the captaincy to Alvin Martin in 1984, after a decade of leading West Ham, Bonds remained a valuable member of the first-team squad and in 1987, when he signed a new contract, he was still making vital contributions to the all-round effectiveness of the Upton Park set-up, not least by passing his vital experience and bubbling enthusiasm to all around him. That year he was awarded the MBE for services to football. John Lyall appointed him youth coach in 1988 and he was ideally placed to take over from Lou Macari in February 1990 (see *Hammers' Manager*).

BILLY BONDS MBE

	LEAGUE		FA CUP		FL CUP		EUROPE		TOTAL	
	App	Gls	App	Gls	App	Gls	App	Gls	App	Gls
1967-68	37	1	3	0	2	0	0	0	42	1
1968-69	42	1	3	0	2	0	0	0	47	1
1969-70	42	3	1	0	2	0	0	0	45	3
1970-71	37	0	1	0	2	0	0	0	40	0
1971-72	42	3	4	0	10	2	0	0	56	5
1972-73	39	3	2	0	2	0	0	0	43	3
1973-74	40	13	2	0	1	0	0	0	43	13
1974-75	31	7	8	0	3	2	0	0	42	9
1975-76	17/1	1	0	0	5	1	9	2	31/1	4
1976-77	41	3	2	0	3	0	0	0	46	3
1977-78	29	1	3	1	0	0	0	0	32	2
1978-79	39	4	1	0	1	0	0	0	41	4
1979-80	34	1	5	0	9	0	0	0	48	1
1980-81	41	0	3	0	8	1	6	1	58	2
1981-82	29	1	2	1	4	0	0	0	35	2
1982-83	34	3	1	0	4	0	0	0	39	3
1983-84	27	0	0/1	0	2	0	0	0	29/1	0
1984-85	19/3	3	0	0	4	0	0	0	23/3	3
1986-87	13/4	0	3/1	0	1/2	0	0	0	17/7	0
1987-88	22	0	2	0	0	0	0	0	24	0
	655/8	48	46/2	2	65/2	6	15	3	781/12	59

110

They called Ron Boyce 'Ticker' because his work-rate was like clockwork — he never stopped. He was all over the field prompting his forwards, and never was his stamina more evident than in the last moments of the 1964 FA Cup Final. The scores were level and cramp-ridden players were cursing the prospect of extra-time as Peter Brabrook's cross hung in the air. But Boyce had covered ground where others might not have done. A nudge of the head sent the ball across Kelly, and it was time to celebrate the fact that West Ham had lifted the FA Cup for the first time. An England Schoolboy international, he made his League debut in October 1960 when only 17 years old. He was another Hammer selected for the England Youth team, following in the footsteps of Cartwright, Kirkup, Lyall, John Smith, Walker, Reader, Moore, Tony Scott, Andy Smillie, Woodley, Hurst and Peters — with many more to come later. He was never a

goalscoring inside-forward, but he weighed in with two goals in the 1964 semi-final before the dramatic Wembley winner. He was a push-and-run player, an ideal midfielder for the 4-2-4 system. At Wembley again, in 1965, he engineered the 2-0 win over TSV München 1860 which brought a European trophy. After retiring from playing, he joined the coaching staff at Upton Park.

RON BOYCE

	LEAGUE		FA CUP		FL CUP		EUROPE		TOTAL	
	App	Gls	App	Gls	App	Gls	App	Gls	App	Gls
1960-61	3	0	0	0	0	0	0	0	3	0
1961-62	4	1	0	0	0	0	0	0	4	1
1962-63	27	3	5	2	1	0	0	0	33	5
1963-64	41	6	7	3	7	2	0	0	55	11
1964-65	41	4	2	0	1	0	9	1	53	5
1965-66	16	2	1	0	2	0	4	0	23	2
1966-67	37	4	1	0	5	0	0	0	43	4
1967-68	38	0	1	0	3	0	0	0	42	0
1968-69	37/2	0	2/1	0	3	0	0	0	42/3	0
1969-70	18/2	1	1	0	1	0	0	0	20/2	1
1970-71	13	0	0	0	0	0	0	0	13	0
1971-72	0/1	0	0	0	0	0	0	0	0/1	0
1972-73	0/2	0	0	0	0	0	0	0	0/2	0
	275/7	21	20/1	5	23	2	13	1	331/8	29

Despite being born not far from Upton Park, playing schoolboy soccer for East Ham, Essex and London, and supporting West Ham, Peter Brabrook cost the Hammers £35,000 when he eventually signed for the club. By then he was almost 25, and had won most of the game's representative honours while with his first club — Chelsea. Tall and speedy for a winger, Brabrook signed professional forms for Chelsea in March 1955. Quickly in the first team, that same season, he became an England Youth international and Under-23 cap. Then he was chosen in the England World Cup squad which went to Sweden in 1958. His full England debut came in a group play-off against Russia. Brabrook hit a post twice and England lost 1-0. He went on to win nine Under-23 caps and three full caps and also represented the Football League. West Ham offered their money for him in October 1962 and in the first minute of his debut game, he scored a goal. Brabrook played in the 1964 FA Cup Final win, and he was in the teams that took on West Brom in the two-legged 1966 League Cup Final. In 1968, he left for Orient, with whom he spent three seasons. And in 1969-70, when Orient were Third Division

Champions, Brabrook played in all but five of the games. The next season, though, he left for Romford, thus ending a career of 488 League games (85 goals).

	LEAGUE		FA CUP		FL CUP		EUROPE		TOTAL	
	App	Gls	App	Gls	App	Gls	App	Gls	App	Gls
1962-63	29	7	5	0	0	0	0	0	34	7
1963-64	38	8	7	2	6	2	0	0	51	12
1964-65	22	3	0	0	1	1	1	0	24	4
1965-66	32	8	4	1	8	2	6	1	50	12
1966-67	32	5	1	0	5	0	0	0	38	5
1967-68	14	2	0	0	3	1	0	0	17	3
	167	33	17	3	23	6	7	1	214	43

PETER BRABROOK

111

Probably the most popular 'Arsenal-schooled' player ever to appear at Upton Park, Liam Brady's past connections were soon forgotten when it became evident that, despite his years, his ability had diminished little. Born in Dublin, Brady's talents had already been recognised by the Republic's Schools Association, even before he joined Arsenal as an apprentice in the summer of 1971. Making his debut at Highbury against Birmingham City in October 1973, he went on to play 340 senior games for the North London club. He was a member of the three Arsenal sides that contested FA Cup Finals between 1978-1980, the last of which was a humiliating defeat at the hands of Second Division West Ham United. On the international field he collected 72 caps, 26 as an Arsenal player, 11 with Hammers and the remainder whilst attached to Italian clubs. Brady had a highly successful career in the Italian League, making over 180 appearances in that competition spread among four clubs. The Irishman's most successful association was with Juventus, who captured the Italian title in each of the two seasons he was with them. Following spells with Sampdoria, Inter-Milan and Ascoli, Brady returned to the UK in 1986. He then surprised the soccer world by rejecting his former club, Arsenal, and choosing to join West Ham. His style fitted in with Hammers' methods and he made over 100 senior appearances whilst with the Upton Park club. Brady announced his intention to retire at the end of the 1989-90 season and on the final day of his playing career he scored a goal against Wolves in the closing minutes. In July 1991, Brady took on the manager's job at Glasgow Celtic.

Trevor Brooking started as an apprentice on 24 July 1965 and played his last game almost 19 years later. During his one-club career, he made a strong impression on the British public. He was upright,

TREVOR BROOKING MBE

LIAM BRADY

	LEAGUE		FA CUP		FL CUP		TOTAL	
	App	Gls	App	Gls	App	Gls	App	Gls
1986-87	12	2	0	0	0	0	12	2
1987-88	21/1	2	2	1	2	0	25/1	3
1988-89	21/1	3	7	0	4/1	0	32/2	3
1989-90	25/8	2	0	0	8/2	0	33/10	2
	79/10	9	9	1	14/3	0	102/13	10

	LEAGUE		FA CUP		FL CUP		EUROPE		TOTAL	
	App	Gls	App	Gls	App	Gls	App	Gls	App	Gls
1967-68	24/1	9	3	0	0	0	0	0	27/1	9
1968-69	29/3	7	2	0	3	1	0	0	34/3	8
1969-70	20/1	4	0	0	2	0	0	0	22/1	4
1970-71	17/2	2	0	0	1	0	0	0	18/2	2
1971-72	40	6	4	0	10	1	0	0	54	7
1972-73	40	11	2	0	2	0	0	0	44	11
1973-74	38	6	0	0	2	0	0	0	40	6
1974-75	36	3	8	1	3	1	0	0	47	5
1975-76	34	5	1	0	4	1	7	3	46	9
1976-77	42	4	2	0	3	0	0	0	47	4
1977-78	37	4	2	0	0	0	0	0	39	4
1978-79	21	2	1	0	0	0	0	0	22	2
1979-80	37	3	7	2	8	1	0	0	52	6
1980-81	36	10	3	0	7	0	4/1	0	50/1	10
1981-82	34	8	2	0	5	1	0	0	41	9
1982-83	1	0	0	0	0	0	0	0	1	0
1983-84	35	4	3	0	5	2	0	0	43	6
	521/7	88	40	3	55	8	11/1	3	627/8	102

honest and polite, and above all he could really play the game. His tall strong physique had a gentleness caused by his abundance of skill, yet he also worked hard. He was the modern midfield player. A handsome man, and a natty dresser, he was nicknamed 'Hadleigh' after a television character of similar appearance. Born in Barking, he grew up a West Ham supporter and was pleased to join the club straight from school. He was capped for England Youth, and in the same year (1967) made his First Division debut — against Burnley. He played initially as a striker, but settled down as a left-sided midfield player, two-footed, capable of twisting and turning either way. Capped once at Under-23 level, Brooking won 47 full England caps. None was more satisfying than the crucial World Cup qualifying game in Hungary in 1981 when his two goals — the second a rasping left-footer — sealed a 3-1 victory and England's place in the Finals. At club level he won two FA Cup winners' medals and, on the second occasion, in 1980, scored the only goal of the game; he dived forward to meet Stuart Pearson's attempt at a cross-shot and headed an early goal. Brooking won runners-up medals in the European Cup-winners' Cup (1976) and the League Cup (1981). And he won a Second Division championship medal in 1980-81, when he was probably at his peak. That year he was awarded the MBE. He retired in May 1984 and became a well-known voice on the radio, providing expert comment during live match commentaries.

Ken Brown was one of those centre-halves who was often described as 'cool, calm and collected'. He was also consistent and commanding, through a career of more than 15 years at Upton Park. Brown was born at Forest Gate, on 16 February 1931, though his family moved to Dagenham. He played for Dagenham Boys when a pupil at Lymington Secondary Modern School. He played with a Dagenham side, Neville United, before signing professional for the Hammers in October 1951. Brown's first appearances, in the 1952-3 season, came while he was still serving in the army. His League debut was at Rotherham on 21 February 1953, but most of his early days were spent in the reserves, where he shared in the Football Combination League and Cup success of the mid-1950s. Taking over from Malcolm Allison, he was a pivotal force in the 1957-8 Second Division title-winning side. Two years later, he was selected for England against Northern Ireland. Brown went on to play a central part during the mid-1960s, the Hammers' best-ever bounty-hunting period. Eventually he moved to Torquay for a couple of seasons, then Hereford United and Bournemouth (as trainer-coach). A playing partnership with John Bond continued into the managerial and coaching side of the game. When Bond left Norwich City for Manchester City in November 1980, Brown graduated from assistant to manager. He took Norwich to their 1985 Milk Cup success, and twice into the First Division but was dismissed after a poor start to 1987-8. He spent a very brief period with Shrewsbury Town, a longer spell with Plymouth Argyle, and now manages a leisure centre in Norwich. One of life's most affable characters, his infectious humour brings pleasure to all those around him.

KEN BROWN

	LEAGUE		FA CUP		FL CUP		EUROPE		TOTAL	
	App	Gls	App	Gls	App	Gls	App	Gls	App	Gls
1952-53	3	0	0	0	0	0	0	0	3	0
1953-54	0	0	0	0	0	0	0	0	0	0
1954-55	23	0	0	0	0	0	0	0	23	0
1955-56	2	0	0	0	0	0	0	0	2	0
1956-57	5	0	0	0	0	0	0	0	5	0
1957-58	41	0	3	0	0	0	0	0	44	0
1958-59	42	0	1	0	0	0	0	0	43	0
1959-60	40	0	2	0	0	0	0	0	42	0
1960-61	42	0	2	0	2	0	0	0	46	0
1961-62	38	0	1	0	2	0	0	0	41	0
1962-63	40	2	5	0	2	0	0	0	47	2
1963-64	36	0	7	0	6	0	0	0	49	0
1964-65	33	1	2	0	1	0	9	0	45	1
1965-66	23	1	3	0	9	0	6	0	41	1
1966-67	18	0	0	0	6	0	0	0	24	0
	386	4	26	0	28	0	15	0	455	4

Yet another local boy, and yet another product of the West Ham youth policy, Jack Burkett staked a regular place in the first team in the 1962-3 season, playing his way into the FA Cup-winning side when he was at the tender age of 21. He was a left-back of 1960s style, quick-tackling and not afraid to make forays down the wing. Supporters were no longer panic-stricken if they saw a full-back advancing over the halfway line — others could cover. When Burkett signed professional in October 1959, it must have been dispiriting to see full-backs like John Bond, Noel Cantwell and Joe Kirkup ahead of him in the queue. Two of these — Cantwell and Kirkup — were to fetch transfer fees of over £30,000. Burkett stood 5ft 9in, and his style was never going to give him the media attention of a Byrne or a Moore. But he was a key element in the Cup-winning team, and the European Cup-winners' Cup team of 1965. Nothing in football is permanent, however, and in 1966-7 injury led to him losing his place to John Charles. At the age of

24 he was no longer a first-teamer. He moved to Charlton Athletic for £10,000 in June 1968, but played very few games. He was later on the books of Millwall and Southend, without playing a League game, and was player-manager of St Patrick's Athletic.

JACK BURKETT

	LEAGUE		FA CUP		FL CUP		EUROPE		TOTAL	
	App	Gls	App	Gls	App	Gls	App	Gls	App	Gls
1961-62	1	0	0	0	0	0	0	0	1	0
1962-63	38	0	5	0	2	0	0	0	45	0
1963-64	40	1	7	0	7	0	0	0	54	1
1964-65	24	0	0	0	1	0	5	0	30	0
1965-66	19	2	4	0	4	0	2	0	29	2
1966-67	11/1	1	2	0	2	0	0	0	15/1	1
1967-68	8	0	0	0	1	0	0	0	9	0
	141/1	4	18	0	17	0	7	0	183/1	4

Capped for England Under-23 as a Fourth Division player, subjected to the ordeal of a record transfer fee between English clubs, Johnny Byrne more than lived up to his potential during his four years at West Ham. They called him 'Budgie', supposedly because he was a constant chatterer on the field, but he could also make a football talk. He had silky skills in the deep, but he could finish too. His record of a goal every two games (on average) was excellent, and in Cup matches he was even more prolific, scoring 28 times in 34 ties for West Ham. 'Budgie' Byrne was born at West Horsley in Surrey of Irish parents. An England Youth international, he joined Crystal Palace in July 1956. He was the first-ever Fourth Division player capped for England Under-23; and in 1961, he helped Crystal Palace out of the Fourth by scoring 30 goals. The next season he played for England against Northern Ireland. The 1964 West Ham team might have had Moore, Hurst and Peters (although not in the Cup Final) but Byrne was the star. He cost £65,000 and in March 1962 had impressed enough to have a long run in the England team. In 1963-4, when he won a Cup winners' medal, he played seven times for England. In one game, against Portugal, he scored three, including an 87th-minute winner. He missed the 1965 European Cup-winners' Cup Final after injuring

a knee in an England-Scotland international a few weeks before, but Byrne played in the 1966 League Cup Final. He returned to Crystal Palace for a £45,000 fee in February 1967, and a year later Fulham beat the transfer deadline for his signature — too late to save them from relegation. He later played for the South African club, Durban City, who promoted him to manager.

JOHNNY BYRNE

	LEAGUE		FA CUP		FL CUP		EUROPE		TOTAL	
	App	Gls	App	Gls	App	Gls	App	Gls	App	Gls
1961-62	11	1	0	0	0	0	0	0	11	1
1962-63	30	9	5	2	2	3	0	0	37	14
1963-64	33	24	7	4	5	5	0	0	45	33
1964-65	34	25	2	1	1	0	7	3	44	29
1965-66	23	9	3	0	6	5	5	3	37	17
1966-67	25	11	1	0	5	2	0	0	31	13
	156	79	18	7	19	15	12	6	205	107

After he took over at left-half from Jack Tresadern in 1923, Albert Cadwell had spells in and out of West Ham's team. But by the end of a ten-season career with Hammers, which began with a match against Chelsea at Stamford Bridge on 20 October 1923, he had made almost 300 appearances for the club. Cadwell was born at Edmonton on 1 November 1900. He was strong in the tackle, skilful on the ball, and an energetic player whose eye-catching performance lit up many a Saturday afternoon at Upton Park throughout the second half of the 1920s. He was perhaps lucky that his career with West Ham coincided with a relatively long spell in the First Division and on that platform he performed consistently well enough to earn a major representative honour when he was selected to play for the Football League against the Irish League in 1930. Albert Cadwell died on 13 July 1944, aged only 43.

	LEAGUE		FA CUP		TOTAL	
	App	Gls	App	Gls	App	Gls
1923-24	29	0	3	0	32	0
1924-25	40	0	6	0	46	0
1925-26	18	0	0	0	18	0
1926-27	13	0	0	0	13	0
1927-28	27	0	2	0	29	0
1928-29	40	0	5	0	45	0
1929-30	38	0	4	0	42	0
1930-31	31	0	1	0	32	0
1931-32	26	1	2	0	28	1
1932-33	10	0	2	0	12	0
	272	1	25	0	297	1

ALBERT CADWELL

Thick set and skilful, Republic of Ireland international Noel Cantwell was valued higher than any full-back in history when he was transferred to Manchester United for £29,500 in November 1960. Thus ended his eight years with the Hammers, much of which had been spent in the first team in a stable full-back partnership with John Bond. Cantwell, who was born in Cork on 28 February 1932, was one of a new era of full-backs who could stamp their authority on the whole of the pitch. He had started with Cork United, after gaining junior honours in several positions. At West Ham, he went from the 'A' team to the Second Division team in one season making his League debut at Fulham in April 1953. He played mainly as a left-back, but was occasionally moved further upfield. He was capped 36 times by the Republic of Ireland, including 17 whilst at West Ham. In 1963, he collected the FA Cup at Wembley as captain of the Manchester United team which beat Leicester City 3-1. However, he played only a few games in each of United's two Championship teams of the mid-1960s. Cantwell's managerial career started with five years at First Division Coventry City, whom he took to sixth place in 1969-70. He enjoyed success at his next club, taking Peterborough United into Division Three. He also managed the New England Tea Men in the North American Soccer League.

NOEL CANTWELL

	LEAGUE		FA CUP		TOTAL	
	App	Gls	App	Gls	App	Gls
1952-53	4	0	0	0	4	0
1953-54	23	0	0	0	23	0
1954-55	17	0	2	0	19	0
1955-56	40	0	6	0	46	0
1956-57	39	1	2	0	41	1
1957-58	33	4	2	0	35	4
1958-59	42	3	1	0	43	3
1959-60	40	3	2	0	42	3
1960-61	10	0	0	0	10	0
	248	11	15	0	263	11

In Alf Chalkley's era as a West Ham full-back — he played 200 games during the 1930s — the full-back's role in the team was clearly defined — to win the ball, clear it upfield and stay covering when your team was on the attack. A goalscoring full-back was such a rarity that the whole nation sat up on 2 March 1932, when Chalkley's clearance, from near his own penalty-area, led to a goal for West Ham against Manchester City after goalkeeper Len Langford misjudged the flight of the ball. Chalkley had started as an outside-left in schools soccer around his Plaistow home. He played for England Boys, and also represented the London FA and London Combination. He made his League debut for West Ham at Burnden Park, Bolton, in August 1931.

	LEAGUE		FA CUP		TOTAL	
	App	Gls	App	Gls	App	Gls
1931-32	29	1	2	0	31	1
1932-33	34	0	6	0	40	0
1933-34	37	0	2	0	39	0
1934-35	42	0	2	0	44	0
1935-36	32	0	2	0	34	0
1936-37	14	0	0	0	14	0
	188	1	14	0	202	1

ALF CHALKLEY

Joe Cockroft was a small, consistent wing-half of the 1930s, an enduring Yorkshireman who was a great loss to West Ham when he returned to his native county during the war. He was born in Barnsley on 20 June 1911 and played for Wombwell, Rotherham and Gainsborough before he signed for West Ham at the back-end of the 1932-3 season. He helped save the club from relegation to the Third Division South and never looked back. Between 1932 and 1937 he established a club record of 217 consecutive League and Cup appearances. Cockroft, who made his League debut at Chesterfield in April 1933, was a member of the team which beat Blackburn to win the League War Cup at Wembley, and earlier he had played in an international trial for England against The Rest. However, in 1941 his home was hit in the London Blitz, and he decided to move back to Yorkshire. He joined Sheffield Wednesday and became their captain. Cockroft was 37 when he played in the First Division for the first time. He was signed for £4,000 by Sheffield United, who were desperate to stay in Division One. Despite Cockroft's efforts — he played 12 games for United in the 1948-9 season — they went down anyway, and a fine Football League career reached its close. Cockroft became player-manager of Wisbech Town. He is still living in Yorkshire and goes to see Hammers when they play in Sheffield.

	LEAGUE		FA CUP		TOTAL	
	App	Gls	App	Gls	App	Gls
1932-33	6	0	0	0	6	0
1933-34	42	0	2	0	44	0
1934-35	42	0	2	0	44	0
1935-36	42	1	2	0	44	1
1936-37	42	1	2	0	44	1
1937-38	38	0	1	0	39	0
1938-39	39	1	3	0	42	1
	251	3	12	0	263	3

JOE COCKROFT

Born in Brentford, James Frederick Arthur Collins
was a long-serving West Ham wing-half in the late-
1920s and early-1930s. Captain of East Ham Boys,
he was selected for England Schoolboys but never won
a cap as the game wasn't played. He was born in June
1919 and followed a familiar kind of route —
Chelmsford, Clapton and Leyton — before joing West
Ham as an amateur in 1921. He was forced to change
from inside-forward to wing-half to establish himself
in the first team after making his League debut against
Spurs at Upton Park in February 1924. In the First
Division days of the mid-1920s, he played 160
consecutive games, an exceptionally fine performance
for a player who was always at the heart of the action.
In his spare time he trained and owned greyhounds.
He was the owner of Golden Hammer, a dog which
finished second in the 1931 Greyhound Derby. He was
also a horticulturalist. He died in May 1977.

	LEAGUE		FA CUP		TOTAL	
	App	*Gls*	*App*	*Gls*	*App*	*Gls*
1923-24	5	1	0	0	5	1
1924-25	2	0	1	0	3	0
1925-26	24	0	1	0	25	0
1926-27	42	1	3	0	45	1
1927-28	42	0	2	0	44	0
1928-29	39	1	5	0	44	1
1929-30	21	0	4	0	25	0
1930-31	38	0	1	0	39	0
1931-32	35	0	2	0	37	0
1932-33	33	0	6	0	39	0
1933-34	17	0	0	0	17	0
1934-35	12	0	0	0	12	0
1935-36	1	0	0	0	1	0
	311	3	25	0	336	3

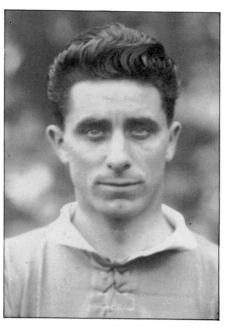

JIMMY COLLINS

Bill Cope was a robust full-back recruited by Hammers
just before World War One. Born at Stoke-on-Trent
in 1885, Cope's first senior club was Port Vale, whom
he joined in 1904-05, and he spent three seasons with
them before they resigned from the Football League
Second Division. He joined Stoke in 1907-08 and
played 25 times before that club also resigned from
the League. Undaunted, Cope moved to Oldham
Athletic, then embarking on their second season of
League football, but never established himself at
Boundary Park, averaging only about ten games a
season between 1908 and 1914. In May 1914 he
transferred to West Ham and made his debut at home
to Gillingham at the start of the following season. A
rugged player, Cope often fell foul of referees and was
sent off at least twice, once with Oldham Reserves
and once at Bristol City when he was playing for
Hammers. His tally of wartime games for Hammers
was exceeded only by Puddefoot and in 1919 he was
made skipper, a position he held until the end of
1921-2. He lacked speed but kicked strongly, which
was considered an admirable quality in the 1920s. His
final game was against Blackpool at Upton Park on
29 April 1922 and at the age of 36 he moved to Third
Division North club, Wrexham.

	LEAGUE		FA CUP		TOTAL	
	App	*Gls*	*App*	*Gls*	*App*	*Gls*
1914-15	31	0	2	0	33	0
1919-20	29	0	4	0	33	0
1920-21	36	0	1	0	37	0
1921-22	41	0	3	0	44	0
	137	0	10	0	147	0

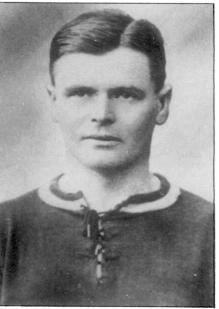

WILLIAM COPE

117

A wing-half who also played in the forward line in the more flexible days of wartime football, Norman Corbett had a whirlwind start to his football career. Born at Falkirk in June 1919, he was captain of Falkirk Boys when they won the Scotland Schools Trophy, and he won Scotland Schoolboy and Junior international honours. He was signed by West Ham from Heart of Midlothian in April 1937 and was a regular in the Hammers' team after making his League debut against Sheffield United the month after arriving at Upton Park. His older brother, David, had been a West Ham player in the 1930s and was also a well-known competitor in the Highland Games. A third brother, Willie, guested for West Ham during World War Two, when he also won a Scotland wartime cap when with Celtic. Norman Corbett stayed at Upton Park into the 1950s, playing in the reserve team and coaching. He later joined Clapton FC.

	LEAGUE		FA CUP		TOTAL	
	App	Gls	App	Gls	App	Gls
1936-37	1	0	0	0	1	0
1937-38	6	0	0	0	6	0
1938-39	31	1	4	0	35	1
1946-47	35	0	1	0	36	0
1947-48	42	1	2	0	44	1
1948-49	39	1	1	0	40	1
1949-50	12	0	0	0	12	0
	166	3	8	0	174	3

NORMAN CORBETT

Perhaps West Ham United, more than any other club, has a history of employing footballers who are already supporters. Tony Cottee, born in West Ham, had followed the Hammers when a young boy, and there is evidence of him watching players like 'Pop' Robson and Trevor Brooking. Although only 5ft 8in tall, he is strong, muscular and supple, and while still a young man he produced a sustained spell of goalscoring power. Cottee came to Upton Park as an apprentice, having been spotted by scout Ronnie Gale while playing for Chase Cross United. He played for England Youth and worked his way through the West Ham teams. He made his first-team debut on New Year's Day 1983, heading a goal against Tottenham. He was still 17. The next season, 1983-4, Cottee started and finished the campaign as the Hammers demanded the nation's attention with the way they won their first five games and shot to the top of the League. From that point, Cottee was set to score around 20 goals a season. He was capped for the England Under-21 team and in

July 1988 moved to Everton for a British record fee of £2.2 million.

	LEAGUE		FA CUP		FL CUP		TOTAL	
	App	Gls	App	Gls	App	Gls	App	Gls
1982-83	3/5	5	1	0	0	0	4/5	5
1983-84	37/2	15	4	0	4	4	45/2	19
1984-85	40/1	17	5	4	4	3	49/1	24
1985-86	41/1	20	7	4	3	2	51/1	26
1986-87	42	22	5	1	6	5	53	28
1987-88	40	13	2	2	2	0	44	15
	203/9	92	24	11	19	14	246/9	117

TONY COTTEE

118

The much-migrated striker David Cross, a man of ten clubs, had by far the best time of his exciting career when he was at West Ham in the late-1970s and early-1980s. He helped the Hammers win the FA Cup, reach the League Cup Final and climb to the First Division. Tall, lean and handsome, Cross came from Heywood, which is equidistant from Rochdale (his first club in August 1969) and Bury (where he went on loan in January 1986). In his career of over 550 League games, he came close to scoring 200 goals. Rochdale were a successful Third Division side during his time with the club, and Cross was bought by Norwich City in October 1971. He scored eight goals in 32 League games that season — Graham Paddon also scored eight — and Norwich became Second Division champions. Norwich struggled in the top flight on that occasion, but his next club, Coventry City, were more established. West Ham almost signed Cross in November 1976, but failed to agree terms with the player. Instead, he went to West Brom, where his goals helped Albion to seventh place in the First Division. Finally, in December 1977, for a record club fee (at the time) of £180,000, the Hammers at last signed him. Although Cross scored seven goals in his last seven games that season, he could not help prevent Hammers going down to the Second Division. When promotion was achieved, in 1980-81, Cross was top goalscorer with 27 League and League Cup goals, including four in a game at Grimsby, and the second-half winner against Spurs which put the Hammers in the League Cup semi-final.

After leaving West Ham he had spells with Manchester City, Vancouver Whitecaps, Oldham Athletic, West Brom (again), and Bolton Wanderers.

	LEAGUE		FA CUP		FL CUP		EUROPE		TOTAL	
	App	Gls	App	Gls	App	Gls	App	Gls	App	Gls
1977-78	21	9	3	0	0	0	0	0	24	9
1978-79	40	18	1	0	1	0	0	0	42	18
1979-80	38/1	12	5	1	9	5	0	0	52/1	18
1980-81	41	22	3	0	9	5	6	6	59	33
1981-82	38	16	2	1	5	2	0	0	45	19
	178/1	77	14	2	24	12	6	6	222/1	97

DAVID CROSS

Billy Dare was born in Willesden in February 1927 and played as an amateur with Hendon, Arsenal and Brentford. He signed professional with Brentford and spent six seasons with them, playing over 200 games, moving to West Ham for a £5,000 fee. He made his League debut against Leeds United at Upton Park in March 1955. Playing centre-forward alongside the much taller John Dick, Dare scored regularly and played a vital role in the 1957-8 Second Division title-winning season. In his earlier days, Dare played for an FA XI against the Combined Universities. He joined West Ham on 27 January 1955, shortly after Brentford had been relegated to the Third Division South. He was able to add considerable Second Division experience to the West Ham line-up before moving to non-League Yiewsley soon after the Hammers had risen to the First Division.

	LEAGUE		FA CUP		TOTAL	
	App	Gls	App	Gls	App	Gls
1954-55	13	2	0	0	13	2
1955-56	40	18	6	4	46	22
1956-57	30	9	2	1	32	10
1957-58	26	14	0	0	26	14
1958-59	2	1	0	0	2	1
	111	44	8	5	119	49

BILLY DARE

England Youth international goalkeeper Mervyn Day was born at Chelmsford on 26 June 1955 and became a West Ham apprentice in July 1971, making his League debut on a rain-lashed night in August 1973 when he played in a 3-3 draw with Ipswich Town. After only his second game in the first team, Ron Greenwood announced that Day would be Hammers' goalkeeper for the next ten years, but that was not to be, although Day did manage almost 250 League and Cup appearances in the next five and a half years. In his first season, he found himself in a struggling team and he played his part in Hammers avoiding relegation. His biggest moment came when he appeared in the 1975 FA Cup Final and was chosen as the Young Footballer of the Year. Day is a cool, composed goalkeeper with excellent positional sense but another, this time unsuccessful, relegation battle in 1977-8 did little for his confidence. After the signing of Phil Parkes, he moved to Orient in the summer of 1979 and made 170 appearances for them before returning to the First Division with Aston Villa. From Villa Park he went to Leeds United and with his old confidence restored, he was a great influence in Leeds reaching the 1986-7 FA Cup semi-finals and the play-off final for Division One.

	LEAGUE		FA CUP		FL CUP		EUROPE		TOTAL	
	App	Gls	App	Gls	App	Gls	App	Gls	App	Gls
1973-74	33	0	2	0	2	0	0	0	37	0
1974-75	42	0	8	0	3	0	0	0	53	0
1975-76	41	0	1	0	5	0	9	0	56	0
1976-77	42	0	2	0	3	0	0	0	47	0
1977-78	23	0	0	0	1	0	0	0	24	0
1978-79	13	0	1	0	0	0	0	0	14	0
	194	0	14	0	14	0	9	0	231	0

MERVYN DAY

The storming, evasive running and dribbling of slightly-built Alan Devonshire was one of the most exciting spectacles in British football during the late 1970s and early '80s. Had it not been for a bad knee injury early in 1984, he might have won far more than eight England caps. He joined West Ham from Isthmian League club, Southall, for £5,000 in October 1976, when he was in his 21st year. His father, Les, had been an outside-left with Chester and Crystal Palace in '50s. Alan established himself in the Hammers' first team soon after signing professional. He had the confidence to carry the ball at times when many players dare not. His seemingly fragile physique withstood substantial punishment, but it was inevitable that he would miss games through injury. Devonshire was a star of the

various Cup campaigns circa 1980, a provider rather than striker, and it was with much all-round relief that he returned to the team in 1985. His last appearance was as substitute in the 6-0 defeat by Oldham in the 1990 League Cup semi-finals. He moved to Watford for 1990-91.

	LEAGUE		FA CUP		FL CUP		EUROPE		TOTAL	
	App	Gls	App	Gls	App	Gls	App	Gls	App	Gls
1976-77	27/1	0	0	0	1	0	0	0	28/1	0
1977-78	32/2	3	3	0	1	0	0	0	36/2	3
1978-79	41	5	1	0	1	0	0	0	43	5
1979-80	34	5	8	1	7	0	0	0	49	6
1980-81	39	6	3	0	9	0	4	0	55	6
1981-82	35	1	1	0	5	0	0	0	41	1
1982-83	39	3	1	0	6	0	0	0	46	3
1983-84	22	1	1	0	4	2	0	0	27	3
1984-85	0	0	2	0	0	0	0	0	2	0
1985-86	38	3	6	0	3	0	0	0	47	3
1986-87	20	2	3	0	4	0	0	0	27	2
1987-88	1	0	0	0	0	0	0	0	1	0
1988-89	14/6	0	7	0	4	0	0	0	25/6	0
1989-90	3/4	0	0	0	0/3	0	0	0	3/7	0
	345/13	29	36	1	45/3	2	4	0	430/16	32

ALAN DEVONSHIRE

Only three players have scored more goals for West Ham than John Dick, the tall Glaswegian inside-left of the 1950s. Born in Govan in March 1930, close to the Glasgow Rangers ground, Dick won a Scottish Junior cap with Maryhill. While on National Service at Colchester, he played for Crittall Athletic, which was where the Hammers spotted him. He signed in July 1953 and made his League debut against Lincoln the following month. In his second season, he equalled Bill Robinson's post-war record of 26 League goals in a season, and people expected him to soon gain international honours to add to his Scotland 'B' cap (March 1954). He had to wait until he had helped West Ham into the First Division and proved his goalscoring ability in the upper echelons. Twenty-seven League goals in 1958-9 saw him drafted into the Scotland team against England at Wembley. Dick was transferred to Brentford in September 1962 and his 23 goals that season brought him a Fourth Division Championship medal and Brentford full value for their £17,500 outlay. In 1965 he moved to Southern League Gravesend and later returned to Upton Park for a couple of seasons in charge of the juniors.

	LEAGUE		FA CUP		FL CUP		TOTAL	
	App	Gls	App	Gls	App	Gls	App	Gls
1953-54	39	13	3	0	0	0	42	13
1954-55	39	26	2	0	0	0	41	26
1955-56	35	8	6	6	0	0	41	14
1956-57	36	8	2	1	0	0	38	9
1957-58	41	21	3	2	0	0	44	23
1958-59	41	27	1	0	0	0	42	27
1959-60	24	11	1	1	0	0	25	12
1960-61	34	16	2	1	2	2	38	19
1961-62	35	23	1	0	2	0	38	23
1962-63	2	0	0	0	0	0	2	0
	326	153	21	11	4	2	351	166

JOHN DICK

A pugnacious and determined defender (and attacker) Julian Dicks has the qualities that might be thought unappealing to a West Ham faithful brought up on cultured soccer. But Dicks has proved that his raw aggression has a part to play in West Ham's methods. His fierce shooting has settled many a match, for since assuming the duties of penalty-taker he has been successful with 17 spot-kicks. Born at Bristol in August 1968, Dicks graduated through schools football in the Midlands and joined Birmingham City on a YTS scheme in 1984. Within 12 months he had signed professional forms and went on to play 89 League games for the Blues before being transferred to West Ham for £400,000 in March 1988. Dicks, a regular member of the Hammers' side relegated from Division One at the end of 1988-9, was only five games short of a century of League appearances for Hammers when a knee injury sustained in a game at Swindon put a temporary halt to his career. If Dick could only have controlled his disciplinary problems he would surely have won a place in the full England squad.

	LEAGUE		FA CUP		FL CUP		TOTAL	
	App	Gls	App	Gls	App	Gls	App	Gls
1987-88	8	0	0	0	0	0	8	0
1988-89	34	2	6	0	7	0	47	2
1989-90	40	9	1	0	9	4	50	13
1990-91	13	4	0	0	2	1	15	5
1991-92	23	3	6	2	0	0	29	5
1992-93	34	11	1	0	1	0	36	11
	152	29	14	2	19	5	185	36

JULIAN DICKS

121

Full-back Alf Earl served West Ham United well throughout the latter part of the 1920s and early '30s. Earl was born at Earlsfield on 19 March 1903 and joined the Hammers from Summerstown in 1925. He made his debut in the 5-2 win over Aston Villa at Upton Park on Christmas Day that year, a match in which his near-namesake, Stan Earle, netted a hat-trick. In those days Alf operated at left-back, although in his second season he was restricted to only one League appearance — the opening game of the season at home to Leicester City. Thereafter his fortunes changed and, in 1927-8, he missed only nine games. Indeed, Earl was a regular in the Hammers' defence for the next four seasons, during which time he showed some versatility in playing on either flank. Later, Earl settled into the right-back spot in a now struggling West Ham team. His last full season was a dreadful one for the Hammers and at the end of it they were relegated to the Second Division when he was part of a defence which conceded 107 League goals. He began 1932-3 — a season in which Hammers went perilously close to Division Three South — but by the time the club met Everton in the FA

Cup semi-final at Molineux, he had played his last game in West Ham's colours. The same year, Earl joined Streatham Town. He died at Carshalton, Surrey, on 17 August 1951.

ALF EARL

	LEAGUE		FA CUP		TOTAL	
	App	Gls	App	Gls	App	Gls
1925-26	8	0	1	0	9	0
1926-27	1	0	0	0	1	0
1927-28	33	0	2	0	35	0
1928-29	32	0	5	0	37	0
1929-30	38	0	4	0	42	0
1930-31	38	0	1	0	39	0
1931-32	30	0	2	0	32	0
1932-33	11	0	0	0	11	0
	191	0	15	0	206	0

Stan Earle was 6ft 1½in tall, weighed 12st 7lb and was an impressive athlete during his days as a West Ham inside-forward. Born in Stratford, East London, in September 1897, Earle was an established England Amateur international when he first joined West Ham in August 1924, being eventually persuaded to turn professional. Later he captained the West Ham team, and played almost 300 League and Cup games for the club, despite his late start which came at home to Preston on 30 August 1924. An England Schoolboy international (in 1912), Earle played for Clapton, where he won his two Amateur caps and played alongside Vivian Gibbins (later West Ham, too) in Clapton's 1924 FA Amateur Cup-winning team. Gibbins and Earle played together in a full international against France in 1924. Before his long career with West Ham, Earle played a few games for Arsenal. As his playing days drew to a close, he slipped into the Second Division. Earle moved to Clapton Orient for a season and later coached Waltamstow Avenue and managed Leyton. He died at Brightlingsea in September 1971.

	LEAGUE		FA CUP		TOTAL	
	App	Gls	App	Gls	App	Gls
1924-25	18	6	0	0	18	6
1925-26	37	9	1	0	38	9
1926-27	42	13	3	0	45	13
1927-28	31	11	1	0	32	11
1928-29	41	6	5	2	46	8
1929-30	36	3	4	0	40	3
1930-31	36	8	1	0	37	8
1931-32	17	0	0	0	17	0
	258	56	15	2	273	58

STAN EARLE

For all the sarcastic remarks English people have made about Scottish goalkeepers, it remains a fact that English clubs are more than willing to sign them. And West Ham United have no cause to regret their Scottish goalies of the 1960s, first Lawrie Leslie, then Bobby Ferguson. Ferguson had enjoyed huge success with Kilmarnock. He was an ever-present when the Rugby Park club reached third place in the League (1965-6) and had played a few games in the Scottish League Championship of 1964-5, understudy to Campbell Forsyth. In 1966-7, Ferguson took part in Kilmarnock's incredible run in the Inter-Cities Fairs Cup. West Ham knew they were in line to sign the brilliant Scottish goalkeeper but they had to wait until Kilmarnock were eliminated from the competition. It didn't happen until 24 May, when the Killies could only draw the second leg of their semi-final, losing 4-2 on aggregate to Leeds United. Inside a year, Ferguson had won seven Scotland caps (playing under three different managers), and he was valued at £65,000 when he made the move south. It was a record British fee for a goalkeeper. Ferguson came to West Ham as a 22-year-old and stayed for

13 years. Surprisingly, he was never capped again, although he had erratic spells while at Upton Park, and was under pressure from goakeepers like Peter Grotier and Mervyn Day. He had a short period on loan to Sheffield Wednesday in 1973, and later emigrated to Australia to join Port Elizabeth.

BOBBY FERGUSON

	LEAGUE		FA CUP		FL CUP		TOTAL	
	App	Gls	App	Gls	App	Gls	App	Gls
1967-68	39	0	3	0	2	0	44	0
1968-69	39	0	3	0	3	0	45	0
1969-70	30	0	1	0	2	0	33	0
1970-71	23	0	1	0	0	0	24	0
1971-72	36	0	4	0	10	0	50	0
1972-73	31	0	2	0	0	0	33	0
1973-74	9	0	0	0	0	0	9	0
1974-75	0	0	0	0	0	0	0	0
1975-76	1	0	0	0	0	0	1	0
1976-77	0	0	0	0	0	0	0	0
1977-78	19	0	3	0	0	0	22	0
1978-79	11	0	0	0	1	0	12	0
1979-80	2	0	0	0	1	0	3	0
	240	0	17	0	19	0	276	0

A forward who served West Ham from 1934 right into wartime football, Stan Foxall began his career with Gainsborough Trinity, 20 miles from his Lincolnshire birthplace of Crowle, where he first saw the light of day on 8 October 1914. He once scored 70 goals in a season of junior football but it was not until a little while after he became established in Hammers' first team — he made his League debut at Bradford in September 1934 — that his great goalscoring ability came to fruition in the Football League. He was the hero of the 1939 FA Cup saga against Tottenham Hotspur when he scored in all three games. His total of 241 League, Cup and wartime games for West Ham included their 1940 League War Cup Final win against Blackburn Rovers at Wembley. His last game for West Ham was against Queen's Park Rangers in September 1944, a game in which he suffered the knee injury which ended his long career at Upton Park. Stan Foxall died, aged 76, on 12 August 1991.

STAN FOXALL

	LEAGUE		FA CUP		TOTAL	
	App	Gls	App	Gls	App	Gls
1934-35	4	2	0	0	4	2
1935-36	1	1	0	0	1	1
1936-37	25	11	2	0	27	11
1937-38	36	10	0	0	36	10
1938-39	40	14	5	5	45	19
	106	38	7	5	113	43

Tall central defender Tony Gale was an experienced professional when he was signed by the Hammers in the summer of 1984; although he was not yet 24, he had played almost 300 League games for his first club, Fulham. Gale was also the veteran of a relegation season (1979-80) and a promotion season, when Fulham earned third place in the Third Division in 1981-2. London-born Gale had his transfer fee set by a tribunal when he signed for West Ham. Capped for England Youth and England Under-21s while with Fulham, he swiftly settled into the West Ham team, forming a well-balanced central defensive pairing with Alvin Martin. He played in all 52 League and Cup games in the 1985-6 season, when the Hammers achieved their best-ever position in the Football League — third in Division One.

	LEAGUE		FA CUP		FL CUP		TOTAL	
	App	Gls	App	Gls	App	Gls	App	Gls
1984-85	36/1	0	0	0	3	0	39/1	0
1985-86	42	0	7	0	3	0	52	0
1986-87	32	2	4	1	4	0	40	3
1987-88	17/1	0	2	0	0	0	19/1	0
1988-89	31	0	5	0	6	1	42	1
1989-90	36	1	1	0	7	0	44	1
1990-91	23/1	1	7	0	0/1	0	30/2	1
1991-92	24/1	0	2	0	3/1	0	29/2	0
1992-93	21/2	1	0	0	0	0	21/2	1
	262/6	5	28	1	26/2	1	316/8	7

TONY GALE

One of the last amateurs to play in a full England international, Vivian Gibbins averaged close to a goal every other game when he assisted West Ham. For England he scored three goals in two games. V.W.T.Gibbins was a centre-forward who could also play inside-forward. Born in Forest Gate in 1903, he played with Clapton before he made his first appearance for West Ham at Nottingham Forest in December 1923, during the first season back in Division One. His professional career was as a schoolmaster, progressing to the headmaster's job from which he retired in the 1970s. His football was solely amateur. He won eight England Amateur international caps between 1925 and 1932, and he played for Clapton when they won the FA Amateur Cup in successive years in the mid-1920s. His appearances in the Amateur Cup often meant he was unavailable for the Hammers, and it says a lot for the abilities of Gibbins that a club like West Ham would persist in asking him to play on an irregular basis. After leaving West Ham he played with Brentford, Bristol Rovers, Southampton and Leyton. He died at Herne Bay, Kent, on 21 November 1979.

	LEAGUE		FA CUP		TOTAL	
	App	Gls	App	Gls	App	Gls
1923-24	3	1	0	0	3	1
1924-25	1	0	0	0	1	0
1925-26	1	2	0	0	1	2
1926-27	22	4	1	0	23	4
1927-28	25	14	2	2	27	16
1928-29	29	11	2	0	31	11
1929-30	18	3	3	2	21	5
1930-31	21	18	1	1	22	19
1931-32	9	5	0	0	9	5
	129	58	9	5	138	63

VIVIAN GIBBINS

Born in Harlington, Middlesex, in October 1959, Paul Goddard was signed by QPR as an apprentice. He was 18 when he made his first appearance in the First Division, playing in the same team as Phil Parkes when coming on as substitute against Arsenal in April 1978. However, Rangers were back in the Second Division before Goddard made a major impact. Playing up front alongside Clive Allen, he hit 16 goals in 1979-80 and early the next season, Hammers parted with a club record £800,000 to obtain his signature. Goddard looked small alongside David Cross, his co-striker at West Ham, but his muscular legs were full of running and his sharpness in the penalty area helped the Hammers out of Division Two. He also scored vital goals in the League Cup, an aggregate equaliser in the semi-final against Coventry and one in the Final replay at Villa Park. In the end, though, it was a runners-up medal. Goddard was Hammers' top scorer in 1982-3, but problems with injuries, combined with the form of Tony Cottee and the arrival of Frank McAvennie, meant he was often third-choice striker. He moved to Newcastle in 1986-7 and helped them retain their First Division status with a series of goals in the latter part of the season. He was again showing the form that had brought him an England cap in 1982, when he came on as substitute against Iceland and scored a goal. Derby bought him £425,000 in August 1988 and he surprisingly moved to Millwall for £800,000 in December 1989. After a miserable time at The Den he helped Ipswich, managed by his former Hammers' boss John Lyall, back to the top flight.

PAUL GODDARD

	LEAGUE		FA CUP		FL CUP		EUROPE		TOTAL	
	App	Gls	App	Gls	App	Gls	App	Gls	App	Gls
1980-81	37	17	3	0	9	4	6	0	55	21
1981-82	38/1	15	2	0	5	2	0	0	45/1	17
1982-83	39	10	0	0	7	2	0	0	46	12
1983-84	3/2	1	0	0	1	1	0	0	4/2	2
1984-85	38/2	9	5	3	3	2	0	0	46/2	14
1985-86	1/5	1	0/1	0	0	0	0	0	1/6	1
1986-87	3/1	1	0	0	1	1	0	0	4/1	2
	159/11	54	10/1	3	26	12	6	0	201/12	69

For two years just before World War Two, Len Goulden was first-choice England inside-left, despite playing with a middle-of-the-table Second Division side. His magnificent England performances included a spectacular goal in a 6-3 win in Germany, and a fine display when England beat Scotland at Hampden in 1939. Altogether Goulden won 14 peacetime England caps and played six internationals during the war. He was born in Hackney in July 1912, and brought up in Plaistow. He played for West Ham and England Schoolboys, and had short spells on loan to Chelmsford and Leyton after signing amateur forms for West Ham in 1931. By the end of 1933-4, he was a fixture in the Hammers' first team after making his League debut against Charlton Athletic at The Valley in April 1933. He played over 400 times for West Ham, and there is no telling how much he would have achieved had it not been for the war. He played in the Hammers team which won the War League Cup in 1940, but, strangely, he never won a major club honour, either at West Ham or his post-war club, Chelsea, who paid £5,000 for his transfer. He played 111 times for Chelsea, scoring 19 goals. Goulden managed Watford between 1952 and 1956, and later had a period in charge of Banbury Town. His son Roy, also an England Schoolboy international, played for Arsenal and Southend United.

LEN GOULDEN

	LEAGUE		FA CUP		TOTAL	
	App	Gls	App	Gls	App	Gls
1932-33	7	1	0	0	7	1
1933-34	40	7	2	1	42	8
1934-35	40	3	2	0	42	3
1935-36	38	15	2	0	40	15
1936-37	42	15	2	0	44	15
1937-38	35	9	1	0	36	9
1938-39	37	4	5	0	42	4
	239	54	14	1	253	55

Born at Larbert, Scotland, in November 1880, inside-forward Billy Grassam first played for the junior club, Redcliffe Thistle, and later, Glasgow Maryhill. In the close season of 1899, Grassam came south to play for Port Vale but after one season in the Potteries moved to London for his first spell with Hammers. He scored four goals on his debut, against Gravesend, and was a regular on the score-sheet thereafter. After three full seasons at the Memorial Grounds he signed for Manchester United but by 1905-06 was back in East London via spells at Glasgow Celtic and Leyton. His re-appearance in Hammers' colours had nothing like the impact of his first game back in September 1900 but he and Harry Stapley, who arrived with him, made a considerable contribution over the next couple of seasons.

	LEAGUE		FA CUP		TOTAL	
	App	Gls	App	Gls	App	Gls
1900-01	20	12	3	3	23	15
1901-02	29	10	1	0	30	10
1902-03	29	19	1	0	30	19
1905-06	14	3	0	0	14	3
1906-07	37	10	2	0	39	10
1907-08	32	9	2	0	34	9
1908-09	8	2	1	0	9	2
	169	65	10	3	179	68

WILLIAM GRASSAM

The stark statistics of Jimmy Greaves' goalscoring career speak for themselves — 357 First Division goals, 35 in the FA Cup, seven in the League Cup, 44 for England (in 57 internationals). His slight physique and nonchalant air belied his abilities in opposition penalty areas, which was where he earned virtually all his wages. He would dart off the mark, and snaffle half-chances from all angles, mainly with his left foot. In short, he was the best. Strangely though, he scored more goals against West Ham than for them — 16 as opposed to 13. He spent just over a season at Upton Park before his retirement in the summer of 1971, when he was 31. Greaves had a remarkable knack for scoring debut goals. He never failed: Chelsea Juniors, Chelsea Reserves, England Youth, Chelsea, England Under-23, England, AC Milan, Spurs Reserves, Spurs — and West Ham. His Hammers' debut brought two goals in the 5-1 win over Manchester City. But that was his West Ham high spot. He spent the summer co-driving in the World Cup rally with Tony Ford (in a Ford Escort) then the next season playing below par as he began to take alcohol too seriously. There was a rumpus when he and three other Hammers players stayed out late before a game against Blackpool. Late in the season, there was examples of vintage Greaves — a winner at Coventry and a late goal against West Brom — which helped Hammers avoid relegation. Valued at £99,999 when he came back from Italy — not quite the first £100,000 player — Greaves was top scorer for Tottenham in each of his eight seasons with the club. He won two FA Cup winners' medals (1962 and 1967) and was in the team which won the European Cup-winners' Cup in 1963. He came to West Ham in the £200,000 deal which took Martin Peters to White Hart Lane. Today, Greaves has carved out a new career as a television soccer pundit.

	LEAGUE		FA CUP		FL CUP		TOTAL	
	App	Gls	App	Gls	App	Gls	App	Gls
1969-70	6	4	0	0	0	0	6	4
1970-71	30/2	9	1	0	1	0	32/2	9
	36/2	13	1	0	1	0	38/2	13

JIMMY GREAVES

The story of Ernie Gregory reads like a latter-day story of West Ham United itself. A local boy, a loyal servant of the club for over 50 years, Gregory helped Hammers back into Division One in the mid-1950s and after retiring from goalkeeping, he stayed on as a coach, being responsible for several generations of players with good football habits at Upton Park. Born at Stratford on 10 November 1921, Gregory played in the 1936 West Ham Boys team which shared the English Schools Trophy. He won an Isthmian League championship medal as an amateur with Leytonstone, and in May 1939 signed professional forms for Hammers. He was forced to wait until December 1946 for his Football League debut — against Plymouth at Upton Park — and was by then the veteran of a long campaign in the army. Until 1959 he was West Ham's regular 'keeper, apart from 1954-5 when he was injured and George Taylor stepped in. It was fitting that Gregory should end his career in Division One. His honours were a Second Division championship medal and an England 'B' cap, against France in 1952. Gregory played his last game on 5 September 1959, against Leeds United at Upton Park, and was awarded a testimonial match in October the following year, against the LDA club of Costa Rica. After retirement, Ernie Gregory became one of those vitally important unsung heroes. He played an important role in Ron Greenwood's new coaching plan, giving the club an element of 'boot-room stability' that is evident at other successful clubs like Liverpool. Gregory coached the reserves and then the first team; obviously his greatest value came when he worked with the goalkeepers, passing on the specialist skills he had learned through 406 League and Cup games with Hammers. He retired from Upton Park in May 1987, after 51 years splendid service with his only League club.

Jack Hebden, who was born at Castleford, Yorkshire, on 12 November 1900, played for Bradford City before joining West Ham in May 1921. A strong and dependable full-back, who was good in the air despite standing only 5ft 8in tall, Hebden made his Hammers debut against South Shields shortly after signing and went on to captain the club in 1926-7 when Hammers finished a creditable sixth in the First Division. That was his best season. The following season, however, he joined Fulham in a joint-move with another West Ham full-back, George Horler, for £850, bowing out of West Ham's story with an appearance at White Hart Lane on 5 November 1927. Hebden was not a success at Craven Cottage and after only 24 League appearances he was on the move again, this time to Thames Association, in August 1929 when they began their ill-fated career in Division Three South. In 1932, Thames did not seek re-election and Hebden joined

ERNIE GREGORY

	LEAGUE		FA CUP		TOTAL	
	App	Gls	App	Gls	App	Gls
1946-47	9	0	0	0	9	0
1947-48	42	0	2	0	44	0
1948-49	27	0	1	0	28	0
1949-50	42	0	2	0	44	0
1950-51	30	0	2	0	32	0
1951-52	28	0	3	0	31	0
1952-53	42	0	1	0	43	0
1953-54	27	0	3	0	30	0
1954-55	0	0	0	0	0	0
1955-56	36	0	6	0	42	0
1956-57	29	0	0	0	29	0
1957-58	37	0	3	0	40	0
1958-59	32	0	1	0	33	0
1959-60	1	0	0	0	1	0
	382	0	24	0	406	0

Clapton Orient. The following year he signed for Halifax Town before retiring to find work with the electricity company in East Ham.

	LEAGUE		FA CUP		TOTAL	
	App	Gls	App	Gls	App	Gls
1920-21	1	0	0	0	1	0
1921-22	19	0	0	0	19	0
1922-23	9	0	0	0	9	0
1923-24	2	0	0	0	2	0
1924-25	4	0	3	0	7	0
1925-26	24	0	0	0	24	0
1926-27	39	0	3	0	42	0
1927-28	12	0	0	0	12	0
	110	0	6	0	116	0

JACK HEBDEN

127

When Billy Henderson was West Ham's regular right-back, his playing colleagues included Hufton, Hebden, Horler and Hodgson. There were almost as many aitches dropped in the 1920s as there were bees blurted out in 1960, when Bond, Boyce *et al* were in action. Henderson was born at Whitburn, County Durham, on 5 January 1900 and signed for West Ham from Aberdare Athletic in January 1922. He made his League debut at home to Crystal Palace in March that year and went on to prove a reliable full-back who partnered both George Hebden and Jack Young. In those days, full-backs had more responsibility for taking care of the opposition's central attackers, releasing the centre-half for more roving link-man and attacking duties. Henderson won an FA Cup runners-up medal in 1923. He was ever-present in 1923-4 and played for the FA XI against the Army, and for the Professionals against the Amateurs. He would have made many more appearances for West Ham, but for a knee injury which kept him out of action for over a year. He left West

Ham in 1928 and suffered a tragically early death, from tuberculosis, in January 1934.

BILLY HENDERSON

	LEAGUE		FA CUP		TOTAL	
	App	Gls	App	Gls	App	Gls
1921-22	12	0	0	0	12	0
1922-23	34	0	9	0	43	0
1923-24	42	0	3	1	45	1
1924-25	41	0	6	0	47	0
1925-26	17	0	1	0	18	0
1926-27	0	0	0	0	0	0
1927-28	16	0	2	0	18	0
	162	0	21	1	183	1

Born at Bromley-by-Bow in August 1885, George Hilsdon was a pupil at Marner Street School at the same time as Bill Bridgeman who later became his colleague at West Ham and Chelsea. The Hildson family moved to East Ham where young George switched to Plashet Lane School and skippered East Ham Boys to victory in the 1900-01 Corinthian Shield. After playing for the South West Ham and Boleyn Castle clubs he made several appearances in the Hammers' reserve team whilst still an amateur. He signed professional forms in 1904-05 and in a Western League match that season scored four goals against Bristol Rovers. In 1905-06, a foot injury restricted his appearances and in the close season he joined the infant Chelsea club. It was at Stamford Bridge that his career blossomed. He scored five on his debut, against Glossop in a Second Division game, and a hat-trick for the Football League against the Irish League was the prelude to eight England caps. After scoring over 100 goals in 160 appearances for Chelsea, Hilsdon returned to Upton Park in 1912, shortly after helping Chelsea to promotion for a second time. The high-spot of his second spell with Hammers came when he scored two goals in an FA Cup first-round, second replay, against West Brom at Stamford Bridge; in the

first replay two goals from Hilsdon had saved Hammers from defeat. War ended his League career but he later played for Chatham in the Kent League. He died on 10 September 1941, aged 55.

GEORGE HILSDON

	LEAGUE		FA CUP		TOTAL	
	App	Gls	App	Gls	App	Gls
1904-05	7	4	0	0	7	4
1905-06	9	3	2	0	11	3
1912-13	32	13	4	4	36	17
1913-14	17	6	0	0	17	6
1914-15	20	5	1	0	21	5
	85	31	7	4	92	35

Tommy Hodgson was born at Hetton-le-Hole, County Durham, in 1902. He joined Hammers as a full-back in 1922 and made his debut at Blackpool on May 6 that year. Hodgson never really established himself in the side, although he managed 33 appearances in 1928-9. In 1930, he signed for Luton Town, joining his old West Ham colleague, George Kay, at Kenilworth Road. Hodgson made 67 League appearances for the Hatters before his career was ended by a serious leg injury in 1933. Hodgson was not finished with football, however, and in 1950 he returned to Luton as a junior director. Nine years later he found himself leading out the team at Wembley when he was acting manager. Luton lost that FA Cup Final to Nottingham Forest, but Hodgson carried on his association with Luton, becoming chairman of the club in 1964, and later being elected president. His last game for West Ham was at home to Blackburn Rovers on 28 December 1929.

	LEAGUE		FA CUP		TOTAL	
	App	Gls	App	Gls	App	Gls
1921-22	1	0	0	0	1	0
1922-23	11	0	0	0	11	0
1923-24	5	0	0	0	5	0
1924-25	1	0	0	0	1	0
1925-26	16	0	0	0	16	0
1926-27	16	0	0	0	16	0
1927-28	5	0	0	0	5	0
1928-29	28	0	5	0	33	0
1929-30	4	0	0	0	4	0
	87	0	5	0	92	0

TOMMY HODGSON

One of the quieter heroes of the late-1970s was midfielder Pat Holland, who played in the 1975 FA Cup Final triumph and was unlucky to be injured when the Hammers reached the 1980 FA Cup Final and 1981 League Cup Final. Holland was another player who was highly motivated to play for his local club. Born at Poplar, he was an apprentice at West Ham, and turned professional in April 1969. Two years later, he had a spell on loan to Bournemouth, who were busy gaining promotion to the Third Division. In those days he was a more orthodox right winger. Although Holland scored a couple of key goals in the FA Cup run of 1974-5 — the winner at Swindon and at home to Queen's Park Rangers — he had not been in the starting line-up for the sixth round or semi-final, and was in competition with Bobby Gould and Keith Robson. In the event, Holland proved as much a Wembley match-winner as Alan Taylor. His passes set up the two shots, by Jennings and Paddon, which led to Taylor's sensational goal poaching. The next season,

Holland was a regular as the Hammers sped to the European Cup-winners' Cup Final. He scored in the Final but had to settle for a runners-up medal. His last game for West Ham was against Notts County on 17 January 1981, when he received a serious injury whilst scoring a goal. Having seen the Hammers through to the semi-final of the League Cup, he was forced to miss the run-in, and he was limited to playing in the reserves thereafter. He later coached at Orient and Queen's Park Rangers.

	LEAGUE		FACUP		FLCUP		EUROPE		TOTAL	
	App	Gls	App	Gls	App	Gls	App	Gls	App	Gls
1968-69	1	0	0	0	0	0	0	0	1	0
1969-70	8	1	0	0	0	0	0	0	8	1
1970-71	2/1	0	0	0	0	0	0	0	2/1	0
1971-72	4	0	0	0	0	0	0	0	4	0
1972-73	30/2	1	2	1	2	0	0	0	34/2	2
1973-74	20/3	2	1/1	1	0/2	0	0	0	21/6	3
1974-75	18/4	4	4/3	2	1/1	0	0	0	23/8	6
1975-76	35	2	1	0	5	0	7	2	48	4
1976-77	6	0	0	0	1	0	0	0	7	2
1977-78	18/3	3	1	0	0	0	0	0	19/3	3
1978-79	39	3	0	0	1	0	0	0	40	3
1979-80	21/5	4	1	0	8	1	0	0	30/5	5
1980-81	25	3	2	0	4	0	3	0	34	3
	227/18	23	12/4	4	22/3	3	10	2	271/25	32

PAT HOLLAND

Born at Durham on 14 June 1933, the son of a professional footballer, also called Harry Hooper, Harry Hooper junior, was a fast right winger who fetched £25,000 when signed by Wolves in March 1956. It was the most a club had paid for a wing forward. It was a shrewd move when West Ham appointed Harry Hooper, senior, as a trainer in November 1950, for it meant he brought with him his son, who had played for Hylton Colliery in the Durham League and as an amateur for Sunderland. Within months Harry Hooper junior was in the West Ham first team, making his debut against Barnsley at Upton Park in February 1951. His father had played for 15 years with Sheffield United, skippering their 1936 FA Cup Final side. He came to West Ham after three seasons with Hartlepool United, and immediately made an impact, taking charge of the Football Combination team which won Cup and League honours in 1953-4. Harry Hooper junior, was his father's footballing *alter ego* — a winger as opposed to a full-back — and his speed brought

him into the limelight. He had been a Durham youth sprint champion. After representative honours in the army — he started National Service in 1951 — young Harry played six times for England 'B', twice for England Under-23s and for the Football League. He was in the full squad while with West Ham but never played a full international. At Wolves, he scored 19 goals in 39 games but before the end of their 1957-8 Championship season he moved to Birmingham. He played out his career with Sunderland — a local boy going home. But to Londoners he was at his best when he was 'Arry 'Ooper of the 'Ammers.

HARRY HOOPER

	LEAGUE		FA CUP		TOTAL	
	App	Gls	App	Gls	App	Gls
1950-51	11	3	0	0	11	3
1951-52	2	0	0	0	2	0
1952-53	12	4	0	0	12	4
1953-54	23	6	3	2	26	8
1954-55	41	11	2	2	43	13
1955-56	30	15	6	1	36	16
	119	39	11	5	130	44

Ted Hufton, who joined West Ham at the age of 25 in 1919, played 401 League and Cup games for the Hammers. One wonders how many more appearances this England international goalkeeper might have made, had it not been for the war and football injuries. Born at Southwell, Nottinghamshire, on 25 November 1892, Hufton moved from Atlas & Norfolk to his first League club, Sheffield United, in 1913. A broken nose in a trial game at the start of 1914-15 put him out of action and lost him a place in the United team. Harold Gough kept goal for the Blades in that season's FA Cup Final. Hufton was wounded serving with the Coldstream Guards in World War One, and whilst recuperating he played as a guest for West Ham. He was bought for £350 in May 1919, to take over from Joe Hughes, and made his League debut at home to Lincoln City on 30 August 1919, which was Hammers' first game as a Football League club. Hufton endured the regular batterings that were a goalkeeper's lot in the 1920s and helped West Ham to promotion from Division Two and to the first Wembley Cup Final. Between May

1923 and May 1929, he made more appearances for England than any of the other 15 goalkeepers his country had tried. But for injuries in the mid-1920s he would have won far more than his six caps. Hufton was something of a 'penalty-king', saving 11 out of 18 spot kicks in a two-season spell. He was almost 40 when he left West Ham for Watford at the end of the 1932-3 season. Later he managed a West End firm in the motor trade and worked part-time for Hammers. He died in Swansea in February 1967.

TED HUFTON

	LEAGUE		FA CUP		TOTAL	
	App	Gls	App	Gls	App	Gls
1919-20	38	0	4	0	42	0
1920-21	38	0	1	0	39	0
1921-22	33	0	3	0	36	0
1922-23	39	0	9	0	48	0
1923-24	15	0	0	0	15	0
1924-25	7	0	0	0	7	0
1925-26	38	0	1	0	39	0
1926-27	40	0	3	0	43	0
1927-28	25	0	2	0	27	0
1928-29	31	0	4	0	35	0
1929-30	30	0	4	0	34	0
1930-31	14	0	0	0	14	0
1931-32	22	0	0	0	22	0
	370	0	31	0	401	0

Ron Greenwood needed a strong player up front, someone to take punishment, work hard and perhaps knock in a few goals. His decision to switch Geoff Hurst, then a wing-half, into the attack proved a masterstroke. For ten seasons, Hurst was West Ham's best hope for a goal. Strong in the shoulder, thick in the thigh, he had all-round talent, as indicated by his legendary three goals in the 1966 World Cup Final — one with his head, one with his right foot, the last with his left. His father, Charlie Hurst, had played for Oldham, Bristol Rovers and Rochdale in the League, moving south to play with Chelmsford City after Geoff had been born in Lancashire in December 1941. Geoff Hurst became an England Youth international, and made his First Division debut in February 1960. He proved a marked man after his success in the mid-1960s — FA Cup Final win, League Cup Final, European trophy and the World Cup — but he fulfilled his goalscoring potential. He was a pioneering near-post goalscorer, he unselfishly ran and provided for others, his penalty-taking style was typical of the way he reacted in the area — powerful and explosive rather than subtle and dainty. The second-highest Hammers goalscorer of all-time — but by far the highest in Cup competitions — Hurst moved to Stoke for £80,000 in August 1982, spending three years with the Potteries club. Then came a short spell with West Brom, a season with Seattle Sounders and the player-manager's job at Telford United. His career brought him four England Under-23 caps and 49 full England caps. He scored 24 England goals. After a period as assistant manager of Chelsea, he took over as manager for two seasons, narrowly failing to take them into Division One in the first season (1979-80). He left Stamford Bridge in 1981, ironically after the team was suffering a goal famine, and now works in the insurance business.

GEOFF HURST

	LEAGUE		FACUP		FLCUP		EUROPE		TOTAL	
	App	Gls	App	Gls	App	Gls	App	Gls	App	Gls
1959-60	3	0	0	0	0	0	0	0	3	0
1960-61	6	0	0	0	0	0	0	0	6	0
1961-62	24	1	1	0	2	0	0	0	27	1
1962-63	27	13	0	0	2	2	0	0	29	15
1963-64	37	14	7	7	6	5	0	0	50	26
1964-65	42	17	1	2	1	0	9	0	53	19
1965-66	39	23	4	4	10	11	6	2	59	40
1966-67	41	29	2	3	6	9	0	0	49	41
1967-68	38	19	3	1	3	5	0	0	44	25
1968-69	42	25	3	2	3	4	0	0	48	31
1969-70	38/1	16	1	0	2	2	0	0	41/1	18
1970-71	39	15	0	0	2	1	0	0	41	16
1971-72	34	8	4	4	10	4	0	0	48	16
	410/1	180	26	23	47	43	15	2	498/1	248

Twelve years after George Kay failed to agree re-signing terms with Bolton Wanderers, he was facing his old club in the famous first Wembley FA Cup Final of 1923. Kay was centre-half and captain of West Ham. He was born in Manchester on 21 September 1891 and Bolton had been his first club. When he fell out with them he moved to Ireland to play for Belfast Celtic. He was the first Englishman to skipper an Irish League side. During the war he served with the Royal Garrison Artillery, and he signed for West Ham in 1919, making his debut at home to Barnsley in September that year. Kay's consistency — and the increase in the League programme — enabled him to be the first Hammers' player to play more than 200 League games. After leaving Upton Park in the mid-1920s, he had a spell with Stockport. His managerial career was particularly successful. He kept Southampton stable in Division Two for five seasons (1931-6) and was the man who signed Vic Watson from West Ham, a big surprise at the time. Then Kay took over at Liverpool, masterminding a League Championship success when football resumed after the war. He stayed with the Merseyside club until he retired in February 1951. He died in April 1954.

	LEAGUE		FA CUP		TOTAL	
	App	Gls	App	Gls	App	Gls
1919-20	27	3	4	0	31	3
1920-21	36	1	1	0	37	1
1921-22	39	5	3	0	42	5
1922-23	36	0	5	0	41	0
1923-24	40	3	3	1	43	4
1924-25	41	2	6	1	47	3
1925-26	18	1	0	0	18	1
	237	15	22	2	259	17

GEORGE KAY

Born in Colchester in 1930, Vic Keeble grew into a strong centre-forward who won a Cup winners' medal with Newcastle United before joining West Ham in time to ensure the Hammers returned to the First Division in 1958. Keeble played with King George Youth Club in Colchester before being signed for the first time by Ted Fenton, then Colchester United manager. Newly elected to the Football League, Colchester were helped to establish themselves by Keeble's goalscoring power — 23 goals in 46 League games before his £15,000 transfer to Newcastle United in February 1952. He did not play for the Magpies in that season's Cup Final, but he played a big part in the 3-1 Wembley win over Manchester City in 1955. Fenton's second signing of Keeble came in October 1957, when the Hammers were a mid-table Second Division team. Keeble hit 19 goals in 29 League games, and his feared partnership with John Dick was crucial to West Ham's progress into the First Division. A back injury caused his retirement, and later he worked on the staff of Colchester United and Chelmsford City.

	LEAGUE		FA CUP		TOTAL	
	App	Gls	App	Gls	App	Gls
1957-58	29	19	3	4	32	23
1958-59	32	20	1	0	33	20
1959-60	15	6	0	0	15	6
	76	45	4	4	80	49

VIC KEEBLE

Harry Kinsell was born at Cannock on 3 May 1921, and joined his local club, West Bromwich Albion, in the 1930s. He then established himself as a top-class left-back during the war, when he also guested for Blackpool and played in their side which won the Football League North. In 1946, he played for England in two Victory internationals and was a key member of Albion's 1948-9 promotion-winning side, lining up once at outside-left, incidentally, which he no doubt enjoyed since he was a fast, intelligent defender in the days when full-backs were not supposed to stray far from their goal. His career received a jolt when Len Millard won his place and Kinsell had short stays with Bolton Wanderers and Reading before Ted Fenton signed him for Hammers in January 1951, when the player was in his 30th year. Over the next five seasons his experience proved valuable to West Ham who must have been satisfied with their £5,250 outlay. His job at Upton Park done, Kinsell was eventually given a free-transfer and moved into the Southern League to play for Bedford Town.

| | LEAGUE | | FA CUP | | TOTAL | |
	App	Gls	App	Gls	App	Gls
1950-51	16	1	1	0	17	1
1951-52	32	1	3	0	35	1
1952-53	25	0	0	0	25	0
1953-54	10	0	0	0	10	0
1954-55	18	0	0	0	18	0
	101	2	4	0	105	2

HARRY KINSELL

North-easterner Joe Kirkup, who was born at Sunderland on 17 December 1939, played rugby for Northumberland Schools but switched to soccer when his family moved south. Kirkup was yet another product of the West Ham youth policy and represented the London FA before winning England Youth honours. He was a member of the Hammers team that lost to Manchester United in the 1956-7 FA Youth Cup Final and, after a number of games at centre-half in the reserve team, made his League debut against Manchester City in December 1958. Kirkup developed into a classy, footballing full-back who won England Under-23 honours. He looked less like one's idea of a traditional full-back, and more like an all-round athlete, and his speed helped him to play an overlapping game in support of his forwards. Although he missed West Ham's first-ever FA Cup triumph, over Preston in 1964, he reached the pinnacle of his career 12 months later when he played in the magnificent European Cup-winners' Cup Final at Wembley. In March 1966, Kirkup was transferred to Chelsea, and later gave Southampton five years' service before leaving The Dell in 1974 to play in South Africa.

| | LEAGUE | | FACUP | | FLCUP | | EUROPE | | TOTAL | |
	App	Gls	App	Gls	App	Gls	App	Gls	App	Gls
1958-59	11	0	0	0	0	0	0	0	11	0
1959-60	16	0	0	0	0	0	0	0	16	0
1960-61	20	1	1	0	0	0	0	0	21	1
1961-62	41	1	1	0	2	0	0	0	44	1
1962-63	27	1	5	0	0	0	0	0	32	1
1963-64	18	0	0	0	1	0	0	0	19	0
1964-65	15	2	1	0	0	0	5	0	21	2
1965-66	17	1	0	0	4	0	2	0	23	1
	165	6	8	0	7	0	7	0	187	6

JOE KIRKUP

Goalkeeper George Kitchen was also a professional golfer when he arrived at Upton Park from Everton in 1905. Born at Fairfield, near Buxton, Derbyshire, in 1876, he played for Stockport County, then in the Lancashire League, and once helped them beat Manchester City — Meredith and all — in a Manchester Cup Final replay. He signed for Everton in 1898 but made only three first-team appearances in as many seasons before becoming established for the next three seasons. After Everton signed two well-known 'keepers, L.R.Roose (Stoke) and Billy Scott (Linfield), Kitchen collected his share of a benefit and joined Hammers, making his debut against Swindon Town on 2 September 1905 — and scored a goal. His late penalty ensured that Hammers, fielding seven new faces, started off on the right note. Kitchen was often quite superb in an otheriwse 'leaky' West Ham defence. In 1906, in a Cup game at Woolwich, he played

brilliantly in goal, denying a rampant home forward line, before scoring a penalty. A serious injury in a Cup match at Newcastle in 1908 almost ended his career but he bounced back to enjoy three more seasons with Hammers and two with Southampton, for whom he played between 1912-14. After his football career was over he became a golf professional with a club near Bournemouth.

	LEAGUE		FA CUP		TOTAL	
	App	Gls	App	Gls	App	Gls
1905-06	29	3	2	1	31	4
1906-07	37	0	2	0	39	0
1907-08	23	0	2	0	25	0
1908-09	35	0	6	0	41	0
1909-10	36	0	5	0	41	0
1910-11	24	2	4	0	28	2
	184	5	21	1	205	6

GEORGE KITCHEN

For 15 seasons, Frank Lampard was a virtual fixture at left-back in the West Ham team. Only Billy Bonds has played in more Cup ties for the Hammers. Fleet of foot, strong in the tackle, Lampard's enthusiasm was a tremendous influence throughout the 1970s and early 1980s. He won FA Cup winners' medals in 1975 and 1980, and played in the 1981 League Cup Final and 1976 European Cup-winners' Cup Final, the latter appearance marred by a serious pelvic injury he received during the game. Perhaps his most dramatic Cup tie moment came at the end of extra-time when the Hammers played Everton in the 1980 semi-final replay. David Cross headed the ball across and Lampard ducked to head the winning goal. Some moments in professional soccer still defy logic, and this was one to savour. Born in East Ham, Lampard was an apprentice before he established himself in the first team in the 1967-8 season. A broken leg in the

1968-9 season was a major set-back but he recovered to establish himself again. An England Youth international, he went on to win four England Under-23 caps. His two full international caps were almost eight years apart. After his free transfer in 1985 he spent a season with Southend United.

	LEAGUE		FACUP		FLCUP		EUROPE		TOTAL	
	App	Gls	App	Gls	App	Gls	App	Gls	App	Gls
1967-68	19	0	3	0	0	0	0	0	22	0
1968-69	1	0	0	0	0	0	0	0	1	0
1969-70	30	0	1	0	2	1	0	0	33	1
1970-71	41	1	1	0	2	0	0	0	44	1
1971-72	39	1	4	0	10	0	0	0	53	1
1972-73	38	0	2	0	2	0	0	0	42	0
1973-74	42	2	2	0	2	0	0	0	46	2
1974-75	40	4	8	1	3	0	0	0	51	5
1975-76	37	3	1	0	4	0	9	1	51	4
1976-77	36	1	2	0	1	0	0	0	39	1
1977-78	40	0	3	0	1	0	0	0	44	0
1978-79	28/1	3	1	0	1	0	0	0	30/1	3
1979-80	35/1	0	7	1	6	0	0	0	48/1	1
1980-81	38/1	1	2	0	8	0	6	0	54/1	1
1981-82	27/1	0	2	0	5	0	0	0	34/1	0
1982-83	37	2	1	0	4	0	0	0	42	2
1983-84	17/1	0	3	0	3	0	0	0	23/1	0
1984-85	1	0	0	0	0	0	0	0	1	0
	546/5	18	43	2	54	1	15	1	658/5	22

FRANK LAMPARD

Edinburgh-born Lawrie Leslie won five caps as Scotland's goalkeeper during his career with his first professional club, Airdrie. He also played three times for the Scottish League. For a fee of £15,000, in June 1961, the Hammers signed one of the most fearless goalkeepers of all time. Thick-set, crew-cut, Leslie was a brave last line of defence. Unfortunately he received his fair share of injuries. One of these injuries, a broken leg in the 1962-3 season, prompted West Ham to sign Jim Standen, and thereafter Leslie was competing for his place. He moved to Stoke City in October 1963 — the fee was again £15,000 — and played regularly for their First Division side. Leslie finished his playing career with Millwall and Southend, and coached Millwall in the early 1970s.

	LEAGUE		FA CUP		FL CUP		TOTAL	
	App	Gls	App	Gls	App	Gls	App	Gls
1961-62	37	0	1	0	1	0	39	0
1962-63	20	0	0	0	2	0	22	0
	57	0	1	0	3	0	61	0

LAWRIE LESLIE

When World War Two ended, West Ham's Archie Macaulay was one of the greats of British football. He had won four wartime Scotland caps and there were more honours to come. But sadly for Hammers, by the time Macaulay won his first full peacetime cap, he was a Brentford player, having moved to Griffin Park in October 1946. At that end of that first post-war season he moved again, this time to Arsenal where he won six more caps and a League Championship medal as well reaching the pinnacle of his career when he was selected to play for Great Britain against the Rest of the World. Falkirk-born, red-haired Macaulay was signed by West Ham from Glasgow Rangers in the close season of 1937 and made his League debut for the Hammers at Villa Park in August that year. He came to West Ham as an inside-forward who could both make and score goals, but during wartime football he made the switch to wing-half. Macaulay won a Football League War Cup medal in 1940 and then served with the Essex Regiment Territorials. After ending his playing career with Fulham, he took up managership and went on to enjoy an excellent record. After working for non-League Guildford, and then a spell as trainer-coach at Dundee, he took Norwich City from a re-election place in the Third Division South to an FA Cup semi-final appearance and into Division Two. He stayed a little over a year at his next club, West Brom, but at Brighton he managed the Seagulls team that won the Fourth Division title.

	LEAGUE		FA CUP		TOTAL	
	App	Gls	App	Gls	App	Gls
1937-38	39	10	0	0	39	10
1938-39	36	16	5	2	41	18
1945-46	0	0	2	0	2	0
1946-47	8	3	0	0	8	3
	83	29	7	2	90	31

ARCHIE MACAULAY

135

Frank McAvennie arrived from St Mirren in the summer of 1985 and made an immediate impact on English soccer. In his first season he scored 26 goals and only Gary Lineker did better in the First Division. Born in Glasgow, McAvennie joined St Mirren from St Johnstone Boys' Club in 1980 and scored 50 goals in 135 Scottish League games. The blond striker, who evoked comparisons with Denis Law, was valued at £340,000 when West Ham bought him. He had won five Under-21 caps at St Mirren — three as an over-age player — and his move to West Ham brought him full international recognition. Late in 1985, he played twice for Scotland against Australia, seeing his country safely into the World Cup finals. By mid-December, McAvennie had manifold reasons for elation. As well as Scotland's success — he had scored a vital goal at Hampden Park — West Ham were unbeaten for 12 League games, the last nine of which had been won. McAvennie's 11 goals in those 12 games was an incredible record in the tight-marking modern age. His goals, and partnership with Tony Cottee, were key factors in West Ham's best-ever season — third in Division One.

Eventually Celtic made West Ham an offer they couldn't refuse and McAvennie helped them to the Scottish League and Cup in 1987-8 before returning to Upton Park, but a broken leg at Stoke on the first day of 1989-90 sidelined him for some time. After signing off with a hat-trick he played briefly for Villa, Cliftonville and in Hong Kong before returning to Celtic, linking up with former Hammers colleague Stuart Slater.

	LEAGUE		FA CUP		FL CUP		TOTAL	
	App	Gls	App	Gls	App	Gls	App	Gls
1985-86	41	26	7	1	3	1	51	28
1986-87	36	7	5	4	5	0	46	11
1987-88	8	0	0	0	1	0	9	0
1988-89	8/1	0	0	0	0	0	8/1	0
1989-90	1/4	0	0	0	0	0	1/4	0
1990-91	24/10	10	3/1	1	0/1	0	27/12	11
1991-92	16/4	6	4	0	2/1	1	22/5	7
	134/19	49	19/1	6	11/2	2	164/22	57

FRANK McAVENNIE

John McDowell's career had a familiar ring which says such a lot for the Hammers' scouting policy and youth-coaching schemes — born in East Ham, apprentice professional and a Youth international. Added to this came a long-serving career which had cost West Ham nothing in transfer fees. McDowell could play in any defensive position, but he was at his best at right-back, the position he played in the 1975 FA Cup Final. He was quick and acrobatic, a strong tackler who always gave everything. He played 13 times for the England Under-23 team — only six players have made more appearances — but the expected full international cap never materialised. A knee injury kept him out of the Hammers team in 1976-7 and proved a niggling handicap in the years to come. He moved to Norwich City in August 1979 and played in their first team for a couple of seasons.

	LEAGUE		FA CUP		FL CUP		EUROPE		TOTAL	
	App	Gls	App	Gls	App	Gls	App	Gls	App	Gls
1970-71	25	0	0	0	0	0	0	0	25	0
1971-72	40	0	4	0	10	0	0	0	54	0
1972-73	38	2	2	0	2	1	0	0	42	3
1973-74	33	2	1	0	2	0	0	0	36	2
1974-75	33/1	1	8	0	2	0	0	0	43/1	1
1975-76	36/1	0	0	0	5	0	7	0	48/1	0
1976-77	0	0	0	0	0	0	0	0	0	0
1977-78	12/2	1	3	0	0	0	0	0	15/2	1
1978-79	26/2	2	1	0	0	0	0	0	27/2	2
	243/6	8	19	0	21	1	7	0	290/6	9

JOHN McDOWELL

Wing-half Roddy MacEachrane hailed from Inverness and came to Canning Town to work at the Thames Ironworks and play for the football team. He began his career with Inverness Thistle and if his workmates found his thick Scots accent was hard to understand, they were in no doubt about his intentions on the football field. He stood barely 5ft 6in tall, yet he was a splendid tackler and his consistent performances made him a great favourite at the Memorial Grounds. He was with the Irons when the club embraced professionalism and thus became one of the first paid players. In 1901-02, MacEachrane became the first Ironworks-Hammers player to make 100 appearances but at the end of the season he joined Woolwich Arsenal. He was a great asset to the Plumstead club and made an important contribution to their promotion to the Football League Division One in 1903-04. MacEachrane played his final senior game for Arsenal in 1913-14. He died in 1952, aged 74.

RODERICK MacEACHRANE

	LEAGUE		FA CUP		TOTAL	
	App	Gls	App	Gls	App	Gls
1900-01	28	1	6	0	34	1
1901-02	25	4	1	0	26	4
	53	5	7	0	60	5

Andy Malcolm, born just a few minutes from the Upton Park ground, was raised mainly in Romford, where he played for his local schoolboy representative teams and also captained England Schoolboys. He later became an England Youth international. He joined the West Ham groundstaff, turned professional in July 1950 and continued to serve a long apprenticeship typical of the 1950s. In fact he had played 82 reserve-team games and had a tour of National Service in the Forces before he was called up for his Football League debut in the 1953-4 season, against Notts County at Upton Park. His biting play at right-half was a major factor in the Hammers' Second Division championship season of 1957-8, when Malcolm was an ever-present. In November 1961, he moved to Chelsea in an exchange deal involving Ron Tindall, and less than 12 months later he was on the move again — to Queen's Park Rangers for another five-figure fee. He also played in South Africa. Malcolm later became a publican at Maldon, Essex.

	LEAGUE		FA CUP		FL CUP		TOTAL	
	App	Gls	App	Gls	App	Gls	App	Gls
1953-54	14	0	3	0	0	0	17	0
1954-55	38	0	2	0	0	0	40	0
1955-56	22	0	6	0	0	0	28	0
1956-57	37	0	2	0	0	0	39	0
1957-58	42	3	3	0	0	0	45	3
1958-59	42	0	1	0	0	0	43	0
1959-60	40	0	2	0	0	0	42	0
1960-61	40	1	2	0	2	0	44	1
1961-62	8	0	0	0	0	0	8	0
	283	4	21	0	2	0	306	4

ANDY MALCOLM

Born in Avonbridge, Stirlingshire, on 3 January 1908, Dr James Marshall was the only medical practitioner of his era who forged a career as a footballer at the highest levels. During his long spell with Glasgow Rangers, which started in the 1925-6 season and ended with his transfer to Arsenal nine seasons later, Marshall won Scottish Cup and League medals. He also played for Scotland three times — all against England. On his League debut for Hammers, at Port Vale in March 1935, he scored in a 2-2 draw. Throughout his career he was an inside-right. He was signed by the Hammers around the time that Vic Watson was transferred to Southampton and Dave Mangnall was signed from Birmingham as the new centre-forward. The thought of former coalminer Mangnall partnering the elegant Scottish doctor in attack is intriguing. When Marshall retired, in the close season of 1937, he took up a post with Bermondsey Borough Council. He died in December 1977.

	LEAGUE		FA CUP		TOTAL	
	App	Gls	App	Gls	App	Gls
1934-35	10	2	0	0	10	2
1935-36	36	10	2	0	38	10
1936-37	11	2	0	0	11	2
	57	14	2	0	59	14

JIMMY MARSHALL

A towering central defender, with a scoring record of which some midfielders would be proud, Alvin Martin took over a key position from Tommy Taylor and his career parallels Hammers' steady rise from the late 1970s. He signed as an apprentice in 1974 and turned full-time in the summer of 1976. He played a few games in the relegation season, but established himself in the 1978-9 season. A Youth international, he was capped for the full England side when 22, the first of many such honours. He played in the 1980 FA Cup Final win, and through the lengthy League Cup campaign the following season. His partnership with Billy Bonds was an excellent blend in the centre of defence. Later, alongside Tony Gale, he was solidarity itself, especially in 1985-6, when the Hammers finished third. That season he scored three goals in a home game against Newcastle — against three goalkeepers after Thomas was injured, then Beardsley replaced Hedworth. Injury restricted his appearances after 1987 and he was given a free transfer late in 1991-2, but recalled during an injury crisis in April he impressed and earned another year's contract. A recurrence of a foot injury in April 1992 signalled another long lay-off however.

ALVIN MARTIN

	LEAGUE		FA CUP		FL CUP		EUROPE		TOTAL	
	App	Gls	App	Gls	App	Gls	App	Gls	App	Gls
1977-78	5/2	1	0	0	0	0	0	0	5/2	1
1978-79	22	1	1	0	0	0	0	0	23	1
1979-80	40	2	7	0	8	1	0	0	55	3
1980-81	41	1	3	0	9	1	6	0	59	2
1981-82	28	4	2	0	5	0	0	0	35	4
1982-83	38	3	0	0	7	0	0	0	45	3
1983-84	29	3	1	0	5	1	0	0	35	4
1984-85	40	1	5	0	4	0	0	0	49	1
1985-86	40	4	7	0	3	0	0	0	50	4
1986-87	16	2	1	0	3	0	0	0	20	2
1987-88	15	0	0	0	2	0	0	0	17	0
1988-89	27	1	5	0	5	2	0	0	37	3
1989-90	31	0	1	0	10	1	0	0	42	1
1990-91	20	1	0	0	3	0	0	0	23	1
1991-92	7	0	0	0	0	0	0	0	7	0
1992-93	23	1	1	0	2	0	0	0	26	1
	422/2	25	34	0	66	6	6	0	528/2	31

A deserving winner of the 1991 Hammer of the Year award, goalkeeper Ludek Miklosko's popularity at Upton Park is such as to make him a serious candidate for the trophy for the foreseeable future. Many times Hammers' saviour in defence, the giant Czech's huge kicking often threatens the other goal. Indeed, some of his wind-assisted kicks, on hard grounds, give opposing 'keepers real problems. Born in Ostrava (also the home town of Ivan Lendl) in December 1961, Miklosko cost the Hammers £300,000 in the winter of 1990. To make this important capture, West Ham had to convince Home Office officials that 'Ludo' was worthy of being granted a work permit. This took several months but, since making his League debut at Swindon in February 1990, the Czech has more than justified the trouble taken to obtain his services. In his first full season at Upton Park, Miklosko almost eclipsed Phil Parkes' club record of 21 clean sheets. He has appeared for Czeckoslovakia a number of times but his selection to face England at Wembley in April 1990 is the highlight of his international career to date. He was ever-present in the 1992-3 promotion season.

	LEAGUE		FA CUP		FL CUP		TOTAL	
	App	Gls	App	Gls	App	Gls	App	Gls
1989-90	18	0	0	0	1	0	19	0
1990-91	46	0	7	0	3	0	56	0
1991-92	36	0	3	0	4	0	43	0
1992-93	46	0	2	0	2	0	50	0
	146	0	12	0	10	0	168	0

LUDEK MIKLOSKO

Billy Moore, who was born at Newcastle-upon-Tyne on 6 October 1894, was on West Ham's books for 38 years — seven as a player, three as assistant trainer and the rest as trainer. He came from Newcastle and after winning England Amateur international caps against Belgium, Denmark and Sweden, he signed professional for Sunderland. An inside-left, small and slim, Moore arrived at West Ham in the summer of 1922 and his first season was sensational. He played in every one of the 51 games which saw the Hammers back in Division One and into the first Wembley Cup Final. That May, he made his only appearance for England, scoring twice in Sweden, three days after his semi-final namesake, Derby's Jimmy Moore, had played against the same opposition. After under-studying Charles Paynter for a few years, Moore became chief of the training staff. Having seen the Hammers safely back in the First Division he retired in May 1960, when 65 years old. He died in September 1968, in Plaistow, East London.

	LEAGUE		FA CUP		TOTAL	
	App	Gls	App	Gls	App	Gls
1922-23	42	15	9	5	51	20
1923-24	36	9	3	1	39	10
1924-25	32	10	6	0	38	10
1925-26	30	4	0	0	30	4
1926-27	12	2	1	0	13	2
1927-28	23	2	1	0	24	2
1928-29	6	0	1	0	7	0
	181	42	21	6	202	48

BILLY MOORE

BOBBY MOORE

In February 1993, the football world was shattered when it was announced that Bobby Moore had died of cancer. Standing tall in the heart of the West Ham team, looking unhurried and calm in every situation, Moore was the pin-up boy of the 1960s, the idol of '70s and a legend in the '80s. Captain of the England World Cup winners in 1966, a record 108 England international appearances and more games for the Hammers than any other player, Moore won everlasting fame. He was a controlled player. He seemed to have control over the ball and control over his emotions, and he never appeared to be in a hurry, mopping up loose balls at the back of the defence, springily jumping to direct a header. In the South, he was pure gold in claret and blue, making natural progress through England Youth and England Under-23 teams to the World Cup side in Chile in 1962. In the North they said he could not tackle or battle, or step up his game. But in March 1964, Moore won the ball from a Manchester United player, fought through the Hillsborough mud and set up a super goal for Geoff Hurst to seal a place in the Cup Final. By then Moore had been captaining England for almost a year. Footballer of the Year in 1964, an FA Cup winners' medal that same year, Cup-winners' Cup trophy the next, League Cup runners-up in 1966, the victory over West Germany in 1966, the football world lay at his feet. But Moore did not add to his medals until 1975, when he played against West Ham for his new club, Fulham, in the FA Cup Final. By then there had been the Bogota bracelet incident, the beautifully-timed tackles on Pelé and Jairzinho in Mexico, five weeks out of the West Ham side after being seen in a Blackpool night-club on a Friday night, the slip in Poland that cost a goal, and the dive to his right that saved Mickey Bernard's penalty in a League Cup semi-final replay (only for Bernard to score the rebound against the deputy 'keeper). More than anything, though, there were those million moments of composure — a light touch to kill the ball, a lift of the blond hair and a long pass to clear the ball. After such a playing career — which ended at Seattle Sounders — Moore had little need to prove himself as a manager, but he had spells with Oxford City and Southend United. Moore was born in Barking, Essex, on 12 April 1941, and signed for West Ham in June 1958, making his League debut a few weeks later when he played against Manchester United at Upton Park on 8 September. In January 1967, in the wake of his triumph in leading the World Champions, Moore was awarded the OBE in the New Year's Honours List. It was perhaps strange that, after such a glittering career, he should now bow out of West Ham's first team against relatively unglamourous opposton in Hereford United, in an FA Cup match in January 1974. In fact, Moore's final appearance in the claret and blue of West Ham was in even more humble circumstances, a reserve game against Plymouth. When he finally bowed out with Fulham, he had taken his total of League games to 900.

	LEAGUE		FACUP		FLCUP		EUROPE		TOTAL	
	App	Gls	App	Gls	App	Gls	App	Gls	App	Gls
1958-59	5	0	0	0	0	0	0	0	5	0
1959-60	13	0	0	0	0	0	0	0	13	0
1960-61	38	1	2	0	2	1	0	0	42	2
1961-62	41	3	1	0	2	0	0	0	44	3
1962-63	41	3	5	0	1	0	0	0	47	3
1963-64	37	2	7	0	6	0	0	0	50	2
1964-65	28	1	0	0	0	0	7	0	35	1
1965-66	37	0	4	0	9	2	6	0	56	2
1966-67	40	2	2	0	6	0	0	0	48	2
1967-68	40	4	3	0	3	0	0	0	46	4
1968-69	41	2	3	0	3	0	0	0	47	2
1969-70	40	0	1	0	2	0	0	0	43	0
1970-71	38/1	2	1	0	2	0	0	0	41/1	2
1971-72	40	1	4	0	10	0	0	0	54	1
1972-73	42	3	2	0	2	0	0	0	46	3
1973-74	22	0	1	0	1	0	0	0	24	0
	543/1	24	36	0	49	3	13	0	641/1	27

Born in Sheffield, in July 1914, John Morton, also known as 'Jimmy', signed as a professional for Gainsborough Trinity at the age of 17. Three months later he was transferred to West Ham for the princely sum of £600, and made his League bow at home to Arsenal in March 1932. Morton, who could play on either wing, had a long spell as a West Ham regular, interrupted only by the war. He played outside-right for England against Scotland in the 1935 Jubilee international. In 1937, he won his only full cap, scoring in the 5-4 victory at White Hart Lane, over Czechoslovakia at White Hart Lane, a game in which Stanley Matthews scored a hat-trick. During the war, Morton served in the Royal Air Force and afterwards became a bookmaker. He died in March 1986.

JACKIE MORTON

	LEAGUE		FA CUP		TOTAL	
	App	Gls	App	Gls	App	Gls
1931-32	5	1	0	0	5	1
1932-33	36	11	6	2	42	13
1933-34	42	6	2	0	44	6
1934-35	40	7	2	0	42	7
1935-36	26	5	0	0	26	5
1936-37	39	14	2	0	41	14
1937-38	39	3	1	0	40	3
1938-39	31	7	4	1	35	8
	258	54	17	3	275	57

The catalyst which changed Malcolm Musgrove from a Lynemouth Colliery Welfare amateur in his native North-East — he was born at Durham on 8 July 1933 — to a professional footballer in London was his RAF National Service. After trials for West Ham he signed professional forms in November 1953. Not bad for someone who had played rugby for his county schools side. Musgrove, who made his League debut at Brentford in February 1954, ousted Ken Tucker from the Hammers' left-wing spot in the mid-1950s and proved a high-scoring winger who rarely missed a game. He won a Second Division championship medal in 1957-8. After nine years at West Ham, he joined Leyton Orient, too late in 1962-3 to save Orient's relegation from the First Division. And his last appearances came in the season (1965-6) Orient dropped to the Third. Musgrove was chairman of the PFA between 1963 and 1966, then a coach with Dave Sexton at Leyton Orient, and assistant to Frank O'Farrell at both Leicester and Manchester United. He was manager at Torquay in the mid-1970s and later held managerial or coaching posts with Charlton, Villa, Exeter, Plymouth and Shrewsbury.

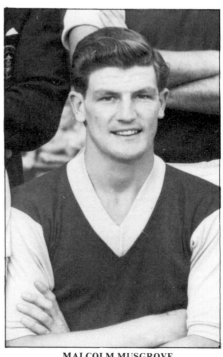

MALCOLM MUSGROVE

	LEAGUE		FA CUP		FL CUP		TOTAL	
	App	Gls	App	Gls	App	Gls	App	Gls
1953-54	4	0	0	0	0	0	4	0
1954-55	21	8	1	0	0	0	22	8
1955-56	8	0	1	0	0	0	9	0
1956-57	39	8	2	1	0	0	41	9
1957-58	39	9	3	0	0	0	42	9
1958-59	40	7	1	0	0	0	41	7
1959-60	41	15	2	1	0	0	43	16
1960-61	40	17	2	0	2	1	44	18
1961-62	36	13	1	0	1	1	38	14
1962-63	15	7	0	0	2	1	17	8
	283	84	13	2	5	3	301	89

Frank O'Farrell was born in Cork, 9 October 1927, and his first club was Cork United. His predecessor in the Cork team, Tommy Moroney, had been signed by West Ham, and O'Farrell followed him to Upton Park in January 1948. After over 50 Football Combination games, he made his Football League debut in December 1950 at Notts County. A polished wing-half, O'Farrell was a regular for six years, part of the famous West Ham soccer academy which produced a generation of managers — Malcolm Allison, Dave Sexton, John Bond, Noel Cantwell, Jimmy Andrews, Ken Brown and Malcolm Musgrove (with whom O'Farrell later worked). After having played for the Football Combination (against the Brussels League) O'Farrell impressed his national selectors. He won the first seven of his nine Republic of Ireland caps while at West Ham, and he was reserve on other occasions. His last two caps came as a player at Preston North End, who signed him in exchange for Eddie Lewis, seven years O'Farrell's junior. O'Farrell went into management with Southern League Weymouth as a player-manager, then had spells at Torquay United, Leicester City, Manchester United,

the Iran national team, Cardiff City and Torquay again. His major success came at Leicester, whom he took to the FA Cup Final and the Second Division championship.

FRANK O'FARRELL

	LEAGUE		FA CUP		TOTAL	
	App	Gls	App	Gls	App	Gls
1950-51	18	0	2	0	20	0
1951-52	41	2	3	1	44	3
1952-53	41	1	1	0	42	1
1953-54	22	0	0	0	22	0
1954-55	28	1	1	0	29	1
1955-56	40	1	6	0	46	1
1956-57	7	1	0	0	7	1
	197	6	13	1	210	7

Born at Colchester in June 1926, Derek Parker joined West Ham from Grays Athletic in October 1944. He appeared briefly for the club in wartime, then fought through the competition in the immediate post-war period to earn a regular place in the early 1950s. His League debut was on 21 September 1946, against Millwall in the Second Division. He made occasional appearances during the next three seasons, some as an inside-forward, before becoming the regular right-half. In 1951, he was chosen to tour Australia with an FA XI. He played his last game for the club in December 1956, scoring in the 3-3 draw against Bury. Three months later he joined his home-town club, Colchester United, hoping to help them to promotion from the Third Division South. They failed by a single point, but the next season became founder members of the newly-structured Third Division. Parker played 130 League games for Colchester, and as his career came to an end, Colchester dropped to the Fourth Division.

	LEAGUE		FA CUP		TOTAL	
	App	Gls	App	Gls	App	Gls
1946-47	10	1	0	0	10	1
1947-48	2	0	0	0	2	0
1949-50	32	2	2	0	34	2
1950-51	38	1	2	0	40	1
1951-52	30	3	3	0	33	3
1952-53	39	0	1	0	40	0
1953-54	28	1	0	0	28	1
1954-55	7	0	0	0	7	0
1955-56	8	0	0	0	8	0
1956-57	5	1	0	0	5	1
	199	9	8	0	207	9

DEREK PARKER

"If you want quality you have to pay for it," said John Lyall in February 1979, explaining why a Second Division club should splash out £525,000, the highest-ever fee for a goalkeeper. In the years that followed, West Ham fans were undoubtedly grateful for the signing of Phil Parkes, whose size, ability and technique engendered trust. One of the travesties of modern times is that Parkes won only one England cap — against Portugal in 1974 while still a QPR player. He also won six Under-23 caps, and played once for the Under-21s as an over-age player. Sedgley-born Parkes started with Third Division Walsall, signing professional in January 1968 and making his debut the following season. He went to QPR in June 1970, for a small fee, and stayed for over eight seasons, covering the eras of Marsh and Bowles. He helped Rangers into Division One, then to runners-up in 1975-6. He played the maximum 42 League games in eight seasons (four times ever-present with Hammers) and in a further six seasons he appeared in all but one or two League games. A knee injury in 1984-5 was a hindrance, but Parkes nursed himself through the next season as Hammers finished third in Division One. He played in Cup Finals for West Ham in 1980 and 1981,

collecting a winners' medal in 1980. By the end of 1986-7 he had joined the select band of players who have appeared in over 700 League games. His last Hammers appearance was in the League Cup semi-final disaster at Oldham in February 1990, a game which also saw the end of Lou Macari as West Ham manager. Parkes' total of 344 League games for Hammers is exactly the same as the number he made for QPR. Before the following season John Lyall, his former manager at Upton Park, snapped up 40-year-old Parkes as goalkeeping cover at Ipswich.

PHIL PARKES

	LEAGUE		FA CUP		FL CUP		EUROPE		TOTAL	
	App	Gls	App	Gls	App	Gls	App	Gls	App	Gls
1978-79	18	0	0	0	0	0	0	0	18	0
1979-80	40	0	8	0	8	0	0	0	56	0
1980-81	42	0	3	0	9	0	6	0	60	0
1981-82	39	0	2	0	4	0	0	0	45	0
1982-83	42	0	1	0	7	0	0	0	50	0
1983-84	42	0	4	0	5	0	0	0	51	0
1984-85	10	0	0	0	0	0	0	0	10	0
1985-86	42	0	7	0	3	0	0	0	52	0
1986-87	33	0	5	0	6	0	0	0	44	0
1987-88	1	0	0	0	0	0	0	0	1	0
1988-89	13	0	3	0	1	0	0	0	17	0
1989-90	22	0	1	0	9	0	0	0	32	0
	344	0	34	0	52	0	6	0	436	0

Eric Parsons, born at Worthing on 9 November 1923, was one of the speediest wingers in the game, valued at £23,000 when West Ham transferred him to Chelsea in November 1950. West Ham was his first club. He was spotted when playing for Worthing Boys against West Ham Boys at Upton Park. He played regularly as an outside-right in the post-war Second Division days, after making his debut at Leicester in January 1947, then made the transition to the First Division — and more. He won two England 'B' caps and a League Championship medal with Chelsea in 1954-5, when he played in all the games, scoring 11 goals and setting up many more for the likes of Roy Bentley. Parsons' pace and style was direct. He was the kind of winger who could 'catch pigeons' or 'chase greyhounds' and not unnaturally he took his fair share of punishment. Despite cartilage operations early in his career, and a broken leg at his last club, Brentford, Parsons made 423 League appearances in total.

	LEAGUE		FA CUP		TOTAL	
	App	Gls	App	Gls	App	Gls
1946-47	12	4	1	0	13	4
1947-48	42	11	2	1	44	12
1948-49	42	9	1	0	43	9
1949-50	38	7	2	0	40	7
1950-51	11	3	0	0	11	3
	145	34	6	1	151	35

ERIC PARSONS

Joe Payne scored only six goals during his short stay with West Ham — four less than he managed in an incredible 63-minute spell in his first game as a centre-forward. Payne's remarkable ten-goals-in-a-game were scored for Luton Town against Bristol Rovers on 11 April 1936, in the Third Division South, and it is yet another of those football records which were set in the days of attacking football and which will now presumably never be beaten. A Derbyshire coalminer — he was born at Brimington on 17 January 1914 — Payne played for his local club, Bolsover, and then moved south to Biggleswade Town before being signed by Luton. He was a 22-year-old reserve wing-half when he was drafted in to play at centre-forward in that record-breaking game which Luton went on to win 12-0. In 1936-7 his 55 goals helped Luton win the Third Division South title, and at the end of that season he won his only England cap, scoring twice in the 8-0 victory over Finland. In March 1938, he signed for Chelsea for £2,000, but during wartime football he twice broke an ankle. He was almost 33 when West Ham signed him in December 1946 and he scored on his debut, against Southampton at The Dell, but stayed only until the end of that season. Troubled by injuries Payne did not manage a League game for his last club, Millwall. He died at Luton in April 1975.

Tall, sleek and slender, Martin Peters was a classic model for midfield players in the 1960s and 1970s. He would prompt with delicate touches and beautifully clipped passes, and then appear on the end of crosses with headers — finely-judged at the near post or thumped from a distance — or shots. According to one television commentator, he 'came from nowhere' (which, in effect, meant out of camera-shot). During his career of 722 Football League matches, Peters never won a Championship medal, and the nearest he came to an FA Cup Final was in 1963-4, when Ron Greenwood was forced to omit him from the team after using him as a utility player for most of the season. Otherwise, though, Peters won most of what football had to offer. He was born at Plaistow on 8 November 1943 and made his Hammers debut at Cardiff in April 1962. He had followed his England Schoolboys honours — in the same cohort as Brian Dear — with England Youth caps. He played five times for England Under-23s and 67 times for the full national team. The first 33 caps were as a West Ham player — the rest with Tottenham after his transfer, valued at £200,000, in March 1970 — and none was more famous than the 4-2 victory over West Germany in 1966 when England won the World Cup. Peters scored the second England goal that day, smashing home a dropping ball from the edge of the goal area. "Ten years ahead of his time," Sir Alf said, some months later. In Mexico, in 1970, Peters again scored a second goal against West Germany; this time, though, England slumped from 2-0 ahead to lose 3-2, and the goal did not bring Peters the glamour it might have done. His club achievements were many: European Cup-winners' Cup medal (1965) and a League Cup runners-up medal (1966) with West Ham; two League Cup Final wins (1971 & 1973) and two UEFA Cup Final triumphs (1972 & 1974) whilst with Spurs, who paid £150,000 plus Jimmy Greaves. He moved to Norwich in March 1975, for £50,000, and after his first ten games, the Canaries were pushing for a promotion place. The next

JOE PAYNE

	LEAGUE		FA CUP		TOTAL	
	App	Gls	App	Gls	App	Gls
1946-47	10	6	1	0	11	6
	10	6	1	0	11	6

season was Norwich's best ever — tenth in Division One. Peters stayed for five years before spending a short time as Sheffield United's manager. Later he teamed up with Geoff Hurst again, this time working for a motor insurance company.

MARTIN PETERS

	LEAGUE		FA CUP		FL CUP		EUROPE		TOTAL	
	App	Gls	App	Gls	App	Gls	App	Gls	App	Gls
1961-62	5	0	0	0	0	0	0	0	5	0
1962-63	36	8	1	0	2	1	0	0	39	9
1963-64	32	3	0	0	4	0	0	0	36	3
1964-65	35	5	2	0	1	0	9	1	47	6
1965-66	40	11	4	0	10	3	6	3	60	17
1966-67	41	14	2	0	6	2	0	0	49	16
1967-68	40	14	3	2	3	2	0	0	46	18
1968-69	42	19	3	3	3	2	0	0	48	24
1969-70	31	7	1	0	2	0	0	0	34	7
	302	81	16	5	31	10	15	4	364	100

Frank Piercy was a well-known figure at centre-half in West Ham's teams between 1904-11. Upton Park regulars knew him as 'the old war-horse' and his robust style often fell foul of referees. In the opening match of 1907-08 he was sent off against Swindon Town and suspended for a month. Apparently learning little from the experience he was dismissed again in February the same season and punished again. Born at Haverton Hill, Middlesbrough, Piercy did not take up football until he was 16 and remained in his trade as a blacksmith until signing professional for Middlesbrough. After the Teessiders found themselves in the Football League First Division in 1902, he failed to make a first-team appearance for two seasons and in 1904 signed for West Ham, making his debut in the first match at Upton Park, against Millwall. A great favourite, he was made captain when Dave Gardner moved to Croydon Common in 1907 but surrendered the job to George Kitchen when injuries began to plague him. An all-round sportsman, Piercy spent 20 years as Hammers' assistant trainer. He died in 1931, aged 51.

	LEAGUE		FA CUP		TOTAL	
	App	Gls	App	Gls	App	Gls
1904-05	33	2	1	0	34	2
1905-06	24	0	2	0	26	0
1906-07	37	0	2	0	39	0
1907-08	23	0	2	0	25	0
1908-09	26	2	0	0	26	2
1909-10	29	0	5	0	34	0
1910-11	32	2	4	0	36	2
1911-12	10	1	1	0	11	1
	214	7	17	0	231	7

FRANK PIERCY

In the topsy-turvy world of professional football it is refreshing to discover that there still exists men like Geoff Pike. An industrious, muscular midfielder, Pike contributed much to restoring Hammers to the First Division after relegation in 1978. He was born at Clapton on 28 September 1956 and joined West Ham in July 1973. He enjoyed some early success and was a member of the team which reached the 1975 FA Youth Cup Final. By his mid-20s, he had gained an FA Cup winners' medal, a League Cup runners-up award and a Second Division championship medal. In that promotion season of 1980-81, Pike was ever present and runner-up in the club's Hammer of the Year award. He made his League debut at home to Birmingham in March 1976, and after playing over 350 games for the club he joined Notts County for £35,000 in July 1987 and scored 17 goals in 82 League games for them.

A hat-trick against Southend was the only one of his career. Pike moved to Orient in September 1989 and made 44 League appearances for the Os.

	LEAGUE		FACUP		FLCUP		EUROPE		TOTAL	
	App	Gls	App	Gls	App	Gls	App	Gls	App	Gls
1975-76	0/3	0	0	0	0	0	0	0	0/3	0
1976-77	20	6	1	1	0	0	0	0	21	7
1977-78	25/3	2	0/1	0	1	0	0	0	26/4	2
1978-79	10/4	1	0	0	0/1	0	0	0	10/5	1
1979-80	27/4	5	7/1	1	6	1	0	0	40/5	7
1980-81	42	6	3	0	9	1	6	1	60	8
1981-82	34	2	2	0	5	0	0	0	41	2
1982-83	40	6	1	0	7	0	0	0	48	6
1983-84	27/1	2	2	1	5	1	0	0	34/1	4
1984-85	30	2	4	1	4	0	0	0	38	3
1985-86	10	0	5	1	0	0	0	0	15	1
1986-87	10/1	0	4	0	1	0	0	0	15/1	0
	275/16	32	29/2	5	38/1	3	6	1	348/19	41

GEOFF PIKE

145

Syd Puddefoot, whose entire first-class career spanned 20 years between March 1913 and March 1933, was Hammers' best-known player of the inter-war years. A product of Park School, West Ham, which also produced England international Harold Halse, he excelled at most sports and later played county cricket for Essex. Puddefoot had an early disappointment when he missed an England Schoolboy cap because he was four days over-age but in 1912-13, after playing for East London junior sides, Condor Athletic and Limehouse Town, he signed for West Ham and made his debut in a South-Eastern League game at Watford. Two goals from 18-year-old Puddefoot that day helped Hammers' reserves turn a 3-1 deficit into a 4-3 win. By the end of February he had scored 16 goals and early in March was given his first-team debut, against Norwich. It took him three more games to score his first League goal and he had to wait until November for his first goal of 1913-14, when he scored in the 3-1 win over Gillingham. Thereafter, Puddefoot was rarely out of the side and ten goals in four consecutive matches, in December and January, included three against Bristol Rovers and five in a Cup game against Chesterfield. Eventually, an ankle injury sustained in an abandoned game at Watford temporarily halted his progress. Throughout wartime football, Puddefoot rediscovered his scoring ability and he netted prolifically for Hammers and as a guest player for other clubs. In one extraordinary game against Crystal Palace in November 1918 he scored a London Combination record of seven goals. Capped in the 1919 Victory internationals, Puddefoot was Hammers' leading scorer for three seasons, 1919-22, which made him a target for other clubs. Yet when he left Upton Park it was for the unlikely destination of Scottish League club, Falkirk. He scored 45 goals in over 100 appearances for the Brockville Park club before signing for Blackburn in 1925. He was now 30 but in 1925-6 won two full England caps and in 1928 was involved in a Cup Final upset when he helped Rovers beat hot favourites Huddersfield Town at Wembley. In February 1932, after more than 230 League appearances for the Ewood Park club, Puddefoot, now 36, rejoined Hammers but could not help arrest their slide to Division Two. His playing career ended in 1932-3 and two spells coaching in Turkey were interrupted by a period as Northampton Town manager (1935-7). His first period in Turkey, with the Galatasaray club, ended unhappily when he was badly manhandled trying to calm down excited players and spectators. Seventeen players were suspended and Puddefoot returned to England. In 1963 he was connected with Southend United in a scouting capacity. Syd Puddefoot died on 2 October 1972, aged 78.

SYDNEY PUDDEFOOT

	LEAGUE		FA CUP		TOTAL	
	App	Gls	App	Gls	App	Gls
1912-13	4	1	0	0	4	1
1913-14	16	9	4	7	20	16
1914-15	35	18	2	0	37	18
1919-20	39	21	4	5	43	26
1920-21	38	29	1	0	39	29
1921-22	26	14	3	0	29	14
1931-32	7	0	0	0	7	0
1932-33	15	3	0	0	15	3
	180	95	14	12	194	107

Born at Barking in 1886, Randall's early football was with Ethelburgers and Barking St Andrew's. A three-month spell with Barking FC in the South Essex League and an appearance in the Essex county team against Suffolk led to a trial at Upton Park, in November 1905 in a London League game against Willesden. Randall then operated mostly on the wing and sometimes at inside-left and his first goal for Hammers was also in a London League game, against Woolwich Arsenal Reserves. Illness restricted him in 1905-06 but he was back late the following season. Contrary to popular belief it was not during this season that he converted to wing-half. In November 1906 he scored twice from inside-right as Woolwich Arsenal were beaten in Charlie Paynter's benefit match. Randall had to wait until the final match of that season for his Southern League debut. Deputising for the sick Billy Grassam against champions Fulham, he scored to help a ten-man Hammers team complete a remarkable double over the Cottagers. Infrequent appearances followed in 1907-08 and the fans nicknamed him 'Old Mother Randall' because of his pedantic style. By November 1908 he had made only 12 first-team

appearances in three years at the club. He returned for a game at Northampton and, despite Hammers losing 6-0, retained his place. Polished displays saw him represent the Southern League five times and under his captaincy Hammers finished sixth and fourth in consecutive seasons. A serious knee injury restricted him to only five appearances in 1914-15 and his last game was at home to Plymouth on 5 December 1914.

	LEAGUE		FA CUP		TOTAL	
	App	Gls	App	Gls	App	Gls
1906-07	1	1	0	0	1	1
1907-08	7	1	0	0	7	1
1908-09	17	1	0	0	17	1
1909-10	39	1	5	1	44	2
1910-11	34	1	4	0	38	1
1911-12	23	1	0	0	23	1
1912-13	35	2	4	0	39	2
1913-14	28	1	3	0	31	1
1914-15	5	0	0	0	5	0
	189	9	16	1	205	10

THOMAS RANDALL

With 23 Division Two goals in 1949-50, then a further 26 the following season, Bill Robinson proved a popular centre-forward when he ended his playing career at West Ham. Born at Whitburn on 4 April 1919, Robinson joined Charlton Athletic from Sunderland for £1,000 in May 1946. With Charlton he won an FA Cup winners' medal in 1947, playing a major part in the move which led to Chris Duffy scoring the game's only goal. In January 1949, West Ham paid out £7,000 for his signature, and Robinson rewarded them with some sterling displays. He retired from playing at the end of the 1952-3 season, taking charge of the West Ham junior sides, working with Wally St Pier. In November 1957, he became Ted Fenton's assistant, midway through the Second Division championship season. He later had a spell as manager of Hartlepools United in his native North-East. Bill Robinson died on 7 October 1992, aged 72.

	LEAGUE		FA CUP		TOTAL	
	App	Gls	App	Gls	App	Gls
1948-49	17	10	0	0	17	10
1949-50	40	23	2	1	42	24
1950-51	40	26	2	0	42	26
1951-52	4	1	0	0	4	1
	101	60	4	1	105	61

BILL ROBINSON

Bryan 'Pop' Robson scored over 250 goals in his exciting career of almost 700 League matches, and Hammers' fans were fortunate to see him during two spells with the club. He was signed in February 1971, for a club record £120,000 fee from Newcastle United, where he had poached goals alongside Wyn Davies. Not particularly tall — Robson stood 5ft 8in — he was acrobatic, strong, sharp in the penalty area and had a powerful shot from long range. At Newcastle, he won a Second Division championship medal, a Fairs Cup winners' medal and two England Under-23 caps. He also played for the Football League. Robson's 28 League goals for West Ham in the 1972-3 season made him the League's equal top-scorer (joint with Fred Binney of Exeter). A move to Sunderland saw him win another Second Division championship medal, and then West Ham bought him back for £80,000 in October 1976. His 24 League goals in the 1978-9 season was the best individual performance in the Second Division. By this time the balding Robson was into his mid-30s, and one might have expected his career to be on the wane. However, he again joined Sunderland, then Carlisle and, in the 1982-3 season, he was playing for Chelsea, helping along John Neal's Second Division youngsters. Turning to coaching, he did not immediately relinquish his playing skills, turning out for Carlisle (in two spells) and Sunderland. He came on as a substitute for Carlisle a few weeks before his 40th birthday. Robson, who was born at Sunderland on 11 November 1945, managed a scoring debut for West Ham, against Nottingham Forest in February 1971.

BRYAN ROBSON

	LEAGUE		FA CUP		FL CUP		TOTAL	
	App	Gls	App	Gls	App	Gls	App	Gls
1970-71	14	3	0	0	0	0	14	3
1971-72	42	9	4	1	10	4	56	14
1972-73	42	28	2	0	2	0	46	28
1973-74	22	7	0	0	1	1	23	8
1976-77	30	14	2	0	0	0	32	14
1977-78	37	9	3	2	1	0	41	11
1978-79	40	24	1	1	1	1	42	26
	227	94	12	4	15	6	254	104

Although born in Doncaster, Yorkshire, on 8 August 1900, Jimmy Ruffell, one of the most famous players in Hammers' history, was an adopted Londoner. His first clubs were Fullers FC, Chadwell Heath United, Manor Park Albion, East Ham and Wall End United. He joined West Ham in March 1920, made his debut at home to Burnley in December 1921, and stayed for over 18 years. And for many years he stayed held the record for West Ham League appearances — until his 505 games were surpassed by Bobby Moore in 1973. Capitalising on the change in the offside law in 1925, Ruffell was a raiding left winger with a good goalscoring record. His crosses contributed to countless goals by Vic Watson. Ruffell played six times for England, three of them in the 1928-9 season, when

he was approaching his peak. He had earlier received an FA Cup runners-up medal, when the Hammers lost to Bolton in 1923. After leaving Upton Park, he spent part of a season (1938-9) at Aldershot, his career eventually ending through injury. Later he worked as a brewery representative and as a licensee in Essex.

JIMMY RUFFELL

	LEAGUE		FA CUP		TOTAL	
	App	Gls	App	Gls	App	Gls
1921-22	14	0	1	0	15	0
1922-23	33	6	9	1	42	7
1923-24	39	2	3	0	42	2
1924-25	42	9	6	3	48	12
1925-26	40	12	1	0	41	12
1926-27	37	13	3	1	40	14
1927-28	39	18	2	1	41	19
1928-29	37	20	5	0	42	20
1929-30	40	13	4	0	44	13
1930-31	37	13	1	0	38	13
1931-32	39	15	2	0	41	15
1932-33	8	0	0	0	8	0
1933-34	22	8	2	0	24	8
1934-35	36	20	2	0	38	20
1935-36	30	10	2	1	32	11
1936-37	12	0	0	0	12	0
	505	159	43	7	548	166

Two goals, speared into a Wembley net from close range in May 1965, made Alan Sealey the talk of the nation. They were the only goals of the European Cup-winners' Cup Final against TSV München 1860. For only the second time, a European soccer trophy came to Britain. Sealey had been unlucky not to play in the FA Cup Final the previous season. A Hammers regular in the early 1960s, Sealey in fact played more League games than John Sissons in the 1963-4 Cup winning season. A strong front-runner, he was born in Canning Town and started his Football League career with Leyton Orient. He moved to West Ham in March 1961, in the deal which took Dave Dunmore to Orient, and made his debut at Leicester the following month. A freak accident soon after the European Cup-winners' Cup Final success seriously hampered the progress of his career. He broke a leg when playing a knock-about cricket game in pre-season training. This caused him to miss the next season (1965-6) and play only four more League games for West Ham. He had a short spell with Plymouth before joining Romford.

	LEAGUE		FA CUP		FL CUP		EUROPE		TOTAL	
	App	Gls	App	Gls	App	Gls	App	Gls	App	Gls
1960-61	6	1	0	0	0	0	0	0	6	1
1961-62	32	11	0	0	2	0	0	0	34	11
1962-63	26	6	5	0	0	0	0	0	31	6
1963-64	18	2	0	0	4	1	0	0	22	3
1964-65	21	2	2	0	0	0	7	3	30	5
1965-66	0	0	0	0	0	0	0	0	0	0
1966-67	4	0	1	0	0	0	0	0	5	0
	107	22	8	0	6	1	7	3	128	26

ALAN SEALEY

A quiet giant of the modern-day soccer world, Dave Sexton was associated with nine Football League clubs as a player or manager before being appointed assistant to England manager Bobby Robson in July 1983. His four-year spell at West Ham was during their Second Division days but undoubtedly the experience helped develop the mind of one of the finest coaches of recent years. Born at Islington, on 6 April 1930, Sexton was the son of a Southern Area middleweight boxing champion, and Dave Sexton himself boxed in the army. His first soccer club was Chelmsford City, moving from there to Luton Town. An attacking inside-forward, occasionally centre-forward, he was signed by West Ham in March 1953 and made his debut against Fulham that April. While with the Hammers he played for the FA against the RAF (October 1953). He moved to Orient, and then, for £2,000, to Brighton, where he played in the Division Three South championship team, and for Division Three South against Division Three North. But these were small pickings compared with his successes after his playing career had ended with a knee injury (while with Crystal Palace). As manager of Chelsea (1967-74) he helped them to the FA Cup (1970), the European Cup-winners' Cup (1971) and runners-up spot in the League (1971-2). At his next two clubs, QPR and Manchester United, he again came within one place of managing the Champions. Although dismissed from his next club, Coventry City, his reputation was such that he was soon recruited to the England set-up. He is now chief coach to Aston Villa, the 1993 FA Premier League runners-up.

	LEAGUE		FA CUP		TOTAL	
	App	Gls	App	Gls	App	Gls
1952-53	3	1	0	0	3	1
1953-54	31	12	3	2	34	14
1954-55	25	12	0	0	25	12
1955-56	15	2	0	0	15	2
	74	27	3	2	77	29

DAVE SEXTON

Forward Danny Shea was West Ham's first home-grown personality. Born at Wapping in November 1887 and employed in a shipping office, he played for Manor Park Albion in the South Essex League, twice on Sundays (thus violating FA rules) and in the Tufnell Park Thursday League. He made his Southern League debut for West Ham as an amateur, at Norwich in December 1907, and by the start of 1908-09 had ousted long-serving Billy Grassam. West Ham's top scorer for the next five seasons, Shea won Southern League representative honours and finished his last Hammers season still leading scorer despite moving to Blackburn Rovers halfway through the campaign. With Herbert Ashton he gave Hammers a formidable wing partnership and Shea himself was the Southern League's leading marksman in 1909-10 and 1910-11. At Blackburn he continued to score regularly and won three full England caps and Football League representative honours. His 27 goals helped Rovers win the League Championship in 1913-14. As a wartime guest he scored prolifically for Hammers again and spells with Fulham, Birmingham and Nottingham Forest were followed by one more season at Blackburn before he returned to Upton Park again. Hammers were now in the Football League and Shea was in his 33rd year. He scored once in 16 games — that match being one of only four in which Puddefoot, Shea and Vic Watson appeared together for Hammers — and early in 1921 moved to Fulham. Shea later played for Coventry (1923), Clapton Orient (1925) and finally Sheppey United (1926). He died on Christmas Day 1960.

John Sissons became the youngest player to score in an FA Cup Final when in 1964, aged 17, he netted against Preston. He was born at Hayes, Middlesex, on 30 September 1945. West Ham first spotted him playing for Middlesex and England Schoolboys and he scored four goals on his England debut. He signed for Hammers in October 1962 and made his League debut in May 1963, against Blackburn Rovers. The following year Sissons played in every FA Cup tie when West Ham won the trophy. Great things were expected of him as he had a rare talent, a brilliant left foot, and a burst of speed. He played a big part in Hammers' European campaign the following year which culminated in that wonderful exhibition of football with the Germans, TSV München 1860. International honours followed and he won ten England Under-23 caps in the next three years. But Sissons' early talents did not blossom and in August 1970, after 265 games, he left for Sheffield Wednesday. A further 115 League appearances were made in the Owls' colours before, in December 1973, he signed for his former teammate, John Bond, at Norwich. Seventeen League games and two goals later, he was on his travels again and returned

DANIEL SHEA

	LEAGUE		FA CUP		TOTAL	
	App	Gls	App	Gls	App	Gls
1907-08	13	3	2	0	15	3
1908-09	35	16	6	4	41	20
1909-10	38	28	5	3	43	31
1910-11	35	25	4	3	39	28
1911-12	36	24	5	0	41	24
1912-13	22	15	0	0	22	15
	179	111	22	10	201	121

to London with Chelsea in August 1974. He failed to establish himself in their struggling side which was relegated that year and had played in only ten games when his contract was cancelled. John Sissons then left England for the sunshine of South Africa to play for Cape Town City. He still lives there and works for a motor product company.

JOHN SISSONS

	LEAGUE		FA CUP		FL CUP		EUROPE		TOTAL	
	App	Gls	App	Gls	App	Gls	App	Gls	App	Gls
1962-63	1	0	0	0	0	0	0	0	1	0
1963-64	14	3	7	3	1	0	0	0	22	6
1964-65	38	8	2	1	1	0	9	2	50	11
1965-66	36	5	2	1	9	1	4	1	51	8
1966-67	34/1	7	2	1	6	3	0	0	42/1	11
1967-68	37	8	3	2	2	0	0	0	42	10
1968-69	31/1	4	1	0	2	1	0	0	34/1	5
1969-70	19/1	2	1	0	0	0	0	0	20/1	2
	210/3	37	18	8	21	5	13	3	262/3	53

As the players left the Upton Park pitch following Hammers' 5-0 defeat of Sheffield United on 21 March 1990, Blades' defender Chris Wilder shook Stuart Slater's hand, remarking, "That's the closest I've been to you all evening." Slater had just given one of those performances that can only be described as 'magic'. Sheffield United, eventually promoted from the Second Division, had been tormented for 90 minutes by Slater's pace and close control. Suffolk-born Slater learned those skills in the footballing backwater of Sudbury and before coming to London to join West Ham he supported Ipswich Town. Within two years of his arrival at Upton Park, Slater was an established first-teamer but at the end of his first season had to share with his colleagues the shattering disappointment of relegation. Used as a striker in his early days, Slater's talents were switched to the wings during 1989-90. His 40 appearances that term yielded seven goals, plus a couple in a ten-match run to the Littlewoods Cup semi-final. Five League and Cup goals during the following campaign included a gem against Everton in an FA Cup sixth-round tie. Along with Ian Bishop, Slater was selected for the England 'B' game against Switzerland at Walsall in May 1991. In 1991-2, however, he failed to score a single goal for West Ham and his old clubmate and agent, Liam Brady, took him to Celtic for £1.5 million.

	LEAGUE		FA CUP		FL CUP		TOTAL	
	App	Gls	App	Gls	App	Gls	App	Gls
1987-88	0/2	0	0	0	0	0	0/2	0
1988-89	16/2	1	3	1	1	0	20/2	2
1989-90	40	7	0	0	9/1	2	49/1	9
1990-91	37/3	3	7	2	2	0	46/3	5
1991-92	41	0	6	0	4	0	51	0
	134/7	11	16	3	16/1	2	166/8	16

STUART SLATER

In all games for West Ham, centre-forward Sam Small scored 123 goals in 293 appearances, but the vast majority of these came during World War Two. Small was at his peak in the middle of the conflict. His most sensational contribution to the Hammers' history was the goal that won the Cup — the one he scored against Blackburn Rovers when a 1-0 victory secured the League War Cup at Wembley in 1940. Born in Birmingham, on 15 May 1912, Small joined West Ham from Birmingham in 1937, and he left for Brighton in March 1948. By this time, in his mid-30s, his role was necessarily changing and he played 60 times for Brighton without scoring a goal.

	LEAGUE		FA CUP		TOTAL	
	App	Gls	App	Gls	App	Gls
1936-37	18	11	0	0	18	11
1937-38	18	7	0	0	18	7
1938-39	19	11	4	0	23	11
1945-46	0	0	4	0	4	0
1946-47	39	7	1	0	40	7
1947-48	14	3	1	0	15	3
	108	39	10	0	118	39

SAM SMALL

151

Jim Standen was an experienced goalkeeper who signed for West Ham in 1962, when regular 'keeper Lawrie Leslie was injured. Standen was born at Edmonton on 30 May 1935 and joined his first club, Arsenal, in 1953. After 35 League appearances for the Gunners, he moved to Luton for a couple of seasons and played in 36 League games for the Hatters. His best days, however, were reserved for Hammers, and Liverpool players in particular would testify to his courage and agility, for Standen always seemed to play well against the Merseysiders. One brilliant display came in September 1963 helping to ensure victory against Liverpool at Anfield when he defied Hunt and St John, and also saved a Moran penalty. During his six years at Upton Park, Standen collected FA Cup and European Cup-winners' Cup medals, followed by a runners-up award in the 1966 League Cup Final. He was also a fine cricketer and was a member of the Worcestershire side which won the County Championship. After leaving West Ham in 1968, Standen had a brief spell with Millwall (eight League appearances) and Portsmouth (13). His playing career finally ended in 1971 and in recent years he has coached in the United States.

	LEAGUE		FA CUP		FL CUP		EUROPE		TOTAL	
	App	Gls	App	Gls	App	Gls	App	Gls	App	Gls
1962-63	18	0	5	0	0	0	0	0	23	0
1963-64	39	0	7	0	7	0	0	0	53	0
1964-65	42	0	2	0	1	0	8	0	53	0
1965-66	37	0	4	0	8	0	6	0	55	0
1966-67	39	0	2	0	6	0	0	0	47	0
1967-68	3	0	0	0	1	0	0	0	4	0
	178	0	20	0	23	0	14	0	235	0

JIM STANDEN

Centre-forward Harry Stapley was an amateur throughout his career. Born on 29 April 1883, he became a teacher and worked in various parts of the country. He played for Bromley, Norwich CEYMS and Reading (no first-team games) before, around 1904, leaving Reading Collegiate School for Woodford College in Essex. He became captain of Woodford Town before accepting an invitation to play for West Ham in 1905. Although he was small, slight and had no Southern League experience, Stapley prospered. He shunned the physical aspect of the game and instead relied on skill and guile. He was 22 when he made his Hammers debut, on the same day that Grassam returned to the club from Leyton, and scored the only goal of the game against Portsmouth. Stapley's arrival meant that Hilsdon had to make way, although the new man's availability was governed by his teaching duties. Stapley won 15 England Amateur caps, five as a Hammer, and helped Great Britain win the first-ever Olympic football title in 1908. He ended each of his two and a half seasons at Upton Park as leading scorer and repeated that feat in four out of five seasons with Glossop. A useful cricketer who played for Manor Park Constitutional Club whilst in East London, Harry Stapley died at his home in Glossop on his 54th birthday in 1937.

	LEAGUE		FA CUP		TOTAL	
	App	Gls	App	Gls	App	Gls
1905-06	13	9	0	0	13	9
1906-07	35	20	2	2	37	22
1907-08	23	10	2	0	25	10
	71	39	4	2	75	41

HARRY STAPLEY

152

When Ray Stewart made his debut for West Ham in September 1979 they were in the Second Division relegation zone. Nine months later they were winning the FA Cup and Stewart's hard-driven passes, strong tackling and ferocious shooting had much to do with that and with subsequent achievements in the '80s. He was top scorer in that Cup run, with two goals from midfield against Orient and a late penalty to put out Villa. Although he has appeared as a central defender and midfielder, he was best known for his displays on the right side of defence. His expertise as a penalty-taker was also invaluable, his technique generally relying on power rather than accuracy. He was born at Stanley, Perthshire, on 7 September 1959 and it took courage for a Second Division club to pay £430,000 for an uncapped Dundee United player, as West Ham did in 1979. He was only 20, yet less than two years later he was in the Scotland team. This meant Stewart had represented Scotland at all levels and he captained Hammers in the absence of Alvin Martin. During his latter days at Upton Park, Stewart endured long absences due to injury and in 1991 he moved to his home-town club, St Johnstone, on a free transfer. He played 17 times in 1991-2 before becoming community development officer and coaching the youngsters at McDiarmid Park.

RAY STEWART

	LEAGUE		FA CUP		FLCUP		EUROPE		TOTAL	
	App	Gls	App	Gls	App	Gls	App	Gls	App	Gls
1979-80	38	10	8	3	8	1	0	0	54	14
1980-81	41	5	3	1	9	2	6	1	59	9
1981-82	42	10	2	0	5	3	0	0	49	13
1982-83	39	8	1	0	6	3	0	0	46	11
1983-84	42	7	4	1	5	1	0	0	51	9
1984-85	37	6	4	1	4	0	0	0	45	7
1985-86	39	6	6	1	3	3	0	0	48	10
1986-87	23	4	3	0	3	0	0	0	29	4
1987-88	33	4	2	0	0	0	0	0	35	4
1988-89	5/1	2	2	0	1	1	0	0	8/1	3
1990-91	5	0	0/1	0	0	0	0	0	5/1	0
	344/1	62	35/1	7	44	14	6	1	429/2	84

Alan Taylor became a household name in 1975 when his goals swept West Ham to Wembley glory. Two goals in each of the quarter-final, semi-final and Wembley games earned Hammers the FA Cup, and Taylor a 'Roy of the Rovers' tag. He was born at Hinckley on 14 November 1953 and joined Rochdale from non-League Morecambe in May 1953. After 55 League games for the Spotland club, in which he scored seven goals, Taylor joined Hammers in November 1974 and made his debut a month later, against Leeds. A year after his remarkable FA Cup scoring record, he played in the team which lost the 1976 Cup-winners' Cup Final to Anderlecht. Injuries cost him his place and in 1979, he moved to Norwich, for whom he made 23 appearances before joining NASL club Vancouver Whitecaps. After returning to England in 1980, he had short spells with Cambridge City and Hull City. He later played for Burnley and Bury, and made a brief return to Division One with Norwich in 1988-9.

	LEAGUE		FA CUP		FLCUP		EUROPE		TOTAL	
	App	Gls	App	Gls	App	Gls	App	Gls	App	Gls
1974-75	11/3	2	4	6	0	0	0	0	15/3	8
1975-76	33/2	13	1	0	4	1	6/1	3	44/3	17
1976-77	24/1	5	1	0	2	1	0	0	27/1	6
1977-78	10/1	2	0/1	0	1	0	0	0	11/2	2
1978-79	10/3	3	1	0	1	0	0	0	12/3	3
	88/10	25	7/1	6	8	2	6/1	3	109/12	36

ALAN TAYLOR

Born in Hornchurch on 26 September 1951, Tommy Taylor won England Schoolboy, Youth and Under-23 honours and for a time looked a candidate for full caps. Tall, well-built with curly fair hair, his potential as a 'golden boy' matched that of Bobby Moore, his partner in the centre of the defence when Taylor arrived in October 1970 to make his debut against Spurs. After first appearing for Orient as a 16-year-old, he helped the Os to the Third Division title in 1969-70. Early the next season, Hammers agreed a fee of about £80,000 and for nine years Taylor was a regular last line of defence, taking over from Alan Stephenson. In his first five full seasons at Upton Park, he played in 48 Cup ties, helping Hammers to the League Cup semi-final, the FA Cup Final win over Fulham and the Cup-winners' Cup Final. After a decade of stability, Taylor was replaced by Alvin Martin. In the summer of 1979, he returned to Orient and his last season with the Os saw them return to the Third Division. His career of almost 600 Football League games had gone the full circle. Taylor went to Antwerp, and later coached the

Charlton Athletic youth team. After three years in New Zealand soccer management, Taylor took up a coaching post with Football League new boys Maidstone United in 1989.

TOMMY TAYLOR

	LEAGUE		FA CUP		FL CUP		EUROPE		TOTAL	
	App	Gls	App	Gls	App	Gls	App	Gls	App	Gls
1970-71	30	1	1	0	0	0	0	0	31	1
1971-72	42	0	4	0	10	0	0	0	56	0
1972-73	37	3	2	0	2	0	0	0	41	3
1973-74	40	0	2	0	2	0	0	0	44	0
1974-75	39	0	7	0	3	0	0	0	49	0
1975-76	42	2	0	0	5	0	9	0	56	2
1976-77	36	0	2	0	3	0	0	0	41	0
1977-78	42	2	3	0	0	0	0	0	45	2
1978-79	32	0	0	0	1	0	0	0	33	0
	340	8	21	0	26	0	9	0	396	8

'An impertinent little fellow, he seems to steal the ball rather than win it in an honest, straight-forward fashion' — that was how the *Daily Chronicle* soccer correspondent summed up West Ham's dapper, terrier-like wing-half, Jack Tresadern on the morning of the 1923 FA Cup Final. Born at Leytonstone in September 1893, Tresadern was a successful schoolboy footballer. From Harold Halse's old club, Wanstead, he became a regular with Barking after refusing an offer to follow in Halse's footsteps and join Southend United. In January 1913 he began to play occasional reserve team games for West Ham. Eventually he signed professional forms and made his senior debut in a 6-0 defeat at Watford. Alf Fenwick and then Dan Woodards restricted his appearances to just six games before Tresadern joined the Royal Artillery. Lieutenant Tresadern made few wartime appearances for Hammers but he won a regular place when peacetime football resumed and Hammers joined the Football League. In the wake of Hammers' 1923 Cup Final appearance, Tresadern, Watson and Moore were capped for England but then his club form slumped

and in October 1924 he joined ailing Burnley. Later he became player-manager, then manager of Northampton. He also managed Crystal Palace, Spurs, Plymouth, Hastings and Tonbridge. He was still in football, as Tonbridge manager, when he died on Boxing Day 1959, aged 66.

JACK TRESADERN

	LEAGUE		FA CUP		TOTAL	
	App	Gls	App	Gls	App	Gls
1913-14	4	0	0	0	4	0
1014-15	2	0	0	0	2	0
1919-20	35	0	4	0	39	0
1920-21	30	0	1	0	31	0
1921-22	28	3	2	0	30	3
1922-23	37	2	9	0	46	2
1923-24	10	0	0	0	10	0
1924-25	4	0	0	0	4	0
	150	5	16	0	166	5

Londoner Ken Tucker who was born on 2 October 1925, played for East Ham Boys and Finchley before signing for West Ham in May 1946. Initially as a part-time professional, and later full time, Tucker was a strong-running left winger who made a dream debut, scoring a hat-trick against Chesterfield in October 1947. Yet, incredibly, Tucker failed to establish himself as a first-team regular until he had turned 30. Careers were slow to progress in the 1950s, with clubs sporting large playing staffs and players often temporarily absent on National Service, but Tucker was unusually restricted to the reserves. He played around 200 Football Combination games for the Hammers and won Championship and Cup medals with the second team. Only in 1955-6 was he chosen regularly for the Second Division team, scoring 14 times in 37 League games. In March 1957, he left for a season at Notts County, and he later played for Margate.

KEN TUCKER

	LEAGUE		FA CUP		TOTAL	
	App	Gls	App	Gls	App	Gls
1947-48	5	3	0	0	5	3
1948-49	2	0	0	0	2	0
1949-50	2	0	0	0	2	0
1950-51	3	0	0	0	3	0
1951-52	7	5	3	0	10	5
1952-53	15	3	1	0	16	3
1953-54	2	0	1	0	3	0
1955-56	37	14	5	0	42	14
1956-57	10	6	0	0	10	6
	83	31	10	0	93	31

Between September 1975 and May 1978, Anderlecht played a maximum 27 games in the European Cup-winners' Cup, twice winning the trophy. One of their stars was the dynamic and skilful Francois Van der Elst, who scored two goals in the 1976 Final to help the Belgium team to a famous 4-2 victory — against West Ham. Six years later he was a player at Upton Park. He was signed in January 1982 from New York Cosmos, a deal which cost West Ham £400,000. He played himself back into the Belgium squad in time for the World Cup Finals in Spain, and he appeared a couple of times as a substitute in those Finals. The next season he played regularly for the Hammers, and was equal highest goalscorer (in all competitions) as the club ended the season in eighth place in the First Division. Soon afterwards, however, Van der Elst returned to Belgium, joining Lokeren. His West Ham debut came at Brighton on 16 January 1982.

FRANCOIS VAN DER ELST

	LEAGUE		FA CUP		FL CUP		EUROPE		TOTAL	
	App	Gls	App	Gls	App	Gls	App	Gls	App	Gls
1981-82	21/1	5	1	0	0	0	0	0	22/1	5
1982-83	40	9	1	0	5/1	3	0	0	46/1	12
	61/1	14	2	0	5/1	3	0	0	68/2	17

Albert Walker spent six seasons as a Hammers full-back in the late-1930s, then returned to work for a further 28 years on the backroom staff before retiring in 1980. Born in Little Lever, Walker grew up in an area of Lancashire which had a strong football tradition and had been the centre of debates about professionalism in the 1880s. He played for Little Lever United, Southport, Bolton Wanderers and Barrow without making any real impact. In the summer of 1932, he joined West Ham, who were rebuilding after relegation to Division Two. Walker's full-back partnership with Albert Chalkley began and he became a great favourite with Hammers fans, after making his League debut at home to Oldham in October 1932. He found himself in a side struggling to avoid relegation to the Third Division South — Hammers finished 20th — but helped steady the ship and in 1934-5, when West Ham finished third, Walker was an ever-present at left-back. He missed only one game the next season, when Hammers again looked promotion favourites.

He left Upton Park in 1938 and his next two clubs, either side of the war, were Doncaster and Colchester. At the latter he worked with Ted Fenton, soon to become West Ham manager. In 1952, Fenton sent for Albert Walker, who became manager of the 'B' team in the Metropolitan League. This was the start of a second career at Upton Park, during which he assisted teams at all levels. He died in April 1993, aged 83.

ALBERT WALKER

	LEAGUE		FA CUP		TOTAL	
	App	Gls	App	Gls	App	Gls
1932-33	33	0	6	0	39	0
1933-34	37	0	2	0	39	0
1934-35	42	0	2	0	44	0
1935-36	41	0	2	0	43	0
1936-37	8	0	0	0	8	0
1937-38	1	0	0	0	1	0
	162	0	12	0	174	0

The bare statistics of Dick Walker's career with West Ham — 311 League and Cup games and two goals — underestimate his value to the club in a playing career which spanned almost 25 years. After playing as an amateur for West Ham's 'A' team, Becontree Athletic and Park Royal, Hackney-born Walker became a professional and made his debut in August 1934 against Burnley. He had the unenviable task of taking over from England international Jim Barrett, at a time when the centre-half role was changing. Walker made nearly 100 appearances for the Hammers during the war, including the game against Blackburn Rovers which saw West Ham win the League War Cup. He served in a paratroop regiment during the war, and played for the British Army in representative games in the Middle East. When the war ended, Walker became the Hammers' captain, a regular and reliable general in the first five post-war seasons. By the time he retired, at the end of 1956-7, Walker had chalked

up another 200 plus appeararances in the Reserves, acting as coach and setting a fine example to the club's younger players. He later coached Dagenham and worked for Tottenham Hotspur as a scout. He died in February 1988, aged 75.

DICK WALKER

	LEAGUE		FA CUP		TOTAL	
	App	Gls	App	Gls	App	Gls
1934-35	3	0	0	0	3	0
1935-36	2	0	0	0	2	0
1936-37	27	0	2	0	29	0
1937-38	32	0	1	0	33	0
1938-39	38	0	5	0	43	0
1945-46	0	0	4	0	4	0
1946-47	34	0	1	0	35	0
1947-48	39	1	1	0	40	1
1948-49	40	1	1	0	41	1
1949-50	39	0	2	0	41	0
1950-51	33	0	2	0	35	0
1951-52	4	0	0	0	4	0
1952-53	1	0	0	0	1	0
	292	2	19	0	311	2

One of the very few Cambridgeshire men to make a career in professional football, and probably the most famous of those who did, Vic Watson was an astonishingly productive centre-forward. Some of his West Ham records are unlikely to be beaten: 298 League goals in his career, 42 League goals in a season (1929-30) and six goals in a game (against Leeds in February 1929). Watson played for Girton, Cambridge Town, Peterborough & Fletton United and Brotherhood Engineering Works. He joined West Ham in March 1920 and in 13 of the next 15 seasons he reached double figures in the goal charts, nine times scoring over 20 in a League programme after making his debut at Cardiff in September 1920. It is strange that he was limited to five England caps. He scored four times in those games, of which four were drawn and one won. His most famous season was 1929-30, soon after he had passed his 30th birthday. He scored 42 League goals, eight in four FA Cup matches, and ended the season with two for England against Scotland in a notable 5-2 victory. He had one season with

Southampton before retiring to Cambridgeshire where he died on 3 August 1988, in his 91st year.

VIC WATSON

	LEAGUE		FA CUP		TOTAL	
	App	Gls	App	Gls	App	Gls
1920-21	9	2	0	0	9	2
1921-22	37	12	3	1	40	13
1922-23	41	22	9	5	50	27
1923-24	11	3	0	0	11	3
1924-25	41	22	6	1	47	23
1925-26	38	20	1	0	39	20
1926-27	42	34	3	3	45	37
1927-28	33	16	2	0	35	16
1928-29	34	29	5	1	39	30
1929-30	40	42	4	8	44	50
1930-31	18	14	0	0	18	14
1931-32	38	23	2	2	40	25
1932-33	35	23	6	4	41	27
1933-34	30	26	2	3	32	29
1934-35	15	10	0	0	15	10
	462	298	43	28	505	326

Strong and speedy with a fierce shot, George Webb was an amateur international who also appeared in the full England team. Born in the East End, Webb was the stepson of George Hone, one of the early adminstrators of Thames Ironworks and a director of West Ham United. He went to school less than half a mile from Upton Park and in August 1905 took part in a pre-season trial, aged 18. Later that season he made his Southern League debut in a Division Two match against Reading, although his main obligations at that time were to Ilford Alliance FC. Later he played for Wanstead, the main amateur club in the district. Webb, a toy manufacturer and freemason, remained an amateur throughout his career and his appearances were always restricted by his business committments. In six years with Hammers he never played more than six matches in succession and George Shea once said that Webb led too crowded a life. He scored on his senior debut, against Leyton, but reserved his best displays for FA Cup games and internationals. He hit

two of Hammers' five at Wolves in 1910 and all three against First Division Preston the following season. Illness ruled him out of the latter part of 1911-12 and he began the next season with Manchester City but after injury and then a financial dispute with City, he dropped out of League football. In March 1915, George Webb died of consumption, aged 28.

GEORGE WEBB

	LEAGUE		FA CUP		TOTAL	
	App	Gls	App	Gls	App	Gls
1908-09	4	2	0	0	4	2
1909-10	18	7	4	5	22	12
1910-11	19	10	4	3	23	13
1911-12	11	4	2	1	13	5
	52	23	10	9	62	32

Born in East Ham, on 11 December 1919, winger Terry Woodgate made his West Ham debut as a 21-year-old on Good Friday 1939, against Bradford. He was forced to wait over seven years before experiencing regular Second Division football. During the war he served with the Essex Regiment and the Royal Artillery. He managed 73 wartime appearances for the Hammers and guested for other clubs. Then he established himself as a regular in the post-war Second Division seasons, not missing a game in 1950-51. Woodgate, who could play on either wing, eventually found his place threatened by the likes of Harry Hooper and Malcolm Musgrove. In March 1954, he moved to Midland League Peterborough United, who had recently caused a sensation by reaching the FA Cup third round and were destined to become famous Cup fighters. After retiring from football he became landlord of a pub in March, Cambridgeshire. He died, aged 65, on 26 April 1985.

	LEAGUE		FA CUP		TOTAL	
	App	Gls	App	Gls	App	Gls
1938-39	4	0	0	0	4	0
1945-46	0	0	4	0	4	0
1946-47	41	5	1	1	42	6
1947-48	38	7	2	0	40	7
1948-49	38	9	1	0	39	9
1949-50	29	4	2	2	31	6
1950-51	42	12	2	0	44	12
1951-52	38	8	3	1	41	9
1952-53	29	3	1	0	30	3
	259	48	16	4	275	52

TERRY WOODGATE

With his fashionable crew-cut hairstyle, his sleek, slender appearance and his innovative approach to the game, Welsh-international Phil Woosnam oozed class. As inside-forwards went he was craft rather than graft, brain rather than brawn. Born in Montgomeryshire, on 22 December 1932, Woosnam played as an amateur with Sutton United and Manchester City while obtaining a university degree. Such an education made him a rarity in the 1950s professional-football game, and he was increasingly looked upon as a man of ideas. Generally modelled around players like Johnny Haynes, Woosnam knew about wall-passes, near-post crosses, and, when the Hammers introduced a 4-2-4 system, Woosnam was the creative link man to play alongside the then attacking Bobby Moore. His first professional experience was with Leyton Orient, whom he had previously helped win Division Three South. West Ham signed him for £30,000 in November 1958. At that time only three British players had been valued higher in the transfer market. Woosnam made his League debut for Hammers at home to Arsenal in November 1958. He played for Wales at Schoolboy and Amateur levels, and then won 17 full international caps during his career with Leyton Orient, West Ham and Aston Villa. It was inevitable he would turn to coaching, and in 1966 he emigrated to the USA to become player-coach of Atlanta Chiefs. His greatest soccer success, however, came as an administrator. In January 1969, he took over as Commissioner of the North American Soccer League, setting about the task of gaining media attention and public enthusiasm for a sport which was hitherto unknown to most Americans. Leading the way by example, Woosnam succeeded. By the mid-1970s Americans were talking of Pelé, Beckenbauer and Best; and Phil Woosnam could claim full credit.

PHIL WOOSNAM

	LEAGUE		FA CUP		FL CUP		TOTAL	
	App	Gls	App	Gls	App	Gls	App	Gls
1958-59	13	2	0	0	0	0	13	2
1959-60	38	11	2	0	0	0	40	11
1960-61	38	6	2	0	1	0	41	6
1961-62	34	6	1	0	2	1	37	7
1962-63	15	1	0	0	1	0	16	1
	138	26	5	0	4	1	147	27

In 1922-3, the season the Hammers won promotion to the First Division on goal average and also earned a Cup Final appearance at Wembley, there was a small but significant backroom happening: Tommy Yews made the move from Hartlepools United to West Ham. His sparkling displays in the Third Division North led the Hammers to pay £150 for his services, and he quickly won a first-team place on the right wing of the First Division team. His League debut came at Cardiff in September 1923 and his runs and crosses were soon an asset to the foraging power of centre-forward Vic Watson. Yews was a provider rather than a prolific goalscoring winger, but, in contrast to most wingers, he improved his goalscoring record as he developed. He was essentially a corner-flag type winger, but he learned to put his 5ft 8in frame where it hurt. He joined Clapton Orient in 1933, and later became an engineer at Briggs Motor Bodies and a charge-hand at the Ford Motor Co. Born at Wingate, County Durham, in February 1902, Tommy Yews died at Ilford on 19 August 1966.

TOMMY YEWS

	LEAGUE		FA CUP		TOTAL	
	App	Gls	App	Gls	App	Gls
1923-24	12	1	0	0	12	1
1924-25	33	1	6	1	39	2
1925-26	32	1	1	0	33	1
1926-27	39	8	3	0	42	8
1927-28	42	11	2	0	44	11
1928-29	41	10	5	3	46	13
1929-30	41	3	4	1	45	4
1930-31	37	7	1	0	38	7
1931-32	23	2	2	0	25	2
1932-33	32	2	5	0	37	2
	332	46	29	5	361	51

Matches to Remember

Hammers 7   Gravesend United 0

PLAYING under their new title for the first time, West Ham United got off to a splendid start in cold and drizzly weather which made life uncomfortable for players and spectators alike in this Southern League Division One game.

The Kent club had not originally been given any fixtures after refusing to pay a league fine at the end of the previous season. However, they relented and opened the season against the re-formed Ironworks club at the Memorial Grounds.

Within five minutes Hammers' new inside-right Billy Grassam scored but the real danger for Gravesend came from Hammers' wingers, Fergus Hunt and Fred Fenton. Fenton, in particular, was very fast and on one occasion left his colleagues as well as opponents behind. When he crossed, Kaye missed it by yards but Hunt, on the other wing, retrieved the ball and scored from an acute angle.

Kaye missed yet another Fenton cross and when he finally connected with a third, succeeded only in putting it into the side netting. By half-time, however, Hammers were 3-0 ahead. Wilcox, a Gravesend reserve, was having a poor game in goal and although he managed to stop one shot from Jimmy Reid, the same player soon found the back of the net.

Almost from the restart Hunt provided Grassam with a pass for goal number-four and after Fenton and Hunt had continually harrassed the Gravesend defence, Reid made it 5-0 from a mêlée in front of the posts. Henderson forced Hammers' goalkeeper, Monteith, to a good save but West Ham were soon on the attack again and two more from Grassam completed the scoreline.

It was an outstanding team performance and besides Grassam with his four goals, and the two wingers, skipper Roddy MacEachrane and Len Raisbeck both had outstanding games.

West Ham United: Monteith; Tranter, Craig, Dove, Raisbeck, MacEachrane, Hunt, Grassam, Reid, Kaye, Fenton.
Gravesend United: Wilcox; Lockie, Woodhams, Gitins, McAvoy, Parkinson, Penney, Howell, Henderson, Pugh, Jury.
Referee: H.Walker (Leicester)   *Attendance: 2,000*

Hammers 11   Crystal Palace 0

THE *Sportsman* described West Ham's scoring as 'extraordinary' and Syd Puddefoot as 'outstanding' after Hammers recorded the biggest victory in the three-year history of the London Combination.

Syd Puddefoot, who scored seven goals in the rout of Crystal Palace during World War One.

Puddefoot's seven goals equalled Bob Thomson's feat for Chelsea against Luton Town two years earlier but no team had ever managed to score 11 goals in a single Combination fixture.

Palace's woefully inept rearguard left goalkeeper Rae helpless as the goals rained in. The scoring began in only the third minute when Puddefoot netted, and in the 15th minute Rae could only parry Macksey's shot for Cunningham to finish it off. After Burke missed a simple chance Puddefoot took the ball half the length of the field for Hammers' third, and then dashed through to make it 4-0 as Palace appealed for offside.

Burke made it 5-0 inside two minutes of the second half and although Rae then made a superb save from Piggott he could not stop Puddefoot's follow-up shot for goal number-six.

Fifteen minutes later Puddefoot made it 7-0 and when Burke got the eighth it was also Hammers' 100th goal of the season.

A minute later Puddefoot made it 9-0 and then followed an incident between Macksey and a visiting defender. Macksey ended up on the floor and when he recovered was suprisingly sent off.

Hammers soon recovered from the shock of Macksey's dismissal and Puddefoot found his seventh goal of the afternoon after good work by Ashton. Ashton himself scored Hammers' 11th goal after Rae dropped a difficult shot from Cunningham.

West Ham United: Cpl E.Hufton; Gnr J.Hodson, A.Tirrell, Bmdr W.Johnstone, Lt A.C.Bell, Gnr Piggott, A.Mech H.Ashton, Dvr F.Burke, S.Puddefoot, Cadet A.Cunningham, J.Macksey.
Crystal Palace: Gnr C.Rae; Sgt P.Dodd, F.Hudspeth (RND), CSM Wm.Keeble, Cpl W.Blain, Pte H.Tanner, Sgt.W.Wiggins, A.S.Illsley, Sgt J.Jameson, Cpl W.Busby, P.Keene.
Referee: A.G.Neale (Southgate) *Attendance: 4,000*

Match to Remember 3   7 March 1927

Hammers 7   Arsenal 0

HAMMERS swept to their biggest win of the season against injury-hit Arsenal in this First Division match at Upton Park. Lacking Buchan, Hulme and Baker of the side which had won through to the FA Cup semi-finals the previous week, the Gunners were overwhelmed by a full-strength Hammers side bent on all-out attack.

By half-time West Ham were 4-0 ahead and centre-forward Vic Watson had a hand in all of them. In only the second minute he won a race with Arsenal 'keeper Dan Lewis to flick the ball home with the outside of his right foot after good work by Ruffell and Johnson.

In the 17th minute Watson's speculative screw-shot was turned past Lewis by the Gunners' right-back Tom Parker, and after Lewis failed to hold a fierce shot by Ruffell, there was Watson to tap the ball home. A second own-goal shortly before the interval was again preluded by Watson. This time it was left-back Bob John who deflected the centre-forward's shot past poor Lewis.

Soon after the restart, inside-left Johnson made it 5-0, wriggling past two defenders before slipping the ball home. The pitch was becoming heavier by the minute but Watson shrugged it off to score his third and Hammers' sixth 'with a calm and judicious kick after a perfect pass by Ruffell', according to one writer. It was Ruffell who was rewarded with the seventh goal, with almost the last kick of the game.

Hammers finished sixth in Division One to win the unofficial accolade of 'London's top team'. For Arsenal 'keeper Dan Lewis there was more misery to follow and the following month his fateful fumble at Wembley allowed Cardiff to take the FA Cup out of England for the first time.

West Ham United: Baillie; Hebden, Horler, Collins, Barrett, Cadwell, Yews, Earle, Watson, Johnson, Ruffell.
Arsenal: Lewis; Parker, John, Seddon, Butler, Barley, Hoar, Shaw, Brain, Blyth, Haden. *Attendance: 28,000*

162

Vic Watson, who hit six goals against Leeds United in a First Division game.

Hammers 8   Leeds United 2

ALMOST as remarkable as Vic Watson's six goals in this First Division match was the fact that far from being overwhelmed, Leeds were still on level terms and looking the more likely victors with half an hour to play.

Hammers had certainly started the game with a rush and their progressive approach made it seem certain that there would be no shortage of goals. Jimmy Collins laid the foundations for Watson's first goal, and Jimmy Ruffell set up another for the England centre-forward to make it 2-0.

But Leeds struck back through their England forward, Russell Wainscoat. The scheming inside-left made it 2-1 and then Scotsman Tom Jennings equalised past Ted Hufton who had hurt his wrist in an earlier scrimmage.

With nearly an hour played, and England centre-half Ernie Hart commanding a rock-like presence in the Leeds defence, there was no hint of the goal-glut that was about to happen.

The complexion of the game changed dramatically in the 59th minute, however, when Vivian Gibbins had a simple task of putting Hammers back in front following a superb pass from Stan Earle. Watson completely deceived the goalkeeper, Wilson, feinting to shoot with his left foot then cracking the ball home with his right, and the floodgates were open.

The Leeds 'keeper made a fine diving save from Watson but could not prevent the same player pouncing on a loose ball to make it 5-2, and Tommy Yews ended a daring dribble with the sixth goal.

Watson completed the rout with the seventh and eighth goals to set an individual Hammers' record which stood alone until 39 years later when Geoff Hurst equalled the feat.

West Ham United: Hufton; Hodgson, Earle, Collins, Smailes, Cadwell, Yews, Earle, Watson, V.Gibbins, Ruffell.
Leeds United: Wilson; Townsley, Roberts, Edwards, Hart, Reed, Turnbull, Keetley, Jennings, Wainscoat, Mitchell. *Attendance: 18,055*

Footnote: Vic Watson proved a real scourge to Leeds and on 16 November the same year he scored a hat-trick at Elland Road. Four goals in an FA Cup match in January 1930 and another hat-trick two months later made Watson's tally 16 goals in only four games against United.

Match to Remember 5 1 September 1930

Hammers 7 Liverpool 0

MAKING good use of the early play, Hammers were two goals ahead in the first ten minutes through well-worked efforts from Stan Earle and Vic Watson — and well on the way to an unexpected 7-0 win over the Merseysiders.

Upton Park was not Liverpool's favourite ground at this time. Twelve months earlier they had been beaten 4-1 there. But in 1928 they managed a 1-1 draw, thanks to this goal from Jimmy McDougall. The Hammers goalkeeper is David Baillie, who got a hand to the ball but could not stop it.

In the face of such a shock start Liverpool, who fielded Robert Done at right-back instead of the injured James Jackson, strove hard to get back in the game but their graft in midfield was let down by some poor finishing and further hampered by the fine form of Hammers' centre-half Jim Barrett.

West Ham's forwards were quicker to the ball but at half-time there had been no further score. Indeed, Liverpool looked capable of getting back in the game until three goals left them devastated.

Watson began it with a goal from Albert Cadwell's pass, then Earle got his own second after dribbling through a confused Liverpool rearguard, leaving Welsh inside-left Wilf James to complete the goal-burst. James' goal came after Earle and Tommy Yews had drawn out Liverpool's South African-born 'keeper, Arthur Riley, leaving an open net.

Almost inevitably it was that prolific scorer, Watson, who found the sixth and seventh goals to finish with a personal tally of four.

Strangely, Hammers themselves went down 6-1 at Villa Park only five days later and finished the season in 18th place, ten rungs below Liverpool. Hammers' plight was not helped by a 2-0 defeat at Anfield on the last day of the season.

West Ham United: Dixon; Earl, Wade, Collins, Barrett, Cadwell, Yews, Earle, Watson, James, Ruffell.
Liverpool: Riley; Done, Lucas, Morrison, Bradshaw, McDougall, Edmed, Hodgson, Smith, McPherson, Hopkin.

Attendance: 14,000

Match to Remember 6   8 June 1940

Hammers 1   Blackburn Rovers 0

HAMMERS progressed to this League War Cup Final at Wembley with some fine performances in a competition played out in the eerie atmosphere of the so-called 'Phoney War', although in the semi-final at Stamford Bridge they had allowed Fulham to pull back to 4-3 from 4-0. There had been some nail-biting minutes for West Ham supporters before the final whistle there.

Although the Final lacked some of the prestige of a peacetime Wembley game, the pomp and ceremony were still apparent, albeit in subdued form. Perhaps the biggest cheer was reserved for the men of the British Expeditionary Force who, with their wounded comrades dressed in hospital uniform of blue jackets, white shirts and red ties, had their own special section of seating.

The Band of the Irish Guards played the National Anthems of Britain and France, the First Lord of the Admiralty, Mr A.V.Alexander, met the teams, and the game began.

Blackburn forced a corner in the opening minute but it was largely West Ham's first half and Foreman (twice) and Foxall forced spectacular saves from Barron in the Blackburn goal.

Eventually abandoning their down-the-middle approach in the face of Rovers' mounting offside tactics, Hammers attacked down the wings and it was a ploy which brought the only goal of the game in the 34th minute.

Foxall began the move, Goulden and Foreman took it on, and Barron could only touch Foreman's shot to Sam Small who ran in to score an easy goal.

Both sides had their chances in the second half but there was no questioning Hammers' right to the handsome trophy which still helps to adorn the Upton Park boardroom.

West Ham United: Conway; Bicknell, C.Walker, E.Fenton, R.Walker, Cockroft, Small, Macaulay, Foreman, Goulden, Foxall.
Blackburn Rovers: Barron; Hough, Crook, Whiteside, Pryde, Chivers, Rogers, Butt, Weddle, Clarke, Guest.
Referee: G.Dutton (Warwick)   *Attendance: 43,000*

Match to Remember 7   26 December 1963

Hammers 2   Blackburn Rovers 8

BLACKBURN came to Upton Park as League leaders who were unbeaten in their last ten games. Even so, few people would have tipped them to inflict upon Hammers their record home defeat. Yet from the ashes of this humiliation, the Londoners picked themselves up and finished the season in glory.

The main tormentor of West Ham was little England winger, Bryan Douglas, who twisted and teased his way through the Hammers' defence and laid on a hat-full of goals.

The rout began after only five minutes when Fred Pickering scored with an 18-yard drive. Ten minutes later Johnny Byrne wriggled past three defenders before equalising, and when Byrne then hit the bar and Hurst missed a good chance from the rebound, the Upton Park faithful perhaps thought that their side could get back in the game.

They reckoned without Douglas, however. With as many as three defenders chasing him at any one time, the winger restored Blackburn's lead after 29 minutes and then laid on goals for McEvoy (36 minutes) and Ferguson (40) to give Rovers a 4-1 half-time lead.

In the second half Hammers plunged deeper into the mire of muddy mistakes and again it was Douglas who plotted their downfall. McEvoy made it 5-1, Pickering completing his hat-trick with two more goals. And then it was McEvoy's turn to score his third and Rovers' eighth.

Byrne got another consolation goal for Hammers after 61 minutes and the Boxing Day crowd streamed home to dwell on the result. Yet two days later Hammers won 3-1 at Ewood Park to begin a splendid revival that was to end at Wembley.

West Ham United: Standen; Bond, Burkett, Peters, Brown, Moore, Brabrook, Boyce, Byrne, Hurst, Sissons.
Blackburn Rovers: Else; Bray, Newton, Clayton, England, McGrath, Ferguson, McEvoy, Pickering, Douglas, Harrison.
Referee: J.Osborne (Ipswich)   *Attendance: 20,500*

Johnny Byrne scrambles the ball over the line for the Hammers' second goal at Ewood Park.

Match to Remember 8   **2 May 1964**

Hammers 3   Preston North End 2

BEFORE this timely triumph, West Ham had been branded by many, even their own fans, as a 'team that would never win anything'. Victory over Preston changed all that and ensured that programme editors had something other than the 1923 Cup Final to write about when Hammers were the visitors.

Wembley must have seemed a distant dream when West Ham lost 8-2 at home to Blackburn on Boxing Day 1963, but with only one team change — Bovington

Johnny Byrne (left) throws his hands in the air as he sees teammate Ronnie Boyce head what proved to be the winning goal in the 1964 FA Cup Final.

for Peters — Hammers not only gained revenge at Ewood Park two days later, they discovered a Cup-winning combination which eventually eliminated Manchester United to reach Wembley.

Preston, who had just missed promotion from Division Two, caused a sensation in Cup Final week by suspending left-half Ian Davidson for an alleged breach of discipline. Howard Kendall thus became the youngest player ever to appear in an FA Cup Final.

Kendall, then 17, belied his age and started the tenth-minute move which led to Doug Holden putting Preston ahead after Jim Standen had failed to hold Alex Dawson's shot. Hammers hit straight back, however, when Sissons and Byrne interchanged passes before Sissons levelled the scores with a cross-shot.

Byrne missed a great opportunity to put Hammers ahead and five minutes before half-time Preston regained the lead through a powerful Dawson header after Kendall had won a corner.

After 52 minutes Hammers were level again when Hurst headed home, the ball spinning down off the bar and over the line. The pace was now frantic and there were chances at both ends before West Ham sealed the game in the dying moments.

Hurst rode several tackles to get the ball out to Brabrook who swung over a centre. Boyce rose high to head wide of Kelly — and West Ham had won the Cup for the first time.

West Ham United: Standen; Bond, Burkett, Bovington, Brown, Moore, Brabrook, Boyce, Byrne, Hurst, Sissons.

Preston North End: Kelly; Ross, Smith, Lawton, Singleton, Kendall, Wilson, Ashworth, Dawson, Spavin, Holden.
Referee: A.Holland (Barnsley)

Attendance: 100,000

Hammers 2   TSV München 1860 0

RANKED by many as the finest of all Wembley Finals, this European Cup-winners' Cup game restored the public's faith in football after the boring Liverpool-Leeds FA Cup Final three weeks earlier.

In front of a capacity crowd and an estimated 30 million television viewers throughout Europe, the sides thrilled everyone with a match full of football's finer arts and packed with excitement.

West Ham began at a furious pace but at half-time there was still no score despite chances at both ends. In the 12th minute Sissons had put the ball wide of the far post from only three yards out; Dear brought goalkeeper Radenkovic to a brilliant save, one of several he made in that first half; Sealey and Dear both just missed a Sisson cross; and at the other end Kuppers narrowly failed to put Munich ahead.

The second half began in similar vein with Dear and Sissons (whose shot hit

West Ham's triumphant European Cup-winners' Cup team. Back row (left to right): Brown, Peters, Kirkup, Standen, Dear, Moore. Front row: Sealey, Boyce, Hurst, Burkett, Sissons.

169

an upright) both going close for Hammers, and Brunnenmeier, Grosser and Kuppers each bringing fine saves from Standen.

In the 69th minute, however, Hammers broke the deadlock. Boyce pushed a perfect pass between two German defenders and Sealey crashed home a rocket of a shot from a difficult angle.

Hammers fans were still celebrating when the issue was put beyond doubt. Two minutes after Sealey's goal, Dear was fouled and the Germans failed to clear the free-kick. Moore put over a cross, the goalkeeper failed to collect it — and there was Sealey again to make it 2-0.

East Enders were still celebrating a week later. Ron Greenwood contented himself with this appraisal: "This was our greatest game . . .a tremendous advertisement for football."

West Ham United: Standen; Kirkup, Burkett, Peters, Brown, Moore, Sealey, Boyce, Hurst, Dear, Sissons.
TSV München 1860: Radenkovic; Wagner, Kohlars, Bena, Reich, Luttrop, Heiss, Kuppers, Brunnenmeier, Grosser, Rebele.
Referee: I. Zolt (Hungary)   *Attendance: 100,000*

Match to Remember 10   7 November 1966

Hammers 7   Leeds United 0

FRESH from a 6-1 thrashing of London rivals, Fulham, only 48 hours earlier, cock-a-hoop Hammers went one better against Leeds and recorded their biggest-ever victory in the Football League Cup.

David Harvey made saves from Johnny Byrne and Ken Brown in the opening minute but he could not prevent Hammers opening the scoring a minute later when Byrne slipped the ball out to Sissons on the left flank and his cross-shot curled into the net.

Thus, with 88 minutes still to play Leeds were forced to come forward in this fourth round tie. That suited West Ham just fine and the rest of the goals came as follows:

24 minutes: Byrne put Brabrook clear with a brilliant reverse pass and the winger went past Willie Bell before squaring the ball for Sissons to score his and Hammers' second.

35 minutes: In a remarkably similar move, this time Peters fed Brabrook who again found Sissons. A low shot past Harvey completed his hat-trick and put Hammers 3-0 ahead.

41 minutes: This time Sissons began the move. His long cross was only half cleared and Brabrook found Peters. His header got the ball to Byrne and the centre-forward's first-time shot went via Reaney and Charlton, although Hurst was credited with the goal.

59 minutes: Byrne displayed magnificent control before sending Hurst away. This time there was no argument about ownership of the goal as Hurst drove home a hard, low shot after rounding a defender.

79 minutes: Peters dribbled past two defenders before sending a superb right-foot shot crashing past the disconsolate Harvey.

170

81 minutes: Goalkeeper Standen punted the ball downfield and Byrne judged Brabrook's header-on to perfection. The ball came over and Hurst hammered it home.

West Ham United: Standen; Bovington, Charles, Peters, Brown, Moore, Brabrook, Boyce, Byrne, Hurst, Sissons.
Leeds United: Harvey; Reaney, Bell, Bremner, Charlton, Hunter, Madeley, Belfitt, Greenhoff(Bates), Giles, O'Grady.
Referee: E.Jennings (Stourbridge)   *Attendance: 27,474*

Match to Remember 11   12 November 1966

Tottenham Hotspur 3   Hammers 4

'THE Match of the Year'. . .'Magnificent magic'. . .'One of the greatest exhibitions of attacking football ever' . . .'Thriller of the season' . . .These were just a few of the superlatives which a grateful media heaped on this seven-goal feast.

After absorbing tremendous pressure early in the game, Hammers scored against the run of play when Peters and Boyce combined before Brabrook's cross found Johnny Byrne perfectly poised to clip his shot past Pat Jennings.

In the 24th minute Spurs were level through a Jimmy Greaves penalty after he

Johnny Byrne (extreme right) scores West Ham's first goal against Spurs. England, Knowles and Mullery can only watch as Jennings is beaten.

171

had been felled by Bovington. And they might have gone ahead four minutes later but Gilzean's shot hit an upright.

Spurs were still bemoaning their luck when Hammers restored their lead 60 seconds later. Jennings could only beat out Moore's shot and Brabrook gleefully snapped up the gift.

Three minutes later West Ham went 3-1 ahead when Sissons ran from deep inside his own half and, instead of making the expected pass to Hurst, scored himself with a cracking drive from outside the penalty area.

The game was back in the melting pot almost immediately when Terry Venables crashed home a stunning 25-yard shot. Two minutes before half-time Spurs should have been level after Moore handled but Greaves lofted the penalty over the Hammers' crossbar.

Undaunted, Tottenham continued to press forward and their pressure paid off after 61 minutes when Jimmy Robertson's cross was back-headed past Standen by Alan Gilzean.

At 3-3, the issue was wide open and with 13 minutes remaining Moore began a move deep in his own half. Peters took it up, put Brabrook away down the right and the winger's cross was headed on by Sissons to where Hurst was waiting to head a classic winner.

It was heart-stopping stuff for the remaining minutes but Hammers held out for their third successive win with a goals tally of 17-4.

Tottenham Hotspur: Jennings; Beal, Knowles, Mullery, England, Mackay, Robertson, Greaves, Gilzean, Venables, Jones.
West Ham United: Standen; Bovington, Charles, Peters, Brown, Moore, Brabrook, Boyce, Byrne, Hurst, Sissons.
Referee: R. Tinkler (Boston)   *Attendance: 57,137*

Match to Remember 12   17 December 1966

Chelsea 5   Hammers 5

ONLY West Ham and Chelsea, the unpredictable teams of London football, could have served up a see-sawing ten-goal spectacular like this. In a match of wildly fluctuating fortunes Hammers twice let their hosts off the hook and eventually had to share the spoils of this pre-Christmas cracker at Stamford Bridge.

After Johnny Byrne had a goal disallowed for offside, Hammers took the lead in the 24th minute when Brabrook, the former Chelsea winger, headed home Sissons' corner. Five minutes later it was 2-0 when Byrne and Hurst set up a goal for Peters, but just before the interval, Tommy Baldwin made it 2-1 with a scrambled effort.

Five minutes into the second half Tony Hateley caught Standen napping to level the scores with a snap 25-yard drive, and four minutes after that Chelsea took the lead for the first time when Charlie Cooke finished off a Baldwin-Hateley move.

Inside a minute Hammers were level when Peter Bonetti was beaten by Sissons' wickedly swerving drive. And on the hour Bonetti was holding his head after allowing a hopeful 40-yard shot from Sissons to beat him.

Little more than a minute later Hammers regained their two-goal lead when Ron

Bonetti saves Byrne's penalty but the Hammers' striker restored their two-goal lead from the rebound.

Harris handled. Bonetti made a fine save form Byrne's penalty but the Irons' leader pounced on the rebound, dribbled around McCreadie and ex-Hammer Joe Kirkup, and made amends for his miss.

After 80 minutes it was Hammers' turn to pay the penalty. Moore felled Hateley and Tambling scored from the spot. In a grandstand finish, Tambling created a Chelsea record when he equalised with almost the last kick of the game.

Chelsea: Bonetti; Kirkup, McCreadie, Hollins, Hinton, Harris, Boyle, Baldwin, Hateley, Cooke, Tambling.
West Ham United: Standen; Bovington, Charles(Burnett), Peters, Brown, Moore, Brabrook, Boyce, Byrne, Hurst, Sissons.
Referee: H.Richards (Oldham)   *Attendance: 47,805*

Match to Remember 13   19 October 1968

Hammers 8   Sunderland 0

SUNDERLAND had every reason to be apprehensive after losing 5-1 to West Ham at Roker Park 12 months earlier. Even so, they could hardly have expected the hammering they received in this match, nor to have been on the receiving end of a remarkable piece of individual scoring from Geoff Hurst.

One man who Sunderland could not blame was goalkeeper Jim Montgomery whose defenders were left chasing shadows before him. Montgomery survived only until the 19th minute when he could do nothing to stop Hurst opening the scoring

Geoff Hurst heads home a goal in the 8-0 defeat of Sunderland.

from Peters' cross. Hurst later admitted that he had helped the ball home with his hand.

Four minutes later Bobby Moore thundered home a glorious free-kick after Hurley had been penalised, and a 35th-minute far-post header from Hurst made it 3-0. Just before half-time Redknapp's corner found Hurst who completed his first hat-trick of the afternoon.

Sissons, Brooking and Peters combined to give Hurst his fourth goal early in the second half and 13 minutes later he netted his fifth — and ended up in the net with the ball.

More slack Sunderland defending allowed Brooking to score the seventh and one minute later, a shocking pass from Herd went straight to Brooking. He sent Redknapp away and the winger's cross was met by Hurst who scored his sixth goal.

The Observer columnist at the match wrote: 'Hurst was allowed to keep the match-ball which was only proper since he had it for most of the afternoon'.

West Ham United: Ferguson; Bonds, Charles, Peters, Stephenson, Moore, Redknapp, Boyce, Brooking, Hurst, Sissons.
Sunderland: Montgomery; Irwin, Palmer, Hurley, Harvey, Porterfield, Herd, Harris, Brand, Suggett, Mulhall.
Referee: K. Burns (Dudley)   *Attendance: 24,718*

Match to Remember 14   3 May 1975

Hammers 2   Fulham 0

FOR the second time in 11 years West Ham won the FA Cup with an all-English team and by beating Second Division opponents. Adding to the attraction of this

Fulham's Mellor is beaten by Alan Taylor's shot and the Hammers are 1-0 ahead. Bobby Moore is the Cottagers' number-6.

all-London Cup Final was the appearance in a Fulham shirt of Bobby Moore, making what proved to be his last appearance on the Wembley stage.

Fulham started the competition as 500-1 outsiders and, with replays, played more games (11) and more hours of Cup football (18) than any other club in a single season.

Hammers had enjoyed a less fraught passage to the Final and from their programme emerged Alan Taylor, a man who was to become something of an East End folk hero. Signed from Rochdale for £40,000 earlier that season, Taylor had totalled a mere 65 minutes of substitute appearances before scoring two goals against Arsenal in the quarter-final.

The whippet-like striker repeated the feat in the semi-final replay against Ipswich Town at Stamford Bridge and now stood on the threshold of completing a story-book transition from the Fourth Division.

Fulham won the toss and kicked off — their only moment of good fortune all day. A rare error by Bobby Moore almost let in Jennings, and then Jennings brought Fulham 'keeper Mellor to a fine save. Then Taylor headed just over and Bonds lofted the ball wide after Lampard and Brooking had set him up.

Fulham had looked the more polished side in the first half but Hammers were marginally ahead 'on points' and on the hour they went ahead.

When Jennings' powerful shot was blocked by Mellor, it was Taylor who swooped to flash the ball between the goalkeeper's legs and into the net. Five minutes later, Paddon set up a shot which Mellor fumbled and there was the lightning fast Taylor to stab the ball high into the net.

West Ham United: Day; McDowell, Lampard, Bonds, T.Taylor, Lock, Jennings, Paddon, A.Taylor, Brooking, Holland.
Fulham: Mellor; Cutbush, Fraser, Mullery, Lacy, Moore, Mitchell, Jim Conway, Busby, Slough, Barrett.
Referee: P.Partridge (Durham)   *Attendance: 100,000*

Match to Remember 15   5 May 1976

Hammers 2   Anderlecht 4

ROARED on by 10,000 of their own supporters in the Heysel Stadium, Brussels, West Ham were confident that they could lift the European Cup-winners' Cup for the second time.

Trevor Brooking fights off a challenge by Dockx in the Heysel Stadium.

And when Pat Holland put them into the lead after 28 minutes there seemed little doubt that Hammers would indeed win their second European Final.

But that was before tragedy struck. Just before half-time Frank Lampard misjudged a back-pass to goalkeeper Mervyn Day, allowing Ressel to nip in. He switched the ball to Rensenbrink who hammered home the equaliser.

That, however, was not the real tragedy of the incident. Lampard, in attempting the back-pass, tore a stomach muscle which ruled him out for the rest of the game. Forced to re-adjust, Hammers never recovered from that double blow although they still made an immense contribution to a superb game of football.

Two minutes before half-time Rensenbrink, who was having a fine game, laid on a goal for Van der Elst. Hammers still showed great character by equalising through Keith Robson after Brooking had curled in a good cross, but the Dutch World Cup stars, Haan and Rensenbrink were in irrepressible form.

In the 76th minute referee Wurtz awarded a dubious penalty after Holland had apparently robbed Rensenbrink with a fair tackle and slid the ball for what everyone thought was a corner. Rensenbrink himself slammed the spot kick past Mervyn Day.

Time was running out for West Ham and, as they pushed up in search of the goal that would put them back in the game, they were caught out by the brilliance of Van der Elst. With two minutes remaining he streaked through to put the game beyond Hammers' reach.

West Ham United: Day; Coleman, Lampard(A.Taylor), Bonds, T.Taylor, McDowell, Holland, Paddon, Jennings, Brooking, Robson.
Anderlecht: Ruiter; Lomme, Broos, Van Binst, Thissen, Dockx, Coeck(Vercauteren), Van der Elst, Ressel, Haan, Rensenbrink.
Referee: R.Wurtz (France)

Attendance: 58,000

Match to Remember 16   10 May 1980

Hammers 1   Arsenal 0

THE sight of Paul Allen coming down the steps from Wembley's Royal Box after collecting his FA Cup winners' medal in 1980 is a memory which will linger for a long time in the minds of those who saw it.

Allen had just become the youngest footballer ever to appear in an FA Cup Final and his reward had been to play an important part in Hammers' victory over Arsenal in the so-called 'Cockney Cup Final'.

It had taken Arsenal seven hours of football to beat Liverpool in the semi-final and their tiredness showed on the Wembley stage. Indeed, the first ten minutes was all slow-motion stuff and the teams weighed each other up like championship boxers at the start of a big fight.

After 13 minutes, however, the game came to life when a David Cross shot rebounded off the giant Arsenal centre-half Willie Young. Stuart Pearson tried another shot which proved off target but Trevor Brooking stooped low to steer a header past Pat Jennings and into the Arsenal net.

Arsenal's recovery was slow but, prompted by Liam Brady, who later became a Hammers player, they eventually got forward and Brady made chances which Rix and then Stapleton headed wide.

177

Trevor Brooking bends to head home the only goal of the 1980 FA Cup Final.

For 30 minutes of the second half Hammers were thrown back and had to rely on counter-attacks. But Bonds and Martin stood firm in their defence and then Devonshire and Brooking began to run at defenders, pulling them out of position.

Arsenal became frustrated and it showed when Allen was clean through only to be brought down by Young. The centre-half was booked, Arsenal's frustration continued, and the Cup came back to the East End.

Arsenal: Jennings; Rice, Devine(Nelson), Talbot, O'Leary, Young, Brady, Sunderland, Stapleton, Price, Rix.

West Ham United: Parkes; Stewart, Lampard, Bonds, Martin, Devonshire, Allen, Pearson, Cross, Brooking, Pike.

Referee: G.Courtney (Spennymoor) *Attendance: 100,000*

Match to Remember 17 25 October 1983

Hammers 10 Bury 0

TEENAGER Tony Cottee led the massacre of Bury with four goals in this Milk Cup second round match at Upton Park. With midfield stars Trevor Brooking and

Alan Devonshire scoring two apiece, West Ham were on their way to their biggest-ever win — watched, ironically, by their smallest-ever crowd for a home Cup game.

Leading 2-1 from the first leg at Gigg Lane, Hammers soon put the issue beyond doubt when Swindlehurst headed down for Cottee to whip the ball home after only two minutes.

Five minutes later Bury should have drawn level on the night when they were awarded a penalty but Bramhall's spot kick rebounded off a post. Thereafter it was all West Ham.

Alvin Martin rose majestically to make it 2-0, and after 23 minutes Bonds released Brooking on the left and the England schemer dummied past two defenders before squeezing the ball inside the far post. Ten minutes later Bonds headed on a cross for Cottee to dive and force the ball home.

Cottee completed his hat-trick five minutes later with a superb header from Paul Allen's cross and then Brooking made it 5-0 before Cottee got Hammers' sixth after Martin headed on Devonshire's cross.

Swindlehurst put Devonshire through for goal number-seven, then Stewart got the eighth from a penalty after Devonshire had been fouled.

Nine minutes from time Brooking made it 9-0 with a deflected shot from the edge of the penalty area and the fans' cries of 'We want ten', were rewarded when Devonshire flicked home Brooking's pass five minutes from time.

West Ham United: Parkes; Stewart, Walford, Bonds(Orr), Martin, Devonshire, Allen, Cottee, Swindlehurst, Brooking, Pike.
Bury: Brown; Gardner, Pashley, Coleman, Hilton, Bramhall, Potts, Entwhistle, Spence, Jakub, Deacy.
Referee: D.Letts (Basingstoke)

Attendance: 10,896

Match to Remember 18   30 November 1988

Hammers 4   Liverpool 1

WEST Ham were struggling in the League when they met the Merseysiders in this Littlewoods Cup game and a big Cup tie under the lights at Upton Park is a different proposition, as many opponents have discovered.

From the start the Hammers were confident and their passing was sharp. Wave after wave of attacks flooded towards the North Bank goal. Then, in the 20th minute, Brady sent over a curling cross which was spectacularly volleyed into the net by Paul Ince.

Three minutes later, Liverpool were stunned when Ince again dashed in to head Devonshire's corner wide of Hooper.

After 34 minutes, however, Liverpool were back in the game when referee Ashworth awarded them a debatable penalty. Alvin Martin was adjudged to have held Aldridge, who took the penalty himself and beat McKnight.

On 57 minutes, an aimless cross by Kelly dropped into the Liverpool penalty area and Staunton decided to head it back to goalkeeper Hooper but misdirected his effort into the net.

Liverpool became disheartened and their misery was complete after 76 minutes. A free-kick was awarded to West Ham and Tony Gale curled the ball over the wall and beyond Hooper's grasping fingertips. The 4-1 scoreline stunned the footballing world, for it was Liverpool's heaviest cup defeat since February 1939. It was also a night to savour for the Hammers' ecstatic fans.

West Ham United: McKnight; Potts, Dicks, Gale, Martin, Devonshire, Ward, Kelly, Rosenior, Dickens, Ince.
Liverpool: Hooper; Ablett, Venison, Nicol(Watson), Whelan, Spackman, Beardsley, Aldridge, Staunton, Houghton, McMahon(Durnin).
Referee: J.Ashworth (Luffenham) *Attendance: 26,971*

Match to Remember 19 8 May 1993

Hammers 2   Cambridge United 0

UPTON Park was not the place for faint-hearted Hammers supporters on the last day of the regular 1992-3 season, for West Ham needed all three points to win promotion — and even then goals scored came into it — whilst Cambridge United needed victory to avoid relegation.

The gates were closed half an hour before kick-off with the Hammers' biggest attendance of the season wedged inside, eagerly awaiting the contest. Before the start, Steve Potts was presented with the Hammer of the Year trophy, with Kevin Keen the runner-up.

In the first half, Cambridge played with a fierce commitment, although their spoiling, time-wasting tactics angered Hammers fans.

All around the stadium one could almost touch the tension and it was partially relieved only when a large roar told everyone that close rivals Portsmouth had gone behind to Grimsby Town.

Two minutes into the second half, Hammers' on-loan striker David Speedie volleyed home the opening goal to ease the tension further. In the 63rd minute, Leadbitter fired a shot past Miklosko but to the huge relief of the crowd, the linesman's flag was raised for offside against Bartlett.

The tension became almost unbearable as word spread that Portsmouth were now leading 2-1, but two minutes from the end, Julian Dick battled through on the left and his pass left substitute Clive Allen a simple tap-in for the second goal.

This, alas, sparked a pitch invasion and the players urged the fans to leave and allow the game to be finished.

There was just a minute left on referee Elleray's watch and then the celebrations began in earnest. Thousands of fans swarmed on to the pitch to form a sea of claret and blue in front of the main stand. The club's anthem, *Bubbles* echoed around the ground. West Ham were now members of the Premier League.

West Ham United: Miklosko; Breacker, Dicks, Potts, Gale, Bishop, Robson(C.Allen), Butler, Speedie(M.Allen), Morley, Keen.
Cambridge United: Filan; Heathcote, Kimble(Fensome), Rayner, Chapple, O'Shea, Dennis(Bartlett), Claridge, Butler, Clayton, Leadbitter.
Referee: D.Elleray (Middlesex) *Attendance: 27,399*

David Speedie volleys home the opening goal against Cambridge United and Hammers are on their way back to the top flight.

1895-96

Thames Ironworks

All home games played at Hermit Road

Friendlies

Sep	7	(h)	Royal Ordnance	D	1-1
	14	(h)	Dartford	W	4-0
	28	(a)	Manor Park	W	8-0
Oct	5	(a)	Streatham	W	3-0
	16	(a)	Old St Stephens	W	4-0
	19	(h)	Erith United	L	1-2
Nov	2	(h)	Reading	L	2-3
	9	(h)	Grenadier Guards	W	4-0
	16	(h)	Charlton United	W	4-0
	23	(h)	West Croydon	W	2-0
	30	(h)	Coldstream Guards	W	3-1
Dec	7	(a)	Dartford	L	0-2
	14	(a)	Millwall	L	0-6
	16	(h)	Old St Stephens	W	3-1
	21	(h)	Grenadier Guards	L	1-4
	25	(h)	South West Ham	W	4-1
	26	(h)	Wandsworth	W	5-1
	28	(h)	Lewisham St Marys	W	7-1
Jan	4	(h)	Novacastrians	W	6-1
	18	(h)	Upton Park	W	2-1
	20	(h)	Barking Woodville	W	6-2

	25	(h)	Civil Service	W	5-0
Feb	1	(h)	Manor Park	W	7-2
	6	(h)	Royal Ordnance	W	2-1
	8	(h)	Hornsey United	W	4-0
	17	(h)	Vampires	L	1-3
	22	(h)	St Lukes	W	1-0
	29	(a)	Reading	L	2-4
Mar	7	(h)	Fulham	W	5-1
	9	(h)	West Croydon	W	5-0
	14	(a)	St Lukes	L	1-3
	16	(h)	Woolwich Arsenal	L	3-5
	20	(h)	West Bromwich Albion	L	2-4
	28	(h)	Leyton	W	3-0
	30	(h)	Royal Ordnance	L	0-4
Apr	3	(h)	St Lukes	D	1-1
	4	(h)	Liverpool Casuals	W	3-1
	6	(h)	Vampires	W	6-2
	11	(h)	Commercial Athletic	W	3-1
	18	(h)	South West Ham	W	3-0
	25	(h)	Millwall Athletic	D	1-1

FA Cup

Oct 12	(a)	Chatham	L	0-5

1st Qualifying round

West Ham Charity Cup

Feb 15	(a)	Park Grove	W	1-0

Park Grove protested and forced a replay

Mar 7	(a)	Park Grove	W	3-0
	21	(a)	Barking	D	2-2
	28	(a)	Barking	D	0-0
Apr 20	(a)	Barking	W	1-0

1896-97

Thames Ironworks

London League

Sep	19	(h)	Vampires	W	3-0
Oct	8	(h)	1st Scots Guards *	W	2-0
	22	(a)	3rd Grenadier Guards	L	1-4
	24	(a)	Crouch End	W	1-0
Nov	28	(a)	Ilford	D	2-2
Feb	27	(a)	Vampires	W	2-1
Mar	6	(h)	Ilford	W	3-2
	13	(a)	Barking Woodville	L	0-1
Apr	1	(h)	3rd Grenadier Guards	L	0-5
	3	(h)	Crouch End	W	4-1
	8	(h)	Barking Woodville	D	1-1

	P	W	D	L	F	A	Pts
3rd Grenadier Gds	12	9	1	2	32	13	19
Thames Ironworks	12	7	2	3	17	17	16
Barking Woodville	12	6	3	3	20	11	15
Ilford	12	7	1	4	26	14	15
Crouch End	12	4	2	6	14	19	10
Vampires	12	3	1	8	10	28	7
London Welsh	12	0	2	10	9	26	2

FA Cup

Oct 10	(a)	Sheppey U	L	0-8

1st Qualifying round

West Ham Charity Cup

Mar 11	(h)	Manor Park	W	2-0
	20	(n)	West Ham Garfield	L	0-1

London Senior Cup

Oct	17	(a)	West Norwood	W	2-1
Nov	7	(a)	Marcians	W	4-0
Jan	9	(h)	Wandsworth	W	3-1
	16	(h)	Barking Woodville	W	2-0
	30	(h)	Bromley	D	3-3
Feb	6	(a)	Bromley	D	2-2
	13	(a)	Bromley	L	0-2

Essex Senior Cup

Dec 5	(a)	Leyton	L	2-3

* The 1st Scots Guards withdrew during the season and their record was deleted. London Welsh were suspended near the end of the season and as a result Thames Ironworks were awarded two wins.

1897-98

Thames Ironworks
All home games played at Memorial Grounds

London League

Sep 11	(h)	Brentford	W	1-0
Oct 2	(h)	Leyton	W	4-0
23	(a)	3rd Grenadier Guards	W	1-0
30	(a)	Leyton	W	3-1
Nov 13	(h)	Barking Woodville	W	3-0
Dec 2	(h)	2nd Grenadier Guards	W	5-1
11	(a)	Ilford	D	3-3
Jan 1	(h)	Ilford	W	4-0
8	(h)	Stanley	W	4-2
15	(h)	Bromley	W	7-3
Feb 26	(a)	Stanley	D	1-1
Mar 12	(a)	Barking Woodville	D	0-0
19	(a)	Bromley	W	5-1
Apr 2	(h)	3rd Grenadier Guards	W	3-1
23	(a)	Brentford	L	0-1
30	(a)	2nd Grenadier Guards	W	3-1

FA Cup

Sep 18	(h)	Redhill	W	3-0
25	(h)	RE Training Battalion	W	2-1
Oct 16	(a)	St Albans	L	0-2

London Senior Cup

Nov 27	(a)	Novacastrians	W	1-0
Jan 15	(h)	2nd Grenadier Guards	W	*

Walk-over after Guards withdrew

22	(h)	Ilford	L	1-3

	P	W	D	L	F	A	Pts
Thames Ironworks	16	12	3	1	47	15	27
Brentford	16	12	2	2	43	17	26
Leyton	16	8	4	4	41	33	20
3rd Grenadier Gds	16	7	3	6	34	33	17
Ilford	16	5	7	4	33	25	17
Stanley	16	5	4	7	22	22	14
Barking Woodville	16	2	6	8	16	37	10
Bromley	16	4	2	10	20	49	10
2nd Grenadier Gds	16	0	3	13	17	42	3

Thames Ironworks in the FA Cup 1895-96 to 1897-98

1895-96
1st Qualifying Round
Oct 12 v Chatham (a) 0-5
Watson; Tull, Williams, Stewart, French, Parks, Woods, Sage, Lindsay, Freeman, Darby.
Att: 3,000

1896-97
1st Qualifying Round
Oct 10 v Sheppey United (a) 0-8
Southwood; Stevenson, Holstock, Bird, Dandridge, Davie, Nicholls, H.Rossiter, Hatton, Gresham, Morrison.
Att: 800

1897-98
Sep 18 v Redhill (h) 3-0
Chisholm 2, Opp own-goal
Furnell; Chalkley, Tranter, Dove, Dandridge, Chisholm, Older, Hatton, J.Reid, Gresham, Edwards.
Att: 1,000
Sep 25 v RE Training Battalion (h) 2-1
Hatton, Reid
Furnell; Chalkley, Tranter, Dove, Dandridge, Chisholm, Older, Hatton, J.Reid, Gresham, Edwards.
Att: 1,000
Oct 16 v St Albans (a) 0-2
Furnell; Chalkley, Taylor, Dove, Dandridge, Gillies, Hird, Gresham, Hatton, J.Reid, Edwards.
Att: 1,000

1898-99

1	Sep	10	(a)	Shepherd's Bush	W	3-0	Atkinson 2, Adams		1,500
2		24	(h)	Brentford	W	3-1	Hay 2, Dove		1,200
3	Oct	8	(a)	Uxbridge	L	1-2	Gresham		2,000
4		29	(a)	Wycombe	L	1-4	Reid		1,000
5	Nov	5	(h)	Shepherd's Bush	W	1-0	Wenham		1,000
6		12	(a)	St Albans	W	4-1	Lloyd 3, Reid		800
7		26	(a)	Watford	D	0-0			1,000
8	Dec	3	(h)	Fulham	W	2-1	Reynolds, Gresham		2,000
9		17	(h)	Watford	W	2-1	Lloyd 2		1,500
10		24	(a)	Chesham	W	3-0	Hird 2, Hounsell		1,000
11		31	(a)	Maidenhead	W	4-0	McEwan, Hird, Reynolds, Reid		2,000
12	Jan	14	(h)	Wycombe	W	4-1	McEwan, Lloyd 2, Opp own-goal		1,000
13		21	(a)	Wolverton	W	4-3	Dove, Chisholm, Leonard 2		200
14		28	(h)	Chesham	W	8-1	Lloyd, Reid, Reynolds 2, Dove, MacEachrane, Gresham 2		2,000
15	Feb	11	(a)	Brentford	W	2-0	Reynolds, Leonard		2,000
16		18	(h)	Uxbridge	W	4-0	Henderson 4		1,500
17	Mar	4	(a)	Southall	W	2-0	Henderson 2		4,000
18		11	(h)	St Albans	W	1-0	J.Reid		2,000
19		18	(a)	Wolverton	W	2-1	J.Reid 2		1,000
20		25	(h)	Southall	W	2-0	G.Reid, Gilmore		3,000
21	Apr	8	(a)	Fulham	W	1-0	Lloyd		3,000
22		15	(h)	Maidenhead	W	10-0	Lloyd 3, Leonard 4, J.Reid 2, Henderson		3,000

P	W	D	L	F	A	W	D	L	F	A	Pts	Pos	Div	
22	11	0	0	39	6	8	1	2	25	10	39	1st	SL	Appearances
														Goals

FA Cup

1Q	Oct	1	(h)	RE Training Battn	W	2-0	MacEachrane, Gresham		1,000
2Q		15	(a)	Brighton U	D	0-0			2,000
R		19	(h)	Brighton U	L	1-4	Hird		2,000

Appearances
Goals

Championship Decider (played at Millwall)

	Apr	22	(n)	Cowes	W	3-1	Lloyd, Henderson, Leonard	1,000

Appearances
Goals

Test Match (played at Chatham)

	Apr	29	(n)	Sheppey U	D	1-1	Lloyd	2,000

Appearances
Goals

Player appearance and goalscoring grid (shirt numbers by match).

	Moore	Tranter	Marjeram	Chisholm	Dove	MacEachrane	Hird	Brett	Atkinson	Adams	Foss	Lloyd	Hitch	Hay	Gresham	Hounsell	Cobb	Reid J	Buller	McEwan	Reynolds	Wenham	Niel	Dunn	Leonard	Henderson	Reid G	McManus	Bird	Gilmore	
	1	2	3	4	5	6	7	8	9	10	11																				1
	1	2		4	11	6	7		9			3	5	8	10																2
	1			4	3	6	7			9		2	5	8	10		11														3
	1	2		4	3	6	7						5	9	10			8	11												4
	1	2	3		4	6									10		11	8		5	7	9									5
	1	2	3	6			11	7							9			10		8	5						4				6
	1	2	3	4		6	7								9	10		8		5											7
	1	2	3	6	4		11	7							9	10				5	8										8
	1	2	3	4			11	8							9		6	10		5	7										9
	1	2	3		4	6	7								9		11	10		5	8										10
		2		1	6	5									9		11	8		10	4	7		3							11
	1	2			6	4									9		10			8	5	7			3	11					12
	1	2		5	4	6	8								9		10				7				3	11					13
	1	3		4	5	6									9		8				11			2	7						14
	1	2		5	4	6											8				7			3	11	9	10				15
	1	2		5	6	4											8				7			3	11	10	9				16
	1	2		4	5	6											8				7			3	11	9	10				17
	1	2		4		6	7										8							3	11	9	10	5			18
	1	2		4		6	7										8							3	11	9	10	5			19
	1	2			4	6	7																	3		9	10	5	8	11	20
	1	2		4		6	7				8					10								3	11	9		5			21
	1	2		4		6	7				8										10			3	11	9		5			22
Apps	21	20	8	15	14	22	19	1	2	2	1	11	3	6	14	2	2	13	1	8	12	1	2	11	10	8	6	5	1	1	
Goals		1	3	1	3		2	1					12		2	4	1		9		2	5	1		7	7	1		1		

1 own-goal

	Moore	Tranter	Marjeram	Chisholm	Dove	MacEachrane	Hird	Brett	Atkinson	Adams	Foss	Lloyd	Hitch	Hay	Gresham	Hounsell	Cobb	Reid J	Buller	McEwan	Reynolds	Wenham	Niel	Dunn	Leonard	Henderson	Reid G	McManus	Bird	Gilmore	
	1	2		4		6	7			10		3		8	9		11			5											1Q
	1	3		6	2	4	8		9			7	5		11		10														2Q
	1	3		4	2	6	7		9			8	5		10		11														R
	3	3		3	2	3	3		3			3	2	1	3		3			1											
												1																			

	Moore	Tranter	Marjeram	Chisholm	Dove	MacEachrane	Hird	Brett	Atkinson	Adams	Foss	Lloyd	Hitch	Hay	Gresham	Hounsell	Cobb	Reid J	Buller	McEwan	Reynolds	Wenham	Niel	Dunn	Leonard	Henderson	Reid G	McManus	Bird	Gilmore	
	1	2		4	5	6								8				10			7			3	11	9					
	1	1		1	1	1								1				1			1			1	1	1					
														1											1	1					

	Moore	Tranter	Marjeram	Chisholm	Dove	MacEachrane	Hird	Brett	Atkinson	Adams	Foss	Lloyd	Hitch	Hay	Gresham	Hounsell	Cobb	Reid J	Buller	McEwan	Reynolds	Wenham	Niel	Dunn	Leonard	Henderson	Reid G	McManus	Bird	Gilmore	
	1	2		4		6								8	10						7			3	11	9	5				
	1	1		1		1								1	1						1			1	1	1	1				
														1											1	1					

1899-1900

#					Result	Scorers	Att.
1	Sep	16	(a)	Reading	L 0-1		3,000
2		18	(h)	Chatham	W 4-0	McKay 2, Carnelly 2	1,000
3	Oct	7	(h)	Bedminster	W 1-0	Joyce	3,000
4	Nov	4	(a)	Tottenham H	L 0-7		7,000
5		11	(h)	New Brompton	D 0-0		2,000
6		25	(h)	Swindon T	W 1-0	Adams	2,000
7	Dec	2	(a)	Bristol C	L 0-2		3,000
8		16	(a)	Southampton	L 1-3	McKay	4,000
9		23	(h)	Millwall	L 0-2		12,000
10		25	(a)	Queen's Park R	L 0-2		4,000
11		30	(h)	Queen's Park R	L 1-2	McKay	4,000
12	Jan	6	(a)	Chatham	L 1-3	Carnelly	5,000
13		13	(h)	Reading	L 0-1		4,000
14		15	(a)	Bristol R	D 1-1	McKay	6,000
15		20	(a)	Sheppey U	W 3-0	McKay, Carnelly, Joyce	4,000
16		24	(a)	Gravesend	L 1-2	Carnelly	1,200
17	Feb	10	(a)	Bedminster	L 1-3	Carnelly	2,000
18		17	(h)	Bristol R	D 0-0		4,000
19		24	(a)	Portsmouth	L 0-2		2,000
20	Mar	10	(h)	Tottenham H	D 0-0		9,000
21		17	(a)	New Brompton	L 1-3	Opp own-goal	2,000
22		24	(h)	Gravesend	W 2-1	Carnelly 2	3,500
23		31	(a)	Swindon T	L 1-3	Opp own-goal	3,000
24	Apr	5	(h)	Portsmouth	L 2-4	Joyce 2	5,000
25		7	(h)	Bristol C	D 0-0		5,000
26		9	(h)	Southampton	W 4-1	Joyce 3, Allan	4,000
27		17	(h)	Sheppey U	W 4-2	McKay, Joyce, Taylor, Opp own-goal	3,000
28		28	(a)	Millwall	W 1-0	McKay	8,000

P	W	D	L	F	A	W	D	L	F	A	Pts	Pos	Div	Appearances
28	6	4	4	19	13	2	1	11	11	32	21	14th	SL	Goals

FA Cup

#					Result	Scorers	Att.
P	Sep	23	(h)	Royal Engineers	W 6-0	Joyce 3, McKay, MacEachrane, Reid	1,000
1Q		30	(a)	Grays U	W 4-0	Joyce, McKay, Carnelly, McManus	750
2Q	Oct	14	(h)	Sheppey U	W 4-2	Carnelly 2, Joyce 2	2,000
3Q		28	(a)	Dartford	W 7-0	Carnelly 2, McKay 2, Joyce, MacEachrane, Bradshaw	1,200
4Q	Nov	18	(a)	New Brompton	D 0-0		3,000
R		23	(h)	New Brompton	W 2-0	Carnelly, McKay	3,000
5Q	Dec	9	(h)	Millwall	L 1-2	Bradshaw	13,000

Appearances
Goals

Test Match (played at Tottenham)

					Result	Scorers	Att.
	Apr	30	(n)	Fulham	W 5-1	Joyce 3, Stewart, Opp own-goal	600

Appearances
Goals

Player appearance / shirt-number grid (league season).

Moore	Dunn	King	Dove	McManus	MacEachrane	Corbett	McKay	Joyce	Carnelly	Bradshaw	Hird	Craig	Gentle	Janes	Reid	Bigden	Adams	Walker	Sunderland	Allan	Gilmore	Turner	Stewart	Taylor	#
1	2	3	4	5	6	7	8	9	10	11															1
1	2	3	4	5	6	7	8	9	10	11															2
1	2	3	4	5	6		8	9	10	11	7														3
1	2	3	4	5	6		8	9	10	11		7													4
1		3	5		6		8		9	11		2	4	7	10										5
1	2	3			6		8	9	10			4				5	7	11							6
		3		5	6	7	8	10	9			2				4		11	1						7
1		4			6		8	10	9			2				5	3	11		7					8
1		4			6		8	10	9			2				5	3	11		7					9
1					6		8	10	9			2				5	3	11		7	4				10
1					6		8	10	9			2					3	11		7	4		5		11
1	2				6		8	9	10								3	11		7	4		5		12
1	2	3			6		8	9	10			4								7			5	11	13
1	2	3			6		8	9				4								7		10	5	11	14
1	2	3	11		6		9	8	7							4						10	5		15
1	2	3	11		6		8	9	10							4				7			5		16
1	2	3			6		8	9	10			4								7			5	11	17
1	2	3	4		6		8	9	10			4								7			5	11	18
1	2	3			6		8	9	10			4								7			5	11	19
1	2				6		8	9	10			4								7	3		5	11	20
1	2				6		8	9	10				7							4	3		5	11	21
1	2		4		6		8	9	10			3								7			5	11	22
1	2		4		6		8	9	10			3								7			5	11	23
1	2		4		6		8	9	10			3								7			5	11	24
1	2		4		6		8	9	10			3								7			5	11	25
1	2		4		6		8	9	10			3								7			5	11	26
1	2		4		6		8	9	10			3								7			5	11	27
1	2		4		6		8	9	10			3								7			5	11	28
27	**21**	**16**	**15**	**5**	**28**	**3**	**28**	**27**	**27**	**5**	**1**	**17**	**1**	**2**	**1**	**11**	**6**	**7**	**1**	**21**	**4**	**4**	**16**	**14**	
							8	8	8							1				1				1	

3 own-goals

Cup matches:

Moore	Dunn	King	Dove	McManus	MacEachrane	Corbett	McKay	Joyce	Carnelly	Bradshaw	Hird	Craig	Gentle	Janes	Reid	Bigden	Adams	Walker	Sunderland	Allan	Gilmore	Turner	Stewart	Taylor	Rd
1	2	3	4	5	6		8	9		11	7				10										P
1	2	3	4	5	6		8	9	10	11	7														1Q
1	2	3	4	5	6		8	9	10	11	7														2Q
1	2	3	4	5	6		8	9	10	11		7													3Q
1	2	3			6		8	9	10	11		4	7				5								4Q
1	2	3			6		8	9	10	11		4					5	7							R
1	2	3	5		6		8	9	10	11		4						7							5Q
7	**7**	**7**	**5**	**4**	**7**		**7**	**7**	**6**	**7**	**3**	**4**	**1**			**1**	**2**	**2**		**1**					
				1	2		5	7	6	2		1													

(own-goal note for cup section)

Moore	Dunn	King	Dove	McManus	MacEachrane	Corbett	McKay	Joyce	Carnelly	Bradshaw	Hird	Craig	Gentle	Janes	Reid	Bigden	Adams	Walker	Sunderland	Allan	Gilmore	Turner	Stewart	Taylor
1		3	6		4		10	9	8			2								11			5	7
1		1	1		1		1	1	1			1								1			1	1
									3														1	

1 own-goal

West Ham in the Southern League 1900-15

IN September 1900, West Ham United began a 15-year association with the Southern League. Although the new club was on the threshold of senior football, most of its players and officials had already experienced at least two years of Southern League football.

Under its old title of Thames Ironworks, the club had made a splendid entry into the Southern League, winning the title by a healthy margin in its first season. The subsequent campaign, however, brought them down to earth when the realities of playing top-class opposition, whilst themselves having only a veneer of comparable ability, was soon exposed.

Following the tragedy of Harry Bradshaw, the club skipper who died on Christmas Day 1899, the side embarked on a downward path that ended only in a Test Match at White Hart Lane. With the situation saved, and given a second chance, the new club began again and for the next 15 years proved to be a singularly average team.

Only once more, in 1909, were they threatened by relegation. They escaped comfortably and, anyway, it proved a false alarm because the division was enlarged for the following season.

At the other end of the table, West Ham seemed equally reluctant to challenge for the top places. The best performance was in 1912-13 when they got to within two points of Plymouth Argyle's Championship-winning 50.

They never managed as many as 70 goals in a season; and only twice in 538 Southern League matches did they exceed six goals in a game. On the other hand, only once, in 1911-12, did the Hammers concede more than 60 goals in a season, and they never let in more than six at one time.

West Ham United in 1907. Back row (left to right): S. Hammond, W. Wildman, D. Clark, G. Kitchen, C. Simmonds, A. Taylor, J. Gault. Middle row: T. Robinson (trainer), D. Woodwards, T. Allison, F. Piercy, E. S. King (secretary-manager), L. Jarvis, R. Young, G. Horn, C. Paynter. Front row: D. Lindsay, T. Randall, W. Brown, A. Reed, W. Grassam, H. Stapley, A. Harwood, L. Watson, F. Blackburn, T. Lee. On ground: A. Featherstone, F. Kemp.

Well-known players to wear Hammers' colours included Dave Gardner, Matt Kingsley, James Jackson and George Kitchen, all familiar names before they came to Upton Park. Some, like Dick Pudan, Bill Yenson, George Hilsdon and Albert Denyer, earned their reputations after leaving the club.

Others — men like Syd Puddefoot, Danny Shea, George Webb and Tommy Randall — earned distinction as West Ham players.

Through this entire period, West Ham's hallmark was that of inconsistency. The players had little trouble raising their game for spirited efforts against the likes of Manchester United, Wolves and West Brom in FA Cup matches, but for ordinary Southern League games they could not find the same inspiration.

The only spell of sustained success almost brought the Southern League title to Upton Park in 1912-13 when a sequence of 15 unbeaten League matches, beginning against Crystal Palace on 25 January, brought 22 points out of 30.

West Ham finished third, behind Plymouth and Swindon. Three more points would have seen them clear Champions and they had certainly not faltered against the top two clubs, taking seven points from them.

To underline that no single player can 'make a team', the sequence began immediately following Danny Shea's transfer to Blackburn Rovers in January 1913.

The Hammers failed to maintain that form but 1914-15, the last one before the war, brought another improvement and in February, West Ham were in second place. They ended the season fourth, but not before beating Watford, the eventual Champions, twice, and taking two points from runners-up Reading.

Crystal Palace were the only visitors to win at Upton Park and, strangely, it was bottom club Gillingham who inflicted Hammers' biggest hiding of the season, winning 4-0 at Priestfield Stadium.

On 24 April 1915, West Ham United played what turned out to be their last game in the Southern League. They drew 1-1 with Norwich, and George Hilsdon missed a penalty. The players trooped off the Boleyn pitch and it would be four years before normal football resumed.

1900-01

1	Sep	1	(h)	Gravesend	W	7-0	Grassam 4, Reid 2, Hunt	2,000
2		8	(a)	Millwall	L	1-3	Reid	10,000
3		15	(h)	Southampton	W	2-0	Reid, Grassam	7,500
4		29	(h)	Bristol C	L	1-2	Kaye	5,000
5	Oct	6	(a)	Swindon T	W	1-0	Corbett	2,000
6		13	(h)	Watford	W	2-0	Corbett, Fenton	4,000
7		20	(a)	Luton T	L	0-2		4,000
8		27	(a)	Tottenham H	D	0-0		6,000
9	Nov	10	(a)	Portsmouth	L	2-3	Reid, Kaye	5,000
10		24	(a)	Bristol R	L	0-2		3,000
11	Dec	1	(h)	Reading	W	1-0	Ratcliffe	4,000
12		15	(a)	Gravesend	D	0-0		1,000
13		29	(a)	Southampton	L	2-3	Fenton, Hunt	4,000
14	Jan	12	(a)	Bristol C	L	0-1		2,500
15		19	(h)	Swindon T	W	3-1	Corbett 2, Grassam	4,000
16		26	(a)	Watford	W	1-0	Grassam	2,000
17	Feb	9	(h)	Luton T	W	2-0	Taylor, Corbett	1,000
18		16	(h)	Tottenham H	L	1-4	Grassam	5,500
19		23	(a)	Queen's Park R	W	2-0	Grassam, Taylor	6,000
20	Mar	2	(h)	Portsmouth	D	1-1	MacEachrane	3,000
21		9	(a)	New Brompton	D	1-1	Hunt	2,000
22		16	(h)	Bristol R	W	2-0	Corbett, Grassam	4,000
23		21	(h)	Millwall	W	1-0	Corbett	2,500
24		23	(a)	Kettering T	W	1-0	Grassam	1,000
25		30	(h)	Kettering T	D	1-1	Taylor	1,000
26	Apr	5	(h)	Queen's Park R	W	2-1	Ratcliffe 2	4,000
27		10	(a)	Reading	L	1-3	Grassam	1,000
28		20	(h)	New Brompton	W	2-0	Ratcliffe, Taylor	2,000

P	W	D	L	F	A	W	D	L	F	A	Pts	Pos	Div	
28	10	2	2	28	10	4	3	7	12	18	33	6th	SL	Appearances
														Goals

FA Cup

3Q	Nov	3	(h)	Olympic	W	1-0	Fenton	3,000
4Q		17	(a)	New Brompton	D	1-1	Corbett	1,200
R		21	(h)	New Brompton	W	4-1	Kaye 2, Corbett, Hunt	4,000
5Q	Dec	8	(h)	Clapton O	D	1-1	Kaye	10,000
R		12	(a)	Clapton O	W	3-2	Grassam 3	5,000
I	Jan	5	(h)	Liverpool	L	0-1		6,000

Appearances
Goals

Appearance grid (shirt numbers worn by each player per match).

Monteith	Tranter	Craig	Dove	Raisbeck	MacEachrane	Hunt	Grassam	Reid	Kaye	Fenton	Moore	Allan	Corbett	King	Neil	Kelly	Walker	Ratcliffe	Pudan	Taylor	Pinder	No.
1	2	3	4	5	6	7	8	9	10	11												
	2	3	4	5	6		8	9	10	11	1	7										1
	2	3		5	6	7	8	9	10	11	1	4										2
1	2	3		5	6	7		9	10	11		4	8									3
1		3		5	6	7		9	10	11		4	8	2								4
		3		5	6	7		9	10	11	1		8	2	4							5
1		3		5	6	7		9	10	11		4	8	2								6
1		3		5	6	7		9	10	11		4	8	2								7
1		3		5	6	7		9	10	11		4	8	2								8
1		3			6	7		9		11		4	8	2		5		10				9
1		3			6	7	8	9		11		4		2		5		10				10
1		3	4		6	7	8	9	10	11				2		5						11
1		3	4		6	7	8		10	11				2		5	9					12
1					6	7	8	9		11		4		2		5		10	3			13
1					6	7	8					4	9	2		5		10	3	11		14
1		3			6	7	8					4	9	2		5		10		11		15
1		3			6	7	8					4	9	2		5		10		11		16
		3			6	7	8				1	4	9	2		5		10		11		17
1					6	7	8					4	9	2		5		10		11	3	18
1		3			6	7	8					4	9	2		5		10		11		19
1		3			6	7	8					4	9	2		5		10		11		20
1		3			6	7	8					4	9	2		5		10		11		21
1		3			6	7	8			11		4	9	2		5		10				22
1		3			6	7	8		11			4	9	2		5		10				23
1		3			6	7	8					4	9	2		5		10		11		24
1		3			6	7	8					4	9	2		5		10		11		25
1	2	3			6	7	8					4	9			5		10		11		26
1	2	3			6	7	8					4	9			5		10		11		27
1	2	3			6	7	8					4	9			5		10		11		28
24	**4**	**25**	**13**	**2**	**28**	**27**	**20**	**13**	**14**	**14**	**4**	**24**	**21**	**22**	**1**	**19**	**1**	**17**	**2**	**12**	**1**	
		1	3	12	5		2	2				7						4	4			(goals)

Monteith	Tranter	Craig	Dove	Raisbeck	MacEachrane	Hunt	Grassam	Reid	Kaye	Fenton	Moore	Allan	Corbett	King	Neil	Kelly	Walker	Ratcliffe	Pudan	Taylor	Pinder	No.
1		3	5	4	6	9	8	10	11		7	2										3Q
1	2	5			6	7	8	10	11			4	9	3								4Q
1	2	5	4		6	7	8	10	11				9	3								R
1		3			6	7	8	9	10	11		4		2		5						5Q
1		3		5	6	7	8	9	10	11				2	4							R
1		3	4		6	7	8	9		11				2		5	10					1
6	**2**	**6**	**3**	**2**	**6**	**6**	**3**	**6**	**6**	**5**	**3**	**2**	**6**	**3**	**1**							
			1	3		3	1					2										(goals)

191

1901-02

1	Sep	7	(a)	Bristol R	W	2-0	Grassam, Corbett	5,000
2		14	(h)	Brentford	W	2-0	Grassam 2	4,500
3		21	(a)	New Brompton	D	0-0		4,000
4		28	(h)	Kettering T	W	1-0	Grassam	6,000
5		30	(h)	Wellingborough T	W	4-2	Corbett 3, Grassam	2,000
6	Oct	5	(a)	Northampton T	W	4-3	Grassam 2, MacEachrane, Opp own-goal	2,000
7		12	(h)	Luton T	W	4-1	Corbett 2, Linward, Ratcliffe	6,000
8		19	(a)	Watford	D	0-0		4,000
9		26	(h)	Millwall	L	0-2		9,000
10	Nov	2	(h)	Tottenham H	L	0-1		17,000
11		9	(a)	Queen's Park R	L	1-2	Linward	4,000
12		23	(a)	Reading	L	0-3		5,000
13	Dec	7	(a)	Southampton	L	0-4		4,000
14		14	(h)	Swindon T	W	2-1	Linward, MacEachrane	2,000
15		21	(h)	Bristol R	W	2-0	McDonald 2	2,000
16		27	(a)	Wellingborough T	W	2-0	MacEachrane, Allan	2,500
17	Jan	4	(h)	New Brompton	D	0-0		2,000
18		11	(a)	Kettering T	L	0-1		2,000
19		18	(h)	Northampton T	L	0-1		5,000
20		25	(a)	Luton T	W	3-0	Hunt 2, Grassam	5,000
21	Feb	1	(h)	Watford	W	3-2	Ratcliffe 2, Grassam	2,000
22		8	(a)	Millwall	D	1-1	Ratcliffe	3,000
23		15	(a)	Tottenham H	W	2-1	MacEachrane, Jenkinson	8,000
24		22	(h)	Queen's Park R	W	4-0	Ratcliffe 2, Hunt 2	4,000
25	Mar	3	(a)	Brentford	W	2-0	Jenkinson, Hunt	500
26		8	(h)	Reading	W	2-1	Ratcliffe, Hunt	6,000
27		15	(a)	Portsmouth	D	0-0		6,000
28		22	(h)	Southampton	W	2-1	Grassam, Ratcliffe	7,000
29		29	(a)	Swindon T	W	1-0	Ratcliffe	1,000
30	Apr	12	(h)	Portsmouth	D	1-1	Ratcliffe	6,000

P	W	D	L	F	A	W	D	L	F	A	Pts	Pos	Div	Appearances
30	10	2	3	27	13	7	4	4	18	15	40	4th	SL	Goals

FA Cup

3Q	Nov	2	(a)	Leyton	W	1-0	Taylor	2,000
4Q		16	(h)	Grays	L	1-2	Linward	2,000

Appearances
Goals

192

Football appearances and goals grid (player shirt-number chart).

No.	Monteith	King	Craig	Bigden	Kelly	MacEachrane	Allan	Grassam	Corbett	Ratcliffe	Linward	Yenson	Hitchens	Jenkinson	Hunt	Ambler	Kyle	Wallace	Pudan	Jones	McDonald	Fair	McGeorge	Pinder	Taylor	Ward
1	1	2	3	4	5	6	7	8	9	10	11															
2	1	2	3	4	5	6	7	8	9	10	11															
3	1	2	3	4	5	6	7	8	9	10	11															
4	1	2	3	4	5	6	7	8	9	10	11															
5	1	2	3	4	5	6	7	8	9	10	11															
6	1	2	3	4	5	6	7	8	9	10	11															
7	1	2	3	4	5	6	7	8	9	10	11															
8	1	2	3	5		6	7	8	9		11	4	10													
9	1	2	3	4	5	6	7	8	9		11		10													
10	1	2	3	4	5	6		8	9	10	11			7												
11		2	3		5	6	4	8	7	10	11				1	9										
12	1	2	3		5	6			7	10	11			4	9		8									
13	1		3	4	5		7	8	9	10	11			6					2							
14	1	2		4		6	7	8		10	11			9					3	5						
15	1	2	3	4		6	7	8			11			10						5	9					
16	1	2	3	4			6	7	8		11			10	9					5						
17	1	2	3	4				7	8		11			6	9					5	10					
18	1	2	3	6			4		8		11			10	7					5	9					
19	1		3	4		6	7	8		10	11								2	5	9					
20	1	2	3	4			7		8		11			10	9				6	5						
21	1	2	3	4			7		8		11			10	9				6	5						
22	1	2	3	4	6		7		8		11			10	9					5						
23	1	2	3	4	6		7		8		11			10	9					5						
24	1	2	3	4	6		7		8		11			10	9					5						
25	1	2	3	4	6		7		8		11	5		10	9											
26	1	2	3	4	6		7		8		11			10	9					5						
27	1	2	3	4	6	7			8		11	5		10	9											
28	1	2	3	4	6		7		8		11			10	9					5						
29	1	2		4	6		7		8		11	3		10	9					5						
30	1	2	3	4	6		7		8		11			10	9					5						
App	29	28	28	28	12	25	18	29	12	24	30	5	1	19	15	1	1	1	5	15	4					
Gls		4		1		10	6	10	3					2	6						2					

1 own-goal

Rd	Monteith	King	Craig	Bigden	Kelly	MacEachrane	Allan	Grassam	Corbett	Ratcliffe	Linward	Yenson	Hitchens	Jenkinson	Hunt	Ambler	Kyle	Wallace	Pudan	Jones	McDonald	Fair	McGeorge	Pinder	Taylor	Ward
3Q						7				5	10			1	9	8	3			2	4		6	11		
4Q	1	2	5			6		8		10	11			9			3			4		7				
	1	1	1			1	1	1		1	1	1	1		1	2	1	2		1	2	1	1	1		
											1										1					

1902-03

Manager: Syd King

1	Sep	6	(h)	Reading	D	1-1	Barnes	7,000
2		13	(a)	Queen's Park R	D	0-0		7,000
3		27	(a)	Wellingborough T	L	1-5	Grassam	4,000
4	Oct	4	(h)	Bristol R	W	1-0	Grassam	6,500
5		11	(a)	Northampton T	L	0-2		3,000
6		18	(h)	Watford	W	3-1	Grassam 2, Barnes	4,000
7		25	(a)	Brentford	W	3-0	Grassam 2, Bigden	3,000
8	Nov	1	(a)	Tottenham H	D	1-1	Grassam	7,000
9		8	(h)	Millwall	L	0-3		10,000
10	Dec	6	(h)	Kettering T	D	1-1	Grassam	2,500
11		20	(a)	Reading	L	0-6		4,000
12		25	(h)	Southampton	L	1-2	Grassam	6,000
13		26	(a)	Portsmouth	L	0-2		18,000
14		27	(h)	Queen's Park R	W	2-0	Grassam, Barnes	2,500
15	Jan	10	(h)	Wellingborough T	W	3-0	Barnes, Davidson, Grassam	4,000
16		17	(a)	Bristol R	D	1-1	Wallace	4,000
17		24	(h)	Northampton T	W	3-2	Davidson, Grassam, Wallace	4,000
18		31	(a)	Watford	L	1-2	Campbell	5,000
19	Feb	7	(h)	Brentford	W	2-0	Grassam 2	3,000
20		14	(h)	Tottenham H	W	1-0	Wallace	8,000
21	Mar	7	(a)	New Brompton	L	0-2		7,000
22		14	(h)	Swindon T	D	1-1	Farrell	4,000
23		23	(h)	New Brompton	D	1-1	Farrell	1,000
24		28	(h)	Luton T	W	4-1	Grassam 2, Farrell, Bigden	800
25	Apr	4	(a)	Swindon T	D	1-1	Grassam	2,500
26		10	(h)	Portsmouth	D	1-1	Grassam	10,000
27		13	(a)	Southampton	L	0-6		6,000
28		15	(a)	Kettering T	D	1-1	Bush	2,000
29		18	(a)	Luton T	L	0-4		2,000
30		25	(a)	Millwall	L	1-2	Grassam	3,000

P	W	D	L	F	A	W	D	L	F	A	Pts	Pos	Div		Appearances
30	8	5	2	25	14	1	5	9	10	35	28	10th	SL		Goals

FA Cup

1	Dec	13	(a)	Lincoln C	L	0-2		3,000

Appearances
Goals

Biggar	Eccles	Dow	Bigden	McAteer	Blythe	Campbell	Grassam	Farrell	Barnes	Linward	Allan	King	Griffiths	Sugden	Kelly	Fair	Yenson	Davidson	Wallace	Miecznikowski	Parkinson	Bush	Evans	
1	2	3	4	5	6	7	8	9	10	11														1
1	2	3	4	5	6	7	8	9	10	11														2
1	2	3	4	5	6		8	9	10	11	7													3
	3		4	5	6		8	9	10	11	7	2	1											4
	3		4	5	6		8	9	10	11	7	2	1											5
	3	2	4	5	6	7	8		10	11			1	9										6
	3	2	10	5	6	7	8	9		11			1		4									7
	3	2	4	5	6	7	8	9	10	11			1											8
	3	2	4	5	6	7	8	9	10	11			1											9
			4	5	6	8	9		10	11	7	2	1			3								10
1	3		8	5	6	10	7	9	11			2					4							11
	3		4		6	7	8	10	11			2	1				5	9						12
	3		4		6	7	8	10	11			2	1				5	9						13
	3		4		6	7	8	9	11				1			2	5	10						14
	3		4		6	7	8		11				1			2	5	9	10					15
	3		4		6	7	8		11			2	1				5	9	10					16
	3		4		6	7	8		11				1			2	5	9	10					17
	3		4		6	7	8		11				1			2	5	9	10					18
		3	4		6	7	8		11				1			2	5	9	10					19
		3	4		6	7	8		11				1			2	5	9	10					20
		3	4		6		8	9	11				1			2	5		10	7				21
	3		4		6		8	9	11		7		1			2	5		10					22
	3	2	4		6		9	8	11		7		1				5		10					23
	3		4		6		9	8	11		7		1			2	5		10					24
1	2		4		6		8	9	11		7	3					5		10					25
	3		4		6		9	8	11		7		1			2	5		10					26
1	2	3	4	7	6	11	9	8									5		10					27
1			4				9	8				3			5		2		10	11	6	7		28
	2		4	5	6				11				1			3			10	7		8	9	29
1	2	3	8		6		9		11		7						5		10		4			30
8	25	13	30	13	29	18	29	20	27	10	10	9	22	1	2	12	19	9	16	3	2	2	1	
			2			1	19	3	4									2	3			1		

	3	2	4		6		8	9	10	11	7		1		5	1
	1	1	1		1		1	1	1	1	1		1		1	

1903-04

Manager: Syd King

							Att
1	Sep	5	(a)	Millwall	L 2-4	Kirby, Satterthwaite	10,000
2		7	(h)	Kettering T	W 4-1	Bigden, Lyon 2, Allison	1,000
3		12	(h)	Queen's Park R	W 1-0	Satterthwaite	6,000
4		19	(a)	Plymouth A	L 0-2		5,000
5		24	(h)	Luton T	D 0-0		3,000
6		26	(h)	Reading	D 1-1	Satterthwaite	10,000
7	Oct	10	(h)	Bristol R	L 1-4	Watts	5,000
8		17	(a)	Brighton & HA	L 2-3	Satterthwaite, Fair	4,000
9	Nov	7	(h)	Brentford	L 0-1		2,000
10		21	(a)	Tottenham H	L 1-2	Kirby	8,000
11	Dec	5	(a)	New Brompton	D 0-0		4,000
12		25	(h)	Southampton	W 2-1	Kirby, Satterthwaite	10,000
13		26	(a)	Portsmouth	L 1-2	Barnes	14,000
14		28	(h)	Fulham	W 2-0	Satterthwaite, Kirby	2,000
15	Jan	2	(h)	Millwall	L 0-1		10,000
16		9	(a)	Queen's Park R	L 1-2	Kirby	7,000
17		16	(h)	Plymouth A	D 1-1	Kirby	8,000
18		30	(h)	Wellingborough T	W 4-1	Kirby 2, Thompson, Satterthwaite	250
19	Feb	6	(a)	Bristol R	L 0-4		2,000
20		13	(h)	Brighton & HA	W 5-0	Satterthwaite 4, Lyon	3,000
21		27	(h)	Northampton T	W 2-0	Lyon, Kirby	4,000
22	Mar	2	(a)	Reading	L 0-1		1,000
23		5	(a)	Brentford	L 0-2		4,000
24		12	(a)	Swindon T	L 0-1		3,000
25		19	(h)	Tottenham H	L 0-2		9,500
26		26	(a)	Luton T	L 0-1		5,000
27	Apr	1	(h)	Portsmouth	W 3-0	Satterthwaite 2, Bridgeman	8,000
28		2	(h)	New Brompton	D 0-0		5,000
29		4	(a)	Southampton	D 1-1	Bridgeman	10,000
30		7	(a)	Northampton T	W 3-1	Mercer, Allison, Kirby	1,000
31		9	(a)	Kettering T	W 1-0	Bridgeman	1,000
32		20	(h)	Wellingborough T	L 0-3		3,000
33		23	(a)	Fulham	D 1-1	Bridgeman	4,000
34		30	(h)	Swindon T	L 0-1		4,000

P	W	D	L	F	A	W	D	L	F	A	Pts	Pos	Div	
34	8	4	5	26	14	2	3	12	13	30	27	12th	SL	Appearances
														Goals

FA Cup

							Att
3Q	Oct	31	(h)	Brighton & HA	W 4-0	Lyon 2, Watts, Satterthwaite	5,000
4Q	Nov	14	(a)	Clapton O	W 3-0	Lyon 2, Satterthwaite	4,500
5Q		28	(a)	Chatham	W 5-0	Satterthwaite 3, Kirby, Lyon	5,000
1	Dec	12	(h)	Fulham	L 0-1		12,000

Appearances
Goals

196

Cotton	Fair	Eccles	Bigden	Watts	Blythe	Kirby	Lyon	Ingham	Satterthwaite	Barnes	Allison	Butchart	Mapley	Hilsdon	Bridgeman	Earl	Griffiths	Birnie	Mercer	Thompson	Oakes	Church	Jarvis	#
1	2	3	4	5	6	7	8	9	10	11														1
1	2	3	4	5		7	9		10	11	6	8												2
1	2	3	4	5		7	9		10	11	6	8												3
1	2	3	4	5		7	9		10	11	6	8												4
1	2	3		5		7	9		10	11	6		3	8										5
1	3	2	4	5		7	8	9	10	11	6													6
1		2	4	5		7	9		10		6		3		8	11								7
1	9	2	8	5	6	7			10	11	4		3											8
		2		5	6	7	9		10	11	4		3				1	8						9
		2	8	5	6	7	9		10	11	4		3				1							10
		2	8	5	6	7	9		10	11	4		3				1							11
		2	8	5	6		9		10	11	4		3		7		1							12
		2	8	5	6		9		10	11	4		3		7		1							13
		2	8	5	6		9		10		4		3		7		1		11					14
		2	4	5	6	7	8		10	11			3				1			9				15
		2	4	5	6	7	8		10	11			3				1			9				16
		2	4		6	7	8		10	11	5		3				1			9				17
		2	4	3	6	7	8		10	11	5						1			9				18
	3	2	4		6	7	8		10	11	5						1			9				19
		2	4		6	7	8		10		5				11		1			9	3			20
		2	4		6	7	8		10		5				11		1			9	3			21
		2	4		6	7	8		10		5				11		1			9	3			22
		2	4		6	7	8		10		5				9		1				3		11	23
		2	4		6	7	8		10		5				9		1				3		11	24
		2	4		6	7	8		10		5				9		1				3			25
		2	4	5	6	7	8		10						9		1		11		3			26
		2	4	5		7	8		10						9		1		11		3	6		27
		2	4	5		7	8		10						9		1		11		3	6		28
		2	4	5	6	7	8		10						9		1		11		3			29
		2	4	5	6	7	8		10						9		1		11		3			30
		2		5	6	7	8		10		4				9		1		11		3			31
		2	4	5	6	7	8		10						9		1		11		3			32
		2	7	5	6		8			11	4				9		1			10	3			33
		2	7	5	6		8			11	4				9		1			10	3			34
8	7	34	33	25	23	33	29	2	32	21	28	3	13	1	18	1	26	1	8	10	14	2	2	
1		1	1						10	4	13	1	2		4				1	1				

Cotton	Fair	Eccles	Bigden	Watts	Blythe	Kirby	Lyon	Ingham	Satterthwaite	Barnes	Allison	Butchart	Mapley	Hilsdon	Bridgeman	Earl	Griffiths	Birnie	Mercer	Thompson	Oakes	Church	Jarvis	#
1		2	8	5	6	7	9		10	11	4		3											3Q
		2	8	5	6	7	9		10	11	4		3				1							4Q
		2	8	5	6	7	9		10	11	4		3				1							5Q
		2	8	5	6		9		10	11	4		3				1		7					1
1		4	4	4	4	3	4		4	4	4		4				3		1					
						1	1		5	5														

1904-05

Manager: Syd King

1	Sep	1	(h)	Millwall	W 3-0	Bridgeman 2, Flynn	10,000
2		3	(a)	Brentford	D 0-0		7,000
3		10	(h)	Queen's Park R	L 1-3	Allison	14,000
4		17	(a)	Millwall	D 1-1	Fletcher	10,000
5		24	(h)	Tottenham H	D 0-0		16,000
6	Oct	1	(a)	Luton T	W 2-0	Fletcher, Bridgeman	4,000
7		8	(h)	Swindon T	W 2-0	Fletcher, Flynn	6,000
8		15	(a)	New Brompton	L 0-3		7,000
9		22	(h)	Wellingborough T	W 4-0	Fletcher 3, Flynn	5,000
10		29	(a)	Southampton	D 2-2	Bridgeman, McCartney	4,000
11	Nov	5	(h)	Fulham	D 0-0		8,000
12		19	(h)	Plymouth A	W 2-1	Simmons 2	10,000
13		26	(h)	Bristol R	L 0-2		7,000
14	Dec	3	(a)	Reading	L 0-1		5,000
15		17	(a)	Northampton T	L 0-1		4,000
16		26	(a)	Portsmouth	L 1-4	Blackwood	16,000
17		27	(h)	Brighton & HA	L 0-1		12,000
18		31	(h)	Brentford	L 0-1		8,000
19	Jan	7	(a)	Queen's Park R	L 0-1		8,000
20		21	(a)	Tottenham H	L 0-1		12,000
21		28	(h)	Luton T	W 6-2	Carrick 3, Bridgeman 2, Simmons	5,000
22	Feb	4	(a)	Swindon T	D 3-3	Fletcher, Piercy, Bridgeman	3,000
23		11	(h)	New Brompton	W 2-0	Simmons, Hilsdon	6,000
24		18	(a)	Wellingborough T	L 0-3		1,500
25		25	(h)	Southampton	W 2-1	McCartney, Hilsdon	1,500
26	Mar	11	(h)	Watford	W 2-0	Carrick, Bridgeman	3,000
27		18	(a)	Plymouth A	L 0-2		7,000
28		25	(a)	Brighton & HA	L 1-3	Bridgeman	5,000
29	Apr	1	(h)	Reading	L 0-2		5,000
30		8	(a)	Bristol R	D 2-2	Carrick, Hilsdon	5,000
31		15	(h)	Northampton T	W 5-1	Carrick, Simmons 2, McCartney, Bridgeman	7,000
32		17	(a)	Fulham	W 3-0	Allison, Hilsdon, Simmons	1,000
33		21	(h)	Portsmouth	D 1-1	Bridgeman	6,000
34		25	(a)	Watford	W 3-0	Simmons, Piercy, Smith	1,000

P	W	D	L	F	A	W	D	L	F	A	Pts	Pos	Div		Appearances
34	9	3	5	30	15	3	3	5	9	18	27	32	11th	SL	Goals

FA Cup

6Q	Dec	10	(h)	Brighton & HA	L 1-2	Flynn	6,000

Appearances
Goals

198

Football appearances and goals grid.

Kingsley	Bamlett	Gardner	Allison	Piercy	Russell	McCartney	Fletcher	Bridgeman	Simmons	Flynn	Jarvis	Carrick	Fair	Milnes	Hamilton	Blackwood	Brunton	Cotton	Hammond	Hilsdon	Smith	
1	2	3	4	5	6	7	8	9	10	11												1
1	2	3	4	5	6	7	8	9	10	11												2
1	2	3	4	5	6	7	8	9	10	11												3
1	2	3	4	5	6	7	8	9	10	11												4
1	2	3	4	5	6	7	8	9	10	11												5
1	2	3	4		6		8	9	10	11		5	7									6
1		3	4	5	6		8	9	10	11			7	2								7
1		3	4	5	6	7	8	9	10	11						2						8
1		3	4	5	6	7	8	9	10	11						2						9
1	2	3		5	6	7	8	9	10	11		4										10
1	2			5	6	7		9	8	11		4	10	3								11
1	2		4	5	6	7		9	8	11			10	3								12
1	2		4	5	6	7	10	9	8	11				3								13
1	2		4	5	6	7	10	9	8	11				3								14
1	2		4	5			8		10	11	6	3		7	9							15
1		3		5			8		10	11	6	2		7	9	4						16
	2	3	4	5		7			10	11	6			8	9		1					17
1	2	3	4	5			8		10	11	6			7	9							18
1		3	4	5		7	8	9	10		6	11						2				19
1		3	4	5		7	8	9	10		6	11						2				20
1	2	3	4	5		7	8	9	10	11	6											21
1	2	3	4	5		7	8		10		6	11							9			22
1	2	3	4	5		7	8		10		6	11							9			23
1		3	4	5		7	8		10		6	11						2	9			24
1		3	4	5		7	8	9	10		6	11						2				25
1		3	4	5		7	8	9	10		6	11						2				26
1		3	4	5		7		9	10		6	11	2						8			27
1		3	4	5		7	8	9	10		6	11										28
1		3	4	5		7		9	10		6	11						2	8			29
		3	4	5		7		9	10		6	11					1	2	8			30
		3	4	5		7		9	10		6	11	2				1	2	8			31
		3	4	5		7		9	10		6	11					1	2	8			32
		3	4	5	6			9	10		4	11		7			1	2	8			33
		3		5	6			9	10		4	11			7		1	2	8			34
29	18	29	30	33	16	28	25	27	34	20	22	18	9	2	5	4	1	5	10	7	2	
	2	2		3	7	11	8	3			6					1			4	1		

Kingsley	Bamlett	Gardner	Allison	Piercy	Russell	McCartney	Fletcher	Bridgeman	Simmons	Flynn	Jarvis	Carrick	Fair	Milnes	Hamilton	Blackwood	Brunton	Cotton	Hammond	Hilsdon	Smith	
1	2		4	5	6	7	8	9	10	11		3										6Q
1	1		1	1	1	1	1	1	1	1		1										
												1										

199

1905-06

Manager: Syd King

1	Sep	2	(h)	Swindon T	W	1-0	Kitchen	10,000
2		9	(a)	Millwall	L	0-1		6,500
3		16	(h)	Luton T	L	1-2	Blackburn	10,000
4		23	(a)	Tottenham H	L	0-2		12,000
5		30	(h)	Brentford	W	2-0	Blackburn, Wilkinson	8,000
6	Oct	7	(a)	Norwich C	L	0-1		6,000
7		14	(h)	Plymouth A	W	2-1	Blackburn, Mackie	5,000
8		21	(a)	Southampton	L	0-1		6,000
9		28	(h)	Reading	L	2-3	Ford, Allison	7,000
10	Nov	4	(a)	Watford	L	1-3	Bridgeman	4,000
11		11	(h)	Brighton & HA	W	2-0	Wilkinson, Mackie	8,000
12		18	(a)	Northampton T	L	1-2	Mackie	5,000
13		25	(a)	Fulham	L	0-1		12,000
14	Dec	2	(h)	Queen's Park R	W	2-0	Hilsdon, Watson	7,500
15		9	(a)	Bristol R	L	1-2	Hilsdon	5,000
16		16	(h)	New Brompton	W	1-0	Jarvis	6,000
17		23	(h)	Portsmouth	W	1-0	Stapley	8,000
18		30	(a)	Swindon T	W	3-2	Watson, Jarvis, Blackburn	4,000
19	Jan	6	(h)	Millwall	W	1-0	Watson	15,000
20		20	(a)	Luton T	D	1-1	Stapley	5,000
21		27	(h)	Tottenham H	L	0-1		16,500
22	Feb	10	(h)	Norwich C	W	6-1	Grassam, Watson 2, Stapley 2, Kitchen	6,000
23		17	(a)	Plymouth A	L	2-4	Kitchen, Grassam	3,000
24		26	(h)	Southampton	W	3-0	Stapley 2, Bridgeman	5,000
25	Mar	3	(a)	Reading	L	1-6	Watson	5,000
26		10	(h)	Watford	D	0-0		7,000
27		17	(a)	Brighton & HA	D	0-0		5,000
28		24	(h)	Northampton T	W	4-1	Stapley 2, Bridgeman 2	4,000
29		31	(h)	Fulham	D	0-0		12,000
30	Apr	7	(a)	Queen's Park R	W	1-0	Stapley	10,000
31		14	(h)	Bristol R	W	2-0	Blackburn, Hilsdon	9,000
32		21	(a)	New Brompton	D	0-0		3,000
33		23	(a)	Brentford	L	1-3	Grassam	2,000
34		28	(a)	Portsmouth	L	0-1		5,000

P	W	D	L	F	A	W	D	L	F	A	Pts	Pos	Div	
34	12	2	3	30	9	2	3	12	12	30	33	11th	SL	Appearances
														Goals

FA Cup

1	Jan	13	(a)	W Arsenal	D	1-1	Kitchen	18,000
R		18	(h)	W Arsenal	L	2-3	Bridgeman, Watson	12,000

Appearances
Goals

Kitchen	McCartney	Gardner	Hindle	Piercy	Jarvis	Bridgeman	Ford	Mackie	Watson	Blackburn	Hammond	Bush	Winterhalder H	Wilkinson	Allison	Hilsdon	Featherstone	Jackson	Grassam	Stapley	Cotton	Milnes	
1	2	3	4	5	6	7	8	9	10	11													1
1	2	3	4	5	6	9	7	8	10	11													2
1		3		5	6	9		8		11	2	4	7	10									3
1		3		5	6	9		8		11	2		7	10	4								4
1		3		5		8				10	2	6	7	11	4	9							5
1		3		5		8				10	2	6	7	11	4	9							6
1	2	3		5		8	7	9		10		6		11	4								7
1	2	3		5		8	7	9		10		6		11	4								8
1	2	3	5			8	7	9		10		6		11	4								9
1	2	3		5	6	8		9		10				11	4		7						10
1		3			5	8		9		10		6		11	4		7	2					11
1		3			5	8		9		10		6		11	4		7	2					12
1		3			5	8			10			6		11	4	9	7	2					13
1		3			5	8			10			6		11	4	9	7	2					14
1		3			5	8			10			6		11	4	9	7	2					15
1		3			5				10	11		6		8	4	9	7	2					16
1		3			5				10	11		6			4		7	2	8	9			17
1		3		6	5				10	11					4		7	2	8	9			18
1		3		6	5				10	11					4		7	2	8	9			19
1		3		6	5				10			4	11				7	2	8	9			20
1		3		6	5				10	11		4					7	2	8	9			21
1		3		6	5	7			10	11					4			2	8	9			22
1		3		6	5	8			10	11					4		7	2	9				23
1		3			5	8			10	11		6			4		7	2		9			24
1		3			5	8			10	11		6			4		7	2		9			25
1		3		6					8	10			11		4	5	7	2		9			26
1		3		5			7		10	11		6				4		2	8	9			27
1		3		5	6	7			10	11					4			2	8	9			28
		3		5	6	7			10	11					4			2	8	9	1		29
1		3		5	6	7			10	11					4			2	8	9			30
		3		5	6	8				10			11		4	9	7	2			1		31
		3		5	6	7			10	11			9		4			2	8		1		32
		3		5	6	9	7			10			11		4			2	8		1		33
		3		5	6	7			10	11			9		4			2	8		1		34
29	6	34	3	24	27	26	7	10	22	30	4	18	10	14	28	9	17	24	14	13	5		
3					2	4	1	3	6	5				2	1	3			3	9			

1		3		6	5	7			10	11		8			4	9						2	1
1		3		6	5	8			10	11				7	4	9						2	R
2		2		2	2	2			2	2		1		1	2	2						2	
1						1			1														

1906-07

Manager: Syd King

1	Sep	1	(a)	Tottenham H	W	2-1	Stapley, Watson	17,000
2		8	(h)	Swindon T	W	2-0	Watson, Stapley	10,000
3		15	(a)	Norwich C	L	2-3	Blackburn, Stapley	10,000
4		22	(h)	Luton T	W	5-1	Watson 3, Stapley, Lindsay	13,000
5		24	(a)	Bristol R	L	0-3		3,000
6		29	(a)	Crystal P	D	1-1	Winterhalder	10,000
7	Oct	6	(h)	Brentford	W	3-1	Allison, Stapley, Grassam	12,000
8		13	(a)	Millwall	D	1-1	Stapley	15,000
9		15	(h)	Bristol R	L	0-1		4,000
10		20	(h)	Leyton	W	3-0	Grassam 2, Stapley	12,000
11		27	(a)	Portsmouth	L	3-4	Grassam 3	12,000
12	Nov	3	(h)	New Brompton	D	1-1	Stapley	7,000
13		10	(a)	Plymouth A	D	0-0		10,000
14		17	(h)	Brighton & HA	D	0-0		5,000
15		27	(a)	Reading	D	2-2	Grassam, Lindsay	4,000
16	Dec	1	(h)	Watford	D	1-1	Stapley	7,000
17		8	(a)	New Brompton	D	2-2	Stapley, Watson	5,000
18		22	(a)	Fulham	W	4-1	Watson 3, Blackburn	10,000
19		25	(h)	Southampton	W	1-0	Stapley	20,000
20		29	(h)	Tottenham H	W	4-2	Winterhalder 3, Stapley	14,000
21	Jan	5	(a)	Swindon T	L	0-2		5,000
22		19	(h)	Norwich C	W	3-1	Stapley 2, Lindsay	7,000
23		26	(a)	Luton T	D	1-1	Stapley	4,000
24	Feb	9	(a)	Brentford	D	0-0		6,000
25		16	(h)	Millwall	L	0-1		16,000
26		23	(a)	Leyton	D	0-0		10,000
27		25	(h)	Queen's Park R	W	2-1	Watson, Grassam	4,000
28	Mar	2	(h)	Portsmouth	W	3-0	Stapley 2, Lindsay	11,000
29		7	(a)	Northampton T	D	0-0		2,000
30		16	(h)	Plymouth A	D	0-0		6,000
31		23	(a)	Brighton & HA	L	0-2		6,000
32		25	(a)	Crystal P	D	1-1	Winterhalder	3,000
33		30	(h)	Reading	W	2-0	Blackburn, Allison	6,000
34	Apr	1	(a)	Southampton	W	3-2	Stapley, Watson, Jarvis	8,000
35		6	(a)	Watford	L	0-2		4,000
36		13	(h)	Northampton T	W	4-0	Stapley 2, Grassam 2	2,500
37		20	(a)	Queen's Park R	L	0-2		5,000
38		27	(h)	Fulham	W	4-1	Watson, Randall, Winterhalder, Blackburn	10,000

P	W	D	L	F	A	W	D	L	F	A	Pts	Pos	Div	
38	12	5	2	39	12	3	9	7	21	29	44	5th	SL	Appearances
														Goals

FA Cup

1	Jan	12	(h)	Blackpool	W	2-1	Stapley, Winterhalder	13,000
2	Feb	2	(h)	Everton	L	1-2	Stapley	14,000

Appearances
Goals

Football season appearance grid. Each cell shows the shirt number (1–11) worn by that player in each match (rows 1–38). Blank cells indicate the player did not appear.

#	Kitchen	Wildman	Gardner	Allison	Piercy	Jarvis	Lindsay	Grassam	Stapley	Watson	Blackburn	Blythe	Winterhalder H	Kemp	Hammond	Taylor	Horn	Featherstone	Clarke	Winterhalder A	Fair	Woodards	Randall	Bourne
1	1	2	3	4	5	6	7	8	9	10	11													
2	1	2	3	4	5	6	7	8	9	10	11													
3	1		3	4	5	6	7	8	9	10	11	2												
4	1	2	3	4	5	6	7	8	9	10	11													
5	1	2	3	4	5	6	7	8		10	11		9											
6	1	2	3	6	5		7	8	9	10		4	11											
7	1	2	3	4	5	6	7	8	9	10				11										
8	1	2		4	5	6	7	8	9	10				11	3									
9	1	2		4	5	6	7	8	9	10				11		3								
10	1	2		4	5	6	7	8	9	10	11					3								
11	1	2	3	4	5	6	7	8	9	10	11													
12	1	2	3	4	5		7	8	9		11	6		10										
13	1	2	3	4	5		7	8	9	10	11				6									
14	1	2	3	4	5	6	7	8	9	10	11													
15	1	2		4	5		7	8	9		11			10	3		6							
16	1	2		4	5		7	8	9		11			10	3		6							
17	1	2	3	4	5		7	8	9	10	11							6						
18	1	2		4	5	6	7	8	9	10	11				3									
19		2		4	5	6	7	8	9	10					3				1	11				
20	1	2		4	5	6		8	9	10					3		7			11				
21	1	2		4	5	6		8	9	10					3		7			11				
22	1	2	3	4	5	6	7	8	9	10										11				
23	1	2	3	4	5	6	7	8	9	10										11				
24	1	2		4	5	6	7	8	9	10					3					11				
25	1	2		4	5	6	7	8	9	10	11				3									
26	1	2		4	5	6		8	9	10	11				3		7							
27	1	2		4	5	6	7	8	9	10	11				3									
28	1	2		4	5	6	7	8	9	5	10				3					11				
29	1	2		4	3	6	7	8	9	5	10									11				
30	1	2			5	6	7	8	9		11			10	3						4			
31	1	2			5	6	7	8	9		11			10	3						4			
32	1	2			5	6	7	8	9	10					3					11	4			
33	1	2		4	5	6	7	8	9	10	11				3									
34	1	2		4	5	6	7	8	9	10	11					3								
35	1	2		4	5	6	7	8	9	10	11					3								
36	1	2		4	5	6	7	8	9	10	11				3									
37	1	2		4	5	6	7	8	9	10	11				3									
38	1	2		4	5		7		9	10					3			6		11		8		
Apps	37	37	14	36	37	30	37	37	35	32	29	3	2	8	16	4	4	2	1	10	3	2	1	1
Goals			2		1	4	10	20	12	4			1							5	1			

#	Kitchen	Wildman	Gardner	Allison	Piercy	Jarvis	Lindsay	Grassam	Stapley	Watson	Blackburn	Blythe	Winterhalder H	Kemp	Hammond	Taylor	Horn	Featherstone	Clarke	Winterhalder A	Fair	Woodards	Randall	Bourne
1	1	2		4	5	6	7	8	9	10					3				11					
2	1	2	3	4	5	6	7	8	9	10									11					
Apps	2	2	1	2	2	2	2	2	2	2					1				1					
Goals								2											1					

1907-08

Manager: Syd King

						Result	Scorers	Attendance
1	Sep	1	(h)	Swindon T		L 1-2	Grassam	8,000
2		7	(h)	Tottenham H		D 1-1	Blackburn	13,000
3		14	(a)	Swindon T		D 1-1	Grassam	5,000
4		21	(h)	Crystal P		W 1-0	Grassam	8,000
5		28	(a)	Luton T		W 3-0	Stapley 2, Grassam	7,000
6	Oct	5	(h)	Brighton & HA		D 0-0		7,000
7		12	(a)	Portsmouth		W 2-0	Watson, Blackburn	12,000
8		19	(h)	Bradford		D 0-0		12,000
9		26	(a)	Millwall		L 0-1		13,000
10	Nov	2	(h)	Brentford		W 4-1	Stapley 2, Randall, Grassam	6,000
11		9	(a)	Bristol R		L 0-1		10,000
12		16	(h)	Leyton		L 0-2		8,000
13		23	(a)	Reading		W 1-0	Watson	6,000
14		30	(h)	Watford		W 2-0	Watson, Stapley	6,000
15	Dec	7	(a)	Norwich C		D 1-1	Grassam	4,500
16		14	(h)	Northampton T		D 1-1	Stapley	4,000
17		21	(a)	Southampton		D 0-0		6,000
18		25	(h)	New Brompton		L 1-2	Opp own-goal	10,000
19		26	(h)	Queen's Park R		W 3-0	Grassam 2, Featherstone	17,000
20		28	(h)	Plymouth A		D 1-1	Shea	10,000
21	Jan	4	(a)	Tottenham H		L 2-3	Stapley 2	12,000
22		18	(a)	Crystal P		W 3-1	Watson, Shea, Stapley	8,000
23		25	(h)	Luton T		W 1-0	Watson	8,000
24	Feb	8	(h)	Portsmouth		W 2-1	Frost, Watson	10,000
25		15	(a)	Bradford		W 1-0	Watson	9,000
26		22	(h)	Millwall		L 0-2		12,000
27		29	(a)	Brentford		L 0-4		4,000
28	Mar	7	(h)	Bristol R		D 0-0		6,000
29		14	(a)	Leyton		D 2-2	Brown 2	11,000
30		21	(h)	Reading		W 2-1	Grassam, Watson	6,000
31		25	(a)	Brighton & HA		L 1-3	Jarvis	1,500
32		28	(a)	Watford		W 3-2	Jarvis, Stapley, Frost	3,000
33	Apr	4	(h)	Norwich C		W 3-0	Young, Blackburn, Frost	6,000
34		11	(a)	Northampton T		L 0-4		6,000
35		17	(a)	New Brompton		L 0-3		6,000
36		18	(h)	Southampton		W 4-2	Brown 2, Blackburn, Shea	8,000
37		20	(a)	Queen's Park R		L 0-4		11,000
38		25	(a)	Plymouth A		L 0-2		4,000

P	W	D	L	F	A	W	D	L	F	A	Pts	Pos	Div	Appearances
38	9	6	4	27	16	6	4	9	20	32	40	10th	SL	Goals

FA Cup

						Result	Scorers	Attendance
1	Jan	11	(h)	Rotherham C		W 1-0	Blackburn	9,500
2	Feb	1	(a)	Newcastle U		L 0-2		47,000

Appearances
Goals

Player appearance and scorers grid (numbers indicate the shirt number worn in each match; row numbers 1–38 at right).

No.	Kitchen	Wildman	Taylor	Allison	Piercy	Jarvis	Lindsay	Grassam	Stapley	Watson	Blackburn	Young	Gault	Brown	Lee	Kemp	Randall	Harwood	Shea	Robertson	Bourne	Horn	Featherstone	Woodards	Frost	Clarke	Hammond
1	1	2	3	4	5	6	7	8	9	10	11																
2	1	2	3	4	5		7	8	9	10	11	6															
3	1		3		5	6	7	8		10	11	4	2	9													
4	1		3	4		6		8	9	10	11	5	2		7												
5	1		3	4				8	9	5	11	6	2		7	10											
6	1		3	4		6	7	8	9	10	11	5	2														
7	1		3	4	5		7	8	9	10	11	6	2														
8	1		3	4	5		7		9	10	11	6	2														
9	1		3	4	5		7		9	10	11	6	2				8										
10	1		3	4	5	6		8	9		11		2			10	7										
11	1			4	3	6		8	9		11	5	2			10	7										
12	1			4	3	6		8	9		11	5	2	10			7										
13	1			4	5		7	8	9	10	11	6	2					3									
14	1			4	5	6	7	8	9	10	11	3	2														
15	1			4	5	6	7	8			10	3	2			11		9									
16	1			4	5	6		7	9		11	3	2			10		8									
17	1		3		5	6	7	8			10	4	2		11				9								
18	1			4		6	7	8	9	10	11	5	2					3									
19	1				6			10	9		11	5	2						8		3	4	7				
20	1							10	9		11	5	2						8		3	4	7	6			
21	1			6				10	9		11	5	2						8		3	4	7				
22	1		3	4	5		7		9	10	11	6	2						8								
23	1		3	4	5				9	10	11	6							8				7				2
24			3		5	6			9	10	11	4	2	8											7	1	
25			3		5	6			9		11	4	2	10					8						7	1	
26			3		5	6			9		11		2	10					8	4					7	1	
27			3		5	6			9		11	4	2	10					8						7	1	
28			3	4	9	6		8			11	5	2	10											7	1	
29			3	4	5	6		8	9			2	10	11											7	1	
30			3	4		6		8	9		11	5	2	10											7	1	
31			3	4		6		8		9	11	5	2	10											7	1	
32			3	4		6		8	9		11	5	2	10											7	1	
33			3	4		6		8		9	11	5	2	10											7	1	
34				4	3	6		8		9	11	5	2	10											7	1	
35				4		6		8		9	11	5	2	10											7	1	3
36			3	4		6		10			11	5	2	9					8				7			1	
37			3	4		6		10			11	5	2	9					10				7			1	
38				4		6		10				5	2	9	7	11	3	8					7			1	
App.	23	2	25	29	23	29	13	32	23	22	36	33	35	17	6	3	7	3	13	1	3	4	5	1	13	15	2
Gls			2		9	10	8	4	1		4			1	3				1				1	3				

1 own-goal

Cup matches:

No.	Kitchen	Wildman	Taylor	Allison	Piercy	Jarvis	Lindsay	Grassam	Stapley	Watson	Blackburn	Young	Gault	Brown	Lee	Kemp	Randall	Harwood	Shea	Robertson	Bourne	Horn	Featherstone	Woodards	Frost	Clarke	Hammond
1	1			5				10	9		11	6	2						8		4	7			3		
2	1		3		5	6		10	9		11	4	2						8			7				1	
App.	2		1		2	1		2	2		2	2	2						2		1	1			1	1	
Gls								1																			

1908-09

Manager: Syd King

1	Sep	1	(h)	Queen's Park R	W 2-0	Foster, Blackburn	7,000
2		5	(a)	Brighton & HA	L 2-3	Foster, Burton	6,000
3		12	(h)	Crystal P	L 0-1		10,000
4		19	(a)	Brentford	L 0-1		6,000
5		26	(h)	Luton T	W 4-0	Foster 2, Piercy, Ashton	3,000
6		30	(a)	Watford	L 1-2	Shea	3,000
7	Oct	3	(a)	Swindon T	L 0-3		6,000
8		10	(h)	Portsmouth	W 3-1	Foster 3	8,000
9		17	(a)	Queen's Park R	L 0-3		6,000
10		24	(h)	Northampton T	W 2-1	Tirrell, Shreeve	9,000
11		31	(a)	New Brompton	L 1-2	Miller	6,000
12	Nov	7	(h)	Millwall	W 1-0	Foster	14,000
13		14	(a)	Southend U	D 0-0		6,000
14		21	(h)	Coventry C	W 2-0	Foster, Randall	6,000
15		28	(a)	Bristol R	L 0-1		8,000
16	Dec	5	(a)	Plymouth A	L 0-2		7,000
17		12	(a)	Norwich C	L 3-6	Burton 2, Grassam	4,500
18		19	(h)	Reading	W 2-1	Grassam, Blackburn	5,000
19		25	(h)	Southampton	W 1-0	Blackburn	15,000
20		26	(a)	Leyton	L 0-1		20,000
21		28	(h)	Plymouth A	W 4-0	Shea 4	10,000
22	Jan	2	(h)	Brighton & HA	D 1-1	Waggott	5,000
23		9	(a)	Crystal P	D 2-2	Shea 2	5,000
24		23	(h)	Brentford	W 3-0	Miller, Waggott, Frost	7,000
25		30	(a)	Luton T	L 0-1		3,000
26	Feb	13	(a)	Portsmouth	L 1-4	Miller	5,000
27		27	(a)	Northampton T	L 0-6		5,000
28	Mar	6	(h)	New Brompton	L 0-1		3,000
29		8	(h)	Swindon T	W 4-2	Shea 3, Costello	4,000
30		13	(a)	Millwall	L 0-3		9,000
31		20	(h)	Southend U	W 4-0	Costello, Piercy, Atkins, Shea	9,000
32		27	(a)	Coventry C	L 1-3	Shea	7,000
33	Apr	1	(h)	Exeter C	W 4-1	Blackburn 2, Miller 2	4,000
34		3	(h)	Bristol R	L 0-2		7,000
35		9	(h)	Leyton	W 1-0	Webb	13,000
36		10	(h)	Watford	W 3-1	Shea 2, Costello	7,000
37		12	(a)	Southampton	D 2-2	Shea, Webb	7,500
38		17	(h)	Norwich C	W 2-1	Shea, Blackburn	5,000
39		21	(a)	Exeter C	L 0-1		7,000
40		24	(a)	Reading	L 0-1		2,500

P	W	D	L	F	A	W	D	L	F	A	Pts	Pos	Div	
40	16	1	3	43	13	0	3	17	13	47	36	17th	SL	Appearances
														Goals

FA Cup

1	Jan	16	(a)	Queen's Park R	D 0-0		17,000
R		20	(h)	Queen's Park R	W 1-0	Shea	11,400
2	Feb	6	(a)	Leeds C	D 1-1	Miller	31,500
R		11	(h)	Leeds C	W 2-1	Shea 2	13,000
3		20	(h)	Newcastle U	D 0-0		17,000
R		24	(a)	Newcastle U	L 1-2	Shea	36,500

Appearances
Goals

206

The following is a dense change‑ringing grid. Each row is a row of eleven bells (a permutation of 1–11) distributed across the named columns. Blank cells are empty.

Kitchen	Gault	Taylor	Yenson	Piercy	Jarvis	Ashton	Dyer	Foster	Burton	Blackburn	Frost	Shea	Waggott	Tirrell	Young	Harwood	Eastwood	Brown	Miller	Shreeve	Grassam	Randall	Allison	Chalkley	Clarke	Dawson	Bourne	Costello	Atkins	Webb	No.
1	2	3	4	5	6	7	8	9	10	11																					1
1	2	3	4	5	6	7	8	9	10	11																					2
1	2	3	4	5	6			9		11	7	8	10																		3
1	2	3	9	5		10				11	7	8			4	6															4
1	2		4	5		7		9	10	11		8			6		3														5
1	2		4	5	6	7		9	10	11		8					3														6
1	2			5	6			9		11		8		4		3	7	10													7
1		2			6				10	11		8		4	5	3	7		9												8
1					6				10	11				4	5	3	7		9	2	8										9
1		3		5	6			9		11	10			4		7				2	8										10
1		3		5						11	10				4	6	7		9	2	8										11
1	2	3		5	6			9		11					4	7					8	10									12
1	2	3		5	6	7		9		11		8			4						10										13
1	2	3		5	6	7		9		11		8			4						10										14
1	2	3		5	6	7		9		11		8			4							10									15
1		3		5	6	7				11	10				4					9	2	8									16
1	2			5	6	7				11	10				4					3	8		9								17
1				5	6	7				11	9			3						2	8	10	4								18
1		2	4		6					11	9			3		7					8	5	10								19
1	2	3	4					9		11	7	8	10	6								5									20
1	2	3	4							11	7	8	10	6					9			5									21
1		3	4							11	7	8	10	6				2	9			5									22
1		3	4							11	7	8	10	6					9	2		5									23
1		3	4							11	7	8	10	6					9	2		5									24
1		3	4					5	7	11		8	10	6					9	2											25
2		5						4	7	11		8	10				3		9			6			1						26
	3	5		4	7				10	11		8							9			6				1	2				27
	3	5		4	7					11		8							9			6				1	2	10			28
	3	5	2	4	7			9		11		8										6				1		10			29
	3	5		4	7				10	11		8								2		6				1		9			30
1		3	4	5		7				11		8								2		6						10	9		31
1		3	4	5		7				11		8								2		6						10	9		32
1		3		5		7				11		8							9	2		6	4					10			33
1		3		5		7				11		8							9	2		6	4					10			34
1		3	5			7				11		8								2		6	4					10	9		35
1		3	4	5		7				11		8								2		6						10	9		36
1		3	4	5		7				11		8								2		6						10	9		37
		3	4	5		7				11		8								2		6				1		10	9		38
	3	4	5					8		11				7					9	2		6				1		10			39
1									10		8	9	6				11									3					40
35	14	34	26	26	23	27	3	15	15	40	7	35	8	13	9	9	6	2	11	19	8	17	5	7	1	4	3	12	2	4	
	2		1					9	3	6	1	16	2	1						5	1	2	1				3	1	2		

Lower block:

Kitchen	Gault	Taylor	Yenson	Piercy	Jarvis	Ashton	Dyer	Foster	Burton	Blackburn	Frost	Shea	Waggott	Tirrell	Young	Harwood	Eastwood	Brown	Miller	Shreeve	Grassam	Randall	Allison	Chalkley	Clarke	Dawson	Bourne	Costello	Atkins	Webb	No.
1		3	4						10	11	7	8						6		9	2							5			1
1		3	4							11	7	8			10	6			9	2							5				R
1		3	4						10	11	7	8						6		9	2							5			2
1		3	4						10	11	7	8						6		9	2							5			R
1		3	5		4	7				11		8							9	2	10	6									3
1		3	5		4	7			10	11		8							9	2		6									R
6		6	6		2	2		4	6	4	6	1	4						6	6	1		4				2				
											4								1												

1909-10

Manager: Syd King

1	Sep	2	(h)	Exeter C	W 2-1	Shea 2	5,000
2		4	(a)	Norwich C	W 3-1	Shea, Blackburn, Haynes	7,000
3		11	(h)	Brentford	W 3-2	Shea 3	10,000
4		13	(h)	Portsmouth	L 0-2		6,000
5		18	(a)	Coventry C	D 2-2	Shea, Haynes	8,000
6		25	(h)	Watford	W 2-0	Shea, Randall	10,000
7		29	(a)	Portsmouth	D 1-1	Haynes	2,000
8	Oct	2	(a)	Reading	W 3-0	Shea 2, Webb	3,000
9		4	(h)	Bristol R	W 5-0	Caldwell 3, Shea, Webb	4,000
10		9	(h)	Southend U	D 0-0		10,000
11		16	(a)	Leyton	W 2-1	Caldwell, Webb	13,000
12		23	(h)	Plymouth A	W 4-1	Webb 2, Shea 2	10,000
13		25	(a)	Bristol R	L 0-1		2,000
14		30	(a)	Southampton	D 2-2	Shea, Haynes	7,000
15	Nov	6	(h)	Croydon Com	W 5-1	Shea 2, Ashton, Caldwell, Whiteman	10,000
16		13	(a)	Millwall	D 0-0		10,000
17		20	(a)	Plymouth A	D 0-0		8,000
18		27	(a)	Northampton T	L 1-3	Webb	7,000
19	Dec	4	(h)	Queen's Park R	L 1-2	Shreeve	12,000
20		11	(a)	Luton T	L 2-4	Ashton, Shea	3,000
21		18	(h)	Swindon T	D 2-2	Blackburn, Shreeve	10,000
22		25	(h)	Brighton & HA	D 1-1	Shea	15,000
23		27	(a)	Brighton & HA	L 0-3		10,000
24	Jan	1	(h)	New Brompton	D 2-2	Caldwell, Shea	7,000
25		8	(h)	Norwich C	W 5-0	Caldwell 2, Shea 2, Cannon	6,000
26		22	(a)	Brentford	D 0-0		4,000
27		29	(h)	Coventry C	W 3-2	Haynes, Ashton, Shea	6,000
28	Feb	12	(h)	Reading	D 1-1	Shreeve	8,000
29		26	(h)	Leyton	D 0-0		10,000
30	Mar	2	(a)	Watford	L 1-2	Butcher	1,000
31		5	(a)	Exeter C	L 0-1		6,500
32		12	(h)	Southampton	D 1-1	Blackburn	4,000
33		19	(a)	Croydon Com	D 1-1	Webb	6,000
34		25	(h)	Crystal P	W 3-1	Shea 2, Opp own-goal	15,000
35		26	(h)	Millwall	L 1-2	Shea	12,000
36		28	(a)	Crystal P	W 4-2	Scanes 2, Ashton, Shea	20,000
37		29	(a)	Southend U	W 1-0	Shea	1,200
38	Apr	2	(a)	New Brompton	L 0-1		5,000
39		9	(h)	Northampton T	W 1-0	Scanes	10,000
40		16	(a)	Queen's Park R	D 3-3	Shea, Waggott, Curtis	7,000
41		23	(h)	Luton T	L 1-2	Curtis	4,000
42		30	(a)	Swindon T	L 0-5		4,000

P	W	D	L	F	A	W	D	L	F	A	Pts	Pos	Div	Appearances
42	10	7	4	43	23	5	8	8	26	33	45	9th	SL	Goals

FA Cup

1	Jan	15	(h)	Carlisle U	D 1-1	Blackburn	11,000
R		20	(h)	Carlisle U	W 5-0	Blackburn 2, Shea, Webb, Randall	7,000
2	Feb	5	(a)	Wolves	W 5-1	Shea 2, Webb 3	17,000
3		19	(a)	Queen's Park R	D 1-1	Webb	31,000
R		24	(h)	Queen's Park R	L 0-1		18,000

Appearances
Goals

Football appearances and goals grid. Columns are players; the right-hand number is the match number.

Kitchen	Shreeve	Fairman	Whiteman	Piercy	Randall	Ashton	Shea	Haynes	Blackburn	Caldwell	Webb	Dawson	Lavery	Wagstaffe	Bourne	Massey	Geggus	Cannon	Butcher	Woodards	Silor	Scanes	Curtis	Waggott	#
1	2	3	4	5	6	7	8	9	10	11															1
1	2	3	4	5	6	7	8	9	10	11															2
1	2	3	4	5	6	7	8	9	10	11															3
1	2	3	4	5	6	7	8	9	10	11															4
1	2	3	4	5	6	7	8	9	10	11															5
1	2	3	4	5	6	7	8		10	11	9														6
1	2	3	4	5	6	7	8	9	10	11															7
1	2	3	4	5	6	7	8		10	11	9														8
1	2	3	4	5	6	7	8		10	11	9														9
1	2	3	4	5	6	7	8		10	11	9														10
1	2	3	4	5	6	7	8		10	11	9														11
1	2	3	4	5	6	7			10	11	9														12
1	2	3	4	5	6	7		9	10	11	8														13
1	2	3	4	5	6	7	8	9	10	11															14
1	2	3	4	5	6	7	8	9	10	11															15
	2	3	4	5	6	7	8		10	11	9	1													16
1	2	3	4	5	6	7	8	9	10	11															17
1	2	3	4	5	6	7	8		10	11	9														18
1	2	3	4	5	6	7	8		10	11	9														19
1		3	4		6	7	8		10	11	9		2	5											20
1	2		4	5		7	8		10	11	9				3	6									21
1	2		4	5		7	8		10	11	9				3	6									22
1	2	3	4	5	6	7	8	9	10	11															23
	2	3		5	6	7	8		10	11						4	1	9							24
1		3		5	6	7	8		10	11			2			4		9							25
1	2			5	6	7	8		10	11				3		4		9							26
1	2			5	6	7	8	9	10	11				3		4									27
1	2	3	4		6	7	8		10	11	9					5									28
1	2	3		5	6	7	8	9	10	11						4									29
1	2	3		5	6	7		9	10	11						4			8						30
	2	3		5	6	7	8		10	11	1					4	9								31
1	2	3			6	7	8		10	11	9			5		4									32
	2	3			6	7			10		9	5				4	1		8					11	33
1	2	3	4		6	7	8		10		9					5					11				34
1	2	3	4		6	7	8		10		9					5					11				35
1	2	3	4		6	7	8		10	11						5						9			36
1	2	3	4		6	7	8		10							5					11	9			37
1	2	3	4		6	7	8		10							5					11		9		38
1	2	3	4		6	7	8		10	11						5					9				39
1	2	3	4		6	7	8		10							5							9	11	40
	2	3	4		6	7	8		10	11						5	1						9		41
	2	3	6			7		9	10							4	1		8	5				11	42
36	41	37	33	29	39	42	38	15	42	35	18	2	2	3	4	20	4	3	3	2	6	3	3	2	
3		1		1	4	28	5	3	8	7						1	1				3	2	1		

1 own-goal

Cup / replay matches:

Kitchen	Shreeve	Fairman	Whiteman	Piercy	Randall	Ashton	Shea	Haynes	Blackburn	Caldwell	Webb	Dawson	Lavery	Wagstaffe	Bourne	Massey	Geggus	Cannon	Butcher	Woodards	Silor	Scanes	Curtis	Waggott	#
1			4	5	6	7	8		10	11			2	3		9									1
1	2			5	6	7	8		10	11	9	3				4									R
1	2	3		5	6	7	8		10	11	9					4									2
1	2	3	4	5	6	7	8		10	11	9					4									3
5	4	3	2	5	5	5	5		5	5	4	2		1		3		1							R
					1		3		3	5															

1910-11

Manager: Syd King

1	Sep	3	(h)	Southend U	D	3-3	Ashton, Webb, Blackburn	15,000
2		10	(a)	Coventry C	L	0-3		6,000
3		12	(a)	Queen's Park R	W	2-0	Shea 2	7,000
4		17	(h)	New Brompton	W	2-0	Shea, Webb	12,000
5		24	(a)	Millwall	W	2-0	Shea, Blackburn	10,000
6	Oct	1	(h)	Queen's Park R	W	3-0	Shea, Curtis 2	20,000
7		8	(a)	Norwich C	L	0-2		8,000
8		15	(a)	Luton T	D	1-1	Shea	8,000
9		22	(h)	Portsmouth	W	3-1	Shea, Ashton, Kitchen	10,000
10		29	(a)	Northampton T	L	0-2		6,000
11	Nov	5	(h)	Brighton & HA	W	3-1	Shea, Kennedy, Kitchen	14,000
12		12	(a)	Exeter C	D	0-0		6,000
13		19	(h)	Swindon T	W	1-0	Shea	12,000
14		26	(a)	Bristol R	D	1-1	Shea	6,000
15	Dec	3	(h)	Crystal P	D	1-1	Shea	10,000
16		10	(a)	Brentford	L	0-3		5,000
17		17	(h)	Leyton	W	3-0	Shea, Ashton 2	7,000
18		24	(a)	Watford	W	3-1	Shea 2, Piercy	2,000
19		26	(h)	Plymouth A	W	4-0	Shea, Webb 2, Rothwell	14,000
20		27	(a)	Plymouth A	L	0-1		8,000
21		31	(a)	Southend U	W	6-0	Shea 4, Kennedy, Caldwell	3,000
22	Jan	7	(a)	Coventry C	D	1-1	Webb	11,000
23		21	(a)	New Brompton	D	1-1	Ashton	5,000
24		28	(h)	Millwall	D	2-2	Randall, Webb	8,000
25	Feb	11	(h)	Norwich C	W	2-1	Webb, Rothwell	12,000
26		18	(h)	Luton T	W	2-0	Kennedy, Piercy	8,000
27	Mar	4	(h)	Northampton T	L	1-2	Butcher	10,000
28		18	(h)	Exeter C	W	4-1	Webb 3, Shea	8,000
29		25	(a)	Swindon T	L	1-4	Kennedy	6,000
30		29	(a)	Portsmouth	D	0-0		2,000
31	Apr	1	(h)	Bristol R	D	2-2	Shea, Caldwell	5,000
32		8	(a)	Crystal P	L	1-4	Shea	10,000
33		14	(h)	Southampton	W	4-1	Shea, Ashton, Harrison, Caldwell	12,000
34		15	(h)	Brentford	W	2-0	Shea, Butcher	8,000
35		17	(h)	Southampton	W	1-0	Harrison	8,000
36		22	(a)	Leyton	L	0-3		10,000
37		26	(a)	Brighton & HA	L	0-3		4,000
38		29	(h)	Watford	D	1-1	Shea	5,000

P	W	D	L	F	A	W	D	L	F	A	Pts	Pos	Div	Appearances
38	12	6	1	44	17	5	5	9	19	29	45	5th	SL	Goals

FA Cup

1	Jan	14	(h)	Nottingham F	W	2-1	Shea 2	12,000
2	Feb	4	(h)	Preston NE	W	3-0	Webb 3	12,000
3		25	(h)	Manchester U	W	2-1	Shea, Caldwell	27,000
4	Mar	11	(h)	Blackburn R	L	2-3	Butcher 2	20,000

Appearances
Goals

210

Kitchen	Shreeve	Fairman	Massey	Piercy	Randall	Ashton	Shea	Webb	Blackburn	Caldwell	Lavery	Curtis	Bourne	Whiteman	Woodards	Butcher	Kennedy	Geggus	Rothwell	Frost	Miellear	Redwood	Harrison	No.
1	2	3	4	5	6	7	8	9	10	11														
1		3	4	5	6	7	8	9	10	11	2													1
1		3	4	5	6	7	8		10	11	2	9												2
1		3	4	5	6	7	8	9	10	11	2													3
1			4	5	6	7	8	9	10	11	2		3											4
1		3	4	5	6	7	8		10	11	2	9												5
1		3	4	5	6	7	8		10	11	2	9												6
1		3			6	7	8	9	10	11	2			4	5									7
1		3			6	7	8	9	10	11	2			4	5									8
1		3			6	7	8	9		11	2			4	5	10								9
1		3		5	6	7	8		10	11	2			4		9								10
1		3		5	6	7	8		10	11	2			4		9								11
		3		5	6	7	8		10	11	2			4		9	1							12
		3		5	6	7	8			11	2			4		10	9	1						13
1		3		5	6	7	8	9		11	2			4		10								14
		3		5	6	7	8	9		11				4		10		1	2					15
		3	4	5	6	7	8	9		11						10		1	2					16
		3	4	5	6	7	8	9		11						10		1	2					17
1		3	4	5	6	7	8	9		11						10			2					18
1		3	4		6	7	8	9		11				5		10			2					19
1	3				6	7	8			11	2			4	5	10	9							20
1		3		5	6	7	8			11				4		10			2					21
1		3		5	6	7	8	9		11				4		10			2					22
1		3		5	6	7	8	9		11				4		10			2					23
1		3	6	5		7	8	9		11				4		10			2					24
1		3		5	6	7				11				4		10	9		2	8				25
1		3	6				8			11				4	5	10	9		2		7			26
1		3		5	6			9		11				4		10			2	8				27
	3			5	6	7	8			11						10	9		2			4		28
	3			5	6	7	8			11				4		10	9	1	2					29
	3			5		7	8		6	11				4		10	9	1	2					30
	3			5	6	7	8	9		11				4		10		1	2					31
	3			5		7	8		6	11				4		10		1	2				9	32
		3		5	6	7	8			11				4		10		1	2				9	33
		3		5	6	7	8			11				4		10		1	2				9	34
		3		5	6	7	8			11				4		10		1	2				9	35
		3		5	6	7				11				4		10		1	2				9	36
1		3		5	6	7		9	10	11				4					2					37
24	5	33	13	32	34	37	35	19	16	38	15	3	1	27	5	26	10	14	22	2	1	1	5	38
2			2	1	6	25	10	2	3		2			2	4		2		2				2	

Kitchen	Shreeve	Fairman	Massey	Piercy	Randall	Ashton	Shea	Webb	Blackburn	Caldwell	Lavery	Curtis	Bourne	Whiteman	Woodards	Butcher	Kennedy	Geggus	Rothwell	Frost	Miellear	Redwood	Harrison	No.
1		3		5	6	7	8	9		11				4		10			2					1
1		3		5	6	7	8	9		11				4		10			2					2
1		3		5	6	7	8	9		11				4		10			2					3
1		3		5	6	7	8	9		11				4		10			2					4
4		4		4	4	4	4	4		4				4		4			4					
						3	3	1						2										

1911-12

Manager: Syd King

#					Result	Scorers	Att
1	Sep	2	(a)	Crystal P	L 0-1		14,000
2		9	(h)	Southampton	D 2-2	Harrison, Kennedy	8,000
3		16	(a)	Plymouth A	D 0-0		9,000
4		23	(h)	Reading	W 5-0	Rothwell, Webb, Shea, Whiteman, Piercy	10,000
5		30	(a)	Watford	L 0-2		6,000
6	Oct	7	(h)	New Brompton	D 0-0		5,000
7		14	(a)	Exeter C	D 3-3	Shea 2, Webb	8,000
8		21	(h)	Brentford	W 7-4	Shea 3, Kennedy 3, Harrison	10,000
9		28	(a)	Queen's Park R	L 1-4	Webb	16,000
10	Nov	4	(h)	Millwall	W 2-1	Harrison 2	23,000
11		11	(h)	Luton T	W 3-0	Webb, Harrison, Shea	9,000
12		18	(a)	Bristol R	D 1-1	Shea	7,000
13		25	(h)	Swindon T	L 0-2		11,000
14	Dec	2	(a)	Northampton T	L 2-3	Harrison, Morrison	6,000
15		9	(h)	Brighton & HA	W 1-0	Shea	7,000
16		16	(a)	Stoke	L 3-4	Kennedy 2, Randall	8,000
17		23	(h)	Coventry C	L 0-1		7,000
18		25	(h)	Leyton	W 2-0	Ashton, Butcher	17,000
19		30	(h)	Crystal P	L 1-6	Shea	8,000
20	Jan	6	(a)	Southampton	W 2-1	Shea 2	3,000
21		20	(h)	Plymouth A	L 0-2		10,000
22		27	(a)	Reading	L 1-3	Ashton	4,000
23	Feb	10	(a)	New Brompton	W 3-0	Shea 2, Butcher	5,000
24		17	(h)	Exeter C	W 3-2	Shea 2, Harrison	10,000
25	Mar	2	(h)	Queen's Park R	W 3-0	Ashton, Caldwell, Shea	10,000
26		9	(a)	Millwall	L 1-5	Harrison	28,400
27		11	(h)	Watford	L 1-3	Rothwell	4,000
28		16	(a)	Luton T	L 1-2	Harrison	6,000
29		23	(h)	Bristol R	W 6-2	Shea 2, Harrison 2, Dawson, Woodards	4,000
30		27	(a)	Brentford	W 2-1	Harrison, Opp own-goal	4,000
31	Apr	5	(h)	Norwich C	W 4-0	Shea 3, Harrison	10,000
32		6	(h)	Northampton T	L 0-2		10,000
33		8	(a)	Norwich C	D 2-2	Woodards, Shea	12,000
34		9	(a)	Leyton	L 1-3	Shea	3,000
35		13	(a)	Brighton & HA	L 0-2		5,000
36		20	(h)	Stoke	D 0-0		8,000
37		22	(h)	Swindon T	L 1-3	Mackesy	2,000
38		27	(a)	Coventry C	L 0-2		5,000

P	W	D	L	F	A	W	D	L	F	A	Pts	Pos	Div	Appearances
38	10	3	6	40	27	3	3	4	12	24	42	33	13th	SL	Goals

FA Cup

#					Result	Scorers	Att
1	Jan	3	(h)	Gainsborough T	W 2-1	Webb, Harrison	14,400
2	Feb	3	(a)	Middlesbrough	D 1-1	Harrison	12,300
R		8	(h)	Middlesbrough	W 2-1	Harrison, Ashton	10,000
3		24	(h)	Swindon T	D 1-1	Butcher	20,000
R		28	(a)	Swindon T	L 0-4		13,328

Appearances
Goals

212

Appearance & goalscoring grid (shirt numbers). Match number shown in the right-hand column of the original.

Match	Geggus	Rothwell	Fairman	Whiteman	Piercy	Randall	Ashton	Shea	Webb	Harrison	Caldwell	Kennedy	Morrison	Glover	Butcher	Woodards	Blackburn	Hughes	Redwood	Massey	Miellear	Frost	Burrill	Walden	Dawson	Bell	Bradford	Mackesy	Bourne
1	1	2	3	4	5	6	7	8	9	10	11																		
2	1	2	3	4	5	6	7	8		10	11	9																	
3	1	2	3	4	5	6	7	8		10		9	11																
4	1	2		4	5	6	7	8	9				11	3	10														
5	1	2		4	3		7	8	9		11				10	5	6												
6	1			4	5	6	7	8	9		11			3	10				2										
7	1		2	4		6	7	8	9	10			11	3						5									
8	1		2	4		6	7	8		10		9	11	3						5									
9	1	2	3	4		6	7	8	9	10			11							5									
10		2		4		6	7	8	9	10			11	3		5		1											
11		2		4		6	7	8	9	10			11	3		5		1											
12		2		4	5	6	7	8		10		9	11	3				1											
13		2		4	5	6	7	8	9	10			11	3				1											
14		2		4	5	6	7	8	9				11	3	10			1											
15		2		4		6	7	8		10		9	11	3		5		1											
16		2		4		6	7	8		10		9	11	3		5		1											
17		2		4			7	8	9	10			11	3		5	6	1											
18		2		4			7	8	9				11	3	10	5	6	1											
19		2		4			7	8		11			9	3	10		6	1	5										
20		2			5	6	7	8		11			9	3	10			1			4								
21		2			5	6	7	8		11			9	3	10			1			4								
22	1	2						8	9				11	3	10	5	6			4			7						
23	1	2						8		9			11	3	10	5	6			4			7						
24		2					7	8					11	3	10	5	6	1	9	4									
25		2					7	8	9				11	3	10	5	6	1		4									
26		2		4				8	9				11	3	10	5	6	1					7						
27		2		4				8	9				11	3	10	5	6	1					7						
28		2		4			7		9					3	10	5	6	1					8		11				
29		2				6			9					3	10	5	4	1					8	7	11				
30		2		4			7		9					3	10	5	6	1					8		11				
31		2		4			7							3	10	5	6	1					8		11	9			
32		2		4			7		9					3	10	5	6	8							11	1	3		
33	1	2		4			7		9	11	3		8		10	5									11				
34		2	3			6			9						10	5	4	8							11	1			
35		2	3			6			9						10	5	4	8	1						11			7	
36		2	3			6			9						10	5	4	8	1						11			9	10
37	1	2				6			9					3	10	5	4	8							11				
38	1	2				6			9					3	10	5	4	8							11				
App	13	24	20	27	10	23	33	36	11	30	11	11	15	29	16	20	22	25	9	5	2	2	7	2	10	2	1	1	1
Gls		2		1	1	1	3	24	4	13	1	6	1			2	2			1					1				

I own-goal

Cup section:

Match	Rothwell	Fairman	Whiteman	Ashton	Shea	Webb	Harrison	Morrison	Glover	Butcher	Woodards	Blackburn	Hughes	Redwood	Massey	
1	2	4	5	7	8	9	11		3	10		6	1			
2	2	4		7	8	11	9	10	3		5	6	1			
R	2			7	8	9	11	10	3		5	6	1	4		
3	2			7	8	9		11	3	10	5	6	1	4		
R	2			7	8			11	3	10	5	6	1	4	9	
App	5	2	1	5	5	2	4	3	2	5	3	4	5	5	3	1
Gls	1			1	3			1					1			

1912-13

Manager: Syd King

1	Sep	2	(h)	Exeter C	W	4-0	Shea 2, Harrison, Dawson	9,000
2		7	(h)	Coventry C	L	1-2	Ashton	12,000
3		14	(a)	Watford	W	2-0	Shea, Harrison	5,000
4		21	(h)	Merthyr T	D	1-1	Shea	7,000
5		28	(a)	Crystal P	D	1-1	Hilsdon	15,000
6	Oct	5	(h)	Plymouth A	W	3-1	Hilsdon, Dawson, Shea	8,000
7		12	(a)	Southampton	W	3-1	Hilsdon, Shea 2	9,000
8		19	(h)	Reading	L	1-2	Hilsdon	15,000
9		26	(a)	Norwich C	L	0-2		7,000
10		30	(a)	Exeter C	D	0-0		2,000
11	Nov	2	(h)	Gillingham	W	4-0	Hilsdon 2, Denyer 2	10,000
12		9	(a)	Northampton T	L	3-4	Casey, Burrill, Shea	6,000
13		16	(h)	Queen's Park R	W	1-0	Denyer	14,000
14		23	(a)	Brentford	L	1-5	Shea	7,000
15		30	(h)	Millwall	D	1-1	Hilsdon	16,000
16	Dec	7	(a)	Bristol R	L	1-2	Ashton	8,000
17		14	(h)	Swindon T	W	4-1	Denyer 2, Hilsdon 2	14,000
18		21	(a)	Portsmouth	W	2-1	Shea, Ashton	10,000
19		25	(h)	Stoke	W	5-0	Shea 2, Ashton, Denyer, Askew	8,000
20		26	(a)	Stoke	W	1-0	Shea	5,000
21		28	(a)	Coventry C	L	1-4	Shea	7,000
22	Jan	4	(h)	Watford	W	2-0	Harrison, Shea	10,000
23		18	(a)	Merthyr T	L	2-6	Butcher 2	4,000
24		25	(h)	Crystal P	D	1-1	Butcher	14,000
25	Feb	8	(a)	Plymouth A	W	2-0	Woodards, Denyer	8,000
26		15	(h)	Southampton	D	1-1	Harrison	5,000
27	Mar	1	(h)	Norwich C	W	2-1	Hilsdon 2	8,000
28		8	(a)	Gillingham	D	2-2	Casey 2	5,000
29		15	(a)	Northampton T	D	0-0		9,000
30		21	(h)	Brighton & HA	D	1-1	Puddefoot	15,000
31		22	(a)	Queen's Park R	W	1-0	Denyer	10,000
32		24	(a)	Brighton & HA	D	0-0		11,000
33		29	(h)	Brentford	W	2-1	Denyer, Hilsdon	7,000
34	Apr	5	(a)	Millwall	W	3-1	Bailey, Ashton, Randall	24,000
35		12	(h)	Bristol R	W	3-1	Randall, Askew, Hilsdon	8,000
36		19	(a)	Swindon T	D	1-1	Denyer	9,000
37		23	(a)	Reading	D	1-1	Denyer	2,000
38		26	(h)	Portsmouth	W	2-1	Ashton, Bailey	8,000

P	W	D	L	F	A	W	D	L	F	A	Pts	Pos	Div	
38	11	6	2	39	15	7	6	6	27	31	48	3rd	SL	Appearances
														Goals

FA Cup

1	Jan	13	(a)	West Brom A	D	1-1	Harrison	20,000
R		16	(h)	West Brom A	D	2-2	Hilsdon 2	15,000
2R		22	(n*)	West Brom A	W	3-0	Hilsdon 2, Denyer	27,075
2	Feb	1	(a)	Aston Villa	L	0-5		50,000

* Played at Stamford Bridge.

Appearances
Goals

214

Player appearance / line-up grid (shirt numbers by match).

No.	Hughes	Irvine	Forster	Woodards	Askew	Randall	Ashton	Shea	Denyer	Harrison	Dawson	Hilsdon	Rothwell	Burton	Whiteman	Burrill	Casey	Blackburn	Caton	Butcher	Mackesy	Carter	Bailey	Puddefoot
	1	2	3	4	5	6	7	8	9	10	11													
1	1	2	3	4	5	6	7	8	9	10	11													
2	1	2	3	4	5	6	7	8		10	11	9												
3	1	2	3	4	5	6	7	8		10	11	9												
4	1		3	4	5	6	7	8	9	11	10		2											
5	1			4	5	6	7	8	9	11	10		2	3										
6	1			4	5	6	7	8	9	11	10		2	3										
7	1	2	3	4	5	6	7	8	9	11	10													
8	1		3	4	5	6	7	8	9	11	10		2											
9	1		3		5	6	7	8	9	11			2		4	10								
10	1		3		5	6	7	8	9		10		2		4		11							
11	1		3		5	6	7	8	9				2		4	10	11							
12	1		3		5	6	7	8	9	11	10		2		4									
13	1		3		5	6	7	8	9	11	10		2		4									
14	1		3	4	5	6	7	8	9		10		2				11							
15	1		3	4		6	7	8	10	9			2	5			11							
16	1		3	4	5	6	7	8	9		10		2				11							
17	1		3	4	5	6	7	8	9		10		2				11							
18	1		3	4	5	6	7	8	9		10		2				11							
19	1		3	4	5	6	7	8	9		10		2				11							
20	1		3	4	5		7	8	9		10		2				11		6					
21	1		3	4	5	6	7	8	10	9			2				11							
22	1		3						9	5		11	2		4		6	7	8	10				
23	1		3	4		6	7		9	5		10	2				11		8					
24			3	4		6			9	5		10	2				11	7	8		1			
25			3	4		6	7		9	5		10	2				11	7	8	1				
26	1		3	4		6	7	8		5		10	2				11							9
27	1		3	4		6	7	8		5		10	2				11							9
28	1		3	4			7			5		10	2				11	6					8	9
29	1		3	4	5	6	7					10	2				11						8	9
30	1		3	4	5	6	7		9			10	2				11						8	
31			3		5	6	7		9			10	2		4		11					1	8	
32			3	4	5	6	7		9			10	2				11					1	8	
33			3	4	5	6	7		9			10	2				11					1	8	
34			3	4	5	6	7		9			10	2				11					1	8	
35			3	4	5	6	7		9			10	2				11					1	8	
36			3	4	5	6	7		9			10	2				11					1	8	
37			3	4	5	6	7		9			10	2				11					1	8	
38			3	4	5	6	7		9			10	2				11					1	8	
Apps	29	16	25	29	30	35	36	22	29	19	12	32	32	5	8	2	24	2	3	4	1	9	10	4
Goals		1	2	2	6	15	11	4	2	13							1	3		3		2	1	

Cup matches:

No.	Hughes	Irvine	Forster	Woodards	Askew	Randall	Ashton	Shea	Denyer	Harrison	Dawson	Hilsdon	Rothwell	Burton	Whiteman	Burrill	Casey	Blackburn	Caton	Butcher	Mackesy	Carter	Bailey	Puddefoot
1	1		3	4	5	6	7	8	9			10	2				11							
R	1		3	4	5	6	7		9	8		10	2				11							
2R	1		3	4		6	7		9	5		10	2				11			8				
2	1		3	4		6	7		9	5		10	2				11			8				
Apps	4		4	4	2	4	4		4	4		4	4				4			2				
Goals						1	1		4															

1913-14

Manager: Syd King

1	Sep	1	(a)	Millwall	D	1-1	Hilsdon	12,000
2		6	(h)	Swindon T	L	2-3	Leafe 2	25,000
3		13	(a)	Bristol R	W	2-1	Denyer, Leafe	10,000
4		20	(h)	Merthyr T	W	3-1	Leafe, Casey, Ashton	15,000
5		27	(a)	Queen's Park R	D	2-2	Leafe, Denyer	12,000
6	Oct	4	(a)	Plymouth A	L	0-3		10,000
7		11	(h)	Southampton	W	5-1	Burton, Hilsdon 2, Casey, Ashton	6,000
8		18	(a)	Reading	L	0-2		8,000
9		25	(h)	Crystal P	L	1-2	Casey	13,000
10	Nov	1	(a)	Coventry C	W	4-2	Leafe 3, Denyer	7,000
11		8	(h)	Watford	D	1-1	Denyer	10,000
12		15	(a)	Norwich C	L	0-1		7,000
13		22	(h)	Gillingham	W	3-1	Burrill, Puddefoot, Leafe	10,000
14		29	(a)	Northampton T	D	0-0		5,000
15	Dec	6	(h)	Southend U	L	0-1		10,000
16		13	(a)	Brighton & HA	W	1-0	Leafe	6,000
17		20	(h)	Portsmouth	W	3-2	Puddefoot, Leafe, Denyer	9,000
18		25	(h)	Exeter C	D	1-1	Puddefoot	18,000
19		26	(a)	Exeter C	D	1-1	Leafe	7,000
20		27	(a)	Swindon T	L	1-4	Puddefoot	8,000
21	Jan	3	(h)	Bristol R	W	6-1	Puddefoot 3, Bailey, Casey, Leafe	14,000
22		17	(a)	Merthyr T	W	2-1	Puddefoot, Casey	6,000
23		24	(h)	Queen's Park R	W	4-1	Leafe, Bailey, Casey 2	11,000
24	Feb	7	(h)	Plymouth A	W	2-1	Puddefoot, Leafe	8,000
25		14	(a)	Southampton	W	3-2	Burton, Bailey, Leafe	7,000
26		28	(a)	Crystal P	W	2-1	Bailey, Ashton	12,000
27	Mar	7	(h)	Coventry C	W	1-0	Leafe	14,000
28		21	(h)	Norwich C	D	1-1	Leafe	6,000
29		23	(h)	Reading	D	0-0		5,000
30		28	(a)	Gillingham	L	1-3	Randall	7,000
31	Apr	1	(a)	Watford	L	0-6		4,000
32		4	(h)	Northampton T	D	1-1	Leafe	10,000
33		10	(a)	Cardiff C	L	0-2		12,000
34		11	(a)	Southend U	D	1-1	Bailey	7,000
35		13	(h)	Cardiff C	D	1-1	Leafe	15,000
36		14	(h)	Millwall	W	3-2	Hilsdon 2, Stallard	15,000
37		18	(h)	Brighton & HA	D	1-1	Hilsdon	10,000
38		25	(a)	Portsmouth	L	1-5	Bailey	8,000

P	W	D	L	F	A	W	D	L	F	A	Pts	Pos	Div	Appearances
38	9	7	3	39	22	6	5	8	22	38	42	6th	SL	Goals

FA Cup

1	Jan	10	(h)	Chesterfield	W	8-1	Puddefoot 5, Bailey, Leafe, Ashton	16,000
2		31	(h)	Crystal P	W	2-0	Bailey 2	18,000
3	Feb	21	(h)	Liverpool	D	1-1	Puddefoot	16,000
R		25	(a)	Liverpool	L	1-5	Puddefoot	45,000

Appearances
Goals

216

Player appearance and goalscoring grid.

Hughes	Rothwell	Forster	Woodards	Askew	Randall	Ashton	Bailey	Denyer A	Hilsdon	Casey	Leafe	Brandon	Whiteman	Burton	Lonsdale	Caton	Burrill	Carter	Puddefoot	Irvine	Butcher	Goddard	Tirrell	Denyer F	Beal	Tresardern	Stallard	Bourne	Mackesy	#
1	2	3	4	5	6	7	8	9	10	11																				1
1	2	3	4	5	6	7	8		10	11	9																			1
1		3	4	5	6	7		8	10	11	9	2																		2
1		3	4	5	6	7		8	10	11	9	2																		3
1		3	4	5	6	7		8	10	11	9	2																		4
1		3	4	5	6	7		8	10	11	9	2																		5
1	2	3		5		7		10	8	11	9		4	6																6
1	2	3		5	6	7		10	8	11	9		4																	7
	2	3	4	5	6	7		10	8	11	9				1															8
		3	4	5	6			9		11	10	2			1	7	8													9
1		3	4	5	6			9		11	10	2				7	8													10
1		3	4	5	6	7			9	11	10	2					8													11
		3	4	5	6	7				11	10	2				1	8		9											12
		3	4	5	6	7				11	10	2					8	1	9											13
			4	5	6	11		7	8		10	2			1				9	3										14
			4	5	6	11		7	8		10	2			1				9	3										15
			4	5	6	7	8			11		2			1				9	3	10									16
			4	5	6	7		10	11	8		2			1				9	3										17
			4	5		7	8			11	10	2	6	1					9	3										18
			4	5		7	8			11	10	2	6	1					9			3								19
1	3		4	5		7	8			11	10	2	6						9											20
1	3		4	5			8			11	10	2	6	7					9											21
1	3		4	5		7		8		11	10	2	6						9											22
1	3		4	5		7	8			11	10	2	6						9											23
			4	5	6	7	8				10	2			1				9							3			11	24
			4	5	6	7		8			10	2			1				9							3			11	25
			4	5	6	7	8				10	2			1											3			11	26
			4	5	6	7	10	9				2			1											3	11			27
			4	5	6	7	9			11	10	2			1						8					3	11			28
			4	5	11	7		10				2			1						8				6	3				29
1			4	5	6	7		9	11	10	2			1									2	8	6					30
			5	6	7	8	9			11	10		4	3	1									2						31
			5	6	7	8	9			11	10		2	3	1								4							32
			5	6	7	8				11	10	2	4	3	1				9											33
			5		7	8	10	11				2	4	3	1										6	9				34
			5		7	8	10	11				2	4	3	1										6	9				35
			5		7	8				11	10	2	4	3					9						1	6				36
15	10	15	30	38	28	35	19	17	17	24	33	31	7	19	21	3	8	1	16	5	4	1	1	2	1	4	2	1	3	38
			1	3	6	5	6	7		20		2			1				9			1								

Cup matches:

Hughes	Rothwell	Forster	Woodards	Askew	Randall	Ashton	Bailey	Denyer A	Hilsdon	Casey	Leafe	Brandon	Whiteman	Burton	Lonsdale	Caton	Burrill	Carter	Puddefoot	Irvine	Butcher	Goddard	Tirrell	Denyer F	Beal	Tresardern	Stallard	Bourne	Mackesy	#
1	2		4	5	6	7	8			11	10				3				9											1
1	3		4	5		7	8			11	10	2			6				9											2
1			4	5	6	7	8			11	10	2			3				9											3
1	3		4	5	11	7	8				10	2			6				9											R
4	3		4	4	3	4	4			3	4	3			4				4											
			1	3						1									7											

217

1914-15

Manager: Syd King

								Att
1	Sep	1	(h)	Gillingham	W	2-1	Puddefoot 2	5,000
2		5	(a)	Exeter C	L	1-3	Puddefoot	4,000
3		9	(a)	Gillingham	L	0-4		2,000
4		12	(h)	Luton T	W	3-0	Puddefoot 2, Hilsdon	5,000
5		19	(a)	Portsmouth	L	1-3	Hilsdon	7,000
6		26	(h)	Swindon T	D	1-1	Puddefoot	11,000
7	Oct	3	(a)	Southend U	W	1-0	Leafe	5,000
8		10	(h)	Queen's Park R	D	2-2	Puddefoot, Leafe	12,000
9		17	(a)	Millwall	L	1-2	Puddefoot	15,000
10		24	(h)	Bristol R	W	4-1	Bailey, Leafe, Wright, Burton	10,000
11		31	(a)	Croydon Com	W	2-1	Bailey, Leafe	5,000
12	Nov	7	(h)	Reading	W	3-2	Bailey, Leafe, Puddefoot	10,000
13		14	(a)	Southampton	L	1-3	Leafe	5,000
14		21	(h)	Northampton T	W	1-0	Leafe	8,000
15		28	(a)	Watford	W	1-0	Bailey	2,000
16	Dec	5	(h)	Plymouth A	W	2-0	Butcher, Carr	6,000
17		12	(h)	Crystal P	L	1-2	Mackesy	5,000
18		19	(a)	Norwich C	D	0-0		4,000
19		25	(a)	Brighton & HA	D	0-0		1,000
20		26	(h)	Brighton & HA	W	2-1	Puddefoot 2	9,600
21	Jan	2	(h)	Exeter C	W	4-1	Puddefoot 3, Fenwick	7,000
22		23	(h)	Portsmouth	W	4-3	Leafe 2, Burton, Casey	3,000
23		30	(a)	Swindon T	D	1-1	Casey	3,000
24	Feb	6	(h)	Southend U	W	3-1	Puddefoot 2, Leafe	5,000
25		13	(a)	Queen's Park R	D	1-1	Whiteman	5,000
26		20	(h)	Millwall	D	1-1	Puddefoot	17,000
27		27	(a)	Bristol R	L	0-1		3,000
28	Mar	6	(h)	Croydon Com	W	1-0	Hilsdon	5,000
29		10	(a)	Luton T	W	2-1	Leafe, Bailey	7,000
30		13	(a)	Reading	L	1-3	Leafe	7,000
31		20	(h)	Southampton	W	3-0	Leafe, Hilsdon, Stallard	8,000
32		27	(a)	Northampton T	D	1-1	Stallard	1,500
33	Apr	2	(h)	Cardiff C	W	2-1	Stallard 2	13,000
34		3	(h)	Watford	W	2-0	Puddefoot, Hilsdon	10,000
35		5	(a)	Cardiff C	L	1-2	Stallard	10,000
36		10	(a)	Plymouth A	L	0-1		5,000
37		17	(a)	Crystal P	L	1-2	Stallard	4,000
38		24	(h)	Norwich C	D	1-1	Stallard	3,000

P	W	D	L	F	A	W	D	L	F	A	Pts	Pos	Div	
38	14	4	1	42	18	4	5	10	16	29	45	4th	SL	Appearances
														Goals

FA Cup

1	Jan	9	(h)	Newcastle U	D	2-2	Leafe 2	15,000
R		16	(a)	Newcastle U	L	2-3	Casey, Leafe	28,130
								Appearances
								Goals

218

Player appearance grid (shirt numbers by match). Columns left-to-right: Webster, Cope, Speak, Fenwick, Askew, Randall, Ashton, Bailey, Puddefoot, Leafe, Wright, Woodards, Burton, Whiteman, Hilsdon, Brandon, Tresadern, Tirrell, Caton, Mackesy, Carr, Stallard, Casey, Hughes, Butcher.

#	Web	Cop	Spe	Fen	Ask	Ran	Ash	Bai	Pud	Lea	Wri	Woo	Bur	Whi	Hil	Bra	Tre	Tir	Cat	Mac	Car	Sta	Cas	Hug	But
1	1	2	3	4	5	6	7	8	9	10	11														
2	1	2	3	4	5	6	7	8	9	10	11														
3	1	2	3		5		7	8	9	10	11		4	6											
4	1	2	3	6	5		7	8	9		11		4	10											
5	1		3	6	5		7	8	9		11		4	10	2										
6	1	2		6	5		7	8	9				3	4	10				11						
7	1	2		6	5		7	8	9	10			3	4					11						
8	1	2		6	5		7	8	9	10			3	4					11						
9	1	2			5		7		9	10			3	4	8	6			11						
10	1			6	5			8	9	10			2	4			3	7				11			
11	1			6	5		7	8	9	10			2	4			3					11			
12	1			6	5		7	8	9	10			2	4			3					11			
13	1				5	6	7		9	10			2	4			3					11		8	
14	1				5	6	7		9				2	4			3		10	11				8	
15	1				5	6		7	9				2	4			3		10	11				8	
16	1		3		5	6		7	9				2	4					10	11				8	
17	1	3		10	5				9		7	6	2	4								11		8	
18		3		10	5				9		7	6	2	4								11	1		8
19		3		6	5				9		7		2	4	10							11	1		8
20		3		10	5				9		7	6	2	4	8							11	1		
21		3		8	5				9		7	6	2	4	10							11	1		
22		3			5				9			6	2	4	10	2					7	11	1		8
23		3			5				9	7			2	4	10							11	1		8
24		3			5				9	8			6	2	4	10				7		11	1		
25		3			5				9	8			6	2	4	10				7		11	1		
26		3			5				9	8			6	2	4	10				7		11	1		
27		3			5				8	7			6	2	4	10					9	11	1		
28		3			5					10	8	7	6	2	4						9	11	1		
29		3	6		5					10	8	7		2	4						9	11	1		
30		2	3		5					8	7		6		4	10					9	11	1		
31		2	3		5					8	7		6		4	10					9	11	1		
32		2	3		5					8	7	11	6		4	10					9		1		
33		2	3		5					8	7	11	6	4		10					9		1		
34		2	3		5					8	7	11	6		4	10					9		1		
35		2	3		5					8	7	10	6		4						9	11	1		
36		2	3		5					8	7		6		4	10					9	11	1		
37		2	3		5					8			6	11	4	10					9		1		
38		2	3		5		7	8					6		4	10					9		1		
Tot	17	31	13	19	36	5	14	20	35	30	10	20	26	34	20	2	2	6	8	5	5	11	19	21	9
		1						5	18	13	1			2	1	5					1	1	7	2	1

Cup block (rows labelled I / R):

Web	Cop	Spe	Fen	Ask	Ran	Ash	Bai	Pud	Lea	Wri	Woo	Bur	Whi	Hil	Bra	Tre	Tir	Cat	Mac	Car	Sta	Cas	Hug	But	
	3		10	5				9	7			6	2	4	8						11	1			I
	3		10	5		7		9	8			6	2	4							11	1			R
	2		2	2		1		2	2			2	2	2	1						2	2			
				3																		1			

219

West Ham in the Football League
1919-20 to 1992-93

		HOME					AWAY						
	P	W	D	L	F	A	W	D	L	F	A	Pts	Pos

DIVISION TWO

	P	W	D	L	F	A	W	D	L	F	A	Pts	Pos
1919-20	42	14	3	4	34	14	5	6	10	13	26	47	7th
1920-21	42	13	5	3	38	11	6	5	10	13	19	48	5th
1921-22	42	15	3	3	39	13	5	5	11	13	26	48	4th
1922-23	42	9	8	4	21	11	11	3	7	42	27	51	2nd

DIVISION ONE

	P	W	D	L	F	A	W	D	L	F	A	Pts	Pos
1923-24	42	10	6	5	26	17	3	9	9	14	26	41	13th
1924-25	42	12	7	2	37	12	3	5	13	25	48	42	13th
1925-26	42	14	2	5	45	27	1	5	15	18	49	37	18th
1926-27	42	9	6	6	50	36	10	2	9	36	34	46	6th
1927-28	42	9	7	5	48	34	5	4	12	33	54	39	17th
1928-29	42	11	6	4	55	31	4	3	14	31	65	39	17th
1929-30	42	14	2	5	51	26	5	3	13	35	53	43	7th
1930-31	42	11	3	7	56	44	3	5	13	23	50	36	18th
1931-32	42	9	5	7	35	37	3	2	16	27	70	31	22nd

DIVISION TWO

	P	W	D	L	F	A	W	D	L	F	A	Pts	Pos
1932-33	42	12	6	3	56	31	1	3	17	19	62	35	20th
1933-34	42	13	3	5	51	28	4	8	9	27	42	45	7th
1934-35	42	18	1	2	46	17	8	3	10	34	46	56	3rd
1935-36	42	13	5	3	51	23	9	3	9	39	45	52	4th
1936-37	42	14	5	2	47	18	5	6	10	26	37	49	6th
1937-38	42	13	5	3	34	16	1	9	11	19	36	42	9th
1938-39	42	10	5	6	36	21	7	5	9	34	31	44	11th
1946-47	42	12	4	5	46	31	4	4	13	24	45	40	12th
1947-48	42	10	7	4	29	19	6	7	8	26	34	46	6th
1948-49	42	13	5	3	38	23	5	5	11	18	35	46	7th
1949-50	42	8	7	6	30	25	4	5	12	23	36	36	19th
1950-51	42	10	5	6	44	33	6	5	10	24	36	42	13th
1951-52	42	13	5	3	48	29	2	6	13	19	48	41	12th
1952-53	42	9	5	7	38	28	4	8	9	20	32	39	14th
1953-54	42	11	6	4	44	20	4	3	14	23	49	39	13th
1954-55	42	12	4	5	46	28	6	6	9	28	42	46	8th
1955-56	42	12	4	5	52	27	2	7	12	22	42	39	16th
1956-57	42	12	4	5	31	24	7	4	10	28	39	46	8th
1957-58	42	12	8	1	56	25	11	3	7	45	29	57	1st

DIVISION ONE

	P	W	D	L	F	A	W	D	L	F	A	Pts	Pos
1958-59	42	15	3	3	59	29	6	3	12	26	41	48	6th
1959-60	42	12	3	6	47	33	4	3	14	28	58	38	14th
1960-61	42	12	4	5	53	31	1	6	14	24	57	36	16th

220

		HOME					AWAY						
	P	W	D	L	F	A	W	D	L	F	A	Pts	Pos
1961-62	42	11	6	4	49	37	6	4	11	27	45	44	8th
1962-63	42	8	6	7	39	34	6	6	9	34	35	40	12th
1963-64	42	8	7	6	45	38	6	5	10	24	36	40	14th
1964-65	42	14	2	5	48	25	5	2	14	34	46	42	9th
1965-66	42	12	5	4	46	33	3	4	14	24	50	39	12th
1966-67	42	8	6	7	40	31	6	2	13	40	53	36	16th
1967-68	42	8	5	8	43	30	6	5	10	30	39	38	12th
1968-69	42	10	8	3	47	22	3	10	8	19	28	44	8th
1969-70	42	8	8	5	28	21	4	4	13	23	39	36	17th
1970-71	42	6	8	7	28	30	4	6	11	19	30	34	20th
1971-72	42	10	6	5	31	19	2	6	13	16	32	36	14th
1972-73	42	12	5	4	45	25	5	7	9	22	28	46	6th
1973-74	42	7	7	7	36	32	4	8	9	19	28	37	18th
1974-75	42	10	6	5	38	22	3	7	11	20	37	39	13th
1975-76	42	10	5	6	26	23	3	5	13	22	48	36	18th
1976-77	42	9	6	6	28	23	2	8	11	18	42	36	17th
1977-78	42	8	6	7	31	28	4	2	15	21	41	32	20th
				DIVISION TWO									
1978-79	42	12	7	2	46	15	6	7	8	24	24	50	5th
1979-80	42	13	2	6	37	21	7	5	9	17	22	47	7th
1980-81	42	19	1	1	53	12	9	9	3	26	17	66	1st
				DIVISION ONE									
1981-82	42	9	10	2	42	29	5	6	10	24	28	58*	9th
1982-83	42	13	3	5	41	23	7	1	13	27	39	64	8th
1983-84	42	10	4	7	39	24	7	5	9	21	31	60	9th
1984-85	42	7	8	6	27	23	6	4	11	24	45	51	16th
1985-86	42	17	2	2	48	16	9	4	8	26	24	84	3rd
1986-87	42	10	4	7	33	28	4	6	11	19	39	52	15th
1987-88	40	6	9	5	23	21	3	6	11	17	31	42	16th
1988-89	38	3	6	10	19	30	7	2	10	18	32	38	19th
				DIVISION TWO									
1989-90	46	14	5	4	50	22	6	7	10	30	35	72	7th
1990-91	46	15	6	2	41	18	9	9	5	19	16	87	2nd
				DIVISION ONE									
1991-92	42	6	6	9	22	24	3	5	13	15	35	38	22nd
1992-93†	46	16	5	2	50	17	10	5	8	31	24	88	2nd

	P	W	D	L	F	A
Home	1410	745	347	318	2736	1668
Away	1410	341	341	728	1649	2568
Total	2820	1086	688	1046	4385	4236

*This season three points were awarded for a win.
†Formerly Division Two before the advent of the FA Premier League.

1919-20

Manager: Syd King

1	Aug	30	(h)	Lincoln C	D	1-1	Moyes	20,000
2	Sep	1	(a)	Barnsley	L	0-7		6,000
3		6	(a)	Lincoln C	W	4-1	Puddefoot 2, Burton, Butcher	6,000
4		8	(h)	Barnsley	L	0-2		14,000
5		13	(a)	Rotherham C	W	1-0	Puddefoot	6,000
6		20	(h)	Rotherham C	W	2-1	Butcher, Puddefoot	20,000
7		27	(a)	Stoke	L	1-2	Puddefoot	12,000
8	Oct	4	(h)	Stoke	D	1-1	Puddefoot	23,000
9		11	(a)	Grimsby T	W	1-0	Turner	6,000
10		18	(h)	Grimsby T	W	1-0	Palmer	20,000
11		25	(a)	Birmingham	W	1-0	Kay	25,000
12	Nov	1	(h)	Birmingham	L	1-2	Allen R	20,000
13		8	(a)	Leicester C	D	0-0		14,000
14		15	(h)	Leicester C	W	1-0	Burton	23,000
15		22	(a)	Fulham	W	2-1	Puddefoot 2	20,000
16		29	(h)	Fulham	L	0-1		20,000
17	Dec	6	(a)	Coventry C	D	0-0		15,000
18		13	(h)	Coventry C	W	2-0	Bailey, Butcher	15,000
19		20	(a)	Huddersfield T	L	0-2		6,000
20		25	(h)	Bristol C	W	2-0	Bailey, Butcher	20,000
21		26	(a)	Bristol C	D	0-0		12,000
22		27	(h)	Huddersfield T	D	1-1	Butcher	25,000
23	Jan	3	(a)	Blackpool	D	0-0		7,000
24		17	(h)	Blackpool	W	1-0	Bailey	26,000
25		24	(h)	Bury	W	1-0	Kay	20,000
26	Feb	7	(h)	Port Vale	W	3-1	Puddefoot 3	23,000
27		11	(a)	Bury	L	0-1		5,000
28		14	(a)	Port Vale	L	0-1		15,000
29		28	(a)	Clapton O	L	0-1		25,000
30	Mar	4	(h)	Clapton O	L	0-1		15,000
31		13	(h)	Tottenham H	W	2-1	Puddefoot 2	30,000
32		20	(a)	South Shields	L	0-3		18,000
33		22	(a)	Tottenham H	L	0-2		25,000
34		27	(h)	South Shields	W	1-0	Bailey	18,000
35	Apr	2	(h)	Nottingham F	W	5-1	Puddefoot 4, Bailey	20,000
36		3	(a)	Wolves	D	1-1	Bailey	15,000
37		5	(a)	Nottingham F	L	1-2	Bailey	10,000
38		10	(h)	Wolves	W	4-0	Butcher 2, Puddefoot 2	16,000
39		17	(a)	Hull C	D	1-1	Bailey	8,000
40		24	(h)	Hull C	W	2-1	Bailey, Puddefoot	18,000
41		26	(a)	Stockport C	L	0-1		5,000
42	May	1	(h)	Stockport C	W	3-0	Butcher, Kay, Puddefoot	15,000

P	W	D	L	F	A	W	D	L	F	A	Pts	Pos	Div	Appearances
42	14	3	4	34	14	5	6	10	13	26	47	7th	2	Goals

FA Cup

1	Jan	10	(a)	Southampton	D	0-0		12,000
R		15	(h)	Southampton	W	3-1	Puddefoot 2, Butcher	25,000
2		31	(h)	Bury	W	6-0	Puddefoot 3, Bailey, Butcher, S.Smith	27,000
3	Feb	21	(a)	Tottenham H	L	0-3		47,646

Appearances
Goals

222

Appearances and goalscorers grid (shirt numbers by player and match).

#	Hutton	Cope	Lee	Lane	Fenwick	McCrae	Smith D	Moyes	Puddefoot	Morris	Bradshaw	Tirrell	Leafe	Biggin	Green	Johnson	Burton	Tresadern	Butcher	Murray	Palmer	Kay	Turner	Phipps	Woodburn	Allen P	Allen R	Bailey	Carter	Smith S	Webster	Cumming	Mackesy	Smithurst	Woodards	Birchenough	Roberts	Stanley	Young
	1	2	3	4	5	6	7	8	9	10	11																												
1	1	2		4	5	6			9	10		3	7	8	11																								
2	1	2				3			9				7			4	5	6	8	10	11																		
3	1	2				3			9				7			4		6	8	10	11	5																	
4	1	2	3				11		9				7		10		4	6	8			5																	
5	1	2					3	8	9		11		7		10		4	6				5																	
6	1	3	4						9		11		7		10			6				5	2	8															
7	1	3				6			9		11		7				4		8		10	5	2																
8	1	3				6			9		11		7				4		8		10	5	2																
9	1	2		4					9		11		7				3	6	8		10	5																	
10	1	2		4		6			9		11		7				3		8		10	5																	
11	1	2				6			9		11		7				3		8		10	5				4													
12	1	2		4		6			9		11		7				3		8		10	5																	
13	1	2				6			9		11		7				3	4			10	5						8											
14	1	2				6			9								3	4	8		10	5		7					11										
15	1	2				6			9								3	4	10			5						8	7	11									
16	1	2	3			6			9									4	10			5						8	7	11									
17	1	2	3			6			9									4	10			5						8	7	11									
18	1		3			6			9								2	4	10			5						8	7	11									
19	1	2				6			9		11						3	4	10			5						8	7										
20	1	2				6			9								3	4	10			5						8	7	11									
21		2				6			9								3	4	10			5						8	7	11	1								
22	1	2				6			9								3	4			10	5			8				7	10									
23	1	2				6			9								3	4	10			5						8	7	11									
24	1	2				6			9								3	4	10			5						8	7	11									
25		2				6			9								3	4	10			5						8	7	11	1								
26	1		2			6			9	10							3	4				5		7				8		11									
27	1	2				6			9		11						3	4	8			5						9	7	10									
28	1	2	9			6							7				3	4	10			5						8		11									
29	1	2				6			9								3	4	8		10							11											
30	1		2			6			9								3	4						10		5		8	11	7									
31	1		2						9								3	4								5		8		11		10	6	7					
32	1		2	3					9									4								5		8		11		10	6	7					
33	1		2						9									4	10									8		11			7	6	5				
34	1		2						9								3	4	10									8		11			7	6	5				
35	1		2		6				9								3	4	10									8		11			7	6	5				
36			2			6			9						10		3	4										8		11			7		5				
37	1		2			6			9								3	4										8		11			7		5	1			
38	1		2			6			9				7				3	4	10									8		11					5				
39	1		2			6			9								3	4	10									8		11					5				
40		2				6			9									4	10									8		11			7		5		1	3	
41	1		2			6			9								3	4	10										8				7		5				11
42	1		2			6			9								3	4	10			5						8		7									11
Tot	38	29	17	9	2	35	1	2	39	3	13	1	15	2	3	2	34	35	33	2	12	27	3	1	4	4	1	27	13	23	2	10	5	2	9	1	1	1	1
Gls							1		21						2				8		1	3	1						1	9									

Cup ties / replays:

#	Hutton	Cope	Lee	Lane	Fenwick	McCrae	Smith D	Moyes	Puddefoot	Morris	Bradshaw	Tirrell	Leafe	Biggin	Green	Johnson	Burton	Tresadern	Butcher	Murray	Palmer	Kay	Turner	Phipps	Woodburn	Allen P	Allen R	Bailey	Carter	Smith S	Webster	Cumming	Mackesy	Smithurst	Woodards	Birchenough	Roberts	Stanley	Young
1	1	2				6			9								3	4	10			5							8										7 11
R	1	2				6			9								3	4	10			5						8	7	11									
2	1	2				6			9								3	4	10			5						8	7	11									
3	1	2				6			9		11						3	4	8			5						7		10									
Tot	4	4				4			4		1						4	4	4			4			1			3	3	4									
	5																		2													1	1						

1920-21

Manager: Syd King

No	Month	Date	H/A	Opponent	Result	Scorers	Attendance
1	Aug	28	(h)	Hull C	D 1-1	Puddefoot	28,000
2		30	(a)	Wolves	W 2-1	Puddefoot 2	30,000
3	Sep	4	(a)	Hull C	L 1-2	Simmons	12,000
4		6	(h)	Wolves	W 1-0	Puddefoot	15,000
5		11	(a)	Fulham	D 0-0		30,000
6		18	(h)	Fulham	W 2-0	Kay, Puddefoot	20,000
7		25	(a)	Cardiff C	D 0-0		30,000
8	Oct	2	(h)	Cardiff C	D 1-1	Shea	25,000
9		4	(a)	Coventry C	W 1-0	Watson	6,000
10		9	(a)	Leicester C	L 0-1		17,000
11		16	(h)	Leicester C	L 0-1		25,000
12		23	(a)	Blackpool	L 0-1		9,000
13		30	(h)	Blackpool	D 1-1	Puddefoot	25,000
14	Nov	6	(a)	Sheffield W	W 1-0	Puddefoot	30,000
15		13	(h)	Sheffield W	W 4-0	Puddefoot 4	22,000
16		20	(a)	Stockport C	L 0-2		9,000
17		27	(h)	Stockport C	W 5-0	Leafe 3, Puddefoot 2	20,000
18	Dec	4	(a)	Stoke	L 0-1		10,000
19		11	(h)	Stoke	W 1-0	Puddefoot	20,000
20		25	(h)	Birmingham	D 1-1	Bishop	37,000
21		27	(a)	Birmingham	L 1-2	Puddefoot	60,000
22	Jan	1	(h)	Coventry C	W 7-0	Puddefoot 4, Leafe 2, Bishop	8,000
23		15	(a)	Clapton O	W 1-0	Bishop	20,000
24		22	(h)	Clapton O	W 1-0	James	27,864
25		29	(a)	Leeds U	W 2-1	Carter, Puddefoot	15,000
26	Feb	5	(h)	Leeds U	W 3-0	Puddefoot 3	23,000
27		12	(a)	Bury	L 0-1		10,000
28		19	(h)	Bury	L 0-1		20,000
29		26	(a)	Bristol C	L 0-1		20,000
30	Mar	5	(h)	Bristol C	W 1-0	Puddefoot	25,000
31		12	(a)	Barnsley	D 1-1	Puddefoot	18,000
32		19	(a)	Barnsley	W 2-1	James, Opp own-goal	20,000
33		25	(h)	Notts C	L 0-2		25,000
34		26	(h)	Nottingham F	W 3-0	Puddefoot 2, Leafe	24,000
35		28	(h)	Notts C	D 1-1	Puddefoot	22,000
36	Apr	2	(a)	Nottingham F	L 0-1		8,000
37		9	(h)	Rotherham C	W 1-0	Leafe	20,000
38		16	(a)	Rotherham C	L 0-2		7,000
39		23	(h)	Port Vale	D 1-1	Robinson	15,000
40		30	(a)	Port Vale	W 2-1	James, Watson	12,000
41	May	2	(h)	South Shields	W 2-1	Puddefoot, Opp own-goal	15,000
42		7	(a)	South Shields	D 0-0		10,000

P	W	D	L	F	A	W	D	L	F	A	Pts	Pos	Div	
42	13	5	3	38	11	6	5	10	13	19	48	5th	2	Appearances Goals

FA Cup

No	Month	Date	H/A	Opponent	Result	Attendance
1	Jan	8	(a)	Sheffield W	L 0-1	49,125

Appearances
Goals

Appearances and goals grid (player line-ups by match). Columns are players; cell values are shirt numbers worn; the rightmost number is the match number.

Hufton	Cope	Burton	Tresadern	Kay	McCrae	Cumming	Shea	Puddefoot	Simmons	Young	Crowther	Bradshaw	Watson	Smithurst	Butcher	Lee	Bailey	Lane	Carter	Allen	Leafe	Bishop	Hampson	Woodards	James	Cowell	Robinson	Hart	Smith	Gatland	Hebden	Palmer	Calladine	Brown	#
1	2	3	4	5	6	7	8	9	10	11																									1
1	2	3	4	5	6	7	8	9	10	11																									2
1	2	3	4	5	6	7	8	9	10	11																									3
1	2	3	4	5	6		8	9	7	11	10																								4
1	2	3	4	5	6		8	9	7			10	11																						5
1	2	3	4	5	6		8	9	7	11		10																							6
1	2	3	4	5	6		8	9	7	11				10																					7
1	2	3	4	5	6		8	9	7	11				10																					8
1	2	3	4	5	6		8	9	7	11				10																					9
1	2	3	4	5	6		8	9	7	11				10																					10
1	2	3	4	5	6		8	9		11						7	10																		11
1	2		4	5	6	7	8	9		11						3	8																		12
1		3	4	5	6	7	8	9		11								10	2																13
1		3	5	4	6		8	9		11								10	2	7															14
1		3	5		6		8	9		11								10	2	7	4														15
1		3	5	6			8	9		11								10	2	7	4														16
1		3	6	5			9	8		11									2	7	4	10													17
1		3	6	5			9	8		11									2	7	4	10													18
1	2		6	5				9		11						8			3	7	4	10													19
1		3	6	5			9	8		11									2	7	4	10													20
1	3	2	6	5				9	7	11									4	10	8														21
1	3	2	6	5				9		11									7	4	10	8													22
	3	2		5				9		11									7	4	10	8	1	6											23
1	3	2	6	5				9		11									7	4		8			10										24
1	2	3	6	5				9		11									7	4		8			10										25
1	3	2	6	5				9		11									7	4		8			10										26
1	3	2		5				9		11									7	4		8	6		10										27
1	3	2	6	5				9		11									7	4		8			10										28
1	3	2		5				9		11						8			7	4		6			10										29
1	2	3		5				9	7	11						8				4		6			10										30
1	3	2		5				9	7	11									4			8	6		10										31
1	3	2	6	5			7			11						9				4		8			10										32
1		2	6	5			8			11						9			3	7		4			10										33
1		2		5				9											3	7	4	10	8			6	11								34
	2			5				9											3	7	4	10	8	1	6	11									35
				5															9	3	2	7	4	10	8	1	6	11							36
1				5				9											3	2	7	4	10		6		11	8							37
1	2			5				9											3		7	4	10		6		11	8							38
1	3		6					9											4	7				5	11		8	2	10						39
1	2		6							11					9				3	4	7	5			10		8								40
1	2		6					9							10				3	4	5				11		8				7				41
	3						5	9		11									4			1			8						2	6	7	10	42
38	**36**	**30**	**30**	**36**	**15**	**5**	**16**	**38**	**18**	**34**	**3**	**1**	**9**	**1**	**1**	**9**	**8**	**10**	**20**	**28**	**13**	**21**	**4**	**7**	**18**	**1**	**5**	**1**	**1**	**1**	**1**	**1**	**1**	**1**	
				1			1	29	1				2						1	7	3				3		1								

2 own-goals

Hufton	Cope	Burton	Tresadern	Kay	McCrae	Cumming	Shea	Puddefoot	Simmons	Young	Crowther	Bradshaw	Watson	Smithurst	Butcher	Lee	Bailey	Lane	Carter	Allen	Leafe	Bishop	Hampson	Woodards	James	Cowell	Robinson	Hart	Smith	Gatland	Hebden	Palmer	Calladine	Brown	#
1	3	2	6	5				9		11									7	4	10	8													1
1	1	1	1	1				1		1									1	1	1	1													

1921-22

Manager: Syd King

1	Aug	27	(a)	Stoke	L	0-2	18,000
2		29	(h)	Bradford	W	1-0 Opp own-goal	18,000
3	Sep	3	(h)	Stoke	W	3-0 Allen, Jackson, Puddefoot	20,000
4		5	(a)	Bradford	L	0-2	8,000
5		10	(h)	Port Vale	W	3-0 Puddefoot 2, Watson	15,000
6		17	(a)	Port Vale	L	1-2 Watson	10,000
7		24	(h)	South Shields	D	1-1 Puddefoot	20,000
8	Oct	1	(a)	South Shields	L	0-1	16,000
9		3	(a)	Coventry C	L	0-2	6,000
10		8	(h)	Bristol C	W	3-0 Puddefoot 2, Watson	18,000
11		15	(a)	Bristol C	W	1-0 Bishop	11,000
12		22	(h)	Nottingham F	W	1-0 Watson	20,000
13		29	(a)	Nottingham F	L	0-2	16,000
14	Nov	5	(h)	Wolves	W	2-0 Kay, Thirlaway	16,000
15		12	(a)	Wolves	W	1-0 Bishop	8,000
16		19	(h)	Barnsley	W	4-0 Puddefoot 2, Bishop, Watson	18,000
17		26	(a)	Barnsley	D	1-1 Thirlaway	12,000
18	Dec	10	(h)	Coventry C	W	3-0 Puddefoot 2, Watson	18,000
19		17	(h)	Derby C	W	3-1 Puddefoot 2, James	20,000
20		24	(a)	Derby C	L	1-3 Kay	5,000
21		26	(a)	Bury	W	1-0 Allen	20,000
22		27	(h)	Bury	W	3-2 Puddefoot 2, Bishop	28,785
23		31	(h)	Leicester C	W	1-0 Tresadern	20,000
24	Jan	14	(a)	Leicester C	L	1-2 Watson	16,000
25		21	(a)	Leeds U	D	0-0	7,000
26		28	(h)	Leeds U	D	1-1 James	20,000
27	Feb	4	(a)	Hull C	D	0-0	8,000
28		11	(h)	Hull C	D	1-1 Kay	18,000
29		25	(h)	Notts C	W	2-1 Watson 2	20,000
30	Mar	4	(a)	Crystal P	W	2-1 Allen, Watson	8,000
31		11	(h)	Crystal P	W	2-0 Tresadern, Watson	22,000
32		18	(h)	Rotherham U	L	1-2 Kay	20,000
33		25	(a)	Rotherham U	W	1-0 James	10,000
34		29	(a)	Notts C	D	1-1 Watson	7,000
35	Apr	1	(h)	Sheffield W	W	2-0 Allen, Kay	20,000
36		8	(a)	Sheffield W	L	1-2 Tresadern	4,000
37		14	(h)	Clapton O	L	1-2 James	30,000
38		15	(h)	Fulham	W	1-0 Allen	25,000
39		17	(a)	Clapton O	D	0-0	30,000
40		22	(a)	Fulham	L	0-2	10,000
41		29	(h)	Blackpool	L	0-2	18,000
42	May	6	(a)	Blackpool	L	1-3 Williams	12,000

P	W	D	L	F	A	W	D	L	F	A	Pts	Pos	Div	
42	15	3	3	39	13	5	5	11	13	26	48	4th	2	Appearances
														Goals

FA Cup

1	Jan	7	(a)	Swansea T	D	0-0	26,000
R		11	(h)	Swansea T	D	1-1 Watson	20,000
2R		16	(n*)	Swansea T	L	0-1	8,976

* Played at Bristol City.

Appearances
Goals

226

Football appearance and goalscoring grid (players by shirt number, per match).

Hufton	Hebden	Cope	Allen	Gurkin	Bishop	Brown	Robinson	Puddefoot	James	Young	Kay	Thirlaway	Smith	Jackson	Hampson	Watson	Carter	Tresadern	Turner	Ruffell	Waugh	Leafe	Mackesy	Simmons	Henderson	Hodgson	Williams	Lee	
1	2	3	4	5	6	7	8	9	10	11																			
1	2	3	4		8		10	9	6		5	7	11																1
1	2	3	4		6			9	11		5	7	10	8															2
1	2	3	4		8			9	6		5	7	11	10															3
	2	3	4		6	8		9	11		5	7			1	10													4
	2	3	4		6	8		9	11		5	7			1	10													5
1	2	3	4		6			9	11		5	7				10		8											6
1	2	3	4		6	8		9	11		5	7				10													7
1	2	3	4		6	8		9	11		5	7				10													8
1	2	3	4		8			9	6	11	5	7				10													9
	2	3	4		8			9	6	11	5	7			1	10													10
	2	3	4		6	8			10	11	5	7			1	9													11
	2	3	4		8			9	6	11	5	7			1	10													12
	2	3	4		8			9	11		5	7			1	10		6											13
	2	3	4		8			9	11		5	7			1	10		6											14
1	2	3	4		8			9	11		5	7				10		6											15
1	2	3	4		8			9	11		5	7				10		6											16
1	2	3	4		8			9	11		5	7				10		6											17
1	2	3	4		8			9	11		5	7				10		6											18
1		3	4		8			9	11		5	7				10		6	2										19
1		3	4		8			9	11		5	7				10		6	2										20
1		3	4		8			9				7				10	5	6	2	11									21
1		3	4		5			9	8			7				10		6	2	11									22
1		3	4		8						5					9		6	11	2	7	10							23
1		3	4		10						5					9		6	11	2	7								24
1		3	2	4				9	11		5	7				10		6							8				25
1		3	4		8			9	11		5	7				10		6						2	8				26
		3	4		10				11		5	7			1	9		6						2	8				27
1		3	4		8				10		5					9		6	2	11	7								28
1		3	4		8				10		5					9		6	2	11	7								29
1		3	4		8				10		5					9		6		11	7			2					30
1		3	4		8				10		5					9		6		11	7			2					31
1		3	4		10	8			11		5					9		6			7			2					32
1		3	4		10	8			11		5					9					7			2					33
1		3	4		10	8			11		5					9		6			7		6	2					34
1		3	4		10	8			11		5	7				9		6						2					35
1		3	4		8				10		5	7				9		6						2					36
1		3	4		10	8					5	7				9		6		11				2					37
1		3	4		10	8					5	7				9		6		11				2					38
1		3	4		8				10		5	7				9		6		11				2					39
1		3	4		8	10					5	7				9		6		11				2					40
1		3	4		8	10					5	7				9		6		11				2					41
			4								5	7			1	9	8	6		11					3	2	10		42
33	19	41	42	1	36	7	10	26	36	5	39	33	3	3	9	37	3	28	4	14	6	3	1	9	12	1	1		
	5		4		14	4					5	2	1			12		3						1					

1 own-goal

Hufton	Hebden	Cope	Allen	Gurkin	Bishop	Brown	Robinson	Puddefoot	James	Young	Kay	Thirlaway	Smith	Jackson	Hampson	Watson	Carter	Tresadern	Turner	Ruffell	Waugh	Leafe	Mackesy	Simmons	Henderson	Hodgson	Williams	Lee	
1		2	4		8			9	6		5	7				10		11						3					1
1		2	4		8			9	11		5	7				10	6							3					R
1		2	4		8			9	11		5	7				10	6	3											2R
3		3	3		3			3	3		3	3				3	2	1	1					2					
														1															

1922-23

Manager: Syd King

1	Aug	26	(h)	Bradford C	L 1-2	Watson	25,000
2		28	(h)	Derby C	D 0-0		16,000
3	Sep	2	(a)	Bradford C	W 1-0	Ruffell	20,000
4		4	(a)	Derby C	L 1-2	Moore	9,000
5		9	(h)	Rotherham U	W 4-0	Moore 2, Ruffell, Watson	15,000
6		16	(a)	Rotherham U	D 2-2	Robinson, Watson	9,000
7		23	(h)	Stockport C	L 0-1		18,000
8		30	(a)	Stockport C	L 1-2	Moore	15,000
9	Oct	7	(h)	Southampton	D 1-1	Crossley	20,000
10		14	(a)	Southampton	L 0-2		17,000
11		21	(h)	Blackpool	W 2-0	Watson 2	15,000
12		28	(a)	Blackpool	L 1-4	Moore	14,000
13	Nov	4	(a)	Leeds U	L 1-3	Moore	12,000
14		11	(h)	Leeds U	D 0-0		14,000
15		18	(h)	Clapton O	W 1-0	Watson	20,000
16		25	(a)	Clapton O	W 2-0	Watson 2	20,000
17	Dec	2	(h)	South Shields	W 1-0	Moore	14,000
18		9	(a)	South Shields	D 0-0		7,000
19		16	(a)	Wolves	W 4-1	Brown 2, Moore, Watson	13,000
20		22	(h)	Wolves	W 1-0	Watson	15,000
21		25	(a)	Manchester U	W 2-1	Moore, Brown	17,500
22		26	(h)	Manchester U	L 0-2		20,000
23		30	(a)	Coventry C	W 3-1	Watson 3	14,000
24	Jan	6	(h)	Coventry C	W 1-0	Tresadern	16,000
25		20	(a)	Port Vale	W 3-1	Bishop, Ruffell, Richards	10,000
26		27	(h)	Port Vale	D 0-0		17,000
27	Feb	10	(a)	Leicester C	D 2-2	Richards, Brown	16,000
28		15	(a)	Leicester C	W 6-0	Moore 3, Richards, Ruffell, Tresadern	6,000
29		17	(h)	Barnsley	D 0-0		20,000
30	Mar	3	(h)	Sheffield W	W 2-1	Brown, Moore	16,000
31		17	(a)	Hull C	D 1-1	Ruffell	10,000
32		30	(h)	Bury	D 0-0		30,000
33		31	(a)	Crystal P	W 5-1	Watson 4, Brown	14,000
34	Apr	2	(a)	Bury	W 5-2	Watson 2, Richards, Moore, Ruffell	25,000
35		7	(h)	Crystal P	D 1-1	Watson	25,000
36		9	(h)	Hull C	W 3-0	Brown 2, Richards	10,000
37		14	(a)	Fulham	W 2-0	Bishop, Moore	33,807
38		16	(a)	Barnsley	L 0-2		7,000
39		18	(a)	Notts C	L 0-1		10,000
40		21	(h)	Fulham	W 1-0	Watson	20,000
41		30	(a)	Sheffield W	W 2-0	Brown, Watson	12,000
42	May	5	(h)	Notts C	L 0-1		26,000

P	W	D	L	F	A	W	D	L	F	A	Pts	Pos	Div	Appearances
42	9	8	4	21	11	11	3	7	42	27	51	2nd	2	Goals

FA Cup

1	Jan	13	(a)	Hull C	W 3-2	Watson 2, Moore	14,000
2	Feb	3	(a)	Brighton & HA	D 1-1	Watson	19,531
R		7	(h)	Brighton & HA	W 1-0	Moore	20,000
3		24	(h)	Plymouth A	W 2-0	Moore, Richards	30,525
4	Mar	10	(a)	Southampton	D 1-1	Watson	21,960
R		14	(h)	Southampton	D 1-1	Watson	28,000
2R		19	(n*)	Southampton	W 1-0	Brown	22,184
SF		24	(n†)	Derby C	W 5-2	Brown 2, Moore 2, Ruffell	50,795
F	Apr	28	(n‡)	Bolton W	L 0-2		126,047

* Played at Villa Park. † Played at Stamford Bridge. ‡ Played at Wembley.   Appearances
Goals

228

Hufton	Hodgson	Horler	Allen	Kay	Bishop	Charlton	Crossley	Watson	Moore	Richards	Hebden	Tresadern	Burgess	Ruffell	Robinson	Young	Brown	Henderson	Carter	Williams	Thirlaway	Mackesy	Edwards	Fletcher	Hampson	
1	2	3	4	5	6	7	8	9	10	11																1
1	2		4	5		7	8	9	10	11	3	6														2
1	2			5	4	7		9	10		3	6	8	11												3
1	2			5	4	7		9	10		3	6	8	11												4
1	2		4	5		7		9	10		3	6		11	8											5
1	2			5	4	7		9	10		3	6		11	8											6
1	2			5	4	7		9	10			6		11	8	3										7
1	2			5	4	7		9	10			6		11		3	8									8
1		8	5	7				10	9	11	2	6				3	4									9
1								10	8	11	7	2	6		4	3	5	9								10
1	2			5				10	9	8	7	6		11		3	4									11
1	2			5				10	9	8	7	6		11		3	4									12
1				5	4			10	9	8	7	6		11		3		2								13
1				5	4		8	9	10		2	6		11		3					7					14
1				5	4		8	9	10		2	6		11		3					7					15
1				5	4			9	10	7		6		11		3	8	2								16
1				5	4			9	10	7		6		11		3	8	2								17
1				5	4			9	10	7		6		11		3	8	2								18
1				5	4			9	10	7		6		11		3	8	2								19
1				5	4			9	10	7		6		11		3	8	2								20
1				5	4			9	10	7		6		11		3	8	2								21
1				5	4		8	9	10	7		6		11		3		2								22
1				5	4		8	9	10	7		6		11		3		2								23
1				5	4		8	9	10	7		6		11		3		2								24
1	3			5	4		8	9	10	7		6		11				2								25
1	3	4					11	9	10	7		6					8	2	5							26
1		3					11	9	10	7		6			4			2	5							27
1	3							9	10	7		6		11			8	2	5							28
1	3	4						9	10	7		6		11			8	2	5							29
1			4					9	10	7				11		3	8	2	5	6						30
1				5	4			9	10	7		6		11		3	8	2								31
1				5	4			9	10	11		6				3	8	2			6	7				32
1				5	4			9	10	7		6		11		3	8	2								33
1				5	4			9	10	7		6		11		3	8	2								34
1				5	4			9	10	7				11		3	8	2			6					35
1				5	4				10	7				11		3	8	2			6		9			36
1				5	4			9	11	7		6				3	8	2								37
1				5	4			9	10	11	7	6				3	8	2			11					38
1				5	4			9	10	7		6				3	8	2								39
				5	4			9	10	7		6		11		3	8	2		11				1		40
				5	4			9	10	7		6		11		3	8	2						1		41
				5	4			9	10	7		6		11		3	8	2						1		42
39	11	5	6	36	34	8	15	41	42	34	9	37	2	33	3	25	26	34	10	1	2	4	1	1	3	
			2			1	22	15	5		2		6	1		9										

Hufton	Hodgson	Horler	Allen	Kay	Bishop	Charlton	Crossley	Watson	Moore	Richards	Hebden	Tresadern	Burgess	Ruffell	Robinson	Young	Brown	Henderson	Carter	Williams	Thirlaway	Mackesy	Edwards	Fletcher	Hampson	
1				5	4		8	9	10	7		6		11		3		2								1
1	3			5	4			9	10	7		6		11			8	2								2
1	3							9	10	7		6		11			8	2	5							R
1		4		5				9	10	7		6		11		3	8	2	4							3
1		4						9	10	7		6		11		3	8	2	5							4
1		4						9	10	7		6		11		3	8	2	5							R
1				5	4			9	10	7		6		11		3	8	2								2R
1				5	4			9	10	7		6		11		3	8	2								SF
1				5	4			9	10	7		6		11		3	8	2								F
9		2	1	5	8		1	9	9	9		9		9		7	8	9	4							
								5	5	1				1			3									

1923-24

Manager: Syd King

1	Aug	25	(a)	Sunderland	D	0-0		35,000
2		27	(h)	Arsenal	W	1-0	Fletcher	20,000
3	Sep	1	(h)	Sunderland	L	0-1		25,000
4		8	(h)	Cardiff C	D	0-0		30,000
5		10	(a)	Arsenal	L	1-4	Hodges	40,000
6		15	(a)	Cardiff C	L	0-1		33,000
7		22	(h)	Middlesbrough	D	1-1	Brown	20,000
8		29	(a)	Middlesbrough	W	1-0	Yews	22,000
9	Oct	6	(a)	Newcastle U	D	0-0		25,000
10		13	(h)	Newcastle U	W	1-0	Brown	30,000
11		20	(a)	Chelsea	D	0-0		51,000
12		27	(h)	Chelsea	W	2-0	Kay, Brown	26,000
13	Nov	3	(h)	Birmingham	W	4-1	Brown, Richardson, Kay, Moore	22,000
14		10	(a)	Birmingham	L	0-2		22,000
15		17	(a)	Burnley	L	1-5	Moore	5,000
16		24	(h)	Burnley	D	0-0		20,000
17	Dec	1	(a)	Bolton W	D	1-1	Brown	20,000
18		8	(h)	Bolton W	L	0-1		28,000
19		15	(a)	Nottingham F	L	1-2	Edwards	10,000
20		22	(h)	Nottingham F	W	3-2	Moore 2, Kay	15,000
21		25	(a)	Aston Villa	D	1-1	Richardson	40,000
22		26	(h)	Aston Villa	W	1-0	Moore	26,000
23		29	(a)	Liverpool	L	0-2		24,000
24	Jan	1	(a)	Sheffield U	W	2-0	Gibbins, Brown	30,000
25		5	(h)	Liverpool	W	1-0	Moore	25,000
26		19	(a)	Blackburn R	D	0-0		22,000
27		26	(h)	Blackburn R	L	0-1		20,000
28	Feb	9	(h)	Tottenham H	D	0-0		30,000
29		16	(a)	Huddersfield T	D	1-1	Ruffell	10,000
30	Mar	1	(a)	Notts C	D	1-1	Collins	10,000
31		8	(h)	Notts C	D	1-1	Proctor	20,000
32		15	(h)	Everton	W	2-1	Campbell, Edwards	22,000
33		22	(a)	Everton	L	1-2	Moore	20,000
34		27	(h)	Huddersfield T	L	2-3	Young 2	15,000
35		29	(h)	West Brom A	W	1-0	Ruffell	18,000
36	Apr	5	(a)	West Brom A	D	0-0		12,000
37		12	(h)	Preston NE	W	3-1	Watson, Moore, Edwards	18,000
38		19	(a)	Preston NE	L	1.2	Watson	18,000
39		21	(h)	Sheffield U	D	2-2	Campbell 2	15,000
40		22	(a)	Tottenham H	W	1-0	Campbell	20,000
41		26	(h)	Manchester C	L	1-2	Moore	18,000
42	May	3	(a)	Manchester C	L	1-2	Watson	12,000

P	W	D	L	F	A	W	D	L	F	A	Pts	Pos	Div	Appearances
42	10	6	5	26	17	3	9	9	14	26	41	13th	1	Goals

FA Cup

1	Jan	12	(h)	Aberdare	W	5-0	Brown 2, Henderson, Moore, Williams	23,000
2	Feb	2	(h)	Leeds U	D	1-1	Kay	30,123
R		6	(a)	Leeds U	L	0-1		32,000

Appearances
Goals

Appearances and goals grid (shirt numbers by player and match):

Hufton	Henderson	Hodgson	Bishop	Kay	Tresadern	Richards	Brown	Fletcher	Moore	Ruffell	Hampson	Hodges	Hebden	Yews	Young	Proctor	Watson	Carter	Cadwell	Richardson	Thirlaway	Edwards	Gibbins	Williams	Robinson	Collins	Campbell	No.
1	2	3	4	5	6	7	8		10	11							9											1
	2	3	4	5	6	7	8	9	10	11	1																	2
	2	3	4	5	6	7	8	9	10	11	1																	3
1	2	3	4	5	6	7	8	9	10	11																		4
	2	3	4	5	6	7	8	9	10	11	1		9															5
1	2		4	5	6		8	9	10	11				7	3													6
1		3	4	5	6			9	10	11				7	2	8												7
1	2		4	5	6		8		10	11				7	3		9											8
1	2			5	6		8		10	11				7	3		9	4										9
1	2		4	5	6		8		10	11				7	3		9											10
1	2			5	6		8		10	11				7	3			4		9								11
1	2		4	5			8		10					7	3				6	9	11							12
1	2			5	6		8		10	11				7	3		9	4										13
1	2		4	5			8		10	11					3				6	9		7						14
1	2		4	5			8		10	11					3				6	9		7						15
	2		4	5			8		10	11	1				3				6	9		7						16
1	2		4	5			8		10	11					3				6	9		7						17
1	2		4	5			8		10	11					3				6			7	9					18
1	2		5	4			8		10	11					3				6			7	9					19
	2		5			11	8		10		1				3			4	6	9		7						20
	2		5			11	8		10		1	3			3			4	6	9		7						21
	2		5				8		10	11	1				3			4	6			7	9					22
	2		5				8		10	11	1				3			4	6	9		7						23
	2		5				8		10	11	1				3			4	6			7	9					24
	2		5				8		10	11	1				3			4	6			7		9				25
	2		5						10	11	1				3			4	6			7		9	8			26
	2		5							11	1				3	9		4	6			7		10	8			27
	2		4	5				9		11	1				3				6			7		10	8			28
	2		4	5			8		10	11	1				3				6			7					9	29
	2		4	5					10	11	1				3	8			6			7					9	30
	2		4	5					10	11	1				3				6			7		8			9	31
	2		4	5					10	11	1				3	8			6			7					9	32
	2		4	5					10	11	1				3	8			6			7					9	33
	2		4	5					10	11	1				3	8			6			7					9	34
	2		4	5			8		10	11	1				3				6			7					9	35
	2		4	5					10	11	1				3	8			6			7					9	36
	2		4						10	11	1				3	8	5	6				7					9	37
	2		4						10	11	1				3	8	5	6				7					9	38
	2		4	5					10	11	1			7	3	8			6								9	39
	2		4	5					10	11	1			7	3	8			6								9	40
	2		4	5					10	11	1			7	3	8			6								9	41
	2		4	5					10	11	1			7	3	8			6								9	42
15	42	5	31	40	10	9	26	7	36	39	27	2	2	12	35	7	11	16	29	10	1	25	3	5	1	5	11	
		3					6	1	9	2			1		1	2	1	3				2		3	1	1	4	

Cup appearances:

Hufton	Henderson	Hodgson	Bishop	Kay	Tresadern	Richards	Brown	Fletcher	Moore	Ruffell	Hampson	Hodges	Hebden	Yews	Young	Proctor	Watson	Carter	Cadwell	Richardson	Thirlaway	Edwards	Gibbins	Williams	Robinson	Collins	Campbell	No.
	2		5				8		10	11	1				3			4	6			7		9				1
	2		5				8		10	11	1				3			4	6			7		9				2
	2		5			7	8		10	11	1				3			4	6	9								R
	3		3	1	3		3	3	3						3	3	1		2	2								
	1			1			2		1											1									

1924-25

Manager: Syd King

1	Aug	30	(h)	Preston NE	W	1-0	Jennings	25,000
2	Sep	6	(a)	Blackburn R	W	1-0	Earle	18,000
3		8	(h)	Newcastle U	D	0-0		22,000
4		13	(h)	Huddersfield T	D	0-0		28,103
5		17	(a)	Newcastle U	L	1-4	Watson	25,000
6		20	(a)	Aston Villa	D	1-1	Watson	30,000
7		22	(a)	Sheffield U	D	1-1	Watson	10,000
8		27	(h)	Arsenal	W	1-0	Earle	31,000
9	Oct	4	(a)	Manchester C	L	1-3	Opp own-goal	45,000
10		11	(h)	Bury	D	1-1	Young	22,000
11		18	(a)	Nottingham F	L	1-2	Jennings	13,000
12		25	(h)	Burnley	W	2-0	Moore, Ruffell	22,000
13	Nov	1	(a)	Leeds U	L	1-2	Watson	17,000
14		8	(h)	Birmingham	L	0-1		28,000
15		15	(a)	West Brom A	L	1-4	Watson	16,000
16		22	(h)	Tottenham H	D	1-1	Watson	26,000
17		29	(a)	Bolton W	L	0-5		33,000
18	Dec	6	(h)	Notts C	W	3-0	Williams 2, Watson	18,000
19		13	(a)	Everton	L	0-1		15,000
20		20	(h)	Sunderland	W	4-1	Watson 2, Moore 2	20,000
21		25	(h)	Cardiff C	W	3-2	Moore, Watson, Kay	25,000
22		26	(a)	Cardiff C	L	1-2	Watson	30,000
23		27	(a)	Preston NE	L	2-3	Watson, Williams	9,000
24	Jan	3	(h)	Blackburn R	W	2-0	Watson, Moore	16,000
25		17	(a)	Huddersfield T	W	2-1	Watson, Ruffell	14,000
26		24	(h)	Aston Villa	W	2-0	Watson, Williams	20,000
27	Feb	7	(h)	Manchester C	W	4-0	Moore 2, Ruffell, Watson	25,000
28		14	(a)	Bury	L	2-4	Watson, Yews	15,000
29		28	(a)	Burnley	L	4-5	Ruffell, Moore, Jennings, Watson	10,000
30	Mar	7	(h)	Leeds U	D	0-0		15,000
31		14	(a)	Birmingham	D	1-1	Campbell	20,000
32		21	(h)	West Brom A	W	2-1	Kay, Ruffell	25,000
33		23	(a)	Arsenal	W	2-1	Ruffell, Campbell	10,000
34		28	(a)	Tottenham H	D	1-1	Watson	35,000
35	Apr	2	(h)	Nottingham F	D	0-0		8,000
36		4	(h)	Bolton W	D	1-1	Campbell	25,000
37		10	(a)	Liverpool	L	0-2		30,000
38		11	(a)	Notts C	L	1-4	Ruffell	10,000
39		13	(h)	Liverpool	L	0-1		12,000
40		14	(h)	Sheffield U	W	6-2	Watson 2, Ruffell 2, Earle, Moore	12,000
41		18	(h)	Everton	W	4-1	Earle 2, Moore, Watson	15,000
42		25	(a)	Sunderland	D	1-1	Earle	10,000

P	W	D	L	F	A	W	D	L	F	A	Pts	Pos	Div	
42	12	7	2	37	12	3	5	13	25	48	42	13th	1	Appearances
														Goals

FA Cup

1	Jan	14	(h)	Arsenal	D	0-0		26,000
R		21	(a)	Arsenal	D	2-2	Ruffell 2	34,160
2R		26	(n*)	Arsenal	W	1-0	Kay	36,955
4		31	(a)	Nottingham F	W	2-0	Ruffell, Yews	10,590
5	Feb	21	(h)	Blackpool	D	1-1	Watson	30,000
R		25	(a)	Blackpool	L	0-3		15,190

* Played at Stamford Bridge

Appearances
Goals

Football appearances & goals grid (player shirt numbers by match). Columns read left to right: Hampson, Henderson, Young, Bishop, Kay, Cadwell, Edwards, Earle, Watson, Jennings, Ruffell, Tresadern, Gibbins, Carter, Horler, Yews, Moore, Cowper, Kaine, Campbell, Hebden, Williams, Collins, Hufton, Hodgson, Barrett, Eastman. Match number shown at right.

No.	Hampson	Henderson	Young	Bishop	Kay	Cadwell	Edwards	Earle	Watson	Jennings	Ruffell	Tresadern	Gibbins	Carter	Horler	Yews	Moore	Cowper	Kaine	Campbell	Hebden	Williams	Collins	Hufton	Hodgson	Barrett	Eastman
1	1	2	3	4	5	6	7	8	9	10	11																
2	1	2	3		5	6	7	8	9	10	11	4															
3	1	2	3		5	6	7	8	10		11	4	9														
4	1	2	3		5	6	7	8	9	10	11	4															
5	1	2	3		5	6	7	8	9		11	4					10										
6	1	2	3		5	6	7	8	9		11			4			10										
7	1	2			5	6		8	9		11			4	3	7	10										
8	1	2			5	6		8	9		11			4	3	7	10										
9	1	2	3		5	6		8	9		11			4		7	10										
10		2	3	6	5			8	9		11			4		7	10		1								
11		2	3		5	6		8	9		11			4		7	10		1								
12		2	3		5	6		8			11			4		7	10		1	9							
13	1	2	3		5	6		8			11			4		7	10			9							
14	1	2	3	4	5	6		8			11					7	10			9							
15	1	2	3		5	6		8	9		11			4		7	10										
16	1	2			5	6		8	9		11			4		7	10					3					
17	1	2	3	4	5	6		8	9	10	11					7											
18	1	2	3	4	5	6			9	8	11					7				10							
19	1	2	3	4	5	6			9		11				7	8				10							
20	1	2	3	4	5	6			9		11				7	8				10							
21	1	2	3	4	5	6			9		11				7	8				10							
22	1	2	3		5	6		8	9		11			4		7				10							
23	1	2	3		5	6			9		11			4		7	8			10							
24	1	2	3		5	6			9		11			4		7	8			10							
25	1	2		6	5				9		11			4		7	8			10	3						
26	1	2			5	6			9		11			4		7	8			10	3						
27	1	2			5	6			9		11			4		7	8			10	3						
28	1	2	3		5	6			9	10	11					7	8					4					
29		2			5	6			9		11				3	7	8			10			1				
30		2			5	6					11			4	3	7	8			10			1				
31		2			5	6					11			4	3	7	8		1	9							
32					5	6				10	11				3	7	8		1	9			4	2			
33		2			5	6		8			11				3	7			1	9		10			4		
34		2			5	6			9		11				3	7	8		1			10			4		
35		2			5	6				10	11				3	7	8		1						4		
36		2			5	6				10	11				3	7	8			9			1		4		
37		2			5	6				10	11				3	7	8			9			1		4		
38		2		4	5	6		8	9		11				3	7	10						1				
39		2		4	5	6		8	9		11				3	7	10						1				
40		2		4		6		8	9		11				3	7	10						1				
41		2		4	5	6		8	9		11				3	7	10						1			5	
42		2		4	5	6		8	9		11				3	7	10						1				
Apps	27	41	23	14	41	40	7	18	41	9	42	4	1	19	15	33	32	2	7	10	4	15	2	8	1	5	1
Goals			1		2			6	22	3	9			1		10				3		4					

I own-goal

Cup section:

No.	Hampson	Henderson	Young	Bishop	Kay	Cadwell	Edwards	Earle	Watson	Jennings	Ruffell	Tresadern	Gibbins	Carter	Horler	Yews	Moore	Cowper	Kaine	Campbell	Hebden	Williams	Collins	Hufton	Hodgson	Barrett	Eastman
3	1	2	3		5	6			9		11			4		7	8			10							
R	1	2	3		5	6			9		11			4		7	8			10							
2R	1	2			5	6			9		11			4		7	8			3		10					
4	1	2			5	6			9		11					7	8			3		10					
5	1	2	3		5	6			9		11					7	8					10	4				
R	1	2			5	6			9		11			4		7	8			3		10					
Apps	6	6	3		6	6			6		6			5		6	6			3		6	1				
Goals			1						1		3			1													

1925-26

Manager: Syd King

1	Aug	29	(h)	Manchester U	W	1-0	Earle	29,000
2		31	(h)	Cardiff C	W	3-1	Watson 2, Earle	20,000
3	Sep	5	(a)	Liverpool	D	0-0		30,000
4		7	(a)	Cardiff C	W	1-0	Watson	25,000
5		12	(h)	Burnley	W	2-0	Ruffell 2	28,000
6		19	(a)	Leeds U	L	2-5	Watson 2	16,000
7		21	(a)	Arsenal	L	2-3	Ruffell, Watson	27,000
8		26	(h)	Newcastle U	W	1-0	Watson	30,000
9	Oct	3	(a)	Bolton W	L	0-1		18,068
10		5	(h)	Arsenal	L	0-4		25,000
11		10	(h)	Notts C	W	1-0	Williams	29,500
12		17	(h)	Sheffield U	L	1-3	Earle	22,000
13		24	(a)	West Brom A	L	1-7	Ruffell	20,000
14		31	(h)	Manchester C	W	3-1	Ruffell, Bishop, Earle	23,000
15	Nov	7	(a)	Tottenham H	L	2-4	Yews, Barrett	35,000
16		14	(h)	Blackburn R	W	2-1	Moore, Watson	25,000
17		21	(a)	Sunderland	L	1-4	Watson	12,000
18		28	(h)	Huddersfield T	L	2-3	Ruffell, Watson	18,000
19	Dec	5	(a)	Everton	L	0-2		25,000
20		12	(h)	Birmingham	D	2-2	Watson, Ruffell	18,000
21		19	(a)	Bury	L	1-4	Watson	12,000
22		25	(h)	Aston Villa	W	5-2	Earle 3, Williams, Watson	27,000
23		26	(a)	Aston Villa	L	0-2		55,000
24	Jan	2	(a)	Manchester U	L	1-2	Ruffell	28,000
25		16	(h)	Liverpool	L	1-2	Watson	25,000
26		23	(a)	Burnley	D	2-2	Barrett, Williams	10,000
27		30	(h)	Leeds U	W	4-2	Barrett 3, Moore	22,000
28	Feb	6	(a)	Newcastle U	L	1-4	Barrett	25,000
29		13	(h)	Bolton W	W	6-0	Gibbins 2, Ruffell 2, Watson 2	30,000
30		27	(a)	Sheffield U	D	1-1	Moore	25,000
31	Mar	6	(h)	West Brom A	W	3-0	Watson 2, Moore	25,000
32		13	(a)	Manchester C	L	0-2		40,000
33		20	(h)	Tottenham H	W	3-1	Watson, Ruffell, Kay	35,000
34		22	(a)	Notts C	D	1-1	Ruffell	9,000
35		27	(a)	Blackburn R	L	0-1		15,000
36	Apr	2	(h)	Leicester C	D	1-1	Watson	30,000
37		3	(h)	Sunderland	W	3-2	Campbell 2, Earle	28,000
38		5	(a)	Leicester C	D	1-1	Campbell	20,000
39		10	(a)	Huddersfield T	L	1-2	Earle	20,000
40		17	(h)	Everton	W	1-0	Campbell	25,000
41		24	(a)	Birmingham	L	0-1		15,000
42	May	1	(h)	Bury	L	0-2		18,000

P	W	D	L	F	A	W	D	L	F	A	Pts	Pos	Div	
42	14	2	5	45	27	1	5	15	18	49	37	18th	1	Appearances
														Goals

FA Cup

3	Jan	9	(a)	Tottenham H	L	0-5		49,800

	Appearances
	Goals

234

Appearance and scoring grid (player columns left→right: Hufton, Hodgson, Henderson, Carter, Barrett, Cadwell, Yews, Earle, Watson, Moore, Ruffell, Edwards, Young, Horler, Williams, Campbell, Hebden, Weale, Kay, Bishop, Baillie, Collins, Earl, Kaine, Gibbins, Eastman). The final column is the match number.

Huf	Hod	Hen	Car	Bar	Cad	Yew	Ear	Wat	Moo	Ruf	Edw	You	Hor	Wil	Cam	Heb	Wea	Kay	Bis	Bai	Col	Earl	Kai	Gib	Eas	#
1	2	3	4	5	6	7	8	9	10	11																1
1	2	3	4	5	6	7	8	9	10	11																2
1	2	3	4	5	6		8	9	10	11	7															3
1	2	3	4	5	6	7	8	9	10	11																4
1	2	3	4	5	6	7	8	9	10	11																5
1	2		4	5	6	7	8	9	10	11		3														6
1	2		4	5	6	7	8	9	10	11			3													7
1	2	3	4	5	6	7	8	9		11				10												8
1	2	3	4	5	6	7	8	9		11				10												9
1	2	3	4	5	6		8		10	11	7						9									10
1		3	4	5	6		8	9		11				10			2	7								11
1		3	4	5	6		8	9	10	11							2	7								12
1		3	4	5	6	7		9	10	11						2			8							13
1	2		4	5	6	7		9	10	11						3			8							14
1	2		4	5	6	7		9	10	11						3			8							15
1	2			5	6	7	8	9	10	11						3			4							16
1	2			5	6	7	8	9	10	11						3			4							17
			4	5			8	9	7	11			3	10		2			6	1						18
1			4	5		7	9	8		11			3	10		2			6							19
1			5				8	9		11			3	10		2	7		6	4						20
1	2		5			7	8	9		11				10					6	4	3					21
1	2		5			7	8	9		11				10					6	4	3					22
1	2		5			7	8	9		11				10					6	4	3					23
1	2	6				7	8	9		11				10					6	4	3	1				24
1	2	9		7			8			11				10				5	6	4	3					25
1	2	9		7			8	10		11								5	6	4	3					26
1	2	9		7			8	10		11								5	6	4	3					27
1	2	4		7	8	10		11										5	6	3		9				28
	4	3		7	8			10	11			9	2					5		1	6					29
	4	3		7	8	9	10	11					2					5			6					30
1	4	3		7	8	9				11						2		5	10	6						31
1	4	3		7	8	9							11			2		5	6							32
1	4	3		7	8	9	10	11								2		5	6							33
1	4	3		7	8	9	10	11								2		5	6							34
1	4	3		7	8	9	10	11								2		5	6							35
1	4	3		7	8	9	10	11								2		5	6							36
1	4	3		7	8			10	11				9		2		5	6								37
1	4	3		7	8			10	11				9		2		5	6								38
1	4	3		7	8	9	10	11							2		5	6								39
1	4	3		7	8	10	11						9		2			6			5					40
1	4	3			8	10			11	7			9		2		5	6								41
1	4	3			8	9	10	11	7						2		5	6								42
38	16	17	29	42	18	32	37	38	30	40	4	1	5	12	6	24	3	18	14	3	24	8	1	1	1	
		6		1	9	20	4	12					3	4			1	1			2					

Huf	Hod	Hen	Car	Bar	Cad	Yew	Ear	Wat	Moo	Ruf	Edw	You	Hor	Wil	Cam	Heb	Wea	Kay	Bis	Bai	Col	Earl	Kai	Gib	Eas	#
1		2			5		7	8	9		11			10					6		4	3				3
1		1			1		1	1	1		1			1					1		1	1				

1926-27

Manager: Syd King

1	Aug	28	(h)	Leicester C	D	3-3	Earle, Ruffell, Watson	20,000
2	Sep	4	(a)	Everton	W	3-0	Watson 2, Moore	30,000
3		6	(a)	Sheffield W	L	0-1		20,000
4		11	(h)	Blackburn R	L	1-5	Watson	18,000
5		18	(a)	Huddersfield T	L	1-2	Watson	16,000
6		25	(h)	Sunderland	L	1-2	Yews	27,000
7	Oct	2	(a)	West Brom A	W	3-1	Ruffell, Watson, Earle	18,000
8		4	(h)	Sheffield W	D	1-1	Earle	15,000
9		9	(h)	Bury	L	1-2	Watson	20,000
10		16	(a)	Arsenal	D	2-2	Gibbins, Watson	40,000
11		23	(a)	Sheffield U	W	2-0	Ruffells	20,000
12		30	(h)	Manchester U	W	4-0	Gibbins, Watson, Yews, Opp own-goal	20,000
13	Nov	6	(a)	Bolton W	L	0-2		12,000
14		13	(h)	Aston Villa	W	5-1	Watson 3, Yews, Earle	11,000
15		20	(a)	Cardiff C	W	2-1	Yews, Watson	11,000
16		27	(h)	Burnley	W	2-1	Watson, Gibbins	20,000
17	Dec	4	(a)	Newcastle U	L	0-2		30,000
18		11	(h)	Leeds U	W	3-2	Gibbins, Ruffell, Watson	35,000
19		18	(a)	Liverpool	D	0-0		25,000
20		25	(h)	Birmingham	W	1-0	Earle	30,000
21		27	(a)	Birmingham	W	2-0	Ruffell, Watson	35,000
22		28	(a)	Derby C	L	0-3		22,000
23	Jan	1	(h)	Derby C	L	1-2	Watson	18,000
24		15	(a)	Leicester C	L	0-3		20,000
25		22	(h)	Everton	W	2-1	Moore, Watson	12,000
26	Feb	5	(h)	Huddersfield T	W	3-2	Johnson, Watson, Yews	22,000
27		12	(a)	Sunderland	W	3-2	Earle, Watson, Yews	10,000
28		14	(a)	Blackburn R	L	1-4	Yews	10,000
29		19	(h)	West Brom A	L	1-2	Watson	18,000
30		26	(a)	Bury	W	2-1	Johnson, Yews	15,000
31	Mar	7	(h)	Arsenal	W	7-0	Watson 3, Johnson, Ruffell, Opp own-goals 2	28,000
32		12	(h)	Sheffield U	W	3-0	Earle 2, Watson	18,000
33		19	(a)	Manchester U	W	3-0	Watson 2, Johnson	20,000
34		26	(h)	Bolton W	D	4-4	Ruffell 2, Watson, Earle	20,000
35	Apr	2	(a)	Aston Villa	W	5-1	Watson 2, Earle, Johnson, Ruffell	20,000
36		9	(h)	Cardiff C	D	2-2	Earle, Watson	15,000
37		15	(a)	Tottenham H	W	3-1	Ruffell 2, Earle	40,000
38		16	(a)	Burnley	L	1-2	Watson	18,000
39		18	(h)	Tottenham H	L	1-2	Earle	26,000
40		23	(h)	Newcastle U	D	1-1	Ruffell	36,000
41		30	(a)	Leeds U	L	3-6	Watson 2, Johnson	10,000
42	May	7	(h)	Liverpool	D	3-3	Johnson, Collins, Barrett	15,000

P	W	D	L	F	A	W	D	L	F	A	Pts	Pos	Div	
42	9	6	6	50	36	10	2	9	36	34	46	6th	1	Appearances
														Goals

FA Cup

3	Jan	8	(h)	Tottenham H	W	3-2	Watson 3	44,417
4		29	(h)	Brentford	D	1-1	Ruffell	40,000
R	Feb	2	(a)	Brentford	L	0-2		25,000

Appearances
Goals

236

Player appearance / shirt-number grid (numbers indicate the shirt number worn by each player in each match; blank = did not play). Match numbers are shown in the right-hand column.

Hufton	Hebden	Earl	Bishop	Barrett	Collins	Yews	Earle	Watson	Moore	Ruffell	Carter	Dowsey	Williams	Payne	Gibbins	Hodgson	Kaine	Horler	Johnson	Hull	Cadwell	Baillie	Campbell	No.
1	2	3	4	5	6	7	8	9	10	11														1
1	2		4	3	6	7	8	9	10	11	5													2
1	2		4	3	6		8	9	10		5	7	11											3
1	2		4	3	6		8		10	11	5			7	9									4
1	2		4	3	6	7	8	9		11	5				10									5
1	2		4	3	6	7	8	9		11	5				10									6
1			4	3	6		8	10	7	11	5				9	2								7
1			4	3	6	7	8	9	10	11	5					2								8
1			4	3	6	7	8	9	10	11	5					2								9
1	2		4	5	6	7	8	9		11					10	3								10
1	2			5	6	7	8	9		11	4				10	3								11
1	2			5	6	7	8	9		11	4				10	3								12
1	2			5	6	7	8	9	10	11	4					3								13
1	2			5	6	7	8	9		11	4				10	3								14
1	2			5	6	7	8	9		11	4				10	3								15
1	2			5	6	7	8	9		11	4				10	3								16
1	2			5	6	7	8	9		11	4				10	3								17
1	2			5	6	7	8	9		11	4				10	3								18
1	2			5	6	7	8	9	10	11	4					3								19
1	2			5	6	7	8	9		11	4				10	3								20
1	2			5	6	7	8	9		11	4				10	3								21
1	2			5	6	7	8	9		11	4				10	3								22
	2			5	6	7	8	9		11	4				10		1	3						23
1	2			5	6	7	8	9		11	4				10			3						24
1	2			5	6	7	8	9	10	11	4							3						25
1	2			5	6	7	8	9		11	4							3	10					26
1	2			5	6	7	8	9	10		4							3	11					27
1	2			5	6	7	8	9		11	4							3	10					28
1	2			5	6	7	8	9		11					10			3	4					29
1	2			5	4	7	8	9	10									3		11	6			30
	2			5	4	7	8	9		11								3	10		6	1		31
1	2			5	4	7	8	9		11								3	10		6			32
1	2			5	4	7	8	9	10									3	11		6			33
1	2			5	4	7	8	9		11								3	10		6			34
1	2			5	4	7	8	9		11								3	10		6			35
1	2			5	4	7	8	9		11								3	10		6			36
1	2			5	4	7	8	9		11					10			3			6			37
1	2			5	4	7	8	9		11								3	10		6			38
1	2			5	4	7	8	9		11					10			3			6			39
1	2			5	4	7	8	9		11								3	10		6			40
1	2			5	4	7	8	9		11								3	10		6			41
1	2			5	4	7	8	9		11								3	10		6			42
40	**39**	**1**	**9**	**42**	**42**	**39**	**42**	**42**	**12**	**37**	**26**	**1**	**1**	**1**	**22**	**16**	**1**	**20**	**14**	**1**	**13**	**1**		
				1	1	8	13	34	2	13					4			7						

3 own-goals

FA Cup:

Hufton	Hebden	Earl	Bishop	Barrett	Collins	Yews	Earle	Watson	Moore	Ruffell	Carter	Dowsey	Williams	Payne	Gibbins	Hodgson	Kaine	Horler	Johnson	Hull	Cadwell	Baillie	Campbell	No.
1	2			5	6	7	8	9		11	4				10	3								3
1	2			5	6	7	8	9	10	11	4					3								4
1	2			5	6	7	8		10	11	4					3			9					R
3	**3**			**3**	**3**	**3**	**3**	**3**	**1**	**3**	**3**				**1**	**3**			**1**					
								3	1															

1927-28

Manager: Syd King

1	Aug	27	(a)	Derby C	W	3-2	Barrett, Watson, Gibbins	19,000
2	Sep	1	(h)	Sunderland	L	2-4	Ruffell 2	22,000
3		3	(h)	Huddersfield T	W	4-2	Earle 2, Yews, Loughlin	28,000
4		10	(h)	Portsmouth	W	4-2	Loughlin 2, Earle, Ruffell	25,000
5		17	(a)	Leicester C	W	3-2	Yews, Ruffell, Earle	30,000
6		24	(h)	Liverpool	W	3-1	Earle, Gibbins, Ruffell	32,000
7	Oct	1	(a)	Arsenal	D	2-2	Gibbins, Earle	40,000
8		8	(h)	Burnley	W	2-0	Gibbins 2	10,000
9		15	(a)	Bury	L	1-3	Ruffell	18,000
10		22	(a)	Everton	L	0-7		10,000
11		29	(h)	Manchester U	L	1-2	Watson	28,000
12	Nov	5	(a)	Tottenham H	L	3-5	Barrett, Ruffell, Earle	36,000
13		12	(h)	Cardiff C	W	2-0	Yews, Watson	28,000
14		19	(a)	Blackburn R	L	0-1		15,000
15		26	(h)	Middlesbrough	L	4-5	Yews 2, Gibbins, Watson	15,000
16	Dec	3	(a)	Sheffield W	L	0-2		25,000
17		10	(h)	Bolton W	W	2-0	Watson 2	20,000
18		17	(a)	Birmingham	W	2-1	Yews, Ruffell	30,000
19		24	(h)	Newcastle U	W	5-2	Ruffell 2, Gibbins 3	25,000
20		26	(a)	Sheffield U	L	2-6	Yews, Gibbins	25,000
21		27	(h)	Sheffield U	D	1-1	Yews	20,000
22		31	(h)	Derby C	D	2-2	Watson, Ruffell	22,000
23	Jan	2	(a)	Sunderland	1	2-3	Gibbins 2	23,000
24		7	(a)	Huddersfield T	L	2-5	Watson, Yews	8,000
25		21	(a)	Portsmouth	L	1-2	Gibbins	15,000
26	Feb	4	(a)	Liverpool	W	3-1	Earle, Gibbins, Ruffell	32,000
27		11	(h)	Arsenal	D	2-2	Watson 2	35,000
28		18	(a)	Burnley	D	0-0		12,000
29		25	(h)	Bury	L	1-2	Ruffell	25,000
30	Mar	3	(h)	Everton	D	0-0		32,000
31		10	(a)	Manchester U	D	1-1	Earle	25,000
32		12	(h)	Leicester C	W	4-0	Watson 3, Yews	10,000
33		17	(h)	Tottenham H	D	1-1	Ruffell	35,000
34		24	(a)	Cardiff C	W	5-1	Earle 2, Watson 2, Yews	18,000
35		31	(h)	Blackburn R	W	4-3	Ruffell 2, Moore, Earle	25,000
36	Apr	6	(h)	Aston Villa	D	0-0		36,000
37		7	(a)	Middlesbrough	D	2-2	Moore, Ruffell	25,000
38		9	(a)	Aston Villa	L	0-1		35,000
39		14	(h)	Sheffield W	L	1-2	Barrett	15,000
40		21	(a)	Bolton W	L	0-4		10,000
41		28	(h)	Birmingham	D	3-3	Barrett 2, Loughlin	16,000
42	May	5	(a)	Newcastle U	L	1-3	Gibbins	20,000

P	W	D	L	F	A	W	D	L	F	A	Pts	Pos	Div	
42	9	5	7	48	34	5	5	4	12	33	54	39	17th	1	Appearances
															Goals

FA Cup

3	Jan	14	(a)	Portsmouth	W	2-0	Gibbins, Ruffell	27,692
4		28	(a)	Huddersfield T	L	1-2	Gibbins	27,000

Appearances
Goals

238

Appearance & scorers grid (shirt numbers worn in each match).

Hufton	Hebden	Earl	Collins	Barrett	Cadwell	Yews	Earle	Watson	Gibbins	Ruffell	Moore	Baillie	Loughlin	Johnson	Henderson	Horler	Cox	Smith H	Norrington	Tate	Jackson	Campbell	Smith W	Hodgson	Robson	No.
1	2	3	4	5	6	7	8	9	10	11																1
1	2	3	4	5	6	7	8	9		11	10															2
	2	3	4	5	6	7	8			11		1	9	10												3
1	2	3	4	5	6	7	8	10		11			9													4
1		3	4	5	6	7	8	9		11			10		2											5
1		3	4	5	6	7	8		9	11			10		2											6
1		3	4	5	6	7	8		9	11			10		2											7
1		3	4	5	6	7	8		9	11			10		2											8
1		3	4	5	6	7		9	10	11			8		2											9
		3	4	5	6	7		9	10	11		1	8		2											10
	2		4	5		7	8	9		11			1			3	6	10								11
	2		4	5		7	8	9		11	10		1			3	6									12
	2		4	5		7	8	9	10	11		1					6		3							13
	2		4	5		7	8	9	10	11		1					6		3							14
	2		4	5		7	8	9	10	11		1					6		3							15
	2		4	5		7	8	9	10	11		1					6		3							16
	2		4	5		7	8	9		11	10						6		3	1						17
	2		4	5		7		8	9	11	10						6		3	1						18
	2		4	5		7		8	9	11	10						6		3	1						19
	2		4	5		7		8	9		10						6		3	1	11					20
	2		4	5		7		10	9								6		3	1	11					21
	2		4	5		7		8	10	11							6		3	1			9			22
	2		4	5		7		8	9	11	10						6		3	1						23
1	2		4	5		7	8	9		11	10						6					3				24
1		3	4		6	7	8	9		11	10				2		5									25
1		3	4		6	7	8	9		11	10				2		5									26
1		3	4		6	7	8	9		11	10				2		5									27
1		3	4		6	7	8	9		11	10				2		5									28
1		3	4		6	7	8	9		11	10				2		5									29
1		3	4	5		7	8	9		11	10				2		6									30
1		3	4		6	7	8		9	11	10				2		5									31
		3	4		6	7	8	9		11	10	1			2		5									32
1		4	3		6	7	8	9		11	10				2		5									33
1		3	4	5	6	7	8	9		11	10				2											34
		3	4	5	6	7	8	9		11	10		1											2		35
1		3	4	5	6	7	8	9		11	10													2		36
1		3	4	5	6	7	8	9		11	10													2		37
1		3	4	5	6	7	8	9	10	11														2		38
1		3	4	5	6	7	8	9	10			11												2		39
1	2	4	3		6	7	8	9		11	10						5									40
1	2	4	10		6	7	8			11			9				5		3							41
1	2	4			6	7			10	11			9				5		3						8	42
23	12	33	42	34	27	42	31	33	25	39	23	10	10	1	16	2	26	1	13	7	2	1	1	5	1	
						5	11	11	16	14	18		2		4											
								2	1																	

Hufton	Hebden	Earl	Collins	Barrett	Cadwell	Yews	Earle	Watson	Gibbins	Ruffell	Moore	Baillie	Loughlin	Johnson	Henderson	Horler	Cox	Smith H	Norrington	Tate	Jackson	Campbell	Smith W	Hodgson	Robson	No.
1		3	4		6	7	8	9		11	10				2		5									3
1		3	4		6	7	8	10	9	11					2		5									4
2		2	2		2	2	1	2	2	2	1				2		2									
								2	1																	

239

1928-29

Manager: Syd King

1	Aug	25	(h)	Sheffield U	W 4-0	Ruffell 2, Barrett, Shone	30,000
2	Sep	1	(a)	Bury	W 3-0	Watson 2, Ruffell	16,000
3		3	(a)	Burnley	D 3-3	Watson 2, Yews	22,000
4		8	(h)	Aston Villa	W 4-1	Watson 2, Ruffell, Collins	38,000
5		10	(a)	Cardiff C	L 2-3	Watson, Ruffell	20,000
6		15	(a)	Leicester C	L 0-5		25,000
7		17	(h)	Cardiff C	D 1-1	Watson	18,000
8		22	(h)	Manchester U	W 3-1	Shone 2, Payne	30,000
9		29	(a)	Leeds U	L 1-4	Watson	30,000
10	Oct	6	(h)	Liverpool	D 1-1	Earle	30,000
11		13	(a)	Arsenal	W 3-2	Earle, Shone, Ruffell	48,000
12		20	(h)	Everton	L 2-4	Shone, Gibbins	25,000
13		29	(a)	Blackburn R	L 0-2		20,000
14	Nov	3	(h)	Manchester C	W 3-0	Ruffell 2, Yews	26,000
15		10	(a)	Birmingham	D 2-2	Gibbins, Earle	25,000
16		17	(h)	Portsmouth	L 0-1		18,000
17		24	(a)	Bolton W	L 1-4	Gibbins	10,000
18	Dec	1	(h)	Sheffield W	W 3-2	Yews 2, Watson	25,000
19		8	(a)	Derby C	L 0-6		20,000
20		15	(h)	Sunderland	D 3-3	Ruffell 2, Robson	20,000
21		22	(a)	Huddersfield T	L 0-4		12,000
22		25	(h)	Newcastle U	W 1-0	Gibbins	30,000
23		26	(a)	Newcastle U	L 0-1		40,000
24		29	(a)	Sheffield U	D 3-3	Yews, Watson, Ruffell	25,000
25	Jan	5	(h)	Bury	L 2-3	Yews, Watson	15,000
26		19	(a)	Aston Villa	L 2-5	Watson, Ruffell	30,000
27	Feb	2	(a)	Manchester U	W 3-2	Watson, Gibbins, Ruffell	15,000
28		9	(h)	Leeds U	W 8-2	Watson 6, Gibbins, Yews	18,055
29		23	(h)	Arsenal	L 3-4	Ruffell 2, Watson	35,000
30	Mar	4	(h)	Leicester C	W 2-1	Ruffell, Earle	10,000
31		9	(h)	Blackburn R	D 3-3	Yews 2, Watson	30,000
32		12	(a)	Liverpool	L 1-2	Watson	12,000
33		16	(a)	Manchester C	L 2-4	Ruffell, Watson	30,000
34		23	(h)	Birmingham	W 2-1	Earle, Watson	20,000
35		29	(h)	Burnley	W 4-0	Ruffell 2, Gibbins, Yews	20,000
36		30	(a)	Portsmouth	L 0-3		22,000
37	Apr	6	(h)	Bolton W	W 3-0	Watson, Earle, Gibbins	30,000
38		10	(a)	Everton	W 4-0	Gibbins 3, Opp own-goal	10,000
39		13	(a)	Sheffield W	L 0-6		25,000
40		20	(h)	Derby C	D 2-2	Watson 2	20,000
41		27	(a)	Sunderland	L 1-4	Watson	10,000
42	May	4	(h)	Huddersfield T	D 1-1	Ruffell	20,000

P	W	D	L	F	A	W	D	L	F	A	Pts	Pos	Div	
42	11	6	4	55	31	4	3	14	31	65	39	17th	1	Appearances
														Goals

FA Cup

3	Jan	12	(h)	Sunderland	W 1-0	Earle	35,000
4		26	(h)	Corinthians	W 3-0	Earle, Watson, Yews	42,000
5	Feb	16	(a)	Bournemouth	D 1-1	Yews	11,346
R		20	(h)	Bournemouth	W 3-1	Barrett, Yews, Opp own-goal	30,217
6	Mar	2	(a)	Portsmouth	L 2-3	Barrett 2	39,088

Appearances
Goals

Appearance grid (numbers indicate playing position 1–11 in each match; right-hand column = match number).

#	Hufton	Hodgson	Norrington	Collins	Barrett	Cadwell	Yews	Earle	Watson	Shone	Ruffell	Norris	Tate	Cox	Gibbins	Payne	Baillie	Earl	Moore	Coshall	Robson	Hull	Smith W	Smailes	Dixon
1	1	2	3	4	5	6	7	8	9	10	11														
2	1	2	3	4	5	6	7	8	9	10	11														
3	1	2	3	4	5	6	7	8	9	10	11														
4	1	2	3	4	5	6	7	8	9	10	11														
5	1	2	3	4	5	6	7		9	10	11	8													
6		2	3	4	5	6	7	8	9	10	11		1												
7		2		4	5	6	7	8	9		11		1	3	10										
8		2	3	4		6	7	8	9	10			1	5		11									
9		2	3	4		6	7	8	9	10	11		1	5											
10		2		4	5	6	7	8	9	10	11						1	3							
11	1			4	5	6	7	8		10	11			3	9			2							
12	1			4	5	6	7	8		10	11			3	9			2							
13	1	2		4		6	7	8		10	11			5	9			3							
14	1	2		4		6	7	8			11			5	9			3	10						
15	1	2		4		6	7	8			11			5	9			3	10						
16	1	2		4		6	7	8						5	9	11		3	10						
17	1			4		6	7	8	9		11			5	10			3	2						
18	1	2		4		6	7	8	9		11			5	10			3							
19	1			4		6		8	9		11			5	10	7		3	2						
20	1	2		4			7	5	9		11			6	10			3		8					
21	1			4			7	5	9		11			2	10			3		8	6				
22	1	2		4		6	7	8	9		11			5	10			3							
23	1	2		4		6	7	8	9		11			5	10			3							
24	1		2	4		6	7	8	9		11			5	10			3							
25	1		2	4		6	7	8	9		11			5	10			3							
26	1			4		6	7	8	9		11			5				3	10		2				
27	1	2		4		6	7	8	9		11			5	10			3							
28	1	2		4		6	7	8	9		11				10			3			5				
29		2		4	10	6	7	8	9		11						1	3			5				
30		2		4		6	7	8	9		11		1		10			3			5				
31		2		4		6	7	8	9				1		10			3	11		5				
32		2		4		6	7	8	9				1		10			3	11		5				
33		2		4	10	6	7	8	9		11							3			5		1		
34			3	4	5	6	7	8	9		11							2						10	1
35	1		3	4	5	6	7	8	9		11							2						10	
36	1		3	4	5	6	7	8	9		11							2						10	
37	1			4	2	6	7	8	9		11							3			5			10	
38	1			4	2	6	7	8			11				9			3			5			10	
39	1			4	2	6	7	8			11				9			3			5			10	
40	1	2			5	6	7	8	9		11	4			10			3							
41	1	2			5	6	7	8	9		11	4			10			3							
42	1	2	3		5	6	7	8			11	4			9									10	
Apps	**31**	**28**	**14**	**39**	**22**	**40**	**41**	**41**	**34**	**12**	**37**	**6**	**7**	**20**	**29**	**3**	**2**	**32**	**6**	**2**	**5**	**1**	**1**	**7**	**2**
Goals				1	1		10	6	29	5	20				11	1			1						

1 own-goal

FA Cup

Rd	Hufton	Hodgson	Norrington	Collins	Barrett	Cadwell	Yews	Earle	Watson	Shone	Ruffell	Norris	Tate	Cox	Gibbins	Payne	Baillie	Earl	Moore	Coshall	Robson	Hull	Smith W	Smailes	Dixon
3	1	2		4		6	7	8	9		11			5				3	10						
4	1	2		4		6	7	8	9		11			5	10			3							
5	1	2		4		6	7	8	9		11				10			3			5				
R		2		4	10	6	7	8	9		11						1	3			5				
6	1	2		4	10	6	7	8	9		11							3			5				
Apps	**4**	**5**		**5**	**2**	**5**	**5**	**5**	**5**		**5**			**2**	**2**		**1**	**5**	**1**		**3**				
Goals						3	3	2	1																

1 own-goal

1929-30

Manager: Syd King

1	Aug	31	(a)	Blackburn R	D	3-3	Ball, Watson, Opp own-goal	25,000
2	Sep	4	(a)	Birmingham	L	2-4	Watson 2	20,000
3		7	(h)	Middlesbrough	W	5-3	Ruffell 2, Ball 2, Watson	35,000
4		9	(h)	Newcastle U	W	5-1	Yews 2, Ball 2, Watson	25,000
5		14	(a)	Liverpool	L	1-3	Watson	25,000
6		16	(h)	Birmingham	L	0-1		16,000
7		21	(h)	Derby C	W	2-0	Barrett, Ruffell	35,000
8		28	(h)	Manchester U	W	2-1	Ball, Watson	20,000
9	Oct	5	(a)	Grimsby T	D	2-2	Watson, Ball	15,000
10		12	(h)	Leicester C	L	1-2	Watson	30,000
11		19	(a)	Manchester C	L	3-4	Yews, Ruffell, Ball	25,000
12		26	(h)	Portsmouth	L	0-1		25,000
13	Nov	2	(a)	Arsenal	W	1-0	Watson	50,000
14		9	(h)	Everton	W	3-1	Ruffell 2, Watson	30,000
15		16	(a)	Leeds U	W	3-1	Watson 2, Opp own-goal	15,000
16		23	(h)	Sheffield W	D	1-1	Watson	22,000
17		30	(a)	Burnley	D	1-1	Barrett	6,000
18	Dec	7	(h)	Sunderland	D	1-1	Watson	21,000
19		14	(a)	Bolton W	L	1-4	Watson	8,000
20		21	(h)	Aston Villa	W	5-2	Watson 3, Gibbins, Ruffell	18,000
21		25	(h)	Huddersfield T	L	2-3	Watson, Gibbins	30,000
22		26	(a)	Huddersfield T	L	0-3		20,000
23		28	(h)	Blackburn R	L	2-3	Watson, Ruffell	27,000
24	Jan	1	(a)	Sheffield U	L	2-4	Ball, Ruffell	20,000
25		4	(a)	Middlesbrough	L	0-2		12,000
26		18	(h)	Liverpool	W	4-1	Watson, Robson, Barrett, Opp own-goal	25,000
27	Feb	1	(a)	Manchester U	L	2-4	Earle, Watson	20,000
28		5	(a)	Derby C	L	3-4	Watson 2, Opp own-goal	10,000
29		8	(h)	Grimsby T	W	2-0	Watson, Ruffell	16,500
30		20	(a)	Leicester C	W	2-1	Watson, Wood	10,000
31		22	(h)	Manchester C	W	3-0	Watson, Barrett, Gibbins	28,000
32	Mar	8	(h)	Arsenal	W	3-2	Watson 2, Earle	35,000
33		12	(a)	Portsmouth	L	1-3	Ruffell	10,000
34		15	(a)	Everton	W	2-1	Watson 2	25,000
35		22	(h)	Leeds U	W	3-0	Watson 3	30,000
36		29	(a)	Sheffield W	L	1-2	Watson	30,000
37	Apr	5	(h)	Burnley	W	1-0	Barrett	15,000
38		12	(a)	Sunderland	L	2-4	Barrett, Ruffell	20,000
39		18	(h)	Sheffield U	W	1-0	Watson	30,000
40		19	(h)	Bolton W	W	5-3	Watson 2, Barrett, Ruffell, Earle	18,000
41		26	(a)	Aston Villa	W	3-2	Watson 3	22,000
42	May	3	(a)	Newcastle U	L	0-1		48,000

P	W	D	L	F	A	W	D	L	F	A	Pts	Pos	Div	
42	14	2	5	51	26	5	3	13	35	53	43	7th	1	Appearances
														Goals

FA Cup

3	Jan	11	(h)	Notts C	W	4-0	Watson 2, Barrett, Gibbins	28,384
4		25	(h)	Leeds U	W	4-1	Watson 4	34,000
5	Feb	15	(h)	Millwall	W	4-1	Watson 2, Gibbins, Yews	24,000
R	Mar	1	(a)	Arsenal	L	0-3		40,492

Appearances
Goals

Player appearance and goal-scoring grid (shirt numbers by match). Columns left-to-right: Hufton, Wade W, Earl, Collins, Barrett, Cadwell, Yews, Earle, Watson, Ball, Ruffell, Cox, Pollard, Hodgson, Wood, Norris, St Pier, Gibbins, Robson, Wade R, Dixon. The right-hand number is the match number.

Huf	WaW	Earl	Col	Bar	Cad	Yew	Earle	Wat	Ball	Ruf	Cox	Pol	Hod	Woo	Nor	StP	Gib	Rob	WaR	Dix	№
1	2	3	4	5	6	7	8	9	10	11											
1	2	3	4	5		7	8	9	10	11	6										1
1	2	3	4	5	6	7	8	9	10	11											2
1	2	3	4	5	6	7	8	9	10	11											3
1	2	3	4	5	6	7	8	9		11		10									4
1	2	3	4	5	6	7	8	9	10	11											5
1		3	4	5	6		8	9	10	11			2	7							6
1		3		5	6	7	8	9	10	11			2		4						7
1		3		5	6	7	8	9	10	11			2		4						8
1	2	3		5		7	8	9	10	11	6				4						9
1		2		5	6	7	8	9	10	11	3				4						10
1		2		5	6	7	8	9	10	11	3				4						11
1		2		5	6	7	8	9		11	3				4		10				12
1		2		5	6	7	8	9		11	3				4		10				13
1		2		5	6	7	8	9		11	3				4		10				14
1		2		5	6	7	8	9		11	3				4		10				15
1		2		5	6	7	8	9			3			11	4		10				16
1		2		5	6	7	8	9		11	3				4		10				17
1		2			6	7	8	9		11	3				4	5	10				18
1		2		5	6	7		9		11	3				4		10	8			19
1	2			5	6	7		9		11	3				4		10	8			20
1	2			5	6	7		9		11	3				4		10	8			21
1				5	6	7		9	10	11	3	2			4			8			22
1	2			5	6	7			10	11	3				4		9	8			23
1		2		5	6	7		9		11	3				4		10	8			24
1	2		4	5	6	7	8	9		11							10		3		25
	2		4	5	6	7	8	9		11	3						10			1	26
1		2		5	6	7	8	9		11	3				4		10				27
1		2	4	5	6	7	8	9		11	3						10				28
	2				6	7	8	9	10		3		11		4		5			1	29
	2		4	5	6	7	8	9		11	3						10			1	30
1	2		4	5	6	7	8	9		11	3						10				31
1	2		4	5	6	7	8	9	10	11	3										32
	2		4	5	6	7	8	9		11	3						10			1	33
	2		4	5	6	7	8	9		11	3						10			1	34
	2		4	5	6		8	9		11	3			7			10			1	35
	2		4	5	6	7	8			11	3	10					9			1	36
	2		4	5	6	7	8	9		11	3	10								1	37
	2		4	5	6	7	8	9		11	3	10								1	38
	2		4	5	6	7	8	9		11	3	10								1	39
	2		4	5	6	7	8	9		11		10							3	1	40
	3	2	4			7	8	9		11	6	10				5				1	41
	3	2	4			7	8	9		11	6	10				5				1	42
30	**11**	**38**	**21**	**40**	**38**	**41**	**36**	**40**	**15**	**40**	**32**	**7**	**4**	**4**	**19**	**4**	**18**	**10**	**2**	**12**	
			7			3	3	42	9	13					1		3	1			

4 own-goals

Cup ties (rounds 3, 4, 5, Replay):

Huf	WaW	Earl	Col	Bar	Cad	Yew	Earle	Wat	Ball	Ruf	Cox	Pol	Hod	Woo	Nor	StP	Gib	Rob	WaR	Dix	Rd
1	2		4	5	6	7	8	9		11	3						10				3
1	2		4	5	6	7	8	9		11	3							10			4
1	2		4	5	6	7	8	9		11	3						10				5
1	2		4	5	6	7	8	9		11	3						10				R
4	**4**		**4**	**4**	**4**	**4**	**4**			**4**	**4**						**3**	**1**			
			1		1			8									2				

1930-31

Manager: Syd King

1	Aug	30	(h)	Huddersfield T	W	2-1	Watson 2	24,000
2	Sep	1	(h)	Liverpool	W	7-0	Watson 4, Earle 2, James	14,000
3		6	(a)	Aston Villa	L	1-6	Watson	40,000
4		8	(h)	Middlesbrough	L	0-3		12,000
5		13	(h)	Chelsea	W	4-1	Watson 2, Earle, James	35,201
6		17	(a)	Middlesbrough	D	2-2	James, Watson	20,000
7		20	(a)	Newcastle U	L	2-4	Earle, Watson	18,000
8		27	(h)	Sheffield W	D	3-3	Gibbins, Ruffell, James	32,000
9	Oct	4	(a)	Grimsby T	L	0-4		17,000
10		11	(h)	Manchester U	W	5-1	Gibbins 3, Ruffell, Barrett	26,000
11		18	(h)	Blackburn R	W	4-3	Yews 2, Gibbins, Ruffell	28,000
12		25	(a)	Arsenal	D	1-1	Pollard	56,000
13	Nov	1	(h)	Sheffield U	W	4-1	Gibbins 2, Earle, Barrett	25,000
14		8	(a)	Birmingham	W	2-0	Yews 2	25,000
15		15	(h)	Leeds U	D	1-1	Norris	20,000
16		22	(a)	Derby C	D	1-1	Gibbins	12,324
17		29	(h)	Leicester C	W	2-0	Ruffell 2	25,000
18	Dec	6	(a)	Blackpool	W	3-1	Ruffell, Earle, Gibbins	12,000
19		13	(h)	Manchester C	W	2-0	Ruffell 2	22,000
20		20	(a)	Sunderland	L	1-6	Gibbins	20,000
21		25	(h)	Portsmouth	W	4-3	Gibbins 2, James, Norris	32,000
22		26	(a)	Portsmouth	L	0-2		30,000
23		27	(h)	Huddersfield T	L	0-2		12,000
24	Jan	3	(h)	Aston Villa	D	5-5	Barrett, Yews, Gibbins 2, Horris	25,000
25		17	(a)	Chelsea	L	1-2	Gibbins	50,000
26		26	(h)	Newcastle U	W	3-2	Earle, Gibbins, James	10,000
27		31	(a)	Sheffield W	L	3-5	Yews, James, Watson	12,000
28	Feb	7	(h)	Grimsby T	L	3-4	Ruffell 3	18,000
29		14	(a)	Manchester U	L	0-1		10,000
30		21	(a)	Blackburn R	L	0-1		10,000
31		28	(h)	Arsenal	L	2-4	Watson, Earle	35,000
32	Mar	7	(a)	Sheffield U	W	2-1	Yews, Ruffell	12,000
33		16	(h)	Birmingham	L	1-2	Watson	12,000
34		21	(a)	Leeds U	L	0-3		10,000
35		28	(h)	Derby C	L	0-1		20,000
36	Apr	3	(h)	Bolton W	L	1-4	Wood	18,000
37		4	(a)	Leicester C	D	1-1	Gamble	18,000
38		6	(a)	Bolton W	L	2-4	Barrett, Gamble	20,000
39		11	(h)	Blackpool	W	3-2	Musgrave, Gibbins, Ruffell	15,000
40		18	(a)	Manchester C	D	1-1	Gibbins	15,000
41		25	(h)	Sunderland	L	0-3		12,000
42	May	2	(a)	Liverpool	L	0-2		25,000

P	W	D	L	F	A	W	D	L	F	A	Pts	Pos	Div		Appearances
42	11	3	7	56	44	3	3	5	13	23	50	36	18th	1	Goals

FA Cup

3	Jan	10	(h)	Chelsea	L	1-3	Gibbins	21,000

Appearances
Goals

Appearances grid (shirt numbers worn per match):

Dixon	Earl	Cox	Collins	Barrett	Cadwell	Yews	Earle	Watson	James	Ruffell	Wade	Hufton	St Pier	Gibbins	Evans	Norris	Pollard	Harris	Robson	England	Goodacre	Musgrave	Fryatt	Wood	Gamble	No.
1	2	3	4	5	6	7	8	9	10	11																
1	2		4	5	6	7	8	9	10	11	3															1
1	2		4	5	6	7	8	9	10	11	3															2
1	2		4	5	6	7	8	9	10	11	3															3
	2		4	3	6	7	8	9	10	11		1	5													4
	2		4	3	6	7	8	9	10	11		1	5													5
	2	3	4		6	7	8	9	10	11		1	5													6
	2		4	3	6	7	8		10	11		1	5	9												7
	2		4	3	6		8		10	11		1	5	9	7											8
1	2		4	5	6	7	8		10	11	3			9												9
1	2		4	5	6	7	8		10	11	3			9												10
1	2			5	6	7	8	9		11	3					4	10									11
1	2			5	6	7	8		10	11	3			9		4										12
1	2			5	6	7	8		10	11	3			9		4										13
1	2		4	5	6	7	8		10	11	3			9												14
1	2		4	5	6		8		10	11	3			9		7										15
1	2		4	5		7	8		10	11	3			9		6										16
1	2		4	5	6	7	8		10	11	3			9												17
1	2		4	9	6	7	8		10	11	3					5										18
1	2		4	5	6	7	8		10	11	3			9												19
1	2		4	5	6	7		9			3			8		11	10									20
1	2		4	5	6	7		10			3			9			11	8								21
1	2		4	5	6	7	8	10			3			9			11									22
1	2		4	5	6	7	8	10						9			11	3								23
1	2		4			7	8		10	11	3			9		6										24
	2		4	5		7	8		10	11		1		9		6		3								25
1	2		4	5	6	7	8	9	10	11	3															26
1	2			5	6	7		9	10	11				8		4		3								27
			4	5		7	8	9	10	11	3	1										2	6			28
1	2		4		6	7	8	9	10	11	3		5													29
1	2		4	5	6	7	8	9	10	11	3															30
1	2		4	5		7	8	9	10	11	3										6					31
1			4	5		7	8	9	10	11	2							3			6					32
1			4	5		7	8	9	10	11									3		6	2				33
			4	5	6	7	8		10	11				9				3				2				34
		3	4	5	6		8	9	10	11		1										2	7			35
		3	4	5	6	7	8			11		1				10						2		9		36
		3	4	5	6			10		11		1							8	11		2	7	9		37
	2		4	5		7	8			11	3	1		9		6					10					38
	2		4	5		7				11	3	1		9		6				8	10					39
1	2		4	5		7				11	3			9		6				8	10					40
	2		4	5			8	9	10	11	3	1											7			41
28	**38**	**2**	**38**	**40**	**31**	**37**	**36**	**18**	**36**	**37**	**28**	**14**	**6**	**21**	**1**	**16**	**5**	**5**	**1**	**5**	**6**	**7**	**1**	**3**	**2**	
			4		7	8	14	7	13					18		2	1	1		1				1	2	

Additional match:

Dixon	Earl	Cox	Collins	Barrett	Cadwell	Yews	Earle	Watson	James	Ruffell	Wade	Hufton	St Pier	Gibbins	Evans	Norris	Pollard	Harris	Robson	England	Goodacre	Musgrave	Fryatt	Wood	Gamble	No.
1	2		4	5	6	7	8		10	11	3			9												3
1	1		1	1	1	1	1		1	1	1			1												
														1												

1931-32

Manager: Syd King

No	Month	Day		Opponent	Result	Scorers	Attendance
1	Aug	29	(a)	Bolton W	W 1-0	Watson	12,000
2		31	(h)	Chelsea	W 3-1	Weldon, Watson, Norris	35,000
3	Sep	5	(h)	Middlesbrough	L 0-2		20,000
4		7	(a)	Sheffield U	L 0-6		12,000
5		12	(a)	Huddersfield T	L 1-3	Watson	12,000
6		19	(h)	Newcastle U	W 1-2	Watson, Ruffell	28,000
7		21	(h)	Sheffield U	L 1-2	Ruffell	15,000
8		26	(a)	Aston Villa	L 2-5	Wood, Opp own-goal	40,000
9	Oct	3	(h)	Leicester C	L 1-4	Gibbins	25,000
10		10	(a)	Liverpool	D 2-2	Gibbins, Weldon	25,000
11		17	(a)	Manchester C	W 1-0	Ruffell	18,000
12		24	(h)	Portsmouth	W 2-1	Gibbins 2	20,000
13		31	(a)	Derby C	L 1-5	Watson	10,000
14	Nov	7	(h)	West Brom A	L 1-5	Ruffell	20,000
15		14	(a)	Arsenal	L 1-4	Watson	45,000
16		21	(h)	Blackpool	D 1-1	Ruffell	16,000
17		28	(a)	Blackburn R	W 4-2	Barrett, Gibbins, Phillips, Watson	10,000
18	Dec	5	(h)	Everton	W 4-2	Ruffell 3, Wood	40,000
19		12	(a)	Birmingham	L 1-4	Watson	22,000
20		19	(h)	Sunderland	D 2-2	Watson, Barrett	10,000
21		25	(a)	Grimsby T	L 1-2	Watson	14,000
22		26	(h)	Grimsby T	W 3-1	Ruffell 2, Watson	30,000
23	Jan	2	(h)	Bolton W	W 3-1	Watson 2, Ruffell	20,000
24		16	(a)	Middlesbrough	L 2-3	Watson 2	6,000
25		30	(a)	Newcastle U	D 2-2	Watson, Cadwell	28,000
26	Feb	1	(h)	Huddersfield T	D 1-1	Watson	10,000
27		6	(h)	Aston Villa	W 2-1	Phillips, Yews	30,000
28		18	(a)	Leicester C	L 1-2	Ruffell	12,000
29		20	(h)	Liverpool	W 1-0	Ruffell	18,000
30	Mar	2	(h)	Manchester C	D 1-1	Chalkley	18,000
31		5	(a)	Portsmouth	L 0-3		15,000
32		12	(h)	Derby C	W 2-1	Ruffell, Watson	24,000
33		19	(a)	West Brom A	L 1-3	Phillips	16,000
34		25	(h)	Sheffield W	L 1-2	Ruffell	38,000
35		26	(h)	Arsenal	D 1-1	Watson	40,000
36		28	(h)	Sheffield W	L 1-6	Watson	18,000
37	Apr	2	(a)	Blackpool	L 2-7	Morton, Watson	12,000
38		9	(h)	Blackburn R	L 1-3	Watson	16,000
39		16	(a)	Everton	L 1-6	Opp own-goal	35,000
40		23	(h)	Birmingham	L 2-4	Wheldon, Watson	12,000
41		30	(a)	Sunderland	L 0-2		10,000
42	May	7	(a)	Chelsea	L 2-3	Barrett, Yews	30,000

P	W	D	L	F	A	W	D	L	F	A	Pts	Pos	Div	Appearances
42	9	5	7	35	37	3	2	16	27	70	31	22nd	1	Goals

FA Cup

Round	Month	Day		Opponent	Result	Scorers	Attendance
3	Jan	9	(a)	Charlton A	W 2-1	Watson 2	26,500
4		23	(a)	Chelsea	L 1-3	Weldon	36,657

Appearances
Goals

Player appearance and goal-scoring grid (positions 1–11 shown for each match). Column headers, left to right:

Hufton, Earl, Chalkley, Norris, Barrett, Cadwell, Yews, Earle, Watson, Weldon, Ruffell, Pollard, Cox, Collins, Wood, Dixon, Gibbins, Wade W, St Pier, James, Goodacre, Phillips, Harris, Puddefoot, Wade R, Musgrave, Morton.

No.	Hufton	Earl	Chalkley	Norris	Barrett	Cadwell	Yews	Earle	Watson	Weldon	Ruffell	Pollard	Cox	Collins	Wood	Dixon	Gibbins	Wade W	St Pier	James	Goodacre	Phillips	Harris	Puddefoot	Wade R	Musgrave	Morton
1	1	2	3	4	5	6	7	8	9	10	11																
2	1	2	3	4	5	6	7		9	10	11	8															
3	1	2	3	4	5	6	7		9	10	11	8															
4	1	2	3	4	5	6	7	8	9	10	11																
5	1	2		4	5		7		9	10	11	8	3	6													
6	1	2		4	5		7	8	9	10	11		3	6													
7	1	2		4	5			8	9	10	11		3	6	7												
8		2		4	5			8	9	10	11		3	6	7	1											
9	1	2		4	5		7	8		10	11		3	6			9										
10	1	2		4						10	11			6	7		9	3	5	8							
11	1			6		8				10	11			4	7		9	3	5		2						
12	1			6						10	11	8		4	7		9	3	5		2						
13	1			6				8	9	10	11			4	7			3	5		2						
14	1			6				8	9	10	11	3		4	7				5		2						
15	1	3		6					9	8	11			4	7				5	10	2						
16		2			5			8		10	11		6	4	7	1	9	3									
17		2	3		5	6				10	11			4	7	1	9					8					
18		2	3		5	6			9		11			4	7	1	10					8					
19		2	3		5	6			9		11			4	7	1	10					8					
20		2	3		5	6			9		11			4	7	1	10					8					
21		2	3		5	6			9		11			4	7	1				10		8					
22		2	3		5	6	7		9		11			4		1				10		8					
23		2	3		5	6	7		9	10	11			4		1						8					
24		2	3		5	6	7		9	10	11			4		1						8					
25		2	3		5	6	7		9	10	11			4		1						8					
26		2	3		5	6	7	8	9					4		1					10	11					
27		2	3		5	6	7	8	9					4		1					10	11					
28		2	3		5	6	7	8	9		11			4		1					10						
29		2	3		5	6	7	8	9		11			4		1					10						
30			3		5	6	7	8	9		11			4		1					2	10					
31			3		5	6	7		9		11			4		1					2	10		8			
32		2	3		5	6	7		9		11			4		1						10		8			
33			3		5	6	7		9		11			4		1					2	10		8			
34	1		3		5				9		11			4							10	8	2				
35	1		3		5				9		11	8		4							10				2	6	7
36	1	2	3		5	6		8	9		11			4							10						7
37	1	2	3		5	6			9					4	8												7
38	1		3	4	5	6	7		9											8	2	10	11				
39	1	2	3	4	5		7	8	9	10	11		6														
40		2	3	4	5	6	7		9	10	11	8	1														
41	1	2	3	4	10		7		9		11			8					5							6	
App.	**22**	**30**	**29**	**17**	**38**	**26**	**23**	**17**	**38**	**20**	**39**	**7**	**9**	**35**	**17**	**20**	**9**	**5**	**7**	**4**	**10**	**21**	**2**	**7**	**2**	**3**	**5**
Goals		1	1	3	1	2			23	3	15			2	5						3						1

2 own-goals

No.	Hufton	Earl	Chalkley	Norris	Barrett	Cadwell	Yews	Earle	Watson	Weldon	Ruffell	Pollard	Cox	Collins	Wood	Dixon	Gibbins	Wade W	St Pier	James	Goodacre	Phillips	Harris	Puddefoot	Wade R	Musgrave	Morton
		2	3		5	6	7		9	10	11			4		1						8					
3		2	3		5	6	7		9	10	11			4		1						8					
4		2	2		2	2	2		2	2	2			2		2						2					
									2	1																	

1932-33

Manager: Charlie Paynter

1	Aug	27	(a)	Swansea T	L 0-1		15,000
2		29	(h)	Bradford C	L 2-4	Mills, Pollard	15,000
3	Sep	3	(h)	Notts C	D 1-1	Puddefoot	15,000
4		7	(a)	Bradford C	L 1-5	Watson	17,000
5		10	(a)	Port Vale	L 0-4		8,000
6		17	(h)	Millwall	W 3-0	Watson 2, Morton	30,000
7		24	(a)	Southampton	L 3-4	Morton 2, Watson	10,000
8	Oct	1	(h)	Bury	L 0-1		10,000
9		8	(a)	Lincoln C	L 0-6		10,000
10		15	(h)	Oldham A	W 5-2	Norris 3, Morton, Watson	18,000
11		22	(a)	Preston NE	L 1-4	Mills	8,000
12		29	(h)	Burnley	D 4-4	Watson 3, Morton	14,000
13	Nov	5	(a)	Bradford	L 0-3		13,000
14		12	(h)	Grimsby T	W 5-2	Wilson 2, Yews, Watson, Opp own-goal	16,000
15		19	(a)	Stoke C	D 0-0		10,000
16		26	(h)	Charlton A	W 7-3	Wilson 2, Watson 2, Barrett, Yews, Morton	23,000
17	Dec	3	(a)	Nottingham F	D 2-2	Watson, Wilson	7,000
18		10	(a)	Manchester U	W 3-1	Watson 2, Wilson	15,000
19		17	(a)	Tottenham H	D 2-2	Morton, Opp own-goal	46,250
20		24	(h)	Plymouth A	D 2-2	Barrett, Morton	20,000
21		26	(a)	Fulham	L 2-4	Pollard, Puddefoot	27,861
22		27	(h)	Fulham	D 1-1	Watson	40,000
23		31	(h)	Swansea T	W 3-1	Watson 2, Barrett	18,000
24	Jan	7	(a)	Notts C	L 0-2		11,000
25		21	(h)	Port Vale	W 5-0	Watson 2, Wilson 2, Barrett	18,000
26		30	(a)	Millwall	L 0-1		5,000
27	Feb	4	(h)	Southampton	W 3-1	Watson, Wilson 2	20,000
28		11	(a)	Bury	L 1-6	Barrett	7,000
29	Mar	6	(h)	Preston NE	D 1-1	Puddefoot	12,000
30		11	(a)	Burnley	L 0-4		10,000
31		13	(a)	Oldham A	L 2-3	Mills, Wood	6,000
32		20	(h)	Bradford	W 2-1	Watson 2	12,000
33		25	(a)	Grimsby T	L 1-2	Wilson	12,000
34		27	(h)	Lincoln C	D 0-0		12,000
35	Apr	1	(h)	Stoke C	L 1-2	Barrett	23,000
36		8	(a)	Charlton A	L 1-3	Barrett	30,000
37		14	(a)	Chesterfield	L 0-1		11,000
38		15	(h)	Nottingham F	W 4-3	Barrett, Goulden, Morton, Wood	20,000
39		17	(h)	Chesterfield	W 3-1	Morton, Pollard, Watson	21,000
40		22	(a)	Manchester U	W 2-1	Morton, Wilson	18,000
41		29	(h)	Tottenham H	W 1-0	Wilson	35,000
42	May	6	(a)	Plymouth A	L 1-4	Opp own-goal	12,000

P	W	D	L	F	A	W	D	L	F	A	Pts	Pos	Div	Appearances
42	12	6	3	56	31	1	3	17	19	62	35	20th	2	Goals

FA Cup

3	Jan	14	(a)	Corinthians	W 2-0	Pollard, Watson	16,421
4		28	(h)	West Brom A	W 2-0	Watson, Wilson	37,222
5	Feb	18	(a)	Brighton & HA	D 2-2	Musgrave, Watson	32,310
R		22	(h)	Brighton & HA	W 1-0	Morton	36,742
6	Mar	4	(h)	Birmingham	W 4-0	Wilson, Morton, Pollard, Opp own-goal	44,232
SF		18	(n*)	Everton	L 1-2	Watson	37,936

* Played at Molineux

Appearances
Goals

Dixon	Earl	Chalkley	Collins	Barrett	Musgrave	Yews	Wilson	Mills	Puddefoot	Ruffell	Watson G	Pollard	Deacon	Fenton	Watson V	Norris	St Pier	Morton	Fryatt	Cadwell	Walker A	Johnson	Goodacre	Wood	McMahon	Goulden	Cockroft	
1	2	3	4	5	6	7	8	9	10	11																		1
	2	3	4	5	6	7		9		11	1	8	10															2
1	2	3	4	5	6	7		9	10	11		8																3
1	2	3	4	5	6	7			10	11				8	9													4
	2	3	4	5	6	7			10	11	1			8	9													5
	2	3			6	7			10		1			8	9	4	5	11										6
	2	3			6	7			10		1			8	9	4	5	11										7
	2		4		6	7			10		1			8	9		5	11	3									8
	2		4	5			8		10	11	1				9			7	3	6								9
	2				6	7		9			1				10	8	4	11		3	5							10
	2				6	7		9			1				10	8	4	11		3	5							11
	2			5		7		9			1				10	8		11	6	3	4							12
	2			5		7			10		1	8			9			11		3	4							13
	2			5	6	7	8		10		1				9			11		3	4							14
	2		4	5	6	7			10		1	8			9			11		3								15
	2		4	5	6	7			10		1	8			9			11		3								16
	2			5	6	7			10		1	8			9	4		11		3								17
	2		4	5	6	7			10		1	8			9			11		3								18
	2		4	5	6	7		9	10		1	8						11		3								19
	2		4	5	6	7			10		1	8			9			11		3								20
			4	5	6	7			10		1	8			9			11		3	2							21
			4	5	6	7			10		1	8			9			11		3	2							22
			4	5	6				10		1	8			9			11		3	2	7						23
			4	5	6				10		1	8			9			11		3	2	7						24
	2		4	5	6	7			10	11	1	8			9					3								25
	2		4	5		7			10		1	8			9			11	6	3								26
	2		4	5		7			10		1	8			9			11	6	3								27
	2		4	5		7			10		1	8			9			11	6	3								28
	2		4	5	6	7			10			8			9			11		3				1				29
	2		4	5	6	7			10						9	8		11		3				1				30
	2			5	6				10				8		9		4	11		3		7		1				31
	2		4	5		7			10						9			11	6	3		8	1					32
	2		4	5		7			10						9			11	6	3		8	1					33
	2		4	5		7			10				8		9			11	6	3			1					34
	2		4	5		7			10			8			9			11	6	3			1					35
	2		4				8			11					9		5	7	6	3					1	10		36
	2		4	5			8								9			11		3				7	1	10	6	37
	2		4	5			8								9			11		3				7	1	10	6	38
	2		4	5									8		9			11		3				7	1	10	6	39
	2		4	5			8								9			11		3				7	1	10	6	40
	2		4	5			8								9			11		3				7	1	10	6	41
	2		4	5									9					11		3				7	1	10	6	42
3	11	34	33	40	23	32	27	7	15	8	26	18	3	6	35	7	7	36	2	10	33	5	4	11	13	7	6	
							8	2	13	3	3	3		3	23	3		11						2	1			

3 own-goals

	Earl		Collins	Barrett	Musgrave	Yews			Puddefoot		Watson G	Pollard			Watson V			Morton	Fryatt	Cadwell	Walker A	Johnson	Goodacre					
	2		4	5	6	7			10		1	8			9			11		3								3
	2		4	5		7			10		1	8			9			11	6	3								4
	2		4	5	6	7			10		1	8			9			11		3								5
	2		4	5	6	7			10		1	8			9			11		3								R
	2		4	5	6	7			10			8			9			11		3		1						6
	2		4	5					10		1	8			9			11	6	3	7							SF
	6		6	6	4	5			6		5	6			6			6	2	6	1	1						
					1	2			2			4			2													

1 own-goal

1933-34

Manager: Charlie Paynter

1	Aug	26	(h)	Bolton W	W	4-2	Watson 2, Morton, Opp own-goal	26,000
2		30	(a)	Plymouth A	D	4-4	Goulden 3, Barrett	25,000
3	Sep	2	(a)	Brentford	L	1-4	Wilson	24,000
4		4	(h)	Plymouth A	W	5-1	Tippett 2, Watson 2, Landells	20,000
5		9	(h)	Burnley	L	1-2	Tippett	26,000
6		16	(a)	Oldham A	L	1-4	Tippett	7,000
7		23	(h)	Preston NE	W	6-0	Watson 3, Goulden, Morton, Tippett	20,000
8		30	(a)	Bradford	D	0-0		12,000
9	Oct	7	(h)	Grimsby T	W	3-1	Morton, Watson, Opp own-goal	25,000
10		14	(a)	Nottingham F	W	1-0	Wood	10,000
11		21	(a)	Millwall	D	2-2	Barrett, Watson	32,000
12		28	(h)	Lincoln C	W	4-1	Watson 3, Opp own-goal	23,851
13	Nov	4	(a)	Bury	L	1-2	Watson	11,000
14		11	(h)	Hull C	W	2-1	Landells, Watson	23,591
15		18	(a)	Fulham	L	1-3	Landells	18,000
16		25	(h)	Southampton	D	0-0		23,160
17	Dec	2	(a)	Blackpool	D	1-1	Ruffell	15,000
18		9	(h)	Bradford C	L	1-2	Barrett	20,211
19		16	(a)	Port Vale	D	0-0		8,000
20		23	(h)	Notts C	W	5-3	Ruffell 2, Watson, Morton, Goulden	20,000
21		25	(h)	Swansea T	D	1-1	Watson	28,000
22		26	(a)	Swansea T	D	1-1	Goulden	20,000
23		30	(a)	Bolton W	L	1-5	Mills	8,000
24	Jan	6	(h)	Brentford	W	3-2	Watson 2, Tippett	26,449
25		20	(a)	Burnley	L	2-4	Barrett, Watson	7,000
26	Feb	3	(a)	Preston NE	L	1-3	Ette	15,000
27		7	(h)	Oldham A	L	1-4	Watson	10,000
28		10	(h)	Bradford	L	0-1		16,500
29		17	(a)	Grimsby T	D	1-1	Morton	10,000
30		24	(h)	Nottingham F	W	2-1	Ruffell 2	16,500
31	Mar	3	(h)	Millwall	D	1-1	Watson	26,400
32		10	(a)	Lincoln C	W	2-0	Ruffell, Wood	6,000
33		17	(h)	Bury	W	3-1	Fenton 3	17,400
34		24	(a)	Hull C	L	0-2		7,000
35		30	(a)	Manchester U	W	1-0	Fenton	32,000
36		31	(h)	Fulham	W	5-1	Watson 3, Goulden, Morton	26,050
37	Apr	2	(h)	Manchester U	W	2-1	Wood 2	18,000
38		7	(a)	Southampton	L	2-3	Barrett, Watson	8,000
39		14	(h)	Blackpool	L	1-2	Watson	16,600
40		21	(a)	Bradford C	D	2-2	Fenton, Ruffell	9,000
41		28	(h)	Port Vale	W	1-0	Ruffell	12,000
42	May	5	(a)	Notts C	W	2-1	Tippett 2	5,000

P	W	D	L	F	A	W	D	L	F	A	Pts	Pos	Div	
42	13	3	5	51	28	4	8	9	27	42	45	7th	2	Appearances
														Goals

FA Cup

3	Jan	13	(h)	Bradford C	W	3-2	Watson 2, Goulden	28,426
4		27	(a)	Tottenham H	L	1-4	Watson	51,747

Appearances
Goals

250

Match	McMahon	Thorpe	Robson	Anderson	Barrett	Cockroft	Tippett	Landells	Watson V	Goulden	Morton	Mills	Watson G	Collins	Wilson	Chalkey	Walker A	Rutherford	Wood	Ruffell	Inns	Musgrave	Ette	Fenton	Young
1	1	2	3	4	5	6	7	8	9	10	11														
2	1	2	3	4	5	6	7	8		10	11		9												
3		2	3		5	6	7		9	10	11		1	4	8										
4					5	6	7	8	9	10	11		1	4		2	3								
5	1			4	5	6	7	8	9	10	11					2	3								
6				4	5	6	7	8	9	10	11					2	3	1							
7				4	5	6	7	8	9	10	11					2	3	1							
8				4	5	6	7	8	9	10	11					2	3	1							
9				4	5	6	10	8	9		11					2	3	1	7						
10				4	5	6	7	8	9	10	11					2	3	1							
11				4	5	6	7	8	9	10	11					2	3	1							
12				4	5	6	7	8	9	10	11					2	3	1							
13				4	5	6	7	8	9	10	11					2	3	1							
14				4	5	6	7	8	9	10	11					2	3	1							
15				4	5	6		8	9	10	7					2	3	1		11					
16				4	5	6		8	9	10	7					2	3	1		11					
17				4	5	6		8	9	10	7					2	3	1		11					
18				4	5	6		8		10	7	9				2	3	1		11					
19				4	5	6	7		9	10		8				2	3	1		11					
20				4	5	6	7		9	10		8				2	3	1		11					
21					5	6		8		10	7	9				2		1		11	3	4			
22				4	5	6	7	10	8	9			1			2				11	3				
23				4	5	6	7		9	10	8					2	3	1		11					
24				4	5	6		8	9	10	7					2	3	1		11					
25				4	5	6			9	10	7					2	3	1		11	8				
26					5	6			9	10	7			4	8	2	3	1		11					
27				4		6		8	9	10	11						3	1	7		2		5		
28					5	6		8		10				4			3	1	7	11	2			9	
29					5	6		8	9	10				4		2	3	1	7	11				9	
30					5	6		8	9	10				4		2	3	1	7	11					
31					5	6		8	9	10				4		2	3	1	7	11					
32					5	6		8		10				4		2	3	1	7	11				9	
33					5	6		8		10				4		2	3	1	7	11				9	
34					5	6		8		10				4		2	3	1	7	11				9	
35					5	6			9	10	11			4		2	3	1	7					8	
36					5	6			9	10	11			4		2	3	1	7					8	
37					5	6			9	10	11			4		2	3	1	7					8	
38				4	5	6			9	10	11					2	3	1	7					8	
39				4	5	6			9	10	11					2	3	1	7					8	
40						6		8		10			1	4		2	3		7	11				9	5
41						6		8		10			1	4		2	3		7	11				9	5
42						6		8	9	10				4		2	3	1	7	11					5
Total	3	3	3	24	38	42	21	21	30	40	42	4	6	17	2	37	37	33	16	22	4	1	1	12	3
Goals					5		8	3	26	7	6	1		1					4	8			1	5	

3 own-goals

	McMahon	Thorpe	Robson	Anderson	Barrett	Cockroft	Tippett	Landells	Watson V	Goulden	Morton	Mills	Watson G	Collins	Wilson	Chalkey	Walker A	Rutherford	Wood	Ruffell	Inns	Musgrave	Ette	Fenton	Young
3				4	5	6	7		9	10	8					2	3	1		11					
4				4	5	6		8	9	10	7					2	3	1		11					
Total				2	2	2	1	1	2	2	2					2	2	2		2					
Goals									3	1															

251

1934-35

Manager: Charlie Paynter

1	Aug	27	(h)	Burnley	L	1-2	Watson	20,000
2	Sep	1	(h)	Nottingham F	W	3-1	Wood 2, Morton	21,000
3		3	(a)	Burnley	L	2-5	Fenton 2	13,000
4		8	(a)	Brentford	L	1-4	Fenton	24,000
5		15	(h)	Fulham	W	2-1	Morton, Ruffell	20,000
6		17	(a)	Hull C	L	0-4		5,000
7		22	(a)	Bradford	W	3-1	Mills 2, Fenton	7,000
8		29	(h)	Plymouth A	W	2-1	Barrett, Mills	22,400
9	Oct	6	(a)	Norwich C	W	2-1	Foreman, Mills	17,000
10		13	(h)	Newcastle U	W	3-2	Barrett, Mills, Ruffell	29,000
11		20	(h)	Swansea T	W	2-0	Mills, Morton	22,000
12		27	(a)	Manchester U	L	1-3	Mills	30,000
13	Nov	3	(h)	Port Vale	W	3-1	Mills 2, Ruffell	22,400
14		10	(a)	Barnsley	D	1-1	Mills	8,000
15		17	(h)	Sheffield U	W	2-0	Goulden, Mills	22,500
16		24	(a)	Bradford C	W	2-0	Foreman, Morton	8,000
17	Dec	1	(h)	Notts C	W	4-0	Watson 3, Ruffell	21,000
18		8	(a)	Southampton	D	2-2	Ruffell, Watson	12,000
19		15	(h)	Bolton W	W	4-1	Ruffell 2, Watson 2	32,000
20		22	(a)	Oldham A	W	2-1	Ruffell, Watson	5,000
21		25	(a)	Bury	W	4-2	Ruffell 2, Watson, Wood	15,000
22		26	(h)	Bury	W	3-0	Ruffell 2, Watson	40,000
23		29	(h)	Hull C	L	1-2	Ruffell	31,000
24	Jan	5	(a)	Nottingham F	L	0-2		16,000
25		19	(h)	Brentford	W	2-0	Ruffell, Tippett	30,000
26		26	(a)	Fulham	L	0-3		26,000
27	Feb	2	(h)	Bradford	W	2-1	Morton, Ruffell	26,000
28		9	(a)	Plymouth A	W	1-0	Foreman	11,000
29		18	(h)	Norwich C	W	1-0	Ruffell	13,700
30		23	(a)	Newcastle U	L	0-3		25,000
31	Mar	2	(a)	Swansea T	L	4-5	Foxall 2, Morton, Tippett	10,000
32		9	(h)	Manchester U	D	0-0		25,000
33		16	(h)	Port Vale	D	2-2	Mangnall, Marshall	10,000
34		23	(h)	Barnsley	W	4-3	Barrett, Goulden, Marshall, Ruffell	25,000
35		30	(a)	Sheffield U	W	2-1	Mangnall 2	17,000
36	Apr	6	(h)	Bradford C	W	1-0	Mangnall	30,000
37		13	(a)	Notts C	W	2-0	Ruffell, Morton	11,000
38		19	(a)	Blackpool	L	2-3	Fenton, Barrett	30,000
39		20	(h)	Southampton	W	2-1	Fenton, Ruffell	31,000
40		22	(h)	Blackpool	W	2-1	Mangnall, Ruffell	38,000
41		27	(a)	Bolton W	L	1-3	Goulden	35,000
42	May	4	(h)	Oldham A	W	2-0	Barrett, Mangnall	25,000

P	W	D	L	F	A	W	D	L	F	A	Pts	Pos	Div		Appearances
42	18	1	2	46	17	8	3	10	34	46	56	3rd	2		Goals

FA Cup

3	Jan	12	(h)	Stockport C	D	1-1	Mills	26,400
R		16	(a)	Stockport C	L	0-1		17,911

Appearances

Goals

Conway	Chalkley	Walker A	Walker R	Barrett	Cockroft	Wood	Morton	Watson V	Goulden	Ruffell	Collins	Fenton E	Young	Mills	Foxall	Foreman	Anderson	Tippett	Gall	Marshall	Mangnall	Watson G	Wallbanks	
1	2	3	4	5	6	7	8	9	10	11														1
1	2	3		5	6	7	8	9	10	11	4													2
1	2	3	4	5	6	7	11		10			8		9										3
1	2	3		5	6	7	8		10	11	4	9												4
1	2	3		5	6	7	8		10	11	4	9												5
1	2	3		5	6	7		9	10	11	4	8												6
1	2	3		5	6	7			10			8	4	9	11									7
1	2	3		5	6		8		10	11	4	9		7										8
1	2	3	5		6		8		10	11	4	9		7										9
1	2	3		5	6		8		10	11	4	9		7										10
1	2	3		5	6		8	10		11	4	9		7										11
1	2	3		5	6		8		10	11	4	9		7										12
1	2	3		5	6		8		10	11	4	9		7										13
1	2	3		5	6			9	10	11	4	8		7										14
1	2	3		5	6		8		10	11	4	9		7										15
1	2	3		5	6		8		10	11	4	9		7										16
1	2	3		5	6		8	9	10	11	4			7										17
1	2	3		5	6		8	9	10	11	4			7										18
1	2	3		5	6	7	8	9	10	11	4													19
1	2	3		5	6	7	8	9	10	11	4													20
1	2	3		5	6	7	8	9	10	11	4													21
1	2	3		5	6	7	8	9	10	11	4													22
1	2	3		5	6		8	9	10	11	4			7										23
1	2	3		5	6		8		10	11	4					7	4	9						24
1	2	3		5	6		8		10	11						7	4	9						25
1	2	3		5	6		8		10	11	4					7		9						26
1	2	3		5	6		8	9	10	11	4					7								27
1	2	3		5	6		8	9	10	11	4					7								28
1	2	3		5	6		8		10		4			9		7		11						29
1	2	3		5	6		8		10		4			9		7	11							30
1	2	3		5	6		11	9	10		4			8		7								31
1	2	3		5	6	7			10	11	4									8	9			32
1	2	3		5	6	7			10	11	4									8	9			33
1	2	3		5	6	7			10	11	4									8	9			34
1	2	3		5	6		11		10		4					7				8	9			35
1	2	3		5	6	7			10	11	4									8	9			36
1	2	3		5	6	7			10	11	4									8	9			37
	2	3		5	6	7			10	11	4									8	9	1		38
1	2	3		5	6	7			10	11	4							1		8	9			39
1	2	3		5	6	7			10	11	4									8	9			40
1	2	3		5	6	7			10	11	4									8	9			41
1	2	3		5	6	7			10	11	4									8	9			42
41	42	42	3	41	42	12	40	15	40	36	12	32	1	10	4	21	2	4	1	10	10	1		
					5		3	7	10	3	20			6	11	2	3		2		2	6		

Conway	Chalkley	Walker A	Walker R	Barrett	Cockroft	Wood	Morton	Watson V	Goulden	Ruffell	Collins	Fenton E	Young	Mills	Foxall	Foreman	Anderson	Tippett	Gall	Marshall	Mangnall	Watson G	Wallbanks	
1	2	3		5	6		8		10	11	4	9		7										3
1	2	3		5	6		8		10	11	4	9		7						4				R
2	2	2		2	2		2		2	2	2	2		2						1				
												1												

253

1935-36

Manager: Charlie Paynter

1	Aug	31	(a)	Norwich C	L 3-4	Marshall, Morton, Ruffell	29,779
2	Sep	2	(a)	Bradford	L 0-2		16,000
3		7	(h)	Nottingham F	W 5-2	Mangnall 3, Ruffell 2	30,000
4		9	(h)	Bradford	W 1-0	Goulden	21,000
5		14	(a)	Blackpool	L 1-4	Marshall	25,000
6		16	(h)	Sheffield U	W 3-2	Goulden, Mangnall, Marshall	30,000
7		21	(h)	Doncaster R	L 1-2	Mangnall	30,000
8		28	(a)	Bury	L 0-3		9,000
9	Oct	5	(h)	Barnsley	W 2-0	Mangnall 2	25,000
10		12	(h)	Swansea T	W 4-0	Goulden 2, Marshall, Opp own-goal	25,000
11		19	(a)	Plymouth A	L 1-4	Marshall	19,000
12		26	(h)	Bradford C	D 1-1	Mangnall	20,000
13	Nov	2	(a)	Newcastle U	D 3-3	Mangnall 2, Ruffell	20,000
14		9	(h)	Tottenham H	D 2-2	Mangnall, Ruffell	41,000
15		16	(a)	Manchester U	W 3-2	Fenton, Foreman, Simpson	25,000
16		23	(h)	Hull C	W 4-1	Ruffell 2, Conwell, Mangnall	25,000
17		30	(a)	Fulham	L 2-4	Mangnall, Opp own-goal	27,000
18	Dec	14	(a)	Charlton A	D 2-2	Barrett, Goulden	35,000
19		21	(h)	Port Vale	W 4-0	Goulden 2, Foreman, Mangnall	18,000
20		25	(h)	Southampton	D 0-0		30,000
21		26	(a)	Southampton	W 4-2	Mangnall 2, Goulden, Opp own-goal	18,989
22		28	(h)	Norwich C	W 3-2	Mangnall 3	26,000
23	Jan	4	(a)	Nottingham F	W 2-0	Goulden, Ruffell	16,000
24		18	(h)	Blackpool	W 2-1	Foreman, Marshall	15,000
25		25	(a)	Doncaster R	W 2-0	Lewis, Simpson	12,000
26	Feb	1	(h)	Bury	W 6-0	Lewis 3, Cockroft, Morton, Simpson	27,000
27		3	(h)	Burnley	D 0-0		10,000
28		8	(a)	Barnsley	W 2-1	Goulden, Morton	12,000
29		15	(a)	Swansea T	W 1-0	Mangnall	10,000
30		22	(h)	Plymouth A	W 4-2	Barrett, Fenton, Goulden, Morton	20,000
31		29	(a)	Burnley	L 0-1		6,000
32	Mar	7	(h)	Manchester U	L 1-2	Goulden	31,000
33		14	(a)	Tottenham H	W 3-1	Goulden, Marshall, Simpson	58,426
34		21	(h)	Newcastle U	W 4-1	Marshall 2, Ruffell, Simpson	40,000
35		28	(a)	Hull C	W 3-2	Goulden, Ruffell, Simpson	5,000
36	Apr	4	(h)	Fulham	D 0-0		33,000
37		10	(h)	Leicester C	W 3-2	Fenton, Goulden, Simpson	39,000
38		11	(a)	Bradford C	L 1-3	Morton	12,000
39		13	(a)	Leicester C	D 1-1	Simpson	25,000
40		18	(h)	Charlton A	L 1-3	Simpson	41,500
41		25	(a)	Port Vale	W 3-2	Mangnall 2, Foxall	9,000
42	May	2	(a)	Sheffield U	L 2-4	Foreman, Marshall	24,000

P	W	D	L	F	A	W	D	L	F	A	Pts	Pos	Div	Appearances
42	13	5	3	51	23	9	3	9	39	45	52	4th	2	Goals

FA Cup

3	Jan	11	(h)	Luton T	D 2-2	Mangnall, Ruffell	42,000
R		15	(a)	Luton T	L 0-4		17,527

Appearances
Goals

254

#	Blore	Chalkley	Walker A	Fenton E	Barrett	Cockroft	Morton	Marshall	Simpson	Goulden	Ruffell	Tonner	Mangnall	Parker	Foreman	Collins	Walker R	Lewis	Conway	Tippett	Conwell	Musgrave	Bicknell	Foxall	Dowen
1	1	2	3	4	5	6	7	8	9	10	11														
2	1	2	3	4	5	6	7	8	9	10	11														
3	1		3	4	5	6	7	8		10	11	2	9												
4	1		2		4	5	6	7	8	10	11		9	3											
5	1		2		4	5	6	11	8	10			9	3	7										
6	1	2	3			6	7	8		10	11		9			4	5								
7	1	2	3	4		6	7			10	11		9				8	5							
8		2	3	4	5	6	7	8		10	11		9						1						
9		2	3	4	5	6		8		10	11		9		7				1						
10	1	2	3	4	5	6		8		10	11		9		7										
11	1	2	3	4	5	6		8		10	11		9		7										
12		2	3	4	5	6				10	11		9		7				1		8				
13		2	3	4	5	6				10	11		9		7				1		8				
14		2	3	4	5	6			9	10	11				7				1		8				
15		2	3	4	5	6				10	11		9		7				1		8				
16		2	3	4	5	6				10	11		9		7				1		8				
17		2	3	4	5	6				10	11		9		7				1		8				
18		2	3	4	5	6		8		10	11		9		7				1						
19		2	3	4	5	6		8		10	11		9		7				1						
20		2	3	4	5	6	7	8		10	11		9						1						
21		2	3	4	5	6	7	8		10	11		9						1						
22		2	3	4	5	6	7	8		10	11		9						1						
23		2	3	4	5	6		8	9	10					7				1	11					
24		2	3	4	5	6		8	9	10					7				1	11					
25		2	3	4	5	6	7	8	9		11							10	1						
26		2	3	4	5	6	7	8	9		11							10	1						
27		2	3	4	5	6	11	8		10			9		7				1						
28		2	3	4	5	6	11	8		10			9		7				1						
29		2	3	4	5	6	7	8		10	11		9						1						
30		2	3	4	5	6	11	8		10			9		7				1						
31		2	3	4	5	6	7	8	9	10	11								1						
32		2	3	4	5	6	7	8	9	10	11								1						
33		2	3	4	5	6	7	8	9	10	11								1						
34			3	4	5	6	7	8	9	10	11								1				2		
35			3	4	5	6	7	8	9	10	11								1				2		
36			3	4	5	6	11	8	9	10					7				1				2		
37			3	4	5	6	11	8	9	10					7				1				2		
38			3	4	5	6	11	8	9	10					7				1				2		
39		2	3	4	5	6	7	8	9	10	11								1						
40			3	4	5	6	11	8		10					7				1				2		9
41				4	5	6	11	8	9	10					7				1			2		3	
42		2	3	4	5	6	7	8	9	10	11								1						
	9	32	41	41	40	42	26	36	20	38	30	1	25	2	20	1	2	4	33	2	6	2	7	1	1
		3	2	1	5	10	9	15	10	22			4		4				1				1		

3 own-goals

	Blore	Chalkley	Walker A	Fenton E	Barrett	Cockroft	Morton	Marshall	Simpson	Goulden	Ruffell	Tonner	Mangnall	Parker	Foreman	Collins	Walker R	Lewis	Conway	Tippett	Conwell	Musgrave	Bicknell	Foxall	Dowen
3		2	3	4	5	6	8		7	10	11		9						1						
R		2	3	4	5	6	8		7	10	11		9						1						
		2	2	2	2	2	2		2	2	2		2						2						
										1			1												

1936-37

Manager: Charlie Paynter

#	Month	Date		Opponent	Result	Scorers	Attendance
1	Aug	29	(h)	Tottenham H	W 2-1	Goulden 2	35,000
2		31	(h)	Newcastle U	L 0-2		23,200
3	Sep	5	(a)	Blackpool	L 0-1		25,000
4		9	(a)	Newcastle U	L 3-5	Maring 3	22,000
5		12	(h)	Blackburn R	W 3-1	Goulden, Martin, Morton	28,000
6		14	(a)	Sheffield U	L 0-2		15,000
7		19	(a)	Bury	D 1-1	Martin	16,000
8		26	(h)	Leicester C	W 4-1	Marshall 2, Goulden, Martin	26,000
9	Oct	3	(a)	Nottingham F	L 0-1		20,000
10		10	(a)	Norwich C	D 3-3	Barrett, Cockroft, Martin	15,000
11		17	(h)	Plymouth A	D 1-1	Morton	28,000
12		24	(a)	Coventry C	L 0-4		24,000
13		31	(h)	Doncaster R	W 1-0	Guest	15,000
14	Nov	7	(a)	Fulham	L 0-5		20,000
15		14	(h)	Burnley	L 0-2		25,000
16		21	(a)	Southampton	W 2-0	Adams, Foxall	16,000
17		28	(h)	Swansea T	W 2-0	Foxall, Goulden	19,000
18	Dec	5	(a)	Bradford C	L 1-2	Goulden	7,000
19		19	(a)	Chesterfield	D 1-1	Morton	10,000
20		25	(a)	Bradford	L 1-2	Green	17,203
21		26	(a)	Tottenham H	W 3-2	Simpson 2, Foxall	34,000
22		28	(h)	Bradford	W 1-0	Morton	16,000
23	Jan	2	(h)	Blackpool	W 3-0	Foxall, Simpson, Opp own-goal	28,000
24		9	(a)	Blackburn R	W 2-1	Goulden, Morton	8,000
25		23	(a)	Bury	W 5-1	Small 2, Fenton, Foxall, Goulden	21,000
26	Feb	4	(a)	Leicester C	D 2-2	Goulden, Foxall	7,000
27		6	(h)	Nottingham F	D 2-2	Morton 2	20,000
28		13	(h)	Norwich C	W 4-1	Foxall 2, Morton 2	22,000
29		20	(a)	Plymouth A	L 0-2		19,000
30		27	(h)	Coventry C	W 4-0	Foxall, Green, Morton, Small	15,000
31	Mar	6	(a)	Doncaster R	W 4-1	Foxall, Goulden, Morton, Small	8,000
32		13	(h)	Fulham	D 3-3	Goulden, Morton, Small	35,000
33		20	(a)	Burnley	L 1-2	Small	8,000
34		26	(h)	Barnsley	D 0-0		31,000
35		27	(h)	Southampton	W 4-0	Goulden 2, Morton, Small	20,000
36		29	(a)	Barnsley	D 0-0		20,000
37	Apr	3	(a)	Swansea T	D 0-0		12,000
38		10	(h)	Bradford C	W 4-1	Small 2, Foxall, Goulden	18,000
39		17	(a)	Aston Villa	W 2-0	Kirkcaldie, Small	15,000
40		24	(h)	Chesterfield	D 1-1	Small	12,000
41		26	(h)	Aston Villa	W 2-1	Goulden, Green	12,000
42	May	1	(h)	Sheffield U	W 1-0	Morton	15,000

P	W	D	L	F	A	W	D	L	F	A	Pts	Pos	Div		
42	14	5	2	47	18	5	6	10	26	37	49	6th	2	Appearances	Goals

FA Cup

#	Month	Date		Opponent	Result		Attendance
3	Jan	16	(h)	Bolton W	D 0-0		42,300
R		20	(a)	Bolton W	L 0-1		21,539

Appearances
Goals

1937-38

Manager: Charlie Paynter

#					Result	Scorers	Attendance
1	Aug	28	(a)	Aston Villa	L 0-2		45,000
2		30	(h)	Swansea T	W 2-1	Fenton, Foxall	16,000
3	Sep	4	(h)	Bradford	W 3-1	Goulden 2, Macaulay	20,000
4		6	(a)	Swansea T	D 0-0		14,000
5		11	(a)	Stockport C	D 0-0		18,000
6		13	(h)	Chesterfield	W 5-0	Goulden 2, Small 2, Morton	17,000
7		18	(a)	Southampton	D 3-3	Small 2, Foxall	20,000
8		25	(h)	Blackburn R	W 2-0	Foxall, Goulden	30,000
9	Oct	2	(a)	Sheffield W	L 0-1		20,000
10		9	(h)	Fulham	D 0-0		35,000
11		16	(h)	Barnsley	W 4-1	Goulden 2, Foxall, Macaulay	31,000
12		23	(a)	Luton T	D 2-2	Small, Opp own-goal	18,000
13		30	(h)	Newcastle U	W 1-0	Morton	34,000
14	Nov	6	(a)	Nottingham F	D 0-0		15,000
15		13	(h)	Coventry C	D 0-0		40,000
16		20	(a)	Tottenham H	L 0-2		47,691
17		27	(h)	Burnley	W 1-0	Williams	27,000
18	Dec	4	(a)	Bury	L 3-4	Foxall 2, Williams	5,000
19		11	(h)	Sheffield U	L 0-2		22,000
20		27	(a)	Norwich C	D 2-2	Williams 2	19,000
21		28	(h)	Norwich C	D 3-3	Barrett, Green, Williams	27,000
22	Jan	1	(h)	Aston Villa	D 1-1	Opp own-goal	32,000
23		15	(a)	Bradford	L 1-2	Macaulay	6,000
24		22	(h)	Stockport C	W 1-0	Macaulay	25,000
25		29	(h)	Southampton	W 3-1	Foxall, Macaulay, Small	21,000
26	Feb	5	(a)	Blackburn R	L 1-2	Small	13,000
27		12	(h)	Sheffield W	W 1-0	Macaulay	19,000
28		19	(a)	Fulham	D 1-1	Goulden	23,000
29		23	(a)	Manchester U	L 0-4		10,000
30		26	(a)	Barnsley	L 0-1		10,000
31	Mar	5	(h)	Luton T	D 0-0		20,000
32		12	(a)	Newcastle U	D 2-2	Foxall 2	20,000
33		19	(h)	Nottingham F	W 2-1	Macaulay 2	24,000
34		26	(a)	Coventry C	D 1-1	Opp own-goal	20,000
35	Apr	2	(h)	Tottenham H	L 1-3	Morton	32,300
36		9	(a)	Burnley	L 0-2		8,000
37		15	(h)	Plymouth A	L 0-1		23,000
38		16	(h)	Bury	W 3-1	Fenton, Green, Macaulay	17,000
39		18	(a)	Plymouth A	L 1-2	Foxall	22,000
40		23	(a)	Sheffield U	L 1-3	Fenton	30,000
41		30	(h)	Manchester U	W 1-0	Goulden	17,000
42	May	7	(a)	Chesterfield	W 1-0	Macaulay	7,000

P	W	D	L	F	A	W	D	L	F	A	Pts	Pos	Div	
42	13	5	3	34	16	1	9	11	19	36	42	9th	2	Appearances
														Goals

FA Cup

3	Jan	8	(a)	Preston NE	L 0-3		30,198
							Appearances
							Goals

Player appearances and goals grid (27 players):

Weare	Bicknell	Walker C	Fenton E	Walker R	Cockroft	Foxall	Macaulay	Small	Goulden	Morton	Green	Barrett	Fenton B	Young	Williams	Roberts	Kirkcaldie	Walker A	Conway	Turner	Wood	Corbett N	Dell	Forde	Black	Attwell	No.
1	2	3	4	5	6	7	8	9	10	11																	1
1	2	3	4	5	6	7	8	9		11	10																2
1	2	3	4		6	7	8	9	10	11		5															3
1	2	3	4		6	7	8	9	10	11		5															4
1	2	3	4		6	7	8	9	10	11		5															5
1	2	3	4		6	7	8	9	10	11		5															6
1	2	3	4		6	7	8	9	10	11		5															7
1	2	3	4	5	6	7	8	9	10	11																	8
1	2	3	4	5	6	7	8	9	10	11																	9
1	2	3	4	5	6	7	8		10	11				9													10
1	2	3	4	5	6	7	8	9	10	11																	11
1	2	3	4		6	7	8	9	10	11			5														12
1	2	3	4		6	7	8	9	10	11		5															13
1	2	3	4	5	6	7	8	9	10	11																	14
1	2	3	4	5	6	7	8		10	11					9												15
1	2	3	4	5	6	7	8		10	11					9												16
1	2	3		5	6	7	8		10	11					9	4											17
1	2	3		5	6	7	8		10	11	4				9												18
1	2	3	4	5	6	11	8		10						9		7										19
1	2			5	6		8			11	10				9		7										20
1	2			5	6		8			11	10	4			9		7	3									21
1	2	3		5	6	7			10	11	8	4			9												22
	2	3	4	5	6	7	8		10	11					9				1								23
	2	3	4	5	6	7	8			11	10				9				1								24
	2	3	4	5	6	7	8	9	10	11									1								25
	2	3	4	5	6	7	8	9	10	11									1								26
	2	3	4		6	7	8	9	10	11									1	5							27
	2	3		5	6	7	8	9	10	11									1	4							28
	2	3	4		6		8	9	10	7									1	5	11						29
	2	3	4	5	6		8			7	10				9				1		11						30
	2	3	4	5	6	9	8		10								7		1		11						31
	2	3		5	6	9			10		8						7		1		11	4					32
	2	3		5	6		9		10	7	8								1		11	4					33
	2	3			6	7	9		10	11									1	5		4	8				34
	2		4			7	9		10	11	8								1	5		6		3			35
	2					9		7	10										1	5	11	6	8	3	4		36
	2		4	5	6		9		10	11	8			7					1					3			37
	2		4	5	6	7	9		10	11	8								1					3			38
	2		4	5	6	7	9		10	11	8								1					3			39
	2		6	5		7	9		10	11	8								1					3		4	40
	2	3	4	5	6	7	9		10	8									1		11						41
1	2	3	4	5		7	8		9	10										6	11						42
23	42	35	32	32	38	36	39	18	35	39	15	8	3	1	9	1	6	1	19	6	8	6	2	6	1	1	
		3						10	10	7	9	3	2	1	5												

3 own-goals

Weare	Bicknell	Walker C	Fenton E	Walker R	Cockroft	Foxall	Macaulay	Small	Goulden	Morton	Green	Barrett	Fenton B	Young	Williams	Roberts	Kirkcaldie	Walker A	Conway	Turner	Wood	Corbett N	Dell	Forde	Black	Attwell	No.
	2	3	4	5	6			10	11	8					9		7		1								3
	1	1	1	1	1			1	1	1					1		1		1								

1938-39

Manager: Charlie Paynter

1	Aug	27	(a)	Fulham	L	2-3	Macaulay 2	25,000
2		29	(h)	Blackburn R	L	1-2	Macaulay	15,000
3	Sep	3	(h)	Sheffield W	L	2-3	Fenton, Morton	23,000
4		7	(a)	Manchester C	W	4-2	Foxall 2, Fenton, Morton	18,000
5		10	(a)	Bury	D	1-1	Small	10,000
6		17	(h)	Coventry C	W	4-1	Fenton 2, Macaulay 2	30,000
7		19	(a)	Blackburn R	L	1-3	Fenton	20,000
8		24	(h)	Tranmere R	W	6-1	Macaulay 3, Cockroft, Corbett, Foxall	24,000
9	Oct	1	(a)	Chesterfield	L	0-1		15,000
10		8	(h)	Swansea T	W	5-2	Small 2, Morton 2, Foxall	23,000
11		15	(a)	Nottingham F	D	0-0		17,000
12		22	(h)	Newcastle U	D	1-1	Opp own-goal	30,200
13		29	(a)	Tottenham H	L	1-2	Foxall	52,304
14	Nov	5	(h)	Norwich C	W	2-0	Fenton, Macaulay	24,600
15		12	(a)	Luton T	W	2-1	Macaulay, Small	18,000
16		19	(h)	Plymouth A	W	2-1	Goulden, Macaulay	25,000
17		26	(a)	Sheffield U	L	1-3	Foxall	18,000
18	Dec	3	(h)	Burnley	W	1-0	Morton	22,400
19		10	(a)	West Brom A	L	2-3	Macaulay, Small	25,000
20		17	(h)	Southampton	L	1-2	Small	16,500
21		24	(h)	Fulham	W	1-0	Macaulay	8,000
22		27	(h)	Millwall	D	0-0		41,300
23		31	(a)	Sheffield W	W	4-1	Foxall 2, Morton, Small	30,000
24	Jan	14	(h)	Bury	D	0-0		20,000
25		28	(a)	Tranmere R	D	2-2	Fenton, Foxall	10,000
26	Feb	4	(h)	Chesterfield	D	1-1	Macaulay	23,400
27		16	(a)	Swansea T	L	2-3	Green, Macaulay	8,000
28		18	(h)	Nottingham F	W	5-0	Fenton 2, Foxall, Goulden, Macaulay	16,200
29		25	(a)	Newcastle U	L	0-2		30,000
30	Mar	4	(h)	Tottenham H	L	0-2		26,400
31		11	(a)	Norwich C	W	6-2	Small 3, Foxall 2, Morton	15,000
32		18	(h)	Luton T	L	0-1		23,000
33		25	(a)	Plymouth A	D	0-0		19,000
34		27	(a)	Millwall	W	2-0	Foreman, Proudlock	10,000
35	Apr	1	(h)	Sheffield U	D	0-0		21,400
36		7	(h)	Bradford	L	0-2		25,000
37		8	(a)	Burnley	L	0-1		8,000
38		11	(a)	Bradford	W	2-1	Gore, Small	8,000
39		15	(h)	West Brom A	W	2-1	Bell, Foxall	16,400
40		22	(a)	Southampton	W	2-0	Foxall, Goulden	9,931
41		24	(a)	Coventry C	D	0-0		10,000
42	May	6	(h)	Manchester C	W	2-1	Goulden, Hubbard	26,004

P	W	D	L	F	A	W	D	L	F	A	Pts	Pos	Div	
42	10	5	6	36	21	7	5	9	34	31	44	11th	2	Appearances
														Goals

FA Cup

3	Jan	7	(a)	Queen's Park R	W	2-1	Foxall, Morton	22,408
4		21	(h)	Tottenham H	D	3-3	Foxall 2, Macaulay	42,716
R		30	(a)	Tottenham H	D	1-1	Foxall	50,798
2R	Feb	2	(n*)	Tottenham H	W	2-1	Foxall, Macaulay	50,468
5		11	(a)	Portsmouth	L	0-2		47,614

*Played at Highbury Stadium, London.

Appearances
Goals

Appearance grid (shirt numbers by player and match). Player columns left→right; match numbers in the right‑hand column.

#	Conway	Bicknell	Walker C	Fenton E	Turner	Cockroft	Foxall	Wood	Macaulay	Goulden	Morton	Kirkcaldie	Corbett	Fenton B	Barrett	Walker R	Small	Medhurst	Green	Forde	Foreman	Proudlock	Woodgate	Gore	Bell	Banner	Burton	Hubbard
1	1	2	3	4	5	6	7	8	9	10	11																	
2	1	2	3	4	5	6		8	9	10	11	7																
3	1	2	3		5	6	7		9	10	11		4	8														
4	1	2	3			6	7		9	10	11		4	8		5												
5	1	2	3			6	7		8	10	11		4			5	9											
6	1	2	3			6	7		9	10	11		4	8		5												
7	1	2	3			6	7		9	10	11		4	8		5												
8	1	2	3			6	7		9	10	11		4	8		5												
9	1	2	3			6	7		9	10	11		4	8		5												
10	1	2	3			6	7		9	10	11		4			5	8											
11	1	2	3			6	7		9	10	11		4			5	8											
12	1	2	3			6	7				11		4	10		5	8											
13	1	2	3			6	7		9	10	11		4	8		5												
14	1	2	3			6	7		8		11		4	10		5	9											
15	1	2	3			6	7		8		11		4	10		5	9											
16	1	2	3			6	7		9	10	11		4	8		5												
17	1	2	3			6	7		9	10	11		4	8		5												
18	1	2	3			6	7		8	10	11		4			5	9											
19	1	2	3			6	7		8	10	11		4			5	9											
20		2	3			6	7		8	10	11		4			5	9	1										
21		2	3			6	7		8	10	11		4			5	9	1										
22		2	3	4			7		8	10	11		6			5	9	1										
23		2	3	4			7		8	10	11		6			5	9	1										
24	1		3	4					9		11		7	6	10	5								8	2			
25		2	3			6	7		9	10	11		4	8		5		1										
26		2	3	4		6	7		9	10			11			5	8	1										
27		2	3	4		6	7		9	10				8		5		1										
28		2	3			6	7		9	10	11		4	8		5		1										
29		2	3			6	7		9	10	11		4	8		5		1										
30		2	3			6	7		8	10	11		4			5	9	1										
31		2	3			6	7		8	10	11		4			5	9	1										
32		2	3			6	7		8	10	11		4			5	9	1										
33		2	3			6	11		8	10			4			5	7	1		9								
34		2	3			6	11		8				4			5	7	1			9	10						
35		2	3			6	11		8				4			5	7	1			9	10	7					
36		2	3	4		6	11		8							5		1			9	10	7					
37		2	3	4		6	11		8	10						5		1			9		7					
38		2	3	4		6			8	10						5	9	1					7	11				
39		2	3	4		6	7		8							5	9	1						11	10			
40		2		4		6	7		8	10						5		1			9			11		3		
41		2	3	4		6	7			10						5		1				9	8	11				
42		2	3	4		6			8	10						5		1						11			7	9
Totals	21	41	41	12	5	39	40	2	36	37	31	2	31	18	1	38	19	21	3	1	6	4	4	5	1	1	1	1
Goals				1	14		16	4	7				1	9		11			1			1	1	1				1

1 own-goal

FA Cup:

Rd	Conway	Bicknell	Walker C	Fenton E	Turner	Cockroft	Foxall	Wood	Macaulay	Goulden	Morton	Kirkcaldie	Corbett	Fenton B	Barrett	Walker R	Small	Medhurst	Green	Forde	Foreman	Proudlock	Woodgate	Gore	Bell	Banner	Burton	Hubbard
3		2	3	4			7		8	10	11		6			5	9	1										
4		2	3	4			7		8	10	11		6			5	9	1										
R		2	3	4		6	7		8	10	11					5	9	1										
2R		2	3			6	7		8	10	11		4			5	9	1										
5		2	3			6	7		8	10			4	11		5	9	1										
Totals		5	5	3		3	5		5	5	4		4	1		5	4	5										1
Goals							5		2	1																		

1946-47

Manager: Charlie Paynter

#		Date		Venue	Opponent	Result	Scorers	Attendance
1	Aug	31	(a)	Plymouth A		L 1-3	Wood	26,000
2	Sep	2	(h)	Fulham		W 3-2	Small, Macaulay 2	28,000
3		7	(h)	Leicester C		L 0-2		28,000
4		9	(a)	Fulham		L 2-3	Wood 2	19,913
5		14	(a)	Chesterfield		L 1-3	Small	16,000
6		21	(h)	Millwall		W 3-1	Dunn, Small, Opp own-goal	30,400
7		28	(a)	Bradford		W 1-0	Wood	21,360
8	Oct	5	(h)	Manchester C		W 1-0	Macaulay	30,000
9		12	(a)	Burnley		L 1-2	Small	24,000
10		19	(h)	Tottenham H		D 2-2	Small, Bainbridge	34,200
11		26	(a)	Swansea T		L 1-2	Bainbridge	34,000
12	Nov	2	(h)	Newcastle U		L 0-2		32,000
13		9	(a)	West Brom A		W 3-2	Woodgate, Parker, Wood	20,000
14		16	(h)	Birmingham C		L 0-4		25,000
15		23	(a)	Coventry C		L 1-2	Wright	12,000
16		30	(h)	Nottingham F		D 2-2	Proudlock, Hall	10,000
17	Dec	7	(a)	Southampton		L 2-4	Payne, Bainbridge	17,000
18		21	(a)	Barnsley		W 2-1	Hall, Payne	10,000
19		25	(h)	Luton T		W 2-1	Payne, Woodgate	20,000
20		26	(a)	Luton T		L 1-2	Payne	24,000
21		28	(h)	Plymouth A		W 4-1	Bicknell, Small, Payne, Wood	17,000
22	Jan	1	(a)	Sheffield W		D 1-1	Bainbridge	32,000
23		4	(a)	Leicester C		L 0-4		25,000
24		18	(h)	Chesterfield		W 5-0	Wood 2, Hall, Payne, Small	24,000
25		25	(a)	Millwall		D 0-0		22,000
26	Feb	1	(h)	Bradford		D 1-1	Bainbridge	16,845
27		8	(h)	Newport C		W 3-0	Neary 2, Woodgate	12,500
28	Mar	1	(h)	Swansea T		W 3-0	Neary 2, Hall	21,000
29		15	(h)	West Brom A		W 3-2	Neary 3	24,000
30		22	(a)	Birmingham C		L 0-3		30,000
31		29	(h)	Coventry C		L 1-2	Neary	32,000
32	Apr	4	(a)	Bury		L 0-4		15,000
33		5	(a)	Nottingham F		L 3-4	Neary 2, Parsons	20,000
34		7	(h)	Bury		D 3-3	Neary 2, Bainbridge	22,400
35		12	(h)	Southampton		W 4-0	Neary 2, Parsons, Wood	22,000
36		19	(a)	Newport C		D 1-1	Bainbridge	15,000
37		26	(h)	Barnsley		W 4-0	Parsons 2, Bainbridge, Woodgate	17,000
38	May	3	(h)	Sheffield W		W 2-1	Neary, Woodgate	25,000
39		17	(a)	Tottenham H		D 0-0		37,500
40		24	(a)	Manchester C		L 0-2		28,000
41		26	(a)	Newcastle U		W 3-2	Hall, Wood, Bainbridge	35,000
42		31	(h)	Burnley		L 0-5		30,000

P	W	D	L	F	A	W	D	L	F	A	Pts	Pos	Div	
42	12	4	5	46	31	4	4	13	24	45	40	12th	2	Appearances
														Goals

FA Cup

3	Jan	11	(h)	Leicester C	L 1-2	Woodgate		26,000

Appearances
Goals

Football appearances and goals grid (shirt numbers by player and match):

Medhurst	Bicknell	Cater	Corbett N	Walker R	Attwell	Woodgate	Hall	Small	Macaulay	Wood	Banner	Wright	Taylor	Dunn	Proudlock	Parker	Bainbridge	Forde	Sadler	Payne	Gregory	Wilson	Parsons	Neary	Devlin	Travis	
1	2	3	4	5	6	7	8	9	10	11																	1
1	2	3	4	5	6	7	8	9	10	11																	2
1	2		4	5		7	8	6	10	11	3	9															3
	2		4	5	6	7		9		11	3			1	8	10											4
	2		4	5	6	7		9		11	3			1	8	10											5
	2	3	6	5		7		9	10					1	8	4	11										6
	2	3	6	5		7		9	10					1	8	4	11										7
	2	3	6	5		7	8		10					1	9	4	11										8
	2	3	6	5		7	9	8	10					1		4	11										9
	2	3	6	5		7	9	8	10					1		4	11										10
	2	3	6	5		7	9	8	10					1		4	11										11
	2		6	5		7	9	8	10	3				1		4	11										12
	2		6	5		7	9	4		10	3			1		8	11										13
	2		6	5		7	9	4		10				1		8	11	3									14
	2		4	5		7	9	8				10		1		6	11	3									15
	2		4			7	9	6			5	10	1		8		11	3									16
		4		5		7	8	6		2	10	1				11		3	9								17
		4		5		7	8	6		2	10	1				11	3		9								18
		4		5		7		6		2	10	1	8			11	3		9								19
2		4		5		7	8			10						11	3		9	1	6						20
2		4		5		7		6		10				1	8	11	3		9								21
2		4		5		7		6		10				1		11	3		9		8						22
		4	2			7	8	6		10	5			1		11	3		9								23
		4	2			7	8	6		10	5			1		11	3		9								24
		4	2	6		7	8			10	5			1		11	3		9								25
		4	2	6		7	8			10	5			1		11	3						9				26
		4	2	5		7	8	6		10				1		11	3						9				27
		4	2	5		7	8	6		10				1		11	3						9				28
		4	2	5		7	8	6		10				1		11	3						9				29
		4	2			7	8	6		10	5			1		11	3						9				30
		4	2	5		7	10	6						1		11	3						9				31
		4	2	5		7	10	6						1		11	3		8	9							32
		4	2	5			8	6					1		10	11	3		7	9							33
		4	2			7		6		10	5			1		11	3		8	9							34
		4	2			7		6		10	5			1		11	3		8	9							35
		4	2			7		6		10	5			1		11	3		8	9							36
		4	2			7	10	6			5			1		11	3		8	9							37
		4	2	5		7		6		10	11			1					8	9	3						38
		4	2	5		7		6		10				1		11			8		3	9					39
		4	2	5		7	9	6		10	3			1		11			8								40
		4	2	5		7	10	6		11	3			1					8	9							41
3	19	34	35	34	4	41	24	39	8	33	21	7	30	7	4	10	35	24	1	10	9	1	12	14	2	1	42
1						5	5	7	3	10			1			1	1	1	9				6	4	15		

I own-goal

		4	2	5		7	10	6					1			11	3		9		8						3
	1	1	1			1	1	1					1			1	1		1								
		1																									

1947-48

Manager: Charlie Paynter

					Result		Attendance
1	Aug	23	(a)	Bradford	L 1-4	Walker	15,000
2		25	(h)	Millwall	D 1-1	Woodgate	25,000
3		30	(h)	Nottingham F	W 2-1	Parsons, Opp own-goal	25,000
4	Sep	1	(a)	Millwall	D 1-1	Small	15,814
5		6	(a)	Doncaster R	L 0-1		19,953
6		8	(h)	Tottenham H	D 1-1	Parsons	25,600
7		13	(h)	Southampton	W 2-0	Hall, Wood	20,400
8		15	(a)	Tottenham H	D 2-2	Parsons, Wood	35,000
9		20	(a)	Bury	W 2-1	Proudlock, Wood	16,498
10		27	(h)	Coventry C	W 1-0	Proudlock	25,000
11	Oct	4	(h)	Chesterfield	W 4-0	Tucker 3, Proudlock	26,000
12		11	(a)	Newcastle U	L 0-1		55,777
13		18	(h)	Birmingham C	D 0-0		32,000
14		25	(a)	West Brom A	W 2-1	Wright 2	40,000
15	Nov	1	(h)	Barnsley	W 2-1	Moroney, Small	28,000
16		8	(a)	Plymouth A	D 1-1	Parsons	29,111
17		15	(h)	Luton T	D 0-0		31,000
18		22	(a)	Brentford	D 1-1	Small	24,161
19		29	(h)	Leicester C	D 1-1	Woodgate	23,000
20	Dec	6	(a)	Leeds U	L 1-2	Wright	21,500
21		13	(h)	Fulham	W 3-0	Moroney, Parsons, Wright	25,000
22		20	(h)	Bradford	D 0-0		25,000
23		26	(a)	Sheffield W	L 3-5	Corbett, Woodgate, Parsons	37,343
24		27	(h)	Sheffield W	L 1-4	Stephens	20,000
25	Jan	3	(a)	Nottingham F	L 1-2	Woodgate	26,138
26		24	(h)	Doncaster R	W 2-1	Parsons 2	16,000
27		31	(a)	Southampton	L 1-3	Wright	22,000
28	Feb	7	(a)	Bury	W 2-0	Forde, Woodgate	19,000
29		14	(a)	Coventry C	W 1-0	Wright	34,000
30		28	(h)	Newcastle U	L 0-2		30,000
31	Mar	6	(a)	Birmingham C	W 1-0	Dunn	44,000
32		13	(h)	West Brom A	L 0-2		25,000
33		20	(a)	Barnsley	D 1-1	Parsons	18,000
34		26	(a)	Cardiff C	W 3-0	Stephens 3	45,000
35		27	(h)	Plymouth A	D 1-1	Stephens	22,000
36		29	(h)	Cardiff C	W 4-2	Wright 2, Stephens, Parsons	34,000
37	Apr	3	(a)	Luton T	D 0-0		15,000
38		7	(a)	Chesterfield	L 0-6		11,554
39		10	(h)	Brentford	L 0-1		22,000
40		17	(a)	Leicester C	W 3-1	Woodgate, Hall, Wade	34,856
41		24	(h)	Leeds U	W 2-1	Woodgate, Parsons	14,000
42	May	1	(a)	Fulham	D 1-1	Hall	20,000

P	W	D	L	F	A	W	D	L	F	A	Pts	Pos	Div		Appearances
42	10	7	4	29	19	6	7	8	26	34	46	6th	2		Goals

FA Cup

					Result		Attendance
3	Jan	10	(a)	Blackburn R	D 0-0		32,500
R		17	(h)	Blackburn R	L 2-4	Parsons, Stephens	30,000

Appearances

Goals

Football season appearance and goalscoring chart. Shirt numbers are shown in each player's column for every match (rows 1–42), with appearance and goal totals beneath.

#	Gregory	Yeomanson	Forde	Corbett	Banner	Walker	Woodgate	Parsons	Neary	Wright	Bainbridge	Wood	Cater	Small	Hall	Moroney	Proudlock	Parker	Travis	Tucker	Wilson	Stephens	Wade	Devlin	Armstrong	Dunn
1	1	2	3	4	5	6	7	8	9	10	11															
2	1	2	3	4	5	6	7	8	9		11	10														
3	1	2	3	6		5	7	8			11				4	9	10									
4	1	2	3	4		5	7	8		11				9		6	10									
5	1	2	3	4		5	7	8		11				9		6	10									
6	1	2	3	4		5	7	8			11			9		6	10									
7	1	2	3	4		5	7	8	9	11			10			6										
8	1	2	3	4		5		8		11						6	10	7	9							
9	1	2	3	4		5	7	8		11				9		6	10									
10	1	2	3	4		5	7	8		11				9		6	10									
11	1	2	3	4		5	7	8		11				9		6	10									
12	1	2	3	4		5	7	8						9		6	10	11								
13	1	2	3	4		5	7	8		11				9		6	10									
14	1	2	3	4		5	7	8		11			10	9		6										
15	1	2	3	4		5	7	8		11			10	9		6										
16	1	2	3	4		5	7	8		11			10			6				9						
17	1	2	3	4		5	7	8		11			10			6				9						
18	1	2	3	4		5	7	8							9	10	6			11						
19	1	2	3	4		5	7	8		11						10	6				9					
20	1	2	3	4	5	6	7	8					10		11						9					
21	1	2	3	4		5	7	8					10			6						9	11			
22	1	2	3	4		5	7	8					10			6						9	11			
23	1	2	3	4	5		7	8					10			6						9	11			
24	1	2	3	4	5		7	8								6	10					9	11			
25	1		3	4		5	7	8								6	10					9	11	2		
26	1	2	3	5				8		11		7		4		9				10			6			
27	1	2	3	4		5	7	8		11						6						9	10			
28	1	2	3	4		5	7	8				10				6						9	11			
29	1	2	3	4		5	7	8				10				6						9	11			
30	1	2	3	4		5	7	8		10						6						9	11			
31	1	2	3	4		5	7	8								6						9	11		10	
32	1	2	3	4		5	7	8		11						6	10					9				
33	1	2	3	4		5	7	8		11						10	6					9				
34	1	2	3	4		5	7	8				10				6						9	11			
35	1		3	4		5	7	8						2		6	10					9				11
36	1	10	3	4		5	7	8						2		6						9				11
37	1	10	3	4		5	7	8						2		6						9				11
38	1	10	3	4		5	7	8						2		6						9				11
39	1	2	3	4		5	7	8		11						6						9	10			
40	1	2	3	4		5	7	8							10	6						9	11			
41	1	2	3	4		5	7	8		11						6						9	10			
42	1	2	3	4		5	7	8		11						10	6					9				
Apps	42	40	42	42	5	39	38	42	3	21	4	12	7	14	9	36	10	2	4	5	2	21	16	1	1	4
Goals		1	1			1	7	11		8		3		3	3	2	3					3	6	1		1

I own-goal

Cup matches (rounds 3 and R = Replay):

#	Gregory	Yeomanson	Forde	Corbett	Banner	Walker	Woodgate	Parsons	Neary	Wright	Bainbridge	Wood	Cater	Small	Hall	Moroney	Proudlock	Parker	Travis	Tucker	Wilson	Stephens	Wade	Devlin	Armstrong	Dunn
3	1	2	3	4		5	7	8							9	6						10	11			
R	1	2	3	5			7	8					4		9	6						10	11			
Apps	2	2	2	2		1	2	2					1		2	2						2	2			
Goals																1										

1948-49

Manager: Charlie Paynter

1	Aug	21	(h)	Lincoln C	D 2-2	Wright, McGowan	31,000
2		23	(a)	Sheffield W	L 0-3		36,000
3		28	(a)	Chesterfield	D 0-0		18,000
4		30	(h)	Sheffield W	D 2-2	Parsons, Bainbridge	28,000
5	Sep	4	(h)	West Brom A	W 1-0	Hall	28,000
6		6	(a)	Coventry C	L 0-1		16,494
7		11	(a)	Bury	L 0-2		23,754
8		13	(h)	Coventry C	D 2-2	Chapman, Opp own-goal	18,000
9		18	(h)	Plymouth A	W 3-0	Yeomanson, Chapman, Wright	22,000
10		25	(h)	Tottenham H	W 1-0	Hall	38,400
11	Oct	2	(a)	Brentford	D 0-0		31,400
12		9	(a)	Blackburn R	D 0-0		23,800
13		16	(h)	Cardiff C	W 3-1	Parsons, Wright, Chapman	30,000
14		23	(a)	Queen's Park R	L 1-2	Wright	27,500
15		30	(h)	Luton T	L 0-1		25,000
16	Nov	6	(a)	Bradford	W 3-2	Parsons, Hall, Woodgate	15,913
17		13	(h)	Southampton	D 1-1	Woodgate	35,000
18		20	(a)	Barnsley	W 3-2	Wright, Walker, Woodgate	20,289
19	Dec	4	(a)	Nottingham F	L 0-3		23,168
20		11	(h)	Fulham	W 1-0	Wright	22,500
21		18	(a)	Lincoln C	L 3-4	Woodgate 2, Parsons	16,000
22		25	(h)	Leeds U	W 3-2	Wright 2, Corbett	21,000
23		27	(a)	Leeds U	W 3-1	Wright 2, Dick	32,500
24	Jan	1	(h)	Chesterfield	L 1-2	Woodgate	17,000
25		15	(a)	West Brom A	L 1-2	Robinson	25,000
26		22	(h)	Bury	W 2-1	Parsons, Robinson	22,000
27	Feb	5	(a)	Plymouth A	L 0-2		17,000
28		12	(h)	Grimsby T	W 1-0	Robinson	15,000
29		19	(a)	Tottenham H	D 1-1	Woodgate	62,980
30	Mar	5	(h)	Blackburn R	W 2-1	Parsons, Wright	18,560
31		12	(a)	Cardiff C	L 0-4		30,000
32		19	(h)	Queen's Park R	W 2-0	Woodgate, Robinson	26,000
33		26	(a)	Luton T	W 1-0	Robinson	15,587
34	Apr	2	(h)	Bradford	W 4-1	Parsons 2, McGowan, Opp own-goal	19,000
35		9	(a)	Southampton	W 1-0	Robinson	25,000
36		15	(h)	Leicester C	W 4-1	Robinson 3, Woodgate	33,000
37		16	(h)	Barnsley	W 2-0	Parsons, McGowan	21,000
38		18	(a)	Leicester C	D 1-1	Robinson	29,700
39		23	(a)	Grimsby T	L 0-3		16,000
40		25	(h)	Brentford	D 1-1	Bainbridge	15,000
41		30	(h)	Nottingham F	L 0-5		15,000
42	May	7	(a)	Fulham	L 0-2		40,000

P	W	D	L	F	A	W	D	L	F	A	Pts	Pos	Div	Appearances
42	13	5	3	38	23	5	5	11	18	35	46	7th	2	Goals

FA Cup

3	Jan	8	(a)	Luton T	L 1-3	Wade	21,629

Appearances
Goals

	Gregory	Yeomanson	Devlin	Corbett	Walker	Moroney	Parsons	Wood	Stephns	McGowan	Wright	Hall	Bainbridge	Woodgate	Carroll	Cater	Chapman	Forde	Dick	Wade	Taylor	Robinson	Tucker	Jackman	
1	1	2	3	4	5	6	7	8	9	10	11														1
2	1	2	3	4	5	6	7	8		10	11	9													2
3	1	2	3	4	5	6	7	8		10	9	11													3
4	1	2	3	4	5	6	8			10		11	7	9											4
5	1	2	3	4	5	10	7					8		11	9	6									5
6	1	2	3	4	5	10	8						7	11	9	6									6
7	1	2	3	4	5	10	7					8		11	9	6									7
8	1	2		4	5	6	7			10	9			11		8		3							8
9	1	2		4	5	6	7			10	9			11		8		3							9
10	1	2	3	4	5	6	7			10	9			11		8									10
11	1	2		4	5	6	7			10	9			11		8		3							11
12	1	2		4	5	6	7			10	9			11		8		3							12
13	1	2		4	5	6	7			10	9			11		8		3							13
14	1	2		4	5	6	7			10	9			11		8		3							14
15	1	2		4	5	6	7				9			11		8		3	10						15
16	1	2		4	5	6	7				9			11		8		3	10						16
17	1	2		4	5	6	7				9			11		8		3	10						17
18	1	2		4	5	6	7				9			11		8		3	10						18
19	1	2		4	5	6	7				9			11		8		3	10						19
20	1	2		4	5	6	7				9			11		8		3	10						20
21	1	2		4	5	6	7				9			11		8		3	10						21
22		2		4	5	6	7				9			11		8		3	10		1				22
23		2		4	5	6	7	8			9			11				3	10		1				23
24		2		4	5	6	7	8			9			11				3	10		1				24
25	1	2		4	5	6	7							11		8		3	10			9			25
26	1	2		4	5	6	7							11		8		3	10			9			26
27	1	2		4	5	6	7	8						11				3	10			9			27
28	1	2		4	5	6	7	8						11				3	10			9			28
29	1	2		4	5	6	7	8						11				3	10			9			29
30	1	2		4	5		7	8						11			6	3	10			9			30
31		2		4	5		7	8						11			6	3	10		1	9			31
32		2		4	5		7	8						11			6	3	10		1	9			32
33		2		4	5		7	8						11			6	3	10		1	9			33
34		2	3		5	6	7	8						11			4		10		1	9			34
35		2		4	5	6	7	8						11				3	10		1	9			35
36		2		4	5	6	7	8						11				3		10	1	9			36
37		2		4	5	6	7	8						11				3	10		1	9			37
38		2		4	5	6	7	8						11				3	10		1	9			38
39		2			5	6	7	8						11			4	3	10		1	9			39
40		2			5	6	7	8						11			4	3	10		1	9			40
41		2		4	5		7	8						11			6	3	10		1	9			41
42		2		4	5	6	7	8						11				3	10		1	9			42
	27	29	20	39	40	36	42	3	1	15	21	17	16	38	5	18	7	31	14	8	15	17	2	1	
		1		1	1		9			3	11	3	2	9		3		1			10				

2 own-goals

	Gregory	Yeomanson	Devlin	Corbett	Walker	Moroney	Parsons	Wood	Stephns	McGowan	Wright	Hall	Bainbridge	Woodgate	Carroll	Cater	Chapman	Forde	Dick	Wade	Taylor	Robinson	Tucker	Jackman	
	1	2		4	5	6		8				11				7		3	9	10					3
	1	1		1	1	1	1					1				1		1	1	1					
																		1							

1949-50

Manager: Charlie Paynter

							Result	Scorers	Attendance
1	Aug	20	(a)	Luton T		D	2-2	Robinson, Parsons	17,000
2		22	(h)	Leeds U		W	3-1	Robinson 2, McGowan	23,000
3		27	(h)	Barnsley		W	2-1	Gazzard, Bainbridge	28,000
4		31	(a)	Leeds U		D	2-2	Robinson, Bainbridge	29,500
5	Sep	3	(a)	Plymouth A		W	3-0	Gazzard, Robinson, Parsons	25,521
6		6	(h)	Southampton		L	1-2	Robinson	25,000
7		10	(a)	Sheffield U		D	0-0		25,000
8		17	(h)	Grimsby T		W	4-3	Bainbridge 2, Robinson 2	28,000
9		24	(a)	Queen's Park R		W	1-0	Robinson	24,000
10	Oct	1	(h)	Preston NE		L	0-3		37,000
11		8	(h)	Chesterfield		D	1-1	Parsons	26,000
12		15	(a)	Bradford		L	1-2	Robinson	13,863
13		22	(h)	Leicester C		D	2-2	Parsons, Bainbridge	23,000
14		29	(a)	Bury		L	1-3	Gazzard	16,399
15	Nov	5	(h)	Tottenham H		L	0-1		32,000
16		12	(a)	Cardiff C		W	1-0	Robinson	17,000
17		19	(h)	Blackburn R		L	0-2		17,400
18		26	(a)	Brentford		W	2-0	Robinson 2	21,930
19	Dec	3	(h)	Hull C		W	2-1	Robinson, Wade	29,500
20		10	(a)	Sheffield W		L	1-2	Wade	24,000
21		17	(h)	Luton T		D	0-0		25,000
22		24	(a)	Barnsley		D	1-1	Parsons	17,295
23		26	(h)	Swansea T		W	3-0	Parsons, Wade, Opp own-goal	24,000
24		27	(a)	Swansea T		L	0-1		30,000
25		31	(h)	Plymouth A		D	2-2	Robinson, Wade	19,000
26	Jan	14	(h)	Sheffield U		D	0-0		23,000
27		21	(a)	Grimsby T		L	0-2		17,000
28	Feb	4	(h)	Queen's Park R		W	1-0	Robinson	26,000
29		18	(a)	Preston NE		L	1-2	Opp own-goal	25,000
30		25	(a)	Chesterfield		L	0-1		3,036
31	Mar	4	(h)	Bradford		W	1-0	Parker	17,000
32		11	(a)	Leicester C		L	1-2	Robinson	28,040
33		18	(h)	Bury		W	4-0	Parker, Woodgate, Gazzard, Parsons	18,000
34		25	(a)	Tottenham H		L	1-4	Robinson	51,124
35	Apr	1	(h)	Brentford		D	2-2	Robinson 2	21,000
36		8	(a)	Hull C		D	2-2	Robinson, McGowan	27,000
37		10	(h)	Coventry C		L	0-1		11,000
38		11	(a)	Coventry C		L	1-5	Woodgate	26,648
39		15	(h)	Cardiff C		L	0-1		15,000
40		22	(a)	Blackburn R		L	0-2		17,400
41		29	(h)	Sheffield W		D	2-2	Woodgate 2	10,500
42	May	6	(a)	Southampton		L	2-3	Robinson 2	24,778

P	W	D	L	F	A	W	D	L	F	A	Pts	Pos	Div	
42	8	7	6	30	25	4	5	12	23	36	36	19th	2	Appearances
														Goals

FA Cup

						Result	Scorers	Attendance
3	Jan	7	(h)	Ipswich T		W	5-1	Woodgate 2, Gazzard, Wade, Robinson	25,000
4		28	(h)	Everton		L	1-2	McGowan	26,800

Appearances
Goals

Player appearances & goals grid (shirt numbers per match).

#	Gregory	Devlin	Forde	Corbett	Walker	Moroney	Parsons	Gazzard	Robinson	McGowan	Bainbridge	Woodgate	Parker	Kearns	Tucker	Wright	Jackman	Wade	Yeomanson	Cater	Barrett
1	1	2	3	4	5	6	7	8	9	10	11										
2	1	2	3	4	5	6	7	8	9	10	11										
3	1	2	3	4	5	6	7	8	9	10	11										
4	1	2	3	4	5	6	7	8	9	10	11										
5	1	2	3	4	5	6	7	8	9	10	11										
6	1	2	3	4	5	6		8	10	9	11	7									
7	1	2	3		5	6	7	8	9	10	11		4								
8	1	2	3		5	6	7	8	9	10	11		4								
9	1	2	3		5	6	7	8	9	10	11		4								
10	1	2		6	5		7	8	9	10	11		4	3							
11	1	2			5	6		8	10	9	11	7	4	3							
12	1	2			5	6		8	10	9	11	7	4	3							
13	1	2		6	5			8	10	9	11	7	4	3							
14	1	2			5	6	7	8		10	11		4	3		9					
15	1	2			5		7	8	9	6	11		4	3					10		
16	1	2			5		7	8	9	6	11		4	3					10		
17	1	2	3		5		7	8	9	6			11	4					10		
18	1	2	3		5		7	8	9	6			11	4					10		
19	1	2			5		7	8	9	6			11	4	5				10	3	
20	1	2	3		5		7	8	9	6			11	4					10		
21	1	2			5		7	8	9	6			11	4					10	3	
22	1	2			5		7	8	9	6			11	4					10	3	
23	1	2			5		7	8	9	6			11	4	3				10		
24	1	2			5		7	8	9	6			11	4					10	3	
25	1	2			5		7	8	9	6			11	4					10	3	
26	1	2			5		7	8	9	10			11	4					3	6	
27	1	2			5		10	8	9	6			7	4					11	3	
28	1		3		5		8	10	9	6			7	4					11		2
29	1		3		5		8	10	9	6			7	4					11		2
30	1		3		5			8	9	10			7	4					11	2	6
31	1		3	5		6		8	9	10	11	7	4						2		
32	1		3		5		8	10	9	6	11	7	4						2		
33	1		3		5		8	10	9	6	11	7	4						2		
34	1		3		5		8	10	9	6	11	7	4						2		
35	1		3		5	6	8		9	10	11	7	4						2		
36	1		3		5	6	8		9	10	11	7	4						2		
37	1		3	5		6	8	10	9	4	11	7							2		
38	1		3	4	5	6	8		9	10	7					11			2		
39	1		3		5	6	7	10	9		11	4							2	8	
40	1		3		5	6		9	10	11	7								2	4	8
41	1		3	5	6		10	9		7	4					11			2		8
42	42	28	27	12	39	21	38	38	40	37	25	29	32	8	2	2	3	12	20	4	3
Goals						7	4	23	2	5	4	2					4				

2 own-goals

#	Gregory	Devlin	Forde	Corbett	Walker	Moroney	Parsons	Gazzard	Robinson	McGowan	Bainbridge	Woodgate	Parker	Kearns	Tucker	Wright	Jackman	Wade	Yeomanson	Cater	Barrett
3	1	2			5		7	8	9	6	11		4					10	3		
4	1	2			5		7	8	9	6	11		4					3	10		
Apps	2	2			2		2	2	2	2	2		2				1	2	1		
Goals								1	1	1	2							1			

1950-51

Manager: Ted Fenton

1	Aug	19	(h)	Hull C	D 3-3	Gazzard, Robinson, Opp own-goal	30,000
2		24	(h)	Luton T	W 2-1	Woodgate, Betts	21,000
3		26	(a)	Doncaster R	L 0-3		23,678
4		28	(a)	Luton T	D 1-1	Gazzard	14,000
5	Sep	2	(h)	Brentford	L 1-2	Parsons	22,000
6		4	(a)	Cardiff C	L 1-2	Johns	32,000
7		9	(a)	Blackburn R	W 3-1	Robinson 2, Johns	25,200
8		16	(h)	Southampton	W 3-0	Gazzard 2, Robinson	22,500
9		23	(a)	Barnsley	W 2-1	Robinson, Woodgate	25,611
10		30	(h)	Sheffield U	L 3-5	Robinson 3	25,500
11	Oct	7	(h)	Queen's Park R	W 4-1	Parsons 2, Woodgate, Robinson	26,500
12		14	(a)	Bury	L 0-3		15,542
13		21	(h)	Leicester C	D 0-0		25,000
14		28	(a)	Chesterfield	W 2-1	Woodgate, Barrett	11,207
15	Nov	4	(h)	Coventry C	W 3-2	Gazzard 2, Parker	26,000
16		11	(a)	Manchester C	L 0-2		35,000
17		18	(h)	Preston NE	W 2-0	Robinson, Gazzard	27,000
18		25	(a)	Notts C	L 1-4	Woodgate	27,078
19	Dec	2	(h)	Grimsby T	W 2-1	Barrett, Robinson	18,500
20		9	(a)	Birmingham C	L 1-3	Robinson	18,000
21		16	(a)	Hull C	W 2-1	Robinson, Woodgate	20,000
22		23	(h)	Doncaster R	D 0-0		16,000
23		25	(h)	Leeds U	W 3-1	Woodgate 3	19,500
24		26	(a)	Leeds U	L 0-2		32,500
25		30	(a)	Brentford	D 1-1	Robinson	19,290
26	Jan	13	(h)	Blackburn R	L 2-3	Robinson 2	23,000
27		20	(a)	Southampton	D 2-2	Robinson, Gazzard	21,000
28	Feb	3	(h)	Barnsley	W 4-2	Robinson 2, Gazzard 2	17,000
29		17	(a)	Sheffield U	D 1-1	Robinson	15,000
30		24	(a)	Queen's Park R	D 3-3	Woodgate 2, McGowan	21,336
31	Mar	3	(h)	Bury	L 2-3	Robinson 2	19,500
32		10	(a)	Leicester C	L 0-1		23,000
33		17	(h)	Chesterfield	W 2-0	Robinson, Gazzard	16,000
34		23	(h)	Swansea T	D 1-1	Hooper	25,500
35		24	(a)	Coventry C	L 0-1		21,881
36		26	(a)	Swansea T	L 2-3	Robinson, Hooper	12,000
37		31	(h)	Manchester C	L 2-4	Barrett, Woodgate	22,000
38	Apr	7	(a)	Preston NE	W 1-0	Barrett	30,000
39		14	(h)	Notts C	W 4-2	Robinson 2, Hooper, Gazzard	26,000
40		21	(a)	Grimsby T	W 1-0	Gazzard	13,000
41		28	(h)	Birmingham C	L 1-2	Kinsell	12,500
42	May	5	(h)	Cardiff C	D 0-0		18,000

P	W	D	L	F	A	W	D	L	F	A	Pts	Pos	Div	Appearances
42	10	5	6	44	33	6	5	10	24	36	42	13th	2	Goals

FA Cup

3	Jan	6	(h)	Cardiff C	W 2-1	Barrett, Gazzard	26,000
4		27	(a)	Stoke C	L 0-1		48,500

Appearances
Goals

Gregory	Devlin	Yeomanson	Parker	Walker	Jackman	Woodgate	Gazzard	Robinson	Foan	Betts	Moroney	Parsons	Tucker	Johns	Forde	Southren	Barrett	O'Farrell	Kearns	Taylor	Kinsell	Hooper	McGowan	Allison	
1	2	3	4	5	6	7	8	9	10	11															1
1	2	3	4	5		7	8	9	10	11	6														2
1	2	3	4	5		7	10	9		11	6	8													3
1	2	3	4	5	6	7	10	9				8	11												4
1	2	3	4	5	6	7	10	9				8	11												5
1	2	3	4	5		11		9	10		6	7		8											6
1	2		4	5		11	10	9			6	7		8	3										7
1	2		4	5		11	10	9			6	7		8	3										8
1	2		4	5		11	10	9			6	7		8	3										9
1	2		4	5		11	10	9			6			8	3	7									10
1		2	4	5		11	10	9			6	7			3		8								11
1		2	4	5		11	10	9	8		6				3	7									12
1		2	4	5		11	10	9			6			8	3	7									13
1		2	4	5		11	10	9			6				3	7	8								14
1		2	4	5		11	10	9			6	7			3		8								15
1		2	4	5		11	10	9			6	7			3		8								16
1	2		4	5		11	10	9			6				3	7	8								17
1	2		4	5		11	10	9				7			3		8	6							18
1	2		4	5		11	10	9							3	7	8	6							19
1		2	4	5		11	10	9							3	7	8	6							20
1			4	5		11	10	9			6				3	7	8		2						21
1			4	5		11	10	9			6				3	7	8		2						22
1		3	4	5		11	10	9			6					7	8		2						23
		3	4	5		7	10	9	8		6		11						2	1					24
		3	4	5		11	10	9								7	8	6	2	1					25
1			4	5		11	10	9								7	8	6	2		3				26
1			4	5		11	10	9							2	7	8	6			3				27
1			4	5		11	10	9							2			6			3	7	8		28
1			4	5		11	10	9							2	7		6			3		8		29
1			4	5		11	10	9			6				2	7					3		8		30
1			4	5		11	10	9			6				2	7					3		8		31
			4	5		11	10	9			6				2	7				1	3		8		32
			4			11	10	9							2			6		1	3	7	8	5	33
			4		9	11	10								2		8	6		1	3	7		5	34
			4	9		11	10								2		8	6		1	3	7		5	35
			4			11	10	9							2		8	6		1	3	7	8	5	36
1		3	4			11	10	9							2		8	6				7		5	37
			4			11	10	9							2		8	6		1	3	7		5	38
						11	10	9			4				2		8	6		1	3	7		5	39
						11	10	9			4				2		8	6		1	3	7		5	40
						11	10	9			4				2		8	6		1	3	7		5	41
						11	10	9			4				2		8	6		1	3	7		5	42
30	13	17	38	33	4	42	41	40	5	3	25	11	3	6	32	17	22	18	6	12	16	11	7	10	
			1			12	13	26		1		3		2			4				1	3	1		

1 own-goal

1			4	5		11	10	9							3	7	8	6	2						3
1			4	5		11	10	9							3	7	8	6			2				4
2			2	2		2	2	2							2	2	2	2	1		1				
							1										1								

1951-52

Manager: Ted Fenton

1	Aug	18	(a)	Queen's Park R	L	0-2		19,443
2		23	(h)	Bury	D	1-1	Robinson	16,000
3		25	(h)	Blackburn R	W	3-1	Barrett 2, Gazzard	19,500
4		29	(a)	Bury	L	0-4		10,442
5	Sep	1	(a)	Hull C	D	1-1	Hawkins	35,000
6		5	(h)	Swansea T	D	2-2	Bing, Barrett	15,500
7		8	(h)	Barnsley	W	2-1	Hawkins 2	20,000
8		13	(a)	Swansea T	L	1-2	Barrett	16,000
9		15	(a)	Sheffield U	L	1-6	Bing	30,000
10		22	(h)	Leeds U	W	2-0	Hawkins, Woodgate	20,000
11		29	(h)	Coventry C	W	3-1	Parker, Hawkins, McGowan	21,000
12	Oct	6	(a)	Rotherham U	L	1-2	Hawkins	20,000
13		13	(h)	Cardiff C	D	1-1	Hawkins	24,000
14		20	(a)	Birmingham C	L	1-2	Woodgate	21,000
15		27	(h)	Leicester C	L	2-3	Woodgate, Bing	21,000
16	Nov	3	(a)	Nottingham F	D	0-0		20,593
17		10	(h)	Brentford	W	1-0	Hawkins	26,500
18		17	(a)	Doncaster R	L	1-4	Gregory	20,000
19		24	(h)	Everton	D	3-3	Kinsell, Woodgate, Gazzard	22,500
20	Dec	1	(a)	Southampton	W	2-1	Hawkins, Williams	17,473
21		8	(h)	Sheffield W	L	0-6		18,000
22		15	(h)	Queen's Park R	W	4-2	Hawkins 3, Woodgate	17,500
23		22	(a)	Blackburn R	L	1-3	O'Farrell	20,000
24		25	(h)	Luton T	W	3-0	Hawkins, Gazzard, Gregory	20,000
25		26	(a)	Luton T	L	1-6	Gregory	19,654
26		29	(h)	Hull C	W	2-0	Parker, Tucker	19,500
27	Jan	5	(a)	Barnsley	D	1-1	Tucker	16,204
28		19	(h)	Sheffield U	W	5-1	Tucker 3, Gazzard 2	21,000
29		26	(a)	Leeds U	L	1-3	Gazzard	32,500
30	Feb	9	(a)	Coventry C	W	2-1	Barrett, Hawkins	19,486
31		16	(h)	Rotherham U	W	2-1	Woodgate, Hawkins	19,000
32	Mar	1	(a)	Cardiff C	D	1-1	Opp own-goal	38,000
33		8	(h)	Birmingham C	L	0-1		24,000
34		15	(a)	Leicester C	L	1-3	Andrews	30,038
35		22	(h)	Nottingham F	W	3-1	Barrett, Gazzard, O'Farrell	23,500
36	Apr	5	(h)	Doncaster R	D	3-3	Gazzard, Barrett, Andrews	18,000
37		11	(h)	Notts C	W	2-1	Gazzard 2	23,000
38		12	(a)	Everton	L	0-2		36,428
39		14	(a)	Notts C	L	0-1		16,306
40		19	(h)	Southampton	W	4-0	Woodgate 2, Barrett, Kearns	18,500
41		21	(a)	Brentford	D	1-1	Parker	13,000
42		26	(a)	Sheffield W	D	2-2	Barrett, Gazzard	44,011

P	W	D	L	F	A	W	D	L	F	A	Pts	Pos	Div	Appearances
42	13	5	3	48	29	2	6	13	19	48	41	12th	2	Goals

FA Cup

3	Jan	12	(h)	Blackpool	W	2-1	Andrews, O'Farrell	38,600
4	Feb	2	(h)	Sheffield U	D	0-0		35,500
R		6	(a)	Sheffield U	L	2-4	Woodgate, Gazzard	39,073

Appearances
Goals

272

Player appearances and goals grid (shirt numbers by match). Player columns, left to right:

#	Gregory E	Forde	Kinsell	Parker	Allison	O'Farrell	Southren	Barrett	Robinson	Gazzard	Woodgate	Taylor	Wright	Moroney	Bing	Hawkins	Foan	McGowan	Devlin	Williams	Gregory J	Andrews	Walker	Hooper	Kearns	Tucker	Bond	Stroud
1	1	2	3	4	5	6	7	8	9	10	11																	
2		2	3	4	5	6	7	8	9	10	11	1																
3		2	3	4	5	6	7	8	9	10	11	1																
4		2	3	4	5	6	7	8	9	10	11	1																
5			3		5	6		8		10	11	1	2	4	7	9												
6			3		5	6		8		10	11	1	2	4	7	9												
7			3		5	6		8		10	11	1	2	4	7	9												
8			3		5	6		8			11	1	2	4	7	9		10										
9			3		5	6		8			11	1	2	4	7	9			10									
10					5	6		8		10	11	1	2	4	7	9			3									
11				8	5	6	7				11	1	2	4		9		10	3									
12			3		5	6					11	1	2	4	7	9	8	10										
13			3	8	5	6					11	1	2	4	7	9		10										
14			3	4	5	6				10	11	1	2		7	9	8											
15			3	4	5						11	1	2	6	7	9	8	10										
16	1		3	4	5	6	7				11		2			9	8	10										
17	1		3	4	5	6	7	8			11		2			9		10										
18	1		3	4	5	6	7	8		10	11		2			9												
19	1			4	5	6	7			10			2			9			3	8	11							
20	1			4	5	6	7						2			9			3	8	10	11						
21	1		3	4		6	7						2			9				8	10	11	5					
22	1		3	4		6						10	2			9				8		11	5	7				
23	1		3	4		6	7					10	2			9				8		11	5					
24	1		3	4		6	7					10	2			9				8		11	5					
25	1			4	5	6	7	8					2					3			10			9	11			
26	1		3	4	5	6		8			7		2			9					10	11						
27	1		3	4	5	6		8			7		2			9					10	11						
28	1		3	4	5	6		8	11		7		2			9					10							
29	1				5	6		8		10	7		2			9		4				11				3		
30	1		3	4	5	6		8			7		2			9					10	11						
31	1		3	4	5	6		8			7		2			9					10	11						
32	1		3	4	5	6		8			7		2			9					10	11						
33	1		3		5	6		8		10	7		2			9		4				11						
34	1		3		5	6		8			7		2	4		9					10	11						
35	1		3		5	6		8			7		2	4		9					10	11						
36	1		3		5	6		8			7		2	4		9					10	11						
37	1		3	4	5	6		8		10	7		2			9						11						
38	1			4	5	6		8		10	7		2									11				3	9	
39	1		3	4	5	6		8		10	7		2									11		9				
40	1		3	4	5	6		8		10	7		2									11		9				
41	1		3	4	5	6		8		10	7		2			9						11						
42	1		3	4	5	6		8		10	7		2			9						11						
Apps	28	7	32	30	38	41	11	23	4	31	38	14	38	12	10	32	3	9	5	5	9	23	4	2	3	7	2	1
Goals		1	3		2			9	1	11	8		3	15	1		1	3	2			1				5		

1 own-goal

#	Gregory E	Forde	Kinsell	Parker	Allison	O'Farrell	Southren	Barrett	Robinson	Gazzard	Woodgate	Taylor	Wright	Moroney	Bing	Hawkins	Foan	McGowan	Devlin	Williams	Gregory J	Andrews	Walker	Hooper	Kearns	Tucker	Bond	Stroud
3	1		3	4	5	6		8	7		2					9					10	11						
4	1		3	4	5	6		8	7		2					9					10	11						
R	1		3	4	5	6		8	7		2					9					10	11						
Apps	3	3	3	3	3			3	3		3					3					3	3						
Goals				1				1	1												1							

1952-53

Manager: Ted Fenton

#	Month	Date		Opponent	Result	Scorers	Attendance
1	Aug	23	(h)	Southampton	W 1-0	Barrett	26,000
2		25	(a)	Hull C	L 0-1		35,964
3		30	(a)	Bury	D 1-1	Andrews	14,000
4	Sep	1	(h)	Hull C	D 0-0		19,600
5		6	(h)	Birmingham C	L 1-2	Moroney	25,000
6		8	(a)	Leicester C	D 0-0		23,382
7		13	(a)	Luton T	D 0-0		16,009
8		15	(h)	Leicester C	W 4-1	Barrett 2, Woodgate, Kearns	15,500
9		20	(h)	Leeds U	D 2-2	Moroney 2	22,500
10		27	(a)	Plymouth A	D 1-1	Barrett	27,000
11	Oct	4	(h)	Rotherham U	L 2-4	Andrews, Opp own-goal	22,000
12		11	(a)	Blackburn R	L 0-3		22,400
13		18	(h)	Nottingham F	W 3-2	O'Farrell, Southren, Allison	21,500
14		25	(a)	Everton	L 0-2		38,416
15	Nov	1	(h)	Brentford	W 3-1	Hawkins, McGowan, Tucker	23,500
16		8	(a)	Doncaster R	D 1-1	Tucker	10,612
17		15	(h)	Swansea T	W 3-0	Kearns, Tucker, Gregory	18,500
18		22	(a)	Huddersfield T	W 1-0	Kearns	22,267
19		29	(h)	Sheffield U	D 1-1	Woodgate	23,000
20	Dec	6	(a)	Barnsley	L 0-2		8,915
21		13	(h)	Lincoln C	W 5-1	Gregory 2, Foan 2, Kearns	14,500
22		20	(a)	Southampton	W 2-1	Woodgate, Kearns	12,274
23		25	(h)	Notts C	D 2-2	Kearns, Foan	24,000
24		27	(a)	Notts C	D 1-1	Allison	24,189
25	Jan	3	(h)	Bury	W 3-2	Kearns 3	18,000
26		17	(a)	Birmingham C	L 0-2		22,000
27		24	(h)	Luton T	L 0-1		23,500
28	Feb	7	(a)	Leeds U	L 2-3	Kearns, Barrett	17,500
29		18	(h)	Plymouth A	L 0-1		8,000
30		21	(a)	Rotherham U	D 1-1	Andrews	14,700
31		28	(h)	Blackburn R	D 0-0		19,500
32	Mar	7	(a)	Nottingham F	D 0-0		17,938
33		14	(h)	Everton	W 3-1	Andrews, Hooper, Moroney	19,000
34		21	(a)	Brentford	W 4-1	Moroney 2, Hooper 2	19,000
35		28	(h)	Doncaster R	L 1-3	Barrett	13,000
36	Apr	3	(h)	Fulham	L 1-2	Barrett	24,500
37		4	(a)	Swansea T	L 1-4	Barrett	20,000
38		6	(a)	Fulham	W 3-2	Dixon 2, Sexton	22,000
39		11	(h)	Huddersfield T	L 0-1		23,000
40		18	(a)	Sheffield U	L 1-3	Dixon	35,000
41		25	(h)	Barnsley	W 3-1	Dixon, Andrews, Hooper	12,500
42	May	1	(a)	Lincoln C	L 1-3	Barrett	14,235

P	W	D	L	F	A	W	D	L	F	A	Pts	Pos	Div	
42	9	5	7	38	28	4	8	9	20	32	39	14th	2	Appearances
														Goals

FA Cup

3	Jan	10	(h)	West Brom A	L 1-4	Kearns	35,150

Appearances
Goals

Gregory E	Wright	Kinsell	Parker	Allison	O'Farrell	Woodgate	Barrett	Moroney	Gazzard	Andrews	Petchey	Tucker	Bond	Gregory J	Kearns	Southren	Foan	McGowan	Hawkins	Hooper	Walker	Brown	Sexton	Dixon	Devlin	Cantwell	Bing	Gunning	
1	2	3	4	5	6	7	8	9	10	11																			1
1	2	3	4	5	6	7	8	9	10	11																			2
1	2	3	4	5	6	7	8	9	10	11																			3
1	2	3	4	5	6	7	8	9	11	10																			4
1	2		4	5	6	7	8	9				11	3	10															5
1	2		4	5	6	7	8	9				11	3	10															6
1	2		4	5	6	7	8	10			11		3		9														7
1	2		4	5	6	7	8	10			11		3		9														8
1	2		4	5	6		8	10			11		3		9	7													9
1	2		4	5	6		8	10			11		3		9	7													10
1	2		4	5	6		8	10			11		3		9	7													11
1	2	3	4	5	6		8	10			11				9	7													12
1	2	3	4	5	6		8	9			11				7	10													13
1	2	3	4	5	6	7					11				10	8	9												14
1	2	3	4	5	6	7					11				10	8	9												15
1	2	3	4	5	6	7					11		8	9		10													16
1	2	3	4	5	6	7					11		8	9		10													17
1	2	3	4	5	6	7					11		8	9		10													18
1	2		4	5	6	7					11	3	8	9		10													19
1	2	3	4	5	6	7					11		8	9		10													20
1	2	3	4	5	6	7					11		8	9		10													21
1	2	3	4	5	6	7					11		8	9		10													22
1	2		4	5	6	7					11	3	8	9		10													23
1	2		4	5	6	7					11	3	8	9		10													24
1	2		4	5	6	7			10	11			3	8	9														25
1	2		4	5	6	7				11			3	8	9	10													26
1	2		4	5	6	7	8		10				3		9			11											27
1	2	3	4		6	7	8		10						9			11	5										28
1		3	4		6	7			10				2	8	9			11	5										29
1	2	3	4	9	6	7			10		11		8						5										30
1	2	3	4		6		8		10					9	7			11	5										31
1	2	3	4	5	6	7	8	9	10									11											32
1	2	3	4	5	6	7	8	9	10									11											33
1	2	3	4	5	6	7	8	9	10	11								11											34
1	2	3	4	5	6		8	9						7				11			10								35
1	2	3	4	5	6		8							7				11			10	9							36
1			5	6					10					7		4		11			8		9	2	3				37
1	2	3	4	5	6		8		10					7				11			9								38
1	2		4	5			8		10					7				11			9		3	6					39
1	2			5	6		8		10					7		4		11			9		3						40
1	2			5	6		8		10					7				11			9		3	7	11				41
42	40	25	39	39	41	29	26	18	8	23	8	2	15	14	15	21	12	13	5	2	12	1	3	6	1	4	2	1	42
		2	1	3	9	6		5		3			3	10	1	3	1	1	4				1	4					

I own-goal

Gregory E	Wright	Kinsell	Parker	Allison	O'Farrell	Woodgate	Barrett	Moroney	Gazzard	Andrews	Petchey	Tucker	Bond	Gregory J	Kearns	Southren	Foan	McGowan	Hawkins	Hooper	Walker	Brown	Sexton	Dixon	Devlin	Cantwell	Bing	Gunning	
1	2		4	5	6	7							11	3	8	9		10											3
1	1		1	1	1	1							1	1	1	1		1											
																1													

1953-54

Manager: Ted Fenton

1	Aug	19	(h)	Lincoln C	W	5-0	Sexton 2, Parker, Dixon, Andrews	17,000
2		22	(h)	Leicester C	W	4-1	Kearns 3, Andrews	22,500
3		24	(a)	Rotherham U	L	0-5		12,750
4		29	(a)	Stoke C	D	1-1	Dixon	22,000
5	Sep	3	(h)	Rotherham U	W	3-0	Sexton 3	22,500
6		5	(h)	Fulham	W	3-1	Andrews 2, Dixon	30,000
7		10	(a)	Swansea T	D	1-1	Southren	20,000
8		12	(a)	Bristol R	D	2-2	Sexton, Dixon	28,736
9		14	(h)	Swansea T	W	4-1	Dixon 3, Sexton	22,500
10		19	(a)	Leeds U	W	2-1	Dixon, Hooper	28,000
11		26	(h)	Birmingham C	L	1-2	Opp own-goal	30,000
12	Oct	3	(a)	Nottingham F	L	0-4		22,715
13		10	(h)	Brentford	L	0-1		25,000
14		17	(a)	Derby C	L	1-2	Dick	17,689
15		24	(h)	Blackburn R	W	2-1	Southren, Gazzard	23,000
16		31	(a)	Doncaster R	L	0-2		15,176
17	Nov	7	(h)	Bury	W	5-0	Dick 3, Sexton, Stroud	19,500
18		14	(a)	Oldham A	L	1-3	Stroud	12,196
19		21	(h)	Everton	D	1-1	Sexton	25,000
20		28	(a)	Hull C	L	1-2	Sexton	20,000
21	Dec	5	(h)	Notts C	L	1-2	Dick	16,000
22		12	(a)	Lincoln C	W	2-1	Dixon, Dick	12,814
23		19	(a)	Leicester C	L	1-2	Dixon	22,976
24		25	(h)	Luton T	W	1-0	Dick	19,500
25		27	(a)	Luton T	L	1-3	Dixon	20,133
26	Jan	16	(a)	Fulham	W	4-3	Dick 2, Dixon, Sexton	30,000
27		23	(h)	Bristol R	D	1-1	Hooper	21,250
28	Feb	6	(h)	Leeds U	W	5-2	Dixon 2, Hooper, Dick, Andrews	15,500
29		13	(a)	Birmingham C	L	0-2		22,704
30		20	(h)	Nottingham F	D	1-1	Dick	20,000
31		27	(a)	Brentford	L	1-3	Sexton	15,500
32	Mar	6	(a)	Derby C	D	0-0		18,500
33		13	(a)	Blackburn R	L	1-4	Andrews	25,400
34		20	(h)	Doncaster R	W	2-1	Hooper, Dick	14,500
35		27	(a)	Everton	W	2-1	Barrett, Dixon	40,718
36	Apr	3	(h)	Hull C	W	1-0	Hooper	13,000
37		10	(a)	Bury	L	0-2		13,370
38		12	(h)	Stoke C	D	2-2	Hooper, Dick	10,500
39		16	(h)	Plymouth A	D	2-2	Arnott 2	16,500
40		17	(h)	Oldham A	L	0-1		13,000
41		19	(a)	Plymouth A	L	1-2	Dixon	20,938
42		24	(a)	Notts C	L	1-3	Dixon	10,000

P	W	D	L	F	A	W	D	L	F	A	Pts	Pos	Div	
42	11	6	4	44	20	4	3	14	23	49	39	13th	2	Appearances
														Goals

FA Cup

3	Jan	9	(h)	Huddersfield T	W	4-0	Hooper 2, Sexton, Dixon	25,250
4		30	(h)	Blackpool	D	1-1	Dixon	37,000
R	Feb	3	(a)	Blackpool	L	1-3	Sexton	27,120

Appearances
Goals

Appearance and goal-scoring grid (player columns left-to-right; match number in right-hand column).

Gregory	Wright	Cantwell	Parker	Allison	O'Farrell	Southren	Sexton	Dixon	Dick	Andrews	Kearns	Hooper	Bing	Foan	Gazzard	Stroud	Kinsell	Tucker	Bond	Malcolm	Chiswick	Barrett	Musgrove	McGowan	Arnott	#
1	2	3	4	5	6	7	8	9	10	11																1
1	2	3	4	5	6	7	8		10	11	9															2
1	2	3	4	5	6	7	8		10	11	9															3
1	2	3	4	5	6	7	8	9	10	11																4
1	2	3	4	5	6	7	8	9	10	11																5
1	2	3	4	5	6	7	8	9	10	11																6
1	2	3	4	5	6	7	8	9	10		11															7
1	2	3	4	5	6	7	8	9	10		11															8
1	2	3	4	5	6	7	8	9	10		11															9
1	2	3	4	5	6	7	8	9	10		11															10
1	2	3	4	5		7	8	9	10		11	6														11
1	2	3	4	5	6	7	8	9		11				10												12
1	2	3	4	5	6	7	8	9	10	11																13
1	2	3	4	5	6	7	8	9		11				10												14
1	2	3	4	5	6	7	8	9	10	11																15
1	2	3	4	5	6	7	8		10	11				9												16
1	2	3	4	5	6	7	8		10	11				9												17
1	2	3	4	5	6	7	8		10	11				9												18
1	2		4	5	6	7	8		10						9	3	11									19
1	2			5	6	7	8		10		9						11	3	4							20
1	2			5		7	8	9	10	11		6						3	4							21
1	2			5		7	8	9	10	11		6						3	4							22
1	2			5		7	8	9	10	11		6						3	4							23
1	2			5				9	10	11		7	6	8				3	4							24
1	2			5			8	9	10	11		7	6					3	4							25
1	2			5			8	9	10	11		7	6					3	4							26
	2		4	5				9	10	11		7	6					3		1	8					27
	2		4	5	6			9	10	11		7						3		1	8					28
		3		5				9	10	11		7	6			2	4			1	8					29
		3		5	6		8	9	10			7				2	4			1		11				30
		3		5			8	9				7	6	10		2	4			1		11				31
		3		5			8		10	11	9	7				2	4			1			6			32
	2		4	5			8		10	11	9	7				3				1			6			33
	2		4	5				9	10	11		7				3				1	8		6			34
	2		4	5				9	10	11		7				3				1	8		6			35
	2		4	5			8		10	11		7	6			3				1				9		36
			4	5					10	11		7	6			3	2			1	8			9		37
				5					10	11		7				3	2	4		1	8		6	9		38
				5					10	11		7				3	2	4		1	8		6	9		39
			4	5				9	10			7	8			3	2			1		11	6			40
				5				9	10			7				3	2	4		1	8	11	6			41
27	33	23	28	42	22	24	31	29	39	31	5	23	12	4	1	4	10	2	18	14	15	9	4	8	4	42
	1				2	12	17	13	6	3	6			1	2				1		2					

1 own-goal

Gregory	Wright	Cantwell	Parker	Allison	O'Farrell	Southren	Sexton	Dixon	Dick	Andrews	Kearns	Hooper	Bing	Foan	Gazzard	Stroud	Kinsell	Tucker	Bond	Malcolm	Chiswick	Barrett	Musgrove	McGowan	Arnott	#
1	2			5			8	9	10	11		7	6				3	4								3
1	2			5			8	9	10			7	6				11	3	4							4
1	2			5			8	9	10	11		7	6				3	4								R
3	3			3			3	3	3	2		3	3				1	3	3							
							2	2		2																

1954-55

Manager: Ted Fenton

#	Month	Date		Opponent	Result	Scorers	Attendance
1	Aug	21	(a)	Swansea T	L 2-5	Dick 2	20,000
2		23	(a)	Blackburn R	L 2-5	Andrews 2	26,500
3		28	(h)	Notts C	W 3-0	Andrews, Dick, Hooper	19,000
4		30	(h)	Blackburn R	L 2-5	Sexton 2	17,500
5	Sep	4	(a)	Liverpool	W 2-1	Sexton, Hooper	37,593
6		6	(h)	Hull C	D 1-1	Hooper	18,500
7		11	(h)	Bristol R	W 5-2	Sexton, Dick, Andrews, Hooper, O'Farrell	22,500
8		13	(a)	Hull C	W 1-0	Bond	25,851
9		18	(a)	Plymouth A	D 1-1	Sexton	18,370
10		25	(h)	Port Vale	W 2-0	Sexton, Dick	25,500
11	Oct	2	(a)	Doncaster R	L 1-2	Sexton	13,841
12		9	(h)	Nottingham F	W 2-0	Hooper, Foan	25,000
13		16	(a)	Leeds U	L 1-2	Dick	23,000
14		23	(h)	Stoke C	W 3-0	Dick 2, Sexton	27,200
15		30	(a)	Middlesbrough	L 0-6		26,000
16	Nov	6	(h)	Birmingham C	D 2-2	Hooper, Dick	25,500
17		13	(a)	Ipswich T	W 3-0	Sexton, Dick, Andrews	18,600
18		20	(h)	Luton T	W 2-1	Dick, Opp own-goal	23,000
19		27	(a)	Rotherham U	D 2-2	Dick 2	13,000
20	Dec	4	(h)	Bury	D 3-3	Musgrove 2, Dick	18,100
21		11	(a)	Lincoln C	L 1-2	Dick	11,056
22		18	(h)	Swansea T	D 3-3	Hooper, Barrett, Opp own-goal	15,000
23		25	(h)	Derby C	W 1-0	Dick	23,500
24		27	(a)	Derby C	D 0-0		20,473
25	Jan	1	(a)	Notts C	L 1-5	Hooper	21,000
26		22	(a)	Bristol R	W 4-2	Dick 3, Hooper	27,552
27	Feb	5	(h)	Plymouth A	W 6-1	Sexton 3, Dick 2, Bennett	18,200
28		12	(a)	Port Vale	D 1-1	Hooper	12,620
29		24	(h)	Doncaster R	L 0-1		4,500
30	Mar	5	(h)	Leeds U	W 2-1	Bennett, Foan	19,500
31		12	(a)	Stoke C	W 2-0	Musgrove 2	20,498
32		19	(h)	Middlesbrough	W 2-1	Dare, Musgrove	22,500
33		26	(a)	Birmingham C	W 2-1	Dick, Musgrove	9,200
34	Apr	2	(h)	Ipswich T	W 4-0	Dick, Dare, Hooper, Musgrove	23,800
35		8	(h)	Fulham	W 2-1	Dick, Musgrove	34,200
36		9	(a)	Luton T	L 0-2		25,000
37		11	(a)	Fulham	D 0-0		22,500
38		16	(h)	Rotherham U	L 1-2	Dick	24,000
39		23	(a)	Bury	L 1-4	Dick	9,746
40		27	(h)	Liverpool	L 0-3		9,000
41		30	(h)	Lincoln C	L 0-1		10,000
42	May	2	(a)	Nottingham F	D 1-1	Andrews	5,675

P	W	D	L	F	A	W	D	L	F	A	Pts	Pos	Div	
42	12	4	5	46	28	6	6	9	28	42	46	8th	2	Appearances
														Goals

FA Cup

Round	Month	Date		Opponent	Result	Scorers	Attendance
3	Jan	8	(h)	Port Vale	D 2-2	Bennett, Hooper	21,000
R		10	(a)	Port Vale	L 1-3	Hooper	12,410
							Appearances
							Goals

278

Player appearance / shirt-number grid (League). Shirt number worn by each player in each match is shown; the final column is the match number.

Chiswick	Bond	Cantwell	Parker	Allison	Bing	Hooper	Sexton	Stroud	Dick	Andrews	Dixon	Foan	Wright	Brown	Arnott	Taylor	Nelson	Malcolm	O'Farrell	Kinsell	Musgrove	Barrett	Bennett	Blackburn	Hallas	Dare	Moore	#
1	2	3	4	5	6	7	8	9	10	11																		1
1	2	3	4	5	6	7	8			11	9	10																2
1	3		4		6	7	8		10	11			2	5	9													3
1	3		4		6	7	8		10	11			2	5	9													4
	2					7	9		10	11		8		5		1	3	4	6									5
	2					7	9		10	11		8		5		1	3	4	6									6
	2					7	9		10	11		8		5		1		4	6	3								7
	2					7	9		10	11		8		5		1		4	6	3								8
	2					7	9		10	11		8		5		1		4	6	3								9
	2					7	9		10	11		8		5		1		4	6	3								10
	2					7	9		10	11		8		5		1		4	6	3								11
	2					7	9		10	11		8		5		1		4	6	3								12
	2					7	9		10	11		8		5		1		4	6	3								13
	2					7	9		10	11		8		5		1		4	6	3								14
	2					7	9		10	11		8		5		1		4	6	3								15
	2					7	9		10	11		8		5		1		4	6	3								16
	2					7	9		10	11		8		5		1		4	6	3								17
	2		6			7	9		10			8		5		1		4		3	11							18
	2		6			7	9		10			8		5		1		4		3	11							19
	2		6			7			10		9			5		1		4		3	11	8						20
	2		6			7			10		9			5		1		4		3	11	8						21
	2		6			7			10		9			5		1		4		3	11	8						22
	2	3			6	7			10	11				5		1		4				8	9					23
	2				6	7			10	11				5		1		4		3		8	9					24
	3		5			7	9		10				2			1		4	6		11		8					25
	3		5			7	9		10				2			1		4	6		11		8					26
	3		5			7	9		10				2			1		4	6		11		8					27
	3		5			7	9		10				2			1		4	6		11		8					28
	3		5			7			10		9	2				1		4	6		11		8	3	10			29
	3		5			7			10			2				1		4	6		11		8			9		30
	3		5			7			10			2				1		4	6		11		8			9		31
	3		5			7			10			2				1		4	6		11		8			9		32
	3		5			7			10			2				1		4	6		11		8			9		33
	3		5			7			10			2				1		4	6		11		8			9		34
	3		5			7			10			2				1		4	6		11		8			9		35
	3		5			7			10			2				1		4	6		11		8			9		36
	3		5			7			10			2				1		4	6		11		8			9		37
	3		5			7			10			2				1		4	6		11		8			9		38
	3		5			7			10			2				1		4	6		11		8			9		39
		6	5			7	8									1		4			11	10		3	9			40
		6	5			7			10							1		4			11	8		3	9			41
	3	6	5						10	11			7	2		1		4					9	8				42
4	**25**	**17**	**7**	**25**	**5**	**41**	**25**	**1**	**39**	**21**	**4**	**19**	**19**	**23**	**2**	**38**	**2**	**38**	**28**	**18**	**21**	**2**	**19**	**2**	**3**	**13**	**1**	App
1						11	12		26	6		2						1		8	1		2				2	Gls

2 own-goals

F.A. Cup:

Chiswick	Bond	Cantwell	Parker	Allison	Bing	Hooper	Sexton	Stroud	Dick	Andrews	Dixon	Foan	Wright	Brown	Arnott	Taylor	Nelson	Malcolm	O'Farrell	Kinsell	Musgrove	Barrett	Bennett	Blackburn	Hallas	Dare	Moore	Rd
	2	3		5	6	7			10	11				1		4					8	9						3
	3			5		7			10			2		1		4	6		11		8	9						R
1	2		2	1	2			2	1		1		2		2	1		1			2	2						App
				2														1										Gls

1955-56

Manager: Ted Fenton

1	Aug	20	(h)	Rotherham U	D	1-1	Dare	19,000
2		22	(a)	Port Vale	L	1-2	Allison	19,241
3		27	(a)	Swansea T	L	2-4	Bennett, Dare	25,000
4		29	(h)	Port Vale	L	0-2		13,000
5	Sep	3	(h)	Notts C	W	6-1	Hooper 2, Dare 2, O'Farrell, Dick	17,000
6		6	(a)	Bristol C	L	1-3	Tucker	25,923
7		10	(a)	Leeds U	D	3-3	Tucker 2, Dare	21,500
8		17	(h)	Fulham	W	2-1	Hooper 2	26,000
9		24	(a)	Bury	D	1-1	Tucker	10,217
10	Oct	1	(h)	Barnsley	W	4-0	Dare 2, Hooper, Opp own-goal	20,500
11		8	(h)	Plymouth A	W	4-0	Tucker 3, Allison	19,750
12		15	(a)	Liverpool	L	1-3	Hooper	32,187
13		22	(h)	Doncaster R	W	6-1	Hooper 3, Dare, Andrews, Tucker	13,500
14		29	(a)	Lincoln C	D	1-1	Dare	11,000
15	Nov	5	(h)	Blackburn R	L	2-3	Hooper, Dare	23,000
16		12	(a)	Hull C	L	1-3	Tucker	24,050
17		19	(h)	Nottingham F	L	1-2	Hooper	17,000
18		26	(a)	Sheffield W	D	1-1	Tucker	21,670
19	Dec	3	(h)	Leicester C	L	1-3	Tucker	17,500
20		10	(a)	Bristol R	D	1-1	Dick	20,728
21		17	(a)	Rotherham U	L	2-3	Moore, Hooper	10,159
22		24	(h)	Swansea T	W	5-1	Dare, Bond, Dick, Hooper, Tucker	15,000
23		26	(a)	Middlesbrough	L	0-2		22,000
24		27	(h)	Middlesbrough	W	1-0	Opp own-goal	21,500
25		31	(a)	Notts C	W	1-0	Dare	19,000
26	Jan	14	(h)	Leeds U	D	1-1	Foan	20,000
27		21	(a)	Fulham	L	1-3	Dare	25,000
28	Feb	11	(a)	Barnsley	D	1-1	Dare	8,367
29		25	(h)	Liverpool	W	2-0	Opp own-goals 2	18,840
30	Mar	10	(h)	Bristol R	W	2-1	Hooper, Tucker	20,000
31		17	(a)	Blackburn R	L	1-4	Matthews	21,600
32		19	(h)	Bury	W	3-2	Hooper, Dare, Dick	14,300
33		24	(h)	Hull C	D	1-1	Allison	12,750
34		26	(a)	Doncaster R	L	1-2	Dick	6,272
35		30	(h)	Stoke C	W	2-0	Tucker, Dare	18,000
36		31	(a)	Plymouth A	W	1-0	Andrews	17,555
37	Apr	2	(a)	Stoke C	L	0-3		17,284
38		7	(h)	Sheffield W	D	3-3	Dick 2, Dare	17,750
39		14	(a)	Leicester C	L	1-2	Blackburn	17,500
40		18	(a)	Nottingham F	D	0-0		15,589
41		21	(h)	Lincoln C	L	2-4	Dare, Dick	13,500
42		28	(h)	Bristol C	W	3-0	Sexton 2, Blackburn	13,000

P	W	D	L	F	A	W	D	L	F	A	Pts	Pos	Div	
42	12	4	5	52	27	2	7	12	22	42	39	16th	2	Appearances
														Goals

FA Cup

3	Jan	7	(h)	Preston NE	W	5-2	Foan 3, Dare 2	29,000
4		28	(h)	Cardiff C	W	2-1	Dare, Dick	35,500
5	Feb	18	(h)	Blackburn R	D	0-0		28,000
R		28	(a)	Blackburn R	W	3-2	Dick 2, Hooper	29,300
6	Mar	3	(a)	Tottenham H	D	3-3	Dick 3	69,111
R		8	(h)	Tottenham H	L	1-2	Dare	36,000

Appearances
Goals

280

Taylor	Wright	Cantwell	Malcolm	Allison	O'Farrell	Stroud	Bennett	Dare	Dick	Musgrove	Moore	Hooper	Andrews	Tucker	Gregory	Sexton	Bond	Brown	Foan	Matthews	Parker	Blackburn	Grice	Smith	Lansdowne	
1	2	3	4	5	6	7	8	9	10	11																
1	2	3	4	5	6	7		9	10	11	8															1
1	2	3	4	5	6			9	10	11	8	7														2
1	2	3	4	5	6			9	10	11		7	8													3
1	2	3	4	5	6			9	10			7	8	11												4
1	2	3	4	5	6			9	10			7	8	11												5
	2	3		5	6		8	9				7	10	11	1	4										6
	2	3		5	6		8	9	10			7		11	1	4										7
		3		5	6			9	10			7	8	11	1	4	2									8
		3		5	6			9	10			7	8	11	1	4	2									9
		3		5	6			9	10			7	8	11	1	4	2									10
		3		5	6			9	10			7	8	11	1	4	2									11
		3		5	6			9	10			7	8	11	1	4	2									12
		3		5	6			10	9			7	8	11	1	4	2									13
		3			6			9	10			7	8	11	1	4	2	5								14
		3		5	6			9	10			7	8	11	1	4	2									15
		3		5	6			9			8	7	10	11	1	4	2									16
	2			5	6			9			8	7	10	11	1	4	3									17
		3	4	5	6			9			8	7	10	11	1		2									18
		3	4	5	6			9	10		8	7		11	1		2									19
		3	4	5	6			9	10		8	7		11	1		2									20
		3	4	5	6			9	10		8	7		11	1		2									21
		3	4	5	6			9	10		8	7		11	1		2									22
		3	4	5	6			9	10			7		11	1	8	2									23
		3	4	5	6			9	10			7		11	1		2		8							24
		3	4	5	6			9	10			7		11	1		2		8							25
	2		4	5	6			9	10			7		11	1		3		8							26
		3	4	5	6			9	10	11		7			1		2		8							27
		3	4	5	6			9	10			7	8	11	1		2									28
		3	4	5	6			9	10			7		11	1	8	2									29
		3	4	5	6			9	10			7		11	1		2		8							30
		3	4	5	6			9	10			7		11	1		2		8							31
		3	4	5	6		7	9						11	1		2		8	10						32
		3	4	5	6			9	10			7		11	1		2		8							33
		3		5	6		7	9						11	1		2			8	4	10				34
		3		5	6			9	10			7	8	11	1		2				4					35
		3		5	6			9						11	1		2			8	4	7	10			36
		3		5	6		7		10					11	1		2			8	4	9				37
		3		5	6		7		10					11	1		2			8	4	9				38
		3		5	6		7		10					11	1		2			8	4	9				39
		3		5			8		10					11	1		2				4	9		7	6	40
		3					7							11	1	8	2	5			4	9	10		6	41
6	10	40	22	40	40	2	7	40	35	8	8	30	16	37	36	15	34	2	5	9	8	6	2	2	2	42
		3	1		1	18	8		1	15	2	14		2	1		1	1		2						

4 own-goals

Taylor	Wright	Cantwell	Malcolm	Allison	O'Farrell	Stroud	Bennett	Dare	Dick	Musgrove	Moore	Hooper	Andrews	Tucker	Gregory	Sexton	Bond	Brown	Foan	Matthews	Parker	Blackburn	Grice	Smith	Lansdowne	
		3	4	5	6		8	9				7		11	1		2			10						3
		3	4	5	6		8	9				7		11	1		2			10						4
		3	4	5	6		8	9		11		7			1		2			10						5
		3	4	5	6		8	9				7		11	1		2			10						R
		3	4	5	6		8	9				7		11	1		2			10						6
		3	4	5	6		8	9				7		11	1		2			10						R
		6	6	6	6		6	6		1		6		5	6		6			6						
							4	6				1								3						

1956-57

Manager: Ted Fenton

1	Aug	18	(a)	Fulham	W	4-1	Dare 2, Grice, Tucker	26,000
2		20	(h)	Blackburn R	L	1-3	Tucker	19,000
3		25	(h)	Swansea T	L	1-2	Tucker	17,000
4		27	(a)	Blackburn R	W	2-0	Blackburn, Dick	15,100
5	Sep	1	(a)	Lincoln C	W	2-0	Stroud 2	13,031
6		3	(h)	Liverpool	D	1-1	O'Farrell	25,000
7		8	(h)	Rotherham U	D	1-1	Dare	19,200
8		15	(a)	Port Vale	D	0-0		17,587
9		22	(h)	Barnsley	W	2-0	Dick, Dare	19,500
10		29	(a)	Sheffield U	L	0-1		24,001
11	Oct	6	(a)	Leyton O	W	2-1	Musgrove, Opp own-goal	24,613
12		13	(h)	Huddersfield T	L	0-2		22,500
13		20	(a)	Bristol R	D	1-1	Dick	24,402
14		27	(h)	Grimsby T	L	0-1		17,500
15	Nov	3	(a)	Doncaster R	L	0-3		13,071
16		10	(h)	Stoke C	W	1-0	Tucker	17,500
17		17	(a)	Middlesbrough	L	1-3	Tucker	32,000
18		24	(h)	Leicester C	W	2-1	Lewis, Tucker	20,000
19	Dec	1	(a)	Bury	D	3-3	Dick, Musgrove, Parker	8,757
20		8	(h)	Notts C	W	2-1	Smith, Dick	15,000
21		15	(h)	Fulham	W	2-1	Bond, Musgrove	18,250
22		22	(a)	Swansea T	L	1-3	Lewis	18,000
23		25	(h)	Nottingham F	W	2-1	Musgrove, Lewis	17,000
24		29	(h)	Lincoln C	W	2-1	Dare 2	16,100
25	Jan	12	(a)	Rotherham U	W	1-0	Musgrove	10,938
26		19	(h)	Port Vale	W	2-1	Smith, Dick	17,250
27	Feb	2	(a)	Barnsley	W	2-1	Dare, Dick	15,861
28		9	(h)	Sheffield U	W	3-2	Smith, Cantwell, Lewis	22,500
29		16	(h)	Leyton O	W	2-1	Lewis, Lansdowne	36,500
30		23	(a)	Huddersfield T	L	2-6	Smith, Lewis	5,878
31	Mar	2	(h)	Bristol R	L	1-2	Lewis	22,500
32		9	(a)	Grimsby T	L	1-2	Allison	13,796
33		16	(h)	Doncaster R	D	1-1	Lewis	15,500
34		23	(a)	Stoke C	W	1-0	Musgrove	19,705
35		30	(h)	Middlesbrough	D	1-1	Allison	15,000
36	Apr	6	(a)	Leicester C	L	3-5	Musgrove 2, Allison	33,388
37		13	(h)	Bury	W	1-0	Dare	9,000
38		15	(a)	Nottingham F	L	0-3		23,107
39		19	(a)	Bristol C	D	1-1	Allison	24,491
40		20	(a)	Notts C	L	1-4	Smith	17,803
41		22	(h)	Bristol C	W	3-1	Dick, Lewis, Dare	9,500
42		27	(a)	Liverpool	L	0-1		36,236

P	W	D	L	F	A	W	D	L	F	A	Pts	Pos	Div	
42	12	4	5	31	24	7	4	10	28	39	46	8th	2	Appearances
														Goals

FA Cup

3	Jan	5	(h)	Grimsby T	W	5-3	Lewis, Dick, Smith 2, Musgrove	24,500
4		26	(a)	Everton	L	1-2	Dare	55,245

Appearances
Goals

282

Gregory	Wright	Cooper	Malcolm	Brown	O'Farrell	Grice	Foan	Dare	Dick	Tucker	Cantwell	Blackburn	Allison	Wragg	Stroud	Musgrove	Smith R	Lansdowne	Smith J	Parker	Bond	Johnstone	Wyllie	Lewis	Newman	Obeney	Pyke	
1	2	3	4	5	6	7	8	9	10	11																		1
1	2	3	4	5	6	7	8	9	10	11																		2
1	2		4	5	6		8	7	10	11	3	9																3
1	2		4		6				10		3	9	5	7	8	11												4
1	2		4		6				10		3		5	7	8	11	9											5
1	2		4		6				10		3	9	5	7	8	11												6
1	2		4		6			9	10		3		5	7	8	11												7
1	2		4			7		9	10		3		5			11		6	8									8
1	2		4			7		9	10		3		5			11		6	8									9
1	2		4			7		9	10		3		5			11		6	8									10
1	2		4					9	10		3		5	7		11		6	8									11
1	2		4			7		9	10		3		5			11		6	8									12
1									10		3	9	5	7		11		6	8	4	2							13
1							8		10		3	9	5	7		11		6		4	2							14
1								9	10		3		5	7		11			8	6	2	4						15
1			4					9	10	11	3		5			7		6	8		2							16
1			4						10	11	3		5	9		7		6	8		2							17
	2		4						10	11			5			7		6		8	3		1	9				18
			4						10	11	3		5			7		6		8	2		1	9				19
			4						10	11	3		5			7	8	6			2		1	9				20
			4						10	11	3		5			7	8	6			2		1	9				21
			4						10	11	3		5			7	8	6			2		1	9				22
			4					7	10		3		5			11		6	8		2		1	9				23
			4					7	10		3		5			11		6	8		2		1	9				24
			4					7	10		3		5			11		6	8		2		1	9				25
			4					7	10		3		5		9	11		6	8		2		1					26
			4					7	10		3		5			11		6	8		2		1	9				27
			4					7	10		3		5			11		6	8		2		1	9				28
			4					7	10		3		5			11		6	8		2		1	9				29
			4					7	10		3		5			11		6	8		2		1	9				30
1			4					7	10		3		5			11		6	8		2			9				31
1			4					7			3	10	5			11			8		2	6		9				32
1			4			7		8			3		5			11			6		2			9	10			33
1			4			7		9			3		5			11			6		2			10	8			34
1			4			7		9			3		5			11			6		2			10	8			35
1			4			7		9			3		5			11			6		2			10	8			36
1			4			7		9	10		3		5			11			6		2			8				37
1			4					9			3		5	7		11		6	8		2			10				38
1			4					9	11		3		5			7		6	8		2			10				39
1			4						11		3		5			7		6	10		2			9		8		40
1				5				7	10		3		6			11			8		2			9			4	41
1				5				7	10		3		6			11			8		2			9			4	42
29	13	2	37	5	7	11	4	30	36	10	39	6	39	10	5	39	4	26	29	5	30	2	13	24	4	1	2	
					1	1		9	8	6	1	1	4		2	8	1	1	4	1	1			9				

1 own-goal

			4					9	10		3		5			11		6	8		2		1	7				3
			4					9	10		3		5			11		6	8		2		1	7				4
			2					2	2		2		2			2		2	2		2		2	2				
								1	1							1			2					1				

1957-58

Manager: Ted Fenton

1	Aug	24	(h)	Lincoln C	D	2-2	Dare, Allison	19,900
2		26	(a)	Blackburn R	L	1-2	Dare	18,800
3		31	(a)	Bristol R	W	3-2	Dare 3	25,910
4	Sep	2	(h)	Blackburn R	D	1-1	Dare	24,000
5		7	(h)	Derby C	W	2-1	Smith, Cantwell	19,000
6		9	(h)	Sheffield U	L	0-3		22,000
7		14	(a)	Swansea T	L	2-3	Dare, Malcolm	25,000
8		16	(a)	Sheffield U	L	1-2	Dare	7,768
9		21	(h)	Fulham	W	3-2	Dare 2, Cantwell	24,000
10		28	(a)	Barnsley	L	0-1		12,119
11	Oct	5	(h)	Leyton O	W	3-2	Smith, Lansdowne, Lewis	26,000
12		12	(a)	Charlton A	W	3-0	Dare, Smith, Musgrove	30,414
13		19	(h)	Doncaster R	D	1-1	Keeble	20,000
14		26	(a)	Rotherham U	W	2-1	Bond, Dick	8,781
15	Nov	2	(h)	Huddersfield T	W	5-2	Musgrove 2, Dick, Keeble, Cantwell	21,500
16		9	(a)	Grimsby T	W	2-1	Smith, Dick	11,878
17		16	(h)	Stoke C	W	5-0	Keeble 3, Dick, Dare	23,250
18		23	(a)	Bristol C	D	1-1	Dick	22,038
19		30	(h)	Cardiff C	D	1-1	Dick	24,000
20	Dec	7	(a)	Liverpool	D	1-1	Dick	34,030
21		14	(h)	Middlesbrough	W	2-1	Musgrove, Bond	21,000
22		21	(a)	Lincoln C	W	6-1	Dick 2, Keeble 2, Musgrove, Newman	8,375
23		25	(h)	Ipswich T	D	1-1	Newman	25,500
24		26	(a)	Ipswich T	L	1-2	Bond	21,891
25		28	(h)	Bristol R	W	6-1	Smith 3, Keeble 2, Dick	28,000
26	Jan	11	(a)	Derby C	W	3-2	Musgrove, Dick, Bond	21,564
27		18	(h)	Swansea T	W	6-2	Keeble 2, Dick, Bond, Cantwell, Lansdowne	27,500
28	Feb	1	(a)	Fulham	D	2-2	Musgrove, Lewis	42,259
29		8	(h)	Barnsley	D	1-1	Lewis	27,000
30		20	(a)	Leyton O	W	4-1	Smith, Dare, Keeble, Dick	25,284
31		22	(h)	Bristol C	W	3-2	Malcolm, Dare, Keeble	23,800
32	Mar	1	(a)	Doncaster R	W	2-1	Keeble, Smith	12,401
33		8	(h)	Rotherham U	W	8-0	Dick 4, Keeble 2, Smith 2	25,000
34		15	(a)	Huddersfield T	L	1-3	Grice	19,093
35		22	(h)	Grimsby T	W	2-0	Musgrove, Opp own-goal	25,200
36		29	(a)	Stoke C	W	4-1	Keeble 2, Grice, Dick	14,514
37	Apr	4	(h)	Notts C	W	3-1	Bond 2, Opp own-goal	30,000
38		5	(h)	Charlton A	D	0-0		30,500
39		8	(a)	Notts C	L	0-1		18,317
40		12	(a)	Cardiff C	W	3-0	Dick 2, Malcolm	22,000
41		19	(h)	Liverpool	D	1-1	Bond	37,750
42		26	(a)	Middlesbrough	W	3-1	Musgrove, Dick, Keeble	30,000

P	W	D	L	F	A	W	D	L	F	A	Pts	Pos	Div	Appearances
42	12	8	1	56	25	11	3	7	45	29	57	1st	2	Goals

FA Cup

3	Jan	4	(h)	Blackpool	W	5-1	Keeble 3, Dick 2	34,000
4		25	(h)	Stockport C	W	3-2	Lewis 2, Keeble	36,000
5	Feb	15	(h)	Fulham	L	2-3	Grice, Bond	37,500

Appearances

Goals

284

Gregory	Bond	Cantwell	Malcolm	Brown	Allison	Grice	Smith	Dare	Dick	Musgrove	Rhodes	Pyke	Lewis	Blackburn	Neville	Wragg	Lansdowne	Cooper	Keeble	Newman	Wright	Nelson	No.
1	2	3	4	5	6	7	8	9	10	11													1
1	2	3	4	5	6	7	8	9	10	11													2
1	2	3	4	5	6	7	8	9	10	11													3
	2	3	4	5		7	8	9	10	11	1	6											4
	2	3	4	5		7	8	9	10	11	1	6											5
	2	3	4	5		7		9		11	1	6	8		10								6
	2	3	4	5	6	7	8	9	10	11	1												7
	2	3	4	5	6	7	8		10	11	1					9							8
1	2	3	4	5			8		10	11		6				9	7						9
1	2	3	4	5			8		10	11						9	7	6					10
1	2		4	5			8	7	10	11			9				6	3					11
1	2	3	4	5		7	8	9	10	11		6											12
1	2	3	4	5		7	8		10	11							6		9				13
1	2	3	4	5			8	7	10	11							6		9				14
1	2	3	4	5			8	7	10	11							6		9				15
1	2	3	4	5			8	7	10	11							6		9				16
1	2	3	4	5			8	7	10	11							6		9				17
1	2	3	4	5			8	7	10	11							6		9				18
1	2	3	4	5			8	7	10	11							6		9				19
1	2	3	4	5			8	7	10	11							6		9				20
1	2	3	4	5				7	10	11							6		9	8			21
1	2	3	4	5			6	7	10	11									9	8			22
1	2		4	5			6	7	10	11									9	8	3		23
1	2		4	5		7	6		10	11			8						9		3		24
1	2		4	5		7	8		10	11							6		9		3		25
1	2		4	5		7	8		10	11							6		9		3		26
1	2	3	4	5		7	8		10	11							6		9				27
1	2	3	4	5		7			10	11		6	8						9				28
1		3	4	5		7		9	10	11		6	8									2	29
1	2	3	4	5		11	8	7	10								6		9				30
1	2	3	4	5		11	8	7	10								6		9				31
1	2		4			7	8		10	11		6							9	5	3		32
1	2		4	5		7	8		10	11		6							9		3		33
1	2		4	5		11	8		10	7							6		9		3		34
1	2		4	5		7	8		10	11							6		9		3		35
1	2	3	4	5		7	8		10	11		6							9				36
1	2	3	4	5		7	8		10	11		6							9				37
1	2	3	4	5		7	8		10	11		6							9				38
1	2	3	4	5		7	8		10	11		6							9				39
1	2	3	4	5		7			10	11			8						9			6	40
1	2	3	4	5		7			10	11		6	8						9				41
1	2	3	4	5		7	8		10	11									9			6	42
37	41	33	42	41	5	29	32	26	41	39	5	15	7	1	3	3	17	2	29	3	8	3	
8	4	3			1	2	11	14	21	9		3					2		19	2			

2 own-goals

Gregory	Bond	Cantwell	Malcolm	Brown	Allison	Grice	Smith	Dare	Dick	Musgrove	Rhodes	Pyke	Lewis	Blackburn	Neville	Wragg	Lansdowne	Cooper	Keeble	Newman	Wright	Nelson	No.
1	2		4	5		7			10	11			6	8					9	3			3
1	2	3	4	5		7			10	11				8			6		9				4
1	2	3	4	5		7			10	11			6	8					9				5
3	3	2	3	3		3			3	3			2	3			1		3	1			
	1					1			2					2					4				

285

1958-59

Manager: Ted Fenton

1	Aug	23	(a)	Portsmouth	W	2-1	Dick, Keeble		40,470
2		25	(h)	Wolves	W	2-0	Dick, Smith		37,485
3		30	(h)	Aston Villa	W	7-2	Keeble 2, Dick 2, Musgrove 2, Lansdowne		30,506
4	Sep	3	(a)	Wolves	D	1-1	Grice		52,317
5		6	(a)	Luton T	L	1-4	Keeble		25,715
6		8	(h)	Manchester U	W	3-2	Dick, Smith, Musgrove		35,672
7		13	(a)	Nottingham F	L	0-4			30,518
8		17	(a)	Manchester U	L	1-4	Bond		53,276
9		20	(h)	Chelsea	W	4-2	Grice, Smith, Keeble, Dick		31,127
10		27	(h)	Blackpool	L	0-2			32,662
11	Oct	4	(h)	Blackburn R	W	6-3	Keeble 4, Cantwell, Opp own-goal		25,280
12		11	(h)	Birmingham C	L	1-2	Musgrove		29,500
13		18	(a)	West Brom A	L	1-2	Keeble		36,991
14		25	(h)	Burnley	W	1-0	Nelson		29,387
15	Nov	1	(a)	Bolton W	W	2-0	Grice, Dick		31,067
16		8	(h)	Arsenal	D	0-0			38,250
17		15	(a)	Everton	D	2-2	Dick, Bond		40,549
18		22	(h)	Leicester C	L	0-3			23,500
19		29	(a)	Preston NE	L	1-2	Dick		19,436
20	Dec	6	(h)	Leeds U	L	2-3	Dick, Keeble		22,022
21		13	(a)	Manchester C	L	1-3	Dick		22,500
22		20	(h)	Portsmouth	W	6-0	Keeble 2, Woosnam, Dick, Smith, Musgrove		31,500
23		25	(h)	Tottenham H	W	2-1	Dick, Keeble		26,178
24		26	(a)	Tottenham H	W	4-1	Dick, Bond, Keeble, Opp own-goal		43,817
25	Jan	3	(a)	Aston Villa	W	2-1	Cantwell, Opp own-goal		33,360
26		31	(h)	Nottingham F	W	5-3	Dick 2, Keeble 2, Woosnam		26,676
27	Feb	7	(a)	Chelsea	L	2-3	Keeble 2		52,968
28		16	(h)	Blackpool	W	1-0	Dick		28,500
29		21	(h)	Blackburn R	W	2-1	Keeble, Musgrove		17,163
30		28	(a)	Birmingham C	L	0-3			21,001
31	Mar	7	(h)	West Brom A	W	3-1	Dick 3		30,157
32		14	(a)	Burnley	L	0-1			17,311
33		21	(h)	Bolton W	W	4-3	Bond 2, Obeney, Dick		27,722
34		27	(h)	Newcastle U	W	3-0	Dick, Musgrove, Obeney		35,000
35		28	(a)	Arsenal	W	2-1	Dick 2		52,452
36		30	(a)	Newcastle U	L	1-3	Obeney		20,911
37	Apr	4	(h)	Everton	W	3-2	Bond, Dick, Grice		28,500
38		11	(a)	Leicester C	D	1-1	Bond		23,825
39		13	(h)	Luton T	D	0-0			27,000
40		18	(h)	Preston NE	D	1-1	Dare		21,500
41		20	(h)	Manchester C	W	5-1	Dick 2, Grice 2, Cantwell		23,500
42		25	(a)	Leeds U	L	0-1			11,257

P	W	D	L	F	A	W	D	L	F	A	Pts	Pos	Div	
42	15	3	3	59	29	6	3	12	26	41	48	6th	1	Appearances
														Goals

FA Cup

3	Jan	10	(a)	Tottenham H	L	0-2		56,252

Appearances

Goals

Appearance and goal chart (shirt numbers by match; appearances and goals totalled at foot).

Gregory	Bond	Cantwell	Malcolm	Brown	Lansdowne	Grice	Smith	Keeble	Dick	Musgrove	Moore	Wragg	Nelson	Woosnam	Kirkup	Smillie	Dare	Dwyer	Obeney	
1	2	3	4	5	6	7	8	9	10	11										1
1	2	3	4	5	6	7	8	9	10	11										2
1	2	3	4	5	6	7	8	9	10	11										3
1	2	3	4	5	6	7	8	9	10	11										4
1	2	3	4	5	6	7	8	9	10	11										5
1	2	3	4	5		7	8	9	10	11	6									6
1	2	3	4	5		7	8	9	10	11	6									7
1	2	3	4	5	6	11	8	9	10			7								8
1	2	3	4	5		11	8	9	10			7	6							9
1	2	3	4	5		7	8	9	10	11			6							10
1	2	3	4	5		7	8	9	10	11			6							11
1	2	3	4	5		7	8	9	10	11			6							12
1	2	3	4	5		7	8	9	10	11			6							13
1	2	3	4	5		7	8	9	10	11			6							14
1	2	3	4	5		7		9	10	11			6	8						15
1	2	3	4	5		7		9	10	11			6	8						16
1	2	3	4	5		7		9	10	11			6	8						17
1	2	3	4	5		7		9	10	11			6	8						18
1	2	3	4	5		7		9	10	11			6	8						19
1	3	6	4	5		7		9	10	11				8	2					20
1	2	3	4	5		7	6	9	10	11				8						21
1	2	3	4	5		7	6	9	10	11				8						22
1	2	3	4	5		7	6	9	10	11						8				23
1	2	3	4	5		7	6	9	10	11						8				24
1	2	3	4	5		7	6	9	10	11				8						25
1	2	3	4	5		7	6	9	10	11				8						26
1	2	3	4	5		7	6	9	10	11				8						27
1	2	3	4	5		7	6	9	10	11				8						28
1	2	3	4	5		7	6	9	10	11						8				29
1	2	3	4	5		7	6	9	10	11				8						30
1	2	3	4	5		7	8		10	11			6			9				31
	9	3	4	5		7	6		10	11					2			1	8	32
	9	3	4	5		7	6		10	11					2			1	8	33
	9	3	4	5		7	6		10	11					2			1	8	34
	9	3	4	5		7	6		10	11					2			1	8	35
	9	3	4	5		7	6		10	11					2			1	8	36
	8	3	4	5		7	6	9		11					2		10	1		37
	9	3	4	5		7	6		10	11					2			1	8	38
	8	3	4	5		7	6		10	11					2		9	1		39
	3	9	4	5		7	8		10	11	6				2			1		40
	3	9	4	5		7	8		10	11	6				2			1		41
	3	9	4	5		7	8		10	11	6				2			1		42
32	42	42	42	42	6	42	36	32	41	40	5	2	12	13	11	4	2	10	6	
	7	3		1	6	4	20	27	7		1	2		1					3	

3 own-goals

Gregory	Bond	Cantwell	Malcolm	Brown	Lansdowne	Grice	Smith	Keeble	Dick	Musgrove	Moore	Wragg	Nelson	Woosnam	Kirkup	Smillie	Dare	Dwyer	Obeney	
1	2	3	4	5		7	6	9	10	11				8						3
1	1	1	1	1		1	1	1	1	1				1						

1959-60

Manager: Ted Fenton

								Attendance
1	Aug	22	(h)	Leicester C	W	3-0	Smith, Keeble, Grice	28,000
2		25	(a)	Preston NE	D	1-1	Musgrove	29,433
3		29	(a)	Burnley	W	3-1	Woosnam, Smillie, Grice	26,783
4		31	(h)	Preston NE	W	2-1	Smillie, Keeble	32,000
5	Sep	5	(h)	Leeds U	L	1-2	Keeble	28,000
6		9	(a)	Tottenham H	D	2-2	Keeble, Musgrove	58,909
7		12	(a)	Bolton W	L	1-5	Keeble	24,191
8		14	(h)	Tottenham H	L	1-2	Bond	37,500
9		19	(a)	Chelsea	W	4-2	Dick 2, Musgrove, Woosnam	54,349
10		26	(h)	West Brom A	W	4-1	Musgrove 2, Woosnam, Grice	30,570
11	Oct	3	(a)	Newcastle U	D	0-0		41,890
12		10	(h)	Luton T	W	3-1	Woodley 2, Keeble	23,500
13		17	(a)	Everton	W	1-0	Musgrove	30,563
14		24	(h)	Blackpool	W	1-0	Musgrove	32,500
15		31	(a)	Fulham	L	0-1		44,695
16	Nov	7	(h)	Manchester C	W	4-1	Cantwell, Obeney, Musgrove, Opp own-goal	25,500
17		14	(a)	Arsenal	W	3-1	Dick, Obeney, Musgrove	49,760
18		21	(h)	Wolves	W	3-2	Dick 3	38,000
19		28	(a)	Sheffield W	L	0-7		38,367
20	Dec	5	(h)	Nottingham F	W	4-1	Woosnam 2, Obeney 2	26,000
21		12	(a)	Blackburn R	L	2-6	Woosnam, Dick	22,400
22		19	(a)	Leicester C	L	1-2	Obeney	20,000
23		26	(a)	Birmingham C	L	0-2		29,745
24		28	(h)	Birmingham C	W	3-1	Musgrove 2, Brett	26,000
25	Jan	2	(h)	Burnley	L	2-5	Woosnam, Cantwell	26,000
26		16	(a)	Leeds U	L	0-3		15,000
27		23	(h)	Bolton W	L	1-2	Dick	21,600
28	Feb	6	(a)	Chelsea	W	4-2	Bond 3, Dick	29,500
29		20	(h)	Newcastle U	L	3-5	Woosnam 2, Dick	25,000
30		27	(a)	Nottingham F	L	1-3	Musgrove	26,317
31	Mar	5	(h)	Everton	D	2-2	Bond, Dick	25,000
32		9	(a)	West Brom A	L	2-3	Grice, Bond	11,980
33		12	(a)	Blackpool	L	2-3	Bond, Brett	14,515
34		19	(h)	Blackburn R	W	2-1	Woosnam, Musgrove	26,000
35		30	(a)	Manchester C	L	1-3	Musgrove	29,572
36	Apr	2	(h)	Arsenal	D	0-0		29,000
37		11	(a)	Wolves	L	0-5		48,086
38		15	(h)	Manchester U	W	2-1	Musgrove, Grice	35,000
39		16	(h)	Fulham	L	1-2	Smillie	24,085
40		18	(a)	Manchester U	L	3-5	Dunmore, Cantwell, Scott	34,676
41		23	(a)	Luton T	L	1-3	Dunmore	11,404
42		30	(h)	Sheffield W	D	1-1	Woosnam	22,000

P	W	D	L	F	A	W	D	L	F	A	Pts	Pos	Div	Appearances
42	12	3	6	47	33	4	3	14	28	58	38	14th	1	Goals

FA Cup

3	Jan	9	(h)	Huddersfield T	D	1-1	Dick	40,526
R		13	(h)	Huddersfield T	L	1-5	Musgrove	22,605

Appearances
Goals

288

Football appearances and goals grid.

Dwyer	Bond	Cantwell	Malcolm	Brown	Smith	Grice	Woosnam	Keeble	Dick	Musgrove	Smillie	Wragg	Brett	Woodley	Moore	Cartwright	Kirkup	Obeney	Rhodes	Lyall	Scott	Hurst	Dunmore	Bovington	Lansdowne	Gregory	#
1	2	3	4	5	6	7	8	9	10	11																	
1	2	3	4	5	6	7	8	9	10	11																	1
1	2	3	4	5	6	7	8	9		11	10																2
1	2	3	4	5	6	7	8	9		11	10																3
	2	3	4	5	6	7	8	9		11	10														1		4
1	2	3	4	5	6	7	8	9		11	10																5
1	2	3	4	5	6	7	8	9		11	10																6
1	2	3	4	5	6		8	9				7	10														7
1	2	3	4	5	6	7	8	9	10	11																	8
1	2	3	4	5	6	7	8	9	10	11																	9
1	2	3	4	5	6	7	8	9	10	11																	10
1	2	3	4	5	6		8	9	10	11				7													11
1	2	3	4	5		7		9		11	10				6	8											12
1	2	9	4	5	6	7	8		10	11							3										13
1		3	4	5	6	7	8	9	10	11							2										14
1		3	4	5	6	7	8		10	11							2	9									15
1		3	4	5	6	7	8		10	11							2	9									16
	2	3	4	5	6	7	8		10	11								9	1								17
1	2	3	4	5	6	7	8		10	11								9									18
1	2	3	4	5	6	7	8		10	11								9									19
1	2	3	4	5	6	7	8		10	11								9									20
1	2	3	4	5	6	7	8		10	11								9									21
1		3	4	5	6		8		10	11		9	7				2										22
1		3	4	5	6				10	11	8	9	7				2										23
1		3	4	5	6	7	8		10	11							2	9									24
	2	3	4	5	8				11	9		7			6	10	1										25
1	3	9		5	6	7	8		10	11					4		2										26
1	9		4	5			8		10	11					6		2	3	7								27
1	9	3	4	5	6		8		10	11							2	7									28
9	10		4	5			8			11							2		1	3	7	6					29
9	3		4	5		7	8		10	11					6		2		1								30
9	3		4	5		7	8		10	11					6		2		1								31
9	3		4	5	6	7	8			11					10		2		1								32
	2	3	4	5		7	8			11					10				1			6	9				33
		3	4	5		7	8			11					10		2		1			6	9				34
	2	3	4	5		7	8		10	11					6				1				9				35
	2	3	4	5		7	8			11	10				6				1				9				36
	2	3	4	5		7	8			11	10				6				1				9				37
	2	3	4	5		7	8			11	10				6				1				9				38
		3								11	6			5	10	8		2	1		7		9	4			39
	2	3	4			7				11	10				6	8	2		1		7		9			5	40
	2	3	4			7				11	10				6	8	2		1		7		9				41
	2	3	4	5		7	8			11	10				6		2		1				9				42
26	35	40	40	40	28	34	38	15	24	41	13	1	7	3	13	3	16	9	15	2	4	3	9	1	1	1	
7	3			1	5	11	6	11	15	3			2	2			5		1			2					

I own-goal

Dwyer	Bond	Cantwell	Malcolm	Brown	Smith	Grice	Woosnam	Keeble	Dick	Musgrove	Smillie	...	Obeney	...	#
1	2	3	4	5	6	7	8		10	11			9		3
1	2	3	4	5	6	7	8			11	10		9		R
2	2	2	2	2	2	2	2		1	2	1		2		
									1	1					

1960-61

Manager: Ted Fenton

1	Aug	20	(a)	Wolves	L	2-4	Dick, Woosnam	37,266
2		22	(h)	Aston Villa	W	5-2	Woosnam, Bond, Dick, Dunmore, Musgrove	28,959
3		27	(h)	Bolton W	W	2-1	Musgrove, Dick	24,283
4		29	(a)	Aston Villa	L	1-2	Dunmore	30,000
5	Sep	3	(a)	Sheffield W	L	0-1		28,359
6		5	(h)	Manchester U	W	2-1	Brett, Musgrove	30,000
7		10	(a)	Chelsea	L	2-3	Dunmore, Grice	37,873
8		14	(a)	Manchester U	L	1-6	Brett	33,695
9		17	(h)	Blackpool	D	3-3	Bond, Musgrove, Woodley	23,521
10		24	(a)	Everton	L	1-4	Beesley	46,291
11	Oct	1	(h)	Blackburn R	W	3-2	Dick 2, Woosnam	17,519
12		8	(h)	Birmingham C	W	4-3	Grice 2, Musgrove, Dunmore	16,000
13		15	(a)	West Brom A	L	0-1		21,300
14		22	(h)	Preston NE	W	5-2	Musgrove 3, Bond, Dick	16,287
15		29	(a)	Fulham	D	1-1	Dunmore	20,809
16	Nov	5	(h)	Arsenal	W	6-0	Dunmore 3, Dick, Woosnam, Malcolm	29,375
17		12	(a)	Manchester C	W	2-1	Dunmore, Grice	33,721
18		19	(h)	Nottingham F	L	2-4	Dunmore, Opp own-goal	21,047
19	Dec	3	(h)	Cardiff C	W	2-0	Musgrove, Dunmore	14,000
20		10	(a)	Newcastle U	D	5-5	Musgrove, Dick, Bond, Dunmore, Opp own-goal	20,100
21		17	(h)	Wolves	W	5-0	Dunmore 2, Musgrove, Dick, Moore	22,336
22		24	(a)	Tottenham H	L	0-2		54,930
23		26	(h)	Tottenham H	L	0-3		34,481
24		31	(a)	Bolton W	L	1-3	Musgrove	15,931
25	Jan	14	(h)	Sheffield W	D	1-1	Dick	20,620
26		21	(h)	Chelsea	W	3-1	Obeney, Woosnam, Dick	21,829
27	Feb	4	(a)	Blackpool	L	0-3		9,947
28		11	(h)	Everton	W	4-0	Obeney 2, Dick, Musgrove	22,322
29		25	(a)	Birmingham C	L	2-4	Musgrove, Scott	16,850
30	Mar	4	(h)	West Brom A	L	1-2	Dick	21,607
31		11	(a)	Preston NE	L	0-4		12,084
32		18	(h)	Fulham	L	1-2	Obeney	18,742
33		20	(a)	Blackburn R	L	1-4	Opp own-goal	14,000
34		25	(a)	Arsenal	D	0-0		27,663
35		31	(h)	Leicester C	W	1-0	Dick	22,010
36	Apr	1	(h)	Newcastle U	D	1-1	Musgrove	17,103
37		3	(a)	Leicester C	L	1-5	Kirkup	23,776
38		8	(a)	Nottingham F	D	1-1	Dick	26,081
39		15	(h)	Manchester C	D	1-1	Sealey	17,982
40		18	(a)	Burnley	D	2-2	Musgrove 2	12,409
41		22	(a)	Cardiff C	D	1-1	Dick	10,000
42		29	(h)	Burnley	L	1-2	Woosnam	18,761

P	W	D	L	F	A	W	D	L	F	A	Pts	Pos	Div	Appearances
42	12	4	5	53	31	1	6	14	24	57	36	16th	1	Goals

FA Cup

3	Jan	7	(h)	Stoke C	D	2-2	Dunmore, Dick	21,545
R		11	(a)	Stoke C	L	0-1		28,914

Appearances
Goals

League Cup

1	Sep	26	(h)	Charlton A	W	3-1	Dick, Musgrove, Moore	12,000
2	Oct	24	(a)	Darlington	L	2-3	Dunmore, Dick	16,911

Appearances
Goals

Player appearance and scorers grid (shirt numbers shown per match).

#	Rhodes	Bond	Cantwell	Malcolm	Brown	Moore	Grice	Woosnam	Dunmore	Dick	Musgrove	Hurst	Smillie	Shearing	Brett	Woodley	Kirkup	Beesley	Lyall	Boyce	Scott	Obeney	Cartwright	Sealey
	1	2	3	4	5	6	7	8	9	10	11													
1	1	2	3	4	5	6	7	8	9	10	11													
2	1	2	3	4	5	6	7	8	9	10	11													
3	1	2	3		5	6	7	8	9		11		4		10									
4		2	3	4	5	6	7	8	9	10	11		1											
5		2	3	4	5	6	7	8	9		11		1		10									
6		2	3	4	5	6	7	8	9		11		1		10									
7		2	3	4	5	6		8	9		11		1		10	7								
8		9	3	4	5	6		8		10	11		1		7	2								
9		2	3	4	5	6		8	9		11		1		7	10								
10	1	2		4	5	6	7	8	9	10	11								3					
11	1	2		4	5	6	7	8	9	10	11								3					
12	1	2		4	5	6	7	8	9	10	11								3					
13	1	2		4	5	6	7		9	10	11								3	8				
14	1	2		4	5	6	11	8	9	10					7				3					
15	1	2		4	5	6	11	8	9						7				3					
16	1	2		4	5	6	7	8	9	10	11								3					
17	1	3		4	5	6	7	8	9	10	11				2									
18	1	2		4	5	6	7	8	9	10	11								3					
19	1	2		4	5	6	7	8	9	10	11								3					
20	1	2		4	5	6	7	8	9	10	11								3					
21	1	2		4	5	6	7	8	9	10	11								3					
22	1	2		4	5	6	7	8	9	10	11								3					
23	1	2		4	5			8	9	10	11	6	7						3					
24	1			4	5	6		8	9	10	11				2				3		7			
25	1			4	5	6		8		10	11				2				3		7	9		
26	1			4	5	6		8	10		11				2				3		7	9		
27	1			4	5	6		8		10	11				2				3		7	9		
28	1			4	5	6		8		10	11				2				3		7	9		
29	1	3		4	5	6		8	9	10	11				2						7			
30	1	3		4	5	6		8		10	11			7	2						9			
31	1	3		4	5	6	7	8		10	11				2						9			
32	1	3		4	5	6	7	8			11				2	9								
33	1	3			5	6	7	8		10	11	4			2						9			
34	1	3		4	5	6	7	8		10	11				2						9			
35	1	3		4	5					10	11	6		7	2						9	8		
36	1	3		4	5					10	11	6			2			8	7			9		
37	1	3		4	5	6		8		10	11				2				7			9		
38	1	3		4	5	6		8		10	11				2				7			9		
39	1			4	5	6				10	11				2	3	8		7			9		
40	1			4	5	6		8		10	11				2	3			7			9		
41	1			4	5			8		10	11	6			2	3			7			9		
42	1			4	5	6		8		10	11				2	3			7			9		
Apps	36	34	10	40	42	38	24	38	27	34	40	6	3	6	5	5	20	2	21	3	12	9	1	6
Goals		4		1		1	4	6	14	16	17				2	1	1	1		1	4		1	

3 own-goals

#	Rhodes	Bond	Cantwell	Malcolm	Brown	Moore	Grice	Woosnam	Dunmore	Dick	Musgrove	Hurst	Smillie	Shearing	Brett	Woodley	Kirkup	Beesley	Lyall	Boyce	Scott	Obeney	Cartwright	Sealey
3	1	2		4	5	6		8	9	10	11				7				3					
R	1			4	5	6	7	8		10	11					9	2		3					
	2	1		2	2	2	1	2	1	2	2				1	1	1		2					
								1	1															

#	Rhodes	Bond	Cantwell	Malcolm	Brown	Moore	Grice	Woosnam	Dunmore	Dick	Musgrove	Hurst	Smillie	Shearing	Brett	Woodley	Kirkup	Beesley	Lyall	Boyce	Scott	Obeney	Cartwright	Sealey
	1	2		4	5	6			9	10	11				7				3				8	
1	1	2		4	5	6	7	8	9	10	11								3					
2	2	2		2	2	2	1	1	2	2	2				1				2				1	
						1			1	2	1													

1961-62

Manager: Ron Greenwood

							Attendance
1	Aug	19	(h)	Manchester U	D 1-1	Dick	32,628
2		23	(a)	Tottenham H	D 2-2	Woosnam, Musgrove	50,214
3		26	(a)	Wolves	L 2-3	Musgrove, Sealey	25,471
4		28	(h)	Tottenham H	W 2-1	Scott, Sealey	36,348
5	Sep	2	(h)	Nottingham F	W 3-2	Scott, Sealey, Musgrove	23,000
6		4	(a)	Blackpool	L 0-2		19,838
7		9	(a)	Aston Villa	W 4-2	Dick 2, Scott, Sealey	32,000
8		16	(h)	Chelsea	W 2-1	Dick, Musgrove	27,000
9		18	(h)	Blackpool	D 2-2	Musgrove, Boyce	26,000
10		23	(a)	Sheffield U	W 4-1	Dick 2, Musgrove, Sealey	21,034
11		30	(h)	Leicester C	W 4-1	Dick 2, Sealey, Woosnam	26,746
12	Oct	7	(a)	Ipswich T	L 2-4	Sealey, Musgrove	28,051
13		14	(h)	Burnley	W 2-1	Crawford, Dick	32,234
14		21	(a)	Fulham	L 0-2		32,275
15		28	(h)	Sheffield W	L 2-3	Bond, Dick	26,463
16	Nov	4	(a)	Manchester C	W 5-3	Dick 2, Sealey 2, Musgrove	18,839
17		11	(h)	West Brom A	D 3-3	Musgrove, Sealey, Bond	18,000
18		18	(a)	Birmingham C	L 0-4		20,645
19		25	(h)	Everton	W 3-1	Dick 2, Crawford	27,100
20	Dec	2	(a)	Arsenal	D 2-2	Tindall 2	47,206
21		9	(h)	Bolton W	W 1-0	Woosnam	19,472
22		16	(a)	Manchester U	W 2-1	Dick 2	29,472
23		18	(a)	Wolves	W 4-2	Moore 2, Hurst, Musgrove	21,261
24		26	(h)	Blackburn R	L 2-3	Tindall, Dick	22,250
25	Jan	13	(a)	Nottingham F	L 0-3		20,359
26		20	(h)	Aston Villa	W 2-0	Woosnam, Dick	20,000
27	Feb	3	(a)	Chelsea	W 1-0	Moore	34,258
28		10	(h)	Sheffield U	L 1-2	Woosnam	21,829
29		17	(a)	Leicester C	D 2-2	Woosnam, Dick	21,312
30		24	(h)	Ipswich T	D 2-2	Dick, Kirkup	27,760
31	Mar	3	(a)	Burnley	L 0-6		24,279
32		17	(a)	Sheffield W	D 0-0		31,403
33		24	(h)	Manchester C	L 0-4		25,808
34		28	(a)	Blackburn R	L 0-1		8,800
35		31	(a)	West Brom A	W 1-0	Musgrove	18,000
36	Apr	6	(h)	Birmingham C	D 2-2	Musgrove 2	22,548
37		14	(a)	Everton	L 0-3		45,171
38		20	(h)	Cardiff C	W 4-1	Sealey, Crawford, Byrne, Opp own-goal	25,459
39		21	(h)	Arsenal	D 3-3	Scott, Dick, Lansdowne	31,912
40		23	(a)	Cardiff C	L 0-3		11,200
41		28	(a)	Bolton W	L 0-1		17,333
42		30	(h)	Fulham	W 4-2	Dick 2, Crawford 2	22,000

P	W	D	L	F	A	W	D	L	F	A	Pts	Pos	Div	Appearances
42	11	6	4	49	37	6	4	11	27	45	44	8th	1	Goals

FA Cup

3	Jan	6	(a)	Plymouth A	L 0-3		26,915
							Appearances
							Goals

League Cup

1	Sep	11	(h)	Plymouth A	W 3-2	Crawford 2, Woosnam	12,170
2	Oct	9	(h)	Aston Villa	L 1-3	Musgrove	17,775
							Appearances
							Goals

Player appearances and goals grid (shirt numbers shown per match; match number in final column).

Leslie	Kirkup	Bond	Malcolm	Brown	Moore	Scott	Woosnam	Sealey	Dick	Musgrove	Hurst	Boyce	Crawford	Rhodes	Tindall	Bovington	Lyall	Byrne	Woodley	Peters	Lansdowne	Dickie	Burkett	#
1	2	3	4	5	6	7	8	9	10	11														1
1	2	3	4	5	6	7	8	9	10	11														2
1	2	3	4	5	6	7	8	9	10	11														3
1	2	3	4	5	6	7	8	9	10	11														4
1	2	3	4	5	6	7	8	9	10	11														5
1	2	3		5	6	11	7	9	10			4	8											6
1	2	3		5	6	7	8	9	10			4	11											7
1	2	3		5	6	7	8	9	10	11	4													8
	2	3		5	6	7		9	10	11	4		8									1		9
	2	3		5	6	7	8	9	10	11	4											1		10
1	2	3		5	6	7	8	9	10	11	4													11
1	2	3		5	6	7	8	9	10	11	4													12
1	2	3	4	5	6			9	10	11		8	7											13
1	2	3	4	5	6		8	9	10	11			7											14
1	2	3	4	5	6		8	9	10	11			7											15
1	2	3		5	6		8	9	10	11	4		7											16
1	2	3		5	6		8	9	10	11	4		7											17
1	2	3		5	6		8		10	11	4		7	9										18
1	2	3		5	6		8		10	11	4		7	9										19
1	2	3		5	6		8	9	10	11	4		7											20
1	2	3		5			8	9	10	11	4		7			6								21
1	2	3		5	6		8		10	11	4		7	9										22
1	2	3		5	6		8		10	11	4		7	9										23
1	2	3		5	6		8		10	11	4		7	9										24
1	2	3		5	6		8		10	11	4		7	9										25
1	2	3		5	6	7	8	9	10	11					4									26
1	2	3		5	6	7	8	9		11					4	10								27
1	2	3		5	6	7	8	9	10	11					4									28
1	2	3		5	6	7	8	9	10	11					4									29
1	2	3		5	6	7		9	10	11		8			4									30
1	2			5	6	7	8	9	10	11					4	3								31
1	2	3		5	6		8	7		11	4							10		9				32
1	2	3		5	6		8			11	4							10	7	9				33
1	2	3		5	6		8			11	4							10	7	9				34
1	2	3		5	6		8			11	4							10	7	9				35
1	2	3		5	6			9		11	4							10	7	8				36
1	2	3		5	6	7			10	11	4							8		9				37
1	2				6	7		9	10	11					3	8	4		5					38
1	2				6	7		9	10	11					3	8	4		5					39
	2			5	6	7	8	9		11	4					3				10	1			40
	2				6	7		9	10	11					3	8	4		5		1			41
	2				6	7		9	10	11						8	4		5		1		3	42
37	41	37	8	38	41	22	34	32	35	36	24	4	19	3	13	7	4	11	4	5	4	2	1	
1	2	3		3	4	6	11	23	13	1	1	5		3				1				1		

1 own-goal

Leslie	Kirkup	Bond	Malcolm	Brown	Moore	Scott	Woosnam	Sealey	Dick	Musgrove	Hurst	Boyce	Crawford	Rhodes	Tindall	Bovington	Lyall	Byrne	Woodley	Peters	Lansdowne	Dickie	Burkett	#
1	2	3		5	6		8		10	11	4		7	9										3
1	1	1		1	1		1		1	1	1		1	1										

Leslie	Kirkup	Bond	Malcolm	Brown	Moore	Scott	Woosnam	Sealey	Dick	Musgrove	Hurst	Boyce	Crawford	Rhodes	Tindall	Bovington	Lyall	Byrne	Woodley	Peters	Lansdowne	Dickie	Burkett	#
	2	3		5	6	7	8	9	10		4		11	1										1
1	2	3		5	6	7	8	9	10	11	4													2
1	2	2		2	2	2	2	2	2	1	2		1	1										
								1			1			2										

293

1962-63

Manager: Ron Greenwood

1	Aug	18	(a)	Aston Villa	L	1-3	Byrne	37,000
2		20	(h)	Wolves	L	1-4	Musgrove	30,020
3		25	(h)	Tottenham H	L	1-6	Woosnam	30,000
4		29	(a)	Wolves	D	0-0		32,000
5	Sep	1	(a)	Leyton O	L	0-2		23,918
6		3	(h)	Liverpool	W	1-0	Scott	22,262
7		8	(a)	Manchester C	W	6-1	Musgrove 2, Scott, Byrne, Peters, Hurst	25,000
8		12	(a)	Liverpool	L	1-2	Byrne	39,261
9		14	(h)	Blackpool	D	2-2	Musgrove, Scott	24,000
10		22	(a)	Blackburn R	W	4-0	Hurst, Musgrove, Byrne, Peters	15,400
11		29	(h)	Sheffield U	D	1-1	Scott	22,707
12	Oct	6	(h)	Birmingham C	W	5-0	Byrne 2, Hurst, Musgrove, Brown	21,039
13		13	(a)	Arsenal	D	1-1	Scott	49,000
14		22	(h)	Burnley	D	1-1	Hurst	34,612
15		27	(a)	Manchester U	L	1-3	Musgrove	29,204
16	Nov	3	(h)	Bolton W	L	1-2	Moore	19,866
17		10	(a)	Leicester C	L	0-2		21,064
18		17	(h)	Fulham	D	2-2	Hurst, Peters	17,668
19		24	(a)	Sheffield W	W	3-1	Brabrook, Peters, Scott	23,764
20	Dec	1	(h)	West Brom A	D	2-2	Moore, Hurst	20,680
21		8	(a)	Everton	D	1-1	Brabrook	38,701
22		15	(h)	Aston Villa	D	1-1	Peters	21,532
23		22	(a)	Tottenham H	D	4-4	Peters, Kirkup, Boyce, Scott	44,106
24		29	(a)	Nottingham F	W	4-3	Brabrook 2, Byrne, Opp own-goal	18,587
25	Feb	16	(a)	Sheffield U	W	2-0	Boyce, Sealey	18,176
26	Mar	2	(h)	Arsenal	L	0-4		31,967
27		9	(a)	Burnley	D	1-1	Byrne	17,287
28		18	(h)	Manchester U	W	3-1	Brown, Sealey, Opp own-goal	28,950
29		23	(a)	Bolton W	L	0-3		19,071
30		30	(h)	Sheffield W	W	2-0	Hurst, Byrne	22,408
31	Apr	6	(a)	Fulham	L	0-2		26,861
32		12	(h)	Ipswich T	L	1-3	Scott	23,170
33		13	(h)	Leicester C	W	2-0	Sealey 2	25,689
34		15	(a)	Ipswich T	W	3-2	Brabrook, Peters, Hurst	21,971
35		20	(a)	West Brom A	L	0-1		11,600
36		22	(h)	Nottingham F	W	4-1	Hurst 2, Peters, Moore	18,179
37		27	(h)	Everton	L	1-2	Opp own-goal	28,461
38	May	1	(a)	Birmingham C	L	2-3	Scott, Hurst	14,392
39		4	(h)	Blackburn R	L	0-1		18,898
40		11	(h)	Leyton O	W	2-0	Brabrook, Scott	16,745
41		13	(a)	Blackpool	D	0-0		12,434
42		18	(h)	Manchester C	W	6-1	Hurst 2, Sealey 2, Boyce, Brabrook	16,600

P	W	D	L	F	A	W	D	L	F	A	Pts	Pos	Div	
42	8	6	7	39	34	6	6	9	34	35	40	12th	1	Appearances
														Goals

FA Cup

3	Feb	4	(h)	Fulham	D	0-0		21,000
R		20	(a)	Fulham	W	2-1	Boyce, Byrne	20,000
4	Mar	4	(h)	Swansea T	W	1-0	Boyce	25,924
5		16	(h)	Everton	W	1-0	Byrne	31,770
6		30	(a)	Liverpool	L	0-1		49,036
								Appearances
								Goals

League Cup

1	Sep	26	(h)	Plymouth A	W	6-0	Byrne 3, Peters, Hurst, Musgrove	9,714
2	Oct	16	(a)	Rotherham U	L	1-3	Hurst	11,581
								Appearances
								Goals

Football appearance grid. Columns are players; rows are matches (numbered at right). Cell values are shirt numbers.

Leslie	Kirkup	Peters	Hurst	Lansdowne	Moore	Crawford	Boyce	Byrne	Dick	Musgrove	Lyall	Brown	Woosnam	Sealey	Burkett	Dear	Bond	Scott	Brabrook	Dickie	Standen	Bovington	Rhodes	Charles	Britt	Sissons	#
1	2	3	4	5	6	7	8	9	10	11																	1
1	2	4			6	7		9	10	11	3	5	8														2
1	2	4			6	7			10	11	3	5	8	9													3
1	2	4			6		11		10			5	8	9	3	7											4
1	2	4			6		11		10			5	8	9	3	7											5
1		4	10		6			9		11		5	8		3		2		7								6
1		4	10		6			9		11		5	8		3		2		7								7
1		4	10		6			9		11		5	8		3		2		7								8
1		4	10		6			9		11		5	8		3		2		7								9
1		4	10		6			9		11		5	8		3		2		7								10
1		4	10		6			9		11		5	8		3		2		7								11
1		4	10		6			9		11		5	8		3		2		7								12
1		4	10		6			9		11		5	8		3		2		7								13
1		4	10		6			9		11		5	8		3		2		7								14
1		4			6				10	11	3	5	8	9			2		7								15
1		4	10		6			9		11		5	8		3		2		7								16
		4	10		6		8	9		11		5			3		2		7		1						17
	2	4	10		6		8					5		9	3			11	7		1						18
	2	4	10		6		8					5		9	3			11	7		1						19
	2	4	10		6		8					5		9	3			11	7		1						20
	2	4			6		8		10			5		9	3			11	7		1						21
	2	4			6		8		10			5		9	3			11	7		1						22
	2	4			6		8		10			5		9	3			11	7		1						23
	2	4			6		8		10			5		9	3			11	7		1						24
	2				6		8		10			5		9	3			11	7		1	4					25
	2				6		8		10			5		9	3			11	7		1	4					26
	2				6		8		10			5		9	3			11	7		1	4					27
	2		10		6		8					5		9	3			11	7			4	1				28
	2		10		6		8					5		9	3			11	7			4	1				29
	2	4			6		8	9	10			5			3			11	7		1						30
	2				6		8		10			5		9	3			11	7		1	4					31
	2	4			6		8	9	10			5			3			11	7		1						32
	2	10	9		6		8					5		7	3			11			1	4					33
	2	10	9		6		8					5		7	3			11			1	4					34
	2	10	9		6		8					5		7	3			11			1						35
	2	4	10		6		8					5		7	3			11			1						36
	2	4	10		6		8	9				5		7	3			11			1						37
	2	4	10		6		8					5		9	3			11	7		1						38
1	2	4					5		8			3						7	11					6	9	10	39
1		4			6		8		10			5		9	3		2	11	7								40
1		4	10		6		8	11				5		9	3		2		7								41
1			10		6		8			11		5		9	3		2		7			4					42
20	**27**	**36**	**27**	**1**	**41**	**5**	**27**	**30**	**2**	**15**	**4**	**40**	**15**	**26**	**38**	**3**	**14**	**27**	**29**	**2**	**18**	**10**	**2**	**1**	**1**	**1**	
	1	8	13				3	3		9		7		2	1	6		10	7								

3 own-goals

Second grid (rows 3, R, 4, 5, 6):

Leslie	Kirkup	Peters	Hurst	Lansdowne	Moore	Crawford	Boyce	Byrne	Dick	Musgrove	Lyall	Brown	Woosnam	Sealey	Burkett	Dear	Bond	Scott	Brabrook	Dickie	Standen	Bovington	Rhodes	#
	2				6		8		10			5		9	3			11	7		1	4		3
	2				6		8		10			5		9	3			11	7		1	4		R
	2				6		8		10			5		9	3			11	7		1	4		4
	2				6		8		10			5		9	3			11	7		1	4		5
	2	4			6		8		10			5		9	3			11	7		1			6
	5	1			5		5		5			5		5	5			5	5		5	4		
					2		2																	

Third grid (rows 1, 2):

Leslie	Kirkup	Peters	Hurst	Lansdowne	Moore	Crawford	Boyce	Byrne	Dick	Musgrove	Lyall	Brown	Woosnam	Sealey	Burkett	Dear	Bond	Scott	Brabrook	Dickie	Standen	Bovington	#
1		4	10		6		8	9		11		5			3		2		7				1
1		6	10					9		11		5	8		3		2	7				4		2
2		2	2		1		1	2		2		2	1		2		2	2	2			1	
		1	2					3		1													

1963-64

Manager: Ron Greenwood

1	Aug	24	(a)	Chelsea	D	0-0	46,298
2		26	(h)	Blackpool	W	3-1 Peters, Boyce, Brabrook	25,533
3		30	(h)	Ipswich T	D	2-2 Byrne, Boyce	27,599
4	Sep	2	(a)	Blackpool	W	1-0 Byrne	18,407
5		7	(h)	Sheffield U	L	2-3 Byrne, Boyce	23,837
6		9	(h)	Nottingham F	L	0-2	26,200
7		14	(a)	Liverpool	W	2-1 Peters, Hurst	45,495
8		17	(a)	Nottingham F	L	1-3 Byrne	25,369
9		21	(h)	Aston Villa	L	0-1	20,346
10		28	(a)	Tottenham H	L	0-3	50,886
11	Oct	5	(h)	Wolves	D	1-1 Byrne	21,409
12		7	(h)	Burnley	D	1-1 Sealey	21,372
13		12	(a)	Sheffield W	L	0-3	23,503
14		19	(h)	Everton	W	4-2 Brabrook 2, Boyce, Hurst	25,163
15		26	(a)	Manchester U	W	1-0 Britt	42,120
16	Nov	2	(h)	West Brom A	W	4-2 Hurst 2, Brabrook, Opp own-goal	22,888
17		9	(a)	Arsenal	D	3-3 Byrne 2, Peters	52,742
18		16	(h)	Leicester C	D	2-2 Britt, Hurst	23,073
19		23	(a)	Bolton W	D	1-1 Hurst	10,864
20		30	(h)	Fulham	D	1-1 Moore	23,715
21	Dec	7	(a)	Birmingham C	L	1-2 Britt	15,357
22		14	(h)	Chelsea	D	2-2 Byrne 2	21,950
23		20	(a)	Ipswich T	L	2-3 Byrne, Brabrook	11,765
24		26	(h)	Blackburn R	L	2-8 Byrne 2	20,500
25		28	(a)	Blackburn R	W	3-1 Byrne 2, Hurst	28,990
26	Jan	11	(a)	Sheffield U	L	1-2 Sissons	18,733
27		18	(h)	Liverpool	W	1-0 Byrne	25,546
28	Feb	1	(a)	Aston Villa	D	2-2 Hurst 2	16,850
29		8	(h)	Tottenham H	W	4-0 Hurst, Sissons, Boyce, Byrne	36,934
30		17	(a)	Wolves	W	2-0 Hurst, Byrne	14,000
31		22	(h)	Sheffield W	W	4-3 Byrne 3, Hurst	24,578
32	Mar	3	(a)	Burnley	L	1-3 Byrne	14,328
33		7	(h)	Manchester U	L	0-2	27,177
34		18	(a)	Leicester C	D	2-2 Hugo, Burkett	11,980
35		21	(h)	Arsenal	D	1-1 Hurst	28,170
36		27	(h)	Stoke C	W	4-1 Moore, Byrne, Boyce, Brabrook	29,484
37		28	(a)	West Brom A	W	1-0 Hugo	16,000
38		31	(a)	Stoke C	L	0-3	24,900
39	Apr	4	(h)	Bolton W	L	2-3 Sealey, Byrne	19,398
40		11	(a)	Fulham	L	0-2	22,020
41		17	(h)	Birmingham C	W	5-0 Brabrook 2, Hurst, Sissons, Byrne	22,106
42		25	(a)	Everton	L	0-2	33,090

P	W	D	L	F	A	W	D	L	F	A	Pts	Pos	Div	Appearances
42	8	7	6	45	38	6	6	5	10	24	36	40	14th	1	Goals

FA Cup

3	Jan	4	(h)	Charlton A	W	3-0 Hurst, Brabrook, Sissons	34,155
4		25	(a)	Leyton O	D	1-1 Brabrook	34,345
R		29	(h)	Leyton O	W	3-0 Hurst 2, Byrne	35,383
5	Feb	15	(a)	Swindon T	W	3-1 Hurst 2, Byrne	28,582
6		29	(h)	Burnley	W	3-2 Byrne 2, Sissons	36,651
SF	Mar	14	(n*)	Manchester U	W	3-1 Boyce 2, Hurst	65,000
F	May	2	(n†)	Preston NE	W	3-2 Sissons, Hurst, Boyce	100,000

* Played at Hillsborough. † Played at Wembley.

Appearances
Goals

League Cup

2	Sep	25	(h)	Leyton O	W	2-1 Scott, Byrne	11,800
3	Oct	16	(a)	Aston Villa	W	2-0 Bond, Britt	11,194
4	Nov	19	(a)	Swindon T	D	3-3 Hurst, Brabrook, Boyce	12,050
R		25	(h)	Swindon T	W	4-1 Hurst, Brabrook, Byrne, Scott	15,778
5	Dec	16	(h)	Workington T	W	6-0 Byrne 3, Boyce, Hurst, Scott	10,160
SF	Feb	5	(a)	Leicester C	L	3-4 Hurst 2, Sealey	14,087
	Mar	23	(h)	Leicester C	L	0-2	27,393

Appearances
Goals

Division One

Standen	Kirkup	Burkett	Peters	Brown	Moore	Brabrook	Boyce	Byrne	Hurst	Scott	Sealey	Bickles	Dear	Bovington	Sissons	Bond	Britt	Hugo	Dickie	Bennett	Charles	No.
1	2	3	4	5	6	7	8	9	10	11												1
1	2	3	4	5	6	7	8	9	10	11												2
1	2	3	4	5	6	7	8	9	10	11												3
1	2	3	4	5	6	7	8	9	10	11												4
1	2	3	4	5	6	7	8	9	10	11												5
1	2	3	4	5	6	7	8	9	11		10											6
1	2	3	4		6	7	8	9	10			5	11									7
1	2	3	4		6	7	8	9	10			5	11									8
1	2	3	6		5	7	8	9	10				11	4								9
1	2	3	9	5	6		8		10	11	7			4								10
1	2	3	9	5	6		8		10	11	7			4								11
1	2	3	9	5	6		8		10	11	7			4								12
1		3	4	5	6	11	8		10	7						2	9					13
1		3	4	5	6	11	8		10	7						2	9					14
1		3	4	5	6	11	8		10	7						2	9					15
1		3	4	5	6	11	8	9	10	7						2						16
1		3	4	5	6	11	8		10	7						2	9					17
1		3	4	5	6	11	8		10	7						2	9					18
1		3	4	5	6	11	8	7	10							2	9					19
1		3	4	5	6	7	8	11	10							2	9					20
1		3	4	5	6	11	8	9	10	7						2						21
1		3	4	5	6	7	8	9	10						11	2						22
1		3	4	5	6	7	8	9	10						11	2						23
1		3		5	6	7	8	9	10					4	11	2						24
1		3		5	6	7	8	9	10					4	11	2						25
1		3		5	6	7	8	9	10					4	11	2						26
1		3		5	6	7	8	9	10					4	11	2						27
1		3		5	6	7	8	9	10					4	11	2						28
1	2		5		6	7	8	9	10					4	11	3						29
1		3		5	6	7	8	9	10					4	11	2						30
1	2	3	5		6	11	8	9	10	7				4								31
1		3		5	6	7	8	9	10					4	11	2						32
1		3	6	5		11	8	9		7				4		2			10			33
1		3		5	6	7	8	9	10					4	11	2						34
1		3	6	5		11	8		9	7				4		2				10		35
	2	3	4	5	6	7	8	9							11				10	1		36
	2		6	5			8	9	10	7				4		3		11	1			37
1		3	5		6	7		9	10					4	11					8		38
1		3	6	5		7	8		10					4	11	2	9					39
1	2	3		5	6	7	8	9	10					4	11							40
1		3	6	5		7	8		10	11						2	9					41
39	**18**	**40**	**32**	**36**	**37**	**38**	**41**	**33**	**37**	**10**	**18**	**2**	**3**	**22**	**14**	**26**	**9**	**3**	**3**	**1**		
	1		3		2	8	6	24	14		2		3		3	2						

1 own-goal

F.A. Cup

Standen	Kirkup	Burkett	Peters	Brown	Moore	Brabrook	Boyce	Byrne	Hurst	Scott	Sealey	Bickles	Dear	Bovington	Sissons	Bond	Britt	Hugo	Dickie	Bennett	Charles	Rd
1		3		5	6	7	8	9	10					4	11	2						3
1		3		5	6	7	8	9	10					4	11	2						4
1		3		5	6	7	8	9	10					4	11	2						R
1		3		5	6	7	8	9	10					4	11	2						5
1		3		5	6	7	8	9	10					4	11	2						6
1		3		5	6	7	8	9	10					4	11	2						SF
1		3		5	6	7	8	9	10					4	11	2						F
7		**7**		**7**	**7**	**7**	**7**	**7**	**7**					**7**	**7**	**7**						
						2	3	4	7						3							

League Cup

Standen	Kirkup	Burkett	Peters	Brown	Moore	Brabrook	Boyce	Byrne	Hurst	Scott	Sealey	Bickles	Dear	Bovington	Sissons	Bond	Britt	Hugo	Dickie	Bennett	Charles	Rd
1	2	3	9		6		8		10	11	7	5		4								2
1		3	4	5	6	11	8		10	7						2	9					3
1		3	4	5		11	8		10	7						2	9		6			4
1		3		5	6	11	8	9	10	7				4		2						R
1		3		5	6	7	8	9	10	11				4		2						5
1		3	4	5	6	11	8	9	10	7						2						SF
1		3		5	6	7	8	9	10					4	11	2						
7	**1**	**7**	**4**	**6**	**6**	**6**	**7**	**5**	**6**	**3**	**4**	**1**		**3**	**1**	**6**	**2**		**2**			
			2	2	5	5	3	1		1	1											

1964-65

Manager: Ron Greenwood

1	Aug	22	(a)	Fulham	W 2-1	Byrne, Sissons		31,200
2		24	(h)	Manchester U	W 3-1	Byrne, Hurst, Sissons		37,070
3		28	(h)	Nottingham F	L 2-3	Byrne, Sissons		26,760
4	Sep	2	(a)	Manchester U	L 1-3	Opp own-goal		45,123
5		5	(a)	Stoke C	L 1-3	Byrne		26,420
6		7	(h)	Wolves	W 5-0	Hurst 2, Byrne, Sissons, Moore		26,879
7		12	(h)	Tottenham H	W 3-2	Byrne 3		36,730
8		14	(a)	Wolves	L 3-4	Brabrook, Byrne, Opp own-goal		16,000
9		19	(a)	Burnley	L 2-3	Byrne, Boyce		13,541
10		26	(h)	Sheffield U	W 3-1	Byrne 2, Sissons		22,526
11	Oct	3	(a)	Everton	D 1-1	Byrne		45,430
12		10	(h)	Aston Villa	W 3-0	Byrne, Boyce, Peters		20,600
13		17	(a)	Liverpool	D 2-2	Hurst 2		36,029
14		24	(h)	Sheffield W	L 1-2	Brabrook		22,800
15		31	(a)	Blackpool	W 2-1	Hurst, Brabrook		14,383
16	Nov	7	(h)	Blackburn R	D 1-1	Sissons		22,725
17		14	(a)	Arsenal	W 3-0	Byrne, Peters, Hurst		36,026
18		21	(h)	Leeds U	W 3-1	Kirkup, Byrne, Peters		28,150
19		28	(a)	Chelsea	W 3-0	Sealey, Peters, Hurst		44,204
20	Dec	5	(h)	Leicester C	D 0-0			20,515
21		12	(h)	Fulham	W 2-0	Byrne 2		21,985
22		19	(a)	Nottingham F	L 2-3	Byrne, Hurst		20,009
23		26	(a)	Birmingham C	L 1-2	Hurst		23,324
24		28	(h)	Birmingham C	W 2-1	Byrne, Kirkup		23,800
25	Jan	2	(h)	Stoke C	L 0-1			23,913
26		16	(a)	Tottenham H	L 2-3	Byrne, Sissons		50,000
27		23	(h)	Burnley	W 3-2	Boyce, Bond, Byrne		25,490
28	Feb	6	(a)	Sheffield U	L 1-2	Sealey		16,265
29		13	(h)	Everton	L 0-1			25,163
30		20	(a)	Sunderland	L 2-3	Byrne, Hurst		32,885
31		27	(h)	Liverpool	W 2-1	Presland, Hurst		25,750
32	Mar	6	(a)	Sheffield W	L 0-2			14,931
33		13	(h)	Sunderland	L 2-3	Dear 2		23,360
34		20	(a)	Blackburn R	L 0-4			8,990
35		27	(h)	Arsenal	W 2-1	Hurst, Byrne		24,000
36		31	(a)	Aston Villa	W 3-2	Hurst, Byrne, Dear		19,900
37	Apr	3	(a)	Leeds U	L 1-2	Dear		41,918
38		12	(h)	Chelsea	W 3-2	Hurst 2, Sissons		33,288
39		16	(h)	West Brom A	W 6-1	Dear 5, Peters		27,706
40		17	(a)	Leicester C	L 0-1			15,880
41		19	(a)	West Brom A	L 2-4	Hurst, Boyce		14,000
42		23	(h)	Blackpool	W 2-1	Brown, Dear		22,762

P	W	D	L	F	A	W	D	L	F	A	Pts	Pos	Div	
42	14	2	5	48	25	5	2	14	34	46	42	9th	1	Appearances
														Goals

FA Cup

3	Jan	9	(h)	Birmingham C	W 4-2	Hurst 2, Byrne, Sissons		31,056
4		30	(h)	Chelsea	L 0-1			37,000
								Appearances
								Goals

League Cup

2	Sep	30	(a)	Sunderland	L 1-4	Brabrook		22,382
								Appearances
								Goals

Standen	Bond	Burkett	Bovington	Brown	Moore	Brabrook	Boyce	Byrne	Hurst	Sissons	Peters	Sealey	Scott	Kirkup	Presland	Dear	Charles	Bickles	Dawkins	Bennett	No.
1	2	3	4	5	6	7	8	9	10	11											1
1	2	3	4	5	6	7	8	9	10	11											2
1	2	3	4	5	6	7	8	9	10	11											3
1	2	3	4	5	6	7	8	9	10	11											4
1	2	3	4	5	6	7	8	9	10	11											5
1	2	3	4		6		8	9	10	11		5	7								6
1	2	3	4		6		8	9	10	11		5	7								7
1	2	3	4		6	11	8	9	10			5	7								8
1	2	3	4		6		8	9	10	11		5	7								9
1	2		4	5	6	7	8	9	10	11		3									10
1	2	3	4	5		7	8	9	10	11		6									11
1	2		4	5	6	7	8	9	10	11		3									12
1	2		4	5	6	7	8	9	10	11		3									13
1	2		4	5	6	7	8		9	10	3	11									14
1	2	3	4	5		7	8	9	10	11		6									15
1	2	3	4	5			8	9	10	11		6	7								16
1		3	4	5			8	9	10	11		6	7	2							17
1	2	3	4	5			8	9	10	11		6	7								18
1	2	3	4	5			8	9	10	11		6	7								19
1	2	3	4	5		7	8	9	10	11		6									20
1	2	3	4	5		7	8	9	10	11		6									21
1	2	3	4	5		7	8	9	10	11		6									22
1			4	5			6	9	8	10	3	7	11	2							23
1		3	4	5		7	8	9	10	11		6		2							24
1	2		4	5			6	9	8	10	3	7	11								25
1	2		4	5			6	9	8	10	3	7	11								26
1		3	4	5			8	9	10	11		6	7	2							27
1	2		4	5	6		8	9	10	11		3	7								28
1	2		4	5	6		8	9	10	11		3	7								29
1			4		5	7	8	9	10	11		6		2	3						30
1			4		5	7	8	9	10	11		6		2	3						31
1			4		5	7	8		9	11	6			2	3	10					32
1				5	6		8		9			7	11	2	3	10	4				33
1				5	6		4	9	8	11	3	7		2		10					34
1		3			6			9	8	11	4	7		2		10		5			35
1		3			6	11	8	9	10		4	7		2		10		5			36
1		3		5	6		8		9	11	4	7		2		10					37
1		3		5	6	7	8		9	11	4			2		10					38
1	2	3		5	6		8		9	11	4	7				10					39
1				5	6		8		9	11	3	7		2	4	10					40
1		3	4	5	6		8		9	11		7		2		10					41
1		3	4	5	6		8		9	11		7		2		10					42
42	**29**	**24**	**33**	**33**	**28**	**22**	**41**	**34**	**42**	**38**	**35**	**21**	**6**	**15**	**4**	**10**	**1**	**2**	**1**	**1**	
	1			1	1	3	4	25	17	8	5	2		2	1	10					

2 own-goals

Standen	Bond	Burkett	Bovington	Brown	Moore	Brabrook	Boyce	Byrne	Hurst	Sissons	Peters	Sealey	Scott	Kirkup	Presland	Dear	Charles	Bickles	Dawkins	Bennett	No.
1	2		4	5	6		9	8	10		3	7	11	2							3
1	3		4	5			8	9	10	11	6	7		2							4
2	2		2	2			2	2	2	2	2	2	1								
	1			2				1													

Standen	Bond	Burkett	Bovington	Brown	Moore	Brabrook	Boyce	Byrne	Hurst	Sissons	Peters	Sealey	Scott	Kirkup	Presland	Dear	Charles	Bickles	Dawkins	Bennett	No.
1	2	3	4	5		7	8	9	10	11	6										2
1	1	1	1	1		1	1	1	1	1	1										
							1														

1965-66

Manager: Ron Greenwood

1	Aug	21	(a)	West Brom A	L 0-3		19,900
2		23	(h)	Sunderland	D 1-1	Peters	34,700
3		28	(h)	Leeds U	W 2-1	Peters, Hurst	27,900
4	Sep	1	(a)	Sunderland	L 1-2	Hurst	48,626
5		4	(a)	Sheffield U	L 3-5	Byrne, Hurst, Kirkup	15,796
6		6	(h)	Liverpool	L 1-5	Peters	32,144
7		11	(h)	Leicester C	L 2-5	Hurst 2	21,400
8		15	(a)	Liverpool	D 1-1	Hurst	44,397
9		18	(a)	Blackburn R	W 2-1	Peters 2	10,178
10		25	(h)	Blackpool	D 1-1	Hurst	21,000
11	Oct	2	(a)	Fulham	L 0-3		22,310
12		9	(a)	Nottingham F	L 0-5		19,262
13		16	(h)	Sheffield W	W 4-2	Britt 2, Sissons, Peters	20,690
14		23	(a)	Northampton T	L 1-2	Brown	15,367
15		30	(h)	Stoke C	D 0-0		21,545
16	Nov	6	(a)	Burnley	L 1-3	Britt	16,802
17		13	(h)	Chelsea	W 2-1	Brabrook, Peters	31,540
18		20	(a)	Arsenal	L 2-3	Hurst, Peters	35,855
19		27	(h)	Everton	W 3-0	Sissons 2, Brabrook	21,920
20	Dec	4	(a)	Manchester U	D 0-0		32,924
21		11	(h)	Newcastle U	W 4-3	Hurst 3, Brabrook	23,758
22		18	(a)	Sheffield W	D 0-0		12,996
23	Jan	1	(h)	Nottingham F	L 0-3		25,131
24		8	(a)	Newcastle U	L 1-2	Byrne	31,600
25		11	(a)	Everton	D 2-2	Hurst, Peters	29,915
26		15	(h)	Northampton T	D 1-1	Hurst	21,000
27		29	(h)	West Brom A	W 4-0	Hurst 2, Sissons, Peters	25,500
28	Feb	5	(a)	Leeds U	L 0-5		33,312
29		7	(a)	Aston Villa	W 2-1	Hurst, Sissons	13,440
30		19	(h)	Sheffield U	W 4-0	Brabrook, Hurst, Peters, Opp own-goal	21,220
31	Mar	5	(h)	Aston Villa	W 4-2	Burkett, Byrne, Brabrook, Hurst	22,058
32		12	(h)	Blackburn R	W 4-1	Dear, Brabrook, Hurst, Burkett	18,566
33		19	(a)	Blackpool	L 1-2	Boyce	10,559
34		26	(h)	Fulham	L 1-3	Hurst	18,977
35	Apr	2	(h)	Burnley	D 1-1	Brabrook	17,635
36		8	(a)	Tottenham H	W 4-1	Redknapp, Hurst, Byrne, Boyce	50,188
37		9	(a)	Chelsea	L 2-6	Bennett, Opp own-goal	35,958
38		16	(h)	Arsenal	W 2-1	Byrne, Brabrook	26,022
39		25	(h)	Tottenham H	W 2-0	Byrne 2	32,231
40		30	(h)	Manchester U	W 3-2	Hurst 2, Byrne	36,416
41	May	7	(a)	Stoke C	L 0-1		15,670
42		9	(a)	Leicester C	L 1-2	Byrne	16,066

P	W	D	L	F	A	W	D	L	F	A	Pts	Pos	Div	
42	12	5	4	46	33	3	3	4	14	24	50	39	12th	1	Appearances
															Sub Appearances
															Goals

FA Cup

3	Jan	22	(a)	Oldham A	D 2-2	Burnett, Hurst	25,035
R		24	(h)	Oldham A	W 2-1	Hurst, Brabrook	35,330
4	Feb	12	(h)	Blackburn R	D 3-3	Bloomfield, Hurst, Sissons	32,350
R		16	(a)	Blackburn R	L 1-4	Hurst	25,547

Appearances
Sub Appearances
Goals

League Cup

2	Sep	21	(a)	Bristol R	D 3-3	Hurst 2, Byrne	18,354
R		29	(h)	Bristol R	W 3-2	Byrne 2, Hurst	13,160
3	Oct	13	(h)	Mansfield T	W 4-0	Hurst 2, Brabrook, Burnett	11,590
4	Nov	3	(a)	Rotherham U	W 2-1	Hurst, Moore	13,902
5		17	(a)	Grimsby T	D 2-2	Hurst, Charles	16,281
R	Dec	15	(h)	Grimsby T	W 1-0	Hurst	17,500
SF		20	(h)	Cardiff C	W 5-2	Hurst, Bovington, Brabrook, Byrne, Sissons	19,980
	Feb	2	(a)	Cardiff C	W 5-1	Hurst 2, Peters 2, Burnett	14,315
F	Mar	9	(h)	West Brom A	W 2-1	Moore, Byrne	28,323
		23	(a)	West Brom A	L 1-4	Peters	31,925

Appearances
Sub Appearances
Goals

The following is an appearance/scorer grid. Player surnames head the columns (left to right); the right-hand number is the match number. Figures are the shirt numbers worn; `*` and `12` denote substitute/noted appearances.

#	Standen	Kirkup	Burkett	Peters	Bovington	Moore	Brabrook	Boyce	Hurst	Bennett	Sissons	Dickie	Bickles	Redknapp	Byrne	Presland	Scott	Brown	Charles	Burnett	Bloomfield	Britt	Dear	Dawkins
1	1	2	3	4	5	6	7	8	9	10	11													
2		2	3	4		6		8	10		11	1	5	7	9									
3	1	2	3*	8	4	6			10	12	11		5	7	9									
4	1	2		8	4	6			10		11		5	7	9	3								
5	1	2		8	4	6	7		10		11		5		9	3								
6	1	2	3	4		6	7	8	10		11		5		9									
7	1	2	3	8	4	6	7		9	10	11		5											
8		2	3	8	4	6	7		9	10	11	1	5											
9		2	3	8	4	6	7		9	10	11	1	5											
10		2	3	8	4	6	7		10		11	1	5		9									
11				4		6	7		10		11	1	5		9	3	2	8						
12	1	2		4	5	6	11		9	10		12		7		3*	8							
13	1			8	4	6	7		10		11							5	3	2		9		
14	1			4		6	7		10		11							5	3	2	8	9		
15	1			8	4	6	7		10		11							5	3	2		9		
16	1			8	4	6	7		10		11							5	3	2		9		
17	1			8	4	6	7		10		11							5	3	2		9		
18	1			8	4	6	7		10		11							5	3	2*	12	9		
19	1	2		8	4	6	7		10		11				9			5	3					
20	1	2		8	4	6	7		10		11				9			5	3					
21	1	2		8	4	6	7		10		11				9			5	3					
22	1	2		8	4	6	7		10		11				9			5	3					
23	1	2		8	4	6	7		10		11				9			5	3					
24	1	2		8	4	6	7		10		11				9			5	3					
25	1		3	8	4	6	7		10									5		2	9	11		
26	1		3	8	4	6	7		10									5		2	9	11		
27	1		3	8	4	6	7		10		11							5		2	9			
28	1		3	8	4	6	7		10		11							5		2	9			
29	1		3	8	4	6	7		9		11							5		2	10			
30	1		3	4		6	7	8	10		11				9			5		2				
31	1		3	4		6	7	8	10						9			5		2		11		
32	1		3	4		6	7		9		11							5		2	8	10		
33	1		3	4		6			9	10	11							5		2	8		7	
34	1		3	4	5	6	7		9	10	11									2	8			
35	1					6	7	11	9				5						3	2	8	10	4	
36	1			4		6	7	8	9	10	11		5						3	2				
37	1		3			6	7		9		11							5		2	8	10	4	
38	1			4		6	7	8	10		11				9			5	3	2				
39	1			4		6	7	8	10		11				9			5	3	2				
40	1			4		6	7	8	10		11				9			5	3	2				
41	1			4		6	7	8	10		11				9			5	3	2				
42	1			4		6	7	8	10		11				9			5	3	2				
Apps	37	17	19	40	31	37	32	16	39	7	36	5	12	7	23	2	2	23	25	24	9	10	7	2
Sub										1											1			
Goals		1	2	11			8	2	23	1	5			1	9				1			3	1	

2 own-goals

#	Standen	Kirkup	Burkett	Peters	Bovington	Moore	Brabrook	Boyce	Hurst	Bennett	Sissons	Dickie	Bickles	Redknapp	Byrne	Presland	Scott	Brown	Charles	Burnett	Bloomfield	Britt	Dear	Dawkins
3	1		3	8	4	6	7		10						9			5		2		11		
R	1		3	8	4	6	7		10		11				9			5		2				
4	1		3	8	4	6	7		9		11							5		2	10			
R	1		3	8	4	6	7	5	9		11									2	10			
Apps	4		4	4	4	4	4	1	4		2				3			3		4	2	1		
Goals				1					4									2			1			

#	Standen	Kirkup	Burkett	Peters	Bovington	Moore	Brabrook	Boyce	Hurst	Bennett	Sissons	Dickie	Bickles	Redknapp	Byrne	Presland	Scott	Brown	Charles	Burnett	Bloomfield	Britt	Dear	Dawkins
2		2	3	8	4	6			9	7	11	1						10				5		
R		2	3	8		4			9	7	11	1						10		5	6			
3	1			8	4	6	7		10		11							5	3	2		9		
4	1			8	4	6	7		10		11							5	3	2		9		
5	1			8	4	6	7		9		11							5	3	2	10			
R	1	2		8	4	6	7		10		11				9			5	3					
SF	1		3	8	4	6	7		10		11							5		2	9			
F	1		3	4		6	7	8	10		11				9			5		2				
Apps	8	4	4	10	9	9	8	2	10	2	9	2			6			9	7	6	4	1		
Goals				3	1	2	2		11		1				5					1	2			

1966-67

Manager: Ron Greenwood

1	Aug	20	(h)	Chelsea	L	1-2	Boyce	36,126
2		23	(a)	Arsenal	L	1-2	Byrne	40,533
3		27	(a)	Leicester C	L	4-5	Brabrook 2, Hurst 2	26,850
4		29	(h)	Arsenal	D	2-2	Moore, Brabrook	34,964
5	Sep	3	(h)	Liverpool	D	1-1	Hurst	33,000
6		7	(a)	Manchester C	W	4-1	Hurst 2, Boyce, Sissons	31,989
7		10	(h)	Stoke C	D	1-1	Hurst	33,292
8		17	(a)	Sheffield W	W	2-0	Boyce, Byrne	29,171
9		24	(h)	Southampton	D	2-2	Hurst, Peters	32,301
10	Oct	1	(a)	Sunderland	W	4-2	Byrne 2, Hurst, Peters	29,277
11		8	(h)	Everton	L	2-3	Peters, Hurst	32,784
12		15	(a)	Fulham	L	2-4	Byrne, Hurst	34,826
13		26	(h)	Nottingham F	W	3-1	Hurst 2, Bovington	23,000
14		29	(a)	Sheffield U	L	1-3	Peters	20,579
15	Nov	5	(h)	Fulham	W	6-1	Hurst 4, Peters 2	22,260
16		12	(a)	Tottenham H	W	4-3	Byrne, Brabrook, Sissons, Hurst	29,227
17		19	(h)	Newcastle U	W	3-0	Peters, Byrne, Hurst	31,285
18		26	(a)	Leeds U	L	1-2	Hurst	37,382
19	Dec	3	(h)	West Brom A	W	3-0	Redknapp, Dear, Peters	22,961
20		10	(a)	Burnley	L	2-4	Hurst 2	19,509
21		17	(a)	Chelsea	D	5-5	Sissons 2, Brabrook, Peters, Byrne	47,805
22		26	(a)	Blackpool	W	4-1	Hurst, Dear, Byrne, Sissons	26,901
23		27	(h)	Blackpool	W	4-0	Byrne, Hurst, Moore, Peters	29,300
24		31	(h)	Leicester C	L	0-1		34,168
25	Jan	7	(a)	Liverpool	L	0-2		48,518
26		14	(a)	Stoke C	D	1-1	Hurst	27,274
27		21	(h)	Sheffield W	W	3-0	Dear, Hurst, Sissons	29,220
28	Feb	4	(a)	Southampton	L	2-6	Hurst, Burkett	30,123
29		11	(h)	Sunderland	D	2-2	Byrne, Hurst	27,965
30		25	(a)	Everton	L	0-4		42,504
31	Mar	18	(a)	Nottingham F	L	0-1		31,426
32		24	(h)	Aston Villa	W	2-1	Boyce, Peters	28,716
33		25	(h)	Burnley	W	3-2	Peters 2, Sissons	24,428
34		28	(a)	Aston Villa	W	2-0	Hurst 2	22,033
35	Apr	1	(a)	Manchester U	L	0-3		61,380
36		4	(h)	Sheffield U	L	0-2		22,006
37		22	(h)	Leeds U	L	0-1		25,429
38		26	(a)	Newcastle U	L	0-1		38,870
39		28	(a)	West Brom A	L	1-3	Bennett	23,219
40	May	6	(h)	Manchester U	L	1-6	Charles	38,424
41		9	(h)	Tottenham H	L	0-2		35,750
42		13	(h)	Manchester C	D	1-1	Peters	17,186

P	W		D		L		F		A		W		D		L		F		A		Pts	Pos	Div	Appearances
42	8		6		7		40		31		6		2		13		40		53		36	16th	1	Sub Appearances
																								Goals

FA Cup

3	Jan	28	(h)	Swindon T	D	3-3	Hurst 3	37,400
R		31	(a)	Swindon T	L	1-3	Sissons	25,789

Appearances
Sub Appearances
Goals

League Cup

2	Sep	14	(h)	Tottenham H	W	1-0	Hurst	34,000
3	Oct	5	(a)	Arsenal	W	3-1	Hurst 2, Peters	33,647
4	Nov	7	(h)	Leeds U	W	7-0	Sissons 3, Hurst 3, Peters	27,474
5	Dec	7	(a)	Blackpool	W	3-1	Hurst 2, Byrne	15,831
SF	Jan	18	(a)	West Brom A	L	0-4		29,796
	Feb	8	(h)	West Brom A	D	2-2	Byrne, Hurst	35,790

Appearances
Sub Appearances
Goals

302

Standen	Burnett	Charles	Peters	Moore	Bovington	Brabrook	Boyce	Byrne	Hurst	Sissons	Bickles	Bennett	Brown	Burkett	Howe	Redknapp	Dear	Sealey	Mackleworth	Dawkins	Andrew	Kitchener	Heffer	Hartley	Eadie	Game
1	2	3	4	5	6	7	8	9	10	11																1
1	2	3	4	5	6	7	8	9	10	11																2
1	2	3	4	5	6	7	8	9	10	11																3
1	2	3	4	5	6	7	8	9	10	11																4
1	2	3	4		6		7	8	9	10	11	5*	12													5
1	2	3	4		6		7	8	9	10	11	5														6
1	2		4		6	8	7		9	10	11	5	3													7
1	2	3	4		6		7	8	9	10	11	5														8
1	2	3	4		6		7*	8	9	10	11	5	12													9
1	2	3	4		6		7	8	9	10	11	5														10
1	2	3	4		6		7	8	9	10	11	5														11
1	2	3	4		6		7	8	9	10	11	5														12
1	2		11	6	4		7	8		10	9	5	3													13
1	2		11	6	4		7	8		10	12	9	5	3*												14
1		3	4	6	2	7	8	9	10	11				5												15
1		3	4	6	2	7	8	9	10	11				5												16
1	12	3	4	6	2	7	8	9	10	11				5*												17
1		3	4	6	2	7	8	9	10	11	5															18
1	2	3	10	6	4		8				5				7	9	11									19
1	2	3	7	6	4		8	9	10	11				5												20
1	12	3*	4	6	2	7	8	9	10	11				5												21
1		3	4	6	2		8	9	10	11				5	7											22
		3	4	6	2	7		9	10	11				5	8	1										23
1	2	3*	4	6	8	7		9	10	11			12	5												24
1	2		4	6	8	7		9	10	11			3	5												25
1	2	3	4*	6		7	8	9	10	11				5	12											26
1		3*	4	6	2	7			10	11	5				9	8	12									27
1			4	6	2	7	8	9	10	11			3	5												28
1	2		11		6		8	9	10				3		7			4	5							29
1	2		3	9	6		10	11				8			7			4	5							30
1			4	6		7	8		10	11	9*		2		12						3	5				31
1			4	6	11	8		9	10				2		7						3	5				32
1	2	9	6	4		8			10	11					7						3	5				33
1	2	9	6	4	7	8			10	11*					12						3	5				34
1	2	9	6	4	11	8			10						7						3	5				35
	2	9	6	4		9			10	11					7					1	3	5				36
1	2	4	5	6	7	8			10	11		9									3					37
1	2	4	6		11	8		9	10				3		7							5				38
		3	4	6				9	10	11	8		2		7							5	9			39
		3	4	6				9	10	11	8		2		7		1					5				40
1	2	3	7	6	4		8	9			5					10							11			41
1		2	4	6			8		10		5				7						3		9	11		42
39	**24**	**31**	**41**	**40**	**28**	**32**	**37**	**25**	**41**	**34**	**8**	**7**	**18**	**11**	**10**	**4**	**4**	**3**	**2**	**2**	**8**	**9**	**2**	**2**		
	2										1		1	1	1	2	1				1					
		1	14	2	1	5	4	11	29	7		1			1		1	3			1					

Standen	Burnett	Charles	Peters	Moore	Bovington	Brabrook	Boyce	Byrne	Hurst	Sissons	Bickles	Bennett	Brown	Burkett	Howe	Redknapp	Dear	Sealey	Mackleworth	Dawkins	Andrew	Kitchener	Heffer	Hartley	Eadie	
1			4	6	2		10	8	9	11	5		3		7											3
1			4	6	2		10	8	9	11	5		3		7											R
2			2	2	2		2	2	2	2	2		2		2											
								3	1																	

Standen	Burnett	Charles	Peters	Moore	Bovington	Brabrook	Boyce	Byrne	Hurst	Sissons	Bickles	Bennett	Brown	Burkett	Howe	Redknapp	Dear	Sealey	Mackleworth	Dawkins	Andrew	Kitchener	Heffer	Hartley	Eadie	
1	2	3	4	6		7	8		10	11		9	5													2
1	2	3	4	6		7	8	9	10	11			5													3
1		3	4	6	2	7	8	9	10	11			5													4
1	2	3	10	6	4		7	9	8	11			5													5
1	2		8	6	4	7		9	10	11			5	3												SF
1			4	6	2	7	8	9	10	11			5	3												
6	4	4	6	6	4	5	5	5	6	6		1	6	2												
			2					2	9	3																

1967-68

Manager: Ron Greenwood

						Result		Scorers	Attendance
1	Aug	19	(h)	Sheffield W		L	2-3	Hurst, Peters	29,603
2		21	(h)	Burnley		W	4-2	Hurst 2, Peters, Redknapp	30,420
3		26	(a)	Tottenham H		L	1-5	Sissons	55,831
4		29	(a)	Burnley		D	3-3	Hurst, Moore, Peters	16,620
5	Sep	2	(h)	Manchester U		L	1-3	Peters	36,562
6		5	(a)	Everton		L	0-2		46,762
7		9	(a)	Sunderland		W	5-1	Hurst 2, Redknapp, Moore, Peters	39,772
8		16	(h)	Wolves		L	1-2	Hurst	30,780
9		23	(a)	Fulham		W	3-0	Hurst, Moore, Sissons	29,234
10		30	(h)	Leeds U		D	0-0		29,740
11	Oct	7	(h)	Stoke C		L	3-4	Hurst 2, Peters	24,471
12		14	(a)	Liverpool		L	1-3	Peters	46,951
13		23	(h)	Southampton		L	0-1		32,550
14		28	(a)	Chelsea		W	3-1	Dear, Hurst, Peters	40,303
15	Nov	11	(a)	Newcastle U		L	0-1		32,850
16		18	(h)	Manchester C		L	2-3	Hurst, Peters	25,425
17		25	(a)	Arsenal		D	0-0		42,029
18	Dec	2	(h)	Sheffield U		W	3-0	Sissons 2, Brabrook	22,510
19		8	(a)	Coventry C		D	1-1	Hurst	28,393
20		11	(h)	West Brom A		L	2-3	Brabrook, Hurst	18,340
21		16	(a)	Sheffield W		L	1-4	Dear	24,003
22		23	(h)	Tottenham H		W	2-1	Bonds, Dear	32,116
23		26	(h)	Leicester C		W	4-2	Dear 3, Brooking	26,520
24		30	(a)	Leicester C		W	4-2	Dear 2, Brooking, Sissons	24,589
25	Jan	6	(a)	Manchester U		L	1-3	Brooking	58,498
26		20	(a)	Wolves		W	2-1	Dear, Hurst	32,273
27	Feb	3	(h)	Fulham		W	7-2	Brooking 2, Hurst 2, Dear, Moore, Peters	31,248
28		10	(a)	Leeds U		L	1-2	Dear	41,814
29		26	(a)	Stoke C		L	0-2		16,092
30	Mar	16	(a)	Southampton		D	0-0		27,734
31		23	(h)	Chelsea		L	0-1		36,301
32		29	(h)	Arsenal		D	1-1	Brooking	33,942
33	Apr	6	(h)	Newcastle U		W	5-0	Brooking 3, Sissons 2	27,780
34		12	(h)	Nottingham F		W	3-0	Dear 2, Sissons	36,589
35		13	(a)	Manchester C		L	0-3		38,754
36		16	(a)	Nottingham F		D	1-1	Peters	22,198
37		20	(h)	Liverpool		W	1-0	Peters	33,060
38		24	(h)	Sunderlnd		D	1-1	Dear	29,153
39		27	(a)	Sheffield U		W	2-1	Hurst 2	19,530
40	Mar	1	(a)	West Brom A		L	1-3	Peters	25,009
41		4	(h)	Coventry C		D	0-0		30,180
42		11	(h)	Everton		D	1-1	Peters	28,880

P	W	D	L	F	A	W	D	L	F	A	Pts	Pos	Div	
42	8	5	8	43	30	6	5	10	30	39	38	12th	1	Appearances
														Sub Appearances
														Goals

FA Cup

3	Jan	27	(a)	Burnley		W	3-1	Peters 2, Dear	23,452
4	Feb	17	(a)	Stoke C		W	3-0	Sissons 2, Hurst	36,704
5	Mar	9	(h)	Sheffield U		L	1-2	Dear	38,440

Appearances
Sub Appearances
Goals

League Cup

2	Sep	13	(a)	Walsall		W	5-1	Peters 2, Brabrook, Hurst, Opp own-goal	17,752
3	Oct	11	(h)	Bolton W		W	4-1	Hurst 4	20,510
4	Nov	1	(a)	Huddersfield T		L	0-2		17,729

Appearances
Sub Appearances
Goals

Ferguson	Bonds	Charles	Bovington	Cushley	Moore	Redknapp	Peters	Hurst	Boyce	Sissons	Dear	Brooking	Kitchener	Standen	Brabrook	Burkett	Lampard	Heffer	Bennett	Stephenson	Howe	Match
1	2	3	4	5	6	7	8	9	10	11												
1	2	3		5	6	7	4	9	10	11	8											1
1	2	3		5	6	7	4	9	8	11	10											2
1	2	3		5	6	7	4	9	10	11		8										3
1	2*	3		5	6	7	4	9	10	11	8	12										4
1		2		5	6	7	4	9	10	11	8	3										5
	2			5	6	7	4	9	10		8	3	1	11								6
	2			5	6	7	4	10	8	11		9	3	1								7
1		3	2	5	6	7	4	10	8	11		9										8
1	2	3	4	5	6	7	10	9	8			11										9
1	2	3	8	5	6	7	4	10		11		9										10
1	2	3		5	6	7	4	10	8	11		9										11
1	2	3	8	5	6	7	4	10		11		9										12
1	2	3		5	6		4	10	8		11	9			7							13
1	2	4		5		6	9	10	11		8				7	3						14
1				5	6	7	4	10	8	11					9	3	2					15
1	2			5	6	7	4	9	10	11		8			3							16
	2				6	7	4	10	8	11				1	9	3	5					17
1	5	2			6	7	4	10	8	11					9	3						18
1	5	2			6	7	4	10*	8	11					9	3	12					19
1	4	2	6	5		10	8	11	7	9					3							20
1	2			5	6		4	10	8	11	7	9			3							21
1	2			5	6		4	10	8	11	7	9			3							22
1	2			5	6		4	10	8	11	7	9			3							23
1	2			5	6		4	10	8		7	9			11	3						24
1	2			5	6		4	10	8	11	7	9			3							25
1	2			5	6		4	10	8	11	7	9			3							26
1	2			5	6		4	10		11	7	9			3	8						27
1	2			5	6		4	10		11	7	9			3	8						28
1	2				6		4	10	8	11	7	9			3		5					29
1	2				6		4	10	8	11	7	9			3		5					30
1	2				6	7	4		8	11	10	9			3		5					31
1	2				6	7	4		8	11	10	9			3		5					32
1	2				6	7	4		8	11	10	9			3		5					33
1	2	12			6	7	4	11	8		10	9*			3		5					34
1	2				6	7	4	9	8	11	10				3		5					35
1	2				6	7	4	10	8	11	9				3		5					36
1	2				6	7		10	8	11	9	4			3		5					37
1	2				6	7	4	10	8	11	12	9			3*		5					38
1	2	3		5	6		4	10	8	11	7	9					5					39
1	2				6	7	4	10	8	11	9									5	3	40
1	2				6	7	4		8	11	10	9								5	3	41
1	2				6	7	4		8	11	10	9								5	3	42
39	37	19	6	27	40	28	40	38	38	37	25	24	3	3	14	8	19	1	2	12	12	
	1										1	1					1					
	1			4	2	14	19		8	14	9				2							

Ferguson	Bonds	Charles	Bovington	Cushley	Moore	Redknapp	Peters	Hurst	Boyce	Sissons	Dear	Brooking	Kitchener	Standen	Brabrook	Burkett	Lampard	Heffer	Bennett	Stephenson	Howe	Match
1	2			5	6		4	10	8	11	7	9			3							3
1	2			5	6		4	10		11	7	9			3	8						4
1	2			5	6		4	10		11	7	9			3	8						5
3	3			3	3		3	3	1	3	3	3			3	2						
							2	1		2	2											

Ferguson	Bonds	Charles	Bovington	Cushley	Moore	Redknapp	Peters	Hurst	Boyce	Sissons	Dear	Brooking	Kitchener	Standen	Brabrook	Burkett	Lampard	Heffer	Bennett	Stephenson	Howe	Match
	2			5	6	7	4	10	8	11			3	1	9							
1	2	3		5	6	7	4	10	8	11					9							2
1	2	3		5	6	12	4	10	8*		11				9	7						3
2	2	3		3	3	2	3	3	3	2	1		1	1	3	1						4
							2	5						1								

1 own-goal

1968-69

Manager: Ron Greenwood

1	Aug	10	(a)	Newcastle U	D	1-1	Dear	36,830
2		14	(a)	Stoke C	W	2-0	Peters, Sissons	22,131
3		17	(h)	Nottingham F	W	1-0	Hurst	31,114
4		19	(h)	Everton	L	1-4	Peters	34,895
5		24	(a)	Coventry C	W	2-1	Peters, Brooking	33,716
6		26	(h)	Burnley	W	5-0	Hurst 2, Brooking 2, Peters	28,430
7		31	(h)	West Brom A	W	4-0	Peters 3, Redknapp	29,908
8	Sep	7	(a)	Manchester U	D	1-1	Hurst	63,274
9		14	(h)	Tottenham H	D	2-2	Peters, Hurst	35,802
10		21	(a)	Chelsea	D	1-1	Peters	58,062
11		28	(h)	Sheffield W	D	1-1	Hurst	31,182
12	Oct	5	(h)	Southampton	D	0-0		29,558
13		8	(a)	Burnley	L	1-3	Brooking	13,869
14		12	(a)	Leeds U	L	0-2		40,786
15		19	(h)	Sunderland	W	8-0	Hurst 6, Moore, Brooking	24,718
16		26	(a)	Arsenal	D	0-0		59,533
17	Nov	2	(h)	Queen's Park R	W	4-3	Moore, Peters, Hurst, Redknapp	36,008
18		9	(a)	Wolves	L	0-2		29,704
19		16	(h)	Leicester C	W	4-0	Dear 2, Peters, Opp own-goal	26,328
20		23	(a)	Ipsiwch T	D	2-2	Hurst 2	28,964
21		30	(h)	Manchester C	W	2-1	Hurst, Peters	33,082
22	Dec	7	(a)	Liverpool	L	0-2		48,632
23		14	(h)	Leeds U	D	1-1	Peters	24,718
24		21	(a)	Sunderland	L	1-2	Hurst	23,094
25		26	(a)	Southampton	D	2-2	Hurst 2	27,465
26	Jan	11	(a)	Queen's Park R	D	1-1	Dear	28,645
27	Feb	1	(a)	Leicester C	D	1-1	Dear	31,002
28		22	(h)	Liverpool	D	1-1	Sissons	36,498
29	Mar	1	(h)	Newcastle U	W	3-1	Brooking, Peters, Hurst	26,336
30		8	(a)	Nottingham F	W	1-0	Hurst	24,303
31		14	(h)	Coventry C	W	5-2	Hurst 2, Sissons, Peters, Bonds	29,053
32		21	(h)	Ipswich T	L	1-3	Hurst	32,574
33		24	(h)	Wolves	W	3-1	Peters 2, Brooking	25,221
34		29	(h)	Manchester U	D	0-0		41,546
35	Apr	1	(a)	Everton	L	0-1		37,212
36		5	(a)	Sheffield W	D	1-1	Hurst	24,268
37		8	(h)	Stoke C	D	0-0		26,577
38		12	(h)	Chelsea	D	0-0		32,332
39		14	(a)	West Brom A	L	1-3	Peters	20,092
40		19	(a)	Tottenham H	L	0-1		50,970
41		21	(h)	Arsenal	L	1-2	Sissons	34,941
42		30	(h)	Manchester C	D	1-1	Peters	31,846

P	W	D	L	F	A	W	D	L	F	A	Pts	Pos	Div	
42	10	8	3	47	22	3	10	8	19	28	44	8th	1	Appearances
														Sub Appearances
														Goals

FA Cup

3	Jan	4	(h)	Bristol C	W	3-2	Peters 2, Hurst	32,526
4		25	(a)	Huddersfield T	W	2-0	Peters, Hurst	30,992
5	Feb	26	(a)	Mansfield T	L	0-3		21,117
								Appearances
								Sub Appearances
								Goals

League Cup

2	Sep	4	(h)	Bolton W	W	7-2	Hurst 3, Peters, Sissons, Brooking, Redknapp	24,937
3		25	(h)	Coventry C	D	0-0		27,594
R	Oct	1	(a)	Coventry C	L	2-3	Hurst, Peters	25,988
								Appearances
								Sub Appearances
								Goals

306

Appearances grid (shirt numbers by player and match).

Ferguson	Bonds	Charles	Peters	Stephenson	Moore	Redknapp	Boyce	Dear	Hurst	Brooking	Sissons	Cross	Howe	Lindsay	Hartley	Cushley	Miller	Bennett	Grotier	Holland	Death	Lampard	Heffer	#
1	2	3*	4	5	6	7	8	9	10	11	12													1
1	2	3	4	5	6	7	8	9	10		11													2
1	2	3	4	5	6	7	8	9	10		11													3
1	2	3	4	5	6	7	8	9*	10	12	11													4
1	2	3	4	5	6	7	8		10	9	11													5
1	2	3	4	5	6	7	8		10	9	11*	12												6
1	2	3	4	5	6	7	8		10	9	11													7
1	2	3	4	5	6	7	8		10	9	11													8
1	2	3	4	5	6	7	8		10	9	11													9
1	2		4	5	6	7	8		10	9	11	3												10
1	2	3	4	5	6	7	8		10	9	11													11
1	2	3	4	5	6	7	8		10	9	11													12
1	2	3	4	5	6	7	8		10	9*	11			12										13
1	2	3	4	5	6	7	8		10	9	11													14
1	2	3	4	5	6	7	8		10	9	11													15
1	2	3	4	5	6	7	8		10	9	11*				12									16
1	2	3	4	5	6	7	8		10	9					11									17
1	2	3	4	5	6	7	8		10	9					11									18
1	2	3	7	5	6		8	9	10		11				4									19
1	2	3	7	5	6		8	9	10		11*				4	12								20
1	2	3	11	5	6	7	8	9	10						4									21
1	2	3	11	5	6	7	8	9	10						4									22
1	2	3	11	5	6	7	8	9	10						4									23
1	2	3	11	5	6	7	8	9	10						4									24
1	2	3*	4	5		7	12	11	10	9			8	6										25
1	2	3	4	5	6	7		11	10	9			8											26
1	2	3*	4	5	6	7	12		10	9	11		8											27
1	2		4	5	6	7	8		10	9	11	3												28
1	2		4	5	6	7	8		10	9	11	3												29
1	2		4	5	6	7	8		10	9	11	3												30
1	2		4	5	6	7	8		10	9	11	3												31
1	7	2	4	5	6		8		10	9	11	3												32
1	7	2	4	5	6		8		10	9	11	3												33
1	8*	3	4	5	6	7	9		10	12	11	2												34
1	2	3	4	5	6	7	8		10	9	11													35
1	8	3	4	5	6	7			10	9	11	2												36
1	2	3	10	5	6		8		9		11	4			7									37
1	2	3	11	5	6	7	8		10	9		4												38
	2	3*	10	5	6	7	8		9	12	11	4							1					39
	2		10	5	6				9	8	11	3		4			1	7						40
	2		4	5	6	7	8		10	9	11						1			3				41
	2		4	5	6	7	8		10	9	11													42
39	**42**	**35**	**42**	**42**	**41**	**36**	**37**	**11**	**42**	**29**	**31**	**13**	**5**	**2**	**9**	**1**	**2**	**1**	**1**	**1**				
								2		3	1	1		1	1		1							
1		19			2	2		5	25	7	4													

1 own-goal

Ferguson	Bonds	Charles	Peters	Stephenson	Moore	Redknapp	Boyce	Dear	Hurst	Brooking	Sissons	Cross	Howe	Lindsay	Hartley	Cushley	Miller	Bennett	Grotier	Holland	Death	Lampard	Heffer	#
1	2	3	11	5	6	7	8		9				10		4									3
1	3		4	5	6	7	11	10	9				8						2					4
1	2		4	5	6	7	12	10	9	11		3	8*					1						5
3	**3**	**1**	**3**	**3**	**3**	**3**	**2**		**3**	**2**	**1**		**1**	**3**		**1**			**1**					
								1																
		3					2																	

Ferguson	Bonds	Charles	Peters	Stephenson	Moore	Redknapp	Boyce	Dear	Hurst	Brooking	Sissons	Cross	Howe	Lindsay	Hartley	Cushley	Miller	Bennett	Grotier	Holland	Death	Lampard	Heffer	#
1	2	3	4	5	6	7	8		10	9	11													2
1	2	3	4	5	6	7	8		10	9	11													3
1		3	4		6	7	8	11	10	9		2		5										R
3	**2**	**3**	**3**	**2**	**3**	**3**	**3**	**1**	**3**	**3**	**2**	**1**		**1**										
		2			1			4	1	1														

1969-70

Manager: Ron Greenwood

1	Aug	9	(h)	Newcastle U	W	1-0	Hurst	33,323
2		11	(h)	Chelsea	W	2-0	Hurst, Peters	39,003
3		16	(a)	Stoke C	L	1-2	Lindsay	23,361
4		20	(a)	Chelsea	D	0-0		43,347
5		23	(h)	West Brom A	L	1-3	Peters	32,867
6		25	(h)	Arsenal	D	1-1	Cross	39,590
7		30	(a)	Nottingham F	L	0-1		29,097
8	Sep	6	(h)	Tottenham H	L	0-1		40,561
9		13	(a)	Everton	L	0-2		49,052
10		20	(h)	Sheffield W	W	3-0	Hurst, Redknapp, Opp own-goal	23,487
11		27	(a)	Manchester U	L	2-5	Hurst 2	58,579
12	Oct	4	(h)	Burnley	W	3-1	Best 2, Brooking	26,445
13		6	(h)	Stoke C	D	3-3	Best, Brooking, Sissons	26,860
14		11	(a)	Coventry C	D	2-2	Brooking, Sissons	34,277
15		18	(a)	Wolves	L	0-1		28,762
16		25	(h)	Sunderland	D	1-1	Peters	29,171
17	Nov	1	(a)	Southampton	D	1-1	Brooking	26,894
18		8	(h)	Crystal P	W	2-1	Best, Hurst	31,515
19		15	(a)	Liverpool	L	0-2		39,668
20		22	(h)	Derby C	W	3-0	Hurst 2, Peters	32,485
21		29	(a)	Ipswich T	L	0-1		17,456
22	Dec	6	(h)	Manchester C	L	0-4		27,491
23		13	(h)	Everton	L	0-1		26,689
24		17	(a)	Leeds U	L	1-4	Hurst	30,659
25		20	(a)	Tottenham H	W	2-0	Hurst, Peters	23,375
26		26	(a)	West Brom A	L	1-3	Peters	32,867
27		27	(h)	Nottingham F	D	1-1	Bonds	31,829
28	Jan	10	(a)	Sheffield W	W	3-2	Peters 2, Hurst	28,135
29		17	(h)	Manchester U	D	0-0		41,643
30		31	(a)	Burnley	L	2-3	Eustace, Lindsay	14,454
31	Feb	11	(h)	Coventry C	L	1-2	Hurst	22,723
32		21	(a)	Sunderland	W	1-0	Hurst	16,900
33		28	(h)	Southampton	D	0-0		27,088
34	Mar	2	(a)	Newcastle U	L	1-4	Eustace	27,500
35		7	(a)	Derby C	L	0-3		35,615
36		14	(h)	Ipswich T	D	0-0		20,934
37		21	(a)	Manchester C	W	5-1	Hurst 2, Greaves 2, Boyce	28,353
38		24	(a)	Crystal P	D	0-0		34,801
39		28	(h)	Liverpool	W	1-0	Holland	38,239
40		31	(h)	Wolves	W	3-0	Greaves, Bonds, Howe	26,386
41	Apr	2	(h)	Leeds U	D	2-2	Best, Bonds	26,140
42		4	(a)	Arsenal	L	1-2	Greaves	36,218

P	W	D	L	F	A	W	D	L	F	A	Pts	Pos	Div	
42	8	8	5	28	21	4	4	13	23	39	36	17th	1	Appearances
														Sub Appearances
														Goals

FA Cup

3	Jan	3	(a)	Middlesbrough	L	1-2	Stephenson	31,295

Appearances
Sub Appearances
Goals

League Cup

2	Sep	3	(h)	Halifax T	W	4-2	Hurst 2, Best, Lampard	20,717
3		23	(a)	Nottingham F	L	0-1		20,939

Appearances
Sub Appearances
Goals

Appearance / line-up grid (shirt numbers per match). Columns left-to-right: Ferguson, Bonds, Charles, Peters, Stephenson, Moore, Redknapp, Boyce, Bennett, Hurst, Sissons, Lindsay, Lampard, Cross, Howe, Best, Brooking, Miller, Holland, Eustace, Heffer, Grotier, Cushley, Llewellyn, Greaves.

Fe	Bo	Ch	Pe	St	Mo	Re	By	Be	Hu	Si	Li	La	Cr	Ho	Bs	Br	Mi	Hl	Eu	He	Gr	Cu	Ll	Gv	#
1	2	3	4	5	6	7	8	9	10	11															1
1	2	3	4	5		7	6		9	10	11	8													2
1	2	3	4	5		7	6		9	10	11	8													3
1	2		4	5			6	9	10	11		8	3	7											4
1	2	3	4	5	6		8	9	10	11		7													5
1	2		4	5	6		8		10		3*	11	12	7	9										6
1	2		4	5	6		8		10		3	11*		7	9	12									7
1	2		8	5	6		12		10	11	3		4	7*	9										8
1	2		4	5	6		8		10		3	11		7	9										9
1	2	11		5	6	7	4	9			3	10		8											10
1	2	11		5	6	7			10	8	3		4	9											11
1	2			5	6	7			10*	12	8	3	4	11	9										12
1	2			5		7	6		10	8	3*	12	4	11	9										13
1	2			5	6	7			10	8	3		4	11	9										14
1	2			5	6	7	12		10	8	3		4*	11	9										15
1	2	8		5	6	7			10		3		4	11	9										16
1	2	8		5	6				10	11	3		4	7	9										17
1	2	8		5	6	7			10		3		4	11	9										18
1	2	8		5	6	7			10		3		4	11	9										19
1	2	8		5	6	7			10		3		4	11	9										20
1	2	8		5	6				10		3		4	11	9										21
1	2	8		5*	6		9		10	7	3		4	11	12										22
1	2			5		7	6	8	10	11	3		4		9										23
1	2	8		5		7	6		10	11	3		4		9										24
1	2	11		5		7	6	9	8	10	3		4												25
1	2	8		5		7	6	12	9		3		4	11	10*										26
1	2		4	5	6		8		9		3	11						7	10						27
1	2		4	5	6		8		9		3	11						7	10						28
1	2		4	5	6		8		9		3	11						7*	10	12					29
	2		4	5	6		8		10		3	11	7					9			1				30
	2		4	5	6	7	8		9	11	3							10			1				31
	2		4	5	6	7	8		9	11	3							10			1				32
	2		4	5	6	7	8		9	11	3							10			1				33
	2	8		5	6				9		3	11	7					10			1				34
	2	8		5	6		12		9		3	11	7*					10			1	4			35
	2		4	5	6				9		3	11				7	8*		1			12	10		36
	2		4*	5	6	8			9		3	11				7		1				12	10		37
	2		4	5	6		9				3	11				7	8	1				10			38
	2		4	5	6		9				3	11				7	8	1				10			39
	2	3		5		7			11	8				9		6		4			1	10			40
	2		4	5	6		9	11			3					7	8	1				10			41
30	42	5	31	34	40	23	18	11	38	19	17	30	5	32	24	20	1	8	14		12	2		6	42
			2			1	1	1				1		1	1			1	1				2		
3		7			1	1			16	2	2		1	1	5	4		1	2					4	

1 own-goal

Fe	Bo	Ch	Pe	St	Mo	Re	By	Be	Hu	Si	Li	La	Cr	Ho	Bs	Br	Mi	Hl	Eu	He	Gr	Cu	Ll	Gv	#
1	2		8	5	6	12	7		10	11		3		4	9*										
1	1		1	1	1	1		1	1		1	1		1	1										3
			1			1																			

Fe	Bo	Ch	Pe	St	Mo	Re	By	Be	Hu	Si	Li	La	Cr	Ho	Bs	Br	Mi	Hl	Eu	He	Gr	Cu	Ll	Gv	#
1	2		4	5	6	7			10		8	3		11	9										2
1	2	11		5	6	7	4		9		3	10			8										3
2	2		2	2	2	2	1		2		1	2	1		1	2									
			2			1						1													

309

1970-71

Manager: Ron Greenwood

#					Result	Scorers	Att
1	Aug	15	(a)	Tottenham H	D 2-2	Bennett, Greaves	53,640
2		17	(h)	Arsenal	D 0-0		39,004
3		22	(h)	Chelsea	D 2-2	Howe, Hurst	39,240
4		26	(a)	Leeds U	L 0-3		42,677
5		29	(a)	Manchester U	D 1-1	Hurst	50,643
6		31	(h)	Southampton	D 1-1	Hurst	26,213
7	Sep	5	(h)	Everton	L 1-2	Moore	29,171
8		12	(a)	West Brom A	L 1-2	Howe	24,913
9		19	(h)	Newcastle U	L 0-2		25,841
10		26	(a)	Huddersfield T	D 1-1	Hurst	20,887
11	Oct	3	(h)	Burnley	W 3-1	Hurst 3	23,295
12		10	(a)	Stoke C	L 1-2	Greaves	23,035
13		17	(h)	Tottenham H	D 2-2	Eustace, Hurst	42,322
14		24	(a)	Crystal P	D 1-1	Howe	41,486
15		31	(h)	Blackpool	W 2-1	Greaves, Eustace	26,239
16	Nov	7	(a)	Ipswich T	L 1-2	Hurst	22,990
17		14	(a)	Wolves	D 3-3	Best 2, Moore	23,978
18		21	(a)	Manchester C	L 0-2		28,485
19		28	(h)	Coventry C	L 1-2	Best	22,800
20	Dec	5	(a)	Derby C	W 4-2	Best 2, Greaves, Brooking	30,806
21		12	(h)	Liverpool	L 1-2	Greaves	27,459
22		19	(a)	Chelsea	L 1-2	Lampard	42,075
23	Jan	9	(a)	Arsenal	L 0-2		49,007
24		16	(h)	Leeds U	L 2-3	Brooking, Eustace	34,396
25	Feb	6	(h)	Derby C	L 1-4	Eustace	26,606
26		9	(a)	Coventry C	W 1-0	Greaves	25,083
27		16	(a)	Liverpool	L 0-1		38,032
28		20	(h)	Manchester C	D 0-0		30,168
29		24	(h)	Nottingham F	W 2-0	Hurst, Robson	35,601
30		27	(a)	Blackpool	D 1-1	Hurst	15,639
31	Mar	6	(h)	Crystal P	D 0-0		26,157
32		13	(a)	Wolves	L 0-2		25,066
33		20	(h)	Ipswich T	D 2-2	Greaves 2	25,957
34		30	(a)	Everton	W 1-0	Opp own-goal	28,794
35	Apr	3	(h)	Manchester U	W 2-1	Hurst, Robson	38,507
36		9	(h)	West Brom A	W 2-1	Greaves, Robson	34,981
37		10	(a)	Nottingham F	L 0-1		23,032
38		13	(a)	Burnley	L 0-1		15,822
39		17	(h)	Stoke C	W 1-0	Hurst	26,269
40		24	(a)	Newcastle U	D 1-1	Hurst	22,720
41		27	(a)	Southampton	W 2-1	Taylor, Hurst	19,395
42	May	1	(h)	Huddersfield T	L 0-1		24,983

P	W	D	L	F	A	W	D	L	F	A	Pts	Pos	Div	
42	6	8	7	28	30	4	6	11	19	30	34	20th	1	Appearances
														Sub Appearances
														Goals

FA Cup

3	Jan	2	(a)	Blackpool	L 0-4		21,814
							Appearances
							Sub Appearances
							Goals

League Cup

2	Sep	9	(h)	Hull C	W 1-0	Eustace	19,116
3	Oct	6	(a)	Coventry C	L 1-3	Hurst	19,362
							Appearances
							Sub Appearances
							Goals

	Grotier	Bonds	Lampard	Bennett	Stephenson	Moore	Best	Brooking	Hurst	Greaves	Howe	Eustace	Redknapp	Boyce	Heffer	Ayris	Lindsay	Taylor	Dear	McDowell	Holland	Ferguson	Llewellyn	Robson	
	1	2	3	4	5	6	7	8	9	10	11														
	1	2	3	4	5	6	7	8	9	10	11														1
	1	2	3	4	5	6	7	8	9	10	11														2
	1	2	3	4	5	6	7	8	9	10	11														3
	1	2	3	4	5	6	7	8	9	10	11														4
	1	2	3	4*	5	6	7	8	9	10	11	12													5
	1	2	3		5	6	7*	8	9	10	11	4	12												6
	1	2	3	4	5	6	9	7		10	11	8													7
	1	2	3	4	5	6	11	12	9	10		8	7*												8
	1	2	3		5	6	7	8	9		11	10		4											9
	1	2	3			6	10	8	9		11	5		4*	12	7									10
	1	2	3		5	6	8	10	9		11	12	7*	4											11
	1	2	3			6	9	10						4		7	8	5	11						12
	1	2	3			6	9	10			7			4			8	5	11						13
	1		3			6	9	10						4*	12	7	8	5	11	2					14
	1		3			6	10	11			7			4*			8	5		2	12				15
	1		3			6	9	10			11			4		7	8	5		2					16
			3			6	11	10	9			12		4			8*	5		2	7	1			17
			3			6	9	10	11	8		4						5		2	7	1			18
		2	3			6	9	8	10	11		4					7	5				1			19
		2	3			6	9	8	10	11		4				12	7*	5				1			20
		2	3*			6	12	8		11		4				7	10	5	9			1			21
	1	4	3		9*	10		6	11	7							8	5		2		1	12		22
	1	4	3			10	9	6	11	7							8	5		2		1			23
	1	4	3	12		10	9	6*	11	7							8	5		2		1			24
		4	3			6	9	10*		11	7	8				12		5		2		1			25
		4	3			6	9	11		10	7	8						5		2		1			26
		4	3			6	9	11		10	7	8						5		2		1			27
		4	3			6	9	11		10*	7			12				5		2		1		8	28
		4	3			6	9	12		10*	7	8						5		2		1		11	29
		4	3			6	9	11			7	8						5		2		1		10	30
		4	3			6	9	12		11	7*	10						5		2		1		8	31
		4	3			6	12	9	11			8	7					5		2		1		10*	32
		4	3			6	9	11			7	8						5		2		1		10	33
		4	3			6	9	11			7	8						5		2		1		10	34
		4	3			6	12	9	11		7	8*						5		2		1		10	35
		4	3*	12		6	9	11			7					8		5		2		1		10	36
		4				6	11	9		3	8	7						5		2		1		10	37
		8	3	4	6		9				7							5		2		1		10	38
		8	3	4	6		9		11		7							5		2		1		10	39
		8	3	4	6		9		11									5		2		1	7	10	40
		8	3	4	6		9	11			7							5		2		1		10	41
		8	3	4	6		9	11			7							5		2		1		10	42
Apps	19	37	41	8	15	38	20	17	39	30	20	25	20	13	1	6	14	30	4	25	2	23	1	14	
Sub				1	1		2	2		2		1	2	1		2	1	2					1	1	
Gls		1	1				2	5	2	15	9	3	4					1						3	

1 own-goal

	Grotier	Bonds	Lampard	Bennett	Stephenson	Moore	Best	Brooking	Hurst	Greaves	Howe	Eustace	Redknapp	Boyce	Heffer	Ayris	Lindsay	Taylor	Dear	McDowell	Holland	Ferguson	Llewellyn	Robson	
		2	3			6	9			10	11	4				7*	8	5	12		1				
		1	1			1	1			1	1	1				1	1	1			1				3
																		1							

	Grotier	Bonds	Lampard	Bennett	Stephenson	Moore	Best	Brooking	Hurst	Greaves	Howe	Eustace	Redknapp	Boyce	Heffer	Ayris	Lindsay	Taylor	Dear	McDowell	Holland	Ferguson	Llewellyn	Robson	
	1	2	3		5	6	7		9	10	11	4	8												
	1	2	3		5	6	8	10	9		11					7	4								2
	2	2	2		2	2	2	1	2	1	2	1	1			1	1								3
									1																

1971-72

Manager: Ron Greenwood

1	Aug	14	(h)	West Brom A	L	0-1		27,420
2		18	(a)	Derby C	L	0-2		30,583
3		21	(a)	Nottingham F	L	0-1		17,185
4		23	(h)	Ipswich T	D	0-0		25,714
5		28	(h)	Everton	W	1-0	Best	26,878
6		30	(h)	Coventry C	W	4-0	Best 2, Hurst, Robson	28,176
7	Sep	4	(a)	Newcastle U	D	2-2	Hurst, Robson	31,910
8		11	(h)	Chelsea	W	2-1	Best 2	36,866
9		18	(a)	Manchester U	L	2-4	Best, Brooking	53,334
10		25	(h)	Stoke C	W	2-1	Best, Moore	29,193
11	Oct	2	(a)	Leeds U	D	0-0		30,942
12		9	(h)	Leicester C	D	1-1	Hurst	31,060
13		16	(a)	West Brom A	D	0-0		20,740
14		23	(h)	Wolves	W	1-0	Best	33,883
15		30	(a)	Crystal P	W	3-0	Best, Bonds, Coker	41,540
16	Nov	6	(h)	Sheffield U	L	1-2	Robson	36,595
17		13	(a)	Huddersfield T	L	0-1		14,177
18		20	(h)	Manchester C	L	0-2		33,694
19		27	(a)	Liverpool	L	0-1		43,399
20	Dec	4	(h)	Arsenal	D	0-0		35,155
21		11	(a)	Southampton	D	3-3	Best, Bonds, Brooking	20,506
22		18	(h)	Newcastle U	L	0-1		21,991
23		27	(a)	Tottenham H	W	1-0	Best	53,888
24	Jan	1	(h)	Manchester U	W	3-0	Best, Hurst, Robson	41,892
25		8	(a)	Everton	L	1-2	Hurst	38,482
26		22	(h)	Derby C	D	3-3	Brooking, Lampard, Robson	31,045
27		29	(a)	Ipswich T	L	0-1		22,766
28	Feb	12	(a)	Wolves	L	0-1		26,852
29		19	(h)	Crystal P	D	1-1	Best	28,209
30		29	(a)	Sheffield U	L	0-3		24,034
31	Mar	4	(h)	Huddersfield T	W	3-0	Best 2, Robson	18,521
32		11	(a)	Leicester C	L	0-2		23,345
33		18	(h)	Nottingham F	W	4-2	Robson 2, Brooking, Hurst	20,960
34		21	(a)	Coventry C	D	1-1	Best	18,640
35		25	(a)	Chelsea	L	1-3	Best	45,137
36		31	(h)	Leeds U	D	2-2	Bonds, Hurst	41,003
37	Apr	1	(h)	Tottenham H	W	2-0	Brooking, Coker	30,763
38		4	(a)	Stoke C	D	0-0		24,688
39		8	(a)	Manchester C	L	1-3	Hurst	38,491
40		15	(h)	Liverpool	L	0-2		32,660
41		22	(a)	Arsenal	L	1-2	Brooking	42,251
42	May	1	(h)	Southampton	W	1-0	Robson	18,479

P	W	D	L	F	A	W	D	L	F	A	Pts	Pos	Div		Appearances
42	10	6	5	31	19	2	6	13	16	32	36	14th	1		Sub Appearances
															Goals

FA Cup

3	Jan	15	(h)	Luton T	W	2-1	Hurst, Best	32,099
4	Feb	9	(a)	Hereford U	D	0-0		15,000
R		14	(h)	Hereford U	W	3-1	Hurst 3	42,271
5		26	(a)	Huddersfield T	L	2-4	Robson, Best	27,080

Appearances
Sub Appearances
Goals

League Cup

2	Sep	8	(h)	Cardiff C	D	1-1	Bonds	24,432
R		22	(a)	Cardiff C	W	2-1	Hurst 2	30,100
3	Oct	6	(h)	Leeds U	D	0-0		35,890
R		20	(a)	Leeds U	W	1-0	Best	26,504
4		27	(h)	Liverpool	W	2-1	Hurst, Robson	40,878
5	Nov	17	(h)	Sheffield U	W	5-0	Robson 3, Best 2	36,834
SF	Dec	8	(a)	Stoke C	W	2-1	Hurst, Best	36,400
		15	(h)	Stoke C	L	0-1		38,771
R	Jan	5	(n*)	Stoke C	D	0-0		46,916
2R		26	(n†)	Stoke C	L	2-3	Bonds, Brooking	49,247

*Played at Hillsborough, Sheffield.   †Played at Old Trafford, Manchester.

Appearances
Sub Appearances
Goals

Ferguson	McDowell	Lampard	Bonds	Stephenson	Moore	Ayris	Best	Hurst	Taylor	Robson	Howe	Brooking	Redknapp	Durrell	Coker	Eustace	Llewellyn	Grotier	Heffer	Lock	Holland	Charles	Boyce	No.
1	2	3	4	5	6	7	8	9	10	11														1
1	2	3	4	5	6	7*	8	9	10	11	12													2
1	2	3	4		6	7		9	5	8	11	10												3
1	2	3	4		6	7*	8	9	5	11	12	10												4
1	2	3	4		6	7	8	9	5	11		10												5
1	2	3	4		6	7	8	9	5	11		10												6
1	2	3	4		6	7	8	9	5	11		10												7
1	2	3	4		6	7*	8	9	5	11	12	10												8
1	2	3	4		6		8	9	5	11		10	7											9
1	2	3	4		6		8	9	5	11		10	7											10
1	2	3	4		6		8	9	5	11		10	7											11
1	2	3	4		6		8	9	5	11		10	7											12
1	2	3	4		6		8	9	5	11	12	10*	7											13
	2	3	4		6		8		5	11		10	7		9			1						14
1	2*	3	4		6	12	8	9	5	11		10	7											15
1	2	3	4		6		8		5	11		10	7		9									16
1		3	2		6		8		5	11		10	7	12	9*	4								17
1	2	3	4		6		8	9	5	11		10	7											18
1	2	3	4		6		8	9	5	11		10	7											19
1	2	3	4		6		8	9	5	11		10*	7				12							20
1	2	3	4		6	7	8	9	5	11		10												21
1	2	3	4		6		8	9	5	11		10	7											22
1	2	3	4		6		8	9	5	11		10	7											23
1	2	3	4		6		8	9	5	11		10	7											24
1	2	3	4		6		8	9	5	11		10	7											25
	2	3	4		6		8	9	5	11		10	7					1						26
1	2	3*	4	12	6	7	8	9	5	11		10												27
1	2*	3	4		6		8	9	5	11		10	7				12							28
1	2	3	4		6		8		5	11		10			7	9*	12							29
1	2	3	4		6		8	9	5	11		10	7											30
1	2	3	4		6		8	9	5	11		10	7											31
1	2	3	4		6		8	9	5	11		10												32
1	2		4		6		8	9	5	11		10								7				33
1	2	3	4		6		8	9	5	11		10								7	3			34
1	2	3	4		6		8	9	5	11		10								7				35
	2	3	4		6	7*	8		5	11		10					9	1		12	3			36
	2	3	4		6				5	11		10	7				9	1						37
	2	3	4		6		8	9	5	11		10	7					1						38
1	2	3	4		6		8	9	5	11		10	7											39
1	2		4				8		5	11		10	7	9						6		3		40
1	2		4				8			11		10*	7								9	3	12	41
1			2				8		6	11		10*	7								9	3	12	42
36	40	39	42	3	40	11	42	34	42	42	1	40	22	5	5	2	1	6		1	4	4		
		1		1									4	1		1	1		1	2		1		
		1	3		1		17	8		9		6			2									

Ferguson	McDowell	Lampard	Bonds	Stephenson	Moore	Ayris	Best	Hurst	Taylor	Robson	Howe	Brooking	Redknapp	Durrell	Coker	Eustace	Llewellyn	Grotier	Heffer	Lock	Holland	Charles	Boyce	No.
1	2	3	4		6*		8	9	5	11		10	7	12										3
1	2	3	4		6		8	9	5	11		10	7											4
1	2	3	4		6		8	9	5	11		10	7											R
1	2	3	4		6		8	9*	5	11		10	7				12							5
4	4	4	4		4		4	4	4	4		4	4											
															1		1							
					2		4			1														

Ferguson	McDowell	Lampard	Bonds	Stephenson	Moore	Ayris	Best	Hurst	Taylor	Robson	Howe	Brooking	Redknapp	Durrell	Coker	Eustace	Llewellyn	Grotier	Heffer	Lock	Holland	Charles	Boyce	No.
1	2	3	4		6	7	8	9	5	11		10												2
1	2	3	4		6		8	9	5	11		10	7											R
1	2	3	4		6		8	9	5	11		10	7											3
1	2	3	4		6		8	9	5	11		10	7											R
1	2	3	4		6		8	9*	5	11	12	10	7											4
1	2	3	4		6		8	9*	5	11	12	10	7											5
1	2	3	4		6		8	9	5	11		10	7											SF
1	2	3	4		6		8	9	5	11		10	7											
1	2	3	4		6		8	9	5	11		10	7											R
1	2	3	4		6		8	9	5	11		10	7*		12									2R
10	10	10	10		10	1	10	10	10	10		10	9											
											2													
			2				4	4		4					1									

313

1972-73

Manager: Ron Greenwood

1	Aug	12	(a)	West Brom A	D 0-0		21,509
2		14	(h)	Coventry C	W 1-0	Best	27,498
3		19	(h)	Leicester C	W 5-2	Robson 2, Coker, Moore, Tyler	25,490
4		22	(a)	Wolves	L 0-3		21,958
5		26	(a)	Liverpool	L 2-3	Robson 2	50,491
6		29	(a)	Arsenal	L 0-1		43,802
7	Sep	2	(h)	Manchester U	D 2-2	Robson 2	31,939
8		9	(a)	Chelsea	W 3-1	Bonds, Moore, Taylor	34,392
9		16	(h)	Norwich C	W 4-0	Robson 2, Brooking, Taylor	27,780
10		23	(a)	Tottenham H	L 0-1		51,700
11		30	(h)	Birmingham C	W 2-0	Bonds, Best	26,482
12	Oct	7	(a)	Ipswich T	D 1-1	Best	22,377
13		14	(h)	Sheffield U	W 3-1	Robson 2, Brooking	25,379
14		21	(a)	Manchester C	L 3-4	Ayris, Best, Moore	30,890
15		28	(h)	Crystal P	W 4-0	Brooking 2, McDowell, Robson	28,894
16	Nov	4	(h)	Wolves	D 2-2	Brooking, Robson	29,524
17		11	(a)	Coventry C	L 1-3	McDowell	27,189
18		18	(h)	Derby C	L 1-2	Robson	28,154
19		25	(a)	Everton	W 2-1	Best, Brooking	27,558
20	Dec	2	(h)	Newcastle U	D 1-1	Brooking	23,785
21		9	(a)	Leeds U	L 0-1		30,270
22		16	(h)	Stoke C	W 3-2	Robson 2, Best	23,269
23		23	(a)	Southampton	D 0-0		19,429
24		26	(h)	Tottenham H	D 2-2	Robson 2	37,397
25		30	(a)	Leicester C	L 1-2	Brooking	19,341
26	Jan	6	(h)	Liverpool	L 0-1		34,480
27		20	(a)	Manchester U	D 2-2	Best, Robson	50,878
28		27	(h)	Chelsea	W 3-1	Robson 2, Taylor	35,336
29	Feb	10	(a)	Norwich C	W 1-0	Robson	32,597
30		17	(h)	West Brom A	W 2-1	Bonds, Robson	26,079
31		24	(a)	Stoke C	L 0-2		21,885
32	Mar	2	(h)	Ipswich T	L 0-1		37,004
33		10	(a)	Sheffield U	D 0-0		24,024
34		17	(h)	Manchester C	W 2-1	Macdougall, Robson	30,156
35		24	(a)	Crystal P	W 3-1	Brooking, Macdougall, Robson	36,915
36		31	(h)	Everton	W 2-0	Lock, Robson	25,531
37	Apr	7	(a)	Newcastle U	W 2-1	Macdougall 2	24,030
38		14	(h)	Leeds U	D 1-1	Holland	38,804
39		20	(h)	Southampton	W 4-3	Robson 3, Brooking	33,039
40		21	(a)	Derby C	D 1-1	Lutton	28,727
41		23	(a)	Birmingham C	D 0-0		36,942
42		28	(h)	Arsenal	L 1-2	Brooking	37,366

P	W	D	L	F	A	W	D	L	F	A	Pts	Pos	Div	
42	12	5	4	45	25	5	5	7	9	22	28	46	6th	1	Appearances
															Sub Appearances
															Goals

FA Cup

3	Jan	13	(a)	Port Vale	W 1-0	Holland	20,619
4	Feb	3	(a)	Hull C	L 0-1		32,290

Appearances
Sub Appearances
Goals

League Cup

2	Sep	6	(h)	Bristol C	W 2-1	McDowell, Best	17,688
3	Oct	4	(a)	Stockport C	L 1-2	Best	13,410

Appearances
Sub Appearances
Goals

Appearance and scoring grid (shirt numbers by player and match). Columns left-to-right: Ferguson, McDowell, Lampard, Bonds, Taylor, Moore, Tyler, Best, Coker, Brooking, Robson, Holland, Grotier, Lock, Charles, Ayris, Boyce, Lutton, Macdougall. Rows numbered 1–42 (match number at right).

#	Ferguson	McDowell	Lampard	Bonds	Taylor	Moore	Tyler	Best	Coker	Brooking	Robson	Holland	Grotier	Lock	Charles	Ayris	Boyce	Lutton	Macdougall
1	1	2	3	4	5	6	7	8	9	10	11								
2	1	2	3	4	5	6	7	8	9	10	11								
3	1	2	3	4	5	6	7	8	9	10	11								
4	1	2	3	4	5	6	7	8		10	11	9							
5		2	3	4	5	6	7	8		10	11*	9	1	12					
6		2	3	4	5	6	7	8		10	11	9	1						
7		2	3	4	5	6	7	8		10	11	9	1						
8		2	3	4	5	6	7	8		10	11	9	1						
9		2*	3	4	5	6	7	8		10	11	9	1	12					
10			3	4	5	6	7	8		10	11	9	1		2				
11		2		4	5	6	7	8		10	11	9	1		3				
12		2	3	4	5	6	7	8		10	11	9	1						
13		2	3	4	5	6		8		10	11	9	1			7			
14	1	2	3		5	6		8		10	11	9		4		7			
15	1	2	3		5	6	7*	8		10	11	9		4		12			
16	1	2	3	4	5	6	7	8		10	11	9							
17	1		3	4	5	6	7	12		10	11	9			2	8*			
18	1	2	3*	4	5	6	7	8		10	11	9		12					
19	1	2		4	5	6		8		10	11	9			3	7			
20	1	2		4	5	6		8		10	11	9			3	7*	12		
21	1	2	3	4	5	6		8		10	11	9				7			
22	1	2*	3	4	5	6		8		10	11	9		12		7			
23	1	2	3	4	5	6		8		10	11	9				7			
24	1	2	3	4	5	6		8		10*	11	9		12		7			
25	1	2	3		5	6	10	8			11	9		4*	12	7			
26	1	2		4	5	6	10	8			11	9			3	7			
27	1	2	3	4	5	6	7	8		10	11	9							
28	1	2	3	4	5	6		8		10	11					7	9		
29	1	2	3	4	5	6		8		10	11	9				7			
30	1	2	3	4	5	6		8		10	11	9		12		7*			
31	1	2	3	4	5	6		8		10	11	9							
32	1	2	3	4	5	6	7			10	11							8	9
33	1	2	3*	4	5	6	7			10	11				12			8	9
34	1	2		4	5	6	7			10	11				3			8	9
35	1	2	3	4*	5	6		8		10	11				12	7			9
36	1	2	3	4	5	6	7			10	11							8	9
37	1*	2	3	4		6	7			10	11	8		5				12	9
38		2*	3	4		6	7			10	11	8	1	5				12	9
39			3	4		6	7			10	11		1	5	2	8			9
40	1	2	3	4		6	7			10	11			5		8			9
41	1	2	3	4		6	7			10	11			5		8			9
42	1	2	3	4		6	7*			10	11				12	8			9
Apps	31	38	38	39	37	42	21	41	4	40	42	30	11	14	7	13		4	10
Sub	1						1				2			4	2	2	2	2	
Goals		2		3	3	3	1	7	1	11	28	1		1		1		1	4

#	Ferguson	McDowell	Lampard	Bonds	Taylor	Moore	Tyler	Best	Coker	Brooking	Robson	Holland	Grotier	Lock	Charles	Ayris
3	1	2	3*	4	5	6	7	8		10	11	9			12	
4	1	2	3	4	5	6	7*	8		10	11	9	12			
	2	2	2	2	2	2	2	2		2	2	2				
													1	1		
								1								

#	McDowell	Lampard	Bonds	Taylor	Moore	Tyler	Best	Brooking	Robson	Holland	Grotier
2	2	3	4	5	6	7	8	10	11	9	1
3	2	3	4	5	6	7	8	10	11	9	1
	2	2	2	2	2	2	2	2	2	2	2
	1					2					

1973-74

Manager: Ron Greenwood

1	Aug	25	(h)	Newcastle U	L	1-2	Robson	28,169
2		27	(h)	Ipswich T	D	3-3	Best, Bonds, Brooking	23,335
3	Sep	1	(a)	Norwich C	D	2-2	Best, Robson	25,706
4		4	(a)	Queen's Park R	D	0-0		28,360
5		8	(h)	Tottenham H	L	0-1		30,888
6		10	(h)	Queen's Park R	L	2-3	Bonds, Robson	26,042
7		15	(a)	Manchester U	L	1-3	Bonds	44,757
8		22	(h)	Leicester C	D	1-1	Robson	23,567
9		29	(a)	Stoke C	L	0-2		16,395
10	Oct	6	(h)	Burnley	L	0-1		23,604
11		13	(a)	Everton	L	0-1		34,708
12		20	(a)	Coventry C	W	1-0	McDowell	21,097
13		27	(h)	Derby C	D	0-0		31,237
14	Nov	3	(a)	Leeds U	L	1-4	Macdougall	36,869
15		10	(h)	Sheffield U	D	2-2	Bonds, Brooking	21,243
16		17	(a)	Wolves	D	0-0		19,587
17		24	(h)	Arsenal	L	1-3	Bonds	28,287
18	Dec	1	(a)	Liverpool	L	0-1		34,857
19		8	(h)	Manchester C	W	2-1	Brooking, Opp own-goal	20,790
20		15	(a)	Birmingham C	L	1-3	Gould	23,787
21		22	(h)	Stoke C	L	0-2		16,513
22		26	(a)	Chelsea	W	4-2	Best 2, Gould, Lampard	26,982
23		29	(a)	Tottenham H	L	0-2		33,172
24	Jan	1	(h)	Norwich C	W	4-2	Paddon 2, Brooking, Gould	32,259
25		12	(h)	Manchester U	W	2-1	Bonds, Holland	34,147
26		19	(a)	Newcastle U	D	1-1	Holland	27,216
27	Feb	2	(h)	Birmingham C	D	0-0		27,948
28		5	(a)	Ipswich T	W	3-1	Best, McDowell, Opp own-goal	25,747
29		9	(a)	Leicester C	W	1-0	Best	27,032
30		16	(h)	Everton	W	4-3	Best 2, Bonds, Paddon	29,347
31		23	(a)	Burnley	D	1-1	Paddon	18,216
32	Mar	2	(h)	Chelsea	W	3-0	Bonds 3	34,043
33		9	(a)	Derby C	D	1-1	Bonds	24,684
34		16	(h)	Coventry C	L	2-3	Bonds 2	26,502
35		23	(a)	Sheffield U	L	0-1		19,467
36		30	(h)	Leeds U	W	3-1	Best, Brooking, Robson	38,416
37	Apr	6	(a)	Arsenal	D	0-0		37,868
38		12	(h)	Southampton	W	4-1	Best 2, Robson 2	34,163
39		13	(h)	Wolves	D	0-0		29,488
40		15	(a)	Southampton	D	1-1	Best	26,515
41		20	(a)	Manchester C	L	1-2	Gould	29,700
42		27	(h)	Liverpool	D	2-2	Brooking, Lampard	36,160

P	W	D	L	F	A	W	D	L	F	A	Pts	Pos	Div	
42	7	7	7	36	32	4	8	9	19	28	37	18th	1	Appearances
														Sub Appearances
														Goals

FA Cup

3	Jan	5	(h)	Hereford U	D	1-1	Holland	23,087
R		9	(a)	Hereford U	L	1-2	Best	17,423

Appearances
Sub Appearances
Goals

League Cup

2	Oct	8	(h)	Liverpool	D	2-2	MacDougall, Robson	25,840
R		29	(a)	Liverpool	L	0-1		26,002

Appearances
Sub Appearances
Goals

	Ferguson	Lampard	Charles	Bonds	Taylor	Moore	Best	Lutton	Macdougall	Brooking	Robson	Holland	Day	Lock	Ayris	McDowell	Tyler	Coker	Coleman	Gould	McGiven	Paddon	Wooler
1	1	2	3	4	5	6	7*	8	9	10	11	12											
2		2		4	5	6	7		9	10	11	8	1	3									
3	1	2		4	5	6	7		9	10	11	8		3									
4	1	2		4	5	6	7			10	11	8		3	9								
5	1	3		4	5	6	7		9*	10	11	12		8		2							
6	1	3		4	5	6		9		10	11			8		2	7						
7	1	3		4	5			12	9	10	11	8		6		2	7*						
8	1	3		4	5	6			9*	10	11			8		2	7	12					
9	1	3		4	5	6			9	10	11			8		2	7						
10		3		4		6		7*	9	10	11	8	1	12		5			2				
11		3		4	5	6	8		9	10	11		1		7				2				
12		3		4	5	6	9			10	11*		1	12		8	7		2				
13		3		4	5	6	9			10			1	11		8	7		2				
14		3		4	5	6	9		11	10			1			8	7		2				
15	1	3		4	5	6			11	10	9					8	7		2				
16		3		4	5	6	7		9	10	11		1			8			2				
17		3		4	5	6			9	10	11		1			8			2	7			
18		3		4		6			9	10		11	1			8			2	7	5		
19		3		4	5	6	11			10*			1		7	2			12	9		8	
20		3		4	5	6	11						1		7	2			10	9		8	
21		3			5		11					4	1		7*	2			10	9	6	8	12
22		3			5	6	11			10			1			4			2	9	7	8	
23		3		4	5	6	11					12	1			2			10*	9	7	8	
24		3		4	5	6	11			10*			1			2			12	9	7	8	
25		3		4	5		11	9				10	1						2		7	8	6
26		3		4	5		11	12		6		10	1						2	9*	7	8	
27		3		4	5		11			10		7	1			9			2		6	8	
28		3		4	5		11			10		7	1			9			2		6	8	
29		3		4	5		11			10		7	1			9			2		6	8	
30		3		4	5		11			10		7	1			9			2		6	8	
31		3		4	5		11			10		7	1			9			2		6	8	
32		3		4	5		11			10		7	1			9			2		6	8	
33		3		4	5		11			10		7	1			9			2		6	8	
34		3		4	5		11			10	9	7	1						2		6	8	
35		3		4	5		11			10	9	7	1						2		6	8	
36		3		4	5		11			10	9		1			7			2		6	8	
37		3		4	5		11			10	9		1			7			2		6	8	
38		3		4	5		11			10	9		1			7			2		6	8	
39		3		4	5		11			10	9		1			7			2		6	8	
40		3		4	5		11			10	9		1			7			2	12	6*	8	
41		3		4	5		11			10		6	1			7			2	9		8	
42		3		4	5		11			10		7	1			6			2	9		8	
	9	42	1	40	40	22	34	4	14	38	22	20	33	9	5	33	8		31	11	21	24	1
								2				3		2				1	2	1			1
		2		13			12		1	6	7	2				2				4		4	

2 own-goals

	Ferguson	Lampard	Charles	Bonds	Taylor	Moore	Best	Lutton	Macdougall	Brooking	Robson	Holland	Day	Lock	Ayris	McDowell	Tyler	Coker	Coleman	Gould	McGiven	Paddon	Wooler
3		3		4	5	6*	11					12	1			2		10		9	7	8	
R		3		4	5		11	9				10	1						2		7	8	6
		2		2	2	1	2	1				1	2			1		1	1	1	2	2	1
												1											
							1					1											

	Ferguson	Lampard	Charles	Bonds	Taylor	Moore	Best	Lutton	Macdougall	Brooking	Robson	Holland	Day	Lock	Ayris	McDowell	Tyler	Coker	Coleman	Gould	McGiven	Paddon	Wooler
2		3			5		8		9	10	11	12	1	6*	7	2			4				
R		3		4	5	6	9			10		12	1	11*		8	7		2				
		2		1	2	1	2		1	2	1		2	2	1	2	1		2				
												2											
									1		1												

1974-75

Manager: Ron Greenwood

					Result	Scorers	Attendance
1	Aug	17	(a)	Manchester C	L 0-4		30,240
2		19	(h)	Luton T	W 2-0	Bonds, Lampard	23,182
3		24	(h)	Everton	L 2-3	Bonds, McDowell	22,486
4		28	(a)	Luton T	D 0-0		16,931
5		31	(a)	Newcastle U	L 0-2		30,780
6	Sep	7	(h)	Sheffield U	L 1-2	Jennings	20,977
7		14	(a)	Tottenham H	L 1-2	Lampard	27,959
8		21	(h)	Leicester C	W 6-2	Gould 2, Jennings 2, Bonds, Robson	21,377
9		25	(h)	Birmingham C	W 3-0	Jennings, Paddon, Robson	25,495
10		28	(h)	Burnley	W 5-3	Robson 2, Bonds, Brooking, Jennings	17,613
11	Oct	5	(h)	Derby C	D 2-2	Bonds, Robson	32,938
12		12	(a)	Coventry C	D 1-1	Gould	22,519
13		15	(a)	Everton	D 1-1	Gould	31,855
14		19	(h)	Ipswich T	W 1-0	Jennings	33,543
15		26	(a)	Arsenal	L 0-3		41,004
16	Nov	2	(h)	Middlesbrough	W 3-0	Paddon, Robson, Opp own-goal	28,915
17		9	(a)	Carlisle U	W 1-0	Lampard	14,141
18		16	(h)	Wolves	W 5-2	Bonds, Brooking, Lampard, Gould, Jennings	31,708
19		23	(a)	Liverpool	D 1-1	Robson	46,346
20		30	(a)	Queen's Park R	W 2-0	Jennings, Paddon	28,357
21	Dec	7	(h)	Leeds U	W 2-1	Gould, Jennings	39,562
22		14	(a)	Manchester C	D 0-0		33,908
23		21	(a)	Chelsea	D 1-1	Gould	34,969
24		26	(h)	Tottenham H	D 1-1	Robson	37,682
25		28	(a)	Stoke C	L 1-2	Holland	33,493
26	Jan	11	(a)	Leeds U	L 1-2	Robson	40,099
27		18	(h)	Queen's Park R	D 2-2	Bonds, Jennings	28,772
28	Feb	1	(h)	Carlisle U	W 2-0	Holland, Jennings	26,805
29		8	(a)	Middlesbrough	D 0-0		29,179
30		19	(h)	Liverpool	D 0-0		40,256
31		22	(a)	Wolves	L 1-3	Gould	24,794
32		28	(h)	Newcastle U	L 0-1		32,753
33	Mar	15	(h)	Burnley	W 2-1	Robson, A.Taylor	28,830
34		18	(a)	Birmingham C	D 1-1	A.Taylor	34,000
35		22	(a)	Sheffield U	L 2-3	Gould, Jennings	25,527
36		28	(h)	Stoke C	D 2-2	Brooking, Jennings	29,811
37		29	(h)	Chelsea	L 0-1		31,025
38	Apr	1	(a)	Leicester C	L 0-3		30,408
39		12	(a)	Derby C	L 0-1		31,336
40		19	(h)	Coventry C	L 1-2	Holland	27,431
41		26	(a)	Ipswich T	L 1-4	Holland	31,592
42		28	(h)	Arsenal	W 1-0	Paddon	30,195

P	W	D	L	F	A	W	D	L	F	A	Pts	Pos	Div	
42	10	6	5	38	22	3	7	11	20	37	39	13th	1	Appearances
														Sub Appearances
														Goals

FA Cup

					Result	Scorers	Attendance
3	Jan	4	(a)	Southampton	W 2-1	Lampard, Gould	24,615
4		25	(h)	Swindon T	D 1-1	Jennings	35,679
R		28	(a)	Swindon T	W 2-1	Brooking, Holland	27,749
5	Feb	15	(h)	Queen's Park R	W 2-1	Holland, Robson	39,193
6		8	(a)	Arsenal	W 2-0	A.Taylor 2	56,742
SF	Apr	5	(n*)	Ipswich T	D 0-0		58,000
R		9	(n†)	Ipswich T	W 2-1	A.Taylor 2	45,344
F	May	3	(n‡)	Fulham	W 2-0	A.Taylor 2	100,000

* Played at Villa Park. † Played at Stamford Bridge. ‡ Played at Wembley.

Appearances
Sub Appearances
Goals

League Cup

					Result	Scorers	Attendance
2	Sep	11	(a)	Tranmere R	D 0-0		8,638
R		18	(h)	Tranmere R	W 6-0	Gould 3, Bonds 2, Ayris	15,854
3	Oct	3	(a)	Fulham	L 1-2	Brooking	29,611

Appearances
Sub Appearances
Goals

Appearance / team-selection grid (player numbers by match).

League

Day	Coleman	Lampard	Bonds	Taylor T	McDowell	Holland	Paddon	Gould	Brooking	Best	Lock	Ayris	Jennings	Robson	Taylor A	Curbishley	Wooler	No.
1	2*	3	4	5	6	7		8	9	10	11	12						1
1		3	4	5	2	7	8			10	11	6	9					2
1	2	3	4	5	10	7	8	9		11	6							3
1	2	3	4	5	10	7	8	9		11	6							4
1	2	3	4	5	10	7	8	9*		11	6	12						5
1		3	4	5	2	10	8			11	6	7	9					6
1		3	4	5	2	12	8	9	10		6		7*	11				7
1		3	4	5	2		8	9	10		6		7	11				8
1		3	4	5	2		8	9	10		6		7	11				9
1		3	4	5	2*	12	8	9	10		6		7	11				10
1	2	3	4	5			8	9	10		6		7	11				11
1	2	3	4	5			8	9	10		6		7	11				12
1	2	3	4	5			8	9	10		6		7	11				13
1	12	3	4	5	2*		8	9	10		6		7	11				14
1	2	3	4	5			8	9	10		6		7	11				15
1	2	3	4	5			8	9	10		6		7	11				16
1	2	3	4	5			8	9	10		6		7	11				17
1	2	3	4	5			8	9	10		6		7	11				18
1	2	3	4*	5		12	8	9	10		6		7	11				19
1	2	3	4	5	10		8	9			6		7*	11	12			20
1	2	3	4	5	12		8	9	10		6		7*	11				21
1	2	3	4*	5	7		8	9	10	12	6			11				22
1	2	3		5	4		8	9	10		6		7*	11	12			23
1	2	3		5	10	4	8	9		11	6	12	7*					24
1	2	3	4	5		7	8		10	9	6			11				25
1	2*	3	4	5	9		8		10	12	6		7	11				26
1		3	4	5	2	11	8	10*	12		6		7	9				27
1	12	3	4*	5	2	11	8	10	9		6		7					28
1		3	4	5	2	11	8	10			6		7	9				29
1	2*	3		5	4	11	8	12	10		6		7	9				30
1		3		5	2	11*	8	9	10		6		7	4	12			31
1		3	4*	5	2		8	12	10		6		7	11	9			32
1	2	3		5	4		8	7	10		6			11	9			33
1	2	3		5	4		8	11	10		6		7	9				34
1	2	3*		5	4		8	11	10		6	12	7	9				35
1	2			5	3		8	11	10		6	12	7*	9	4			36
1	2			5	3	4		11	10	7	6			9		8		37
1		3	4	5	2	12	8	11	10		6		7	9*				38
1	2	3		5	4		8*	11	10		6		7	9	12			39
1	2	3		5	4			11	10	8	6		7	9				40
1		3	4	5	2	11	8	12	10		6		7*	9				41
42	27	40	31	39	33	18	40	31	36	12	41	2	32	25	11	1	1	42
	2			1	4			3			3	1	4	3	1			
	4	7		1	4	4		9	3				13	10	2			

1 own-goal

FA Cup

Day	Coleman	Lampard	Bonds	Taylor T	McDowell	Holland	Paddon	Gould	Brooking	Best	Lock	Ayris	Jennings	Robson	Taylor A			Rd
1	2	3	4	5		12	8	9*	10		6		7	11				3
1		3	4	5	2	11	8		10	9	6		7					4
1		3	4	5	2	11	8		10	9	6		7					R
1		3	4	5	2	11	8		10		6		7	9				5
1		3	4	5	2		8		10		6		7	11	9			6
1		3	4	5	2	12	8	11*	10		6		7	9				SF
1		3	4	5	2	12	8	11	10		6		7*	9				R
1		3	4	5	2	11	8		10		6		7	9				F
8	1	8	8	7	8	4	8	3	8	2	8		8	3	4			
								3										
								2		1	1		1	1	6			

League Cup

Day	Coleman	Lampard	Bonds	Taylor T	McDowell	Holland	Paddon	Gould	Brooking	Best	Lock	Ayris	Jennings	Robson				Rd
1		3	4	5	2	9	8		10	11	6		7					2
1		3	4	5	2		8	9	10		6		7	11				R
1	2	3	4	5		12	8	9	10		6		7*	11				3
3	1	3	3	3	3	2	3	2	3	1	3		3	2				
		2				1			3	1			1					

319

1975-76

Manager: Ron Greenwood

1	Aug	16	(a)	Stoke C	W	2-1	Gould, A.Taylor	23,744
2		19	(a)	Liverpool	D	2-2	A.Taylor 2	40,564
3		23	(h)	Burnley	W	3-2	A.Taylor 2, Paddon	28,048
4		25	(h)	Tottenham H	W	1-0	Robson	36,567
5		30	(a)	Queen's Park R	D	1-1	Jennings	28,408
6	Sep	6	(h)	Manchester C	W	1-0	Lampard	29,752
7		13	(a)	Leicester C	D	3-3	Bonds, Holland, Lampard	21,413
8		20	(h)	Sheffield U	W	2-0	Best, T.Taylor	28,744
9		27	(a)	Wolves	W	1-0	Paddon	18,455
10	Oct	4	(h)	Everton	L	0-1		31,005
11		11	(h)	Newcastle U	W	2-1	Curbishley, A.Taylor	30,400
12		18	(a)	Middlesbrough	L	0-3		25,831
13		25	(h)	Manchester U	W	2-1	Gould, A.Taylor	38,528
14	Nov	1	(a)	Birmingham C	W	5-1	A.Taylor 2, Brooking, Lampard, Opp own-goal	28,474
15		8	(h)	Coventry C	D	1-1	Robson	29,501
16		15	(a)	Derby C	L	1-2	Brooking	31,172
17		22	(h)	Middlesbrough	W	2-1	Holland, Jennings	26,914
18		29	(h)	Arsenal	W	1-0	A.Taylor	31,012
19	Dec	6	(a)	Norwich C	L	0-1		27,020
20		13	(a)	Burnley	L	0-2		14,907
21		20	(h)	Stoke C	W	3-1	Jennings 3	21,135
22		26	(a)	Aston Villa	L	1-4	Jennings	51,300
23		27	(h)	Ipswich T	L	1-2	T.Taylor	32,741
24	Jan	10	(h)	Leicester C	D	1-1	A.Taylor	24,615
25		17	(a)	Manchester C	L	0-3		32,147
26		24	(h)	Queen's Park R	W	1-0	A.Taylor	26,677
27		31	(h)	Liverpool	L	0-4		26,741
28	Feb	7	(a)	Tottenham H	D	1-1	Brooking	32,832
29		14	(a)	Coventry C	L	0-2		16,173
30		21	(h)	Derby C	L	1-2	Brooking	24,941
31		23	(h)	Leeds U	D	1-1	A.Taylor	28,025
32		28	(a)	Manchester U	L	0-4		57,240
33	Mar	6	(h)	Birmingham C	L	1-2	Curbishley	19,868
34		9	(a)	Leeds U	D	1-1	Jennings	28,453
35		13	(a)	Newcastle U	L	1-2	Jennings	32,842
36		20	(a)	Arsenal	L	1-6	Jennings	34,011
37		27	(h)	Norwich C	L	0-1		20,628
38	Apr	3	(h)	Wolves	D	0-0		16,769
39		10	(a)	Sheffield U	L	2-3	Jennings 2	18,797
40		17	(h)	Aston Villa	D	2-2	Brooking, Robson	21,642
41		19	(a)	Ipswich T	L	0-4		28,217
42		24	(h)	Everton	L	0-2		26,101

P	W	D	L	F	A	W	D	L	F	A	Pts	Pos	Div	
42	10	5	6	26	23	3	5	13	22	48	36	18th	1	Appearances
														Sub Appearances
														Goals

FA Cup

3	Jan	3	(h)	Liverpool	L	0-2		32,363

Appearances
Sub Appearances
Goals

League Cup

2	Sep	9	(h)	Bristol C	D	0-0		19,837
R		24	(a)	Bristol C	W	3-1	Brooking, Best, A.Taylor	19,643
3	Oct	8	(h)	Darlington	W	3-0	Bonds, Paddon, Robson	19,844
4	Nov	12	(a)	Tottenham H	D	0-0		49,125
R		24	(h)	Tottenham H	L	0-2		38,443

Appearances
Sub Appearances
Goals

Day	McDowell	Lampard	Holland	Taylor T	Lock	Taylor A	Paddon	Gould	Brooking	Robson	Jennings	Ayris	Bonds	Best	Coleman	Curbishley	Orhan	McGiven	Wooler	Pike	Ferguson	
1	2	3	4	5	6	7	8	9	10	11												1
1	2	3	4	5	6	7	8	9*	10	11	12											2
1	2	3	4	5	6	7	8		10	11	9*	12										3
1	2	3	4	5	6	7	8		10	11	9											4
1	2	3	4	5	6	7	8		10	11	9											5
1	2	3	4	5	6	7*	8		10	11	9		12									6
1	2	3	7	5	6		8		10	11	9		4									7
1	2	3	11	5	6	7*	8		10		9		4	12								8
1	2	3	11	5	6	7	8		10				4	9								9
1	2	3	11	5	6	12	8		10	7			4	9*								10
1	2	3	11	5		7	8						4	9	6	10						11
1	2	3*	11	5		7	8		10				4	9	6	12						12
1	2	3	4	5		7	8	9	10	11					6							13
1	2	3	9	5		7	8		10	11			4		6							14
1	2		9	5	3	7	8	12	10	11		4*			6							15
1	2	3	9	5	4	7	8*		10	11					6							16
1	2		4	5	3	7	8		10	11	9				6							17
1	2	3	9	5	6	7	8			11	10				4							18
1	2	3	9	5	6	7	8		10	11					4							19
1		3	9	5	6	7	8		10		11	12			2	4*						20
1	4	3	9	5	6	7	8			11	10				2							21
1	4	3	9	5	6	7	8			11	10				2							22
1	3		4	5	6	7	8		9	11	10				2*	12						23
1	2	3	4	5	6	7		9		10			8			11						24
1	2	3	4	5	6	7*	8		10		9		12			11						25
1	2	3	4	5		7	8	9		10					6	11						26
1	2	3	4	5		7	8		10	12	9*				6	11						27
1		3	4	5		7	8		10	11	9				2		6					28
1	2	3	4	5		7	8		10	11	9						6					29
1	7	3	4	5			8		10	11	12		2			9*	6					30
1	2	3*		5	3	7*	8		10	11	12		4				6					31
1		3		5		7	8			11		4			2	9	10*	6	12			32
1		3		5		6	8			11	9	7*	4		2	10			12			33
1	12	3*		5		6	8			11	9	7	4		2	10						34
1		3		5	6	7			10	11	9		4		2*	8	12					35
1	10	3		5	6		7			11	9		4		2	8						36
1	4	3	7	5	6*		8		10	11	9	12			2							37
1	6	3	7	5			8		10	11*	9	12	4		2							38
	6	3	7	5	4*		8		10	11	9	12		2						1		39
1	3			5			8		10	11		7	2		4	9*	6		12			40
1	6	3	7	5				12	8	10	11*	9		2								41
1	6	3	7	5					8	10	11*	9		2								42
41	36	37	35	42	26	33	39	4	34	33	26	3	17	5	26	12	5	6	1	1		
	1			2	1		1	4	6	1	2		2		1		3					
	3	2	2	13	2	2	5	3	11	1	1		2									

1 own-goal

Day	McDowell	Lampard	Holland	Taylor T	Lock	Taylor A	Paddon	Gould	Brooking	Robson	Jennings	Ayris	Bonds	Best	Coleman	Curbishley	Orhan	McGiven	Wooler	Pike	Ferguson	
1		3	4		6	7	8		9		10			2	11		5					3
1		1	1		1	1	1		1		1			1	1		1					

Day	McDowell	Lampard	Holland	Taylor T	Lock	Taylor A	Paddon	Gould	Brooking	Robson	Jennings	Ayris	Bonds	Best	Coleman	Curbishley	Orhan	McGiven	Wooler	Pike	Ferguson	
1	2	3	7*	5	6		8		10	11	9	12	4									2
1	2	3	11	5	6	7	8		10				4	9								R
1	2	3	11	5	6*	10	8			7	12		4	9								3
1	2		9	5	3	7	8		10	11			4		6							4
1	2	3	9	5	6	7	8		10*	11	12		4									R
5	5	4	5	5	5	4	5		4	4	1		5	2	1							
											2	1										
			1	1		1	1		1	1			1	1								

321

1976-77

Manager: Ron Greenwood

1	Aug	21	(a)	Aston Villa	L	0-4		39,012
2		23	(h)	Queen's Park R	W	1-0	Paddon	31,668
3		28	(h)	Leicester C	D	0-0		24,960
4	Sep	4	(a)	Stoke C	L	1-2	A.Taylor	19,131
5		11	(h)	Arsenal	L	0-2		31,965
6		18	(a)	Bristol C	D	1-1	A.Taylor	28,932
7		25	(h)	Sunderland	D	1-1	Jennings	24,319
8	Oct	2	(a)	Manchester C	L	2-4	A.Taylor, Opp own-goal	37,795
9		6	(h)	Leeds U	L	1-3	Jennings	21,909
10		16	(h)	Ipswich T	L	0-2		24,534
11		23	(a)	Everton	L	2-3	Bonds, Opp own-goal	23,163
12		30	(a)	West Brom A	L	0-3		19,856
13	Nov	6	(h)	Tottenham H	W	5-3	B.Robson, Jennings, Bonds, Brooking, Curbishley	28,997
14		10	(a)	Norwich C	L	0-1		24,762
15		20	(h)	Newcastle U	L	1-2	B.Robson	21,324
16		27	(a)	Manchester U	W	2-0	Brooking, Jennings	55,366
17	Dec	4	(h)	Middlesbrough	L	0-1		20,184
18		18	(h)	Liverpool	W	2-0	Brooking, Jennings	24,175
19		27	(a)	Birmingham C	D	0-0		39,978
20	Jan	1	(a)	Tottenham H	L	1-2	Brooking	44,972
21		3	(h)	West Brom A	D	0-0		25,236
22		22	(h)	Aston Villa	L	0-1		27,577
23	Feb	5	(a)	Leicester C	L	0-2		16,201
24		12	(h)	Stoke C	W	1-0	B.Robson	20,160
25		19	(a)	Arsenal	W	3-2	A.Taylor 2, Jennings	38,221
26		26	(h)	Bristol C	W	2-0	Bonds, Jennings	29,713
27	Mar	5	(a)	Sunderland	L	0-6		35,357
28		12	(h)	Manchester C	W	1-0	B.Robson	24,974
29		22	(a)	Ipswich T	L	1-4	B.Robson	27,315
30	Apr	2	(h)	Everton	D	2-2	B.Robson 2	22,518
31		4	(a)	Queen's Park R	D	1-1	B.Robson	24,930
32		8	(h)	Birmingham C	D	2-2	Jennings, Pike	28,167
33		9	(a)	Coventry C	D	1-1	B.Robson	15,816
34		11	(h)	Norwich C	W	1-0	Pike	27,084
35		16	(a)	Newcastle U	L	0-3		30,967
36		20	(a)	Derby C	D	1-1	Pike	21,380
37		26	(a)	Leeds U	D	1-1	B.Robson	16,891
38		29	(a)	Middlesbrough	D	1-1	B.Robson	16,500
39	May	4	(h)	Coventry C	W	2-0	B.Robson, Pike	25,461
40		7	(h)	Derby C	D	2-2	Jennings, Pike	32,079
41		14	(a)	Liverpool	D	0-0		55,675
42		16	(h)	Manchester U	W	4-2	B.Robson 2, Lampard, Pike	29,311

P	W	D	L	F	A	W	D	L	F	A	Pts	Pos	Div	
42	9	6	6	28	23	2	8	11	18	42	36	17th	1	Appearances
														Sub Appearances
														Goals

FA Cup

3	Jan	4	(h)	Bolton W	W	2-1	Jennings, Pike	24,147
4		29	(a)	Aston Villa	L	0-3		46,954

Appearances
Sub Appearances
Goals

League Cup

2	Sep	1	(h)	Barnsley	W	3-0	Holland 2, Paddon	17,889
3		21	(a)	Charlton A	W	1-0	A.Taylor	32,898
4	Oct	27	(h)	Queen's Park R	L	0-2		24,565

Appearances
Sub Appearances
Goals

Day	Coleman	Lampard	Taylor T	Green	Bonds	Taylor A	Paddon	Holland	Brooking	Curbishley	McGiven	Jennings	Orhan	Lock	Ayris	Robson B	Robson K	Devonshire	Pike	Otulakowski	Radford	#
1	2	3	4	5	6	7	8	9	10	11												1
1	2	3	7	5	6	9	8	4	10	11												2
1	2		7	5	6	9	8	4	10		3	11										3
1	2	3	7*	5	6	9	8	11	10		4	12										4
1	2*	3	7	5	4	9	8	11	10		6		12									5
1	2	3*	6	5	4	9	8	11	10		12	7										6
1	2		6	5	4	9	8		10		11	7		3								7
1	2		6	5	4	9	8		10		11*	7		3	12							8
1	2		6	5	4	9	8		10			7		3				11				9
1	2		6	5	4	9*	8		10			7		3			12	11				10
1		3	6	5*	2		8		10	4		7		12		9		11				11
1		3	6		2		8		10	4	12	5				9		11*	7			12
1		3	6		2				10	4		9		5				11	7	8		13
1	12	3	6		2				10	4		9		5*				11	7	8		14
1		3	6*		2				10	4		9		5		12		11	7	8		15
1		3	5		6				10			9		2				11	7	8	4	16
1		3	5		6				10		12	9*		2				11	7	8	4	17
1		3	5	4	6				10			9		2				11	7	8		18
1		3	5	4	6				10			9		2				11	7	8		19
1		3	5	4	6				10			9		2				11	7	8		20
1		3	5	4	6				10		7	9		2				11	12	8*		21
1		3	5		2	7			10			9		6				11	4	8		22
1		3	5		2	7			10			9		6			12	11*	4	8		23
1		3	5		2	7			10			11		6		9			4	8		24
1		3	5		2	7			10			11		6		9			4	8		25
1		3	5		2				10			11		6		9			4	8		26
1		3	5*		2				10		12	11		6		9		8	7	4		27
1		3	5		2				10			11		6		8		9	7	4		28
1		3	5		2				10			11		6		8		9	4	7		29
1		3	5		2				10			11		6		8		9*	4	12	7	30
1		3	5		2			12	10			11		6		8		9*	4		7	31
1		3	5		2	7			10			11		6		8		9	4			32
1		3	5		2	11			10					6		8		9	4		7	33
1		3	5		2	11*			10		12			6		8		9	4		7	34
1		3	5		2*	11			10		12			6		8		9	4		7	35
1	2	3	5			11			10					6		8		9	4		7	36
1		3	5		2	11			10					6		8		9	7	4		37
1		3	5		2	11			10					6		8		9	4		7	38
1		3	5		2	11			10		12			6*		8		9	4		7	39
1		3	5		2	11			10					6		8		9	7	4		40
1		3	5		2	11			10					6		8		9	4		7	41
1		3	5		2	11			10					6		8		9	4		7	42
42	12	36	36	22	41	24	12	6	42	8	15	27	1	25	1	30	7	27	20	10	18	
	1				1						2	1	4	2	1	2		2	1		2	
	1			3	5	1		4	1	9			14			6						

2 own-goals

Day	Coleman	Lampard	Taylor T	Green	Bonds	Taylor A	Paddon	Holland	Brooking	Curbishley	McGiven	Jennings	Orhan	Lock	Ayris	Robson B	Robson K	Devonshire	Pike	Otulakowski	Radford	#
1		3	5	4	6				10	7		9		2		11				8		3
1		3	5	4	6	7			10			9		2		11			8			4
2		2	2	2	2	1			2	1		2		2		2			1	1		
														1					1			

Day	Coleman	Lampard	Taylor T	Green	Bonds	Taylor A	Paddon	Holland	Brooking	Curbishley	McGiven	Jennings	Orhan	Lock	Ayris	Robson B	Robson K	Devonshire	Pike	Otulakowski	Radford	#
1	2		7	5	6	9	8	4	10		3	11										2
1	2		6	5	4	9	8		10		3	7		11								3
1		3	6		2		8		10	4		7	5		11	9						4
3	2	1	3	2	3	2	3	1	3	1	2	2	1	2		1	1					
				1	1	2																

323

1977-78

Manager: John Lyall

1	Aug	20	(h)	Norwich C	L 1-3	Robson	28,178
2		24	(a)	Leicester C	L 0-1		18,310
3		27	(h)	Manchester C	L 0-1		25,278
4	Sep	3	(a)	Newcastle U	W 3-2	Jennings, A.Taylor, Robson	26,983
5		10	(h)	Queen's Park R	D 2-2	Holland, Lock	26,922
6		17	(a)	Bristol C	L 2-3	Pike, Robson	21,180
7		24	(h)	Everton	D 1-1	Opp own-goal	25,296
8	Oct	1	(a)	Arsenal	L 0-3		41,245
9		3	(h)	Middlesbrough	L 0-2		26,508
10		8	(h)	Nottingham F	D 0-0		26,128
11		15	(a)	Wolves	D 2-2	Pike, Robson	19,360
12		22	(h)	Aston Villa	D 2-2	Hales, T.Taylor	26,598
13		29	(a)	Ipswich T	W 2-0	Hales 2	27,308
14	Nov	5	(a)	Coventry C	L 0-1		23,276
15		12	(h)	West Brom A	D 3-3	Devonshire 2, Robson	23,601
16		19	(a)	Derby C	L 1-2	Bonds	23,273
17		26	(h)	Leeds U	L 0-1		26,883
18	Dec	3	(a)	Liverpool	L 0-2		39,659
19		10	(h)	Manchester U	W 2-1	Brooking, Hales	20,759
20		17	(a)	West Brom A	L 0-1		18,868
21		26	(h)	Birmingham C	W 1-0	Curbishley	25,577
22		27	(a)	Chelsea	L 1-2	Robson	44,093
23		31	(h)	Leicester C	W 3-2	Cross, Hales, McDowell	25,455
24	Jan	2	(a)	Norwich C	D 2-2	Devonshire, Hales	29,480
25		14	(a)	Manchester C	L 2-3	Brooking, Cross	43,627
26		21	(h)	Newcastle U	W 1-0	Hales	25,461
27	Feb	11	(h)	Bristol C	L 1-2	Robson	19,934
28		18	(a)	Everton	L 1-2	Hales	33,862
29		25	(h)	Arsenal	D 2-2	Cross, A.Taylor	31,675
30	Mar	4	(a)	Nottingham F	L 0-2		33,924
31		11	(h)	Wolves	L 1-2	Hales	23,525
32		14	(a)	Queen's Park R	L 0-1		20,394
33		18	(a)	Aston Villa	L 1-4	Brooking	28,275
34		24	(h)	Ipswich T	W 3-0	Cross 3	23,867
35		25	(a)	Chelsea	W 3-1	Brooking, Green, Holland	24,987
36		28	(a)	Birmingham C	L 0-3		23,554
37	Apr	1	(h)	Coventry C	W 2-1	Holland, T.Taylor	19,260
38		8	(h)	Leeds U	W 2-1	Hales, Martin	22,953
39		15	(h)	Derby C	W 3-0	Robson 2, Cross	25,424
40		22	(a)	Manchester U	L 0-3		54,089
41		25	(a)	Middlesbrough	W 2-1	Cross 2	13,247
42		29	(h)	Liverpool	L 0-2		37,448

P	W	D	L	F	A	W	D	L	F	A	Pts	Pos	Div	Appearances
42	8	6	7	31	28	4	2	15	21	41	32	20th	1	Sub Appearances
														Goals

FA Cup

3	Jan	7	(h)	Watford	W 1-0	Robson	36,745
4		28	(h)	Queen's Park R	D 1-1	Bonds	35,566
R		31	(a)	Queen's Park R	L 1-6	Robson	24,057
							Appearances
							Sub Appearances
							Goals

League Cup

2	Aug	30	(a)	Nottingham F	L 0-5		18,224
							Appearances
							Sub Appearances
							Goals

Day	Brush	Lampard	Pike	Taylor T	Lock	Taylor A	Robson B	Radford	Brooking	Devonshire	Curbishley	Otulakowski	Holland	Jennings	McGiven	Hales	Bonds	McDowell	Cross	Ferguson	Green	Martin	
1	2	3	4	5	6	7	8	9	10	11													1
1	2	3	4	5	6	7	8	9		11*	10	12											2
1	3	2	4	5	6	7*	8	9		11	10	12											3
1	3	2		5	6	7	8			11	10		4	9									4
1	3	2	7	5	6		8			11	10	12	4	9*									5
1	3	2	12	5	6	7	8		10	11*	9		4										6
1	3	2		5		7	8		10	11	9		4		6								7
1	3	2	12	5		7	8		10	11	9*		4		6								8
1	3	2	11	5		7	8		10		12		4		6	9*							9
1	3	2	6	5			8	9	10	7						11	4						10
1	3	2	6	5			8	9	10	7						11	4						11
1	3	2	6	5			8	9	10	7						11	4						12
1	3	2	6	5			8	9	10	7						11	4						13
1	3	2	6	5			8		10	7	9					11	4						14
1	3	2	6	5			8	9	10	7						11	4						15
1	3	2	6	5			8	9*	10	7	12					11	4						16
1	3	2	6	5*			8		10	7	9					11	4						17
1	3	2*	6	5			8		10	7	9					11	4	12					18
1	3		6	5			8		10	7						11	4	2	9				19
1		3	6	5			8		10	7						11	4	2	9				20
1		3	6	5			8		10	7	11						4	2	9				21
		3		5					10	7	6					11	4	2	9	1			22
	2	3		5			8		10	7	6					11	4		9	1			23
		3		5			8		10	7	6					11	4	2	9	1			24
		3	8	5					10	7*	6		12			11	4	2	9	1			25
1		3	12	5			8		10	7						11*	4	2	9		6		26
		3	4	5			8		10	7						11	2*	12	9	1	6		27
		3	12	5		11	8		10	7							4	2*	9	1	6		28
		3		5			8		10	7	4	12				11		2	9	1	6*		29
		3		5			8		10	7	4	12			6	11		2*	9	1			30
		3	11	5			8		10	7					6		4	2	9	1			31
		3		5			8		10	7*	4				6	11		2	9	1		12	32
		3	7	5			8		10		4					11	2		9	1	6		33
		3	7	5	11				10		4					8	2		9	1	6		34
		3	7	5	11				10		4				12	8	2		9	1	6*		35
		3	7*	5	11				10		4					8	2		9	1	6	12	36
	3			5	11				10	7						9	2			1	6	4	37
	3	2		5	11		8		10	7*	12					9				1	6	4	38
12	3			5	11		8		10	7							2		9	1	6	4*	39
	3			5	11		8		10	7							2		9	1	6	4	40
	3			5	11		8		10	7	12						2		9	1	6	4	41
	3		5*		11		8		10	7	12						2		9	1	6	4	42
23	23	40	25	42	6	10	37	10	37	32	31		18	2	4	23	29	12	21	19	13	5	
	1		3				1			2	1	5	3		1		2					2	
		2	2	1	2	9		4	3	1		3	1			10	1	1	9			1	1

1 own-goal

Day	Brush	Lampard	Pike	Taylor T	Lock	Taylor A	Robson B	Radford	Brooking	Devonshire	Curbishley	Otulakowski	Holland	Jennings	McGiven	Hales	Bonds	McDowell	Cross	Ferguson	Green	Martin	
		3	12	5			8		10	7	6*						4	2	9	1			3
		3		5			8		10	7	6						4	2	9	1			4
		3		5	12	8			7*	6			10			11	4	2	9	1			R
		3		3			3		2	3	3		1			1	3	3	3	3			
		1		1						2										1			

Day	Brush	Lampard	Pike	Taylor T	Lock	Taylor A	Robson B	Radford	Brooking	Devonshire	Curbishley	Otulakowski	Holland	Jennings	McGiven	Hales	Bonds	McDowell	Cross	Ferguson	Green	Martin	
1	3	2	4		6	7	8	9		11	10				5								2
1	1	1	1		1	1	1	1		1	1				1								
															1								

1978-79

Manager: John Lyall

1	Aug	19	(h)	Notts C	W 5-2	Cross 3, Devonshire, Opp own-goal	25,387
2		23	(a)	Newcastle U	W 3-0	Cross, Devonshire, Robson	27,233
3		26	(a)	Crystal P	D 1-1	A.Taylor	32,611
4	Sep	2	(h)	Fulham	L 0-1		25,778
5		9	(a)	Burnley	L 2-3	Cross 2	12,308
6		16	(h)	Bristol R	W 2-0	Brooking, Robson	22,189
7		23	(h)	Sheffield U	W 2-0	Robson 2	24,361
8		30	(a)	Sunderland	L 1-2	Cross	23,676
9	Oct	7	(h)	Millwall	W 3-0	Robson 3	22,210
10		14	(a)	Oldham A	D 2-2	Robson 2	10,143
11		21	(h)	Stoke C	D 1-1	Brooking	27,855
12		28	(a)	Brighton & HA	W 2-1	Robson 2	32,634
13	Nov	4	(h)	Preston NE	W 3-1	Cross, Devonshire, Lampard	23,572
14		11	(a)	Notts C	L 0-1		11,002
15		18	(h)	Crystal P	D 1-1	Bonds	31,245
16		21	(a)	Fulham	D 0-0		26,556
17		25	(a)	Leicester C	W 2-1	Cross 2	16,149
18	Dec	2	(h)	Cambridge U	W 5-0	Robson 2, Bonds, Curbishley, A.Taylor	21,379
19		9	(a)	Wrexham	L 3-4	Cross, Lampard, Robson	15,537
20		16	(a)	Charlton A	W 2-0	Cross, Robson	23,833
21		26	(h)	Orient	L 0-2		29,220
22		30	(h)	Blackburn R	W 4-0	Cross, Robson, A.Taylor, Opp own-goal	21,269
23	Jan	20	(a)	Bristol R	W 1-0	Robson	12,418
24	Feb	10	(h)	Sunderland	D 3-3	Cross 2, Robson	24,998
25		24	(h)	Oldham A	W 3-0	Holland, Martin, Robson	26,052
26		26	(a)	Luton T	W 4-1	Cross 2, Devonshire, Robson	14,205
27	Mar	3	(a)	Stoke C	L 0-2		24,912
28		10	(h)	Brighton & HA	D 0-0		35,802
29		17	(a)	Preston NE	D 0-0		15,376
30		24	(h)	Newcastle U	W 5-0	McDowell 2, Devonshire, Lampard, Robson	24,650
31		26	(h)	Leicester C	D 1-1	Robson	23,992
32	Apr	2	(a)	Sheffield U	L 0-3		17,720
33		7	(a)	Cambridge U	D 0-0		11,406
34		9	(h)	Luton T	W 1-0	Opp own-goal	25,498
35		14	(a)	Orient	W 2-0	Holland, Pike	17,517
36		16	(h)	Cardiff C	D 1-1	Holland	29,058
37		21	(a)	Charlton A	D 0-0		22,816
38		24	(h)	Burnley	W 3-1	Bonds, Cross, Robson	24,139
39		28	(h)	Wrexham	D 1-1	Bonds	28,865
40	May	5	(a)	Blackburn R	L 0-1		7,585
41		11	(a)	Cardiff C	D 0-0		13,140
42		14	(a)	Millwall	L 1-2	Robson	11,917

P	W	D	L	F	A	W	D	L	F	A	Pts	Pos	Div	
42	12	7	2	46	15	6	7	8	24	24	50	5th	2	Appearances
														Sub Appearances
														Goals

FA Cup

3	Jan	9	(a)	Newport C	L 1-2	Robson	14,124
							Appearances
							Sub Appearances
							Goals

League Cup

2	Aug	30	(h)	Swindon T	L 1-2	Robson	19,672
							Appearances
							Sub Appearances
							Goals

Ferguson	Lampard	Brush	Holland	Taylor T	Bonds	Curbishley	Devonshire	Cross	Brooking	Robson B	Taylor A	Pike	McDowell	Martin	Jennings	Day	Parkes	Morgan	Lansdowne	Brignull	#
1	2	3	4	5	6	7	8	9	10	11											1
1	2	3	4	5	6	7	8	9	10*	11	12										2
1	2	3	4	5	6	7	8	9		11	10										3
1	2	3	4	5	6	7		9		11	10*	8	12								4
1	2	3	4	5	6	7	8	9		11			10								5
1	2	3	4	5	6	7	8	9	10	11											6
1	2*	3	4	5	6	7	8		10	11	12		9								7
1		3	4	5	6	7	8	9	10	11			2								8
1	2	3	4	5	6	7	8	9	10	11											9
1	2	3	4	5	6	7*	8	9	10	11			12								10
1		3	4	5	6	7	8	9	10	11			2								11
		3	4	5	6	7	8	9	10	11			2			1					12
		3	4	5	6	7	8	9	10	11						1					13
	2	3	4	5	6	7	8	9	10	11						1					14
	2	3	4*	5	6	7	8	9	10	11	12					1					15
	2	3	4	5	6	7	8	9		11	10					1					16
	2	3	4	5	6		8	9		11	10	7				1					17
	2	3	4	5	6	7	8	9		11	10					1					18
	2	3	4	5		7	8	9		11	10		6			1					19
	2	3	4*	5		7	8	9		11	10	12	6			1					20
	2	3		5		7*	8	9		11	10	4	6			1					21
	2	3			4			8	9	10	11	7	6	5		1					22
		3	7		6	4		8	9	10	11*		2	5		1					23
		3	7		6	4		8	9	10	11*		2	5		1					24
		3	7		6	4		8	9	10	11		2	5			1				25
		3	7		6	4		8	9	10	11		2	5			1				26
		3	7		6	4		8	9	10	11		2	5			1				27
	2	3	7		6	4		8		11	10			5			1				28
	2	3	7		6			8	9	10	11		4	5			1				29
	2	3	7		6			8	9	10*	11	12	4	5			1				30
	2	3	7		6	12		8	9	11	10		4*	5			1				31
	2	3	7		6			8	9	11	10		4	5			1				32
	2*	3	7		6	4		8	9	11	12	10		5			1				33
		3	7		6	4		8		11	10		2	5			1	9			34
		3	7		6	4		8	9	11	10		2	5			1				35
		3	7		6	4		8	9	11	10		2	5			1				36
12		3	7		6	4		8	9	11*	10		2	5			1				37
		3	7		6	4		8	9	11	10		2	5			1				38
		3	7		6	4		8	9	11	10*		2	5			1		12		39
	2	3	7		6	4		8	9	11	10*	12		5			1		11	12	40
	2	3	7		6	4		8	9		10*			5			1		11	12	41
	2	3	7		6	4		8	9	10	11			5			1				42
11	28	42	39	32	39	26	41	40	21	40	10	10	26	22	2	13	18	2			
1					1						3	4	2		2				1	1	
3		3		4	1	5	18	2	24	3	1		2	1							

3 own-goals

Ferguson	Lampard	Brush	Holland	Taylor T	Bonds	Curbishley	Devonshire	Cross	Brooking	Robson B	Taylor A	Pike	McDowell	Martin	Jennings	Day	Parkes	Morgan	Lansdowne	Brignull	#
	2	3			4			8	9	10	11	7	6	5		1					3
	1	1			1			1	1	1	1	1	1	1		1					
														1							

Ferguson	Lampard	Brush	Holland	Taylor T	Bonds	Curbishley	Devonshire	Cross	Brooking	Robson B	Taylor A	Pike	McDowell	Martin	Jennings	Day	Parkes	Morgan	Lansdowne	Brignull	#
1	2	3	4	5	6	7	8	9		11	10*	12									2
1	1	1	1	1	1	1	1	1		1	1										
													1								

1979-80

Manager: John Lyall

#	Month	Date		Opponent	Result	Scorers	Attendance
1	Aug	18	(a)	Wrexham	L 0-1		13,036
2		20	(h)	Chelsea	L 0-1		31,627
3		25	(h)	Oldham A	W 1-0	Holland	18,319
4	Sep	1	(a)	Watford	L 0-2		23,329
5		8	(a)	Preston NE	D 1-1	Cross	10,460
6		15	(h)	Sunderland	W 2-0	Cross, Pearson	24,021
7		22	(a)	Queen's Park R	L 0-3		24,692
8		29	(h)	Burnley	W 2-1	Lansdowne, Stewart	18,327
9	Oct	6	(h)	Newcastle U	D 1-1	Cross	23,206
10		13	(a)	Leicester C	W 2-1	Cross, Martin	22,472
11		20	(a)	Luton T	L 1-2	Allen	25,049
12		27	(a)	Notts C	W 1-0	Holland	12,256
13	Nov	3	(h)	Wrexham	W 1-0	Pike	20,595
14		10	(a)	Fulham	W 2-1	Cross, Stewart	16,476
15		14	(a)	Chelsea	L 1-2	Holland	30,859
16		17	(h)	Swansea C	W 2-0	Brooking, Cross	21,210
17		24	(h)	Cardiff C	W 3-0	Stewart 2, Cross	20,242
18	Dec	1	(a)	Charlton A	L 0-1		19,021
19		8	(h)	Bristol R	W 2-1	Cross 2	17,763
20		15	(a)	Shrewsbury T	L 0-3		8,513
21		21	(h)	Cambridge U	W 3-1	Neighbour, Pearson, Stewart	11,721
22	Jan	1	(a)	Orient	W 4-0	Pearson 2, Devonshire, Pike	23,885
23		12	(h)	Watford	D 1-1	Bonds	23,553
24		19	(h)	Preston NE	W 2-0	Allen, Stewart	17,603
25	Feb	9	(h)	Queen's Park R	W 2-1	Pearson, Opp own-goal	26,037
26		19	(a)	Burnley	W 1-0	Devonshire	10,610
27		23	(h)	Leicester C	W 3-1	Cross, Holland, Pike	27,762
28	Mar	1	(a)	Luton T	D 1-1	Stewart	20,040
29		11	(h)	Notts C	L 1-2	Pike	24,844
30		15	(a)	Newcastle U	D 0-0		25,431
31		22	(h)	Fulham	L 2-3	Devonshire, Stewart	30,030
32		29	(a)	Swansea C	L 1-2	Devonshire	13,275
33	Apr	1	(a)	Cambridge U	L 0-2		8,863
34		5	(h)	Orient	W 2-0	Brooking, Opp own-goal	22,066
35		7	(a)	Birmingham C	D 0-0		28,377
36		19	(a)	Cardiff C	W 1-0	Stewart	12,076
37		22	(h)	Birmingham C	L 1-2	Martin	37,167
38		26	(h)	Shrewsbury T	L 1-3	Brooking	19,765
39		29	(a)	Oldham A	D 0-0		8,214
40	May	3	(a)	Bristol R	W 2-0	Cross, Devonshire	9,824
41		5	(h)	Charlton A	W 4-1	Cross, Morgan, Pike, Stewart	19,314
42		12	(a)	Sunderland	L 0-2		47,000

P	W	D	L	F	A	W	D	L	F	A	Pts	Pos	Div	
42	13	2	6	37	21	7	5	9	17	22	47	7th	2	Appearances
														Sub Appearances
														Goals

FA Cup

Rd	Month	Date		Opponent	Result	Scorers	Attendance
3	Jan	5	(a)	West Brom A	D 1-1	Pearson	20,572
R		8	(h)	West Brom A	W 2-1	Pike, Brooking	30,689
4		26	(a)	Orient	W 3-2	Stewart 2, Opp own-goal	21,521
5	Feb	16	(h)	Swansea C	W 2-0	Allen, Cross	30,497
6	Mar	8	(h)	Aston Villa	W 1-0	Stewart	36,393
SF	Apr	12	(n*)	Everton	D 1-1	Pearson	47,685
R		16	(n†)	Everton	W 2-1	Devonshire, Lampard	40,720
F	May	10	(n‡)	Arsenal	W 1-0	Brooking	100,000

*Played at Villa Park, Birmingham. †Played at Elland Road, Leeds. ‡Played at Wembley Stadium.

Appearances
Sub Appearances
Goals

League Cup

Rd	Month	Date		Opponent	Result	Scorers	Attendance
2	Aug	28	(h)	Barnsley	W 3-1	Brooking, Pearson, Cross	12,320
	Sep	4	(a)	Barnsley	W 2-0	Cross 2	15,898
3		25	(h)	Southend U	D 1-1	Cross	19,658
R	Oct	1	(a)	Southend U	D 0-0		22,497
2R		8	(h)	Southend U	W 5-1	Lansdowne 3, Holland, Stewart	19,718
4		31	(a)	Sunderland	D 1-1	Pike	30,302
R	Nov	5	(h)	Sunderland	W 2-1	Martin, Cross	24,454
5	Dec	4	(h)	Nottingham F	D 0-0		35,856
R		12	(a)	Nottingham F	L 0-3		25,462

Appearances
Sub Appearances
Goals

Parkes	Lampard	Brush	Pike	Martin	Bonds	Holland	Devonshire	Cross	Brooking	Pearson	Banton	Morgan	Lansdowne	Stewart	Neighbour	Allen	Ferguson	Smith	No.
I	2	3	4	5	6	7	8	9	10	11									1
I	2	3	7	5	4	6	11	9	10	8*	12								2
I	2	3	7	5	4	6	11	9	10		8		12						3
I	2	3	7		4	6	11	9	10	8*		12							4
I	2	3	7			4	6	9	10		8	11		5					5
I	2	3		5	4		11	9	10	8					6	7			6
I	2	3	8*	5	4	12	11	9	10						6	7			7
I		3		5	4		11	9	10				8	2	7	6			8
I		3		5	4	12	11	9	10				8	2	7*	6			9
I	3		5	4	6		9	10				8	2	11	7				10
I	3		10	5	4	6		9				8	2	11	7				11
I	3		8	5	4	6		9	10			12	2	11	7				12
I	3		8	5	4	6	10*	9				12	2	11	7				13
	3		8	5	4	6	8	9	10				2	11	7	1			14
	3			5	4	6	8	9	10			12	2	11	7*	1			15
I			5	4	6	8	9	10				11	2		7			3	16
I	3		5	4	6	11	9	10	8			2		7					17
I	3		5	4	6*	11	9	10	8			2	12	7					18
I	3		5	4		11	9	10	8			2	7	6					19
I	3	6	5	4			9	10	8			2	11	7					20
I	3	12	5	4		6	9*	10	8			2	11	7					21
I	3	9	5	4		6		10	8			2	11	7					22
I	3	9	5	4		6		10	8			2	11	7					23
I	2	3	9	5	4*	6			8	12		10	11	7					24
I	2	3	11	5		6	9	10	8			4		7					25
I	2	3	11	5		6	9	10				4	8	7					26
I	2	3	11	5	8	6	9	10				4		7					27
I	2	3	11	5	8*	6	9	10	12			4		7					28
I	2*	3	11	5		12	6	9	10	8			4		7				29
I	2	3	11*	5		12	6	9	10	8			4		7				30
I	2	3*	12	5		11	6	9	10	8			4		7				31
I		3	9	5	4	11	6	12	10	8				2	7*				32
I	2	3		5	4	11	6	9	10	8					7				33
I	2*	3	12	5	4	11	6	9	10	8					7				34
I		3		5	4	11	6	9	10	8				2	7				35
I	2	3	11		5		6	9	10	8				4	7				36
I	2	3	12	5	4		6	9	10	8				11	7*				37
I	2	3	11	5		9*			10	8	12			4	6	7			38
I	2	3	8*	5	4			9	10		12			11	7	6			39
I	2		10	5	4	6	9			8				3	11	7			40
I	12	3	8	5	4		9*		10				6	11	2	7			41
I		3	11	5	4	12	6	9	10	8*				2		7			42
40	35	27	27	40	34	21	34	38	37	24	2	4	5	38	22	31	2	I	
	1		4				5			1		1	2	2	3		1		
			5	2	1	4	5	12	3	5		1	1	10	1	2			

Parkes	Lampard	Brush	Pike	Martin	Bonds	Holland	Devonshire	Cross	Brooking	Pearson	Banton	Morgan	Lansdowne	Stewart	Neighbour	Allen	Ferguson	Smith	2 own-goals
I		3	9	5	4		6		10	8				2	11	7			3
I	3	4	9	5			6			10	8			2	11	7			R
I	3	2	9	5	4		6			8				10	11	7			4
I	2	3	11	5			6	9	10	8*				4	7	12			5
I	2	3	11	5			6	9	10	8				4		7			6
I		3	12	5	4	11	6	9	10	8*				2		7			SF
I	2	3	11				6	9	10	8				4		7			R
I	3		11	5	4		6	9	10	8				2		7			F
8	7	6	7	7	5	1	8	5	7	8				8	4	7			
			1													1			
	1		1				1	1	2	2				3		1			

Parkes	Lampard	Brush	Pike	Martin	Bonds	Holland	Devonshire	Cross	Brooking	Pearson	Banton	Morgan	Lansdowne	Stewart	Neighbour	Allen	Ferguson	Smith	1 own-goal
I	2	3	7	5	4	6	11	9	10	8									2
I	2	3	7		4	6		9	10		8	11		5						
I		3		5	4	6	11	9	10			8	5		7					3
I		3		5	4	6	11	9	10			8	2		7			3		R
I	3		8	5	4	6	11	9	10*			12	2		7					2R
	3		8	5	4	6	10	9				11	2		7	1				4
I	3			5	4	6	11	9	10	8			2		7					R
I	3		6	5	4		11	9	10	8			2		7					5
8	6	4	6	8	9	8	7	9	8	3	1	1	4	8		7	1	1	R
													1						
			1	1		1		5	1	1			3	1					

329

1980-81

Manager: John Lyall

1	Aug	16	(h)	Luton T	L	1-2	Stewart	28,033
2		19	(a)	Bristol C	D	1-1	Cross	13,554
3		23	(a)	Preston NE	D	0-0		9,063
4		30	(h)	Notts C	W	4-0	Goddard 2, Cross, Stewart	21,769
5	Sep	6	(a)	Chelsea	W	1-0	Opp own-goal	32,669
6		13	(h)	Shrewsbury T	W	3-0	Cross, Goddard, Opp own-goal	22,339
7		20	(h)	Watford	W	3-2	Barnes, Brooking, Cross	24,288
8		27	(a)	Cambridge U	W	2-1	Cross, Goddard	8,591
9	Oct	4	(a)	Newcastle U	D	0-0		24,848
10		7	(h)	Cardiff C	W	1-0	Neighbour	20,402
11		11	(h)	Blackburn R	W	2-0	Cross 2	32,402
12		18	(a)	Oldham A	D	0-0		8,344
13		25	(h)	Bolton W	W	2-1	Pike, Opp own-goal	25,277
14	Nov	1	(a)	Bristol R	W	1-0	Goddard	6,328
15		8	(h)	Grimsby T	W	2-1	Cross 2	25,468
16		11	(h)	Bristol C	W	5-0	Goddard 2, Brooking, Martin, Cross	25,210
17		15	(a)	Luton T	L	2-3	Brooking 2	17,031
18		22	(h)	Swansea C	W	2-0	Cross, Goddard	27,376
19		26	(a)	Derby C	L	0-2		18,446
20		29	(a)	Wrexham	D	2-2	Devonshire, Goddard	8,941
21	Dec	6	(h)	Sheffield W	W	2-1	Brooking, Holland	30,476
22		13	(a)	Blackburn R	D	0-0		13,279
23		20	(a)	Derby C	W	3-1	Brooking, Cross, Goddard	24,671
24		26	(a)	Queen's Park R	L	0-3		23,811
25		27	(h)	Orient	W	2-1	Allen, Holland	34,408
26	Jan	10	(a)	Swansea C	W	3-1	Brooking, Cross, Pike	22,110
27		17	(a)	Notts C	D	1-1	Holland	13,718
28		31	(h)	Preston NE	W	5-0	Devonshire 2, Pike, Goddard, Lampard	26,413
29	Feb	7	(a)	Shrewsbury T	W	2-0	Cross, Devonshire	9,201
30		14	(h)	Chelsea	W	4-0	Brooking 2, Cross, Devonshire	35,164
31		21	(h)	Cambridge U	W	4-2	Stewart 2, Devonshire, Goddard	36,002
32		28	(a)	Watford	W	2-1	Cross 2	20,786
33	Mar	7	(h)	Newcastle U	W	1-0	Cross	26,274
34		21	(a)	Oldham A	D	1-1	Goddard	24,394
35		28	(a)	Bolton W	D	1-1	Brooking	13,271
36	Apr	4	(h)	Bristol R	W	2-0	Goddard, Pike	23,544
37		11	(a)	Grimsby T	W	5-1	Cross 4, Pike	17,924
38		18	(a)	Orient	W	2-0	Neighbour, Pike	14,592
39		21	(h)	Queen's Park R	W	3-0	Goddard 3	24,599
40	May	2	(h)	Wrexham	W	1-0	Stewart	30,515
41		6	(a)	Cardiff C	D	0-0		10,558
42		8	(a)	Sheffield W	W	1-0	Morgan	21,067

P	W	D	L	F	A	W	D	L	F	A	Pts	Pos	Div	
42	19	1	1	53	12	9	9	3	26	17	66	1st	2	Appearances
														Sub Appearances
														Goals

FA Cup

3	Jan	3	(h)	Wrexham	D	1-1	Stewart	30,137
R		6	(a)	Wrexham	D	0-0		13,643
2R		19	(a)	Wrexham	L	0-1		14,615

		Appearances
		Sub Appearances
		Goals

League Cup

2	Aug	26	(a)	Burnley	W	2-0	Goddard, Cross	6,818
	Sep	2	(h)	Burnley	W	4-0	Stewart, Goddard, Pike, Opp own-goal	15,216
3		23	(a)	Charlton A	W	2-1	Cross 2	17,884
4	Oct	28	(h)	Barnsley	W	2-1	Martin, Cross	21,548
5	Dec	2	(h)	Tottenham H	W	1-0	Cross	36,003
SF	Jan	27	(a)	Coventry C	L	2-3	Bonds, Opp own-goal	35,468
	Feb	10	(h)	Coventry C	W	2-0	Goddard, Neighbour	36,551
F	Mar	14	(n*)	Liverpool	D	1-1	Stewart	100,000
R	Apr	1	(n†)	Liverpool	L	1-2	Goddard	36,693

*Played at Wembley Stadium. †Played at Villa Park, Birmingham.

		Appearances
		Sub Appearances
		Goals

West Ham United appearance and goalscoring grid.

League

Parkes	Stewart	Brush	Bonds	Martin	Devonshire	Holland	Goddard	Lampard	Cross	Brooking	Pike	Neighbour	Morgan	Barnes	Allen	Pearson	No.
1	2	3	4	5	6	7	8*	12	9	10	11						1
1	2	3	4	5	6	7	8		9	10	11						2
1	4	3		5	6	7	8	2	9	10	11						3
1	2		4	5	6	7	8	3	9	10	11						4
1	2		4	5	6	7	8	3	9	10	11						5
1	2		4	5	6		8	3	9	10	11	7*	12				6
1	2		4	5	6		8	3	9	10	11		7				7
1	2		4	5	6	7	8	3	9	10	11						8
1	2	12	4	5	6	7	8*	3	9		11	10					9
1	2		4	5	6	7		3	9		11	10	8				10
1	2		4	5	6	7	8	3	9		11	10					11
1	2		4	5	6*	7		3	9		11	10	8	12			12
1	2	3	4	5	6	7	8		9		11	10					13
1	2	12	4	5	6*	7	8	3	9		11	10					14
1		2	4	5		7	8	3	9	10	11		6				15
1	2		4	5	6	7	8	3	9	10	11						16
1	2		4	5	6	7	8	3	9	10	11						17
1	2		4	5	6*	7	8	3	9	10	11	12					18
1	2		4	5	6	7	8	3	9	10	11						19
1	2		4	5	6	7	8	3	9	10	11						20
1	2		4	5	6	7	8	3	9	10	11						21
1	2		4	5	6	7	8	3	9	10	11						22
1	2		4	5	6	7	8	3	9	10	11						23
1	2		4	5	6	7	8	3	9*	10	11	12					24
1	2		4	5	6	7	8	3*		10	11		9	12			25
1	2		4	5	6	7	8	3	9	10	11						26
1	2	3	4	5	6	7*	8		9	10	11		12				27
1	2		4	5	6		8	3	9	10	11	7					28
1	2		4	5	6		8*	3	9	10	11	7	12				29
1	2		4	5	6		8	3	9	10	11	7					30
1	2		4	5	6		8	3	9	10	11	7					31
1	2		4	5	6		8	3	9	10	11	7					32
1	2		4	5			8	3	9	10	11	7		6*	12		33
1	2	6*	4	5			8	3	9	10	11		12		7		34
1	2		4	5*	6		8	3	9	10	11	7			12		35
1	2	5	4		6		8	3	9	10	11	7					36
1	2		4	5	6		8	3	9	10	11	7					37
1	2		4	5	6			3	9	10	11	7	12		8*		38
1	2		4	5	6		8	3	9	10*	11	7	12				39
1	2		4	5	6		8*	3	9	10	11	7			12		40
1	2		4	5	6			3	9	10	11	7	8				41
1	2	12	4	5*	6			3	9	10	11	7	8				42
42	41	8	41	41	39	25	37	38	41	36	42	22	5	1	1	2	
		3						1				2	1	5	2	3	
	5		1		6	3	17	1	22	10	6	2	1	1	1		

3 own-goals

FA Cup

Parkes	Stewart	Brush	Bonds	Martin	Devonshire	Holland	Goddard	Lampard	Cross	Brooking	Pike	Neighbour	Morgan	Barnes	Allen	Pearson	Rd
1	2		4	5	6	7	8	3	9	10	11						3
1	2		4	5	6	7	8	3	9	10	11						R
1	2	3	4	5	6		8		9	10	11	12	7*				2R
3	3	1	3	3	3	2	3	2	3	3	3		1				
												1					

League Cup

Parkes	Stewart	Brush	Bonds	Martin	Devonshire	Holland	Goddard	Lampard	Cross	Brooking	Pike	Neighbour	Morgan	Barnes	Allen	Pearson	Rd
1	2		4	5	6	7	8	3	9	10	11						2
1	2		4	5	6	7*	8	3	9	10	11		12				
1	2	10	4	5	6		8	3	9		11		7				3
1	2	4		5	6	7	8	3*	9		11	10	12				4
1	2		4	5	6	7	8	3	9	10	11						5
1	2	3	4	5	6		8		9	10	11	7					SF
1	2		4	5	6		8	3	9	10	11	7					
1	2		4	5	6		8*	3	9	10	11	7		12			F
1	2		4	5	6		8	3	9	10	11*	7		12			R
9	9	3	8	9	9	4	9	8	9	7	9	4	1	1			
															2	2	
	2		1	1		4		5			1	1					

2 own-goals

331

1981-82

Manager: John Lyall

1	Aug	29	(h)	Brighton & HA	D	1-1	Stewart	30,468
2	Sep	2	(a)	Tottenham H	W	4-0	Cross 4	41,200
3		5	(a)	Sunderland	W	2-0	Cross, Goddard	28,347
4		12	(h)	Stoke C	W	3-2	Goddard 2, Stewart	28,774
5		19	(a)	West Brom A	D	0-0		19,516
6		22	(h)	Southampton	W	4-2	Goddard 3, Pike	34,026
7		26	(h)	Liverpool	D	1-1	Pike	30,802
8	Oct	3	(a)	Birmingham C	D	2-2	Cross 2	22,290
9		10	(h)	Everton	D	1-1	Martin	31,608
10		17	(a)	Aston Villa	L	2-3	Brooking, Cross	32,064
11		24	(a)	Notts C	D	1-1	Brooking	12,505
12		31	(h)	Middlesbrough	W	3-2	Goddard, Neighbour, Stewart	27,604
13	Nov	7	(a)	Nottingham F	D	0-0		26,327
14		21	(h)	Coventry C	W	5-2	Martin 2, Brooking, Neighbour, Stewart	26,065
15		28	(a)	Leeds U	D	3-3	Brooking 2, Cross	25,637
16	Dec	5	(a)	Arsenal	L	1-2	Pearson	33,833
17	Jan	5	(a)	Liverpool	L	0-3		28,427
18		16	(a)	Brighton & HA	L	0-1		22,620
19		27	(h)	Manchester U	L	0-1		41,291
20		30	(h)	West Brom A	W	3-1	Cross 2, Goddard	24,423
21	Feb	2	(h)	Manchester C	D	1-1	Bonds	26,552
22		6	(a)	Stoke C	L	1-2	Van der Elst	11,987
23		13	(h)	Birmingham C	D	2-2	Orr, Stewart	22,512
24		20	(a)	Southampton	L	1-2	Stewart	24,026
25		27	(a)	Everton	D	0-0		28,618
26	Mar	2	(h)	Ipswich T	W	2-0	Devonshire, Van der Elst	24,846
27		6	(h)	Aston Villa	D	2-2	Stewart, Van der Elst	26,894
28		13	(h)	Notts C	W	1-0	Stewart	22,145
29		20	(a)	Middlesbrough	W	3-2	Goddard 2, Van der Elst	12,134
30		27	(h)	Nottingham F	L	0-1		24,633
31		30	(a)	Swansea C	W	1-0	Van der Elst	20,272
32	Apr	3	(a)	Manchester C	W	1-0	Goddard	30,875
33		6	(h)	Wolves	W	3-1	Goddard 2, Martin	20,651
34		10	(h)	Swansea C	D	1-1	Goddard	26,566
35		13	(h)	Ipswich T	L	2-3	Cross 2	28,767
36		17	(a)	Coventry C	L	0-1		13,398
37		24	(h)	Leeds U	W	4-3	Brooking 2, Cross, Stewart	24,748
38	May	1	(a)	Arsenal	L	0-2		34,997
39		4	(h)	Sunderland	D	1-1	Stewart	17,310
40		8	(h)	Manchester U	D	1-1	Cross	26,337
41		10	(h)	Tottenham H	D	2-2	Brooking, Goddard	27,677
42		15	(a)	Wolves	L	1-2	Cross	13,283

P	W	D	L	F	A	W	D	L	F	A	Pts	Pos	Div	
42	9	10	2	42	29	5	6	10	24	28	58	9th	1	Appearances
														Sub Appearances
														Goals

FA Cup

3	Jan	2	(h)	Everton	W	2-1	Bonds, Cross	24,431
4		23	(a)	Watford	L	0-2		27,004

Appearances
Sub Appearances
Goals

League Cup

2	Oct	7	(a)	Derby C	W	3-2	Cross, Brooking, Stewart	13,764
		27	(h)	Derby C	W	2-0	Goddard 2	21,043
3	Nov	10	(h)	West Brom A	D	2-2	Stewart, Cross	24,168
R		24	(a)	West Brom A	D	1-1	Stewart	15,869
2R	Dec	1	(h)	West Brom A	L	0-1		24,760

Appearances
Sub Appearances
Goals

Parkes	Stewart	Lampard	Bonds	Martin	Devonshire	Neighbour	Goddard	Cross	Allen	Pike	Pearson	McAlister	Brooking	Brush	Barnes	Banton	Van der Elst	Orr	Cowie	La Ronde	Houghton	No.
1	2	3	4	5	6	7	8	9	10	11												1
1	2	3	4	5	6	7	8	9	10	11												2
1	2	3	4	5	6	7	8*	9	10	11	12											3
1	2	3	4	5	6	7	8	9	10	11												4
1	2	3	4	5	6	7	8	9	10	11												5
1	2	3	4	5	6	7	8	9	10	11												6
1	2	3	4	5	6	7	8	9	10	11												7
	2	3	4	5	6	7	8	9		11		1	10									8
	2	3	4	5	6	7	8	9		11		1	10									9
	2	3	4	5	6	7*	8	9		11		1	10	12								10
1	2	3	4	5	6		8	9		11			10	7								11
1	2	3	4	5	6	7	8	9		11			10									12
1	2	3		5	6	7	8	9	4*	11			10	12								13
1	2	3	4	5	6	7	8	9		11			10									14
1	2	3	4	5	6	7*	8	9	12	11			10									15
1	2	3	4	5	6			9		11	8		10	7*	12							16
1	2	3	4	5	6*	7		9		11	8		10	12								17
1	8	3*	4	5			12	9		11			10	2			7	6				18
1	2		4	5			8	9		11			10	3			7	6				19
1	2		4	5			8	9		11	12		10	3*			7	6				20
1	2		4	5			8	9		11			10	3			7	6				21
1	5	2	4			12	8	9		11			10	3*			7	6				22
1	2		4			7	8	9		11			10	3			6	5				23
1	2	12	4			7*	8		6	11			10	3			9	5				24
1	2		4		6		8		7	11			10	3			9	5				25
1	2		4		6		8		7	11			10	3			9	5				26
1	2	3	4		6		8	9	7	11							10	5				27
1	2	3	4		6	12	8		7	11*			10				9	5				28
1	2	3	4		6	12	8		9	11*			10				7	5				29
1	2	3		5	6		8	9		11			10				7	4				30
1	2	3		5	6		8	9		11			10				7	4				31
1	2	3		5	6		8	9		11			10				7	4				32
1	2	3*		5	6	12	8	9		11			10				7	4				33
1	2			5	6	11*	8	9	3				10				7	4				34
1	2		5*		6		8	9		11			10				7	4	3	12		35
1	2				6		8	9	4	11			10				7	5	3			36
1	2				6			9	4	11			10				7	5	8*	3	12	37
1	2				6		8	9	4	11			10				7	5		3		38
1	2				6		8	9	4	11			10				7	5		3		39
1	2				6		8	9	4	11			10					5	7	3		40
1	2				6		8	9	4	11			10				12	5	7*	3		41
1	2				6		8	9*	4	11			10				12	5	7	3		42
39	42	27	29	28	35	19	38	38	27	34	2	3	34	10	1		21	24	5	6		
	1					4	1				2			3	2	1	1		1	1	1	
	10		1	4	1	2	15	16	2	1			8				5	1				

Parkes	Stewart	Lampard	Bonds	Martin	Devonshire	Neighbour	Goddard	Cross	Allen	Pike	Pearson	McAlister	Brooking	Brush	Barnes	Banton	Van der Elst	Orr	Cowie	La Ronde	Houghton	No.
1	2	3	4	5	6	7	8*	9		11	12		10									3
1	2	3	4	5		7*	8	9		11	12		10		6							4
2	2	2	2	2	1	2	2	2		2			2		1							
											2											
				1				1														

Parkes	Stewart	Lampard	Bonds	Martin	Devonshire	Neighbour	Goddard	Cross	Allen	Pike	Pearson	McAlister	Brooking	Brush	Barnes	Banton	Van der Elst	Orr	Cowie	La Ronde	Houghton	No.
	2	3	4	5	6	7	8	9		11		1	10									2
1	2	3	4	5	6	7	8	9		11			10									
1	4	3		5	6	7	8	9		11		2	10									3
1	2	3	4	5	6	7	8*	9	12	11			10									R
1	2	3	4	5	6	7	8	9*	12	11			10									2R
4	5	5	4	5	5	5	5	5		5		1	5	1								
								2														
	3				2	2							1									

1982-83

Manager: John Lyall

#	Month	Date		Opponent	Result	Scorers	Attendance
1	Aug	28	(h)	Nottingham F	L 1-2	Stewart	24,796
2		31	(a)	Luton T	W 2-0	Bonds, Goddard	13,403
3	Sep	4	(a)	Sunderland	L 0-1		19,239
4		7	(h)	Ipswich T	D 1-1	Lampard	21,963
5		11	(h)	Birmingham C	W 5-0	Clark, Stewart, Goddard, Van der Elst, Martin	18,754
6		18	(a)	West Brom A	W 2-1	Clark, Van der Elst	15,321
7		25	(h)	Manchester C	W 4-1	Clark 2, Goddard, Van der Elst	23,833
8	Oct	2	(a)	Arsenal	W 3-2	Goddard, Martin, Van der Elst	30,484
9		9	(h)	Liverpool	W 3-1	Clark, Martin, Pike	32,500
10		16	(a)	Southampton	L 0-3		19,840
11		23	(a)	Brighton & HA	L 1-3	Devonshire	20,490
12		30	(h)	Manchester U	W 3-1	Goddard, Pike, Stewart	31,684
13	Nov	6	(a)	Stoke C	L 2-5	Pike, Stewart	17,589
14		13	(h)	Norwich C	W 1-0	Clark	22,463
15		20	(a)	Tottenham H	L 1-2	Van der Elst	41,960
16		27	(h)	Everton	W 2-0	Bonds, Opp own-goal	21,424
17	Dec	4	(a)	Aston Villa	L 0-1		24,658
18		11	(h)	Coventry C	L 0-3		19,321
19		18	(a)	Notts C	W 2-1	Dickens, Opp own-goal	8,457
20		27	(h)	Swansea C	W 3-2	Goddard, Stewart, Van der Elst	23,843
21		29	(a)	Watford	L 1-2	Stewart	24,870
22	Jan	1	(h)	Tottenham H	W 3-0	Cottee, Pike, Stewart	33,383
23		4	(h)	Luton T	L 2-3	Clark, Cottee	21,435
24		15	(a)	Nottingham F	L 0-1		17,031
25		22	(h)	West Brom A	L 0-1		19,887
26	Feb	5	(a)	Birmingham C	L 0-3		12,539
27		26	(h)	Southampton	D 1-1	Lampard	19,626
28	Mar	5	(h)	Brighton & HA	W 2-1	Cottee, Dickens	16,850
29		12	(a)	Liverpool	L 0-3		28,551
30		19	(h)	Stoke C	D 1-1	Opp own-goal	16,466
31		22	(a)	Manchester U	L 1-2	Devonshire	30,277
32		26	(a)	Norwich C	D 1-1	Dickens	18,582
33	Apr	2	(h)	Watford	W 2-1	Swindlehurst, Van der Elst	22,647
34		5	(a)	Swansea C	W 5-1	Dickens 2, Pike 2, Devonshire	13,303
35		9	(h)	Sunderland	W 2-1	Dickens, Goddard	20,053
36		16	(a)	Manchester C	L 0-2		23,015
37		23	(h)	Aston Villa	W 2-0	Bonds, Swindlehurst	21,822
38		30	(a)	Everton	L 0-2		16,355
39	May	3	(a)	Ipswich T	W 2-1	Goddard, Stewart	18,690
40		7	(h)	Notts C	W 2-0	Goddard, Van der Elst	17,534
41		10	(h)	Arsenal	L 1-3	Van der Elst	28,930
42		14	(a)	Coventry C	W 4-2	Cottee 2, Goddard, Swindlehurst	10,919

P	W	D	L	F	A	W	D	L	F	A	Pts	Pos	Div	
42	13	3	5	41	23	7	1	13	27	39	64	8th	1	Appearances
														Sub Appearances
														Goals

FA Cup

3	Jan	8	(a)	Manchester U	L 0-2		44,143

Appearances
Sub Appearances
Goals

League Cup

2	Oct	6	(a)	Stoke C	D 1-1	Stewart	18,079
		26	(h)	Stoke C	W 2-1	Goddard, Clark	18,270
3	Nov	10	(a)	Lincoln C	D 1-1	Goddard	13,899
R		29	(h)	Lincoln C	W 2-1	Stewart, Clark	13,686
4	Dec	7	(a)	Notts C	D 3-3	Van der Elst 3	7,525
R		21	(h)	Notts C	W 3-0	Stewart, Clark, Allen	13,140
5	Jan	18	(a)	Liverpool	L 1-2	Allen	23,953

Appearances
Sub Appearances
Goals

334

Player appearance and goalscoring grid. Columns left to right: Parkes, Stewart, Lampard, Bonds, Martin, Devonshire, Van der Elst, Goddard, Clark, Allen, Pike, Neighbour, Morgan, Orr, Brush, Gallagher, Dickens, Cottee, Cowie, Swindlehurst, Brooking, Barnes. Match numbers shown in the right-hand margin (reproduced here as the first column).

#	Parkes	Stewart	Lampard	Bonds	Martin	Devonshire	Van der Elst	Goddard	Clark	Allen	Pike	Neighbour	Morgan	Orr	Brush	Gallagher	Dickens	Cottee	Cowie	Swindlehurst	Brooking	Barnes
1	1	2	3	4	5	6	7	8	9	10	11											
2	1	2	3	4	5	6	7	8	9	10		11*	12									
3	1	2	3	4	5	6	7	8	9	10	11											
4	1	2	3	4	5	6	7	8	9	10	11											
5	1	2	3	4	5	6	7	8	9	10	11											
6	1	2	3	4	5	6	7	8	9	10	11											
7	1	2*	3	4	5	6	7	8	9	10	11		12									
8	1	2	3	4	5	6	7*	8	9	10	11		12									
9	1	2	3	4*	5	6		8	9	10	11	7	12									
10	1	2	3	4	5	6	7	8	9	10	11											
11	1	2	3	4	5	6	7	8	9	10	11											
12	1	2	3	4	5	6	7	8	9	10	11											
13	1	2		4	5	6	7*	8	9	10	11		12	3								
14	1	2	3	4	5		7	8	9	10	11	6										
15	1	2	3	4	5	6*	7	8	9	10	11	12										
16	1	2	3		5		7	8	9	10	11			4	6							
17	1	2	3			6*	7	8		10	11	12		4	9	5						
18	1	2					7	8	9	10	11			4	3	5	6					
19	1	2			5	6	7	8	9	10	11			4	3							
20	1	2	3		5	6	7	8	9	10	11			4								
21	1	2	3		5	6	7	8	9	10	11					4						
22	1	2			5	6	7		9	10	11			4	3		8					
23	1	2			5*	6	7		9	10	11		12	4	3		8					
24	1	2*	3	4	5	6	7	8	9	10	11		12									
25	1	2		4	5	6	7*	8	9	10	11			3			12					
26	1	2		4	5	6	7	8	9	10*				3			12			11		
27	1	2	3	4	5	6	7	8	9*	10	11						12					
28	1	2*	3		5	6	7			10	11	8		4		12	9					
29	1	2	3	4	5	6	7		9	10	11						8					
30	1	2	3	4	5	6	7	8		10	11						9					
31	1	2	3	4	5	6		8			11		7				10			9		
32	1	2	3	4	5	6	7	8			11						10	12		9*		
33	1	2	3	4	5	6	7	8			11						10	12		9*		
34	1	2	3	4	5	6	7	8			11						10	12		9*		
35	1	2	3	4	5	6	7	8			11						10	12		9*		
36	1	2	3	4		6	7	8*	9		11					5	10	12				
37	1	2	3*	4	5	6	7	8			11		12				10			9		
38	1	2		4	5	6	7	8			11			3			10			9		
39	1	2	3	4	5	6	7	8			11						10			9		
40	1	2	3	4	5	6	7	8			11						10			9		
41	1	2	3	4	5	6	7	8			11									9	10	
42	1	2	3	4		6	7	8		10	11*					5		12		9		
Apps	42	39	37	34	38	39	40	39	26	33	40	3	3	9	6	8	12	3	1	9	1	
Sub												4	5			1	3	5	1			
Goals		8	2	3	3	3	9	10	7		6						6	5		3		

3 own-goals

#	Parkes	Stewart	Lampard	Bonds	Martin	Devonshire	Van der Elst	Goddard	Clark	Allen	Pike	Neighbour	Morgan	Orr	Brush	Gallagher	Dickens	Cottee	Cowie	Swindlehurst	Brooking	Barnes
3	1	2	3	4		6	7		9	10	11			5		8						
Apps	1	1	1	1		1	1		1	1	1			1		1						

#	Parkes	Stewart	Lampard	Bonds	Martin	Devonshire	Van der Elst	Goddard	Clark	Allen	Pike	Neighbour	Morgan	Orr	Brush	Gallagher	Dickens	Cottee	Cowie	Swindlehurst	Brooking	Barnes
2	1	2	3		5	6		8	9	10	11	7		4								
3	1	2	3	4	5	6	7	8	9	10	11*		12									
R	1	2		4	5	6	12	8	9	10	11		7*	3								
4	1	2	3	4	5		7	8	9	10	11	6*							12			
R	1	2	3		5	6*	7	8	9	10	11			4	12							
5	1	2			5	6	7	8	9	10	11			3		2						
Apps	7	6	4	4	7	6	5	7	7	7	7	2		4	2	1			1			
Sub	3				3	2	3	2			1			1		1						
Goals		3																				

1983-84

Manager: John Lyall

1	Aug	27	(h)	Birmingham C	W 4-0	Cottee 2, Martin, Swindlehurst		19,729
2		29	(a)	Everton	W 1-0	Walford		20,375
3	Sep	3	(a)	Tottenham H	W 2-0	Swindlehurst, Whitton		38,042
4		6	(h)	Leicester C	W 3-1	Cottee, Swindlehurst, Walford		22,131
5		10	(h)	Coventry C	W 5-2	Swindlehurst 3, Whitton 2		22,195
6		17	(a)	West Brom A	L 0-1			15,161
7		24	(h)	Notts C	W 3-0	Brooking, Goddard, Stewart		20,613
8	Oct	1	(a)	Stoke C	L 1-3	Stewart		13,852
9		15	(h)	Liverpool	L 1-3	Devonshire		32,555
10		22	(h)	Norwich C	D 0-0			18,958
11		29	(a)	Watford	D 0-0			14,559
12	Nov	5	(h)	Ipswich T	W 2-1	Swindlehurst 2		20,682
13		12	(a)	Wolves	W 3-0	Brooking, Cottee, Swindlehurst		12,062
14		19	(a)	Sunderland	W 1-0	Swindlehurst		19,921
15		27	(h)	Manchester U	D 1-1	Swindlehurst		23,355
16	Dec	3	(a)	Aston Villa	L 0-1			21,297
17		10	(h)	Arsenal	W 3-1	Brooking, Pike, Opp own-goal		25,118
18		17	(a)	Nottingham F	L 0-3			14,544
19		26	(h)	Southampton	L 0-1			22,221
20		27	(a)	Luton T	W 1-0	Cottee		16,343
21		31	(h)	Tottenham H	W 4-1	Brooking, Cottee, Stewart, Martin		30,939
22	Jan	2	(a)	Notts C	D 2-2	Swindlehurst, Stewart		8,667
23		14	(a)	Birmingham C	L 0-3			10,334
24		21	(h)	West Brom A	W 1-0	Cottee		17,213
25	Feb	4	(h)	Stoke C	W 3-0	Barnes, Cottee, Stewart		18,775
26		7	(h)	Queen's Park R	D 1-1	Cottee		20,102
27		11	(a)	Coventry C	W 2-1	Cottee, Opp own-goal		13,271
28		21	(h)	Watford	L 2-4	Barnes, Swindlehurst		19,241
29		25	(a)	Norwich C	L 0-1			16,294
30	Mar	3	(a)	Ipswich T	W 3-0	Cottee, Hilton, Opp own-goal		17,297
31		10	(h)	Wolves	D 1-1	Cottee		18,111
32		17	(a)	Leicester C	L 1-4	Stewart		13,533
33		31	(h)	Queen's Park R	D 2-2	Cottee, Pike		21,099
34	Apr	7	(a)	Liverpool	L 0-6			38,359
35		14	(a)	Sunderland	L 0-1			16,558
36		17	(h)	Luton T	W 3-1	Cottee 2, Martin		15,430
37		21	(a)	Southampton	L 0-2			20,846
38		28	(a)	Manchester U	D 0-0			44,124
39	May	5	(h)	Aston Villa	L 0-1			17,393
40		7	(a)	Arsenal	D 3-3	Whitton 2, Hilton		33,347
41		12	(h)	Nottingham F	L 1-2	Stewart		18,468
42		14	(h)	Everton	L 0-1			25,452

P	W	D	L	F	A	W	D	L	F	A	Pts	Pos	Div	
42	10	4	7	39	24	7	5	9	21	31	60	9th	1	Appearances
														Sub Appearances
														Goals

FA Cup

3	Jan	7	(h)	Wigan A	W 1-0	Stewart	16,000
4		28	(a)	Crystal P	D 1-1	Swindlehurst	27,590
R		31	(h)	Crystal P	W 2-0	Barnes, Pike	27,127
5	Feb	18	(a)	Birmingham C	L 0-3		29,570

Appearances
Sub Appearances
Goals

League Cup

2	Oct	4	(a)	Bury	W 2-1	Orr, Goddard	8,050
		25	(h)	Bury	W 10-0	Stewart, Martin, Devonshire 2, Cottee 4, Brooking 2	10,896
3	Nov	8	(h)	Brighton & HA	W 1-0	Swindlehurst	17,082
4		30	(h)	Everton	D 2-2	Pike, Opp own-goal	19,702
R	Dec	6	(a)	Everton	L 0-2		21,609

Appearances
Sub Appearances
Goals

336

Player appearance and goalscoring grid (shirt numbers by match; * denotes substituted/substitute).

Parkes	Stewart	Walford	Bonds	Martin	Devonshire	Whitton	Cottee	Swindlehurst	Brooking	Pike	Orr	Goddard	Dickens	Allen	Lampard	Donald	Brush	Barnes	Hilton	#
1	2	3	4	5	6	7	8	9	10*	11	12									1
1	2	3	4	5	6	7	8	9		11	10									2
1	2	3	4	5	6	7	8	9	10	11										3
1	2	3	4	5	6	7	8	9	10	11										4
1	2	3	4	5	6		8	9	10	11	7*	12								5
1	2	3	4	5	6		8	9	10	11	7									6
1	2	3	4	5	6	7		9	10	11	8									7
1	2	3	4	5	6	7	12	9	10	11	8*									8
1	2	3	4	5	6	7*	8	9	10	11		12								9
1	2	3	4	5	6		8	9	10		11		7							10
1	2	3	4*	5	6		8	9		11	7	10		12						11
1	2	4		5	6		8	9	10	11	7				3					12
1	2	4		5	6	7	8	9	10	11					3					13
1	2	4		5	6	7	8	9	10	11					3					14
1	2	4		5	6	7	12	9	10	11	8*				3					15
1	2	4		5	6	7		9	10	11	8				3					16
1	2	4		5	6	7		9	10	11*	8	12			3					17
1	2	4		5	6	9	8		10		7	11		3*	12					18
1	2	4		5	6	7	9		10		8				3			11		19
1	2	4		5	6	7	8	9	10		11				3					20
1	2	4		5	6	7	8	9	10		11				3					21
1	2	4		5		7	8	9	10		11				3			6		22
1	2	4					8	9	10	11	5				3		6	7		23
1	2	4					8	9			5		11	10	3		6	7		24
1	2	4					8	9			5		11	10	3		6	7		25
1	2	4					8	9			5		11	10	3		6	7		26
1	2	6	4				8	9					11	10	3			7	5	27
1	2	5	4				8	9					11	10	3			7	6	28
1	2	5	4				8	9	10		7		11		3			6		29
1	2	5	4				8	9	10		6		12	11	3	7*				30
1	2	5	4				8	9	10	11	6*			7	3	12				31
1	2	3	4	5			8	9	10	11	6			7						32
1	2	3	4	5		9	8		10	11	6			7						33
1	2		4	5			8	9	10	11	6*			7	3	12				34
1	2	3	4	5			8	9	10	11				7		6				35
1	2	3	4	5			8	9	10	11				7		6*	12			36
1	2	3	4	5			8		10	11	9			7		6				37
1	2*	3	4				8	9	10	11	5	12		7		6				38
1	2	5	4			11	8		10		9			7	3	6				39
1	2	5	4			11	8		10	12	9			7	3*	6				40
1	2	5	4			9	8	12	10	11*	3			7		6				41
42	42	41	27	29	22	22	37	35	35	27	28	3	7	19	17	1	10	11	7	42
						2	1			1	1	2	3		1	1		2	1	
	7	2		3	1	5	15	13	4	2		1			2	2				

3 own-goals

Parkes	Stewart	Walford	Bonds	Martin	Devonshire	Whitton	Cottee	Swindlehurst	Brooking	Pike	Orr	Goddard	Dickens	Allen	Lampard	Donald	Brush	Barnes	Hilton	
1	2	4		5	6*	7	8	9	10		11				3	12				3
1	2	4					8	9	10	11	5		12	3	6*	7				4
1	2	4					8	9	10	11*	5		12	3	6	7				R
1	2	4	12				8	9			5	11	10	3	6*	7				5
4	4	4		1	1	1	4	4	3	2	4	1	1	3	4	3				
		1										2			1					
	1						1	1							1					

Parkes	Stewart	Walford	Bonds	Martin	Devonshire	Whitton	Cottee	Swindlehurst	Brooking	Pike	Orr	Goddard	Dickens	Allen	Lampard	Donald	Brush	Barnes	Hilton	
1	2	3*	4	5	6	7		9	10	11	12	8								2
1	2	3	4*	5	6		8	9	10	11	12		7							3
1	2	4		5	6		8	9	10	11	7			3						4
1	2	4		5	6	7	8*	9	10	11	6			3						R
1	2	4		5		7	8*	9	10	11	6	12		3						
5	5	5	2	5	4	3	4	5	5	5	2	1		1	3					
											3		1							
	1		1	2		4	1	2	1	1	1									

1 own-goal

337

1984-85

Manager: John Lyall;

									Attendance
1	Aug	25	(h)	Ipswich T	D	0-0			19,032
2		27	(a)	Liverpool	L	0-3			32,633
3	Sep	1	(a)	Southampton	W	3-2	Goddard 2, Dickens		18,442
4		4	(h)	Coventry C	W	3-1	Stewart 2, Cottee		14,949
5		8	(h)	Watford	W	2-0	Barnes, Opp own-goal		19,677
6		15	(a)	Chelsea	L	0-3			32,411
7		22	(h)	Nottingham F	D	0-0			17,434
8		29	(a)	Newcastle U	D	1-1	Allen		29,452
9	Oct	6	(h)	Leicester C	W	3-1	Bonds, Cottee, Stewart		15,306
10		13	(a)	Manchester U	L	1-5	Goddard		47,559
11		20	(a)	Stoke C	W	4-2	Allen, Cottee, Goddard, Opp own-goal		9,945
12		27	(h)	Arsenal	W	3-1	Cottee, Goddard, Pike		33,218
13	Nov	3	(a)	Aston Villa	D	0-0			15,709
14		10	(h)	Everton	L	0-1			24,089
15		17	(h)	Sunderland	W	1-0	Cottee		15,204
16		24	(a)	Luton T	D	2-2	Martin, Whitton		10,789
17	Dec	1	(h)	West Brom A	L	0-2			15,572
18		8	(a)	Norwich C	L	0-1			13,908
19		15	(h)	Sheffield W	D	0-0			14,896
20		22	(h)	Southampton	L	2-3	Cottee 2		14,221
21		26	(a)	Tottenham H	D	2-2	Cottee, Goddard		37,198
22		29	(a)	Coventry C	W	2-1	Cottee 2		10,775
23	Jan	1	(h)	Queen's Park R	L	1-3	Brush		20,857
24	Feb	2	(h)	Newcastle U	D	1-1	Allen		17,723
25		23	(a)	Aston Villa	L	1-2	Goddard		14,845
26	Mar	2	(a)	Arsenal	L	1-2	Cottee		25,818
27		15	(h)	Manchester U	D	2-2	Stewart, Opp own-goal		16,674
28		23	(a)	Leicester C	L	0-1			11,375
29		30	(a)	Nottingham F	W	2-1	Cottee, Goddard		13,560
30	Apr	2	(a)	Watford	L	0-5			17,884
31		6	(h)	Tottenham H	D	1-1	Dickens		24,435
32		8	(a)	Queen's Park R	L	2-4	Cottee 2		16,085
33		13	(h)	Chelsea	D	1-1	Cottee		19,003
34		20	(a)	Sunderland	W	1-0	Goddard		15,622
35		27	(h)	Luton T	D	0-0			17,303
36	May	4	(a)	West Brom A	L	1-5	Stewart		8,878
37		6	(h)	Norwich C	W	1-0	Barnes		16,223
38		8	(a)	Everton	L	0-3			32,657
39		11	(a)	Sheffield W	L	1-2	Cottee		24,314
40		14	(h)	Stoke C	W	5-1	Bonds 2, Hilton, Pike, Stewart		13,362
41		17	(a)	Ipswich T	W	1-0	Cottee		19,296
42		20	(h)	Liverpool	L	0-3			22,408

P	W	D	L	F	A	W	D	L	F	A	Pts	Pos	Div	Appearances
42	7	8	6	27	23	6	4	11	24	45	51	16th	1	Sub Appearances
														Goals

FA Cup

								Attendance
3	Jan	5	(h)	Port Vale	W	4-1	Dickens, Goddard 3	11,452
4	Feb	4	(h)	Norwich C	W	2-1	Stewart, Pike	20,098
5	Mar	4	(a)	Wimbledon	D	1-1	Cottee	13,500
R		6	(h)	Wimbledon	W	5-1	Cottee 3, Dickens, Allen	20,258
6		9	(a)	Manchester U	L	2-4	Allen, Opp own-goal	46,769

Appearances
Sub Appearances
Goals

League Cup

								Attendance
2	Sep	25	(a)	Bristol C	D	2-2	Walford, Cottee	15,894
	Oct	9	(h)	Bristol C	W	6-1	Walford, Whitton, Goddard 2, Cottee 2	11,376
3		31	(a)	Manchester C	D	0-0		20,510
R	Nov	6	(h)	Manchester C	L	1-2	Whitton	17,461

Appearances
Sub Appearances
Goals

338

Players (columns left→right): McAlister, Stewart, Walford, Allen, Martin, Gale, Whitton, Cottee, Goddard, Dickens, Pike, Hilton, Barnes, Bonds, Swindlehurst, Campbell, Orr, Brush, Potts, Parkes, McPherson, Lampard, Parris, Devonshire

No.	McA	Ste	Wal	All	Mar	Gal	Whi	Cot	God	Dic	Pik	Hil	Bar	Bon	Swi	Cam	Orr	Bru	Pot	Par	McP	Lam	Parr	Dev
1	1	2	3	4	5	6	7*	8	9	10	11	12												
2	1	2	3	4	5	6		12	9		11		7	8	10*									
3	1	2	3	4	5	6			9	8*	10	11	12	7										
4	1	2	3	4	5	6			9		10	11	7*	12		8								
5	1	2	3	4	5	6			9		10	11	7	12			8*							
6	1	2	3	4		6			9	8	10	11	7	5										
7	1	2	3	4	5	6			9	8		11	7	10										
8	1	2	3	4	5	6	12		9	8		11	7*	10										
9	1	2	3	4	5	6	7		9	8		11		10										
10	1	2	3	4	5	6	7		9	8	11*			10		12								
11	1	2	3	4	5	6	7		9	8		11		10										
12	1	2	3	4	5	6*	7		9	8		11		10		12								
13	1	2	3	4	5	6*	7		9	8	12	11		10										
14	1	2	3	4	5	6	7		9	8		11		10										
15	1	2	3*	4	5	6	7		9	8		11		10	12									
16	1	2	3	4	5	6	7		9	8		11		10*	12									
17	1	2	3	4	5	6	7		9	8	10	11*	12											
18	1		3	2	5	6	7	10	8	4	11				9									
19	1		3	2	5	6	7	10	8	4*	11				9	12								
20	1			2	5	6		10	12	4	11		8		9*		7	3						
21	1			2	5	6		12	10	9	4	11	8*				7	3						
22	1			2	5	6*		12	10	9	4		8				7	3	11					
23	1	2	6	7	5			10	9	4		11	8					3						
24	1	2	6	7	5			10	9	4		11	8*			12		3						
25	1	2	6	7	5			10	9	4		11					8	3						
26	1	2	4	7	5			10	9	11*	6					12	8	3						
27	1	2	4	7	5			10	9	11*						12	8	3						
28	1	2	4	7	5	6		10	9*		11		8			12		3						
29	1	2	4	7	5	6		10	9		11*		8			12		3						
30	1	2	4	7	5	6		10	9		11		8*			12		3						
31	1*	2	4	7	5	6		10	9		11		12				8	3						
32		2	4	7		6		10	9		11		8				5	3		1				
33		2		7	5	6		10	9		11						4	3		1				
34		2		7	5	6		10	9		11					12	8*	4	3	1				
35		2		7	5	6	8	10	9		11						4	3		1				
36		2		7	5	6		10	9	11*			12	8			4	3		1				
37		2		7	5	6		10	9				11	8			4	3		1				
38		2	7*	5	6			10	9		12		11	8			4	3		1				
39		2			5	6		10	9		11	12	7	8			4*	3		1				
40		2	4		5			10	9				11	6	7	8		3		1				
41		2	10		5	12			9				11		7			3		1	4	6*	8	
App	32	37	33	38	40	36	13	40	38	24	30	5	18	19	8	2	17	18	1	10	1	1	1	
Sub					1	4	1	2	1				4	2	3	8	3							
Gls		6	3	1		1	17	9	2	2		1	2	3			1							

3 own-goals

No.	McA	Ste	Wal	All	Mar	Gal	Whi	Cot	God	Dic	Pik	Hil	Bar	Bon	Swi	Cam	Orr	Bru	Pot	Par	McP	Lam	Parr	Dev
3	1		6	2	5			10	9	4		11	8				7	3						
4	1	2	6	7	5			10	9	4		11	8					3						
5	1	2	4	7	5			10	9			11					8	3			6			
R	1	2		7	5			10	9*	11	4					12	8	3			6			
6	1	2	4	7	5			10	9	6	11*	12					8	3						
App	5	4	4	5	5			5	5	4	4	1	2				4	5			2			
Sub												1				1								
Gls		1		2				4	3	2	1													

1 own-goal

No.	McA	Ste	Wal	All	Mar	Gal	Whi	Cot	God	Dic	Pik	Hil	Bar	Bon	Swi	Cam	Orr	Bru	Pot	Par	McP	Lam	Parr	Dev
2	1	2	3	4	5	6			9	8	10	11	7											
—	1	2	3	4	5	6	7		9	8		11	12	10*										
3	1	2	3	4	5	6	7*	9			11		8	10		12								
R	1	2	3	4	5			7	9	8	12	11		10			6*							
App	4	4	4	4	4	3	3		4	3	1	4	1	4		1	1							
Sub																1								
Gls		2						2	3	2														

339

1985-86

Manager: John Lyall

1	Aug	17	(a)	Birmingham C	L	0-1	11,164
2		20	(h)	Queen's Park R	W	3-1 McAvennie 2, Dickens	15,530
3		24	(h)	Luton T	L	0-1	14,004
4		26	(a)	Manchester U	L	0-2	50,773
5		31	(h)	Liverpool	D	2-2 McAvennie 2	19,762
6	Sep	3	(a)	Southampton	D	1-1 McAvennie	14,477
7		7	(a)	Sheffield W	D	2-2 Cottee, McAvennie	19,287
8		14	(h)	Leicester C	W	3-0 Cottee, Devonshire, McAvennie	12,125
9		21	(a)	Manchester C	D	2-2 Cottee, Opp own-goal	22,001
10		28	(h)	Nottingham F	W	4-2 McAvennie 2, Cottee, Dickens	14,540
11	Oct	5	(a)	Newcastle U	W	2-1 Cottee, McAvennie	26,709
12		12	(h)	Arsenal	D	0-0	24,057
13		19	(h)	Aston Villa	W	4-1 Cottee 2, McAvennie 2	15,034
14		26	(a)	Ipswich T	W	1-0 Cottee	16,849
15	Nov	2	(h)	Everton	W	2-1 McAvennie 2	23,844
16		9	(a)	Oxford U	W	2-1 Cottee, Ward	13,140
17		16	(h)	Watford	W	2-1 McAvennie, Ward	21,490
18		23	(a)	Coventry C	W	1-0 McAvennie	11,042
19		30	(h)	West Brom A	W	4-0 Cottee, Devonshire, Orr, Parris	16,325
20	Dec	7	(a)	Queen's Park R	W	1-0 McAvennie	23,836
21		14	(h)	Birmingham C	W	2-0 McAvennie, Stewart	17,481
22		21	(a)	Luton T	D	0-0	14,599
23		26	(a)	Tottenham H	L	0-1	33,835
24	Jan	11	(a)	Leicester C	W	1-0 McAvennie	11,359
25		18	(a)	Liverpool	L	1-3 Dickens	41,056
26	Feb	2	(h)	Manchester U	W	2-1 Cottee, Ward	20,170
27	Mar	15	(a)	Arsenal	L	0-1	31,240
28		19	(a)	Aston Villa	L	1-2 Opp own-goal	11,567
29		22	(h)	Sheffield W	W	1-0 McAvennie	16,604
30		29	(a)	Chelsea	W	4-0 Cottee 2, Devonshire, McAvennie	29,955
31		31	(h)	Tottenham H	W	2-1 Cottee, McAvennie	27,565
32	Apr	2	(a)	Nottingham F	L	1-2 Cottee	17,498
33		8	(h)	Southampton	W	1-0 Martin	22,459
34		12	(h)	Oxford U	W	3-1 McAvennie, Stewart, Opp own-goal	23,956
35		15	(a)	Chelsea	L	1-2 Cottee	29,360
36		19	(a)	Watford	W	2-0 Cottee, McAvennie	16,651
37		21	(h)	Newcastle U	W	8-1 Martin 3, Goddard, McAvennie, Orr, Stewart, Opp own-goal	24,735
38		26	(a)	Coventry C	W	1-0 Cottee	27,251
39		28	(h)	Manchester C	W	1-0 Stewart	27,153
40		30	(h)	Ipswich T	W	2-1 Dickens, Stewart	31,121
41	May	3	(a)	West Brom A	W	3-2 Cottee, McAvennie, Stewart	17,651
42		5	(a)	Everton	L	1-3 Cottee	40,073

P	W	D	L	F	A	W	D	L	F	A	Pts	Pos	Div	
42	17	2	2	48	16	9	4	8	26	24	84	3rd	1	Appearances
														Sub Appearances
														Goals

FA Cup

3	Jan	5	(a)	Charlton A	W	1-0 Cottee	13,037
4		25	(h)	Ipswich T	D	0-0	25,035
R	Feb	4	(a)	Ipswich T	D	1-1 Cottee	25,384
2R		6	(a)	Ipswich T	W	1-0 Cottee	14,515
5	Mar	5	(h)	Manchester U	D	1-1 McAvennie	26,441
R		9	(a)	Manchester U	W	2-0 Pike, Stewart	30,441
6		12	(a)	Sheffield W	L	1-2 Cottee	35,522

	Appearances
	Sub Appearances
	Goals

League Cup

2	Sep	24	(h)	Swansea C	W	3-0 Stewart, McAvennie, Cottee	9,282
2	Oct	8	(a)	Swansea C	W	3-2 Stewart 2, Cottee	3,584
3		29	(a)	Manchester U	L	0-1	32,056

	Appearances
	Sub Appearances
	Goals

Player appearance and goalscoring grid (League season).

Parkes	Stewart	Walford	Gale	Martin	Devonshire	Ward	McAvennie	Goddard	Cottee	Orr	Dickens	Campbell	Parris	Barnes	Potts	Pike	Hilton	No.
1	2	3	4	5	6	7	8	9*	10	11	12							1
1	2	3	4	5	6	7	8		10	11	9							2
1	2	3	4	5	6	7	8		10*	11	9	12						3
1	2	3	4	5	6	7	8		10*	11	9	12						4
1	2	3	4	5	6	7	8		10	11	9							5
1	2	3	4	5	6	7	8	12	11	9	10*							6
1	2	3	4	5		7	8*		10	11	9	6	12					7
1	2	3	4	5	6	7	8		10	11	9							8
1	2	3	4	5	6	7	8		10	11	9							9
1	2	3	4	5	6	7	8		10	11	9							10
1	2	3	4	5	6	7	8		10	11	9							11
1	2	3	4	5	6	7	8		10	11	9*	12						12
1		3	4	5	6*	7	8		10	11	9		2	12				13
1	2	3*	4	5	6	7	8		10	11	9	12						14
1	2	3	4	5	6	7	8		10	11	9							15
1	2	3	4	5	6	7	8		10	11	9							16
1	2	3	4	5	6	7	8		10	11	9							17
1	2	3	4	5	6	7			10	11	9	8						18
1	2	3	4	5	6	7	8		10	11	9							19
1	2	3	4	5	6	7	8		10	11	9	12						20
1	2	3*	4	5	6	7	8		10	11	9	12						21
1	2	3	4	5	6	7	8		10	11	9							22
1	2	3	4	5	6	7	8		10	11	9							23
1	2	3	4	5	6	7	8		10		9			11				24
1	2	3	4	5	6	7	8		10		9			11				25
1		3	4	5	6	7	8		10		9		2	11				26
1	2		4	5	6	7	8		10		9		3	11				27
1		3	4	5		7	8	12	10*	6	9		2	11				28
1	2		4	5		7	8	12	10*	6	9		3	11				29
1	2		4		6*	7	8		10	12	9		3	11	5			30
1	2		4		6	7*	8		10	12	9		3	11	5			31
1	2		4	5		7	8		10	6	9		3	11				32
1	2		4	5	6	7	8		10		9		3	11				33
1	2		4	5	6	7	8		10	12	9		3	11				34
1	2		4*	5	6	7	8		10	12	9		3	11				35
1	2		4	5	6	7	8		10	11	9		3					36
1	2		4	5	6	7	8	12	10	11	9*		3					37
1	2		4	5	6	7	8		10	11	9		3					38
1	2		4	5	6	7	8		10	11	9		3					39
1	2		4	5	6	7	8	12	10	11*	9		3					40
1	2		4	5	6	7	8		10	11	9		3					41
1	2		4	5	6	7	8	12	10	11	9*		3					42
42	39	27	42	40	38	42	41	1	41	33	40	1	23	10	2			
								5	1	3	1	2	3	1	1			
	6			4	3	3	26	1	20	2	4		1					

4 own-goals

Parkes	Stewart	Walford	Gale	Martin	Devonshire	Ward	McAvennie	Goddard	Cottee	Orr	Dickens	Campbell	Parris	Barnes	Potts	Pike	Hilton	Rd
1	2	3	4	5	6	7	8		10		9			11				3
1	2	3*	4	5	6	7	8	12	10		9			11				4
1		3*	4	5	6	7	8		10	12	9		2	11				R
1	2		4	5		7	8		10	6	9		3	11				2R
1	2		4	5	6	7	8		10		9		3	11				5
1	2		4	5	6	7	8		10		9		3	11				R
1	2		4	5	6	7	8		10		9		3	11				6
7	6	3	7	7	6	7	7		7	1	7		5	7				
								1		1								
					1		4				1							

Parkes	Stewart	Walford	Gale	Martin	Devonshire	Ward	McAvennie	Goddard	Cottee	Orr	Dickens	Campbell	Parris	Barnes	Potts	Pike	Hilton	Rd
1	2	3	4	5	6	7	8		10	11	9							
1	2	3	4	5	6	7	8*		10	11	9	12						2
1	2	3	4	5	6	7	8		10	11	*9	12						3
3	3	3	3	3	3	3	3		3	3	3							
												2						
	3					1		2				*						

1986-87

Manager: John Lyall

							Result		Scorers	Attendance
1	Aug	23	(h)	Coventry C	W	1-0	Gale	21,368
2		25	(a)	Manchester U	W	3-2	Devonshire, McAvennie 2	43,306
3		30	(a)	Oxford U	D	0-0		11,684
4	Sep	2	(h)	Nottingham F	L	1-2	McAvennie	21,305
5		6	(h)	Liverpool	L	2-5	Cottee, Stewart	29,807
6		13	(a)	Queen's Park R	W	3-2	Cottee 3	19,257
7		20	(h)	Luton T	W	2-0	Parris, Gale	19,133
8		27	(a)	Sheffield W	D	2-2	Martin, Orr	25,715
9	Oct	4	(a)	Watford	D	2-2	McAvennie, Dickens	17,120
10		11	(h)	Chelsea	W	5-3	Stewart 2, McAvennie, Cottee 2	26,859
11		18	(a)	Norwich C	D	1-1	Goddard	22,884
12		25	(h)	Charlton A	L	1-3	Cottee	24,141
13	Nov	2	(h)	Everton	W	1-0	Dickens	19,094
14		8	(a)	Arsenal	D	0-0		36,084
15		15	(a)	Wimbledon	W	1-0	Cottee	10,342
16		22	(h)	Aston Villa	D	1-1	Cottee	21,959
17		30	(a)	Newcastle U	L	0-4		22,077
18	Dec	6	(h)	Southampton	W	3-1	Devonshire, Ince, Cottee	18,111
19		13	(a)	Manchester C	L	1-3	Martin	19,067
20		20	(h)	Queen's Park R	D	1-1	Cottee	17,290
21		26	(a)	Tottenham H	L	0-4		39,019
22		27	(h)	Wimbledon	L	2-3	Hilton, Cottee	19,122
23	Jan	1	(h)	Leicester C	W	4-1	McAvennie, Dickens, Cottee 2	16,625
24		3	(a)	Liverpool	L	0-1		41,286
25		24	(a)	Coventry C	W	3-1	Cottee 3	14,191
26	Feb	7	(h)	Oxford U	L	0-1		15,220
27		14	(a)	Nottingham F	D	1-1	Stewart	19,373
28		28	(a)	Luton T	L	1-2	Cottee	11,101
29	Mar	7	(a)	Charlton A	L	1-2	Robson	10,100
30		14	(h)	Norwich C	L	0-2		21,531
31		21	(a)	Chelsea	L	0-1		25,386
32		24	(h)	Sheffield W	L	0-2		13,514
33		28	(a)	Watford	W	1-0	Parris	16,485
34	Apr	8	(h)	Arsenal	W	3-1	Cottee 2, Brady	26,174
35		11	(a)	Everton	L	0-4		35,731
36		14	(h)	Manchester U	D	0-0		23,486
37		18	(a)	Leicester C	L	0-2		10,434
38		20	(h)	Tottenham H	W	2-1	Cottee, McAvennie	23,972
39		25	(a)	Aston Villa	L	0-4		13,584
40	May	2	(h)	Newcastle U	D	1-1	Ward	17,844
41		4	(a)	Southampton	L	0-1		16,810
42		9	(h)	Manchester C	W	2-0	Cottee, Brady	18,413

P	W	D	L	F	A	W	D	L	F	A	Pts	Pos	Div	
42	10	4	7	33	28	4	6	11	19	39	52	15th	1	Appearances
														Sub Appearances
														Goals

FA Cup

						Result	Scorers	Attendance
3	Jan	10	(a)	Orient	D	1-1	Hilton	19,225
R		31	(h)	Orient	W	4-1	Parris, Keen, McAvennie, Cottee	19,424
4	Feb	9	(h)	Sheffield U	W	4-0	Gale, McAvennie 2, Robson	17,194
5		21	(a)	Sheffield W	D	1-1	McAvennie	31,134
R		25	(h)	Sheffield W	L	0-2		30,257

Appearances
Sub Appearances
Goals

League Cup

						Result	Scorers	Attendance
2	Sep	23	(a)	Preston NE	D	1-1	Ward	13,153
	Oct	7	(h)	Preston NE	W	4-1	Cottee 3, Dickens	12,742
3		29	(a)	Watford	W	3-2	Ward, Goddard, Dickens	17,523
4	Nov	18	(h)	Oxford U	W	1-0	Cottee	20,530
5	Jan	27	(h)	Tottenham H	D	1-1	Cottee	29,477
R	Feb	2	(a)	Tottenham H	L	0-5		41,995

Appearances
Sub Appearances
Goals

342

Football appearances and goals grid (shirt numbers per match).

Parkes	Stewart	Parris	Gale	Martin	Devonshire	Ward	McAvennie	Dickens	Cottee	Orr	Hilton	Goddard	Pike	Keen	Walford	Bonds	Ince	Potts	Robson	Brady	Strodder	McQueen	McAlister	Dolan	#
1	2	3	4	5	6	7	8	9	10	11															1
1	2	3		5	6	7	8	9	10	11	4														2
1	2	3	4	5	6	7	8	9	10	11															3
1	2	3	4	5	6*	7	8	9	10	11	12														4
1	2	3	4	5		7	8	9	10	11		6*	12												5
1	2	3	4	5			8	9	10	11				7	6										6
1	2	3	4	5			8	9*	10	11	12			7	6										7
1	2	3	4	5		7	8	9	10	11					6										8
1	2	3	4*		7	8	9	10	11	5				12	6										9
1	2	3	4		7	8*	9	10	11	5		6	12												10
1	2	3	4		7*		9	10	11	5	8	6	12												11
1	2	3	4		6*	7		9	10	11	5	8	12												12
1	2	3	4		6	7		9	10		5	8													13
1	2	3	4		6	7	8	9	10		5			11											14
1	2	3	4		6*	7	8	9	10	11	5			12											15
1		3	4		6	7	8	9			5			11*	2	12									16
1		3	4	5	6	7	8	9*	10	11					2										17
1		3	4	5	6	7	8	12	10	11*					9	2									18
1		3	4	5	6	7	8	9	10	11					9	2									19
1		3		5	6	7	8	9	10	11	12			4*		2									20
1		3		5		7	8	12	10		4	11	9*			6	2								21
1		3		5	6	7	8	9	10		4	11			2										22
1		3		5	6		8	9*	10	7		11			2	12									23
1		3		5	6	7	8	9	10		4				2		11								24
1	2	3	4		6	7	8	9*	10		5				12		11								25
1	2	3	4			7	8		10			9		6	5		11								26
1	2		4			7	8	6	10			9		3*	5	12	11								27
1	2	12	4			7	8*	6	10			9		3	5		11								28
1	2	3	5					6	10		9*	12		4	8		11	7							29
1	2	3	4			7	8		10			9					11	6	5						30
1	2*	3	4			7	8	9	10			12					11	6	5						31
1		9	4			7	8	12	10					2			11*	6	5	3					32
		9	4			7		8	10					2			11	6	5	3	1				33
		9	4*				8	10	12		7			2			11	6	5	3	1				34
		2				7	8	9	10					4			11	6	5	3	1				35
		9*	4			7	8	12	10					2			11	6	5	3	1				36
		4		6	7	8			10					2			11	9	5	3	1				37
		4		6	7	8	12	10						2*			11	9	5	3	1				38
				7	8	9	10			12				4	6	2	11		5	3*	1				39
				7	8		10							2	6	4	11	9	5	3	1				40
				7*	8		10	3			4				2	9	6	5			1	12			41
								10	3		4			11	2	9	6	5			1				42
33	**23**	**35**	**32**	**16**	**20**	**37**	**36**	**31**	**42**	**21**	**15**	**3**	**10**	**7**	**13**	**13**	**7**	**8**	**18**	**12**	**12**	**9**	**9**		
	1							5			1	1	1	1	6	1	4	3					1		
	4	2	2	2	2	1	7	3	22	1	1	1					1		1	2					

Parkes	Stewart	Parris	Gale	Martin	Devonshire	Ward	McAvennie	Dickens	Cottee	Orr	Hilton	Goddard	Pike	Keen	Walford	Bonds	Ince	Potts	Robson	Brady	Strodder	McQueen	McAlister	Dolan	#
1		3		5	6	7	8		10		4		11		2		9								3
1		3	4		7	8	9	10	11	5		6	2*	12											R
1	5	3	4		6*	7	8		10		9	12		2		11									4
1	2	3	4		7	8		10		9		6	5		11										5
1	2	3*	4		6	7	8	12	10	9			5		11										R
5	**3**	**5**	**4**	**1**	**3**	**5**	**5**	**5**	**1**	**2**	**4**	**1**	**3**	**3**	**1**	**3**									
	1	1				4		1			1			1			1								

Parkes	Stewart	Parris	Gale	Martin	Devonshire	Ward	McAvennie	Dickens	Cottee	Orr	Hilton	Goddard	Pike	Keen	Walford	Bonds	Ince	Potts	Robson	Brady	Strodder	McQueen	McAlister	Dolan	#
1	2	3	4	5		7	8		10	11		9		6											
1	2	3			7	8	9*	10	11	5		4	6	12											2
1	2	3	4		6	7		9	10	11	5*	8	12												3
1		3	4		6	7	8	9	10	5		11	2*	12											4
1		3		5	6	7	8	9	10	4		2		11											5
1		3*	4	5	6	7	8		10	9	12			2			11								R
6	**3**	**6**	**4**	**3**	**4**	**6**	**5**	**4**	**6**	**4**	**4**	**1**	**1**	**2**	**4**	**1**	**2**								
								2		1	5			1											

1987-88

Manager: John Lyall

1	Aug	15	(h)	Queen's Park R	L	0-3		22,881
2		22	(a)	Luton T	D	2-2	Brady, Stewart	18,073
3		29	(h)	Norwich C	W	2-0	Cottee 2	16,394
4		31	(a)	Portsmouth	L	1-2	Strodder	16,104
5	Sep	5	(h)	Liverpool	D	1-1	Cottee	29,865
6		12	(a)	Wimbledon	D	1-1	Cottee	8,507
7		19	(h)	Tottenham H	L	0-1		27,750
8		26	(a)	Arsenal	L	0-1		40,127
9	Oct	3	(h)	Derby C	D	1-1	Brady	17,226
10		10	(h)	Charlton A	D	1-1	Ince	15,757
11		17	(a)	Oxford U	W	2-1	Cottee, Opp own-goal	9,092
12		25	(h)	Manchester U	D	1-1	Stewart	19,863
13		31	(a)	Watford	W	2-1	Dickens, Cottee	14,427
14	Nov	7	(h)	Sheffield W	L	0-1		16,277
15		14	(a)	Everton	L	1-3	Hilton	29,405
16		21	(h)	Nottingham F	W	3-2	Cottee 2, Stewart	17,216
17		28	(a)	Coventry C	D	0-0		16,740
18	Dec	5	(h)	Southampton	W	2-1	Keen, Dickens	14,975
19		12	(a)	Chelsea	D	1-1	Parris	22,850
20		19	(h)	Newcastle U	W	2-1	Robson, Ince	18,679
21		26	(h)	Wimbledon	L	1-2	Stewart	18,605
22		28	(a)	Tottenham H	L	1-2	Hilton	39,456
23	Jan	1	(a)	Norwich C	L	1-4	Cottee	20,069
24		2	(h)	Luton T	D	1-1	Ince	16,716
25		16	(a)	Queen's Park R	W	1-0	Dickens	14,509
26	Feb	6	(a)	Liverpool	D	0-0		42,049
27		13	(h)	Portsmouth	D	1-1	Cottee	18,639
28		27	(a)	Derby C	L	0-1		16,301
29	Mar	5	(h)	Oxford U	D	1-1	Ward	14,980
30		12	(a)	Charlton A	L	0-3		8,118
31		19	(h)	Watford	W	1-0	Rosenior	16,051
32		26	(a)	Manchester U	L	1-3	Rosenior	37,269
33	Apr	2	(a)	Sheffield W	L	1-2	Rosenior	18,435
34		4	(h)	Everton	D	0-0		21,195
35		12	(h)	Arsenal	L	0-1		26,746
36		20	(a)	Nottingham F	D	0-0		15,775
37		23	(h)	Coventry C	D	1-1	Cottee	17,733
38		30	(a)	Southampton	L	1-2	Cottee	15,652
39	May	2	(h)	Chelsea	W	4-1	Rosenior 2, Hilton, Cottee	28,521
40		7	(a)	Newcastle U	L	1-2	Robson	23,731

P	W	D	L	F	A	W	D	L	F	A	Pts	Pos	Div	Appearances
40	6	9	5	23	21	3	6	11	17	31	42	16th	1	Sub Appearances
														Goals

FA Cup

3	Jan	9	(h)	Charlton A	W	2-0	Brady, Cottee	22,043
4		30	(a)	Queen's Park R	L	1-3	Cottee	23,651

Appearances
Sub Appearances
Goals

League Cup

2	Sep	22	(a)	Barnsley	D	0-0		10,330
	Oct	6	(h)	Barnsley	L	2-5	Keen, Robson	12,403

Appearances
Sub Appearances
Goals

McAlister	Stewart	McQueen	Orr	Martin	Devonshire	Ward	McAvennie	Brady	Cottee	Robson	Dickens	Strodder	Bonds	Ince	Parris	Hilton	Keen	Potts	Dolan	Dicks	Parkes	Slater	Gale	Rosenior	
1	2†	3	4	5	6*	7	8	9	10	11	12	14													1
1	2	3		5		7	8	6	10	11			4	9											2
1	2	3		5		7	8	6	10	11			4	9											3
1	2*	3		5		7	8	6	10	11			4	9		12									4
1	2	3*		5		7	8	6	10	11			4	9		12									5
1	2			5		7	8	6	10	11			4	9	3										6
1	2			5		7	8	6	10	11			4*	9	3	12									7
1	2			5			8	6	10	11			4	9	3		7								8
1	2†	3*		5				6	10	11			4	9	8	12	7					14			9
1	2			5		7		6	10	11	8			9	3		4								10
1	2			5	8			6	10	11	4			9	3		7								11
1	2	11		5		7		6	10		8			9	3		4								12
1	2			5		7		6	10	11	8			9	3		4								13
1	2			5		7		6	10	11	8			9	3		4*		12						14
1			5†			7		6	10	11	8	12	2	9	3*	4	14								15
1	5					7			10	11	8		2	9	3	4	6								16
1	5					7			10	11	8		2	9	3	4	6								17
1	5					7			10	11	8	4	2	9	3		6								18
1	5					7			10	11	8	4	2		3	9	6								19
1	5						7		10	11	8	4	2*	9	3	12	6								20
1	5					7		14	10	11	8†	4	2	9	3*	12	6								21
1	5					7*	8		10	11		12	2	9	3	4	6								22
1	5					7			10	11	8		2	9*	3	4	6†	14				12			23
1	2	3				7	8		10	11	9	5	4										6		24
1	2	12				7	8		10	11	9*	5	4		3								6		25
1	2					7	8		10	11	9	5	4		3								6		26
1	2	14				7	8*		10	11	9†	5	4		3	12							6		27
1	2	3				7			10	11		5	4	9*		12							6		28
1	2	3				7			10	11	8	5	4				12	9					6		29
1	2					7			10	11*	12	5	4				8	3					6	9	30
1	2					7			10		11	5	4				8*	3					6	9	31
1	2					7			10	11	12	5†	4*				8		14	3			6	9	32
1	2*					7			10	11	8	5		12	4					3			6	9	33
1						7			10	11		8	5	12	2*					3	1		6	9	34
						7			10	11		5	4				8	12	2*	3	1		6	9	35
1						7			10	11	8	5	4	2						3			6	9	36
1						7			10		8	5		9*	2	12	4†			3		14	6	9	37
1						7			10		8	5	4	11			2			3			6	9	38
1						7			10	11	8			2	5		4			3			6	9	39
1						7			10	11	8			2	5		4			3			6	9	40
39	33	10	1	15	1	37	8	21	40	37	25	27	22	26	27	9	19	7	1	8	1		17	9	
	2			1				1			3	3		2	3	5	4	1	3		2	1			
	4			1		2	13	2	3	1		3	1	3	1	3	1						5		

1 own-goal

McAlister	Stewart	McQueen	Orr	Martin	Devonshire	Ward	McAvennie	Brady	Cottee	Robson	Dickens	Strodder	Bonds	Ince	Parris	Hilton	Keen	Potts	Dolan	Dicks	Parkes	Slater	Gale	Rosenior	
1		3				7	8*		10	11		5	4	12		9	2						6		3
1	2	3*				7		8	10	11	9	5	4			12							6		4
2	2	1		2		2	2	2	1	2	2						1		1				2		
														1	1										
						1	2																		

McAlister	Stewart	McQueen	Orr	Martin	Devonshire	Ward	McAvennie	Brady	Cottee	Robson	Dickens	Strodder	Bonds	Ince	Parris	Hilton	Keen	Potts	Dolan	Dicks	Parkes	Slater	Gale	Rosenior	
1		12		5		7	8	6	10	11			4	9	3		2*								2
1		3†		5		7		6	10	11	12	4		9	2*	14	8								
2		1		2		2	1	2	2	2		2	2		1	1									
		1								1					1										
										1					1										

1988-89

Manager: John Lyall

					Result		Scorers	Attendance
1	Aug	27	(a)	Southampton	L	0-4		18,407
2	Sep	3	(h)	Charlton A	L	1-3	Keen	19,566
3		10	(a)	Wimbledon	W	1-0	Ward	7,730
4		17	(h)	Aston Villa	D	2-2	Kelly, Opp own-goal	19,186
5		24	(a)	Manchester U	L	0-2		39,941
6	Oct	1	(h)	Arsenal	L	1-4	Dickens	27,658
7		8	(a)	Middlesbrough	L	0-1		19,608
8		15	(a)	Queen's Park R	L	1-2	Kelly	14,566
9		22	(h)	Newcastle U	W	2-0	Dickens, Stewart	17,765
10		29	(h)	Liverpool	L	0-2		30,188
11	Nov	5	(a)	Coventry C	D	1-1	Kelly	14,651
12		12	(h)	Nottingham F	D	3-3	Kelly 2, Rosenoir	21,583
13		19	(a)	Luton T	L	1-4	Martin	9,308
14		26	(h)	Everton	L	0-1		22,176
15	Dec	3	(a)	Millwall	W	1-0	Ince	20,105
16		10	(h)	Sheffield W	D	0-0		16,676
17		17	(h)	Tottenham H	L	0-2		28,365
18		27	(a)	Norwich C	L	1-2	Stewart	17,491
19		31	(a)	Charlton A	D	0-0		11,084
20	Jan	2	(h)	Wimbledon	L	1-2	Rosenior	18,346
21		14	(a)	Derby C	W	2-1	Brady, Kelly	16,796
22		21	(h)	Manchester U	L	1-3	Brady	29,822
23	Feb	4	(a)	Arsenal	L	1-2	Dicks	40,139
24		25	(h)	Queen's Park R	D	0-0		17,371
25	Mar	11	(h)	Coventry C	D	1-1	Ince	15,205
26		25	(a)	Aston Villa	W	1-0	Ince	22,471
27		27	(h)	Norwich C	L	0-2		27,265
28	Apr	1	(a)	Tottenham H	L	0-3		28,376
29		8	(h)	Derby C	D	1-1	Rosenior	16,560
30		11	(h)	Middlesbrough	L	1-2	Keen	16,217
31		15	(h)	Southampton	L	1-2	Brady	14,766
32		22	(h)	Millwall	W	3-0	Dickens, Dicks, Parris	16,603
33	May	3	(a)	Newcastle U	W	2-1	Keen, Ward	14,202
34		6	(h)	Luton T	W	1-0	Dickens	18,606
35		9	(a)	Sheffield W	W	2-0	Dickens, Rosenior	19,905
36		13	(a)	Everton	L	1-3	Slater	21,694
37		18	(a)	Nottingham F	W	2-1	Rosenior 2	20,943
38		23	(a)	Liverpool	L	1-5	Rosenior	41,855

P	W	D	L	F	A	W	D	L	F	A	Pts	Pos	Div	
38	3	6	10	19	30	7	2	10	18	32	38	19th	1	Appearances
														Sub Appearances
														Goals

FA Cup

3	Jan	8	(h)	Arsenal	D	2-2	Dickens, Opp own-goal	22,017
R		11	(a)	Arsenal	W	1-0	Rosenior	44,124
4		28	(a)	Swindon T	D	0-0		18,627
R	Feb	1	(h)	Swindon T	W	1-0	Rosenior	24,723
5		18	(a)	Charlton A	W	1-0	Slater	18,785
6	Mar	18	(h)	Norwich C	D	0-0		29,119
R		22	(a)	Norwich C	L	1-3	Ince	25,785

Appearances
Sub Appearances
Goals

League Cup

2	Sep	27	(a)	Sunderland	W	3-0	Kelly 2, Rosenior	13,691
	Oct	12	(h)	Sunderland	W	2-1	Kelly, Dickens	10,558
3	Nov	1	(h)	Derby C	W	5-0	Martin 2, Stewart, Rosenior, Keen	14,226
4		30	(h)	Liverpool	W	4-1	Ince 2, Gale, Opp own-goal	26,971
5	Jan	18	(a)	Aston Villa	W	2-1	Ince, Kelly	30,110
SF	Feb	12	(h)	Luton T	L	0-3		24,602
	Mar	1	(a)	Luton T	L	0-2		12,020

Appearances
Sub Appearances
Goals

McAlister	Potts	Dicks	Gale	Martin	Keen	Ward	Parris	Slater	Kelly	Robson	Dickens	Hilton	Ince	Devonshire	McKnight	Rosenior	Strodder	Stewart	Brady	Parkes	McAvennie	McQueen	No.
1	2	3	4*	5	6	7	8	9†	10	11	14	12											1
1	2†	3		5	6*	7	8	9	10	11	4		14	12									2
		3		5		7	2	8*	10	11			6	12	1	9	4*						3
		3		5		7	2	8	10	11	5		6	12	1	9	4*						4
		3		5		7	2†	8	10	11	4		6	12	1	9*	14						5
	2†	3	4		14	7		9	8	10	5		11	6	1								6
	2	3	4		14	7	8		10		5		11	6†	1	9							7
		3	4	5	14	7	9	8	10				11	6†	1	2							8
		3	4	5		7	9	8*	10	11			6	12	1	2							9
	2	3	4	5	6	7		8	10	11				12	1	9							10
	2	3	4	5	6	7	14	8*	10	11†				12	1	9		12					11
	2	3	4	5	6†	7	14		10*	11	12				1	9	8						12
	2	3	4	5	6	7*			10	11	12				1	9	8						13
	2	3	4	5				8	10	11			6		1	9	7						14
	2		4	5			3	8	10	11			6		1	9	7						15
	2		4	5	12		3	8	10	11	6*				1	9	7						16
	2		4	5*	14		3	8	10†	11	6				1	9	12	7					17
	2	3	4	5			11	12	8	10					1	9	6	7*					18
	2	3	4	5			11		8	10					1	9	6	7					19
5		3	4		14			8	10	11			6		1	9	12	2*	7†				20
	2	3	4	5	14	10		8*		11			6†	1	9		12		7				21
	2	3	4			7		12		11	8			6*	1	9	5	10					22
	2	3	4	5		7	12	9	8*	11	6							10	1				23
	2	3	4	5		9	7	8	11	6								10	1				24
		3	4		7	2	9	12	5	11	6*							10	1	8			25
		3	4		7	2	9	6	5	11			12					10*	1	8			26
6		3	4		7	2	9	12		11					5*			10	1	8			27
12		3	4*	5		7	2	14	6	11			9					10†	1	8			28
4		3		11		7	2		6	5			9					10	1	8			29
4		3			14	7	2	6†	5	11			9					10*	1	8	12		30
5		3	4	10		7	2	9	6	11*								1	8	12			31
		3	4	5	10	7	2	9	14	6			11					1	8†				32
12		3	4*	5	10	7	2	8	14	6			11	9†				1					33
12		3	4*	5	10	7	2	8		6			11	9				1					34
12		3	4	5	10†	7	2	8	14	6			11*	9				1					35
12		3	4	5	10	7	2	8		6				1	9			11*					36
		3	4	5	14	7	2	8		6			11†	9				10*	12				37
																							38
2	23	34	31	27	16	30	23	16	21	6	34	9	32	14	23	26	4	5	21	13	8		
	5				8			4	2	4		3	2	1	6		2	3	1	1		1	2	
	2		1		3	2	1	1	6		5		3			7			2	3				

1 own-goal

McAlister	Potts	Dicks	Gale	Martin	Keen	Ward	Parris	Slater	Kelly	Robson	Dickens	Hilton	Ince	Devonshire	McKnight	Rosenior	Strodder	Stewart	Brady	Parkes	McAvennie	McQueen	Rd
4	3		5	12			8		10	11	6*		1	9				2	7				3
4	3		5*	14			8		10	11	6		1	9	12	2	7†						R
2	3	4	5		7		8		12	11	6*		1	9		10							4
2	3	4	5*		7		8†		14	11	6		1	9	12	10							R
2		4	5	12	7	3	9		8	11	6*		1			10		1					5
2	3	4		12			9	7	8	11	6*					5		10	1				6
2	3	4		14		9	7†	8	12	11	6*					5		10	1				R
7	6	5	5	5	3	1	3	6	5	7	7	4	4	2	2	7	3						
		5						1			2	1				2							
		1	2	1			4		1		3			2		1							

1 own-goal

McAlister	Potts	Dicks	Gale	Martin	Keen	Ward	Parris	Slater	Kelly	Robson	Dickens	Hilton	Ince	Devonshire	McKnight	Rosenior	Strodder	Stewart	Brady	Parkes	McAvennie	McQueen	Rd
12	3		5*		7	2	8	11	10	4	6			1	9								2
2	3	4		12	7	9		8	10	5	11	6*	1										
		3	4	5	6	7		8*	10	11			1		9		2	12					3
2	3	4	5			8		10	11	6	1	9					7						4
2	3	4		12			8	10*	11	6	1	9					10	1					5
2	3	4	5		7		12	8	11	6	1	9					10*						SF
2	3	4	5		7	8	9	6		11		9					10	1						
5	7	6	5	1	5	3	1	6	1	6	2	7	4	6	5	1	1	4	1				
1			1	1		1									1								
		1	2	1			4		1		3			2		1							

1 own-goal

347

1989-90

Manager: Lou Macari

1	Aug	10	(a)	Stoke C	D	1-1	Keen	16,058
2		23	(h)	Bradford C	W	2-0	Slater 2	19,914
3		26	(a)	Plymouth A	W	3-2	Allen, Keen, Kelly	20,231
4	Sep	2	(a)	Hull C	D	1-1	Ward	9,235
5		9	(h)	Swindon T	D	1-1	Allen	21,469
6		16	(a)	Brighton & HA	L	0-3		12,689
7		23	(h)	Watford	W	1-0	Dicks	20,728
8		26	(a)	Portsmouth	W	1-0	Rosenior	12,632
9		30	(h)	West Brom A	L	2-3	Dolan, Parris	19,842
10	Oct	7	(h)	Leeds U	L	0-1		23,539
11		14	(a)	Sheffield U	W	2-0	Ward 2	20,822
12		18	(h)	Sunderland	W	5-0	Dolan 2, Allen, Keen, Slater	20,901
13		21	(a)	Port Vale	D	2-2	Keen, Slater	8,899
14		28	(h)	Oxford U	W	3-2	Dicks, Parris, Slater	19,177
15	Nov	1	(a)	Bournemouth	D	1-1	Strodder	9,979
16		4	(a)	Wolves	L	0-1		22,231
17		11	(h)	Newcastle U	D	0-0		25,892
18		18	(h)	Middlesbrough	W	2-0	Dicks, Slater	18,720
19		25	(a)	Blackburn R	L	4-5	Brady, Dicks, Slater, Ward	10,215
20	Dec	2	(h)	Stoke C	D	0-0		17,704
21		9	(a)	Bradford C	L	1-2	Ward	9,257
22		16	(h)	Oldham A	L	0-2		14,960
23		26	(a)	Ipswich T	L	0-1		24,365
24		30	(a)	Leicester C	L	0-1		16,925
25	Jan	1	(h)	Barnsley	W	4-2	Keen 2, Allen, Dicks	18,391
26		13	(a)	Plymouth A	D	1-1	Quinn	11,671
27		20	(h)	Hull C	L	1-2	Morley	16,847
28	Feb	10	(h)	Brighton & HA	W	3-1	Quinn 2, Dicks	19,101
29		18	(a)	Swindon T	D	2-2	Quinn 2	16,105
30		24	(h)	Blackburn R	D	1-1	Quinn	20,054
31	Mar	3	(a)	Middlesbrough	W	1-0	Allen	23,617
32		10	(h)	Portsmouth	W	2-1	Allen, Dicks	20,961
33		13	(a)	Watford	W	1-0	Morley	15,683
34		17	(a)	Leeds U	L	2-3	Morley, Opp own-goal	32,536
35		21	(h)	Sheffield U	W	5-0	Quinn 3, Allen, Morley	21,629
36		24	(a)	Sunderland	L	3-4	Quinn 2, Morley	13,896
37		31	(h)	Port Vale	D	2-2	Gale, Morley	20,507
38	Apr	4	(a)	West Brom A	W	3-1	Bishop, Keen, Quinn	11,556
39		7	(a)	Oxford U	W	2-0	Morley, Quinn	8,371
40		11	(h)	Bournemouth	W	4-1	Allen, Bishop, Dicks, Opp own-goal	20,202
41		14	(a)	Barnsley	D	1-1	Morley	10,344
42		17	(h)	Ipswich T	W	2-0	Allen, Keen	25,178
43		21	(a)	Oldham A	L	0-3		12,190
44		28	(a)	Newcastle U	L	1-2	Dicks	31,496
45	May	2	(h)	Leicester C	W	3-1	Keen, Morley, Rosenior	17,939
46		5	(h)	Wolves	W	4-0	Brady, Keen, Morley, Robson	22,509

P	W	D	L	F	A	W	D	L	F	A	Pts	Pos	Div	Appearances
46	14	5	4	50	22	6	7	10	30	35	72	7th	2	Sub Appearances
														Goals

FA Cup

3	Jan	6	(a)	Torquay U	L	0-1		5,342

Appearances
Sub Appearances
Goals

League Cup

2	Sep	19	(a)	Birmingham C	W	2-1	Allen, Slater	10,987
	Oct	4	(h)	Birmingham C	D	1-1	Dicks	12,187
3		25	(a)	Aston Villa	D	0-0		20,989
R	Nov	8	(h)	Aston Villa	W	1-0	Dicks	23,833
4		22	(h)	Wimbledon	W	1-0	Allen	24,746
5	Jan	17	(h)	Derby C	D	1-1	Dicks	25,035
R		24	(a)	Derby C	D	0-0		22,510
2R		31	(h)	Derby C	W	2-1	Slater, Keen	25,166
SF	Feb	14	(a)	Oldham A	L	0-6		19,263
	Mar	7	(h)	Oldham A	W	3-0	Martin, Dicks, Kelly	15,431

Appearances
Sub Appearances
Goals

348

Player appearance and goalscoring grid (shirt numbers worn per match).

Parkes	Potts	Parris	Gale	Martin	Keen	Ward	McAvennie	Slater	Brady	Ince	Kelly D	Strodder	Dicks	Allen	Devonshire	Dolan	Foster	Rosenior	Morley	Bishop	Miklosko	McQueen	Quinn	Robson	Suckling	Fashanu	Kelly P	Milne	#
1	2	3	4	5	6	7	8*	9	10	11	12																		1
1	2	11	4	5	6	7		9	10		8			3															2
1	2	11	4	5	6	7			10		8			3	9														3
1	2		4	5	6	7		11	10†		8			3	9	14													4
1	2	11	4	5	6	7			10*	8†				3	9	12	14												5
1	2	11	4	5	6			8	10					3	9														6
1	2	11	4	5	6			8						3	7			9†	10	14									7
1	2	11	4	5	6			8						3	7				10	9									8
1	2	11	4	5	6			8				9†		3	7	14	10												9
1	2	11	4*	5	6	9		8	12					3	7		10												10
1	2	11		5	6	7		8				4	3			9	10												11
1	2	11		5	6	7		8	12			4	3*	10		9													12
1	2	11		5	6	7		8				4	3	10		9													13
1	2	11		5	6			8	7			4	3	10		9													14
1	2	11		5	6†	14		8	7			4	3	10		9													15
1	2	11		5	6†	14		8	7			4	3	10		9*	12												16
1	2	11		5	6	10		8	7*	14		4	3			12	9†												17
1	2	11		5	6	10		8	7				3	9		4													18
1	2			5		10		8	7				4	3	9	6										11			19
1	2			5	9	10		8	7	14			4	3		6*	12									11†			20
1	2	6		5	9	10		8	7				4		11				3										21
	2	6	5	14	10			8	7				4†	3	11	12	9*								1				22
	2	12	6	5	9	10		8†	7*	14			4	3	11										1				23
	2	11	6	5					10				4	3	7				9	8					1				24
	2	4	6	5	9*				12				3	11			10	8			7				1				25
	2	14	4	5	9†				12				3	7	6*		10	8			11				1				26
2*		6	5		11				7			14	4†				10	8		3	9		1	12					27
1		4*	6	5	11				10	7			9					3	8			12	2						28
		4	6	5	11†				10*	7	14		3	8				12	1			9	2						29
		4	6	5	11				10	7*	14		3	8				12	1			9	2†						30
		4	6	5	11				10	7*		14	3	8				12	1			9†	2						31
		4	6			10		2	7*	11			3	8		5	9†		14	1		12							32
		4	6			10		2					3	8		5		11	7	1		9							33
		4*	6			10		2	12					8		5		11	7	1	3	9							34
		4	6			10		2						8		5		11	7	1	3	9							35
		4	6			10*		2	12		5			8				11	7	1	3	9							36
		4	6			10*	14	2	12				3	8		5		11	7	1		9†							37
		4	6			10		2		5			3	8				11	7	1		9							38
		4	6			10*		2	2				3	8		5		11	7	1	12	9							39
14	4†	6				10		12	2				3	8		5		11*	7	1		9							40
		4	6			7		2	11				3	8		5		10		1		9							41
14	4	6				10		12	2	7†			3	8		5		11*		1	12	9							42
		4	6			10		2	7				3	8		5		11*		1	12	9							43
4	14	6				10		12	2				3	8		5		11†		1		9*	7						44
4		6				10*		2	12				3	8		5	9	11		1		14	7						45
4		6				10*		2	12				3	8		5	9	11†		1		14	7						46
22	30	35	36	31	43	17	1	40	25	1	8	16	40	39	3	8	20	4	18	13	18	5	18	7	6	2			
	2	3			1	2		4	8			8				4	2	2	1	1	4		2	3		1			
	2	1				10	5		7	2			1	1	9	9		3		2	10	2		13	1				

2 own-goals

Parkes	Potts	Parris	Gale	Martin	Keen	Ward	McAvennie	Slater	Brady	Ince	Kelly D	Strodder	Dicks	Allen	Devonshire	Dolan	Foster	Rosenior	Morley	Bishop	Miklosko	McQueen	Quinn	Robson	Suckling	Fashanu	Kelly P	Milne	goals
1	2	4*	6	5	9								3	11				12	10	8			7						3
1	1	1	1	1	1					1	1					1	1			1									
																1													

Parkes	Potts	Parris	Gale	Martin	Keen	Ward	McAvennie	Slater	Brady	Ince	Kelly D	Strodder	Dicks	Allen	Devonshire	Dolan	Foster	Rosenior	Morley	Bishop	Miklosko	McQueen	Quinn	Robson	Suckling	Fashanu	Kelly P	Milne	Rd
1	2	11	4	5	6	7*		8	12				3	9		10													2
1	2	11	4	5	6	10†		8	14	12			3	7	9*														3
1	2	11		5	6			8	7*	12	4	3	10			9													3
1	2	11		5	6	10		8	7			4	3			9													R
1	2	11†		5	6*	10		8	7			4	3	9	14					12									4
1	2	4	6	5	11			12	7			8	3	10			9*												5
1		4	6	5	11			9	7*	8		2		14				3	10*			12							R
1	2*	4	6	5	11			9	7	8		3						12	10				12						2R
1		4	6	5	11			8	7	10	9*	3		12					2										SF
		4	6	5	11			2	7*	10			3	8		9				1	12								
9	7	10	7	10	10	4		9	8	5	5	9	6	4	2		2	1	1	1	3								
								1	2				2		3				2		1	1							
		1	1					2					1	4	2														

1990-91

Manager: Billy Bonds

1	Aug	25	(a)	Middlesbrough	D	0-0	20,680
2		29	(h)	Portsmouth	D	1-1 McAvennie	20,835
3	Sep	1	(h)	Watford	W	1-0 Dicks	19,872
4		8	(a)	Leicester C	W	2-1 Morley, Opp own-goal	14,605
5		15	(h)	Wolves	D	1-1 Martin	23,241
6		19	(h)	Ipswich T	W	3-1 Bishop, Morley, Quinn	18,764
7		22	(a)	Newcastle U	D	1-1 Morley	25,462
8		29	(a)	Sheffield W	D	1-1 Dicks	28,786
9	Oct	3	(h)	Oxford U	W	2-0 Foster, Morley	18,135
10		6	(h)	Hull C	W	7-1 Dicks 2, Quinn 2, Morley, Parris, Potts	19,472
11		13	(a)	Bristol C	D	1-1 McAvennie	16,838
12		20	(a)	Swindon T	W	1-0 McAvennie	13,658
13		24	(h)	Blackburn R	W	1-0 Bishop	20,003
14		27	(h)	Charlton A	W	2-1 Allen 2	24,019
15	Nov	3	(a)	Notts C	W	1-0 Morley	10,781
16		10	(a)	Millwall	D	1-1 McAvennie	20,591
17		17	(h)	Brighton & HA	W	2-1 Foster, Slater	23,082
18		24	(a)	Plymouth A	W	1-0 McAvennie	11,490
19	Dec	1	(h)	West Brom A	W	3-1 McAvennie, Morley, Parris	24,753
20		8	(a)	Portsmouth	W	1-0 Morley	12,045
21		15	(h)	Middlesbrough	D	0-0	23,705
22		22	(a)	Barnsley	L	0-1	10,348
23		26	(h)	Oldham A	W	2-0 Morley, Slater	24,950
24		29	(h)	Port Vale	D	0-0	23,403
25	Jan	1	(a)	Bristol R	W	1-0 Quinn	7,932
26		12	(a)	Watford	W	1-0 Morley	17,172
27		19	(h)	Leicester C	W	1-0 Parris	21,652
28	Feb	2	(a)	Wolves	L	1-2 McAvennie	19,454
29		24	(h)	Millwall	W	3-1 McAvennie 2, Morley	20,503
30	Mar	2	(a)	West Brom A	D	0-0	16,089
31		5	(h)	Plymouth A	D	2-2 Breacker, Opp own-goal	18,933
32		13	(a)	Oxford U	L	1-2 Quinn	8,225
33		16	(h)	Sheffield W	L	1-3 Quinn	26,182
34		20	(h)	Bristol C	W	1-0 Gale	22,951
35		23	(a)	Hull C	D	0-0	9,558
36		29	(a)	Oldham A	D	1-1 Bishop	16,932
37	Apr	1	(h)	Barnsley	W	3-2 Dowie, Foster, McAvennie	24,607
38		6	(a)	Port Vale	W	1-0 Bishop	9,658
39		10	(a)	Brighton & HA	L	0-1	11,904
40		17	(a)	Ipswich T	W	1-0 Morley	20,290
41		20	(h)	Swindon T	W	2-0 Dowie, Parris	25,944
42		24	(h)	Newcastle U	D	1-1 Dowie	24,195
43		27	(a)	Blackburn R	L	1-3 Dowie	10,808
44	May	4	(a)	Charlton A	D	1-1 Allen	16,139
45		8	(h)	Bristol R	W	1-0 Slater	23,054
46		11	(h)	Notts C	L	1-2 Parris	26,551

P	W	D	L	F	A	W	D	L	F	A	Pts	Pos	Div	
46	15	6	2	41	18	9	9	5	19	16	87	2nd	2	Appearances
														Sub Appearances
														Goals

FA Cup

3	Jan	5	(a*)	Aldershot	D	0-0	22,929
R		16	(h)	Aldershot	W	6-1 Morley 2, Slater, Parris, Bishop, Quinn	21,484
4		26	(a)	Luton T	D	1-1 Parris	12,087
R		30	(h)	Luton T	W	5-0 Parris, Bishop, Morley 2, McAvennie	25,659
5	Feb	16	(h)	Crewe A	W	1-0 Quinn	25,298
6	Mar	11	(h)	Everton	W	2-1 Foster, Slater	28,162
SF	Apr	14	(n*)	Nottingham F	L	0-4	40,041

* Played at Villa Park.

Appearances
Sub Appearances
Goals

League Cup

2	Sep	26	(h)	Stoke C	W	3-0 Dicks, Keen, Quinn	15,870
	Oct	10	(a)	Stoke C	W	2-1 Allen 2	8,4411
3		31	(a)	Oxford U	L	1-2 Morley	7,528

Appearances
Sub Appearances
Goals

Miklosko	Potts	Dicks	Foster	Martin	Keen	Bishop	McAvennie	Slater	Allen	Morley	Quinn	Parris	Livett	Rush	Gale	Breacker	Hughton	Clarke	Robson	Carr	Rosenior	Dowie	Stewart	
1	2	3	4	5	6	7	8	9	10	11														1
1	2	3	4	5	6	7	8	9	10	11														2
1	2	3	4	5	6	7	8	9	10†	11*	12	14												3
1	2	3	4	5	6	7	8*	9†	10	11	12	14												4
1	2	3	4	5	6	7	8			10	11	12	9*											5
1	2†	3	4	5	6	7	8*	9	10	11	12	14												6
1	2	3	4	5	6	7	12	9†	10	11	8*	14												7
1	2	3	4	5†	6	7	12	9	10	11	8*	14												8
1	2	3	4	5	6	7		9*	10	11	8	12												9
1	2	3	4	5	6*	7	12		10	11	8†	9		14										10
1	2	3	4	5		7	12	9*	10	11	8	6												11
1	2	3†	4	5		7	12		10	11	8*	6			9	14								12
1		3†	4	5		7	12	14	10	11	8*	6			9	2								13
1			4	5	3	7	8	9*	10	11		6			12	2								14
1			4	5	8	7			10	11	3			9	2	6								15
1			4	5	8	7	9		10*	11	3			12	2	6								16
1			4	5	10	7	8	12		11	3			9*	2	6								17
1			4	5	10	7	8	9		11	3				2	6								18
1			4	5†	10*	7	8	9	12	11	3				2	6								19
1	5					7		8	9	10	11*	12	3		14	2	6							20
1	5					7		8*	9	10	11	12	3		4	2	6							21
1		5				7			9	10	11	8	3		4	2	6							22
1	12	5				7			9	10*	11	8	3		4	2	6							23
1	8	5				7			10		11	9	3		4	2	6							24
1	10	5†				7			8		11	9*	3		4	2	6	12	14					25
1	10					7	5	12	8		11	9*	3		4	2	6							26
1	10					7	5	8	9*	14	11	12	3†		4	2	6							27
1	10					7	5	8	9	14	11		3		4†	2	6							28
1	10					7*	5	8	9	12	11		3			2	6*							29
1	10		4			7	5	8	9	12		11	3			2	6*							30
1	10		5	14	7	8	12			11	3			4	2*	6		9†						31
1	2		5		10	7	8	9	12		11†	3			4		6*		14					32
1	2		5		10	7	8	9*	12		11†	3			4		6			14				33
1	2		5		10†	7	8*		11			3			4		6		14	12	9			34
1	2		5			7	8	10	11			3			4		6				9			35
1	2		5			12	7	8	10	11		3			4		6*				9			36
1	2		5			10	7		8	11		3			4		6				9			37
1	2		5			8	7		11	14	10	12	3				6†				9*	4		38
1	2	5†				10	7	12	8	14	11	3			4		6				9*			39
1	2					10*	7		8	12	11	3			4		6				9	5		40
1	2					10	7		8	12	11	3			4		6				9	5*		41
1	2					8	7	10*	12	11†	14	3			4		6				9	5		42
1	2						7	10	8	11	12	3			4		6				9*	5		43
1	4		5			14	7	12	8	10*	11	3			2		6				9*			44
1	2		5			14	7	12	8	10	11	3			4	6†					9*			45
46	36	13	36	20	36	40	24	37	28	38	16	37	1	2	23	23	32		1		12	5		46
	1				4		10	3	12		10	7		3	1	1		1	1	2	2			
	1	4	3	1		4	10	3	3	12	6	5		1	1						4			

2 own-goals

Miklosko	Potts	Dicks	Foster	Martin	Keen	Bishop	McAvennie	Slater	Allen	Morley	Quinn	Parris	Livett	Rush	Gale	Breacker	Hughton	Clarke	Robson	Carr	Rosenior	Dowie	Stewart	
1	10		5*			7			8	11	9	3	12		4	2	6							3
1	10			7	12			8		11	9	3			4	2	6	5*						R
1	10			7*	5	12	8	9		11		3			4	2	6							4
1	10			7	5	8	9			11		3			4	2	6							R
1	10			7	5	8*	9			11	12	3			4	2	6							5
1	10	5		12	7	8	9				11*	3			4		6				12			6
1	2	5		10	7			8	9*	11†	14	3			4		6				12			SF
7	7	3			6	5	3	7	2	6	3	7			7	6	7	1				1		
					1	1	1			2		1							1					
		1			2	1	2			4	2	3												

Miklosko	Potts	Dicks	Foster	Martin	Keen	Bishop	McAvennie	Slater	Allen	Morley	Quinn	Parris	Livett	Rush	Gale	Breacker	Hughton	Clarke	Robson	Carr	Rosenior	Dowie	Stewart	
1	2	3	4	5	6	7		9	10*	11	8	12												2
1	2	3	4	5	6*	7	14		10	11	9†	8		12										2
1		4	5	3	7		9	10	11	8	6		2											3
3	2	2	3	3	3	3	2	3	3	3	2	1		1		1								
						1				1		1												
		1			2	1	1																	

351

1991-92

Manager: Billy Bonds

No	Month	Date	Venue	Opponent	Result	Scorers	Attendance
1	Aug	17	(h)	Luton T	D 0-0		25,079
2		21	(a)	Sheffield U	D 1-1	Small	21,463
3		24	(a)	Wimbledon	L 0-2		10,081
4		28	(h)	Aston Villa	W 3-1	Small, Rosenior, Brown	23,644
5		31	(h)	Notts C	L 0-2		20,093
6	Sep	4	(a)	Queen's Park R	D 0-0		16,616
7		7	(h)	Chelsea	D 1-1	Small	18,875
8		14	(a)	Norwich C	L 1-2	Small	15,348
9		17	(a)	Crystal P	W 3-2	Thomas, Morley, Small	21,363
10		21	(h)	Manchester C	L 1-2	Brown	25,558
11		28	(a)	Nottingham F	D 2-2	Small 2	25,613
12	Oct	5	(h)	Coventry C	L 0-1		21,817
13		18	(a)	Oldham A	D 2-2	Small, McAvennie	14,365
14		26	(h)	Tottenham H	W 2-1	Small, Thomas	23,946
15	Nov	2	(a)	Arsenal	W 1-0	Small	33,539
16		17	(h)	Liverpool	D 0-0		23,569
17		23	(a)	Manchester U	L 1-2	McAvennie	47,185
18		30	(h)	Sheffield W	L 1-2	Breacker	24,116
19	Dec	7	(a)	Everton	L 0-4		21,563
20		21	(h)	Sheffield U	D 1-1	Dicks	19,287
21		26	(a)	Aston Villa	L 1-3	McAvennie	31,959
22		28	(a)	Notts C	L 0-3		11,163
23	Jan	1	(h)	Leeds U	L 1-3	Dicks	21,766
24		11	(h)	Wimbledon	D 1-1	Morley	18,485
25		18	(a)	Luton T	W 1-0	Small	11,088
26	Feb	1	(h)	Oldham A	W 1-0	Thomas	19,012
27		22	(a)	Sheffield W	L 1-2	Small	24,150
28		29	(h)	Everton	L 0-2		20,976
29	Mar	3	(a)	Southampton	L 0-1		14,548
30		11	(a)	Liverpool	L 0-1		30,821
31		14	(h)	Arsenal	L 0-2		22,640
32		21	(h)	Queen's Park R	D 2-2	Small, Breacker	20,401
33		28	(a)	Leeds U	D 0-0		31,101
34	Apr	1	(a)	Tottenham H	L 0-3		31,809
35		4	(a)	Chelsea	L 1-2	C.Allen	20,684
36		11	(h)	Norwich C	W 4-0	Rush 2, Dicks, Bishop	16,896
37		14	(h)	Southampton	L 0-1		18,298
38		18	(a)	Manchester C	L 0-2		25,601
39		20	(h)	Crystal P	L 0-2		17,710
40		22	(h)	Manchester U	W 1-0	Brown	24,197
41		25	(a)	Coventry C	L 0-1		15,398
42	May	2	(h)	Nottingham F	W 3-0	McAvennie 3	20,629

P	W	D	L	F	A	W	D	L	F	A	Pts	Pos	Div	
42	6	6	9	22	24	3	5	13	15	35	38	22nd	1	Appearances
														Sub Appearance
														Goals

FA Cup

Round	Month	Date	Venue	Opponent	Result	Scorers	Attendance
3	Jan	4	(a*)	Farnborough T	D 1-1	Dicks	23,449
R		14	(h)	Farnborough T	W 1-0	Morley	23,869
4		25	(h)	Wrexham	D 2-2	Dicks, Morley	24,712
R	Feb	4	(a)	Wrexham	W 1-0	Foster	17,995
5		15	(a)	Sunderland	D 1-1	Small	25,475
R		26	(h)	Sunderland	L 2-3	Allen 2	25,830

*Played at home

Appearances
Sub Appearances
Goals

League Cup

Round	Month	Date	Venue	Opponent	Result	Scorers	Attendance
2	Sep	24	(a)	Bradford C	D 1-1	Small	7,034
	Oct	9	(h)	Bradford C	W 4-0	Keen, Morley, Parris, Small	17,232
3		29	(a)	Sheffield U	W 2-0	McAvennie, Small (pen)	11,144
4	Dec	4	(a)	Norwich C	L 1-2	Small	16,325

Appearances
Sub Appearances
Goals

Miklosko	Brown	Thomas	Breacker	Foster	Parris	Bishop	Slater	Small	Rosenior	Allen M	Morley	Keen	Rush	Parks	Hughton	Potts	Gale	Dicks	McAvennie	Atteveld	Allen C	Martin A	Martin D	Clarke	
1	2	3	4	5	6	7*	8	9	10	11		12													1
1	2	3	4	5	6	7	8	9	10*	11†	12	14													2
1	2	3	4	5	6	7	8†	9	10	11*	12		14												3
1	2	3	4	5	6	7	8	9	10	11*		12													4
	2	3	4	5	6	7	8	9	10*		12	11†	1	14											5
	2	3	4	5	6	7	8	9*	14		11†		12	1		10									6
1	2	3	4	5	6	7	8	9		11						10									7
1	2	3	4	5	6*	7	8	9	14		11†		12			10									8
1	2	4	6	5	3	7	8	9		11						10									9
1	2	3	4	5	6	7	8	9	12		11*					10									10
1		3*	2	5	6	7	8	9*	12		11					10	4								11
1	5	3*	2		6	7	8*	9		12	11†	14				10	4								12
1		3	2		6	7	8*	9		12	11†	10				5	4		14						13
1		3	2		6	7	11	9		12		10*				5	4	8							14
1		3	2		6	7	11	9				10				5	4	8							15
1		3	2		6	7	11	9				10				5	4	8							16
1		3	2		6	7	11	9		12		10*				5	4	8							17
1		3	2		6	7	11	9		12		10*				5	4	8							18
1		3	2		6*	7	11	9		10		12				5	4	8							19
1	2			6		7	11	9*		10		12				5	4	3	8						20
1		2		6		7	11	9*			12	10				5	4	3	8						21
1		2	6			7	11	9				10				5	4	3	8						22
1		6	2			7	11	9*			12	10				5	4	3	8						23
1	9	6*	2	5				7	11	14		12	10†				4	3	8						24
1	9	6	2	5				7	11*	14		10	12			4		3	8†						25
	9	6	2	5				11	12		10*	7		1		4		3	8						26
	12		2	5				7	11	9	10	8*		1		4		3		6					27
	8	6	2†	5				7	11*	9	10	12		14	1		4		3						28
	8	6*		5				7	11	9	10	12		14	1		2	4†	3						29
1	2	6*					7	11	9	10		8	12			5	4	3							30
1	2			5	14	7	11	9	10†	12	6					4	3	8*							31
1	2	12	14	5		7*	11	9	10		6†					4	3	8							32
1	2	8	4	5		7	11*	9	10†			12				6	14	3	12						33
1	2	8	6*	5		7	11	9				12				10	4	3	12						34
1	2	9		5		7			12	11*						6	4	3	8	10					35
1		6	2			7	11	9				12	8			4	3			10	5				36
1		2				7	11	9		6	12	8*		4		3			10	5					37
1		2				7	11	9*		10	6			4	8	3		5		12					38
1	12	6	2*			7	11			9	8		4		3			10	5						39
1	10	6				7	11	9			8		2	4	3			5							40
1	10*	6			7†	11	9			12	8	2	4	3			5	14							41
1		6			7	11	9		8			2	4	3	12		5	10							42
36	25	34	33	24	20	41	41	37	5	14	13	20	3	6	34	24	23	16	1	4	7	1			
2	1	1		1					3	4	5	11	9	7		1		1			4		1	1	
3	3	2			1		13	1		2		2				3	6		1						

Miklosko	Brown	Thomas	Breacker	Foster	Parris	Bishop	Slater	Small	Rosenior	Allen M	Morley	Keen	Rush	Parks	Hughton	Potts	Gale	Dicks	McAvennie	Atteveld	Allen C	Martin A	Martin D	Clarke	
1		6	2			7	11	9			12	10				5*	4	3	8						3
1	9	6	2	5		7	11				10					4	3	8							R
1	9	6	2	5			11	12		10	7				4	3	8*								4
	9	6	2	5			11	10†		14	7		1		4	3	8*		12						R
	8		2	5			11	9	10		7	1			4	3		6							5
			2	5		7	11	9	10	12	8		1		4	3		6*							R
3	4	4	6	5		3	6	4	2	2	5	3	5	2	6	4	2								
						1		3						2				1							
		1			1	2	2				2			1	1										

Miklosko	Brown	Thomas	Breacker	Foster	Parris	Bishop	Slater	Small	Rosenior	Allen M	Morley	Keen	Rush	Parks	Hughton	Potts	Gale	Dicks	McAvennie	Atteveld	Allen C	Martin A	Martin D	Clarke	
1	2	4	6	5	3	7	8	9		11*				10	12										2
1		3	2	5	6	7	8	9*		11	10				4	12									
1		3	2		6	7	11	9	12		10				5	4*	8								3
1		3	2		6	7	11	9	10						5	4	8								4
4	1	4	4	2	4	4	4	4	1	2	2				3	3	2								
								1																	
			1				4				1	1				2									

353

1992-93

Manager: Billy Bonds MBE

						Result		Scorers	Attendance
1	Aug	16	(a)	Barnsley		W	1-0	C.Allen	6,761
2		22	(h)	Charlton A		L	0-1		17,054
3		29	(a)	Newcastle U		L	0-2		29,855
4	Sep	5	(h)	Watford		W	2-1	C.Allen, M.Allen	11,921
5		12	(a)	Peterborough U		W	3-1	M.Allen, Morley, Keen	10,657
6		15	(a)	Bristol C		W	5-1	Robson, Morley 2, C.Allen 2	14,130
7		20	(h)	Derby C		D	1-1	Morley	11,493
8		27	(a)	Portsmouth		W	1-0	C.Allen	12,158
9	Oct	4	(a)	Wolves		D	0-0		14,391
10		11	(h)	Sunderland		W	6-0	Martin, Morley, M.Allen, Robson 2, Keen	10,326
11		17	(a)	Bristol R		W	4-0	Dicks, Morley, C.Allen, Keen	6,189
12		24	(h)	Swindon T		L	0-1		17,842
13		31	(a)	Cambridge U		L	1-2	Morley	7,214
14	Nov	3	(a)	Grimsby T		D	1-1	Morley	9,119
15		7	(h)	Notts C		W	2-0	C.Allen, Morley	12,345
16		15	(a)	Millwall		L	1-2	Robson	12,445
17		21	(h)	Oxford U		W	5-3	C.Allen, Breacker, Dicks 2, Morley	11,842
18		28	(h)	Birmingham C		W	3-1	C.Allen 2, Morley	15,004
19	Dec	4	(a)	Tranmere R		L	2-5	C.Allen, Morley	11,782
20		12	(h)	Southend U		W	2-0	C.Allen, Morley	15,739
21		20	(a)	Brentford		D	0-0		11,912
22		26	(a)	Charlton A		D	1-1	Dicks	8,337
23		28	(h)	Luton T		D	2-2	Dicks, Breacker	18,786
24	Jan	10	(a)	Derby C		W	2-0	Robson, Morley	13,737
25		16	(h)	Portsmouth		W	2-0	Morley, Foster	18,127
26		27	(h)	Bristol C		W	2-0	Morley, Robson	12,118
27		30	(a)	Leicester C		W	2-1	Robson, Gale	18,838
28	Feb	6	(h)	Barnsley		D	1-1	Jones	14,101
29		9	(h)	Peterborough U		W	2-1	Butler, Jones	12,537
30		13	(a)	Watford		W	2-1	Robson, Keen	13,115
31		21	(h)	Newcastle U		D	0-0		24,159
32		27	(a)	Sunderland		D	0-0		19,068
33	Mar	6	(h)	Wolves		W	3-1	Morley, Dicks, Holmes	24,679
34		9	(h)	Grimsby T		W	2-1	Dicks 2	13,170
35		13	(a)	Notts C		L	0-1		10,272
36		20	(h)	Tranmere R		W	2-0	Dicks 2	16,369
37		23	(a)	Oxford U		L	0-1		9,506
38		28	(a)	Millwall		D	2-2	Keen, Morley	15,723
39	Apr	3	(a)	Birmingham C		W	2-1	Brown, Bishop	19,053
40		7	(a)	Southend U		L	0-1		12,813
41		11	(h)	Leicester C		W	3-0	Speedie 2, Keen	13,951
42		13	(a)	Luton T		L	0-2		10,959
43		17	(h)	Brentford		W	4-0	Butler, Keen, Morley, M.Allen	16,522
44		24	(h)	Bristol R		W	2-1	Dicks, Speedie	16,682
45	May	2	(a)	Swindon T		W	3-1	Morley, C.Allen, Brown	17,004
46		8	(h)	Cambridge U		W	2-0	Speedie, C.Allen	27,399

P	W	D	L	F	A	W	D	L	F	A	Pts	Pos	Div		Appearances
46	16	5	2	50	17	10	5	8	31	24	88	2nd	1		Sub Appearances
															Goals

FA Cup

3	Jan	4	(a)	West Brom A		W	2-0	C.Allen, Robson	25,896
4		24	(a)	Barnsley		L	1-4	Morley	13,716

Appearances
Sub Appearances
Goals

League Cup

2	Sep	23	(h)	Crewe A		D	0-0		6,981
	Oct	7	(a)	Crewe A		L	0-2		5,427

Appearances
Sub Appearances
Goals

Miklosko	Breacker	Dicks	Potts	Martin	Parris	Robson	Bishop	Butler	Small	Allen C	Keen	Gale	Holmes	Allen M	Morley	Thomas	Brown	Clarke	Foster	Bunbury	Jones	Speedie	No.
1	2	3	4	5	6†	14	7	8	9	10*	11	12											1
1	2	3	4	5	6	12	7*	8	9	10	11												2
1	2	3	4	5		7	8		12	10	11			6*	9								3
1	2	3	4	5	12	7*		8		10	11			6	9								4
1	2		4	5		7	8		12	10*	11			6	9	3							5
1	2		4	5		7*	8		12	10	11			6	9	3							6
1	2		4	5		7*	8		12	10	11			6	9	3							7
1	2	3	4	5		7*	8			10	11		14	6	9								8
1	2	3	4	5		7*	8			10†	11	14	12	6	9								9
1	2	3	4	5		7	8			10	11			6	9								10
1	2	3	4	5		7	8			10	11			6	9								11
1	2		4	5	3	7	8			10	11			6	9								12
1	2		4	5	3	7	8			10	11			6	9								13
1	2		4	5	3	7*	8			10	11	12		6	9								14
1	2		4	5		7	8			10	11			6	9	3							15
1	2		4	5	6	7				10	11*	3		8	9		12						16
1	2	3	4	5	6	7				10	11*	12		8	9								17
1	2	3	4		6	7	12			10	11*	5		8	9								18
1	2	3	4	5		7	8*	12		10	11		14	6†	9								19
1	2	3	4	5	6*	7		12		10	11			8	9								20
1	2	3	4	5		7*	8			10	11			6	9				12				21
1	2	3	4	5		7	8*			10	11			6	9				12				22
1	2	3	4	5		7	8			10	11			6	9								23
1	2	3	4	5†	14	7*	8			10	11			6	9		12						24
1	2	3	4		14	7†	8			10*	11	5	12	6	9								25
1	2		4		14	7†	8				11	5	12	6	9	3	10*						26
1	2		4		12	7*	8				11†	5	10	6	9	3	14						27
1	2	3	4			7	8				11	5		6	9		10						28
1	2	3	4			7	8				11*	5	12	6	9		10						29
1	2	3	4			7*	14	8			11	5	12	6	9		10†						30
1		3	4			7	10	8			11*	5		6	9		2			12			31
1		3	4		12	7†	6	8			11	5	14		9		2			10*			32
1		3	4			7	12	8			11†	5	14		9		2			12			‡33
1		3	4			7	12	8	10*		11	5		6	9		2						34
1		3	4			7*	12	8	10		11	5		6	9		2						35
1		3	4			7*		8			11	5	12	6	10		2			9			36
1		3	4			12		8			11*	5	7	6	10		2			9			37
1	2		4			7	6	8			11	5			10		3			9			38
1	2		4			7*	6	8			11	5	12	3			14		10†	9			39
1	2	3	4			7	6	8			11	5			10					9			40
1	2	3	4			7	6	8			11	5			10					9			41
1	2	3	4				6	8			11	5	12	7*	10					9			42
1	2	3	4			7		8			11	5		6	10					9			43
1	2	3	4			7*	12	8			11	5		6	10					9			44
1	2	3	4			7*	6	8	12		11	5		10†			14			9			45
1	2	3	4			7*	6	8	12		11	5		14	10					9†			46
46	39	34	46	23	10	41	15	39	5	25	46	21	6	33	41	3	13		3	2	4	11	
		6	3	7			4		2		2	12	1		2		1		3	2	2		
	2	11	1			8	1	2		14	7	1	1	4	20		2		1		2	4	

‡ Number-12 shirt used in place of number-6 as a mark of respect to the late Bobby Moore OBE

Miklosko	Breacker	Dicks	Potts	Martin	Parris	Robson	Bishop	Butler	Small	Allen C	Keen	Gale	Holmes	Allen M	Morley	Thomas	Brown	Clarke	Foster	Bunbury	Jones	Speedie	No.
1	2	3	4	5		7		8		10	11			6	9								3
1	2		4			7*		8			11	10	6	9		3		5	12				4
2	2	1	2	1		2		2		1	2	1	1	2	2	1		1					
			1					1			1				1								

Miklosko	Breacker	Dicks	Potts	Martin	Parris	Robson	Bishop	Butler	Small	Allen C	Keen	Gale	Holmes	Allen M	Morley	Thomas	Brown	Clarke	Foster	Bunbury	Jones	Speedie	No.
1	2		4	5		7		8	12	10	11*			6	9								
1	2	3	4	5		7		8		10	11			6	9								2
2	2	1	2	2		2		2		2	2			2	2	1							
								1															

West Ham Against Other League Clubs

West Ham United have played 75 clubs in the Football League since 1919-20. Below is the Hammers' record against each club. Some clubs changed their names (eg Small Heath became Birmingham then Birmingham City) and some clubs modified their titles (eg Leicester Fosse became Leicester City). In all cases the last name used by each club cover all games under previous names.

		HOME					AWAY				
	P	W	D	L	F	A	W	D	L	F	A
AFC BOURNEMOUTH	2	1	0	0	4	1	0	1	0	1	1
ARSENAL	76	12	13	13	57	57	9	12	17	47	66
ASTON VILLA	60	17	9	4	75	38	9	4	17	41	65
BARNSLEY	42	16	4	1	50	19	6	9	6	20	28
BIRMINGHAM CITY	74	15	9	13	70	49	8	7	22	36	68
BLACKBURN ROVERS	68	16	5	13	68	66	9	4	21	43	71
BLACKPOOL	40	12	6	2	37	21	4	4	12	22	40
BOLTON WANDERERS	36	11	2	5	46	29	2	3	13	14	47
BRADFORD	24	8	2	2	16	8	4	1	7	13	21
BRADFORD CITY	14	3	1	3	12	10	2	1	4	9	14
BRENTFORD	20	5	2	3	17	10	2	5	3	12	15
BRIGHTON & HA	10	3	2	0	8	4	1	0	4	3	9
BRISTOL CITY	22	10	0	1	26	5	2	6	3	14	13
BRISTOL ROVERS	20	8	1	1	24	9	7	3	0	20	8
BURNLEY	66	20	6	7	61	41	3	8	22	45	82
BURY	54	14	6	7	58	32	6	5	16	35	63
CAMBRIDGE UNITED	8	4	0	0	14	3	1	1	2	3	5
CARDIFF CITY	36	9	8	1	32	15	7	5	6	22	19
CARLISLE UNITED	2	1	0	0	2	0	1	0	0	1	0
CHARLTON ATHLETIC	20	4	2	4	19	16	1	5	4	9	13
CHELSEA	54	17	5	5	61	31	8	7	12	45	46
CHESTERFIELD	18	5	3	1	23	6	2	2	5	5	14
COVENTRY CITY	66	19	6	8	68	33	12	10	11	34	39
CRYSTAL PALACE	16	3	4	1	11	6	5	3	0	18	7
DERBY COUNTY	48	8	11	5	37	29	5	5	14	27	49
DONCASTER ROVERS	22	4	4	3	18	14	3	1	7	12	20
EVERTON	80	18	9	13	68	53	8	6	26	33	82
FULHAM	62	18	6	7	63	36	8	7	16	39	60
GRIMSBY TOWN	26	11	0	2	30	15	4	3	6	16	21
HUDDERSFIELD TOWN	30	5	4	6	26	23	2	2	11	13	36
HULL CITY	32	8	6	2	32	16	3	7	6	15	23
IPSWICH TOWN	44	8	9	5	33	25	9	2	11	32	36
LEEDS UNITED	74	17	12	8	74	50	5	8	24	43	84
LEICESTER CITY	100	28	13	9	108	61	11	12	27	61	92
LEYTON ORIENT	20	7	0	3	14	9	7	1	2	17	5
LINCOLN CITY	20	4	4	2	23	13	5	1	4	22	19
LIVERPOOL	76	13	12	13	49	53	3	10	25	25	71

	P	HOME					AWAY				
		W	D	L	F	A	W	D	L	F	A
LUTON TOWN	52	11	8	7	29	19	6	10	10	30	43
MANCHESTER CITY	64	18	6	8	58	35	8	3	21	51	73
MANCHESTER UNITED	80	23	10	7	71	49	10	6	24	48	91
MIDDLESBROUGH	34	8	3	6	27	25	5	5	7	18	29
MILLWALL	18	5	4	0	19	6	2	4	3	9	9
NEWPORT COUNTY	2	1	0	0	3	0	0	1	0	1	1
NEWCASTLE UNITED	86	23	11	9	79	43	6	14	23	48	84
NORTHAMPTON TOWN	2	0	1	0	1	1	0	0	1	1	2
NORWICH CITY	34	11	2	4	31	16	3	6	8	26	30
NOTTINGHAM FOREST	90	27	8	10	101	65	6	13	26	32	74
NOTTS COUNTY	52	17	3	6	59	27	6	8	12	23	42
OLDHAM ATHLETIC	20	6	1	3	16	10	1	5	4	11	19
OXFORD UNITED	12	4	1	1	14	8	3	1	2	7	5
PETERBOROUGH UTD	2	1	0	0	2	1	1	0	0	3	1
PLYMOUTH ARGYLE	34	9	6	2	43	21	4	6	7	19	27
PORTSMOUTH	20	6	2	2	22	11	4	0	6	8	16
PORT VALE	26	8	4	1	26	8	4	5	4	16	18
PRESTON NORTH END	24	9	2	1	31	10	1	4	7	10	22
QUEEN'S PARK RANGERS	38	10	6	3	37	26	5	7	7	19	26
ROTHERHAM UNITED	22	6	2	3	26	12	4	3	4	13	18
SHEFFIELD UNITED	70	17	8	10	72	44	8	7	20	46	76
SHEFFIELD WEDNESDAY	72	13	11	12	60	58	8	9	19	42	72
SHREWSBURY TOWN	4	1	0	1	4	3	1	0	1	2	3
SOUTHEND UNITED	2	1	0	0	2	0	0	0	1	0	1
SOUTHAMPTON	64	16	9	7	56	29	8	10	14	47	62
SOUTH SHIELDS	8	3	1	0	5	2	0	2	2	0	4
STOCKPORT COUNTY	8	3	0	1	9	1	0	1	3	1	5
STOKE CITY	58	15	10	4	55	28	6	5	18	28	48
SUNDERLAND	48	8	10	6	52	34	7	3	14	33	51
SWANSEA CITY	42	15	5	1	58	20	4	4	13	31	42
SWINDON TOWN	6	1	1	1	3	2	2	1	0	6	3
TOTTENHAM HOTSPUR	86	19	12	12	66	58	11	11	21	64	83
TRANMERE ROVERS	4	2	0	0	8	1	0	1	1	4	7
WATFORD	22	9	1	1	18	10	6	2	3	13	14
WEST BROMWICH ALBION	66	19	4	10	71	45	8	5	20	35	65
WIMBLEDON	8	0	1	3	5	8	2	1	1	3	3
WOLVERHAMPTON W	52	16	7	3	60	25	7	6	13	29	40
WREXHAM	6	2	1	0	3	1	0	1	2	5	7

Summary

	P	W	D	L	F	A
Home	1410	745	347	318	2736	1668
Away	1410	341	341	728	1649	2568
Total	2820	1086	688	1046	4385	4236

Most, Least, Best, Worst in the League Seasons

Least home goals scored:
19 (1988-89)
Worst total goals scored:
37 (1988-89 & 1991-92)
Most home goals conceded:
44 (1930-31)
Most total defeats:
23 (1931-32)
Most total goals conceded:
107 (1931-32)
Most away goals conceded:
70 (1931-32)
Most away defeats:
17 (1932-33)
Most total goals scored:
101 (1957-58)
Most away goals scored:
45 (1957-58)
Most home goals scored:
59 (1958-59)
Most home defeats:
10 (1988-89)
Most total draws:
18 (1968-69)
Most away draws:
10 (1968-69)
Least total wins:
9 (1987-88 & 1991-92)
Least home wins:
3 (1988-89)
Most home draws:
10 (1981-82)
Least away draws:
1 (1982-83)
Most home wins:
19 (1980-81)
Most total wins:
28 (1980-81)
Least away defeats:
3 (1980-81)
Least away goals conceded:
16 (1990-91)
Least total goals conceded:
29 (1980-81)
Least total defeats:
4 (1980-81)
Least away goals scored:
13 (1919-20, 1920-21, 1921-22)
Least home goals conceded:
11 (1920-21, 1922-23)
Most away wins:
11 (1922-23, 1957-58)
Least away wins:
1 (1925-26, 1932-33, 1937-38, 1960-61)
Least home draws:
1 (1934-35, 1980-81)
Least total draws:
4 (1934-35, 1964-65, 1982-83)
Least home defeats:
1 (1957-58, 1980-81)

Top Ten

League Appearances (including Substitutions)

1.	Billy Bonds	663
2.	Frank Lampard	551
3.	Bobby Moore	544
4.	Trevor Brooking	528
5.	Jimmy Ruffell	505
6.	Vic Watson	462
7.	Jim Barrett	442
8.	Alvin Martin	424
9.	Geoff Hurst	411
10.	Ken Brown	386

League Scorers

1.	Vic Watson	298
2.	Geoff Hurst	180
3.	Jimmy Ruffell	159
4.	John Dick	153
5.	Bryan Robson	94
6.	Tony Cottee	92
7.	Trevor Brooking	88
8.	Malcolm Musgrove	84
9.	Martin Peters	81
10.	Johnny Byrne	79

Geoff Hurst, in top-ten appearances and goals.

Hammers in Wartime 1915-19

LIKE most sporting organisations, West Ham United played a commendable part in providing the public with some diversion during two world wars.

During World War One, the Hammers not only achieved a great deal in taking people's minds, momentarily at least, off the conflict, they earned themselves sufficient status to win a place in the Football League once the fighting was over.

In 1915, Syd King was in his 16th year with the club and he was to skilfully guide Hammers through the testing times ahead. In the summer of that year it was decided that all League and Cup football should be suspended in favour of local, regionalised tournaments for which there would be no prizes and no professionalism.

The suspension of players' contracts for the duration meant that individuals were given virtual freedom to play where they liked and West Ham, in particular, benefited from the arrangement. A host of famous names soon began to appear in Hammers' colours.

From the start of the wartime programme, in September 1915, Syd King took full advantage of the latitude allowed and players from provincial clubs, who now found themselves stationed nearby, were drafted into Hammers' team. The garrisons at Woolwich and Colchester were particularly happy hunting grounds.

The first season Hammers enjoyed the skills of Ted Hufton, Danny Shea (then still a Blackburn player), Bill Masterman (like Hufton from Sheffield United) and Andy Cunningham, the Glasgow Rangers player destined to win a number of caps after the war.

Yet it was a local boy, Syd Puddefoot, who did most to lift Hammers to fourth place in the London Combination Championship. His 24 goals put him amongst the country's leading marksmen.

The new league comprised five Football League clubs and seven from the Southern League and although the players were unpaid, pride was still at stake and Hammers had their share of offenders as vigour sometimes overstepped the mark. Between November 1915 and September 1916, no less than five West Ham players were sent off.

Bill Askew, Danny Shea (along with Clapton Orient's Hinds), Alf Fenwick, and Askew again, all fell foul of the referee, although Askew was exonerated for the second incident. Perhaps the most unlikely wrongdoer was Herbert Ashton who was dismissed in the home game against Watford. Before he reached the dressing-room, however, the visitors goalkeeper, Williams, intervened and won Ashton a reprieve.

On a happier note, Puddefoot scored five in the 8-2 thrashing of Arsenal on Boxing Day and also recorded two hat-tricks that season; and in April, Arthur Stallard hit five in a friendly game.

Amidst all this, of course, the fighting in France and Belgium continued and Hammers fans were given a sharp reminder when the *Athletic News* reported the death of Bill Kennedy who lost his life serving with the London Scottish Regiment. He had spent two years at Upton Park between 1910 and 1912, mainly as understudy to George Webb.

In 1916-17, West Ham won the London Combination title with seven points to spare. They used 49 players in the season, 30 of whom were 'guests'. One 'well-known' (yet still unknown) full-back requested anonimity and appeared under the name, 'J.Day'.

Hammers began the season in blistering style, going nine games before their first defeat, and another 19 before their second. In only three games did they fail to score.

Regular players included four of Everton's 1914-15 Football League Championship winning team — Harrison, Chedgzoy, Macconachie and Kirsopp. Walters and Hodson, members of the Oldham Athletic team which finished runners-up to Everton, also played for Hammers. And Blackburn Rovers, who finished third, provided Danny Shea and Percy Smith.

For the first time West Ham exceeded 100 goals in a season and Puddefoot and Shea between them contributed 56 of the 110 goals West Ham scored in 40 matches.

Soon after the outbreak of war, letters had appeared in newspapers accusing the football authorities of almost treasonable behaviour in allowing the game to continue whilst thousands more, less talented, young men were suffering the horrors of trench warfare. The *Athletic News* responded with regular mentions of sportsmen who had volunteered for military service, and in December 1914, the so-called Footballers' Battalion had been formed as part of the Middlesex Regiment.

Yet not all footballers were fit for the army. Bill Masterman, who had played for Sheffield United in the 1915 FA Cup Final and who turned out for Hammers the following season, was rejected for military service because he was deaf.

Others, including Puddefoot, worked long, exhausting and often dangerous shifts in munitions factories. In November 1915, for instance, a Bromley amateur called Burge made an eventful appearance for West Ham at Stamford Bridge. He scored once, missed two other chances at crucial times, and West Ham went down 5-2. Later it was revealed that he had completed a night shift at the Woolwich Arsenal only hours before the game, and at its conclusion hurried off to begin another.

The course of the war meant that troops were continually on the move and King's task in raising a team became more difficult. In March 1917, scratching around for a side to play an important match against Spurs, heard that MacLachlan (Aberdeen) and McDougal (Liverpool) would be returning from Ireland to their units in Wiltshire.

King wired the mens' CO, requesting their services, and MacLachlan and McDougal arrived just in time to help West Ham end Spurs unbeaten run of 20 games.

One criticism of West Ham was that they had won the title with 'northern imports' but the *Athletic News* congratulated them for taking the Championship despite having to make so many team changes.

In the third wartime season West Ham scored at an even greater rate. Although the 103 goals were fewer than the previous season, they came from a reduced fixture list caused by travelling problems. Southampton, Luton, Portsmouth and Watford were forced out and Hammers' longest journey was now to Brentford. The clubs played each other four times each, giving a 36-match league programme.

West Ham had nothing to show for topping the 100-goal mark again. They used 56 different players and for the third time in four seasons Puddefoot was top scorer, with 35 goals. Shea (16) and Manchester City's Frank Roberts (15 in only 13 appearances) trailed him.

Shea, who ended his association with West Ham after the December fixture with Brentford, scored four in the opening game, against Fulham. Puddefoot netted a hat-trick in the next game, at QPR, and by mid-November, Hammers had scored 36 goals in 11 games. Puddefoot claimed 14 of them and by the season's end he could boast a ten-match scoring sequence, ending with seven against Crystal Palace to equal a Combination record.

In that match, Hammers' outside-left, Jack Macksey, was sent off by referee Albert Neale. Some years later Mr Neale was to collapse and die whilst refereeing a Combination match between Charlton and West Ham at The Valley.

In 1917-18, matches between West Ham and Brentford gave special value for money. One-quarter of Hammers' goals that season were scored against the Bees who themselves contributed 11. The four games between the clubs produced 35 goals.

West Ham used six goalkeepers that season, the best-known being Third Lanark's Scottish international, James Brownlie. The youngest was 16-year-old England Schoolboy international, George Hebden. After the war West Ham lost touch with him and he spent many years with Leicester City and, later, Gillingham.

The saddest event of the 1917-18 was the death of Arthur Stallard who was killed in action in France during the last week of November, seven months after his final game in Hammers' colours.

West Ham called upon 62 players in 1918-19, a club record. Two goalkeepers turned up for one game, against Arsenal in November, but the problem was solved when Hufton, the regular 'keeper, agreed to play at right-back.

The reason for the high number of players was a happy one — nine weeks after the start of the new season, the war came to an end. Servicemen were not released immediately but travel became easier and many more professional players became available.

George Kay, absent from the whole of the previous season recovering from shell-shock, reappeared briefly; and another returnee was Ted Hufton, who had found himself in the front line as the war drew to its close. Of the newcomers, the most important was wing-half James McCrae from Scottish League club, Clyde.

It was McCrae who was the innocent victim of a stone-thrower during a Combination game at Stamford Bridge. McCrae apprehended the miscreant and then himself had to receive police protection from the hostile home supporters.

The fact that West Ham's 1918-19 season was not nearly as impressive as previous campaigns mattered little as the country celebrated the restoration of peace. Only 65 goals were scored and Puddefoot alone reached double figures.

After the Armistice in November 1918, attendances at football matches increased dramatically and by the end of the season almost a quarter of a million people had passed through the Upton Park turnstiles. In January 1919, Hammers beat Clapton Orient 7-0 at home to record their 13th win in 16 wartime matches with the Homerton men.

In the spring of 1919, West Ham applied for the Football League and, with the backing of a significant number of established League clubs, they won their place, finishing second behind Coventry City in the poll. Coventry, incidently, had finished fifth in the Southern League Second Division in 1914-15.

The Southern League clubs and officials themselves were not impressed at Hammers' move and only Swindon Town sent a congratulatory telegram.

Syd King, meanwhile, considered West Ham's elevation as the most important and satisfying achievement of his long career, but even he could not have imagined what feats lay ahead.

1915-16

London Combination Principal Tournament

Manager: Syd King

1	Sep	4	(a)	Brentford	L	1-2	Shea	2,000
2		11	(h)	Chelsea	D	0-0		12,000
3		18	(h)	Tottenham H	D	1-1	Stallard	8,000
4		25	(a)	Crystal P	L	0-2		2,500
5	Oct	2	(h)	Queen's Park R	W	2-1	J Burton, Puddefoot	4,000
6		9	(a)	Fulham	L	0-1		7,000
7		16	(h)	Clapton O	W	5-2	Ashton, Casey, J.Burton, Shea 2	6,500
8		23	(a)	Watford	W	3-2	Bailey, Mackesy, Puddefoot	3,000
9		30	(h)	Millwall	W	2-1	Shea, Stallard	12,000
10	Nov	6	(a)	Croydon	D	1-1	Puddefoot	2,000
11		13	(h)	Brentford	W	4-1	Mackesy, Shea, Puddefoot 2	3,000
12		20	(a)	Chelsea	L	2-5	Puddefoot, Burge	12,000
13		27	(a)	Tottenham H	L	0-3		5,000
14	Dec	4	(h)	Crystal P	W	3-1	Puddefoot 3	3,000
15		11	(a)	Queen's Park R	D	1-1	Casey	2,000
16		18	(h)	Fulham	L	2-3	Puddefoot, Masterman	4,000
17		25	(h)	Arsenal	W	8-2	Puddefoot 5, Masterman 2, Shea	5,500
18		27	(a)	Arsenal	L	2-3	Stallard, Fenwick	8,869
19	Jan	1	(a)	Clapton O	W	2-1	Fenwick, Stallard	2,000
20		8	(h)	Watford	W	5-1	Mackesy, Shea 3, Masterman	5,000
21		15	(a)	Millwall	L	0-1		8,000
22		22	(h)	Croydon	W	3-0	Stallard, Caton, Fenwick	5,000

P	W	D	L	F	A	W	D	L	F	A	Pts	Pos	Div	
22	8	2	1	35	13	2	2	7	12	22	24	4th	LC	Appearances
														Goals

Supplementary Tournament

23	Feb	5	(h)	Tottenham H	W	2-0	Stallard 2	7,000
24		12	(a)	Millwall	L	0-1		6,000
25		19	(h)	Chelsea	W	2-0	Mackesy, Puddefoot	9,000
26	Mar	4	(h)	Brentford	W	4-2	Stallard 3, Shea	2,000
27		11	(a)	Reading	W	4-0	Puddefoot 3, Shea	4,000
28		18	(h)	Millwall	W	2-1	Puddefoot 2	12,000
29		25	(a)	Chelsea	L	0-4		8,000
30	Apr	1	(h)	Watford	D	2-2	Shea 2	8,000
31		8	(a)	Brentford	W	3-1	Mackesy 2, Puddefoot	3,000
32		15	(a)	Reading	W	7-0	Casey, Cunningham 2, Shea 2, Puddefoot 2	5,500
33		21	(a)	Clapton O	L	1-3	Casey	6,000
34		22	(h)	Clapton O	W	2-1	Piggott, Puddefoot	10,000
35		29	(a)	Tottenham H	D	1-1	Stallard	7,000
36	May	6	(a)	Watford	W	2-0	Shea 2	3,500

P	W	D	L	F	A	W	D	L	F	A	Pts	Pos	Div	
14	6	1	0	21	6	3	1	3	11	10	20	2nd	LC	Appearances
														Goals

First grid (matches 1–22):

Leahy	Cope	Burton F	Fenwick	Askew	Woodards	Caton	Shea	Puddefoot	Butcher	Casey	Ashton	Stallard	Mackesy	Piggott	Harold	Speak	Whiteman	Burton J	Bailey	Hughes	Bourne	Appleby	Burge	Tirrell	Hilsdon	Gibbs	Hufton	Tresadern	Masterman	Cross	Burrill	Higgs	McGinn	Cameron	Parker	Cunningham	Tough	#
1	2	3	4	5	6	7	8	9	10	11																												1
1	2	3	4	5	6		8	10			7	9	11																									2
1	2	3		5			8	10		11	7	9		4	6																							3
1	2	6		5		7	8	10		11		9				3	4																					4
1	2			5	6		8	9		11	7					3	4	10																				5
1	2	3	4	5	6		8	9		11	7							10																				6
1	2	3		5	6		8	9		11	7			4				10																				7
1	2		3	5	6		8	10		11	7			4			9																					8
1	2		3	5	6		8	10			7	9	11	4																								9
	2			5	6		8	10			7		11	4					9	1	3																	10
	2	3		5	6	7		10		11				4						1					8	9												11
1										11						10	4		8	9		2																12
1		2		5	6	7		9		11						10	4			3		8																13
		2		5	6	7		9		11				4						1	3				8	10												14
		2		5				9						4							3	8																15
	3	2		5			8	9			7		11	4													1	6	10	11								16
	3	2		5			8	9		11	7			4													1		10									17
		2	3	5			8	9			7	11		4						6							1		10									18
		2	3	5	6	7		8				9	11	4													1		10									19
		2	3	5	6	7	8					9	11	4													1		10									20
		2	3	5	6	7	8					9		4													1		10									21
1	3	2	10	5	6	7				11		9	8	4																								22
12	15	16	16	15	19	9	16	19	1	10	10	11	12	16	1	2	3	4	4	4	6	2	1	1	2	1	6	1	6	1								
	3					1	9	15			2	1	5	3		2	1		1						4													

Second grid (matches 23–36):

Leahy	Cope	Burton F	Fenwick	Askew	Woodards	Caton	Shea	Puddefoot	Butcher	Casey	Ashton	Stallard	Mackesy	Piggott	Harold	Speak	Whiteman	Burton J	Bailey	Hughes	Bourne	Appleby	Burge	Tirrell	Hilsdon	Gibbs	Hufton	Tresadern	Masterman	Cross	Burrill	Higgs	McGinn	Cameron	Parker	Cunningham	Tough	#
	3	2	8	5	6	7				11		9		4													1					10						23
	3	2	6	5		7				11		9	10	4													1					8						24
	3			5	6	7	8	10		11		9		4													1											25
	3	2		5	6	7	8	9						4													1							2				26
	3	2			6	7	8	9		11				4													1						10	11				27
	3	2		5	6	7	8			11				4													1								5			28
	3			5	2	7	8	9						4					6								1										10	29
	3			5	6	2	8	9		11	7			4													1						10	11				30
1	3			5	6	2	8	9		11	7			4																								31
	2			5	6		8			11	7	9	10	4	3												1										10	32
	3	2	5	6			8	9		11	7			4													1									10		33
	3			5	6		8	9			7	11		4													1								10		2	34
	3			5	6		8	9		4	7	11															1						2			10	2	35
	3			5	6		4	7	11																		1									10		36
1	14	6	3	13	13	9	11	12		10	6	6	8	12		1											13					2	3	2	2	1	5	
							8	10		2	6	3	1																					2				

363

1916-17

Managare: Syd King

1	Sep	2	(h)	Arsenal	W 2-1	Chedgzoy, McDougall	3,000
2		9	(a)	Luton T	W 4-3	Shea, Chedgzoy, McDougall, Puddefoot	3,000
3		16	(h)	Reading	W 5-1	Chedgzoy, Shea 4	5,000
4		23	(a)	Millwall	W 4-1	Ashton, McDougall, Wright, Chedgzoy	7,000
5		28	(a)	Tottenham H	W 2-1	Puddefoot, Kay	3,000
6		30	(h)	Watford	D 2-2	McDougall, Wright	8,000
7	Oct	7	(a)	Clapton O	W 4-0	Puddefoot 3, Shea	4,500
8		14	(h)	Fulham	W 2-0	McDougall, Shea	10,000
9		21	(a)	Queen's Park R	W 4-0	McDougall 2, Shea 2	3,000
10		28	(a)	Southampton	L 0-3		5,000
11	Nov	4	(h)	Tottenham H	W 5-1	Kay 3, Shea 2	8,000
12		11	(a)	Crystal P	W 8-1	Shea 3, McDougall 2, Cook, Chedgzoy 2	2,000
13		18	(h)	Brentford	W 4-0	Shea 2, Ashton, Walters	1,800
14		25	(a)	Arsenal	W 2-0	McDougall, Shea	7,000
15	Dec	2	(h)	Luton T	W 2-0	McDougall, Kay	7,000
16		9	(a)	Portsmouth	W 2-1	Stallard, Shea	5,000
17		23	(a)	Watford	W 3-1	Puddefoot, McDougall 2	500
18		25	(a)	Chelsea	D 1-1	McDougall	20,000
19		26	(h)	Chelsea	W 2-0	Puddefoot 2	8,000
20		30	(h)	Clapton O	W 6-1	Shea 3, Mackesy, Puddefoot 2	6,000
21	Jan	6	(a)	Fulham	W 2-0	Puddefoot, Shea	8,000
22		13	(h)	Queen's Park R	W 5-3	Puddefoot 2, Shea 3	4,000
23		20	(a)	Southampton	D 1-1	Shea	3,000
24		27	(a)	Tottenham H	D 0-0		7,000
25	Feb	3	(h)	Crystal P	W 1-0	Puddefoot	3,000
26		10	(a)	Brentford	D 1-1	Harrison	1,500
27		17	(h)	Southampton	W 5-2	Stallard 2, Ashton, Mackesy, Chedgzoy	6,000
28		24	(a)	Clapton O	W 4-3	Chedgzoy 2, Puddefoot, Watson	5,000
29	Mar	3	(a)	Crystal P	L 1-3	Shea	5,000
30		10	(h)	Arsenal	L 2-3	Shea, Stallard	6,000
31		17	(a)	Portsmouth	W 5-2	Harrison 2, Stallard 2, Mackesy	5,000
32		24	(a)	Tottenham H	W 3-0	Shea, Chedgzoy, Puddefoot	12,000
33		31	(a)	Southampton	W 2-1	Shea, Puddefoot	8,000
34	Apr	6	(h)	Brentford	W 2-0	Puddefoot, Opp own-goal	7,000
35		7	(h)	Clapton O	W 2-0	Shea, McDougall	8,000
36		9	(a)	Brentford	W 2-1	Puddefoot, Mackesy	4,000
37		10	(h)	Millwall	L 0-2		6,000
38		14	(h)	Crystal P	W 2-1	Puddefoot 2	7,000
39		21	(a)	Arsenal	L 1-2	Puddefoot	4,000
40		28	(h)	Portsmouth	W 5-2	Puddefoot 2, Casey, McDougall, Shea	5,000

P	W	D	L	F	A	W	D	L	F	A	Pts	Pos	Div	
40	16	2	2	58	20	14	3	3	52	25	65	1st	LC	Appearances
														Goals

The table records the shirt number (1–11) worn by each player in each match. Player names are column headers; match numbers run down the right-hand side. The two bottom rows give total appearances and total goals.

Hufton	Baverstock	Cope	Piggott	Kay	Maclachlan	Chedgzoy	Shea	Puddefoot	McDougal	Knight	Hodson	Woodards	Casey	Maconnachie	Crabtree	Ashton	Wright	Leahy	Burton	Brown	Walters	Smith	Mackesy	Henshall	Cook	Morton	McBean	Day	Fenwick	Stallard	Harrison	Kearns	Kirsopp	Davies	Manning	Feebury	Watson	Taylor	Match
1	2	3	4	5	6	7	8	9	10	11																													1
1	2			5	4	9	11	8	10				3	6	7																								2
1			4		6	7	8					11	5	10	2	3	9																						3
1		3	4	5	6		8	9	10				2			7	11																						4
	2		4	5			11	8	9				6			7		1					10																5
		3			4		8	9	10				2	6	5	7	11	1																					6
		3		5	6	7	8	9	10				2	4		11		1																					7
				5	6	7	8	9	10				2	4		11		1	3																				8
		3	4			7	8	9					2	5		6		1							10	11													9
			4	5			10	9					2	6		7		1					11	8															10
		3		5	6	7	8	9					2	4				1							10	11													11
				5	6	7	8		10				2	4	3			1								11	9												12
				5	6	7	8	9					2	4		11		1	3			10																	13
		3		5	6		8	9	10				2					1	7						4	11													14
		3		5	6	7	8	9	10				2					1					4			11													15
		3			6		8		10				2	11	5										4	7				9									16
		3					8	9	10				2	4	11	7		1				5				6													17
		3		5	6	7	8	9	10				2	4		11		1																					18
		3		5		7	8	9	10					4		11		1	6																				19
		3		5	6		8		10					4		7		1				9	11																20
		3	6	5		7	8	9	10					4		11		1	2																				21
		3	6			7	8	9	10				5	4				1													11								22
		3	6	5			8	9						4		7		1													11	2	10						23
		3	4			7			10									1	5							6				9	11	2		8					24
			6				8	9						4		7		1	3												11	2	10	5					25
								9					2	4		7		1	3				8								11		10	5					26
		3					8						6			7		1					10							9	11		4	5	2				27
		3					8	9					2	6		7		1													11		4	5				10	28
		3					8						6	11		7		1	5				10														2	9	29
		3				7	8						5	6				1					10							9	11		4	2					30
		3					8											1					10							9	11			7		2		5	31
		3	6			7	8	9	10									1	5						2						11		4						32
		3	6				8	9	10										5												11			7	4	2			33
		3	4		6		8	9	10				2					1	5												11			7					34
		3	6				8	9	10							7		1										2	5		11		4						35
			4													7		1	10				8					2		9	11		6	3				5	36
		3					8	9					6			7		1	2				10								11		4	5					37
		3					8	9	10				6		2	4		1	5			7									11								38
		3					8	9	10					4				1													11		7	5		2			39
		3	6				8	9	10				4	11	2	7		1																					40
4	1	31	12	18	20	22	32	34	23	3	16	25	8	6	2	27	2	34	14	2	3	3	11	2	1	2	3	3	2	7	16	3	9	10	4	7	2	3	**Apps**
		5				10	32	24	16					1		3	2		1				4		1					6	3			1					**Goals**

1 own-goal

Divers played number 3 in Match 5 and number 2 in Match 22; Steel played number 3 in Match 10; Ross played number 1 in Match 16; Rothwell played number 2 in Matches 19 and 20; Curry played number 6 in Match 26; Moore played number 4 in Match 29; Carless played number 6 in Matches 31 and 39; Bolton played number 4 in Match 31; Bailey played number 1 in Match 33; Kinnaird played number 5 in Match 40.

365

1917-18

Manager: Syd King

1	Sep	1	(h)	Fulham	W	6-1	Roberts 2, Shea 4	5,000
2		8	(a)	Queen's Park R	W	3-0	Puddefoot 3	5,000
3		15	(h)	Clapton O	L	1-2	Goddard	6,000
4		22	(a)	Millwall	W	3-2	Kirsopp 2, Ashton	10,000
5		29	(h)	Tottenham H	W	1-0	Roberts	6,000
6	Oct	6	(a)	Chelsea	L	3-4	Hamilton, Casey, Puddefoot	12,000
7		13	(h)	Brentford	W	8-3	Roberts 3, Puddefoot, Shea 4	5,000
8		20	(a)	Arsenal	D	2-2	Shea, Puddefoot	6,000
9		27	(a)	Fulham	D	1-1	Puddefoot	10,000
10	Nov	3	(h)	Queen's Park R	W	4-0	Puddefoot 2, Shea 2	4,500
11		10	(a)	Clapton O	W	4-1	Shea 2, Roberts 2	5,000
12		17	(h)	Millwall	D	0-0		7,000
13		24	(a)	Tottenham H	L	0-2		9,000
14	Dec	1	(h)	Chelsea	D	1-1	Shea	8,000
15		8	(a)	Brentford	L	2-3	Puddefoot, Shea	2,000
16		15	(h)	Arsenal	W	3-2	Roberts 2, Puddefoot	5,000
17		22	(h)	Fulham	L	0-3		6,000
18		25	(h)	Crystal P	W	2-1	Puddefoot, Kirsopp	7,000
19		26	(a)	Crystal P	L	0-4		5,000
20		29	(a)	Queen's Park R	D	1-1	Cowless	3,000
21	Jan	5	(h)	Clapton O	W	3-0	Roberts 2, Puddefoot	8,000
22		12	(a)	Millwall	W	1-0	Puddefoot	5,000
23		19	(h)	Tottenham H	D	2-2	Wright, Johnstone	8,000
24		26	(a)	Chelsea	D	2-2	Kirsopp, Puddefoot	8,000
25	Feb	2	(h)	Brentford	W	7-2	Mackesy, Ashton, Roberts, Kirsopp 2, Puddefoot, Opp own-goal	5,000
26		9	(a)	Crystal P	D	1-1	Larcombe	4,000
27		16	(a)	Fulham	L	1-3	Puddefoot	5,000
28		23	(h)	Queen's Park R	W	4-0	Ashton, Tresadern, Cunningham, Puddefoot	5,000
29	Mar	2	(a)	Clapton O	W	3-1	Burke, Tufnell, Puddefoot	4,000
30		9	(h)	Millwall	W	2-0	Cunningham, Puddefoot	6,000
31		16	(a)	Tottenham H	W	5-0	Ashton, Roberts, Puddefoot, Cunningham 2	10,000
32		23	(h)	Chelsea	D	2-2	Puddefoot, Cunningham	14,000
33		29	(h)	Arsenal	W	4-1	Tufnell 2, Puddefoot, Burke	10,000
34		30	(a)	Brentford	W	7-3	Burke, Puddefoot 3, Wright, Ashton, Johnstone	4,000
35	Apr	1	(a)	Arsenal	W	3-1	Puddefoot 2, Burke	6,000
36		6	(h)	Crystal P	W	11-0	Puddefoot 7, Burke 2, Ashton, Cunningham	4,000

P	W	D	L	F	A	W	D	L	F	A	Pts	Pos	Div	
36	12	4	2	61	20	8	5	5	42	31	49	2nd	LC	Appearances
														Goals

366

Players appearances / shirt-number grid (column headers are player surnames; right-hand numbers 1–36 are match numbers; cell numbers are shirt numbers worn).

Match	Leahy	Hodson	Cope	Manning	Campbell	Maconnachie	Ashton	Shea	Roberts	Puddefoot	Hamilton	Ferris	Mackesy	Casey	Goddard	Burton	Kirsopp	Johnstone	Williams	Williams B	Brennan	Massey	Bell	Larcombe	Cunningham	Brown	Wright	Lee	Islip	Temper	Tresadern	Bridgeman	Hebden	Stevenson	Cowless	Hufton	Tirrell	Burke	Tufnell
1	1	2	3	4	5	6	7	8	9	10																													
2	1	2		4			3	7	8			9	5	6	10	11																							
3	1	2		4			3	7	8			9	5				10	11																					
4	1	2	3	4		6	7		9	10			11		5		8																						
5	1	2	3	4		6	7	8	9	10			11					5																					
6	1	2			5		7	8	9		6	3	10	11			4																						
7		2			5		11	8	9	10	6						7	4																					
8		2	3		5		7	8	9		6		11				10	4	1																				
9	1		3		5	2	11	8	9		6						7	4																					
10	1	2	3		5			8	9		6		11				4																						
11	1	2	3		5		7	8	9	10	6		11				4																						
12	1	2	3		5		7	8		10	6		11				4																						
13	1	2			5		7	8	9	10	6						4		11																				
14			3			2	7	8	9		6						4	1	5									10	11										
15	1	2			5		3	7	8	9	10		6							11	4																		
16	1	2	3				7		9	11	5		6				8	4																					
17	1			3	5		7		9	2	10						8	4	11	6																			
18	1	2	3				7		9	5	10						8	4													6	11							
19		2	3				7			4							8						5			6				1									
20		2	3						9	10	8		11				4								1	6								5					
21		3							9	4			11												1									5				2	7
22		3							9	6			8	4											1	10	11							5				2	7
23		3	2						11	8	4		7				10	6							1		9							5					
24		2		4			7		9	10	6		11				8								1									5			3		
25		3		4			11		8								6										9							5				3	
26		2	3		6		7		9	10							4						9						7					5			1	2	10
27		2	3		6		7			10							4						8					11		6				5			1		
28		2	3				7			9	4						4						8					11						5	1		3	7	10
29			2						9	6			11				4										8						5	1		3	7	10
30		2	3		6		7			10							4						9	8					11				5	1				
31		2	3		6		7		10	9			11				4						8										5	1				
32		2	3				7		10	9			11				4				5		8						6					1				
33		2					7		9				11	3		4							6										5	1		8	10	
34		2						3		7			9	6		4					6					11					1		5	1		3	8	10
35		3					7		9				11	5		4					6						1						5	1		3	8	10
36		2					7		9				11			4					5	10											5	1		3	8	

Appearances: 15, 28, 25, 16, 5, 9, 30, 14, 14, 34, 23, 2, 24, 2, 2, 4, 11, 28, 3, 3, 3, 2, 3, 2, 7, 2, 2, 4, 4, 2, 6, 2, 2, 14, 1, 10, 9, 7, 6

Goals: 6, 15, 14, 35, 1, 1, 1, 1, 6, 2, 1, 6, 2, 1, 1, 6, 3

1 own-goal

McDougall played number 11 in Match 1; Woodards played number 6 in Match 3; Lawton played number 1 in Match 7; Tanner played number 3 in Match 7; Butcher played number 10 in Match 9; Kirby played number 7 in Match 10; Hilsdon played number 10 in Match 10; Dodds played number 9 in Match 12; Wray played number 10 in Match 16; Kenlan played number 9 in Match 19; Blythe played number 10 in Match 19; Allen played number 11 in Match 19; Turley played number 7 in Match 21; Langford played number 8 in Match 22; Brownlie played number 1 in Match 27; Pigott played number 6 in Match 36.

1918-19

1	Sep	7	(a)	Brentford	L	0-2		4,000
2		14	(h)	Clapton O	W	3-1	Weir, Best, Ashton	5,000
3		21	(h)	Tottenham H	L	0-1		8,000
4		28	(a)	Chelsea	L	1-3	Puddefoot	12,000
5	Oct	5	(h)	Arsenal	L	1-4	Moyes	6,500
6		12	(a)	Crystal P	D	0-0		4,000
7		19	(h)	Queen's Park R	W	4-1	Moyes, Puddefoot, Kirsopp, Best	7,000
8		26	(a)	Fulham	D	2-2	Kirsopp, Roberts	5,000
9	Nov	2	(h)	Brentford	L	1-3	Roberts	6,000
10		9	(a)	Clapton O	W	5-1	Puddefoot 2, Roberts 2, McCrae	5,000
11		16	(a)	Tottenham H	W	4-1	Best 2, McCrae, Kirsopp	6,000
12		23	(h)	Chelsea	W	3-1	Moyes 2, Cunningham	12,000
13		30	(a)	Arsenal	W	2-0	Best, Kirsopp	7,000
14	Dec	7	(h)	Crystal P	W	2-0	Stevenson, Kirsopp	10,000
15		14	(a)	Queen's Park R	L	0-1		8,000
16		21	(h)	Fulham	W	2-1	Puddefoot 2	10,000
17		25	(a)	Millwall	W	2-0	Dodd, Puddefoot	12,000
18		26	(h)	Millwall	W	2-0	Puddefoot, Dodd	16,000
19		28	(a)	Brentford	L	1-3	Puddefoot	10,000
20	Jan	4	(h)	Clapton O	W	7-0	Burke, Dodd 3, Holmes 2, Campbell	8,000
21		11	(h)	Tottenham H	W	2-0	Dodd, Puddefoot	13,000
22		18	(a)	Chelsea	D	0-0		25,000
23		25	(h)	Arsenal	L	1-2	Kirsopp	18,000
24	Feb	1	(a)	Crystal P	L	0-3		4,000
25		8	(h)	Queen's Park R	L	0-4		12,000
26		15	(a)	Millwall	D	2-2	McCrae, Holmes	25,000
27		22	(h)	Brentford	W	2-1	Dodd, Opp own-goal	16,000
28	Mar	1	(a)	Clapton O	D	0-0		15,000
29		8	(a)	Tottenham H	W	1-0	Puddefoot	17,000
30		15	(h)	Chelsea	D	3-3	Chedgzoy 2, Puddefoot	26,000
31		22	(a)	Arsenal	L	2-3	Bell, Chedgzoy	20,000
32		29	(h)	Crystal P	L	1-3	Dilley	15,500
33	Apr	5	(a)	Queen's Park R	W	3-1	Lewis, Puddefoot, Chedgzoy	7,000
34		12	(h)	Millwall	W	3-2	Butcher 2, Brittan	25,000
35		18	(a)	Fulham	D	1-1	Puddefoot	15,000
36		21	(h)	Fulham	W	2-1	Puddefoot 2	16,000

P	W	D	L	F	A	W	D	L	F	A	Pts	Pos	Div	Appearances
36	11	1	6	39	28	6	6	6	26	23	41	3rd	LC	Goals

	Williams	Cope	Tirrell	Johnstone	Moore	Burke	Kirsopp	Roberts	Hamilton	Best	Cownley	Ashton	McCulloch	Weir	Hodson	Stevenson	Puddefoot	Moyes	Yellop	McCrae	Woods	Allen	Campbell	Tate	Brandon	Britton	Lewis	Hughes	Butcher	Bell	Kay	Chedgzoy	Hufton	Lane	Cunningham	Leafe	Dodd	Tresadern	Holmes	
1	1	2	3		5	6	7	8	9	10	11																													1
2		3	4	6	8						11	2	7	9	10																									2
3	1	3		6		8		4	11			7		10	2	5																								3
4	1	3	4			6	11		7	9			2	5		8	10																							4
5	1	3	4	6	9	10			11	2				5			8	7																						5
6		3	4	6		10			11	2				5	9	8			1	7																				6
7		3		6	8	10	9	5	11	2								1	7																					7
8		3		4	6	7	10	9	8	11			2						1		5																			8
9	3		4	6	7	10	9	8	11			2							1	5																				9
10	3		4		7	8		10							5	9			11		6											1								10
11	2	3			7			11							5		8	6														1	4	10						11
12	2	3	4		7			11							5		8	6														1		10						12
13				4		7	5	11			3				6	1																2		10	9					13
14	2	3			7	9		11							5	8		6														1	4	10	8					14
15	2	3			7	8		11							5			6														1	4	10	9					15
16	2	3	4			8		11	7						5	9		10														1	6							16
17	2	3			8			11	7						5	9		6				4										1			10					17
18	2	3			8			11	7						5	9		6				4										1			10					18
19	3							11			2	5	9			7	6					4										1	8		10					19
20	2	3		9				11	2	7					5							4										1			8	6	10			20
21	2	3			7			11							9			6				5											4		8		10			21
22	2	3			7	10		11							9			6				5										1	4		8					22
23	2	3			7	9		11							5			10				6										1	4		8					23
24	2	3		6	9			7								6						5										1	4		8	10				24
25	2	3													11			5														1	4			10				25
26	2	3							7									5														1	4		8	6	10			26
27	2	3			7													10				5										1	4	10	8	6				27
28	2	3				11									9			10				5										1	4		8	6				28
29	2	3													9			10														1	4			6				29
30	2	3																11				5								5	8	1	4			6				30
31		3						2	7									5									10				8	1	4		7		6			31
32	2	3									9							6					8	1		10	5	7		4							6			32
33	2	3					4									9							9	1	8	10	5										6			33
34	2					9										9				7	3	10		1		8	5	11				6					4			34
35	3															9			10				11	2		1		5	7		6						4			35
36																																								36
	5	26	30	10	9	10	19	6	6	25	7	14	2	2	5	17	14	6	2	22	4	2	14	2	2	1	4	2	4	5	6	21	20	5	5	11	13	3		
		1	6	4		5			1			1			1	16	4			3			1				1	1			2	1		4		1	7		3		

1 own-goal

Turley played number 4 in Match 1; Fisher played number 1 in Match 2; Burkinshaw played number 5 in Match 2; Proctor played number 9 in Match 3; Massey played number 6 in Match 4; Pigott played number 4 in Match 8; Lowe played number 2 in Match 10; Baker played number 9 in Matches 11 and 12; Webster played number 1 in Matches 21 and 31; Smith played number 9 in Match 24; Hilsdon played number 8 in Match 25; Steele played number 11 in Matches 25 and 27; Fenwick played number 5 in Match 25; Walden played number 7 in Matches 26 and 34; Dilley played number 9 in Matches 26, 27, 28 and 32(and scored once); Pearcy played number 11 in Matches 28 and 30; Ashmore played number 7 in Matches 29 and 30; Newton played number 8 in Match 29; Adams played number 10 in Match 30; McDougall played number 9 in Match 31; Harrison played number 11 in Matches 32 and 33; Tyler played number 11 in Match 34; Green played number 8 in Match 36.

1939-46

PREPARATIONS for the 1939-40 football season began in an unreal atmosphere as war loomed once more. The Football League season was only three matches old when everyone's worst fears were realised and this time — unlike 1914 — the League programme was immediately abandoned. There was, of course, a different set of circumstances prevailing in 1939 and, fearing immediate mass air-raids, the Government introduced measures to restrict large gatherings at cinemas, racetracks and, inevitably, football grounds.

Eventually, the restrictions were relaxed and, after a short period of friendly matches, the League began again in a regionalised format. And, as in World War One, West Ham enjoyed considerable success. In June 1940, they beat Blackburn Rovers 1-0 at Wembley to win the League War Cup — the semi-final against Fulham had kicked off at 6.40pm on a Saturday evening to accommodate war-workers — and although they never again tasted wartime Cup triumphs, Hammers were always well placed in the League. In seven competitions between 1939-40 and 1944-5, West Ham finished runners-up on five occasions, even though the format of the competitions was changed often. The nearest they came to further Cup glory was in 1945 when, having won their group from Queen's Park Rangers, Spurs and Aldershot, they found Chelsea too good for them in a White Hart Lane semi-final.

Although able to call on guests — and there were some very impressive ones, too, in the Arsenal trio of Drake, Hapgood and Joy, and Hearts' Tommy Walker — West Ham relied largely on their own players. Some 85 per cent of all wartime appearances were made by men who were already on Hammers' books, or who would be by 1945-6. One of the few guests was Manchester City's Northern Ireland international inside-forward Peter Doherty, who later found great success at Derby.

At first, Charlie Paynter had little difficulty in fielding a strong side. Several players, including Charlie Bicknell, were in the Special Constabulary, and a further group was serving in an Army unit based in East Anglia. Later, it got more difficult to field a regular side, but other clubs suffered far more than Hammers. In January 1941, Millwall's 50-year-old trainer, Bill Voisey, had to turn out against West Ham.

In the late summer of 1944, a V1 flying bomb landed on the pitch at Upton Park, destroying a large part of the South Bank terracing and that end of the Main Stand. Forced to play away from home, Hammers strung together nine consecutive wins — and on their return to Upton Park in December, they lost 1-0 to Spurs. For 1945-6, Hammers found themselves in a more familiar 22-club Football League South, comprising pre-war First and Second Division clubs. Their longest journeys were to Plymouth, Nottingham and Derby and they gained 27 of their 51 points away from home in finishing a respectable seventh.

Nine pre-war players were in the side for the opening game, against Birmingham, and there was a special welcome for Charlie Walker, back home after a long spell in the Far East with the RAF. Joe Cockroft, though, would not return; he decided to remain with Sheffield Wednesday, for whom he had guested during the war. Before the season started, Len Goulden was transferred to Chelsea; and in March, George Foreman joined Tottenham. Before the end of the season, Charlie Walker left to manage Margate, and at the final whistle, Ted Fenton took up a similar post at Colchester United, then in the Southern League.

There were compensations: Derek Parker, Ken Bainbridge, Eric Parsons, Ken Wright and Eddie Chapman had all progressed to the point where they would soon be challenging for a first-team place. Foreman's departure let in 21-year-old Mancunian, Don Travis, who scored four goals in a match against Plymouth; and in the same game, Terry Woodgate emulated Syd Puddefoot's feat in World War One football — a seven-minute hat-trick.

The FA Cup was re-started on a home and away basis up to and including the quarter-finals and Hammers received a plum draw against Arsenal. Some 35,000, the largest Upton Park crowd since January 1939, saw the first-leg when the Gunners were shattered by four goals in the first 30 minutes. Hammers' eventual 6-0 lead gave Arsenal an impossible task. In the fourth round, a 65,000 crowd at Stamford Bridge saw Chelsea win 2-0, and for the return at Upton Park, West Ham dropped Foreman. The game began in a hailstorm and the gates closed on a 31,000 crowd. After only eight minutes they saw former Hammers' favourite, Len Goulden, break his collar-bone, but Chelsea held on and Almeric Hall's goal was not enough to save West Ham. The final match of the season was against Arsenal at White Hart Lane on 4 May 1946. After seven years of 'ersatz' football, everyone connected with the game could now look forward to a return of normality.

1939-40
Football League War Cup

Round 1 (1st leg)
Apr 20 v Chelsea (h) 3-2
Fenton, Macaulay, Opp own-goal
Conway; Bicknell, C.Walker, Cockroft, R.Walker, Masson, Small, Fenton, Foreman, Macaulay, Foxall.
Att: 15,200

Round 1 (2nd leg)
Apr 27 v Chelsea (a) 2-0 (agg 5-2)
Foreman, Small
Medhurst; Bicknell, C.Walker, Corbett, R.Walker, Cockroft, Small, Fenton, Foreman, Goulden, Foxall.
Att: 14,897

Round 2 (1st leg)
May 4 v Leicester C (a) 1-1
Macaulay
Conway; Bicknell, C.Walker, Corbett, R.Walker, Cockroft, Small, Macaulay, Foreman, Wood, Foxall.
Att: 6,320

Round 2 (2nd leg)
May 11 v Leicester C (h) 3-0 (agg 4-1)
Foreman 2, Foxall
Conway; Bicknell, C.Walker, Barrett, R.Walker, Cockroft, Small, Fenton, Foreman, Foxall, Chapman.
Att: 15,500

Round 3
May 18 v Huddersfield T (a) 3-3
Foreman, Foxall, Macaulay
Conway; Bicknell, C.Walker, Barrett, R.Walker, Cockroft, Small, Macaulay, Foreman, Goulden, Foxall.
Att: 7,550

Replay
May 22 v Huddersfield T (h) 3-1
Foreman, Foxall, Macaulay
Conway; Bicknell, Scott, Fenton, R.Walker, Cockroft, Small, Macaulay, Foreman, Goulden, Foxall.
Att: 20,000

Round 4
May 25 v Birmingham (h) 4-2
Foreman, Goulden, Macaulay, Small
Conway; Forde, C.Walker, Fenton, R.Walker, Cockroft, Small, Macaulay, Foreman, Goulden, Foxall.
Att: 18,500

Semi-final
Jun 1 v Fulham (at Stamford Bridge) 4-3
Foxall, Goulden, Small, Opp own-goal
Conway; Forde, C.Walker, Fenton, R.Walker, Cockroft, Small, Macaulay, Foreman, Goulden, Foxall.
Att: 32,799

Final (at Wembley)
Jun 8 v Blackburn R 1-0
Small
Conway; Bicknell, C.Walker, Fenton, R.Walker, Cockroft, Small, Macaulay, Foreman, Goulden, Foxall.
Att: 42,399

1940-41
Football League War Cup

Round 1 (1st leg)
Feb 15 v Norwich C (a) 1-2
Barrett
Medhurst; Bicknell, Savage, Small, Barrett, Corbett, Foxall, Macaulay, Foreman, Goulden, Hobbis.
Att: 4,555

Round 1 (2nd leg)
Feb 22 v Norwich C (h) 4-1 (agg 5-3)
Barrett, Foreman 2, Small
Gregory; Bicknell, Chalkley, Barrett, R.Walker, Corbett, Foxall, Small, Foreman, Goulden, Hobbis.
Att: 5,500

Round 2 (1st leg)
Mar 1 v Southend U (a) 1-2
Foxall
Medhurst; Bicknell, Chalkley, Green, Barrett, Corbett, Foxall, Small, Foreman, Macaulay, Hobbis.
Att: 3,500

Round 2 (2nd leg)
Mar 8 v Southend U (h) 3-1 (agg 4-3)
Small 3
Gregory; Bicknell, Chalkley, Barrett, R.Walker, Corbett, Foxall, Small, Foreman, Wood, Hobbis.
Att: 6,000

Round 3 (1st leg)
Mar 15 v Arsenal (h) 0-1
Gregory; Bicknell, Chalkley, Barrett, R.Walker, Corbett, Foxall, Small, Foreman, Goulden, Hobbis.
Att: 14,000

Round 3 (2nd leg)
Mar 29 v Arsenal (a) 1-2 (agg 1-3)
Foreman
Gregory; Bicknell, Chalkley, Small, R.Walker, Corbett, Foxall, Nieuwenhuys, Foreman, Goulden, Hobbis.

London War Cup 'B' Division

Jan 4 v Millwall (a) 2-1
Foreman, Goulden
Medhurst; Bicknell, Chalkley, Small, Barrett, Fenton, Foxall, Macaulay, Foreman, Goulden, Hobbis.
Att: 2,500

371

Jan 11 v Millwall (h) 2-1
Foreman, Hobbis
Gregory; Bicknell, Chalkley, Small, Barrett, Fenton, Foxall, Macaulay, Foreman, Goulden, Hobbis.
Att: 3,500

Jan 25 v Arsenal (h) 1-3
Bicknell
Gregory; Bicknell, Chalkley, Small, Fenton, Green, Foxall, Macaulay, Foreman, Goulden, Hobbis
Att: 5,000

Feb 1 v Tottenham Hotspur (a) 2-1
Fenton, Small
Medhurst; Bicknell, Savage, Small, Barrett, Green, Foxall, Fenton, Foreman, Goulden, Hobbis.
Att: 4,690

Feb 8 v Tottenham Hotspur (h) 3-2
Foreman, Foxall, Small
Gregory; Bicknell, Savage, Barrett, R.Walker, Green, Foxall, Small, Foreman, Fenton, Hobbis.
Att: 5,200

Mar 22 v Reading (h) 1-1
Hobbis
Medhurst; Bicknell, Banner, Small, Corbett, Lewis, Foxall, Macaulay, Foreman, Goulden, Hobbis.
Att: 4,000

Apr 5 v Reading (a) 1-4
Wood
Medhurst; Bicknell, Chalkley, Small, R.Walker, N.Corbett, Foxall, Wood, Foreman, Goulden, Hobbis.
Att: 5,069

Apr 12 v Clapton Orient (h) 8-1
Chalkley, Corbett, Foreman 2, Foxall, Goulden, Small 2
Gregory; Bicknell, Chalkley, Waller, Barrett, Corbett, Nieuwenhuys, Small, Foreman, Goulden, Foxall.
Att: 3,000

Apr 19 v Clapton Orient (a) 3-2
Foreman 2, Small
Medhurst; Bicknell, Chalkley, Collier, Waller, Lewis, Foxall, Small, Foreman, Goulden, Hobbis.
Att: 1,000

May 17 v Arsenal (a) 0-3
Gregory; Bicknell, Chalkley, Corbett, Barrett, Lewis, Foxall, Chapman, Foreman, Small, Hobbis.
Att: 7,365

1941-42
London War Cup Group One

Mar 21 v Brighton & HA (a) 2-1
Foxall, Foreman
Taylor; Bicknell, Chalkley, Lewis, Fenton, Attwell, Small, Wood, Foreman, Goulden, Foxall.
Att: 4,000

Mar 28 v Arsenal (h) 0-4
Gregory; Bicknell, Chalkley, Corbett, R.Walker, Fenton, Nieuwenhuys, Small, Foreman, Goulden, Foxall.
Att: 19,000

Apr 4 v Brighton & HA (h) 6-2
Fenton, Foreman 3, Mahon 2
Ricketts; Bicknell, Lewis, Waller, Barrett, Fenton, Mahon, Small, Foreman, Goulden, Gore.
Att: 4,000

Apr 6 v Arsenal (a) 4-1
Goulden 2, Small, Fenton
Gregory; Bicknell, Chalkley, Fenton, R.Walker, Corbett, Nieuwenhuys, Small, Foreman, Goulden, Foxall.
Att: 22,000

Apr 11 v Clapton Orient (h) 5-3
Corbett, Foreman 2, Wood 2
Gregory; Bicknell, C.Walker, Corbett, Fenton, Attwell, Small, Wood, Foreman, Goulden, Mahon. *Att: 7,000*

Apr 18 v Clapton Orient (a) 1-0
Foreman
Medhurst; Chalkley, Lewis, Bicknell, Corbett, C.Walker, Mahon, Wood, Foreman, Goulden, Gore.
Att: 8,000

1942-43
Football League (South) Cup
Group One

Mar 6 v Watford (h) 6-1
Dunn 2, Foreman 2, Goulden 2
Medhurst; Chalkley, Lewis, Gladwin, Attwell, Macaulay, Small, Dunn, Foreman, Goulden, Foxall.
Att: 2,000

Mar 13 v Brighton & HA (a) 4-1
Foreman 3, Wood
Gregory; Chalkley, Lewis, Gladwin, Small, Attwell, Foxall, T.Walker, Foreman, Goulden, Wood.
Att: 7,521

Mar 20 v Arsenal (h) 1-3
Foreman
Medhurst; Bicknell, Lewis, Gladwin, Brown, Macaulay, Small, Dunn, Foreman, Goulden, Kippax.
Att: 22,000

Mar 27 v Watford (a) 0-0
Gregory; Bicknell, Lewis, Waller, Page, Gladwin, T.Walker, Wood, Foreman, Goulden, Kippax.
Att: 3,246

Apr 3 v Brighton & HA (h) 7-1
Foreman, Goulden 3, Woodgate, Walker, Opp own-goal
Medhurst; Bicknell, Lewis, Gladwin, W.Corbett, Macaulay, Woodgate, Dunn, Foreman, Goulden, Wood.
Att: 5,500

Apr 10 v Arsenal (a) 1-3
Small
Medhurst; Bicknell, Lewis, Gladwin, Barrett, Small, T.Walker, Macaulay, Foreman, Goulden, Wood.
Att: 31,066

1943-44
Football League (South) Cup
Group B

Feb 19 v Watford (h) 1-2
Weaver
Saunders; Jones, Lewis, N.Corbett, W.Corbett, Weaver, Small, Fenton, Foreman, Goulden, Hobbis.
Att: 4,500

Feb 26 v Southampton (a) 2-1
Dunn, Goulden
Medhurst; Bicknell, Jones, Small, W.Corbett, Fenton, Parsons, Dunn, Foreman, Goulden, Hobbis.
Att: 14,000

Mar 4 v Chelsea (a) 0-4
Medhurst; Bicknell, Jones, Attwell, W.Corbett, Lewis, Small, Fenton, Foreman, Goulden, Hobbis.
Att: 15,520

Mar 11 v Watford (a) 1-2
Wood
Gregory; Bicknell, Jones, N.Corbett, W.Corbett, Lewis, Small, Wood, Dunn, Goulden, Hobbis.
Att: 4,257

Mar 18 v Southampton (h) 5-1
Foreman 2, Small 2, Smith
Medhurst; Bicknell, Jones, Fenton, W.Corbett, Lewis, Small, Smith, Foreman, Goulden, Foxall.
Att: 6,500

Mar 25 v Chelsea (h) 6-1
Bicknell, Fenton 2, Goulden, Small 2
Medhurst; Bicknell, N.Corbett, Small, W.Corbett, Fenton, Chapman, Macaulay, Foreman, Goulden, Lewis.
Att: 11,500

1944-45
Football League (South) Cup
Group 3

Feb 3 v Aldershot (a) 3-1
Goulden, Wood, Woodgate
Medhurst; Banner, Lewis, N.Corbett, Fenton, Wilson, Woodgate, Wood, Foreman, Goulden, Whitchurch.
Att: 5,000

Feb 10 v Tottenham Hotspur (h) 1-0
Goulden
Medhurst; Bicknell, Lewis, N.Corbett, Fenton, Wilson,
Woodgate, Henley, Foreman, Goulden, Buchanon.
Att: 21,000

Feb 17 v Queen's Park R (a) 1-1
Macaulay
Gregory; Bicknell, Lewis, N.Corbett, Fenton, Wilson,
Woodgate, Macaulay, Foreman, Goulden, Whitchuch.
Att: 17,000

Feb 24 v Aldershot (h) 4-0
Goulden 3, Woodgate
Medhurst; Bicknell, Lewis, N.Corbett, Fenton, Banner,
Woodgate, Macaulay, Foreman, Goulden,
Whitchurch.
Att: 10,000

Mar 3 v Tottenham Hotspur (a) 0-4
Medhurst; Bicknell, Lewis, N.Corbett, Fenton, Wilson,
Woodgate, Macaulay, Small, Goulden, Whitchurch.
Att: 29,838

Mar 10 v Queen's Park R (h) 5-0
Goulden 2, Small, Whitchurch 2
Medhurst; Bicknell, Lewis, N.Corbett, Fenton, Wilson,
Woodgate, Dunn, Small, Goulden,Whitchurch.
Att: 20,000

Semi-final (at White Hart Lane)
Mar 17 v Chelsea 1-2
Townsend
Medhurst; Bicknell, Lewis, N.Corbett, Fenton, Wilson,
Woodgate, Dunn, Townsend, Macaulay, Whitchurch.
Att: 35,000

Football League 1939-40
(Abandoned after three games and deleted from the records)

Aug 26 v Plymouth A (a) 3-1
Hubbard 2, Wood
Medhurst; Bicknell, C.Walker, Fenton, R.Walker,
Cockroft, Burton, Macaulay, Hubbard, Goulden,
Wood.
Att: 18,000

Aug 28 v Fulham (h) 2-1
Wood, Fenton
Medhurst; Bicknell, C.Walker, Fenton, R.Walker,
Cockroft, Burton, Macaulay, Hubbard, Goulden,
Wood.
Att: 15,000

Sep 2 v Leicester C (h) 0-2
Medhurst; Bicknell, C.Walker, Fenton, R.Walker,
Cockroft, Burton, Macaulay, Hubbard, Goulden,
Wood.
Att: 13,400

1939-40
South 'A' Division

Manager: Charlie Paynter

1	Oct	21	(h)	Crystal P	L	2-6	Foxall 2	6,700
2		28	(a)	Norwich C	L	3-5	Foreman 2, Foxall	2,000
3	Nov	4	(h)	Tottenham H	W	2-1	Goulden, Macaulay	7,800
4		11	(a)	Millwall	D	2-2	Dunn, Macaulay	8,000
5		18	(a)	Southend U	L	2-3	Dunn, Wood	3,000
6		25	(h)	Watford	W	5-0	Foxall, Goulden, Walker 2, Opp own-goal	5,400
7	Dec	2	(a)	Arsenal	L	0-3		10,000
8		9	(h)	Charlton A	W	4-3	Barrett, Foreman, Small 2	6,850
9		16	(a)	Clapton O	W	6-1	Curtis, Fenton, Foreman 2, Foxall, Small	8,000
10		25	(h)	Norwich C	W	4-1	Barrett, Foreman, Wood 2	6,800
11		26	(a)	Tottenham H	W	1-0	Foreman	4,276
12		30	(h)	Millwall	W	6-2	Foreman 3, Foxall, Small 2	7,200
13	Jan	6	(h)	Southend U	W	4-0	Foreman 2, Small 2	5,200
14		13	(a)	Watford	L	1-3	Foreman	4,000
15		17	(a)	Crystal P	W	3-0	Curtis, Foxall 2	896
16		20	(h)	Arsenal	W	3-0	Barrett, Fenton, Foreman	8,000
17	Feb	8	(a)	Charlton A	W	5-2	Fenton 3, Foxall, Foreman	1,200
18		22	(h)	Clapton O	W	4-1	Fenton, Foreman 2, Foxall	2,300

P	W	D	L	F	A	W	D	L	F	A	Pts	Pos	Div	Appearances
18	8	0	1	34	14	4	1	4	23	19	25	2nd	LS	Goals

'C' Division

19	Feb	10	(h)	Tottenham H	W	2-0	Barrett, Foxall	7,500
20		17	(a)	Brentford	L	3-4	Barrett, Small 2	1,885
21		24	(a)	Portsmouth	W	4-1	Foreman 3, Small	1,800
22	Mar	2	(a)	Millwall	L	0-4		10,857
23		9	(h)	Fulham	W	5-0	Fenton, Foreman 2, Foxall 2	8,000
24		16	(a)	Arsenal	W	3-2	Fenton 2, Foreman	10,731
25		22	(a)	Southampton	W	6-1	Foreman 2, Small 2, Fenton, Goulden	8,000
26		23	(h)	Charlton A	W	2-0	Fenton, Foxall	8,000
27		25	(h)	Southampton	D	2-2	Fenton 2	8,000
28		30	(a)	Chelsea	W	10-3	Fenton 3, Foreman 2, Foxall, Small 4	10,000
29	Apr	6	(a)	Tottenham H	W	6-2	Bicknell, Foreman 4, Goulden	15,000
30		8	(h)	Arsenal	W	2-1	Foreman, Macaulay	8,000
31		13	(h)	Brentford	D	1-1	Foreman	8,000
32		29	(h)	Chelsea	W	4-2	Foreman 2, Goulden, Wilkins	5,500
33	May	13	(a)	Portsmouth	D	1-1	Barrett	3,000
34		27	(a)	Fulham	L	1-2	Barrett	5,000
35	Jun	3	(h)	Millwall	L	1-2	Foreman	5,000
36		5	(a)	Charlton A	D	0-0		4,000

P	W	D	L	F	A	W	D	L	F	A	Pts	Pos	Div	Appearances
18	6	2	1	23	9	4	2	3	30	19	24	2nd	LS	Goals

Medhurst	Bicknell	Forde	Fenton E	Walker R	Cockroft	Small	Macaulay	Foreman	Goulden	Foxall	Walker C	Barrett	Corbett N	Wood	Gregory	Chalkley	Harris	Dunn	Taylor	Attwell	Pearson	Sidey	Cann	Brown W	Griffiths	Curtis	Cater	Flack	Conway	McLeod	Chapman	Masson	Gore	Wilkins	Hobbis	Roles	Robinson	Green	Match
1	2	3	4	5	6	7	8	9	10	11																													
1	2		4				8	9	10	7	3	5	6	11																									1
	2		4		6	7	8	9	10	11		5				1	3																						2
	2					7	8	9				5	6	11		1	3	4	10																				3
	2		4	5				9	10	7	3					11		8			1	6																	4
	2		4			7	8	9	10	11	3	6											5			1													5
	2				6	7	8	9	10	11	3	5														1			4										6
	2		4			7	8	9	10	11	3	6														1	5												7
	2		4			7	8	9	10	11	3	5	6													1			8										8
	2		4			7		9	10	7		5				11		3								1			8				6						9
	2		4			7		9	10	11	6	5						3								1			8				6						10
	2		4	5		7		9	10	11	3	6														1			8										11
1	2		4		6	7		9	10	11	3	5																	8										12
	2		4		6	7		9	10	11	3	5																	8					1					13
	2		4	5				9	10	11		6				3													8					1	7				14
	2		8	5	6			9				7	3	4		11										10								1					15
	2		10	5	6			9				7	3	4		11										8								1					16
	2		8	5	6			9				11		4				1	3							10									7				17
3	18	1	17	10	7	11	4	18	14	17	12	16	3	6	3	6	1	2	1	1	1	1	4	1	1	10	1	2	4	1	1								18
			6	2		7	2	17	2	10				3		3							2			2													

I own-goal

Medhurst	Bicknell	Forde	Fenton E	Walker R	Cockroft	Small	Macaulay	Foreman	Goulden	Foxall	Walker C	Barrett	Corbett N	Wood	Gregory	Chalkley	Harris	Dunn	Taylor	Attwell	Pearson	Sidey	Cann	Brown W	Griffiths	Curtis	Cater	Flack	Conway	McLeod	Chapman	Masson	Gore	Wilkins	Hobbis	Roles	Robinson	Green	Match
	2		8	5	6	7		9		11	3	4		10												1													19
	2		8	5		7		9		11	6	4			3										10	1													20
	2		4	5		7		9	10	11	3		6												8	1													21
	2		10	5	6	8		9			7	3	4			11										1													22
	2		8	5	6	7		9		11	3	4													10	1													23
	2		8	5	6	7		9	10	11	3	4														1													24
1	2		8	5	6	7		9	10	11	3	4																											25
	2		8	5	6	7		9	10	11	3	4													10	1													26
1	2		8	5	6	7		9	10	11	3	4					1																						27
1	2		8	5		7		9	10	11	3		4												10				6										28
1	2		8	5		8	9			7	3	4	6												10				6										29
	2	8	5	6		10	9			7	3															1					11								30
	2		5	6				9	10	7	3	4														1		4	11										31
	2		5	6				9	10	7	3	4														1					8	11							32
	2		5							11		4														1	8	6			8	11				3	7	8	33
	2		5					9	10	11		4													8	1											6		34
												2														1													35
4	16	1	12	17	10	11	2	16	9	17	15	15	3	2	1	1	1								6	12	1	4	2	2	2	1	1	2					36
1	10		9	1	19	3	5		4																								1						

A.R.Brown played number 9 in Match 34; Hapgood played number 3 in Match 35 and number 4 in Match 36; Drake played number 7 in Match 35 and 36; Burke played number 1 in Match 36; E.Smith played number 3 in Match 36; Joy played number 5 in Match 36; Howe played number 6 in Match 36; Richardson played number 8 in Match 36; Jinks played number 9 in Match 36; Jones played number 10 in Match 36; J.Smith played number 11 in Match 36.

375

1940-41
Regional League South

Manager: Charlie Paynter

1	Aug	31	(a)	Tottenham H	W 3-2	Barrett, Fenton 2	5,000
2	Sep	7	(h)	Tottenham H	L 1-4	Goulden	3,000
3		21	(h)	Luton T	W 3-0	Barrett, Fenton, Small	500
4		28	(a)	Clapton O	D 3-3	Foxall 2, Goulden	500
5	Oct	5	(a)	Chelsea	D 1-1	Goulden	2,000
6		12	(h)	Millwall	W 3-2	Fenton, Foreman, Foxall	1,000
7		19	(a)	Millwall	D 2-2	Foreman, Lewis	600
8		26	(h)	Southend U	W 11-0	Foxall 3, Macaulay, Barrett, Fenton, Foreman 4, Goulden	500
9	Nov	2	(a)	Southend U	L 1-3	Foxall	1,000
10		16	(a)	Brentford	W 2-0	Corbett, Goulden	400
11		23	(h)	Charlton A	W 4-0	Fenton, Foreman 2, Foxall	500
12		30	(a)	Charlton A	W 2-1	Foreman, Foxall	300
13	Dec	7	(h)	Chelsea	W 6-2	Goulden, Macaulay, Barrett, Foreman 2, Foxall	1,000
14		14	(h)	Clapton O	W 5-1	Fenton, Foreman 3, Goulden	1,200
15		21	(a)	Fulham	W 2-1	Foreman, Osborne	1,000
16		25	(h)	Arsenal	W 4-2	Chapman, Foreman 2, Foxall	9,000
17		28	(h)	Fulham	D 1-1	Foreman	2,500
18	Apr	14	(h)	Watford	W 2-0	Foreman, Foxall	2,000
19		26	(h)	Fulham	L 0-1		3,000
20	May	3	(h)	Brentford	W 3-2	Foreman, Hobbis, Small	3,000
21		10	(a)	Reading	D 1-1	Barrett	6,000
22		24	(h)	Chelsea	D 3-3	Foxall, Nieuwenhuys 2	2,500
23		31	(a)	Queen's Park R	W 5-1	Foreman 3, Foxall, Goulden	2,000
24	Jun	2	(h)	Millwall	L 0-3		3,500
25		7	(h)	Queen's Park R	L 2-3	Foreman, Small	2,100

P	W	D	L	F	A	W	D	L	F	A	Pts	Pos	Div	Appearances
25	9	2	4	48	24	5	4	1	22	15	34	2nd	LS	Goals

Conway	Chalkley	Walker C	Barrett	Walker R	Cockroft	Small	Fenton E	Foreman	Goulden	Foxall	Medhurst	Corbett N	Woodgate	Macaulay	Chapman	Phypers	Lewis	Savage	Ferris	Bicknell	Gregory	Osborne	Yorston	Waller	Niewenhuys	Hobbis	Hobbins	Penny	Whittaker	Joy	
1	2	3	4	5	6	7	8	9	10	11																					
	3	5		6	9	4		10	11	1	2	7	8																		1
1	2	3	5		6	8	4	9	10	11																					2
1	2	3				4	5	8	9	7					10	6															3
1	2	3	5			7	4		10	11				8	9		6														4
1	2	3	6	5		7	8	9	10	11					4		6														5
1	2	3	5			7	4	9	10	11				8			6														6
1	3		6	5		7	4	9	10	11				8						2											7
1	2			5			4	9	10	11		8			7		6	3													8
1	2			5		7	8	9	10	11							6	3	4												9
1	3			5			8	9	10	11		7					6	4		2											10
1				5		8	4	9	10	11		7					6	3		2											11
1				5		7	4	9	10	11				8			6	3		2											12
1	3			5		7	8	9	10	11							6	4		2											13
	3			5		4	6	9	10	11							7			2	1				8						14
	3			5		4		9	10	11						6	7			2	1				8						15
	3			5		4	6	9	10	11							7			2	1				8						16
	3			5		6		9	10	7										2	1			4	8	11					17
	3			5		6		9	10	7		2								2				4	8	11	1				18
	3		5			8	9		7						10		6			2	1			4		11					19
	3	4	5			8		9	10	7							6			2			1			11					20
	3		6					9	10	7					4					2					8	11	1			5	21
	3	5				4		9	10	7							6			2					8	11	1			5	22
	3		4					9	10	7							6			2	1			5	8	11					23
	3		4			10		9		11					7		6			2					8		1			5	24
13	20	9	21	5	3	22	17	23	23	25	1	6	1	8	10	1	13	6	1	13	6	1	2	4	6	6	5	1	1	1	25
		5				3	7	24	8	14	1			2	1		1			1						2	1				

Match 4 v Clapton Orient, only ten players used.

1941-42
London League

Manager: Charlie Paynter

#	Month	Date		Opponent	Res	Score	Scorers	Att
1	Aug	30	(h)	Portsmouth	L	1-3	Foxall	6,300
2	Sep	6	(a)	Chelsea	W	8-4	Fenton, Foreman 3, Goulden, Foxall 2, Small	6,427
3		13	(a)	Charlton A	D	1-1	Foreman	7,633
4		20	(h)	Clapton O	W	3-1	Foreman, Foxall, Macaulay	4,500
5		27	(a)	Watford	W	8-0	Foreman 3, Nieuwenhuys 2, Foxall 2, Small	4,000
6	Oct	4	(h)	Aldershot	W	3-0	Barrett, Foreman 2	5,500
7		11	(h)	Millwall	W	4-2	Bicknell, Foreman 2, Nieuwenhuys	7,500
8		18	(a)	Arsenal	L	1-4	Foreman	13,419
9		25	(h)	Queen's Park R	W	2-0	Foreman, Macaulay	5,300
10	Nov	1	(a)	Reading	L	2-3	Bicknell, Macaulay	6,000
11		8	(h)	Brighton & HA	W	4-0	Foreman 2, Goulden 2	5,600
12		15	(a)	Brentford	W	5-0	Foxall 2, Goulden, Small 2	5,000
13		22	(h)	Crystal P	L	0-5		7,000
14		29	(a)	Fulham	W	3-1	Small 2, Goulden	4,468
15	Dec	6	(a)	Tottenham H	D	1-1	Foxall	8,493
16		13	(a)	Portsmouth	L	0-1		6,000
17		20	(h)	Chelsea	W	5-0	Fenton, Foreman, Goulden, Foxall, Macaulay	3,800
18		25	(h)	Charlton A	D	2-2	Bicknell, Foxall	4,000
19		27	(a)	Clapton O	L	1-3	Chapman	3,000
20	Jan	3	(h)	Watford	W	4-1	Foxall, Wood 3	4,000
21		10	(a)	Aldershot	W	5-1	Chapman 3, Foreman, Quickenden	3,500
22		17	(a)	Millwall	W	3-1	Chapman, Foxall, Small	4,000
23		24	(h)	Arsenal	W	3-0	Foreman 2, Goulden	20,000
24		31	(a)	Queen's Park R	L	1-2	Small	5,000
25	Feb	14	(a)	Brighton & HA	W	3-1	Foreman, Goulden, Small	3,000
26		21	(h)	Brentford	W	2-1	Goulden, Small	4,000
27		28	(a)	Crystal P	D	1-1	Small	7,790
28	Mar	7	(h)	Fulham	D	1-1	Goulden	2,500
29		14	(h)	Tottenham H	L	2-3	Fenton, Goulden	8,000
30	Apr	25	(h)	Reading	W	2-1	Chapman, Mahon	4,500

P	W	D	L	F	A	W	D	L	F	A	Pts	Pos	Div	
30	10	2	3	38	20	7	3	5	43	24	39	3rd	LL	Appearances
														Goals

378

Medhurst	Bicknell	Chalkley	Fenton E	Walker R	Corbett N	Small	Macaulay	Foreman	Goulden	Foxall	Gregory	Barrett	Lewis	Nieuwenhuys	Attwell	Taylor	Banner	Wood	Walker C	Whatley	Jobling	Waller	Chapman	Ricketts	Sliman	Tann	Quickenden	Dunn	Jones	Mahon	Forde	Pryde	
1	2	3	4	5	6	7	8	9	10	11																							1
	2	3	4			8		9	10	11	1	5	6	7																			2
1	2	3	6	5	4	8		9	10	11				7																			3
	2	3	6		4	8		9	10	11	1	5		7																			4
1	2	3	6	5	4	8		9	10	11				7																			5
	2	3	4			7	8	9	10	11	1	5			6																		6
1	2	3	4	5		8		9	10	11				7	6																		7
	2	3	4	5	6	8		9	10	11	1		5																				8
1	2	3	4		6	7	8	9	10	11			5																				9
	2	3	4	5		7	8	9	10	11	1			6																			10
			4		2	6	8	9	10	11		5		7		1	3																11
	2	3	4	5		7	8	9	10	11	1			6																			12
	2	3	5			8		9	10	11	1	4	7	6																			13
1	2	3	4		6	7		9	10	11		5						8															14
			4	5	6	7	8	9	10	11	1						2	3															15
	2						8	9	10	11	1	5	6							3	4	7											16
1	2		4	5	6	7	8	9	10	11							3																17
	2	3	4		5		8	9	10	11	1			6			7																18
	2		4	10		6	8		9		11	5			3			8				7	1										19
1		4	2			7		9	10	11		3			6			8	5														20
	2	5				6		9	10	11	1	3					8				4	7											21
1	2	4		5		7	6	9	10	11		3					8																22
	2	4				7	6	9	10	11	1			5		3																	23
1	2	5		4		7		9	10	11		6				3																	24
1	3	5		4		7		9	10	11		6				2									8								25
	2	5				7		9	10	11		6				3									8					3	4		26
1	4	2	8	5	6	7		9	10	11						3																	27
1	2	5		4		7		9	10	11		3		6													8						28
		8	5	2		7	6	9	10	11		3		4								6											29
	2		4			5		9	10			6				1	3					7					8		11				30
13	24	18	29	14	16	26	15	30	29	13	10	12	8	9	2	7	3	2	1	1	1	7	1	1	1	1	3	1	1	1	1		
	3		3			11	4	21	11	13		1		3				3				6			1		1						

1942-43

League South

Manager: Charlie Paynter

1	Aug	29	(a)	Portsmouth	W	5-4	Foreman, Foxall, Goulden, Small 2	8,000
2	Sep	5	(h)	Luton T	W	3-1	Barrett, Foreman 2	6,370
3		12	(h)	Crystal P	D	2-2	Dunn, Goulden	7,000
4		19	(h)	Tottenham H	W	3-1	Fenton, Foreman 2	10,160
5		26	(a)	Clapton O	W	5-0	Dunn 2, Foxall, Mahon 2	4,000
6	Oct	3	(h)	Chelsea	L	0-1		10,200
7		10	(a)	Brentford	L	2-6	Foreman, Foxall	7,000
8		17	(a)	Aldershot	L	1-5	Small	7,500
9		24	(h)	Watford	W	3-0	Foreman, Small, Wood	5,000
10		31	(a)	Fulham	W	3-2	Foreman 2, Opp own-goal	5,500
11	Nov	7	(a)	Queen's Park R	L	2-5	Foreman, Foxall	6,852
12		14	(h)	Millwall	W	7-5	Dunn 2, Foreman, Foxall, Goulden 3	5,000
13		21	(a)	Brighton & HA	D	2-2	Foreman, Foxall	3,000
14		28	(h)	Portsmouth	W	2-1	Foxall, Wood	7,000
15	Dec	5	(a)	Luton T	L	2-3	Foreman, Foxall	3,000
16		12	(a)	Crystal P	D	0-0		5,127
17		19	(a)	Tottenham H	L	0-2		9,741
18		25	(h)	Charlton A	L	1-3	Goulden	10,000
19		26	(a)	Charlton A	D	4-4	Foreman, Goulden 3	7,379
20	Jan	2	(h)	Clapton O	W	10-3	Dunn 3, Foreman 3, Macaulay, Trigg 2, Opp own-goal	6,000
21		9	(a)	Chelsea	W	3-1	Fenton, Foreman, Goulden	8,585
22		16	(h)	Brentford	W	4-1	Foreman 2, Kippax, Wood	7,500
23		23	(a)	Aldershot	W	6-3	Dunn 3, Goulden, Small 2	8,000
24		30	(a)	Watford	L	2-3	Goulden, Mahon	2,274
25	Feb	6	(h)	Fulham	W	2-1	Kippax, Small	5,200
26		13	(h)	Queen's Park R	L	1-3	Foreman	6,000
27		20	(a)	Millwall	D	3-3	Dunn, Fenton, Foreman	2,000
28		27	(h)	Brighton & HA	W	2-1	Foreman, Small	3,000

P	W	D	L	F	A	W	D	L	F	A	Pts	Pos	Div	Appearances
28	10	1	3	46	26	4	4	6	34	40	33	6th	LS	Goals

Football appearances and goals grid. Column headers (left to right): Medhurst, Lewis, Banner, Corbett N, Corbett W, Attwell, Small, Dunn, Foreman, Goulden, Foxall, Gregory, Chalkley, Barrett, Macaulay, Mahon, Taylor, Bicknell, Walker R, Fenton E, Chapman, Wood, Aicken, Page, Kippax, Watson-Smith, Davis, Walker T, Trigg, Bartram, Mutitt, Dunkley, Riordan, Woodgate, Wright, Gladwin, Jones.

#	Medhurst	Lewis	Banner	Corbett N	Corbett W	Attwell	Small	Dunn	Foreman	Goulden	Foxall	Gregory	Chalkley	Barrett	Macaulay	Mahon	Taylor	Bicknell	Walker R	Fenton E	Chapman	Wood	Aicken	Page	Kippax	Watson-Smith	Davis	Walker T	Trigg	Bartram	Mutitt	Dunkley	Riordan	Woodgate	Wright	Gladwin	Jones
	1	2	3	4	5	6	7	8	9	10	11																										
1		3		4				8	9	10	11	1	2	5	6	7																					
2		3			5	6	7	8	9	10	11							1	2	4																	
3		3		4			7		9	10	11	1			6				2	5	8																
4	1	3				6	4	8	9	10	11					7				2		5															
5		3		4					9	10	11	1		5		7			2	6		8															
6	1	3				6	4	8	9	10	11					7				2		5															
7		3			5	6	2		9	10	11	1			8	7				4																	
8	1		6	5	3	7			9	10	11				2					4		8															
9	1		3	6			4	8	9	10	11					7				2		5															
10		3						8	9		11	1		5		7			2	4		10	6														
11		3		6	5	2	7	8	9	10	11						1			4																	
12	1	6	3	4					9	10	11					7			2	5		8															
13		3		4	5	6	7		9	10	11	1							2			8															
14		3		4		6			9	10	11	1				7			2	5		8															
15				4		6	7		9	10		1			3	11			2	5		8															
16		3		5		6	2	8	9	10		1				7				4		11															
17	1	3		4			7		9	10					6			2				8					5	11									
18	1	3		4			7		9	10					6			2				8					5	11									
19		3					2	8	9	10					6					5				1	4	7	11										
20		3			5		7		9	10						2			4						8				1	6	11						
21	1	3		4		6	7		9	10							2			5		8															
22		3	6				4	8	9	10		1							2	5						11		7									
23	1	2	3			6	4		9	10					11					5		8						7									
24		3		4		6	7	8	9	10		1	2						5							11											
25	1	3		4		6	8		9			2						5			10				11		7										
26		3		4		8	9					2		1	2			5					11			7											
27		3			6	7		9	10	11				1	2			8															6	7	10		
28	11	25	4	16	8	17	25	11	28	24	16	11	4	5	5	12	4	18	2	21	2	13	1	2	7	1	1	5	1	1	1	1	1	1	1	4	5

Appearances total (row 28): 11 25 4 16 8 17 25 11 28 24 16 11 4 5 5 12 4 18 2 21 2 13 1 2 7 1 1 5 1 1 1 1 1 1 1 1 1

Goals: (Dunn) 8, (Foreman) 12, (Goulden) 23, (Foxall) 12, (Gregory) 8, (Barrett) 1, (Macaulay) 1, (Mahon) 3, (Fenton E) 3, (Wood) 3, (Kippax) 2, (Walker T) 2

2 own-goals

1943-44
League South

Manager: Charlie Paynter

1	Aug	28	(a)	Portsmouth	L 0-2		6,000
2	Sep	4	(h)	Luton T	W 3-2	Foreman, Lowes, Small	6,000
3		11	(h)	Arsenal	D 2-2	Macaulay 2	15,000
4		18	(h)	Tottenham H	D 3-3	Dunn, Foreman, Hobbis	20,000
5		25	(a)	Clapton O	W 4-0	Foreman 2, Foxall, Goulden	6,000
6	Oct	2	(a)	Crystal P	W 6-1	Foreman 2, Foxall 2, Goulden, Wood	7,040
7		9	(h)	Brentford	D 0-0		12,000
8		16	(a)	Southampton	W 4-2	Dunn 2, Fenton, Foreman	9,000
9		23	(h)	Reading	W 1-0	Wood	10,000
10		30	(a)	Fulham	W 6-2	Fenton, Foreman, Goulden 2, Small 2	10,000
11	Nov	6	(h)	Queen's Park R	D 1-1	Wood	16,100
12		13	(h)	Millwall	W 3-0	Foreman, Goulden, Wood	12,000
13		20	(a)	Brighton & HA	W 2-1	Goulden, Foreman	5,000
14		27	(h)	Portsmouth	W 5-1	Foreman, Mahon, Small, Wood, Opp own-goal	8,000
15	Dec	4	(a)	Luton T	W 1-0	Dunn	4,000
16		11	(a)	Arsenal	D 1-1	Foreman	22,497
17		18	(h)	Charlton A	L 0-1		7,000
18		25	(a)	Chelsea	D 3-3	Dunn, Fenton, Wood	16,000
19		27	(h)	Chelsea	W 3-0	Foreman, Wood 2	12,000
20	Jan	1	(a)	Tottenham H	L 0-1		40,067
21		8	(a)	Queen's Park R	L 0-3		11,944
22		22	(h)	Crystal P	W 3-0	Foreman 2, Goulden	9,500
23		29	(a)	Brentford	L 1-2	Foreman	11,220
24	Feb	5	(h)	Southampton	W 4-1	Dunkley, Foreman 2, Goulden	7,500
25		12	(a)	Reading	L 2-3	Foxall, Small	5,574
26	Apr	1	(h)	Fulham	W 3-2	Parsons, Wood 2	5,000
27		10	(h)	Clapton O	W 3-1	Foreman, Goulden, Small	9,000
28		22	(a)	Charlton A	D 1-1	Opp own-goal	8,500
29		29	(a)	Millwall	W 3-1	Foreman 2, Dunn	6,000
30	May	6	(h)	Brighton & HA	W 6-2	Deans, Foreman, Small, Wood, Goulden 2	4,000

P	W	D	L	F	A	W	D	L	F	A	Pts	Pos	Div		Appearances
30	10	4	1	40	16	7	3	5	34	23	41	2nd	LS		Goals

382

Medhurst	Bicknell	Lewis	Corbett W	Morris	Armeson	Small	Wood	Foreman	Goulden	Foxall	Gregory	Corbett N	Dunkley	Lowes	Attwell	Macaulay	Chalkley	Walker T	Dunn	Hobbis	Jones	Cardwell	Wright	Fenton E	Mahon	Hughes	Muttitt	Parsons	Girling	Gibbs	Aldridge	Deans	Wilson	Gillespie	Chapman	Woodgate	Taylor	
1	2	3	4	5	6	7	8	9	10	11																												1
	2	3	5		6	11		9	10		1	4	7	8																								2
1	2	3	5			7	10	9		11		4				6	8																					3
	2	4			6	5		9	10		1						3	7	8	11																		4
1			4		6		8	9	10	7								3		11	2	5																5
	2				6	4	8	9	10	11	1								7		3			5														6
1	2				6	5	8	9	10	7		4								11	3			10														7
	2				6	5		9			1	4						11	8		3			10														8
1	2				6	8	9	10	11			4	7								3			5														9
	2				6	5		7	9	10	1	4	11								3			8														10
1	2	3				7	8	9	10	11		4			6						3			5														11
		3	5			7	11	9	10		1	6					8				2			4														12
1	2				6	5		7	9	10	11	4									3			8														13
		3	5			4	8	9	10		1				7						2			6	11													14
1	2				6	5		7	9	10	11				8						3			4														15
1	2		4			5	8	9	10			7			6						3			11														16
	2				6	5		9	10	11	1				7						8			3														17
	2	4	5			11		9	10		1				7						8			3									6					18
	2				6	5	11	8	9	10	1				7						3			4														19
1		3				4	8	9	10	11					6			7			2			5														20
	2				6	11		9	10		1							7			3			8								4					5	21
1	2				6	5		7	9	10		4						11	3					8														22
	2		5			4	8	9	10		1				7						6	11		3														23
	2					4	8	9	10		7							11	3					5	1	6												24
1	2				6		8	9	10	7		4						11	3					5					7	11								25
	2	3	5		6		8	9	10		1										4			7	11				1	3	4	6	8					26
	2	11				7		9	10					5							1	3	4	6	8							4			7			27
1	2	3			6		8	9	10					5				11			4			7								4				7		28
1	2	3				7		9	10					5				8			4			11								4					11	29
	2	3				7	11	9	10					5				4						8								6					1	30
14	26	27	16	1	4	28	16	30	28	12	13	13	10	1	6	4	3	6	9	6	20	1	1	18	2	1	1	1	1	1	1	4	1	1	1	1	1	
						7	11	22	11	4		1	1		2					6	1			3	1		1					1						

2 own-goals

1944-45

League South

Manager: Charlie Paynter

1	Aug	26	(a)	Tottenham H	D	2-2	Foreman, Wood	14,000
2	Sep	2	(a)	Charlton A	L	2-3	Corbett, Fenton	4,000
3		9	(a)	Watford	D	3-3	Fenton, Foxall, Opp own-goal	3,842
4		16	(a)	Queen's Park R	W	1-0	Goulden	8,000
5		23	(a)	Portsmouth	W	3-1	Dodds, Dunn, Macaulay	16,000
6		30	(a)	Brighton & HA	W	1-0	Dodds	6,000
7	Oct	7	(a)	Aldershot	W	3-2	Dodds, Foreman, Wood	4,500
8		14	(a)	Luton T	W	4-3	Dodds, Dunn, Wood 2	5,000
9		21	(a)	Arsenal	W	3-0	Dodds, Goulden, Opp own-goal	27,800
10		28	(a)	Millwall	W	3-0	Foreman 2, Woodgate	5,000
11	Nov	4	(a)	Clapton O	W	3-0	Dodds 2, Ludford	10,000
12		11	(a)	Fulham	W	7-4	Dodds 3, B.Fenton, Goulden, Ludford 2	10,359
13		18	(a)	Southampton	L	1-2	Dodds	14,000
14		25	(a)	Crystal P	L	0-3		11,600
15	Dec	2	(h)	Tottenham H	L	0-1		25,000
16		9	(h)	Charlton A	W	2-0	Foreman, Woodgate	9,500
17		16	(h)	Watford	W	6-2	Barrett, Foreman, Goulden 2, Wood 2	7,000
18		30	(h)	Queen's Park R	W	4-2	Foreman 3, Woodgate	9,000
19	Jan	6	(h)	Portsmouth	W	4-0	Goulden, Wood, Woodgate 2	9,000
20		13	(h)	Brighton & HA	W	5-4	Bainbridge 2, Foreman 2, Medley	5,000
21		20	(h)	Aldershot	W	8-1	Dunn, Foreman 4, Goulden 3	4,000
22	Mar	24	(h)	Millwall	W	3-1	Wilson 2, Woodgate	8,000
23		31	(h)	Clapton O	W	1-0	Thomas	8,000
24	Apr	2	(a)	Chelsea	W	4-3	Goulden, Mallett, Whitchurch 2	23,827
25		14	(h)	Fulham	W	3-2	Chapman, Fenton, Whitchurch	8,000
26		21	(h)	Southampton	L	3-5	Hall, Lewis, Small	12,000
27		28	(h)	Crystal P	W	5-0	Hall, Small 3, Woodgate	6,257
28	May	5	(a)	Arsenal	D	1-1	Small	9,000
29		12	(h)	Luton T	W	9-1	Cheetham 2, Corbett, Hall 3, Whitchurch 3	5,000
30		19	(h)	Chelsea	W	2-1	Hall, Whitchurch	10,000

P	W	D	L	F	A	W	D	L	F	A	Pts	Pos	Div	Appearances
30	12	1	2	56	21	10	2	3	40	26	47	2nd	LS	Goals

	Gregory	Bicknell	Jones	Deans	Briddon	Lewis	Thomas R	Fenton E	Foreman	Goulden	Wood	Burke	Barrett	Corbett N	Burnett	Macaulay	Medhurst	Attwell	Woodgate	Hubbard	Foxall	Robinson	Dodds	Corbett W	Dunn	Wilson	Hall	Bell	Ludford	Small	Fenton B	Bainbridge	Ferrier	Whitchurch	Medley	Mallett	Chapman	Taylor	Cheetham	
1	1	2	3	4	5	6	7	8	9	10	11																													1
2	1		3	2				11		10	9			4	5	6	7	8																						2
3		3				2		8	10				5	4			1	6	7	9	11																			3
4	1	3	5			2		6		10	11		4					7	8	9																				4
5		2	3			6				10			4		8	1		7		9	5	11																		5
6		2		3		5		10					6		8	1	4	7		9		11																		6
7		2	3		6			11	10	8					1	5		9		4	7																			7
8		2	3			6	5			10		4			1		7		9		8			11																8
9		2		3		5			10	11		6		4	1		7		9		8																			9
10		2	3		6	5	9	10	11		4			1		7			8																					10
11		2	3		6		5		10				1		7		9		8	4		11																		11
12		2		3		5		10		6			1			7		9			4		11	7	8															12
13		2		3		5		10		6		4	1		7		9		8		11																			13
14		2			3			10	11			1	6	7			9	4			5	8																		14
15		2	3		6	5		10	11		4		8	1		7		9																						15
16		2		3		8	9	10	11		4		1		7	5		6																						16
17		2		3		9	10	11	5	4		1		7		8	6																							17
18		2	3		11	5	9	10		4		1		7		8	6																							18
19		2		3		5	9	10	11		4		1		7		8	6																						19
20		2			3		9	10		5	4	1			6			8										8	3	7	11									20
21		2	3		6	5	9	10	11		4		1		7		8																							21
22		2	3		6	5			10		4		1		7				10				9		8		11													22
23		2	3		6	5		10			1		7		4				4					11																23
24		2	3		6			10			1		7		4				4					9		8														24
25		2		3		5		10			4	1		7				6	8		9	11																		25
26		2	3		6	5		10		4	1							9	8				7				11													26
27		2		3		5		10		4			7					6	8		9											1								27
28			3		5			10		2							11		6	8	9											1								28
29		2	3		5			10		4			7					6	8				11									1	9							29
30		2			5			10		4			7					6	8	9			11									1								30
	3	25	17	2	1	28	1	24	11	25	13	1	4	23	1	8	23	4	23	1	2	1	10	2	12	18	7	1	3	7	1	3	1	9	1	1	1	4	1	
		1							3	15	10	7		1	2		1		7				1		11		3	2	6		3	5	1	2		7	1	1	1	2	

2 own-goals

Parker played number 8 in Match 23; D.Thomas played number 9 in Match 23 and dcored a goal; Ridyard played number 5 in Match 24; Pritchard played number 11 in Match 24; Hunt played number 4 in Match 28; Hopkins played number 7 in Match 28; Smith played number 3 in Match 30.

1945-46

League South

Manager: Charlie Paynter

1	Aug	25	(a)	Birmingham C	W	1-0	Bicknell	30,000
2		27	(h)	Arsenal	D	1-1	Whitchurch	25,000
3	Sep	1	(h)	Birmingham C	W	3-2	Foreman 2, Whitchurch	20,000
4		8	(h)	Tottenham H	D	1-1	Foreman	26,000
5		10	(h)	Aston Villa	L	1-2	Foreman	20,000
6		15	(a)	Tottenham H	W	3-2	Hall, Macaulay 2	34,778
7		22	(a)	Brentford	D	1-1	Hall	19,000
8		29	(h)	Brentford	L	0-2		23,000
9	Oct	6	(h)	Chelsea	L	2-4	Foreman, Whitchurch	25,000
10		13	(a)	Chelsea	W	2-1	Bicknell, Hall	45,000
11		20	(a)	Millwall	D	0-0		32,000
12		27	(h)	Millwall	W	3-1	Foreman, Hall, Wood	25,000
13	Nov	3	(h)	Southampton	W	3-1	Small 3	20,000
14		10	(a)	Southampton	D	3-3	Foreman, Woodgate, Wright	17,000
15		17	(a)	Derby C	L	1-5	Hall	20,000
16		24	(h)	Derby C	L	2-3	Small 2	28,000
17	Dec	1	(h)	Leicester C	D	2-2	Macaulay, Small	20,000
18		8	(a)	Leicester C	L	1-4	Woodgate	12,345
19		15	(a)	Coventry C	W	5-2	Hall 2, Woodgate, Wright 2	11,719
20		22	(h)	Coventry C	W	6-3	Foreman 2, Wood, Woodgate, Wright 2	14,000
21		25	(h)	Luton T	L	3-4	Fenton, Foreman, Woodgate	10,000
22		26	(a)	Luton T	W	4-1	Bicknell, Foreman, Small, Woodgate	14,000
23		29	(a)	Aston Villa	D	2-2	Bainbridge, Opp own-goal	30,000
24	Jan	12	(a)	Charlton A	L	0-3		45,000
25		19	(h)	Charlton A	W	2-0	Fenton, Foreman	25,000
26	Feb	2	(a)	Fulham	W	1-0	Hall	30,000
27		9	(a)	Plymouth A	W	2-1	Foreman, Wood	20,000
28		16	(h)	Plymouth A	W	7-0	Travis 4, Woodgate 3	15,000
29		23	(h)	Portsmouth	W	3-1	Bainbridge, Travis, Woodgate	15,000
30	Mar	2	(a)	Portsmouth	W	3-2	Bainbridge, Bicknell, Woodgate	12,000
31		9	(a)	Nottingham F	D	1-1	Fenton	22,000
32		16	(h)	Nottingham F	L	1-3	Small	18,000
33		23	(h)	Newport C	W	4-1	Gray, Hall, Macaulay 2	12,000
34		30	(a)	Newport C	D	2-2	Hall, Macaulay	16,000
35	Apr	6	(a)	Wolves	D	3-3	Macaulay, Wood 2	25,000
36		13	(h)	Wolves	W	2-1	Travis 2	25,000
37		19	(a)	Swansea T	W	3-2	Hall 2, Small	25,000
38		20	(a)	West Brom A	D	1-1	Macaulay	24,600
39		22	(h)	Swansea T	W	3-0	Hall 2, Woodgate	14,959
40		27	(a)	West Brom A	W	2-1	Macaulay, Small	10,000
41		29	(h)	Fulham	L	3-5	Hall 2, Wood	28,000
42	May	4	(a)	Arsenal	L	1-2	Wood	30,000

P	W	D	L	F	A	W	D	L	F	A	Pts	Pos	Div	
42	10	4	7	53	38	10	7	4	41	38	51	7th	LS	Appearances
														Goals

FA Cup

3	Jan	5	(h)	Arsenal	W	6-0	Hall 2, Wood 2, Bainbridge, Foreman	35,000
		9	(a)	Arsenal	L	0-1		22,000
4		26	(a)	Chelsea	L	0-2		65,000
		30	(h)	Chelsea	W	1-0	Hall	31,000

Appearances

Goals

Football appearances and goals grid (players as columns, matches 1–42 as rows):

Medhurst	Bicknell	Walker C	Corbett N	Walker R	Wilson	Woodgate	Fenton E	Foreman	Small	Whitchurch	Hall	Macauley	Wood	Attwell	Hopkins	Forde	Wright	Dunn	Harris	Cater	Powell-Besens	Bainbridge	Travis	Gray	#
1	2	3	4	5	6	7	8	9	10	11															1
1	2	3	4	5	6	7		9	10	11	8														2
1	2	3		5	6	7	4	9		11		8	10												3
1	2	3	4	5		7	6	9		11		8	10												4
1	2		4	3	6		5	9		11	7	8	10												5
1	2		3	6			5	9		11	7	8	10	4											6
1	2		4	3		7	5	9		11	8		10	6											7
1	2	3	4	5		7		9		11	8		10	6											8
1	2	3	4	5	6			9		11	8		10	7											9
1	2	3	4	5	6	7		9		11	8		10												10
1	2		4	3	6	7	5	9		11	8		10												11
1	2		4	5	6	7	8		9	11			10			3									12
1		3	4	2	6	7	5	9		11			8				10								13
1	2	3	4	5	6	7		10	9	11			8												14
1	2	3	4	5		7	6		9	11			10		8										15
1	2	3	4	5		7	6	9				8	10				11								16
1	2	3		6		7	5		9	11	8						10	4							17
1	2		6			7	5	9	4		8		11				10			3					18
1	2		6			7	5	9	4		8		11				10			3					19
1	2		6			7	5	9		11	8									3	4	10			20
1	2	3		6		7	5	9	10		8									4		11			21
1	2	3		6		7	5	9	4	11	8											10			22
1	2			5		7	6	9	4		8	10	11							3					23
1	2			5		7	6	9	10		8	4	11							3					24
1	2			5		7	6	9	4		8	10								3		11			25
1	2	3		5		7	6	9	8			10	11							4					26
1	2	3		5		7	6				8	10								4		11	9		27
1	2		4	5		7	6				8	10								3		11	9		28
1	2		4	5		7	6		9		8	10								3		11			29
1	2	3	4	5		7	10		9		8		11							6					30
1	2		4	5		7	6		9		8	10								3		11			31
1	2			7	5			4		8	10		6							3		11	9		32
1	2		4	3	7	5		9		8	10	11	6							3					33
1	2	3	4			7	5				8	10	11	6								9			34
1	2			5		7	4				8	10	11	6						3		9			35
1	2		6	5		7	4		9		8	10	11							3					36
1	2		6	5		7	4				8	10	11							3					37
1	2			5		7	4		6		8	10	11							3		9			38
1	2		6	5		7	4		9		8	10	11							3		9			39
1	2		6	5		7	4		9		8	10	11							3					40
1	2		6	5		7	4		9		8	10	11							3					41
1	2		6	5		7	4		9		8	10	11							3					42
42	41	19	26	40	11	39	37	23	25	19	33	23	30	7	1	1	5	1	1	21	1	9	6	1	
4			12	3	13	10	3	16	9	7			5				3			7		3	7	1	

1 own-goal

Medhurst	Bicknell	Walker C	Corbett N	Walker R	Wilson	Woodgate	Fenton E	Foreman	Small	Whitchurch	Hall	Macauley	Wood	Attwell	Hopkins	Forde	Wright	Dunn	Harris	Cater	Powell-Besens	Bainbridge	Travis	Gray	#
1	2		5			7	6	9	4		8		10							3		11			
1	2		5			7	6	9	4		8		10							3		11			3
1	2		5			7	6	9	10		8	4	11							3					
1	2		5			7	6		4		8	9	10							3		11			4
4	4		4			4	4	3	4		4	2	4							4		3			
						1			3		2									1					

387

Hammers in Other Competitions

Charity Shield

1964-65
Aug 15 v Liverpool (a) 2-2
Hurst, Byrne
Standen; Bond, Burkett, Bovington, Brown, Moore, Brabrook, Boyce, Byrne, Hurst, Sissons.
Att: 38,858

1975-76
Aug 9 v Derby County (at Wembley) 0-2
Day; McDowell, Lampard, Holland, T.Taylor, Lock, A.Taylor, Paddon, Jennings(Coleman), Brooking, Gould(Robson).
Att: 59,000

1980-81
Aug 9 v Liverpool (at Wembley) 0-1
Parkes; Stewart, Brush, Bonds, Martin, Devonshire, Allen, Holland, Cross, Brooking, Pike(Morgan).
Att: 90,000

Anglo Italian Cup-winners' Cup

1975-76
Sep 3 v Fiorentina (a) 0-1
Day; McDowell, Lampard, Bonds, T.Taylor, Lock, A.Taylor, Paddon, Holland(Jennings), Brooking, Robson.
Att: 35,000
Dec 10 v Fiorentina (h) 0-1
Day; McDowell(Coleman), Lampard, Holland, T.Taylor, Lock, A.Taylor, Paddon, Jennings, Brooking, Ayris(Curbishley).
Att: 14,699

Essex Professional Cup

1950-51
Round 1
Sep 28 v Colchester U (h) 2-1
Gazzard, Robinson
Gregory; B.Nelson, Forde, Parker, Niblett, O'Farrell, Southren, Johns, Robinson, Gazzard, Woodgate.
Semi-final
Mar 5 v Leyton O (a) 0-0
Taylor; Kearns, Kinsell, Jackman, Allison, Moroney, Hooper, McGowan, Robinson, Gazzard, Woodgate.
Replay
Mar 12 v Leyton O (h) 6-1
Gazzard 2, Hooper 2, Parker, Robinson
Taylor; Wright, Kinsell, Parker, Allison, Moroney, Hooper, McGowan, Robinson, Gazzard, Woodgate.
Final
May 7 v Southend U (h) 2-0
Robinson, Moroney
Taylor; Devlin, Forde, Moroney, Allison, O'Farrell, Hooper, Barrett, Robinson, Gazzard, Woodgate.
1951-52
Round 1
Mar 12 v Southend U (h) 2-1
Allison, Andrews
Gregory; Wright, Devlin, Parker, Hawkins, Moroney, Hooper, Barrett, Allison, Gazzard, Andrews.

Semi-final
Apr 3 v Chelmsford C (h) 3-0
Williams 2, Tucker
Taylor; Wright, Devlin, Parker, Allison, McGowan, Woodgate, Williams, Hawkins, Gregory, Tucker.
Final
May 5 v Colchester U (a) 1-3
Barrett
Gregory; Wright, Kinsell, Parker, Allison, McGowan, Woodgate, Barrett, Moroney, Gazzard, Andrews.

1952-53
Round 1
Nov 13 v Colchester U (a) 3-2
Moroney 3
Taylor; Devlin, Cantwell, Armstrong, Allison, McGowan, Southren, Moroney, Dixon, Petchey, Gunning.
Semi-final
Apr 23 v Leyton O (h) 1-1 (Leyton won on toss of coin)
Kearns
Chiswick; Devlin, Bond, Moroney, Brown, Bing, Foan, Gregory, Kearns, Gazzard, Tucker.

1953-54
Round 1
Oct 22 v Colchester U (a) 1-5
Hooper
Chiswick; Bond, Kinsell, Malcolm, Cooper, Bing, Hooper, Matthews, Kearns, Foan, Woodgate.

1954-55
Semi-final
Nov 11 v Colchester U (a) 3-2
Dixon 2, Parker
Gregory; Wright, Cantwell, Bing, Nelson, Noakes, Wragg, Barrett, Dixon, Parker, Tucker.
Final
Aug 31 v Southend U (a) 3-3 (Trophy shared)
Blackburn, Tucker, Moore
Gregory; Bond, Hallas, Sexton, Nelson, Johnstone, Stroud, Moore, Blackburn, Foan, Tucker.

1955-56
Semi-final
Dec 5 v Southend U (h) 2-3
Blackburn, Parker
Taylor; Wright, Cooper, Sexton, Brown, Parker, Musgrove, Bennett, Lawrence, Dick, Blackburn.

1956-57
Round 1
Nov 26 v Chelmsford C (h) 3-1
Dare 2, Bond
Gregory; Wright, Bond, J.Smith, Nelson, Morley, Dare, Matthews, Wragg, Blackburn, Grice.
Semi-final
Feb 25 v Leyton O (h) 0-2
Gregory; Wright, Cooper, Parker, Brown, Morley, Grice, Stroud, Fenn, R.Smith, Tucker.

1957-58
Semi-final
Mar 10 v Southend U (h) 2-1

Smillie, Newman
Rhodes; Kirkup, Cooper, Pyke, Brown, Morley, Fenn, Smillie, Lewis, Newman, Wragg.
Final
May 2 v Chelmsford C (a) 1-5
Lewis
Wyllie; Hayward, Cooper, Morley, Nelson, Lansdowne, Wragg, Newman, Lewis, Dick, Musgrove.

1958-59
Semi-final
Apr 8 v Colchester U (h) 4-3
Bond, Grice, Hills, Opp own-goal
Rhodes; Bond, Smith, Pyke, Brown, Lansdowne, Wragg, Obeney, Dare, Hills, Grice.
Final
Sep 21 v Leyton O (h) 4-1
Brett, Dick, Cantwell, Opp own-goal
Dwyer; Kirkup, Cantwell, Malcolm, Brown, Hurst, Woodley, Woosnam, Brett, Dick, Musgrove.

Southern Floodlight Cup

1955-56
Round 1
Oct 10 v Crystal P (h) 3-0
Tucker, O'Farrell, Dare
Gregory; Bond, Cantwell, Malcolm, Allison, O'Farrell, Hooper, Andrews, Dare, Dick, Tucker.
Att: 6,000
Semi-final
Apr 4 v Reading (a) 3-1
Dare, Grice, Dick
Gregory; Bond, Cooper, Bennett, Nelson, Parker, Grice, Foan, Dare, Dick, Wragg.
Att: 5,000
Final
Apr 23 v Aldershot (h) 2-1
Tucker, Dare
Gregory; Bond, Cantwell, Parker, Nelson, Lansdowne, Grice, Smith, Dare, Dick, Tucker.
Att: 5,000

1956-57
Round 1
Oct 2 v Leyton O (h) 4-1
Musgrove, Dick 3
Gregory; Wright, Bond, Malcolm, Brown, Lansdowne, Grice, Smith, Dare, Dick, Musgrove.
Att: 14,500
Round 2
Nov 12 v Arsenal (h) 1-1
Dick
Gregory; Bond, Cantwell, Malcolm, Allison, Lansdowne, Musgrove, Smith, Dick, Dare, Tucker.
Att: 14,000
Replay
Dec 4 v Arsenal (a) 2-3
Musgrove 2
Wyllie; Bond, Cantwell, Malcolm, Allison, Lansdowne, Musgrove, Smith, Lewis, Dick, Tucker.
Att: 14,156

1957-58
Round 1
Sep 23 v Leyton O (h) 1-0
Dick
Gregory; Bond, Cantwell, Malcolm, Brown, Pyke, Wragg, Dare, Neville, Dick, Musgrove.
Att: 10,000
Round 2
Jan 13 v Reading (h) 3-3
Smith, Keeble, Dick
Gregory; Wright, Cantwell, Malcolm, Brown, Pyke, Grice, Smith, Keeble, Dick, Musgrove.
Att: 5,000
Replay
Jan 29 v Reading (a) 3-5
Dick, Musgrove, Neville
Gregory; Bond, Cantwell, Pyke, Brown, Lansdowne, Grice, Neville, Fenn, Dick, Musgrove.
Att: 13,000

1958-59
Round 1
Oct 27 v Charlton A (h) 5-1
Musgrove 3, Dick 2
Gregory; Bond, Cantwell, Malcolm, Brown, Nelson, Grice, Cartwright, Keeble, Dick, Musgrove.
Att: 8,500
Round 2
Dec 15 v Fulham (h) 3-1
Bond, Keeble, Woosnam
Rhodes; Kirkup, Bond, Smith, Brown, Hurst, Grice, Woosnam, Keeble, Dick, Musgrove.
Att: 4,500
Round 3
Apr 6 v Arsenal (h) 0-2
Dwyer; Kirkup, Lyall, Malcolm, Brown, Nelson, Grice, Obeney, Bond, Smillie, Musgrove.
Att: 15,681

1959-60
Round 1
Oct 13 v Millwall (h) 3-1
Wragg 2, Musgrove
Dwyer; Bond, Cripps, Malcolm, Brown, Boyce, Wragg, Woodley, Keeble, Dick, Musgrove.
Att: 8,250
Round 2
Oct 26 v Reading (h) 6-1
Obeney 4, Smillie, Grice
Dwyer; Kirkup, Cantwell, Malcolm, Brown, Smith, Grice, Woosnam, Obeney, Smillie, Musgrove.
Att: 5,400
Round 3
Dec 7 v Leyton O (h) 4-3
Bond, Musgrove 2, Woosnam
Dwyer; Bond, Cantwell, Malcolm, Brown, Smith, Grice, Woosnam, Obeney, Dick, Musgrove.
Att: 8,606
Semi-final
Apr 5 v Arsenal (a) 3-1
Cartwright 2, Musgrove
Rhodes; Bond, Cantwell, Malcolm, Brown, Moore, Grice, Cartwright, Dunmore, Hurst, Musgrove.
Att: 8,000

Final
Apr 27 v Coventry C (a) 1-2
Cartwright
Rhodes; Bond, Cantwell, Malcolm, Brown, Moore, Grice, Cartwright, Dunmore, Smillie, Musgrove.
Att: 16,921

Watney Cup

1973-74
Round 1
Aug 11 v Bristol R (a) 1-1 (Lost 5-4 on penalties)
MacDougall
Ferguson; McDowell(Lock), Lampard, Bonds, Taylor, Moore, Ayris(Tyler), Holland, MacDougall, Brooking, Robson.
Att: 19,974

Texaco Cup

1974-75
Group Match
Aug 3 v Orient (h) 1-0
Bonds
Day; Coleman, Lampard, Bonds, Taylor, Holland, McDowell, Paddon, Best, Brooking, Gould(Ayris).
Att: 16,338
Group Match
Aug 7 v Luton T (h) 1-2
Bonds
Day; Coleman, Lampard, Bonds, Taylor, McGiven, McDowell(Holland), Paddon, Gould, Brooking, Best.
Att: 14,508
Group Match
Aug 10 v Southampton (a) 0-2
Day; Coleman, Lampard, Bonds, Taylor, McDowell, Holland, Paddon, Gould, Brooking, Best.
Att: 11,364

Full Members' Cup
(Later the Simod Cup and the Zenith Data Systems Cup)
1986-87
Round 3
Nov 25 v Chelsea (h) 1-2
Cottee
Parkes; Walford(Potts), Parris, Gale, Hilton, Ince, Ward, McAvennie, Dickens, Cottee, Keen.
Att: 12,140.

1987-88
Round 1
Nov 10 v Millwall (h) 1-2
Dickens
McAlister; Potts(Keen), Parris, Hilton, Martin, Brady, Ward, Dickens, Ince, Dolan, Robson.
Att: 11,337

1988-89
Round 1
Nov 9 v West Brom A (h) 5-2
Rosenior 4, Kelly
McKnight; Potts, Dicks, Gale, Hilton, Keen, Ward, Kelly, Rosenior, Brady(Parris), Ince.
Att: 5,960
Round 2
Nov 22 v Watford (a) 1-1 (lost 3-1 on penalties)

Ince
McKnight; Potts, Dicks, Gale, Martin(Hilton), Keen, Ward, Brady, Rosenior, Dickens, Ince.
Att: 6,468

1989-90
Round 2
Nov 29 v Plymouth A (h) 5-2
Keen, Dolan, Dicks, Martin, Slater
Parkes; Potts, Dicks, Strodder, Martin, Keen, Devonshire, Slater, Allen, Ward(Dolan), Kelly(Foster).
Att: 5,409
Quarter-final
Dec 22 v Chelsea (a) 3-4
Keen, Slater, Kelly
Parkes; Potts, Dicks, Strodder, Keen, Gale, Brady(Kelly), Slater, Foster, Ward, Allen.
Att: 8,418

1990-91
Round 2
Dec 18 v Luton T (a) 1-5
Keen
McKnight; Kelly, Parris, Gale, Potts, Livett, Allen, Quinn, Slater, Keen, Morley.
Att: 5,759

1991-92
Round 2
Oct 22 v Cambridge U (h) 2-1
Parris, McAvennie
Miklosko; Breacker, Hughton, Gale, Potts, Parris, Bishop, McAvennie, Small, Keen, Allen.
Att: 7,812
Round 3
Nov 25 v Brighton & HA (h) 2-0
McAvennie 2
Miklosko; Breacker, Thomas, Gale, Potts, Parris, Bishop, McAvennie, Small, Keen, Slater.
Att: 8,146
Semi-final
Jan 7 v Southampton (a) 1-2
Bishop
Miklosko; Breacker, Dicks, Gale, Foster, Thomas, Bishop, McAvennie, Brown, Keen(Morley), Slater.
Att: 6,861

Anglo Italian Cup
1992-93
Preliminary Round
Sep 2 v Bristol R (h) 2-2
Dicks 2
Banks; Potts, Dicks, Gale, Martin, M.Allen, Robson(Rush), Butler, Morley, C.Allen, Keen.
Att: 4,809
Sep 30 v Southend U (a) 3-0
Morley, Dicks, Holmes
Miklosko; Breacker, Dicks, Potts, Martin, M.Allen, Robson, Holmes, Morley, C.Allen, Keen.
Att: 6,482
Group Matches
Nov 11 v Cremonese (a) 0-2
Miklosko; Brown, Dicks, Potts, Martin, M.Allen, Robson, Parris(Keen), Morley, C.Allen, Holmes.
Att: 1,639

Nov 24 v AC Reggiana (h) 2-0
C.Allen 2
Miklosko; Breacker, Dicks, Potts, Martin(Brown), M.Allen, Robson(Bishop), Holmes, Morley, C.Allen, Keen.
Att: 6,872
Dec 8 v Cozenza (a) 1-0
C.Allen
Miklosko; Breacker, Dicks, Potts, Martin, M.Allen, Rush, Parris, Jones, C.Allen, Keen(Brown).
Att: 800
Dec 16 v Pisa (h) 0-0
Miklosko; Breacker, Dicks, Potts, Martin, M.Allen, Rush, Bishop, Bunbury, C.Allen(Jones), Keen(Robson).
Att: 7,123

Abandoned League Games

1948
Nov 27 v Grimsby T (h) 1-2
(Abandoned after 50 minutes)
Wright
Gregory; Yeomanson, Forde, Cater, R.Walker,

Moroney, Parsons, Hall, Wright, Dick, Woodgate.
Att: 18,300
1952
Mar 29 v Brentford (a) 1-1
(Abandoned after 45 minutes)
Moroney
Gregory; Wright, Kinsell, McGowan, Allison, O'Farrell, Southren, Barratt, Moroney, Gazzard, Andrews.
Att: 6,000
1954
Jan 2 v Stoke C (h) 4-1
(Abandoned after 83 minutes)
Dick 2, Dixon 2
Gregory; Wright, Bond, Malcolm, Allison, Bing, Hooper, Foan, Dixon, Dick, Andrews.
Att: 15,000
1965
Dec 27 v Aston Villa (a) 0-0
(Abandoned after 30 minutes)
Standen; Kirkup, Charles, Bovington, Brown, Peters, Brabrook, Dear, Byrne, Hurst, Sissons.
Att: 30,382

Hammers in the European Cup-winners' Cup

1964-65
Round 1 (1st leg)
Sep 23 v La Gantoise (a) 1-0
Boyce
Standen; Bond, Peters, Bovington, Brown, Moore, Sealey, Boyce, Byrne, Hurst, Sissons.
Att: 18,000
Round 1 (2nd leg)
Oct 7 v La Gantoise (h) 1-1 (agg 2-1)
Byrne
Dickie; Bond, Peters, Bovington, Brown, Moore, Brabrook, Boyce, Byrne, Hurst, Sissons.
Att: 24,000
Round 2 (1st leg)
Nov 25 v Sparta Prague (h) 2-0
Bond, Sealey
Standen; Bond, Burkett, Bovington, Brown, Peters, Sealey, Boyce, Byrne, Hurst, Sissons.
Att: 27,590
Round 2 (2nd leg)
Dec 9 v Sparta Prague (a) 1-2 (agg 3-2)
Sissons
Standen; Bond, Burkett, Bovington, Brown, Peters, Sealey, Boyce, Byrne, Hurst, Sissons.
Att: 45,000
Round 3 (1st leg)
Mar 16 v Lausanne (a) 2-1
Dear, Byrne
Standen; Kirkup, Peters, Boyce, Brown, Moore, Sealey, Hurst, Byrne, Dear, Sissons.
Att: 20,000
Round 3 (2nd leg)
Mar 23 v Lausanne (h) 4-3 (agg 6-4)

Dear 2, Peters, Opp own-goal
Standen; Kirkup, Peters, Boyce, Brown, Moore, Sealey, Hurst, Byrne, Dear, Sissons.
Att: 31,780
Semi-final (1st leg)
Apr 7 v Real Zaragoza (h) 2-1
Dear, Byrne
Standen; Kirkup, Burkett, Peters, Brown, Moore, Boyce, Dear, Byrne, Hurst, Sissons.
Att: 35,000
Semi-final (2nd leg)
Apr 28 v Real Zaragoza (a) 1-1 (agg 3-2)
Sissons
Standen; Kirkup, Burkett, Peters, Brown, Moore, Boyce, Sealey, Hurst, Dear, Sissons.
Att: 28,000
Final
May 19 v TSV München (at Wembley) 2-0
Sealey 2
Standen; Kirkup, Burkett, Peters, Brown, Moore, Sealey, Boyce, Hurst, Dear, Sissons.
Att: 100,000

1965-66
Round 2 (1st leg)
Nov 24 v Olympiakos (h) 4-0
Hurst 2, Byrne, Brabrook
Standen; Kirkup, Charles, Bovington, Brown, Moore, Brabrook, Peters, Byrne, Hurst, Sissons.
Att: 27,250
Round 2 (2nd leg)
Dec 1 v Olympiakos (a) 2-2 (agg 6-2)
Peters 2

Standen; Kirkup, Charles, Bovington, Brown, Moore, Brabrook, Peters, Byrne, Hurst, Sissons.
Att: 40,000
Round 3 (1st leg)
Mar 2 v FC Magdeburg (h) 1-0
Byrne
Standen; Burnett, Burkett, Peters, Brown, Moore, Brabrook, Boyce, Byrne, Hurst, Sissons.
Att: 30,620
Round 3 (2nd leg)
Mar 16 v FC Magdeburg (a) 1-1 (agg 2-1)
Sissons
Standen; Burnett, Burkett, Bovington, Brown, Moore, Brabrook, Boyce, Hurst, Peters, Sissons.
Att: 35,000
Semi-final (1st leg)
Apr 5 v Borussia Dortmund (h) 1-2
Peters
Standen; Brown, Charles, Peters, Boyce, Moore, Brabrook, Bloomfield, Byrne, Hurst, Dear.
Att: 28,130
Semi-final (2nd leg)
Apr 13 v Borussia Dortmund (a) 1-3 (agg 2-5)
Byrne
Standen; Bovington, Charles, Peters, Brown, Moore, Brabrook, Boyce, Byrne, Hurst, Bloomfield.
Att: 35,000

1975-76
Round 1 (1st leg)
Sep 17 v Lahden Reipas (a) 2-2
Brooking, Bonds
Day; McDowell, Lampard, Bonds, T.Taylor, Lock, Holland, Paddon, A.Taylor, Brooking, Robson (Jennings).
Att: 6,000
Round 1 (2nd leg)
Oct 1 v Lahden Reipas (h) 3-0 (agg 5-2)
Robson, Holland, Jennings
Day; McDowell, Lampard, Bonds, T.Taylor, Lock, A.Taylor(Jennings), Paddon, Robson, Brooking, Holland.
Att: 24,131
Round 2 (1st leg)
Oct 22 v Ararat Erevan (a) 1-1
A.Taylor
Day; McDowell, Lampard, Bonds, T.Taylor, Coleman, A.Taylor, Paddon, Gould, Holland, Robson.
Att: 66,662
Round 2 (2nd leg)
Nov 5 v Ararat Erevan (h) 3-1 (agg 4-2)
Paddon, Robson, A.Taylor
Day; McDowell, Lampard, Bonds, T.Taylor, Coleman, A.Taylor, Paddon, Holland, Brooking, Robson.
Att: 30,399
Round 3 (1st leg)
Mar 3 v FC Den Haag (a) 2-4
Jennings 2
Day; McGiven(Coleman), Lampard, Bonds, T.Taylor, Lock, A.Taylor, Paddon, Jennings, Curbishley, Robson.
Att: 26,000
Round 3 (2nd leg)
Mar 17 v FC Den Haag (h) 3-1 (agg 5-5; won on away goals rule)

A.Taylor, Lampard, Bonds
Day; Coleman, Lampard, Bonds, T.Taylor(McGiven), Lock, A.Taylor, Paddon(Curbishley), Jennings, Brooking, Robson
Att: 29,829
Semi-final (1st leg)
Mar 31 v Eintracht Frankfurt (a) 1-2
Paddon
Day; Coleman, Lampard, Bonds, T.Taylor, McDowell, Holland, Paddon, Jennings, Brooking, Robson.
Att: 45,000
Semi-final (2nd leg)
Apr 14 v Eintracht Frankfurt (h) 3-1 (agg 4-3)
Brooking 2, Robson
Day; Coleman, Lampard, Bonds, T.Taylor, McDowell, Holland, Paddon, Jennings, Brooking, Robson.
Att: 39,202
Final
May 5 v Anderlecht (at Heysel Stadium, Brussels) 2-4
Holland, Robson
Day; Coleman, Lampard(A.Taylor), Bonds, T.Taylor, McDowell, Holland, Paddon, Jennings, Brooking, Robson.
Att: 58,000

1980-81
Round 1 (1st leg)
Sep 17 v Castilla (a) 1-3
Cross
Parkes; Stewart, Lampard, Bonds, Martin, Devonshire(Brush), Morgan(Barnes), Goddard, Cross, Brooking, Pike.
Att: 40,000
Round 1 (2nd leg)
Oct 1 v Castilla (h) 5-1 (agg 6-4)
Cross 3, Pike, Goddard
Parkes; Stewart, Lampard, Bonds, Martin, Devonshire, Holland(Brush), Goddard(Morgan), Cross, Brooking, Pike.
Att: 262
Round 2 (1st leg)
Oct 22 v Poli Timisoara (h) 4-0
Bonds, Cross, Goddard, Stewart
Parkes; Stewart, Lampard, Bonds, Martin, Devonshire, Holland, Goddard(Morgan), Cross, Neighbour, Pike.
Att: 27,257
Round 2 (2nd leg)
Nov 5 v Poli Timisoara (a) 0-1 (agg 4-1)
Parkes; Stewart(Brush), Lampard, Bonds, Martin, Allen, Holland, Goddard, Cross, Neighbour (Brooking), Pike.
Att: 25,000
Round 3 (1st leg)
Mar 4 v Dynamo Tbilisi (h) 1-4
Cross
Parkes; Stewart, Lampard, Bonds, Martin, Devonshire(Allen), Neighbour, Goddard, Cross, Brooking, Pike.
Att: 34,957
Round 3 (2nd leg)
Mar 18 v Dynamo Tbilisi (a) 1-0 (agg 2-4)
Pearson
Parkes; Stewart, Lampard, Bonds, Martin, Brush, Neighbour, Goddard(Pearson), Cross, Brooking, Pike.
Att: 80,000

West Ham Ever-presents in the Football League

Season	Player	Played	Season	Player	Played
1921-22	Percy Allen	42	1971-72	Tommy Taylor	42
1922-23	Billy Moore	42		Bryan Robson	42
1923-24	William Henderson	42	1972-73	Bobby Moore	42
1924-25	Jimmy Ruffell	42		Bryan Robson	42
1925-26	Jim Barrett	42	1973-74	Frank Lampard	42
1926-27	Jim Barrett	42	1974-75	Mervyn Day	42
	Jimmy Collins	42	1975-76	Tommy Taylor	42
	Vic Watson	42	1976-77	Mervyn Day	42
	Stan Earle	42		Trevor Brooking	42
1927-28	Jimmy Collins	42	1977-78	Tommy Taylor	42
	Tommy Yews	42	1978-79	Paul Brush	42
1933-34	Joe Cockroft	42	1980-81	Phil Parkes	42
	John Morton	42		Geoff Pike	42
1934-35	Alf Chalkley	42	1981-82	Ray Stewart	42
	Albert Walker	42	1982-83	Phil Parkes	42
	Joe Cockroft	42	1983-84	Phil Parkes	42
1935-36	Joe Cockroft	42		Ray Stewart	42
1936-37	Joe Cockroft	42	1985-86	Phil Parkes	42
	Len Goulden	42		Tony Gale	42
1937-38	Charlie Bicknell	42		Mark Ward	42
1947-48	Ernie Gregory	42	1986-87	Tony Cottee	42
	Steve Forde	42	1987-88	Tony Cottee	40
	Norman Corbett	42	1990-91	Ludek Miklosko	46
	Eric Parsons	42	1992-93	Ludek Miklosko	46
1948-49	Eric Parsons	42		Steve Potts	46
1949-50	Ernie Gregory	42		Kevin Keen	46
1950-51	Terry Woodgate	42			
1952-53	Ernie Gregory	42			
1953-54	Malcolm Allison	42			
1957-58	Andy Malcolm	42			
1958-59	John Bond	42			
	Noel Cantwell	42			
	Andy Malcolm	42			
	Ken Brown	42			
	Mike Grice	42			
1960-61	Ken Brown	42			
1964-65	Jim Standen	42			
	Geoff Hurst	42			
1968-69	Billy Bonds	42			
	Martin Peters	42			
	Alan Stephenson	42			
	Geoff Hurst	42			
1969-70	Billy Bonds	42			
1971-72	Billy Bonds	42			
	Clyde Best	42			

Martin Peters, ever-present only once.

393

International Hammers

Many players won additional caps with other clubs but the totals given here are solely for appearances made whilst West Ham players. In 1924 the Republic of Ireland began separate international matches; before then there was just one 'Ireland' team and that position is reflected here.

England

Barrett J.W. 1929 v Northern Ireland (1).

Brooking T.D. 1974 v Argentina, Portugal (twice), East Germany, Bulgaria, Yugoslavia, Czechoslovakia (sub); 1975 v Portugal; 1976 v Wales, Brazil, Italy (twice), Finland (twice), Republic of Ireland; 1977 v Holland, Northern Ireland, Wales, Italy; 1978 v West Germany, Wales, Scotland (sub), Hungary, Denmark, Republic of Ireland; 1979 v Northern Ireland (twice), Wales (sub), Scotland, Bulgaria, Sweden (sub), Austria, Denmark; 1980 v Argentina (sub), Wales, Northern Ireland, Scotland, Belgium, Spain, Switzerland; 1981 v Spain, Romania, Hungary (twice); 1982 v Scotland, Finland, Spain (sub) (47).

Brown K. 1959 v Northern Ireland (1).

Brown W. 1923 v Belgium (1).

Byrne J.J. 1963 v Switzerland; 1964 v Scotland, Uruguay, Portugal (twice), Republic of Ireland, Brazil, Argentina, Wales; 1965 v Scotland (10).

Cottee A. 1986 v Sweden (sub), Northern Ireland (sub); 1988 v Hungary (sub) (3).

Devonshire A. 1980 v Australia (sub), Northern Ireland; 1982 v Holland, Iceland, West Germany; 1983 v Wales, Greece, Luxembourg (8).

Earle S.G.J. 1927 v Northern Ireland (1).

Goddard P. 1982 v Iceland (sub) (1).

Goulden L.A. 1937 v Sweden, Norway, Wales, Northern Ireland, Czechoslovakia; 1938 v Germany, Switzerland, France, Wales, Rest of Europe; 1939 v Italy, Scotland, Romania, Yugoslavia (14).

Hufton A.E. 1923 v Belgium; 1927 v Northern Ireland; 1928 v Scotland; 1929 v France, Belgium, Spain (6).

Hurst G.C. 1966 v West Germany (twice), Scotland, Yugoslavia, Finland, Denmark, Argentina, Portugal, Northern Ireland, Czechoslovakia, Wales; 1967 v Scotland, Spain, Austria, Wales, Northern Ireland, Russia; 1968 v Scotland, Sweden (sub), West Germany, USSR, Romania, Bulgaria; 1969 v Romania, France, Northern Ireland, Scotland, Mexico, Uruguay, Brazil, Holland; 1970 v Holland (sub), Belgium, Wales, Northern Ireland, Scotland, Columbia, Ecuador, Romania, Brazil, West Germany, East Germany; 1971 v Greece (twice), Wales, Scotland, Switzerland (twice); 1972 v West Germany (49).

Lampard F.R.G. 1972 v Yugoslavia; 1980 v Australia (2).

Martin A.E. 1981 v Brazil, Scotland (sub), Hungary; 1982 v Finland, Greece, Luxembourg (twice); 1983 v Wales, Greece, Hungary (twice); 1984 v Wales; 1985 v Northern Ireland; 1986 v Israel, Canada, Paraguay (16).

Moore R.F. 1962 v Peru, Hungary, Argentina, Bulgaria, Brazil, France, Northern Ireland, Wales; 1963 v France, Scotland, Brazil, Czechoslovakia, East Germany,

Switzerland, Wales, Rest of the World, Northern Ireland; 1964 v Scotland Uruguay, Portugal (twice), Republic of Ireland, Brazil, Argentina, Northern Ireland, Belgium; 1965 v Scotland, Hungary, Yugoslavia, West Germany, Sweden, Wales, Austria, Northern Ireland, Spain; 1966 v Poland (twice), West Germany (twice), Scotland, Norway, Denmark, Uruguay, Mexico, France, Argentina, Portugal, Northern Ireland, Czechoslovakia, Wales; 1967 v Scotland, Spain, Austria, Wales, Northern Ireland, USSR; 1968 v Scotland, Spain (twice), Sweden, West Germany, Yugoslavia, USSR, Romania, Bulgaria; 1969 v France, Northern Ireland, Wales, Scotland, Mexico, Uruguay, Brazil, Holland, Portugal; 1970 v Belgium, Wales, Northern Ireland, Scotland, Colombia, Ecuador, Romania, Brazil, Czechoslovakia, West Germany, East Germany; 1971 v Greece (twice), Malta, Northern Ireland, Scotland, Switzerland (twice); 1972 v West Germany (twice), Wales (twice), Scotland, Yugoslavia; 1973 v Northern Ireland, Wales (twice), Scotland (twice), Czechoslovakia, Poland, USSR, Italy (twice) (108).

Moore W.G.B. 1923 v Sweden (1).

Morton J.R. 1937 v Czechoslovakia (1).

Peters M.S. 1966 v Yugoslavia, Finland, Poland, Mexico, France, Argentina, Portugal, West Germany, Northern Ireland, Czechoslovakia, Wales; 1967 v Scotland, Wales, Northern Ireland, USSR; 1968 v Scotland, Spain (twice), Sweden, Yugoslavia, USSR, Romania, Bulgaria; 1969 v France, Northern Ireland, Scotland, Mexico, Uruguay, Brazil, Holland, Portugal (sub); 1970 v Holland, Belgium (33).

Ruffell J.W. 1926 v Scotland, Northern Ireland; 1928 v Northern Ireland, Wales; 1929 v Scotland, Wales (6).

Tresadern J. 1923 v Scotland, Sweden (2).

Watson V.M. 1923 v Wales, Scotland; 1930 v Scotland, West Germany, Austria (5).

Webb G.W. 1911 v Wales, Scotland (2).

Scotland

Dick J. 1959 v England (1).

McAvennie F. 1985 v Australia; 1986 v Australia, Denmark (sub), West Germany (sub) (4).

Stewart R.S.M. 1981 v Wales, Northern Ireland, England; 1982 v Northern Ireland, Portugal, Wales; 1984 v France; 1986 v Republic of Ireland, Luxembourg; 1987 v Republic of Ireland (10).

Wales

James W. 1931 v Northern Ireland (twice) (2).

Jones W.J. 1902 v England, Scotland (2).

Richards R.W. 1924 v Scotland, England, Northern Ireland (3).

Woosnam A.P. 1958 v England; 1959 v England, Scotland; 1960 v Northern Ireland, Republic of Ireland, Scotland, England; 1961 v Northern Ireland, Spain, Hungary, England, Scotland; 1962 v Northern Ireland, Brazil (14).

Northern Ireland

Dowie I. 1991 v Yugoslavia, Faeroes (2).
Lutton R.J. 1973 v Cyprus (sub), Scotland (sub), Wales (sub), Portugal (4).
McKnight A. 1989 v Republic of Ireland, Hungary, Spain (twice) (4).
Quinn J. 1990 v Norway; 1991 v Yugoslavia (sub) (2).

Republic of Ireland

Brady L. 1987 v Bulgaria, Belgium, Brazil, Luxembourg; 1988 v Luxembourg, Bulgaria; 1989 v France, Hungary (sub twice); 1990 v West Germany, Finland (11).
Cantwell N. 1953 v Luxembourg; 1955 v Spain; 1956 v Holland, Denmark, West Germany; 1957 v England (twice), Denmark; 1958 v Austria, Poland (twice); 1959 v Czechoslovakia (twice), Sweden; 1960 v Chile, Sweden, Norway (17).
Dwyer N.M. 1959 v Sweden; 1960 v Chile, West Germany, Sweden (4).
Kearns F.T. 1954 v Luxembourg (1).
Kelly D. 1989 v Tunisia (sub) (1).
Hughton C. 1991 v Chile; 1992 v Turkey (2).
McGowan D. 1949 v Portugal, Sweden, Spain (3).
Moroney T. 1948 v Spain; 1949 v Portugal, Sweden, Spain, Finland (twice), England; 1950 v Belgium, Norway; 1951 v Norway; 1952 v West Germany; 1953 v France (12).
O'Farrell F. 1952 v Austria, 1953 v Austria, France; 1955 v Holland, Norway, Yugoslavia; 1956 v Holland (7).
Turner C.J. 1937 v Norway (twice); 1938 v Czechoslovakia, Poland; 1939 v Hungary (5).

Canada

Bunbury A. 1993 v Honduras (twice), El Salvador (twice), Mexico (twice) (6).

Czechoslovakia

Miklosko L. 1990 v Spain, England; 1991 v Albania (twice), Iceland, France; 1992 v England (7).

Under-23 Internationals
England

Bonds W.A. 1969 v Wales, Holland (2).
Brooking T.D. v 1972 v Sweden (1).
Byrne J.J. 1962 v Turkey (1).
Day M.R. 1974 v Yugoslavia, France (sub); 1975 v Scotland, Wales; 1976 v Portugal (5).
Hooper H. 1955 v Italy, Scotland (2).

Hurst G.C. 1964 v Wales, France, Israel, Turkey (4).
Kirkup J. 1962 v Israel, Holland, Turkey (3).
Lampard F.R.G. 1972 v Sweden, East Germany, Poland, USSR (4).
Lock K.J. 1973 v Denmark, Holland, Czechoslovakia; 1976 v Hungary (4).
McDowell J.A. 1973 v Wales, Holland (twice), Scotland, Czechoslovakia, Denmark; 1974 v Poland, Denmark, Scotland, Turkey, Yugoslavia (sub), France (12).
Moore R.F. 1961 v Italy, Wales, Scotland, West Germany; 1962 v Israel, Holland, Scotland, Turkey (8).
Paddon G.C. 1976 v Holland (1).
Sissons J.L. 1965 v Wales, Scotland; 1967 v Wales; 1968 v Hungary, West Germany; 1969 v Wales, Holland, Belgium, Portugal (twice) (10).
Smith J. 1960 v France (1).
Stephenson A. 1968 v Hungary (twice), Italy, West Germany (4).
Taylor T.F. 1972 v East Germany (sub); 1973 v Wales, Holland, Czechoslovakia; 1974 v Poland, Denmark, Wales, Scotland, Turkey, Yugoslavia; 1976 v Portugal (11).

Scotland

Ferguson R. 1968 v England (1).

Wales

Llewellyn D. 1972 v Scotland (1).

Under-21 Internationals
England

Allen P.K. 1985 v Republic of Ireland, Romania (2).
Cottee A. 1985 v Finland (sub), Israel (sub), Republic of Ireland, Romania, Finland; 1987 v Spain, Portugal; 1988 v West Germany (8).
Dickens A. 1985 v Finland (sub) (1).
Dicks J. 1988 v Sweden (sub), Mexico, Morocco, France (4).
Goddard P. 1981 v Norway, Switzerland, Republic of Ireland (sub); 1982 v Norway (sub), Poland, Scotland; 1983 v West Germany (twice) (8).
Ince P. 1989 v Albania; 1990 v Sweden (2).
Slater S. 1990 v Portugal, Czechoslovakia (sub), USSR (sub) (3).
Robson S. 1988 v Spain, Sweden (2).

Scotland

Stewart R.S.M. 1980 v Belgium (twice), England (twice), West Germany; 1981 v Denmark; 1982 v Italy (twice), England (9).

Republic of Ireland

Dolan E. 1987 v Scotland, Belgium (2).
Rush M. 1991 v Poland, Turkey (sub) (2).

Hat-Trick Heroes

6 Goals
League
Vic Watson v Leeds U (h) 9 February 1929.
Geoff Hurst v Sunderland (h) 19 October 1968.

5 Goals
League
Brian Dear v West Brom A (h) 16 April 1965.

FA Cup
Syd Puddefoot v Chesterfield (h) 10 January 1913.

4 Goals
League
Billy Grassam v Gravesend (h) 1 September 1900.
Charles Satterthwaite v Brighton & HA (h) 13 February 1904.
Danny Shea v Plymouth A (h) 28 December 1908.
Danny Shea v Southend U (a) 31 December 1910.
Syd Puddefoot v Nottingham F (h) 2 April 1920.
Syd Puddefoot v Sheffield W (h) 13 November 1920.
Syd Puddefoot v Coventry C (h) 1 January 1921.
Vic Watson v Crystal Palace (a) 31 March 1923.
Vic Watson v Liverpool (h) 1 September 1930.
John Dick v Rotherham U (h) 8 March 1958.
Vic Keeble v Blackburn R (h) 4 October 1958.
Geoff Hurst v Fulham (h) 5 November 1966.
David Cross v Grimsby T (a) 11 April 1981.
David Cross v Tottenham H (a) 2 September 1981.

FA Cup
Vic Watson v Leeds U (h) 25 January 1930.

League Cup
Geoff Hurst v Bolton W (h) 11 October 1967.
Tony Cottee v Bury (h) 25 October 1983.

Zenith Data
Leroy Rosenior v West Brom A (h) 9 November 1988.

3 Goals
League
Fred Corbett v Wellinborough T (h) 30 September 1901.

Jack Fletcher v Wellinborough T (h) 22 October 1904.
Chris Carrick v Luton T (h) 28 January 1905.
Lionel Watson v Luton T (h) 22 September 1906.
Billy Grassam v Portsmouth (a) 27 October 1906.
Lionel Watson v Fulham (a) 22 December 1906.
Arthur Winterhalder v Tottenham H (h) 29 December 1906.
Jack Foster v Portsmouth (h) 10 October 1908.
Danny Shea v Swindon (h) 8 March 1909.
Danny Shea v Brentford (h) 11 September 1909.
Thomas Caldwell v Bristol R (h) 4 October 1909.
George Webb v Exeter C (h) 18 March 1911.
Danny Shea v Brentford (h) 21 October 1911.
William Kennedy v Brentford (h) 21 October 1911.
Danny Shea v Norwich C (h) 5 April 1912.
Alf Leafe v Coventry C (a) 1 November 1913.
Syd Puddefoot v Bristol R (h) 3 January 1914.
Syd Puddefoot v Exeter C (h) 2 January 1915.
Syd Puddefoot v Port Vale (h) 7 February 1920.
Alf Leafe v Stockport C (h) 27 November 1920.
Syd Puddefoot v Leeds U (h) 5 February 1921.
Vic Watson v Coventry C (a) 30 December 1922.
Billy Moore v Leicester C (a) 15 February 1923.
Stan Earle v Aston Villa (h) 25 December 1925.
Vic Watson v Aston Villa (h) 13 November 1926.
Vic Watson v Arsenal (h) 7 March 1927.
Viv Gibbins v Newcastle U (h) 24 December 1927.
Vic Watson v Leicester C (h) 12 March 1928.
Viv Gibbins v Everton (a) 10 April 1929.
Vic Watson v Aston Villa (h) 21 December 1929.
Vic Watson v Leeds U (h) 22 March 1930.
Vic Watson v Aston Villa (a) 26 April 1930.
Viv Gibbins v Manchester U (h) 11 October 1930.
Jimmy Ruffell v Grimsby T (h) 7 February 1931.
Jimmy Ruffell v Everton (h) 5 December 1931.
Fred Norris v Oldham A (h) 15 October 1932.
Vic Watson v Burnley (h) 29 October 1932.
Len Goulden v Plymouth A (a) 30 August 1933.
Vic Watson v Preston NE (h) 23 September 1933.
Vic Watson v Lincoln C (h) 28 October 1933.
Ted Fenton v Bury (h) 17 March 1934.
Vic Watson v Fulham (h) 31 March 1934.
Vic Watson v Notts C (h) 1 December 1934.
Dave Mangnall v Nottingham F (h) 7 September 1935.
Dave Mangnall v Norwich C (h) 28 December 1935.
Harry Lewis v Bury (h) 1 February 1936.

Tudor Martin v Newcastle U (a) 9 September 1936.
Archie Macaulay v Tranmere R (h) 24 September 1938.
Sam Small v Norwich C (a) 11 March 1939.
Frank Neary v West Brom A (h) 15 March 1947.
Ken Tucker v Chesterfield (h) 4 October 1947.
Bill Stephens v Cardiff C (a) 26 March 1948.
Bill Robinson v Leicester C (h) 15 April 1949.
Bill Robinson v Sheffield U (h) 30 September 1950.
Terry Woodgate v Leeds U (h) 25 December 1950.
Bert Hawkins v Queen's Park R (h) 15 December 1951.
Ken Tucker v Sheffield U (h) 19 January 1952.
Fred Kearns v Bury (h) 3 January 1953.
Fred Kearns v Leicester C (h) 22 August 1953.
Dave Sexton v Rotherham U (h) 3 September 1953.
Tommy Dixon v Swansea T (h) 14 September 1953.
John Dick v Bury (h) 7 November 1953.
John Dick v Bristol R (a) 22 January 1955.
Dave Sexton v Plymouth A (h) 5 February 1955.
Ken Tucker v Plymouth A (h) 8 October 1955.
Harry Hooper v Doncaster R (h) 22 October 1955.
Billy Dare v Bristol R (a) 31 August 1957.
Vic Keeble v Stoke C (h) 16 November 1957.
John Smith v Bristol R (h) 28 December 1957.
John Dick v West Brom A (h) 7 March 1959.
John Dick v Wolves (h) 21 November 1959.
John Bond v Chelsea (h) 6 February 1960.
Malcolm Musgrove v Preston NE (h) 22 October 1960.
Dave Dunmore v Arsenal (h) 5 November 1960.
Johnny Byrne v Sheffield W (h) 22 February 1964.
Johnny Byrne v Tottenham H (h) 12 September 1964.
Geoff Hurst v Newcastle U (h) 11 December 1965.
Brian Dear v Leicester C (h) 26 December 1967.
Trevor Brooking v Newcastle U (h) 6 April 1968.
Martin Peters v West Brom A (h) 31 August 1968.
Geoff Hurst v Burnley (h) 3 October 1970.
Bryan Robson v Southampton (h) 20 April 1973.
Billy Bonds v Chelsea (h) 2 March 1974.
Billy Jennings v Stoke C (h) 20 December 1975.

David Cross v Ipswich T (h) 24 March 1978.
David Cross v Notts C (h) 19 August 1978.
Bryan Robson v Millwall (h) 7 October 1978.
Paul Goddard v Queen's Park R (h) 21 April 1981.
Paul Goddard v Southampton (h) 22 September 1981.
Dave Swindlehurst v Coventry C (h) 10 September 1983.
Alvin Martin v Newcastle U (h) 21 April 1986.
Tony Cottee v Queen's Park R (a) 13 September 1986.
Tony Cottee v Coventry C (a) 24 January 1987.
Jimmy Quinn v Sheffield U (h) 21 March 1990.

FA Cup

Billy Grassam v Clapton (a) 12 December 1900.
Charles Satterthwaite v Chatham (a) 28 November 1903.
George Webb v Wolves (a) 5 February 1910.
George Webb v Preston NE (h) 4 February 1911.
Syd Puddefoot v Bury (h) 31 January 1920.
Vic Watson v Tottenham H (h) 8 January 1927.
Albert Foan v Preston NE (h) 7 January 1956.
John Dick v Tottenham H (a) 3 March 1956.
Vic Keeble v Blackpool (h) 4 January 1958.
Geoff Hurst v Swindon T (h) 28 January 1967.
Geoff Hurst v Hereford U (h) 14 February 1972.
Paul Goddard v Port Vale (h) 5 January 1985.
Tony Cottee v Wimbledon (h) 6 March 1985.

League Cup

Johnny Byrne v Plymouth A (h) 26 September 1962.
Johnny Byrne v Workington (h) 16 December 1963.
John Sissons v Leeds U (h) 7 November 1966.
Geoff Hurst v Leeds U (h) 7 November 1966.
Geoff Hurst v Bolton W (h) 4 September 1968.
Bryan Robson v Sheffield U (h) 17 November 1971.
Bobby Gould v Tranmere R (h) 18 September 1974.
Billy Lansdowne v Southend U (h) 8 October 1979.
Francois Van der Elst v Notts C (a) 7 December 1982.
Tony Cottee v Preston NE (h) 7 October 1986.

Europe

David Cross v Castilla (h) 1 October 1980.

Southern League
Appearances & Goalscorers 1900-1915

		LEAGUE		FA CUP	
		App	Gls	App	Gls
ALLAN, Richard	1900-03	52	1	5	0
ALLISON, Tommy	1903-09	156	7	9	0
AMBLER, Charlie	1901-02	1	0	1	0
ASHTON, Herbert	1908-15	224	23	25	1
ASKEW, William	1912-15	104	2	8	0
ATKINS, C	1908-09	2	1	0	0
BAILEY, Daniel	1912-15	49	13	4	3
BAMLETT, Herbert	1904-05	18	0	1	0
BARNES, William	1902-04	48	5	5	0
BEALE, Robert	1913-14	1	0	0	0
BELL, George	1911-12	2	0	0	0
BIGDEN, James	1901-04	91	3	5	0
BIGGAR, William	1902-03	8	0	0	0
BIRNIE, Alexander	1903-04	1	0	1	0
BLACKBURN, Fred	1905-13	217	24	20	4
BLACKWOOD, John	1904-05	4	1	0	0
BLYTHE, Joe	1902-07	55	0	5	0
BOURNE, Stanley	1906-12	13	0	3	0
BOURNE, W	1913-14	1	0	0	0
BRADFORD, T	1911-12	1	0	0	0
BRANDON, Thomas	1913-15	33	0	3	0
BRIDGEMAN, Billy	1903-06	71	19	3	1
BROWN, William	1907-09	19	4	0	0
BRUNTON, Fred	1904-05	1	0	0	0
BURRILL, Frank	1911-14	17	2	0	0
BURTON, John	1908-15	65	7	10	0
BUSH, Robert	1902-06	20	1	1	0
BUTCHART, J	1903-04	3	0	0	0
BUTCHER, George	1909-15	62	9	9	3
CALDWELL, Thomas	1909-12	84	12	12	2
CAMPBELL, John	1902-03	18	1	0	0
CANNON, Frank	1909-10	3	1	1	0
CARR, I	1914-15	5	1	0	0
CARRICK, Christopher	1904-05	18	6	0	0
CARTER, H	1912-14	10	0	0	0
CASEY, Jack	1912-15	74	12	9	1
CATON, Harry	1912-15	14	0	0	0
CHALKLEY, George	1908-09	7	0	4	0
CHURCH, William	1903-04	2	0	0	0
CLARKE, David	1906-09	17	0	0	0
COPE, William	1914-15	31	0	2	0
CORBETT, Fred	1900-02	33	13	2	2
COSTELLO, Frank	1908-09	12	3	0	0
COTTON, Charles	1903-06	18	0	1	0
CRAIG, Charlie	1900-02	53	0	7	0
CURTIS, F	1909-11	6	4	0	0
DAVIDSON, William	1902-03	9	2	0	0
DAWSON, C	1908-10	6	0	0	0
DAWSON, Harold	1911-13	22	3	0	0
DENYER, Albert	1912-14	46	16	4	1
DENYER, Frank	1913-14	2	0	0	0
DOVE, Charles	1900-01	13	0	3	0
DOW, James	1902-03	13	0	1	0
DYER, James	1908-09	3	0	0	0
EARL	1903-04	1	0	0	0
EASTWOOD, H	1908-09	6	0	0	0
ECCLES, George	1902-04	59	0	5	0
EVANS	1902-03	1	0	0	0
FAIR, Aubrey	1901-07	31	1	2	0
FAIRMAN, Robert	1909-12	90	0	12	0
FARRELL, John	1902-03	20	3	1	0
FEATHERSTONE, Arthur	1905-08	24	1	1	0
FENTON, Fred	1900-01	14	2	5	1
FENWICK, Alfred	1914-15	19	1	2	0
FLETCHER, Jack	1904-05	25	7	1	0
FLYNN, Jack	1904-05	20	3	1	1
FORD, William	1905-06	7	1	0	0
FORSTER, Harry	1912-14	40	0	4	0
FOSTER, Jack	1908-09	15	9	0	0
FROST, A	1910-12	4	0	0	0
FROST, James	1907-08	20	4	5	0
GARDNER, Dave	1904-07	77	0	3	0
GAULT, James	1907-09	49	0	2	0
GEGGUS, John	1909-12	31	0	0	0
GLOVER, Victor	1911-12	29	0	5	0
GODDARD, J	1913-14	1	0	0	0
GRASSAM, Billy	1900-09	169	65	10	3
GRIFFITHS, Fred	1902-04	48	0	4	0
HAMILTON	1904-05	5	0	0	0
HAMMOND, Syd	1904-08	32	0	2	0
HARRISON, Fred	1910-13	54	19	8	4
HARWOOD, Alf	1907-09	12	0	0	0
HAYNES, Vincent	1909-10	15	5	0	0
HILSDON, George	1904-15	85	31	7	4
HILSDON, Jack	1903-04	1	0	0	0
HINDLE, Harry	1905-06	3	0	0	0
HITCHENS, J	1901-02	1	0	1	0
HORN, George	1906-08	8	0	1	0
HUGHES, Joseph	1911-15	90	0	15	0
HUNT, Fergus	1900-02	42	9	6	1
INGHAM, William	1903-04	2	0	0	0
IRVINE, George	1912-14	21	0	0	0
JACKSON, James	1905-06	24	0	0	0
JARVIS, Len	1903-09	133	5	7	0
JENKINSON, William	1901-02	19	2	0	0
JONES, William	1901-02	15	0	0	0
KAYE, Albert	1900-01	14	2	6	3
KELLY, William	1900-03	33	0	4	0
KEMP, Fred	1906-08	11	0	0	0
KENNEDY, William	1910-12	21	10	2	0
KING, Syd	1900-03	59	0	7	0
KINGSLEY, Matthew	1904-05	29	0	1	0
KIRBY, William	1903-04	33	10	3	1
KITCHEN, George	1905-11	184	5	21	1
KYLE, Peter	1901-02	1	0	2	0
LAVERY, William	1909-11	17	0	2	0
LEAFE, Alf	1913-15	63	33	6	4
LEE, Tom	1907-08	6	0	0	0
LINDSAY, David	1906-08	50	4	2	0
LINWARD, William	1901-03	40	3	2	1
LONSDALE, Thomas	1913-14	21	0	0	0
LYON, Herbert	1903-04	29	4	4	5
McATEER, T	1902-03	13	0	0	0
McCARTNEY, Alex	1905-06	6	0	0	0
McCARTNEY, William	1904-05	28	3	1	0
McDONALD, Alex	1901-02	4	2	0	0
MacEACHRANE, Rodney	1900-02	53	5	7	0
McGEORGE, Robert	1901-02	0	0	2	0
MACKESY, Jack	1911-15	10	2	0	0
MACKIE, Charles	1905-06	10	3	0	0
MAPLEY, Percy	1903-04	13	0	4	0
MASSEY, Frederick	1909-12	38	0	3	0
MERCER, Frederick	1903-04	8	1	0	0
MIECZNIKOWSKI, W	1902-03	3	0	0	0
MIELLEAR, J	1910-12	3	0	1	0
MILNES, Frederick	1904-06	2	0	2	0
MILLER, Walter	1908-09	11	5	6	1
MONTEITH, Hugh	1900-02	53	0	7	0
MOORE, Thomas	1900-01	4	0	0	0
MORRISON, J	1911-12	15	1	0	0

		LEAGUE		FA CUP	
		App	Gls	App	Gls
NEIL, George	1900-01	1	0	0	0
OAKES, William	1903-04	14	0	0	0
PARKINSON, Harry	1902-03	2	0	0	0
PIERCY, Frank	1904-12	214	7	17	0
PINDER	1900-02	1	0	1	0
PUDAN, Richard	1900-02	7	0	2	0
PUDDEFOOT, Sydney	1912-15	55	28	6	7
RAISBECK, Len	1900-01	2	0	2	0
RANDALL, Tom	1906-15	189	9	16	1
RATCLIFFE, George	1900-02	41	14	2	0
REDWOOD, George	1910-12	10	0	3	0
REID, James	1900-01	13	5	6	0
ROBERTSON	1907-08	1	0	0	0
ROTHWELL, James	1910-14	88	4	11	0
RUSSELL, John	1904-05	16	0	1	0
SATTERTHWAITE, Charles	1903-04	32	13	4	5
SCANES, Albert	1909-10	3	3	0	0
SHEA, Daniel	1907-13	179	111	22	10
SHREEVE, Frederick	1908-11	65	4	10	0
SILOR, William	1909-10	6	0	0	0
SIMMONS, Charles	1904-05	34	8	1	0
SMITH, Sidney	1904-05	2	1	0	0
SPEAK, George	1914-15	13	0	0	0
STAPLEY, Harry	1905-08	71	39	4	2
STALLARD, Arthur	1913-15	13	8	0	0
SUGDEN, Sidney	1902-03	1	0	0	0
TAYLOR, Frank	1900-02	12	4	1	1
TAYLOR, William	1906-09	63	0	7	0
THOMPSON, A	1903-04	10	1	0	0
TIRRELL, Alfred	1913-15	7	0	0	0
TIRRELL, Patrick	1908-09	13	1	4	0
TRANTER, Walter	1900-01	4	0	2	0
TRESADERN, Jack	1913-15	6	0	0	0
WAGGOTT, David	1908-10	10	3	1	0
WAGSTAFFE, George	1909-10	3	0	0	0
WALDEN, George	1911-12	2	0	0	0
WALKER, Len	1900-01	1	0	0	0
WALLACE	1901-03	17	3	1	0
WARD	1901-02	0	0	1	0
WATSON, Lionel	1905-08	76	26	4	1
WATTS, Ernest	1903-04	25	1	4	1
WEBB, George	1908-12	52	23	10	9
WEBSTER, Joseph	1914-15	17	0	0	0
WHITEMAN, Robert	1909-15	136	3	10	0
WILDMAN, William	1906-08	39	0	2	0
WILKINSON, H	1905-06	14	2	1	0
WINTERHALDER, Arthur	1906-07	12	6	2	1
WINTERHALDER, Herbert	1905-06	10	0	0	0
WOODARDS, Daniel	1906-15	109	3	14	0
WRIGHT, P	1914-15	10	1	0	0
YENSON, William	1901-09	50	0	7	0
YOUNG, Robert	1907-09	42	1	2	0

Trevor Brooking

Hammers Career Records

Below are the career records for all Hammers' players in major competitions since 1919

Player	Played	LEAGUE App	Gls	FA CUP App	Gls	LG CUP App	Gls	EUROPE App	Gls	TOTAL App	Gls
ADAMS William	1936-1937	3	1	0	0	0	0	0	0	3	1
ALLEN Clive	1991-	29/2	15	1	1	2	0	0	0	32/2	16
ALLEN Martin	1989-	114/18	16	7	2	12/1	4	0	0	133/19	22
ALLEN Paul	1979-1985	149/3	6	15/3	3	20/4	2	1/1	0	185/11	11
ALLEN Percy	1919-1923	80	5	6	0	0	0	0	0	86	5
ALLEN Robert	1919-1920	1	1	0	0	0	0	0	0	1	1
ALLISON Malcolm	1950-1958	238	10	17	0	0	0	0	0	255	10
ANDERSON Edward	1933-1935	26	0	2	0	0	0	0	0	28	0
ANDREW George	1966-1967	2	0	0	0	0	0	0	0	2	0
ANDREWS Jimmy	1951-1956	114	21	6	1	0	0	0	0	120	22
ARMSTRONG Eric	1947-1948	1	0	0	0	0	0	0	0	1	0
ARNOTT John	1953-1955	6	2	0	0	0	0	0	0	6	2
ATTEVELD Ray	1991-1992	1	0	2	0	0	0	0	0	3	0
ATTWELL Reg	1937-1947	5	0	0	0	0	0	0	0	5	0
AYRIS John	1970-1977	41/16	1	1	0	6/1	1	0	0	48/17	2
BAILEY Dan	1919-1921	35	9	3	1	0	0	0	0	38	10
BAILLIE David	1925-1929	16	0	1	0	0	0	0	0	17	0
BAINBRIDGE Ken	1945-1950	80	16	4	1	0	0	0	0	84	17
BALL John	1929-1930	15	9	0	0	0	0	0	0	15	9
BANNER Arthur	1938-1948	27	0	0	0	0	0	0	0	27	0
BANTON Dale	1979-1982	2/3	0	0	0	1	0	0	0	3/3	0
BARNES Bobby	1980-1986	31/12	5	5/1	1	2/2	0	0/1	0	38/16	6
BARRETT Jim G.	1924-1939	442	49	25	4	0	0	0	0	467	53
BARRETT Jim W.	1949-1955	85	24	2	1	0	0	0	0	87	25
BEESLEY Mike	1960-1961	2	1	0	0	0	0	0	0	2	1
BELL Dick	1938-1939	1	1	0	0	0	0	0	0	1	1
BENNETT Leslie	1954-1956	26	3	2	1	0	0	0	0	28	4
BENNETT Peter	1963-1971	38/4	3	2	0	3	0	0	0	43/4	3
BEST Clyde	1969-1976	178/8	47	12	3	20	8	0	0	210/8	58
BETTS Eric	1950-1951	3	1	0	0	0	0	0	0	3	1
BICKLES Dave	1963-1967	24/1	0	2	0	1	0	0	0	27/1	0
BICKNELL Charlie	1935-1947	137	1	12	0	0	0	0	0	149	1
BIGGIN Horace	1919-1920	2	0	0	0	0	0	0	0	2	0
BING Doug	1951-1955	29	3	4	0	0	0	0	0	33	3
BIRCHENOUGH Frank	1919-1920	1	0	0	0	0	0	0	0	1	0
BISHOP Ian	1989-	109/11	8	9/1	2	7	0	0	0	125/12	10
BISHOP Syd	1920-1927	159	10	13	0	0	0	0	0	172	10
BLACK Robert	1936-1938	2	0	0	0	0	0	0	0	2	0
BLACKBURN Alan	1954-1958	15	3	2	0	0	0	0	0	17	3
BLOOMFIELD Jimmy	1965-1966	9/1	0	2	1	0	0	2	0	13/1	1
BLORE Victor	1935-1936	9	0	0	0	0	0	0	0	9	0
BOND John	1951-1965	381	32	30	1	13	1	4	1	428	35
BONDS Billy	1967-1988	655/8	48	46/2	2	65/2	6	15	3	781/12	59
BOVINGTON Eddie	1959-1968	138	1	19	0	18	1	8	0	183	2
BOYCE Ron	1960-1973	275/7	21	20/1	5	23	2	13	1	331/8	29
BRABROOK Peter	1962-1968	167	33	17	3	23	6	7	1	214	43
BRADSHAW Harold	1919-1921	14	0	1	0	0	0	0	0	15	0
BRADY Liam	1986-1990	79/10	9	9	1	14/3	0	0	0	102/13	10
BREACKER Tim	1990-	95/2	5	14	0	6	0	0	0	115/2	5
BRETT Ron	1959-1961	12	4	1	0	0	0	0	0	13	4
BRIGNULL Phil	1978-1979	0/1	0	0	0	0	0	0	0	0/1	0
BRITT Martin	1962-1966	20	6	4	1	6	1	0	0	26	7
BROOKING Trevor	1967-1984	521/7	88	40	3	55	8	11/1	3	627/8	102
BROWN Billy	1920-1924	60	15	11	5	0	0	0	0	71	20
BROWN Ken	1952-1967	386	4	26	0	28	0	15	0	455	4
BROWN, Ken J.	1991-	38/4	5	5	0	1	0	0	0	44/4	5
BRUSH Paul	1977-1985	144/7	1	17	0	12/1	0	1/3	0	174/11	1

Alan Curbishley

Mervyn Day

Player	Played	LEAGUE App	Gls	FA CUP App	Gls	LG CUP App	Gls	EUROPE App	Gls	TOTAL App	Gls
BUNBURY Alex	1992-	2/2	0	0/1	0	0	0	0	0	2/3	0
BURGESS Dick	1922-1923	2	0	0	0	0	0	0	0	2	0
BURKETT Jack	1961-1968	141/1	4	18	0	17	0	7	0	183/1	4
BURNETT Denis	1965-1967	48/2	0	4	1	10	2	2	0	64/2	3
BURTON Frank	1919-1921	64	2	5	0	0	0	0	0	69	2
BURTON Stan	1938-1939	1	0	0	0	0	0	0	0	1	0
BUTCHER George	1919-1921	34	8	4	2	0	0	0	0	38	10
BUTLER Peter	1992	39	2	2	0	2	0	0	0	43	2
BYRNE Johnny	1961-1967	156	79	18	7	19	15	12	6	205	107
CADWELL Albert	1923-1933	272	1	25	0	0	0	0	0	297	1
CALLADINE John	1920-1921	1	0	0	0	0	0	0	0	1	0
CAMPBELL Greg	1984-1986	3/2	0	0	0	0	0	0	0	3/2	0
CAMPBELL John	1923-1928	28	11	1	0	0	0	0	0	29	11
CANTWELL Noel	1952-1961	248	11	15	0	0	0	0	0	263	11
CARR Franz	1990-1991	1/2	0	0	0	0	0	0	0	1/2	0
CARROLL John	1948-1949	5	0	0	0	0	0	0	0	5	0
CARTER George	1919-1927	136	1	19	0	0	0	0	0	155	1
CARTWRIGHT John	1959-1961	4	0	0	0	1	0	0	0	5	0
CATER Ronald	1945-1950	63	0	7	0	0	0	0	0	70	0
CHALKLEY Alf	1931-1937	188	1	14	0	0	0	0	0	202	1
CHAPMAN Eddie	1948-1949	7	3	0	0	0	0	0	0	7	3
CHARLES Clive	1971-1974	12/2	0	0/1	0	0	0	0	0	12/3	0
CHARLES John	1962-1970	117/1	1	1	0	19	1	4	0	141/1	2
CHARLTON William	1922-1923	8	0	0	0	0	0	0	0	8	0
CHISWICK Peter	1953-1955	19	0	0	0	0	0	0	0	19	0
CLARK Alexander	1982-1983	26	7	1	0	7	3	0	0	34	10
CLARKE Simon	1990-1993	0/3	0	0	0	0	0	0	0	0/3	0
COCKROFT Joe	1932-1939	251	3	12	0	0	0	0	0	263	3
COKER Ade	1971-1974	9/1	3	1	0	0	0	0	0	10/1	3
COLEMAN Keith	1973-1977	96/5	0	3	0	6	0	6/1	0	111/6	0
COLLINS Jimmy	1923-1936	311	3	25	0	0	0	0	0	336	3
CONWAY Herman	1934-1939	121	0	5	0	0	0	0	0	126	0
CONWELL Lawrence	1935-1937	8	1	0	0	0	0	0	0	8	1
COOPER Fred	1956-1958	4	0	0	0	0	0	0	0	4	0
COPE William	1919-1922	106	0	8	0	0	0	0	0	114	0
CORBETT David	1936-1937	4	0	0	0	0	0	0	0	4	0
CORBETT Norman	1936-1950	166	3	8	0	0	0	0	0	174	3
COSHALL John	1928-1929	2	0	0	0	0	0	0	0	2	0
COTTEE Tony	1982-1988	203/9	92	24	11	19	14	0	0	246/9	117
COWELL Herbert	1920-1921	1	0	0	0	0	0	0	0	1	0
COWIE George	1981-1983	6/2	0	0	0	1	0	0	0	7/2	0
COWPER Peter	1924-1925	2	0	0	0	0	0	0	0	2	0
COX William	1927-1932	89	0	8	0	0	0	0	0	97	0
CRAWFORD Ian	1961-1963	24	5	1	0	1	2	0	0	26	7
CROSS David	1977-1982	178/1	77	14	2	24	12	6	6	222/1	97
CROSS Roger	1968-1970	5/2	1	0	0	1	0	0	0	6/2	0
CROSSLEY Charles	1922-1923	15	1	1	0	0	0	0	0	16	0
CROWTHER G.	1920-1921	3	0	0	0	0	0	0	0	3	0
CUMMING James	1919-1921	15	0	0	0	0	0	0	0	15	0
CURBISHLEY Alan	1974-1979	78/7	5	5	0	3	0	1/1	0	87/8	5
CUSHLEY John	1967-1970	38	0	4	0	4	0	0	0	46	0
DARE Billy	1954-1959	111	44	8	5	0	0	0	0	119	49
DAWKINS Trevor	1964-1967	5/1	0	0	0	0	0	0	0	5/1	0
DAY Mervyn	1973-1979	194	0	14	0	14	0	9	0	231	0
DEACON Richard	1932-1933	3	0	0	0	0	0	0	0	3	0
DEAR Brian	1962-1971	67/2	33	6/1	2	3	0	6	4	82/3	39
DEATH Steve	1968-1969	1	0	0	0	0	0	0	0	1	0
DELL Fred	1936-1938	4	0	0	0	0	0	0	0	4	0
DEVLIN Ernie	1946-1953	70	0	2	0	0	0	0	0	72	0
DEVONSHIRE Alan	1976-1990	345/13	29	36	1	45/3	2	4	0	430/16	32
DICK George	1948-1949	14	1	1	0	0	0	0	0	15	1
DICK John	1953-1963	326	153	21	11	4	2	0	0	351	166
DICKENS Alan	1982-1989	173/19	23	19/3	3	14/3	3	0	0	206/25	29
DICKIE Alan	1961-1966	12	0	0	0	2	0	1	0	15	0
DICKS Julian	1987-	152	29	14	2	19	5	0	0	185	36

Alan Devonshire

Jimmy Greaves

Player	Played	LEAGUE App	Gls	FA CUP App	Gls	LG CUP App	Gls	EUROPE App	Gls	TOTAL App	Gls
DIXON Robert	1928-1933	65	0	3	0	0	0	0	0	68	0
DIXON Tommy	1952-1955	39	21	3	2	0	0	0	0	42	23
DOLAN Eamonn	1986-1990	9/6	3	0	0	4	0	0	0	13/6	3
DONALD Warren	1983-1984	1/1	0	0	0	0	0	0	0	1/1	0
DOWEN John	1935-1936	1	0	0	0	0	0	0	0	1	0
DOWIE Ian	1990-91	12	4	0	0	0	0	0	0	12	4
DOWSEY John	1926-1927	1	0	0	0	0	0	0	0	1	0
DUNMORE Dave	1959-1961	36	16	1	1	2	1	0	0	39	18
DUNN Richard	1946-1948	11	2	0	0	0	0	0	0	11	2
DURRELL Joe	1971-1972	5/1	0	0	0	0	0	0	0	5/1	0
DWYER Noel	1958-1960	36	0	2	0	0	0	0	0	38	0
EADIE Doug	1966-1967	2	0	0	0	0	0	0	0	2	0
EARL Alfred	1925-1933	191	0	15	0	0	0	0	0	206	0
EARLE Stan	1924-1932	258	56	15	2	0	0	0	0	273	58
EASTMAN George	1924-1926	2	0	0	0	0	0	0	0	2	0
EDWARDS William	1922-1926	37	3	2	0	0	0	0	0	39	3
ENGLAND Ernest	1930-1931	5	0	0	0	0	0	0	0	5	0
ETTE Cliff	1933-1934	1	1	0	0	0	0	0	0	1	1
EUSTACE Peter	1969-1972	41/2	6	1/1	0	2/1	1	0	0	44/4	7
EVANS Arthur	1930-1931	1	0	0	0	0	0	0	0	1	0
FASHANU Justin	1989-1990	2	0	0	0	0/1	0	0	0	2/1	0
FENTON Benny	1937-1939	21	9	1	0	0	0	0	0	22	9
FENTON Ted	1932-1946	163	18	13	0	0	0	0	0	176	18
FENWICK Alf	1919-1920	2	0	0	0	0	0	0	0	2	0
FERGUSON Bobby	1967-1980	240	0	17	0	19	0	0	0	276	0
FLETCHER Bert	1922-1924	8	1	0	0	0	0	0	0	8	1
FOAN Albert	1950-1957	53	6	7	3	0	0	0	0	60	9
FORDE Steve	1937-1952	170	1	6	0	0	0	0	0	176	1
FOREMAN George	1938-1946	6	1	3	1	0	0	0	0	9	2
FOREMAN John	1934-1937	49	7	2	0	0	0	0	0	51	7
FOSTER Colin	1989-	83/5	4	9	2	5	0	0	0	97/5	6
FOXALL Stan	1934-1939	106	38	7	5	0	0	0	0	113	43
FRYATT Arthur	1930-1933	3	0	0	0	0	0	0	0	3	0
GALE Tony	1984-	262/6	5	28	1	26/2	1	0	0	316/8	7
GALL Tommy	1934-1935	1	0	0	0	0	0	0	0	1	0
GALLAGHER Joe	1982-1983	8/1	0	1	0	1	0	0	0	10/1	0
GAMBLE Fred	1930-1931	2	2	0	0	0	0	0	0	2	2
GATLAND William	1920-1921	1	0	0	0	0	0	0	0	1	0
GAZZARD Gerry	1949-1954	119	29	7	3	0	0	0	0	126	32
GIBBINS Viv	1923-1932	129	58	9	5	0	0	0	0	138	63
GODDARD Paul	1980-1987	159/11	54	10/1	3	26	12	6	2	201/12	71
GOODACRE Reg	1930-1933	20	0	0	0	0	0	0	0	20	0
GORE Reg	1938-1939	5	1	0	0	0	0	0	0	5	1
GOULD Bobby	1973-1976	46/5	15	4	1	2	3	1	0	53/5	19
GOULDEN Len	1932-1939	239	54	14	1	0	0	0	0	253	55
GREAVES Jimmy	1969-1971	36/2	13	1	0	1	0	0	0	38/2	13
GREEN Bill	1976-1978	35	1	2	0	3	0	0	0	40	1
GREEN Thomas	1919-1920	3	0	0	0	0	0	0	0	3	0
GREEN Tommy	1936-1939	40	6	4	0	0	0	0	0	44	6
GREGORY Ernie	1946-1960	382	0	24	0	0	0	0	0	406	0
GREGORY John	1951-1953	24	6	1	0	0	0	0	0	25	6
GRICE Mike	1955-1961	142	18	7	1	1	0	0	0	150	19
GROTIER Peter	1968-1973	50	0	0	0	4	0	0	0	54	0
GUEST Joe	1936-1937	3	1	0	0	0	0	0	0	3	1
GUNNING Harry	1952-1953	1	0	0	0	0	0	0	0	1	0
GURKIN Joe	1921-1922	1	0	0	0	0	0	0	0	1	0
HALES Derek	1977-1978	23/1	10	3	0	0	0	0	0	26/1	10
HALL Almeric	1945-1949	50	11	6	3	0	0	0	0	56	14
HALLAS Geoff	1954-1955	3	0	0	0	0	0	0	0	3	0
HAMPSON Tommy	1920-1925	70	0	9	0	0	0	0	0	79	0
HARRIS Jim	1930-1932	7	1	0	0	0	0	0	0	7	1
HART J	1920-1921	1	0	0	0	0	0	0	0	1	0
HARTLEY Trevor	1966-1969	4/1	0	0	0	0	0	0	0	4/1	0
HAWKINS Bert	1951-1953	34	16	3	0	0	0	0	0	37	16
HEBDEN Jack	1920-1928	110	0	6	0	0	0	0	0	116	0

Pat Holland

Harry Hooper

Player	Played	LEAGUE App	LEAGUE Gls	FA CUP App	FA CUP Gls	LG CUP App	LG CUP Gls	EUROPE App	EUROPE Gls	TOTAL App	TOTAL Gls
HEFFER Paul	1966-1972	11/4	0	1/1	0	0	0	0	0	12/5	0
HENDERSON William	1921-1928	162	0	21	1	0	0	0	0	183	1
HILTON Paul	1983-1989	47/13	7	4/3	1	6/2	0	0	0	57/18	8
HODGES Harry	1923-1924	2	1	0	0	0	0	0	0	2	1
HODGSON Tommy	1921-1930	87	0	5	0	0	0	0	0	92	0
HOLLAND Pat	1968-1981	227/18	23	12/4	4	22/3	3	10	2	271/25	32
HOLMES Jim	1936-1937	2	0	0	0	0	0	0	0	2	0
HOLMES Matt	1992-	6/12	1	1	0	0	0	0	0	7/12	1
HOOPER Harry	1950-1956	119	39	11	5	0	0	0	0	130	44
HORLER George	1922-1928	47	0	5	0	0	0	0	0	52	0
HOUGHTON Ray	1981-1982	0/1	0	0	0	0	0	0	0	0/1	0
HOWE Bobby	1966-1972	68/7	4	3	0	2/2	0	0	0	73/9	4
HUBBARD Cliff	1938-1939	1	1	0	0	0	0	0	0	1	1
HUFTON Ted	1919-1932	370	0	31	0	0	0	0	0	401	0
HUGHTON Chris	1990-1992	32/1	0	7	0	0	0	0	0	39/1	0
HUGO Roger	1963-1964	3	2	0	0	0	0	0	0	3	2
HULL Archie	1926-1929	2	0	0	0	0	0	0	0	2	0
HURST Geoff	1959-1972	410/1	180	26	23	47	43	15	2	498/1	248
INCE Paul	1986-1990	66/6	7	8/2	1	9	3	0	0	83/8	11
INNS Tommy	1933-1934	4	0	0	0	0	0	0	0	4	0
JACKSON Derek	1948-1951	8	0	0	0	0	0	0	0	8	0
JACKSON Tom	1921-1922	3	1	0	0	0	0	0	0	3	1
JACKSON William	1927-1928	2	0	0	0	0	0	0	0	2	0
JAMES Wilf	1930-1932	40	7	1	0	0	0	0	0	41	7
JAMES William	1920-1922	54	7	3	0	0	0	0	0	57	7
JENNINGS Billy	1974-1979	89/10	34	11	2	3/2	0	5/2	3	108/14	39
JENNINGS Sam	1924-1925	9	3	0	0	0	0	0	0	9	3
JOHNS Stan	1950-1951	6	2	0	0	0	0	0	0	6	2
JOHNSON Joe	1926-1928	15	7	0	0	0	0	0	0	15	7
JOHNSON William	1919-1920	2	0	0	0	0	0	0	0	2	0
JOHNSON William	1932-1933	5	0	0	0	0	0	0	0	5	0
JOHNSTONE Gordon	1956-1957	2	0	0	0	0	0	0	0	2	0
JONES Steve	1992-	4/2	2	0	0	0	0	0	0	4/2	2
KAINE Bill	1924-1925	8	0	0	0	0	0	0	0	8	0
KANE Alex	1925-1927	2	0	0	0	0	0	0	0	2	0
KAY George	1919-1926	237	15	22	2	0	0	0	0	259	17
KEARNS Fred	1949-1954	43	14	2	1	0	0	0	0	45	15
KEEBLE Vic	1957-1960	76	45	4	4	0	0	0	0	80	49
KEEN Kevin	1986-	187/32	21	15/7	1	21/1	5	0	0	223/40	27
KELLY David	1988-1990	29/12	7	6	0	11/3	5	0	0	46/15	12
KELLY Paul	1989-1990	0/1	0	0	0	0	0	0	0	0/1	0
KINSELL Harry	1950-1955	101	2	4	0	0	0	0	0	105	2
KIRKCALDIE Jack	1936-1939	11	1	1	0	0	0	0	0	12	1
KIRKUP Joe	1958-1966	165	6	8	0	7	0	7	0	187	6
KITCHENER Bill	1966-1968	11	0	0	0	1	0	0	0	12	0
LAMPARD Frank	1967-1985	546/5	18	43	2	54	1	15	1	658/5	22
LANDELLS Jack	1933-1934	21	3	1	0	0	0	0	0	22	3
LANSDOWNE Bill	1955-1963	57	5	3	0	0	0	0	0	60	5
LANSDOWNE Billy	1978-1980	5/4	1	0	0	4/1	3	0	0	9/5	4
LANE Harry	1919-1921	19	0	0	0	0	0	0	0	19	0
LEAFE Alf	1919-1922	31	7	1	0	0	0	0	0	32	7
LEE Alf	1919-1922	26	0	2	0	0	0	0	0	28	0
LESLIE Lawrie	1961-1963	57	0	1	0	3	0	0	0	61	0
LEWIS Eddie	1956-1958	31	12	5	3	0	0	0	0	36	15
LEWIS Harry	1935-1936	4	4	0	0	0	0	0	0	4	4
LINDSAY Jimmy	1968-1971	36/3	2	4	0	2	0	0	0	42/3	2
LIVETT Simon	1990-1991	1	0	0/1	0	0	0	0	0	1/1	0
LLEWELLYN Dave	1969-1972	2/4	0	0	0	0	0	0	0	2/4	0
LOCK Kevin	1971-1978	122/10	2	11/1	0	13	0	4	0	150/11	2
LOUGHLIN Joe	1927-1928	10	4	1	0	0	0	0	0	11	4
LUTTON Bertie	1972-1974	8/4	1	2	0	2	0	0	0	12/4	1
LYALL John	1959-1963	31	0	0	0	0	0	0	0	31	0
McALISTER Tom	1981-1989	85	0	7	0	7	0	0	0	99	0
MACAULEY Archie	1937-1947	83	29	7	2	0	0	0	0	90	31
McAVENNIE Frank	1985-1992	134/19	49	19/1	6	11/2	2	0	0	164/22	57

Frank Lampard

Alvin Martin

Player	Played	LEAGUE		FA CUP		LG CUP		EUROPE		TOTAL	
		App	Gls	App	Gls	App	Gls	App	Gls	App	Gls
McCRAE James	1919-1921	50	0	4	0	0	0	0	0	54	0
MACDOUGALL Ted	1972-1974	24	5	0	0	1	1	0	0	25	6
McDOWELL John	1970-1979	243/6	8	19	0	21	1	7	0	290/6	9
McGIVEN Mick	1973-1978	46/2	0	3	0	2	0	1/1	0	52/3	0
McGOWAN Danny	1948-1954	81	8	2	1	0	0	0	0	83	9
MACKESY Jack	1919-1923	10	0	0	0	0	0	0	0	10	0
MACKLEWORTH Colin	1966-1967	3	0	0	0	0	0	0	0	3	0
McKNIGHT Alan	1988-1989	23	0	4	0	6	0	0	0	33	0
McMAHON Pat	1932-1934	16	0	1	0	0	0	0	0	17	0
McPHERSON Keith	1984-1985	1	0	0	0	0	0	0	0	1	0
McQUEEN Tommy	1986-1990	24/6	0	1	0	2/3	0	0	0	27/9	0
MALCOLM Andy	1953-1962	283	4	21	0	2	0	0	0	306	4
MANGNALL Dave	1934-1936	35	28	2	1	0	0	0	0	37	29
MARSHALL James	1934-1937	57	14	2	0	0	0	0	0	59	14
MARTIN Alvin	1977-	422/2	25	34	0	66	6	6	0	528/2	31
MARTIN Dean	1991-	1/1	0	0/1	0	0	0	0	0	1/2	0
MARTIN Tudor	1936-1937	11	7	0	0	0	0	0	0	11	7
MATTHEWS Terry	1955-1956	9	1	0	0	0	0	0	0	9	1
MEDHURST Harry	1938-1947	24	0	9	0	0	0	0	0	33	0
MIKLOSKO Ludek	1989-	146	0	12	0	10	0	0	0	168	0
MILLER Keith	1968-1970	1/2	0	0	0	0	0	0	0	1/2	0
MILLS Hugh	1932-1935	21	15	2	1	0	0	0	0	23	16
MILNE Ralph	1989-1990	0	0	0	0	0/1	0	0	0	0/1	0
MOORE Brian	1954-1956	9	1	0	0	0	0	0	0	9	1
MOORE Bobby	1958-1974	543/1	24	36	0	49	3	13	0	641/1	27
MOORE William	1922-1929	181	42	21	6	0	0	0	0	202	48
MORGAN Nicky	1978-1983	14/7	2	0	0	1	0	1/2	0	16/9	2
MORLEY Trevor	1989-	110/12	44	11/3	7	7	2	0	0	128/15	53
MORONEY Tommy	1947-1953	148	8	3	0	0	0	0	0	151	8
MORRIS Robert	1919-1920	3	0	0	0	0	0	0	0	3	0
MORTON John	1931-1939	258	54	17	3	0	0	0	0	275	57
MOYES James	1919-1920	2	1	0	0	0	0	0	0	2	1
MURRAY Albert	1919-1920	2	0	0	0	0	0	0	0	2	0
MUSGRAVE Joe	1930-1936	36	1	4	1	0	0	0	0	40	2
MUSGROVE Malcolm	1953-1963	283	84	13	2	5	3	0	0	301	89
NEARY Frank	1946-1948	17	15	0	0	0	0	0	0	17	15
NEIGHBOUR Jimmy	1979-1983	66/7	5	6/1	0	11/1	1	4	0	87/9	6
NELSON Andy	1957-1959	15	1	0	0	0	0	0	0	15	1
NELSON Bill	1954-1955	2	0	0	0	0	0	0	0	2	0
NEVILLE Bill	1957-1958	3	0	0	0	0	0	0	0	3	0
NEWMAN Mick	1956-1958	7	2	0	0	0	0	0	0	7	2
NORRINGTON Cyril	1927-1929	27	0	0	0	0	0	0	0	27	0
NORRIS Fred	1928-1933	65	6	0	0	0	0	0	0	65	6
OBENEY Harry	1956-1961	25	12	2	0	0	0	0	0	27	12
O'FARRELL Frank	1950-1957	197	6	13	1	0	0	0	0	210	7
ORHAM Yilmaz	1975-1977	6/2	0	0	0	1	0	0	0	7/2	0
ORR Neil	1981-1988	133/13	4	10/1	0	14/4	1	0	0	157/18	5
OTULAKOWSKI Anton	1976-1978	10/7	0	0	0	0	0	0	0	10/7	0
PADDON Graham	1973-1977	115	11	11	0	11	2	9	2	146	15
PALMER James	1919-1921	13	1	0	0	0	0	0	0	13	1
PARKER Derek	1946-1957	199	9	8	0	0	0	0	0	207	9
PARKER Reg	1935-1936	2	0	0	0	0	0	0	0	2	0
PARKES Phil	1978-1990	344	0	34	0	52	0	6	0	436	0
PARKS Tony	1991-1992	6	0	3	0	0	0	0	0	9	0
PARRIS George	1984-1993	211/28	12	21	4	27/3	1	0	0	259/31	17
PARSONS Eric	1946-1951	145	34	6	1	0	0	0	0	151	35
PAYNE Joe	1946-1947	10	6	1	0	0	0	0	0	11	6
PAYNE John	1926-1929	4	1	0	0	0	0	0	0	4	1
PEARSON Stuart	1979-1982	28/6	6	8/2	2	3/2	1	0/1	1	39/11	10
PETCHEY George	1952-1953	2	0	0	0	0	0	0	0	2	0
PETERS Martin	1961-1970	302	81	16	5	31	10	15	4	364	100
PHILLIPS Wilf	1931-1932	21	3	2	0	0	0	0	0	23	3
PHIPPS C	1919-1920	1	0	0	0	0	0	0	0	1	0
PIKE Geoff	1975-1987	275/16	32	29/2	5	38/1	3	6	1	348/19	41
POLLARD Walter	1929-1933	37	4	6	2	0	0	0	0	43	6

Bobby Moore

Player	Played	LEAGUE App	Gls	FA CUP App	Gls	LG CUP App	Gls	EUROPE App	Gls	TOTAL App	Gls
POTTS Steve	1984-	185/10	1	23	0	20/1	0	0	0	228/11	1
PRESLAND Eddie	1964-1966	6	1	0	0	0	0	0	0	6	1
PROCTOR Norman	1923-1924	7	1	0	0	0	0	0	0	7	1
PROUDLOCK George	1938-1949	18	5	0	0	0	0	0	0	18	5
PUDDEFOOT Sidney	1919-1933	125	67	8	5	0	0	0	0	133	72
PYKE Malcolm	1956-1958	17	0	2	0	0	0	0	0	19	0
QUINN Jimmy	1989-1991	34/13	19	4/2	2	3	1	0	0	41/15	22
RADFORD John	1976-1978	28	0	1	0	1	0	0	0	30	0
REDKNAPP Harry	1965-1972	146/3	7	7/1	0	17/1	1	0	0	170/5	8
RHODES Brian	1957-1963	61	0	2	0	3	0	0	0	66	0
RICHARDS Dick	1922-1924	43	5	10	1	0	0	0	0	53	6
RICHARDSON Frank	1923-1924	10	2	1	0	0	0	0	0	11	2
ROBERTS Bill	1937-1938	1	0	0	0	0	0	0	0	1	0
ROBERTS Vivian	1919-1920	1	0	0	0	0	0	0	0	1	0
ROBINSON Bill	1948-1952	101	60	4	1	0	0	0	0	105	61
ROBINSON Leslie	1920-1924	19	2	0	0	0	0	0	0	19	2
ROBSON Bryan	1970-1979	227	94	12	4	15	6	0	0	254	104
ROBSON George	1927-1931	17	2	1	0	0	0	0	0	18	2
ROBSON Keith	1974-1977	65/3	13	3	1	7	1	9	4	84/3	19
ROBSON Mark	1992-	41/3	8	2	1	2	0	0	0	45/3	9
ROBSON Stewart	1986-1991	68/1	4	6	1	8	1	0	0	82/1	6
ROBSON William	1933-1934	3	0	0	0	0	0	0	0	3	0
RONDE Everonde La	1981-1982	6/1	0	0	0	0	0	0	0	6/1	0
ROSENIOR Leroy	1987-1992	44/9	15	4/1	2	7	2	0	0	55/10	19
RUFFELL Jimmy	1921-1937	505	159	43	7	0	0	0	0	548	166
RUSH Matthew	1990-	5/10	2	0	0	1	0	0	0	6//10	2
RUTHERFORD Jack	1933-1934	33	0	2	0	0	0	0	0	35	0
SADLER George	1946-1947	1	0	0	0	0	0	0	0	1	0
ST PIER Wally	1929-1933	24	0	0	0	0	0	0	0	24	0
SCOTT Tony	1959-1966	83	16	7	0	7	3	0	0	97	19
SEALEY Alan	1960-1967	107	22	8	0	6	1	7	3	128	26
SEXTON Dave	1952-1956	74	27	3	2	0	0	0	0	77	29
SHEA Danny	1920-1921	16	1	0	0	0	0	0	0	16	1
SHEARING Peter	1960-1961	6	0	0	0	0	0	0	0	6	0
SHONE Danny	1928-1929	12	5	0	0	0	0	0	0	12	5
SIMMONS Jim	1920-1922	27	1	0	0	0	0	0	0	27	1
SIMPSON Peter	1935-1937	32	12	4	0	0	0	0	0	36	12
SISSONS John	1962-1970	210/3	37	18	8	21	5	13	3	262/3	53
SLATER Stuart	1987-1992	134/7	11	16	3	16/1	2	0	0	166/8	16
SMAILES Matt	1928-1929	7	0	3	0	0	0	0	0	10	0
SMALL Mike	1991-	42/7	13	4/1	1	4/1	4	0	0	50/9	18
SMALL Sam	1936-1948	108	39	10	0	0	0	0	0	118	39
SMILLIE Andy	1958-1961	20	3	3	0	0	0	0	0	23	3
SMITH David	1919-1920	1	0	0	0	0	0	0	0	1	0
SMITH Harold	1928-1929	1	0	0	0	0	0	0	0	1	0
SMITH John	1956-1960	125	20	5	2	0	0	0	0	130	22
SMITH Mark	1979-1980	1	0	0	0	1	0	0	0	2	0
SMITH Roy	1955-1957	6	1	0	0	0	0	0	0	6	1
SMITH Sydney	1919-1922	27	0	4	1	0	0	0	0	31	1
SMITH William	1927-1928	2	0	0	0	0	0	0	0	2	0
SMITHURST Edgar	1919-1921	3	0	0	0	0	0	0	0	3	0
SOUTHREN Tommy	1950-1954	64	3	2	0	0	0	0	0	66	3
SPEEDIE David	1992-	11	4	0	0	0	0	0	0	11	4
STANDEN JIm	1962-1968	178	0	20	0	23	0	14	0	235	0
STANLEY Thomas	1919-1920	1	0	0	0	0	0	0	0	1	0
STEPHENS Bill	1947-1949	22	6	2	1	0	0	0	0	24	7
STEPHENSON Alan	1967-1972	106/2	0	4	1	6	0	0	0	116/2	1
STEWART Ray	1979-1991	344/1	62	35/1	7	44	14	6	1	429/1	84
STRODDER Gary	1986-1990	59/6	2	4/2	0	8	0	0	0	71/8	2
STROUD Roy	1951-1957	13	4	0	0	0	0	0	0	13	4
SUCKLING Perry	1989-1990	6	0	0	0	0	0	0	0	6	0
SWINDLEHURST Dave	1982-1985	52/9	16	4/1	1	5	1	0	0	61/10	18
TATE Isaac	1927-1929	14	0	0	0	0	0	0	0	14	0
TAYLOR Alan	1974-1979	88/10	25	7/1	6	8	2	6/1	3	109/12	36
TAYLOR George	1946-1956	115	0	3	0	0	0	0	0	118	0

Player	Played	LEAGUE		FA CUP		LG CUP		EUROPE		TOTAL	
		App	Gls	App	Gls	App	Gls	App	Gls	App	Gls
TAYLOR Tommy	1970-1979	340	8	21	0	26	0	9	0	396	8
THIRLAWAY William	1921-1924	36	2	3	0	0	0	0	0	39	2
THOMAS Mitchell	1991-	37/1	3	4	0	5	0	0	0	46/1	3
THORPE Peter	1933-1934	3	0	0	0	0	0	0	0	3	0
TINDALL Ron	1961-1962	13	3	1	0	0	0	0	0	14	3
TIPPETT Tommy	1933-1936	27	10	1	0	0	0	0	0	28	10
TIRRELL Alf	1919-1920	1	0	0	0	0	0	0	0	1	0
TONNER Arthur	1935-1936	1	0	0	0	0	0	0	0	1	0
TRAVIS Don	1946-1948	5	0	0	0	0	0	0	0	5	0
TRESADERN Jack	1919-1925	144	5	16	0	0	0	0	0	160	5
TUCKER Ken	1947-1957	83	31	10	0	0	0	0	0	93	31
TURNER Charlie	1937-1939	11	0	0	0	0	0	0	0	11	0
TURNER Cyril	1919-1922	7	1	0	0	0	0	0	0	7	1
TYLER Dudley	1972-1974	29	1	2	0	3	0	0	0	34	1
VAN DER ELST Francois	1981-1983	61/1	14	2	0	5/1	3	0	0	68/2	17
WADE Don	1947-1950	36	5	4	2	0	0	0	0	40	7
WADE Reg	1929-1932	32	0	1	0	0	0	0	0	33	0
WADE William	1929-1931	16	0	0	0	0	0	0	0	16	0
WALFORD Steve	1983-1987	114/1	2	14	0	16/1	2	0	0	144/2	4
WALKER Albert	1932-1938	162	0	12	0	0	0	0	0	174	0
WALKER Charlie	1936-1939	110	0	8	0	0	0	0	0	118	0
WALKER Richard	1934-1953	292	2	19	0	0	0	0	0	311	2
WALLBANKS Fred	1934-1935	0	0	1	0	0	0	0	0	1	0
WARD Mark	1985-1990	163/2	12	17	0	20/1	2	0	0	200/3	14
WATSON George	1932-1935	33	0	5	0	0	0	0	0	38	0
WATSON Victor	1920-1935	462	298	43	28	0	0	0	0	505	326
WAUGH William	1921-1922	6	0	1	0	0	0	0	0	7	0
WEALE Robert	1925-1926	3	0	0	0	0	0	0	0	3	0
WEARE Jack	1936-1938	58	0	2	0	0	0	0	0	60	0
WEBSTER Joe	1919-1920	2	0	0	0	0	0	0	0	2	0
WELDON Tony	1931-1932	20	3	2	1	0	0	0	0	22	4
WHITTON Steve	1983-1985	35/4	6	1	0	6	2	0	0	42/4	8
WILLIAMS Harry	1951-1952	5	1	0	0	0	0	0	0	5	1
WILLIAMS Ron	1937-1938	9	5	1	0	0	0	0	0	10	5
WILLIAMS William	1921-1927	35	8	9	1	0	0	0	0	44	9
WILSON Arthur	1932-1934	29	14	6	2	0	0	0	0	35	16
WILSON Ron	1946-1948	3	0	0	0	0	0	0	0	3	0
WOOD Jackie	1937-1949	58	13	4	2	0	0	0	0	62	15
WOOD Jim	1929-1935	63	13	1	0	0	0	0	0	64	13
WOODARDS Dan	1919-1921	16	0	0	0	0	0	0	0	16	0
WOODBURN J	1919-1920	4	0	0	0	0	0	0	0	4	0
WOODGATE Terry	1938-1953	259	48	16	4	0	0	0	0	275	52
WOODLEY Derek	1959-1962	12	3	0	0	1	0	0	0	13	3
WOOLER Alan	1973-1976	3/1	0	1	0	0	0	0	0	4/1	0
WOOSNAM Phil	1958-1963	138	26	5	0	4	1	0	0	147	27
WRAGG Doug	1956-1960	16	0	0	0	0	0	0	0	16	0
WRIGHT George	1951-1958	161	0	9	0	0	0	0	0	170	0
WRIGHT Ken	1946-1950	51	20	1	0	0	0	0	0	52	20
WYLLIE Robert	1956-1957	13	0	2	0	0	0	0	0	15	0
YEOMANSON Jack	1947-1951	106	1	5	0	0	0	0	0	111	1
YEWS Tommy	1923-1933	332	46	29	5	0	0	0	0	361	51
YOUNG John	1919-1926	124	3	14	0	0	0	0	0	138	3
YOUNG Len	1933-1938	12	0	0	0	0	0	0	0	12	0